THE SCOTTISH
LEGAL SYSTEM

AUSTRALIA
LBC Information Services—Sydney

CANADA and USA
Carswell—Toronto

NEW ZEALAND
Brooker's—Auckland

SINGAPORE and MALAYSIA
Sweet and Maxwell Asia
Singapore and Kuala Lumpur

THE SCOTTISH
LEGAL SYSTEM

AN INTRODUCTION TO THE
STUDY OF SCOTS LAW

BY

DAVID M. WALKER

C.B.E., M.A., Ph.D., LL.D., Hon.LL.D. F.B.A., F.R.S.E., F.S.A.Scot., F.R.S.A.,
One of Her Majesty's Counsel in Scotland,
Of the Middle Temple, Barrister,
Regius Professor Emeritus of Law in the University of Glasgow

EIGHTH EDITION, REVISED

THOMSON

™

SWEET & MAXWELL

First Published 1959
Second edition 1963
Third edition 1969
Fourth edition 1976
Fifth edition 1981
Sixth edition 1992
Seventh edition 1997
Eighth edition 2001
Reprinted 2003, 2005

This edition published in 2001 by W. Green & Son Ltd
21 Alva Street
Edinburgh EH2 4PS

Transferred to Digital Printing 2007

Typeset by LBJ Typesetting Ltd, Kingsclere

Printed and bound in Great Britain by TJI Digital, Padstow, Cornwall

No natural forests were destroyed to make this product;
only farmed timber was used and replanted

A CIP catalogue record for this book is available from the Britain Library

ISBN 978-0-414-01353-7

© D. M. Walker 2001

PREFACE

THIS book was written primarily to provide a textbook for the introductory course in the legal curriculum of Glasgow University, that which is designated Scottish Legal System. Nevertheless I hope that it may prove of interest and utility to other persons concerned to obtain a general conspectus of the subject.

That course, and consequently this book, is intended not as a first or general introductory course on Scots Law itself, but as an attempt to tackle the problem of putting the study of law in its context and teaching the novice law student how to go about the study of law and as an attempt to equip him to do so. It is an introduction to the *study*, not to the law itself. I have tried to put into this book all the kinds of materials which I wish somebody had made available to me when I commenced the study of Scots law. The traditional method of plunging the law student at once into the subject-matter of various branches of the law was quite unsatisfactory, because he did not at that stage have the knowledge or skill necessary to study the law with understanding and effect. This book is therefore not an elementary book on the principles of Scots Law but an attempt to acquaint the student at the very outset of his studies with the background, with the materials of legal study and the methods of working, and with the basic knowledge requisite to enable him intelligently and profitably to pursue legal studies. I hope that some of it will be useful as a reference book at later stages of study.

It is necessary to emphasise that the legal system is constantly developing and changing and that everything discussed and explained herein may be changed, possibly radically, possibly within a short space of time, and that the speed of change in law is accelerating. The reader must be on his guard and watch for developments since the text was printed.

The study of this book is not intended to supersede the necessity for later, closer and more detailed study of each of the topics it covers, as well as of the doctrinal principles of the substantive law. Every topic discussed herein has been deliberately treated in a preliminary and elementary way, and many details, qualifications, subtleties and difficulties have been glossed over. Considerations of space and expense have further severely limited or even prevented altogether the discussion of many points.

I have deliberately avoided the detailed treatment and the full citation of authority which might be expected in a more advanced book, and much bibliographical material has been mentioned in footnotes not so much to vouch the statements in the text as to indicate the sources of further information.

This eighth edition has been completely revised and partially rewritten to take account of developments in the law since the last edition and in the hope of clarifying some of the difficulties.

I am greatly indebted to the publishers and to the printers who have taken such pains and trouble over this book. I have tried to take account of all developments down to the date of this Preface.

D.M.W.

THE UNIVERSITY,
  GLASGOW, G12 8QQ.
January 1, 2001.

CONTENTS

TABLE OF CASES

PAGE

PAGE

PAGE

TABLE OF STATUTES

ABBREVIATIONS

A.C.	Appeal Cases (Law Reports)
All E.R.	All England Law Reports
All E.R. (E.C.)	All England Law Reports European Cases
A.P.S.	Acts of the Parliament of Scotland 1424–1707 (Record edition, 12 vols.)
asp	Acts of the Scottish Parliament, 1999– , number
B.Y.I.L.	British Yearbook of International Law
c.	Chapter (of UK statutes of year)
C.A.	Court of Appeal (England and Wales)
C.A.R.	Criminal Appeal Reports
Camb. Anc. His.	Cambridge Ancient History
Can.Bar.Rev.	Canadian Bar Review
C.J.E.C.	Court of Justice of the European Communities
C.L.	Current Law Monthly Digest
C.L.J.	Cambridge Law Journal
C.L.P.	Current Legal Problems
C.L.Q.	Cornell Law Quarterly
C.L.Y.	Current Law Yearbook
C.M.A.C.	Courts-Martial Appeal Court
C.M.L.R.	Common Market Law Reports
Col. L.R.	Columbia Law Review
Ch.	Chancery Division (Law Reports)
D.C.	Divisional Court (England and Wales)
E.A.T.	Employment Appeal Tribunal
E.C.	European Communities
E.C.J.	European Court of Justice
E.C.R.	European Court Reports (Court of Justice of the European Communities)
E.C.S.C.	European Coal and Steel Community
E.E.C.	European Economic Community
E.H.R.R.	European Human Rights Reports (European Court of Human Rights)
Encyc. Soc. Sc.	Encyclopaedia of Social Sciences
Fam.	Family Division (Law Reports)
G.W.D.	Green's Weekly Digest
H.L.	House of Lords
H.L.R.	Harvard Law Review
I.C.L.Q.	International and Comparative Law Quarterly

I.C.R.	Industrial Cases Reports
Int.Encyc.Soc.Sc.	International Encyclopaedia of Social Sciences
I.R.L.R.	Industrial Relations Law Reports
I.T.R.	Industrial Tribunal Reports
J.	Justice (Judge of the High Court, England and Wales or Northern Ireland)
JJ.	Justices
J.C.	Justiciary Cases, High Court of Justiciary, Scotland, bound in with Session Cases
J.L.H.	Journal of Legal History
J.L.S.S.	Journal of the Law Society of Scotland
J.R.	Juridical Review, Scotland
J.S.P.T.L.	Journal of the Society of Public Teachers of Law
K.B.	King's Bench Division (Law Reports)
K.I.R.	Knight's Industrial Reports
L.C.	Lord Chancellor
L.C.J.	Lord Chief Justice, England and Wales
L.J.	Lord Justice (Judge of the Court of Appeal, England and Wales or Northern Ireland)
L.JJ.	Lords Justices
L.J.R.	Law Journal Reports
L.Q.R.	Law Quarterly Review
L.R.	Law Reports, England and Wales
L.R.R.P.	Law Reports, Restrictive Practices Court
L.V.A.C.	Lands Valuation Appeal Court, Scotland
M.L.R.	Modern Law Review
M.R.	Master of the Rolls, England and Wales
N.I.	Northern Ireland Reports
N.I.L.Q.	Northern Ireland Law Quarterly
O.H.	Outer House, Court of Session
O.J.	Official Journal of the European Communities
O.J.L.S.	Oxford Journal of Legal Studies
P.	Probate, Divorce and Admiralty Division (Law Reports)
P.C.	Privy Council
Pub. L.	Public Law
Q.B.	Queen's Bench Division (Law Reports)
s.	Section of Act of Parliament
S.C.	Session Cases
S.C.C.R.	Scottish Criminal Case Reports
S.C.C.R.Supp.	Scottish Criminal Case Reports Supplement (1950–1980)
S.C.(H.L.)	Session Cases, appeals to the House of Lords
S.C.(J.)	High Court of Justiciary cases, bound in with Session Cases

S.C.L.R.	Scottish Civil Law Reports
S.H.R.	Scottish Historical Review
S.I.	Statutory Instrument
S.L.C.R.	Scottish Land Court Reports
S.L.G.	Scottish Law Gazette
S.L.P.Q.	Scottish Law and Practice Quarterly
S.L.R.	Scottish Law Reporter, 1865–1925
S.L.R.	Scottish Law Review, Sheriff Court Cases, 1885–1963
S.L.T.	Scots Law Times Reports
S.L.T.(Land Ct.)	Scots Law Times (Land Court Reports)
S.L.T.(Lands Tr.)	Scots Law Times (Lands Tribunal Reports)
S.L.T.(Lyon Ct.)	Scots Law Times (Lyon Court Reports)
S.L.T.(News)	Scots Law Times, News Section
S.L.T.(Notes)	Scots Law Times, Notes of Recent Decisions, 1946–81
S.L.T.(Sh.Ct.)	Scots Law Times, Sheriff Court Reports
S.N.	Session Notes
S.R. & O.	Statutory Rules and Orders
S.S.I.	Scottish Statutory Instrument, 1999–
Sc.Jur.	Scottish Jurist
Sh.Ct.Rep.	Sheriff Court Reports, Scottish Law Review, 1885–1963
Traff.Cas.	Railway, Canal and Road Traffic Cases
W.L.R.	Weekly Law Reports (Law Reports)
W.N.	Weekly Notes (Law Reports)
Y.E.L.	Yearbook of European Law
Yale L.J.	Yale Law Journal

CHAPTER 1

THE SCIENCE OF LAW

THE science of law[1] or the systematised knowledge of the principles and rules adopted by societies for regulating the conduct of their members is one of the social sciences, that is, one of the bodies of learning which deal with aspects of human behaviour and the relations and interactions of individuals and groups of individuals.[2] The group of subjects comprises also social and cultural anthropology, sociology, politics, economics, social psychology and social and economic geography.[3] They are all concerned with aspects of Man in Society. Indeed the science of law was one of the first of these to develop as a distinct subject of study and investigation. Some other bodies of learning, such as education and international relations, are sometimes also accounted social sciences. All are concerned with investigating and seeking to understand and explain different aspects of the behaviour of individuals and groups living together and interacting with one another in societies of different kinds, from small tribes up to major nation-states. Law is a social phenomenon, like political, economic, moral and religious phenomena.

Law deals, that is, with one aspect of the relations and interactions of individuals living in societies, namely, with the institutions, machinery and principles which particular societies have developed for the purposes of defining the claims and liabilities of persons against one another in various circumstances, and of providing means for vindicating just claims and peaceably resolving their disputes and controversies in accordance with

---

[1] The word science means knowledge, systematised and rationally ordered, and it is as proper for the social sciences as for the natural sciences. It was only in the 19th century that the word "science" began to be appropriated to the natural sciences (physical, biological and earth sciences). It is used by Justinian in the Prooemium to his *Institutions*.

[2] *cf. Encyclopaedia of the Social Sciences*, I, 3, defining social sciences as "those mental or cultural sciences which deal with the activities of the individual as a member of a group."

[3] The *Encyclopaedia of the Social Sciences* (1930) distinguished the social sciences (politics, economics, law, anthropology, sociology, penology and social work), the semi-social sciences (ethics, education, philosophy and psychology) and the natural sciences with social implications (biology, geography, medicine, linguistics and art). The *International Encyclopaedia of the Social Sciences* (1968), though disclaiming finality in its decision of what are social sciences, deals with anthropology, economics, geography, history, law, political science, psychiatry, psychology, sociology and statistics. The *Encyclopaedia Britannica* (15th ed.) distinguishes Human Society (which embraces social organisation, economics, politics and government, law and education) from History, Philosophy and Religion, and also from the Humanities and the Natural Sciences. Cairns (*Law and the Social Sciences*) considers the relations of law and anthropology, economics, sociology, political science and psychology.

1

the principles accepted as fair and right in the particular community at a given time.[4] Moreover, the content of law is influenced and even determined by the views of society and it has important consequences for society and individuals. The existence of a legal order in society is furthermore presupposed by most other social sciences, so that law and other social sciences are interdependent and, as studies, overlap.

Law is, indeed, a part of human culture, of "that complex whole which includes knowledge, belief, art, morals, law, custom and any other capabilities acquired by man as a member of society."[5] It is both a product of civilisation, in that wherever groups of individuals have attained that stage of organisation and of control over their environment which we call civilisation, some kind of legal ordering of society is found,[6] and it is also an essential of the continuance and development of civilisation, in that without a legal order to regulate conflicting claims and to resolve differences, civilisation would slip back into anarchy. The intimate connection between the legal system and the general culture of our society is well illustrated by the extent to which legal institutions are pictured in English literature[7] and legal phraseology has penetrated into common speech.[8]

The origins of all the social sciences go back to the ancient Greeks and their rationalist inquiries into the nature of man, the state, and morality, but they began to develop more rapidly, and to become increasingly differentiated after the Renaissance and particularly from the eighteenth century. All were affected by the English, American and French Revolutions, the Industrial Revolution, urbanisation, the development of democracy and other similar factors.

Law a True Science

Law, moreover, is truly a science, that is, a systematic body of coherent and ordered knowledge about the institutions, principles and rules regulating human conduct in society.[9] It is "an organised and critically controlled

---

[4] Patterson, *Jurisprudence*, 50, points out that so far as jurists deal with precepts for conduct which *ought to be* followed, law is not a social science but a philosophic discipline, akin to moral philosophy.

[5] Tylor, *Primitive Culture*, 1.

[6] Thus, highly developed legal systems existed in ancient Mesopotamia (see Driver and Miles, *The Babylonian Laws*, 2 vols.; *The Assyrian Laws*), Asia Minor (see Neufeld, *The Hittite Laws*), Palestine (see Kent, *Israel's Law and Legal Precedents*), Greece, Rome and elsewhere in the Ancient World.

[7] See, *e.g.* Underhill, *Shakespeare's England*, Chap. 13; Keeton, *Shakespeare and His Legal Problems*; Holdsworth, *Charles Dickens as a Legal Historian*; McNair, *Dr. Johnson and the Law*; Marshall, *Sir Walter Scott and Scots Law*; Cardozo, "Law and Literature" in *Selected Writings*, 339; Holdsworth, "Literature in Law Books" in *Essays in Law and History*, 219; Lord Macmillan, "Law and Letters" and "Law and Language" in *Law and Other Things*; Windolph, *Reflections on the Law in Literature*; Collins, *Dickens and Crime*.

[8] See, *e.g.* Simon, "English Idioms from the Law" (1960) 76 L.Q.R. 283, 429; (1962) 78 L.Q.R. 245; (1965) 81 L.Q.R. 52.

[9] Lord Atkin once said: "That law is a scientific subject, I suggest, cannot be disputed. I think

body of knowledge both of legal institutions and legal precepts and of the legal order, that is, the legal ordering of society . . . a science of achieving social control by means of or with the aid of laws . . . a science of the adjustment of human relations through the public administration of justice, or, more specifically, a science of the securing of interests in civilised society by means of an ordered judicial and administrative adjustment of relations."[10] Legal science, or jurisprudence (in the wider sense of that word) (*juris prudentia, juris scientia*) covers the whole subject-matter of the study and systematised knowledge of and about law and the administration of justice, including what may be called legal dogmatics, or the study of the actual content of the legal system, of the body of doctrines, principles, rules, propositions and precepts accepted in a particular community and of their applications. In a narrower sense legal science covers the activities of systematic study of, and thinking and writing about, legal topics.[11] Law in a modern community does not consist of a great mass of particular, specific, unrelated rules which have to be looked up, as in a telephone directory, and the study of law does not consist in memorising, or even in learning how to look up, such a directory. The scientific element in law consists in that a system of law comprises a body of reasonably consistent principles and rules, susceptible of arrangement under heads and sub-heads and of systematic study, defining rules for and standards of conduct and the consequences of their non-observance in particular kinds of circumstances. These can be applied to an infinite number and variety of problem-situations, whether known or foreseeable or not, and can solve them in accordance with overriding principles of justice, in the same way as propositions and formulae about the triangle can be applied to any actual triangle.[12] Furthermore, law can

---

it was Burke who said that law is one of the finest and noblest of human sciences: a science which does more to quicken and invigorate the understanding than all the other kinds of learning put together" ("Law as an Educational Subject" (1932) J.S.P.T.L. 27). Stair (*Institutions*, I, 1, 17) affirmed that law could, and should, be handled as a rational discipline, having principles whence its conclusions may be deduced. Alexander Bayne (Professor of Scots Law at Edinburgh, 1722–37, on whom see Menzies, "Alex. Bayne of Rires" (1924) 36 J.R. 60) in *A Discourse on the Rise and Progress of the Law of Scotland*, annexed to his edition of Hope's *Minor Practicks* (1726), wrote that the Science of the Law was of the highest character among the humane sciences, the most useful to mankind, and best entitled to first place among them. Similarly Blackstone (*Commentaries on the Laws of England*, I, 34) wrote: "Law is to be considered not only as a matter of practice, but also as a rational science." (On Blackstone see further: Boorstin, *The Mysterious Science of the Law*, and Hanbury, *The Vinerian Chair and Legal Education*.) *cf.* also Pollock, *First Book of Jurisprudence*, 46; Langdell, Introduction to *Cases on the Law of Contract* (1886).

[10] Pound, *Jurisprudence*, I, 16–17. *cf.* Cairns, *Theory of Legal Science*; Sawer, *Law in Society*.

[11] *cf.* Kantorowicz, *The Definition of Law*, 11–13; Schulz, *History of Roman Legal Science*, 1; Harris, *Law and Legal Science*.

[12] *cf.* Fraser Tytler's *Memoirs of Lord Kames*, I, 114: "The examination of various cases which turn upon one common *ratio decidendi*, familiarises the mind, in all points of doubt to recur immediately to a principle; and this habit of reference will not only be found of the utmost benefit when any abstruse or intricate question is the subject of discussion; but it tends from the

be studied by scientific methods just as can any other science. Experiment, or the observation of phenomena under conditions controlled by the investigator, is possible only to a very limited extent,[13] but observation, classification, analysis and synthesis, inductive and deductive inference, and comparison and analogy are all applicable to legal problems as much as to those of other sciences. Observation and classification in particular are clearly illustrated by the common and centuries-old legal practice of having interesting cases noted or reported under legal headings, so that jurists can subsequently read what the courts have done and said in solving particular problems,[14] and can classify and study together cases relating to similar problems. Analysis involves the breaking down of a legal problem or reported decision into its elements, into the particular factors which constitute it, so as to discern what is unknown or different from other comparable cases, while synthesis is the building up of the legal elements involved in a factual situation which go to impose liability or provide a valid defence or justify a legal remedy in the particular circumstances. Inductive inference consists in drawing a general principle from a number of similar observed instances; deductive inference is the process of applying general principles to suitable particular instances. Both are illustrated repeatedly in the way the courts handle previous reported decisions to help them solve a new problem before them.[15] Comparison and analogy involve the recognition of greater or lesser degrees of similarity between one case and another or others, and again these are techniques regularly resorted to in legal reasoning.[16]

Law must not be thought of solely or even primarily as a body of professional knowledge, the stock-in-trade of the practitioners of certain professions, or as purely a practical or applied science. It is primarily a social science, a pure science, an area in the field of studies of men's relations with one another. The knowledge gained from that study can of course be used to understand and to solve actual everyday problems, as a basis for advice, decision or action; to that extent it forms part of the background knowledge employed by several professions, but the same is true of economics, physiology and many other subjects. The evident utility and manifold applications of the knowledge should not be allowed to

---

agreeable and vigorous exercise it affords to the intellectual powers, to give to jurisprudence that dignity as a science which it merits, and to render the study of the laws, instead of a servile drudgery, the manly employment of a philosophic mind."

[13] It is possible to some extent in such contexts as trying different methods of treatment of criminals, or different methods of control of anti-social activities, such as gambling.

[14] "Case law has a scientific aim, namely, the prediction of events by means of past experience": Pollock, "The Science of Case Law" in *Essays in Jurisprudence and Ethics*, 237, and in *Jurisprudence and Legal Essays*, 169.

[15] *cf.* the inductive inference in *Donoghue v. Stevenson*, 1932 S.C.(H.L.) 31, of the general principle implicit in various particular earlier decisions, and the deduction from that general principle of the particular decision in *Lockhart v. Barr*, 1943 S.C.(H.L.) 1.

[16] See further Levi, *Introduction to Legal Reasoning*.

obscure the status of the subject as a major department of the social sciences, indeed one of the most ancient of them, and one which has in every age and country attracted the attention and devotion of some of the ablest minds of the time.

Relations of Law with other Studies

Legal science deals with only one facet of human conduct and of the relations of people in society, and cannot ignore those other sciences which study other facets of the same relations.[17] One particular piece of conduct may be of interest to the students of many disciplines; an assault by one man on another is to the sociologist a deviation from normal conduct, to the psychologist a problem of motivation, to the philosopher a problem of right and wrong, to the psychiatrist a possible manifestation of a diseased mind, and to the lawyer a breach of a legal duty which is punishable. The relations between law and the principal other social sciences are so close and important as to justify more detailed individual examination.[18]

The various social sciences are not sharply differentiated from one another. They overlap at various points and many topics are of interest and concern to scholars in more than one discipline, examining the topic from different standpoints and with different emphases. Government and the exercise of power over individuals is of concern to the student of politics and also to one of law. Taxation is a concern of the student of economics, of politics, or of law. Crime, its causes, nature and incidence are concerns of some sociologists as well as of many lawyers. But in all such cases the different sciences look at the topic from different standpoints and are more interested in different aspects.

Law and Anthropology

Anthropology is the study of man as a physical and social being as he is found in different environments in the world, and one aspect of this is social anthropology which deals with the life of primitive peoples living in less developed conditions at the present day, and studies their conduct, habits, institutions and attitudes, their beliefs, taboos, class systems, marriage customs, kinship relations, trading relations, reactions to wrongdoing and so on. Such studies seek to discover the origins and evolution of civilisation and culture, and provide important indications of the origins and bases of modern social institutions and the patterns of conduct of

---

[17] *cf.* Lord Kames's Preface to his *Elucidations respecting the Law of Scotland*: "Were law taught as a rational science, its principles unfolded, and its connection with manners and politics, it would prove an enticing study to every person who has an appetite for knowledge." The *Oxford Journal of Legal Studies* stresses interdisciplinary relations of law.

[18] See generally Cairns, *Law and the Social Sciences*; Stone, *Law and the Social Sciences in the Second Half Century*.

civilised peoples. They serve to stimulate, illustrate and modify thinking about law and its origins and nature rather than to influence it today or to provide material to which it is applicable. From such studies it is apparent that means of social control, some approximating in substance to law, can exist without writing or lawyers, without force or formal procedure, in such communities.[19]

Law and Sociology

Sociology is the study of society, social groups and classes, social phenomena, the forms of social institutions, social relationships, social structure, social change and development,[20] and it therefore deals with much that is the background to, and the justification for and explanation of, the legal system. In its study of the interaction and relationships of individuals and groups, it deals with the same subject-matter as does the law, but from a different standpoint. Social institutions, such as the family, marriage and inheritance are in fact regulated in large part by legal rules and are legal institutions as well as sociological.[21] Not least sociology examines such problem groups as criminal classes and their attitude to society, drug-addicts, the poor, and minority groups. Sociology is also concerned with society's reactions to social problems, such as welfare services and prisons.

To the sociologist, law is necessarily a matter of interest because law is, like custom, habit, morals, taboos and fashion, one of the forces of social control which tend to regulate conduct and impose uniformities of behaviour, and is moreover the most widespread and powerful of these forces.[22] Law is also largely a product of social requirements and changes, and of custom and accepted social practices, and develops to take account of such social changes; if it does not, it becomes out of date, out of touch with the requirements and the feelings of the community and to that extent fails to serve its purpose.[23] In the present century there has indeed

---

[19] See further, generally, Boas, "Anthropology" in *Encyc.Soc.Sc.*, I, 73; Greenberg and others, "Anthropology" in *Int.Encyc.Soc.Sc.*, I, 313; Chappel and Coon, *Principles of Anthropology*; Piddington, *Introduction to Social Anthropology* (2 vols.); Lowie, *Primitive Society*; Radcliffe-Brown, *Structure and Function in Primitive Society*; and, on points of legal interest, Hartland, *Primitive Law*; Diamond, *Primitive Law*; Malinowski, *Crime and Custom in Savage Society*; Hogbin, *Law and Order in Polynesia*; Gluckman, *The Judicial Process among the Barotse of Northern Rhodesia; Politics, Law and Ritual in Tribal Society*; Llewellyn and Hoebel, *The Cheyenne Way*; Hoebel, *The Law of Primitive Man*; see also Robson, *Civilisation and the Growth of Law*; Cairns, "Law and Anthropology" (1931) 31 Col.L.R. 32; Sack (ed.), *Law and Anthropology*.

[20] See generally MacIver, "Sociology" in *Encyc.Soc.Sc.*, XIV, 232; Reiss and others, "Sociology" in *Int.Encyc.Soc.Sc.*, XV, 1.

[21] See generally MacIver and Page, *Society, an Introductory Analysis*; Johnson, *Sociology, a Systematic Introduction*; Ogburn and Nimkoff, *Handbook of Sociology*; Ginsberg, *Essays in Sociology and Social Philosophy*, 3 vols.; Michael and Adler, *Crime, Law and Social Science*; Glueck and Hall, *Crime, Theft and Society*.

[22] See Pound, *Social Control Through Law*; "Sociology and Law" in Ogburn and Goldenweiser, *The Social Sciences* (1921), 319.

[23] See further Friedmann, *Law in a Changing Society*; Ginsburg (ed.), *Law and Opinion in England in the 20th Century*; Sawer, *Law in Society*.

developed a branch of study called sociology of law, studying law as a specialised phase of the study of society.[24]

To the student of law, sociology explains much of the society in which his legal system works and for which it exists.[25] It enables him to take account of social facts in the framing of new legislation or the enforcement of existing rules, and requires him to reconsider time-honoured rules or institutions in the light of changed conditions. What is social disorganisation to the sociologist includes what are to the lawyer also problems, such as of crime,[26] divorce, illegitimacy, racial discrimination, street and industrial accidents, and town planning. Sociology both helps to explain the institutions of the legal order, and itself assumes them in its own studies.

Criminology and penology began as particular interests of sociologists and are sometimes now regarded as a subject distinct from sociology; whether distinct or not they overlap with the field of criminal law.[27]

Law and Politics

The relationship in this case is obviously close. Politics is the study of government, of the organisation adopted by the members of a society living in a defined area for their own government in the general interest of peace and order.[28] Politics may be distinguished into political theory, thought or philosophy, the more theoretical study, concerned with the ways in which thinkers have considered that power in a state should be distributed and exercised,[29] and political science, the systematic study of political institutions, behaviour and the operation of political systems.[30]

As studies, jurisprudence and politics are interdependent and almost indistinguishable in origin, and the most profound thinking on the

---

[24] See Timasheff, *The Sociology of Law*; Ehrlich, *Fundamental Principles of the Sociology of Law*; Gurvitch, *Sociology of Law*; Aubert (ed.), *Sociology of Law*; Campbell and Wiles, *Law and Society*; sociology of law is closely related to sociological jurisprudence, which is rather the "applied" aspect of the relations of law and society, examining the legal system functionally, as it works and operates in society. On the latter, see Pound, *Jurisprudence*, I, 291 *et seq.*; Hunt, *The Sociological Movement in Law*; Rokumoto (ed.), *Sociological Theories of Law*.

[25] John Millar, Professor of Law in Glasgow University 1761–1801, wrote on *The Origin of the Distinction of Ranks*, which is important as an early sociological study. It is reprinted with a valuable introduction in Lehmann, *John Millar of Glasgow* (1961). See also Lehmann, "John Millar" (1961) 6 J.R.(N.S.) 218.

[26] Downes and Rock, *Understanding Deviance*; Maguire (ed.), *Oxford Handbook of Criminology*.

[27] See, *e.g.* Garland, *Punishment and Modern Society: A Study in Social Theory*.

[28] See further Heller, "Political Science" in *Encyc.Soc.Sc.*, XII, 207; Brecht and Wolin, "Political Theory" in *Encyc.Soc.Sc.*, XII, 307.

[29] *e.g.* Plato, *Republic*; Aristotle, *Politics*; Hobbes, *Leviathan*; Bentham, *Fragment on Government*; and see generally Sabine, *History of Political Theory*; Bowle, *Politics and Opinion in the Nineteenth Century*; Ebenstein, *Modern Political Thought*.

[30] See, *e.g.* Finer, *Major Governments of Modern Europe*; Wheare, *Federal Government*; Jennings, *Parliament* and *Cabinet Government*; Butler (ed.), *The Law, Politics and the Constitution*.

theoretical side, such as Aristotle's *Politics*, is common to both. In practice the studies of law and politics are inextricably enmeshed and inseparable.[31]

The framework of the political organisation of a community, its constitution, is set out in legal terms and legal forms and secured by legal means, and the subordinate standards, such as the structure and powers of the legislative assembly, the rights and liberties of citizens, the powers and duties of officials, the position of the police and their powers, the system of taxation and so on, are all defined by law. Even in a dictatorial regime, the dictator commonly secures his powers by law; in a democracy every power, control and regulation is a matter of law and effected by legal forms.

Conversely, the political structure of a society has as one of its primary purposes and duties the maintenance of a legal system, of law and order in the community, and in most modern organised societies the modification and reformation of the law in the interests of the community, or possibly of the politically dominant group thereof, is the prerogative of the legislative assembly, which is a part of the political framework, while the application to particular cases and enforcement of the legal principles is the function of other branches of the political organisation. It is clear, therefore, that the nature and content of a legal system may be largely determined by the views of those politically dominant at any given time.[32]

Law and Economics

Law and economics similarly overlap at many points. Economics is the study of human action in relation to the production, exchange, distribution and utilisation of wealth, or of "social phenomena centring about the provision for the material needs of the individual and of organised groups."[33]

As a study economics emerged from ethical, legal and political thinking. Adam Smith lectured and wrote on ethics and legal theory as well as on economics, and only in the nineteenth century did economics become distinct.[34] Like other studies economics is distinguishable into economic theory or economic thought and applied economics.

Much law springs from the necessity of regulating economic relations and exists for that purpose, while economic activities, such as buying and

---

[31] See further Pound, *Jurisprudence*, II, 283; Bryce, *Studies in History and Jurisprudence*, Essay X.

[32] Butler (ed.), *The Law, Politics and the Constitution*.

[33] Seligman, "Economics" in *Encyc.Soc.Sc.*, V, 344; and see Robbins, *Nature and Significance of Economic Science*; Robinson, "Law and Economics" (1938) 2 M.L.R. 257; de Roover and others, "Economic Thought" in *Int.Encyc.Soc.Sc.*, IV, 472.

[34] Adam Smith's works include *The Theory of Moral Sentiments* and *Lectures on Jurisprudence* as well as the *Wealth of Nations*. See further Scott, *Adam Smith as Student and Professor*; Fay, *Adam Smith and the Scotland of His Day*; Cooke, "Adam Smith and Jurisprudence" (1935) 51 L.Q.R. 326; and, more generally, Gide and Rist, *History of Economic Doctrines*; Roll, *History of Economic Thought*. See also Jones, *Historical Introduction to the Theory of Law*, Chap. 10 — "Law and Economic Theory."

selling, transport, manufacture and financial transactions, can flourish only within a regime of law and order and are shaped materially by the legal forms recognised in the community. Associations, such as companies and trade unions, are formed in legal ways and subject to legal regulation for economic ends. The salient economic relations such as sale, hiring, transport and employment are effected within a legal framework. The ancillaries which facilitate such relations, such as credit, bills, cheques, money and other modes of payment, securities for payment and insurances against loss, are all regulated by law.[35] Monopolies,[36] restrictive trading agreements, hire-purchase transactions and the protection of consumers from defective quality are spheres in which law and economics are increasingly interacting. General concepts, such as contract, property and succession on death, taxation and many more, need to be and can profitably be studied from both standpoints.[37] Not merely those engaged in industry or commerce but every individual every day enters into numerous transactions which have both legal and economic significance, the law determining whether it is permissible and in what form it may or must be effected, what its legal effect and consequences are and what can be done to enforce performance, and considerations of economics determining whether that transaction should be entered into or deferred or abandoned, on what terms, and whether completion will give satisfaction or not.

Law and Psychology

Psychology is concerned with investigating the mental processes of the individual, his instincts, beliefs, emotions, means of perception, feeling, remembering and thinking and their influences on his behaviour.[38] In legal contexts it is frequently material to determine such facts as the intention of a party, whether he could have or should have known something, the motive for his conduct, and so on. While the courts normally are content to ignore the underlying mental processes and draw inferences from facts external to the individual, the individual's mental state may be acutely important, as where the issues of insanity or diminished responsibility arise in criminal cases, and psychology may be valuable as giving insight into the springs of the conduct under investigation. In another context, psychology can cast light on the value or fallibility of oral[39] evidence and on the ways by which judges think.[40]

---

[35] See generally Oliver, *Law and Economics*; Coleman (ed.), *Law and Economics* (2 vols.); Prentice, *EEC Directives on Company Law and Financial Markets*.

[36] See, *e.g.* Lewis, "Monopoly and the Law" (1943) 6 M.L.R. 97; Hunter, *Competition and the Law*; Gerber, *Law and Competition in Twentieth Century Europe*.

[37] Weitzman and Maclean, *Economic Consequences of Divorce*.

[38] See Jastrow, "Psychology" in *Encyc.Soc.Sc.*, XII, 588; Bernard, "Social Psychology" in the same, XIV, 151; Waters and others, "Psychology" in *Int.Encyc.Soc.Sc.*; Hollander, *Principles and Methods of Social Psychology*; Farringdon, *Psychology, Law and Legal Processes*; Levine, *Law and Psychology*.

[39] Catler, *Mistaken Identification*.

[40] See Frank, *Law and the Modern Mind* and *Courts on Trial*.

Social psychology is the study of persons' conduct in their interactions with one another in their social and cultural setting, in family, work-group, gang or other group, with reference to the effects of this on their activities, feelings, emotions and habits. It stems from both psychology and sociology. Social conduct, and the person and the group's prejudices, convictions, attitudes, frames of reference and values may all be highly relevant to law and help to explain facts giving rise to legal issues.[41]

In investigating delinquency and criminal behaviour, psychology can sometimes assist by explaining the reasons for criminal conduct, by helping to devise suitable treatment and in persuading the offender to refrain from such conduct in future.[42]

Law and Geography
Much of the data of geography gives rise to legal problems, of landholding, land-use and development, the exploitation of minerals and natural resources, of the oceans and the sea-beds, of transport and communications. In international law frontiers and control of resources give rise to many legal problems. Not least in modern times the law is increasingly invoked in conserving the face of the earth and protecting nature from man.[43]

Overlap of the Social Sciences
The unity and overlap of the social sciences may be seen from the observation that each individual is simultaneously a unit in a number of co-existing systems. He is one in the social system as a male or a female, of the middle class or the working class, of an age group, of a particular religion, and so on; one in the political system as a supporter of one party or another, as a voter or abstainer, possibly as a councillor or party activist; one in the economic system as an employer or employee, a member of a union, a lender to a bank or a borrower from it, a consumer of imported food and so on; one in a social-psychological system as supporter of a football team or a follower of particular fashions; and one in a legal system as a taxpayer, buyer of a house disponed in security to a building society, a criminal who parked on a double yellow line, and so on. Each of the social sciences is interested in the individuals in the territory with which it is concerned but from a different standpoint and interested in different aspects of what he is and does. No one is only an Economic Man or a Political Man; he is both, and also a Legal Man. Justice is an ideal in social, political, economic, moral and legal thought.[44]

---

[41] See further Thouless, *General and Social Psychology*; McDougall, *Introduction to Social Psychology*; Newcomb, *Social Psychology*; Kimball Young, *Handbook of Social Psychology*; Jones, *Historical Introduction to the Theory of Law*, Chap. 7— "The Psychological Theories."

[42] Kapardis, *Psychology and Law*.

[43] See further R.S. Thoman, *Geography of International Trade*; P.H. Wagner, *The Human Use of the Earth*.

[44] *e.g.* Godwin, *Political Justice*; Miller, *Social Justice*; Kelsen, *What is Justice?*; Solomon and Murphy, *What is Justice?*

Relations with other Major Studies

Law and all the other social sciences also have extensive interaction with three other major fields of knowledge, namely history, philosophy and religion.

Law and History

History involves not only the tracing of the order of past happenings but elucidating the causal factors which helped to determine these happenings, and their effects and influence on every facet of the life of the society or institution whose history is being studied.[45] Each of the social sciences has a history of itself as a study or science, and also a history of the subject-matter of that science. The connection of law with history is very close. In the first place, both legal thought and every system of law, international, supranational and national, and every branch of these systems has its own history and course of development which can be traced, and which alone can in many cases provide the explanation for the existence today of apparently peculiar or irrational rules. In the second place, that history itself is only one facet of the general development of international and supranational institutions and relations, of the growth of the structure and organisation of each particular nation-state, and of the communities therein, and has to be related to the other facets, social, political, economic, religious and so on, of that history.[46] Legal history is, moreover, not merely a facet but largely a product of the more general history of the particular society and may repeatedly have been powerfully influenced by important events in other sectors of the general history of the community.[47] A country's legal history is inextricably entangled with its social, political, constitutional, economic and ecclesiastical history, and events primarily within any one of these facets of history may affect legal development. Thus in Scottish legal history important legal changes have been brought about by such events as the struggle for independence, the religious Reformation, the political unions with England under the Commonwealth and Protectorate and since 1707, the Jacobite rebellions, the industrial revolution, the two world wars, and so on.[48]

---

[45] See generally Berr and others, "History and Historiography" in *Encyc.Soc.Sc.*, VII, 357 *et seq.*; Gardiner and others, "History" in *Int.Encyc.Soc.Sc.*, VI, 434.

[46] History, without any explanatory adjective, is usually largely political and diplomatic history.

[47] See further Pound, *Interpretations of Legal History*.

[48] On these points, see further Chap. 4, *infra. cf.* Kames, *Historical Law Tracts*, preface, where he says: "Law in particular becomes then only a rational study, when it is traced historically, from its first rudiments among savages, through successive changes, to its highest improvements in a civilised society." See also Fraser Tytler's *Memoirs of Lord Kames*, I, 208: "There cannot indeed be a more pleasing exercise for the understanding, nor any that affords a greater scope for ingenuity, than the reciprocal elucidation of Law and of History, by the aids which they borrow from each other. Every law is a key to the history of the times in which it was framed, and may, in most instances, be traced up to the political emergency which required its enactment." So, too, Sir Walter Scott in *Guy Mannering*: "A lawyer without history or literature is a mechanic, a mere working mason; if he possesses some knowledge of these, he may venture to call himself an architect."

Historical study of law is of particular importance not only because it can frequently explain what is rationally inexplicable, but because it makes clear that particular rules cannot always be considered as immutable, or as embodying eternal or universal principles; they may proceed only from the prejudices or the exigencies of a particular time; their history explains them but does not justify them, leaving them open to criticism on other grounds.

Law and Philosophy

On its theoretical side, the study of law, as of other social sciences, inevitably impinges on various aspects of philosophy.[49] Philosophy is not a body of knowledge but a body of views on fundamental problems thought out and put forward at different times by very profound thinkers. There are views about the most general and most ultimate problems of every branch of knowledge and human activity, and about how we think and acquire knowledge itself. Originally, as among the Greeks, philosophy covered all subjects; early astronomy and physics grew out of philosophic speculation (hence the phrase "natural philosophy") and the "sciences," a word taken into general use only in the nineteenth century, only gradually separated from philosophy. It is not so much a body of knowledge as a questioning attitude of mind, a seeking for understanding, a critical, reflective activity of examining man's ideas, values, thinking, beliefs, attitudes and conduct. It consists of man's efforts to reflect deeply in a rational, methodical and systematic way on the problems of greatest concern to man. It is consequently central to all intellectual studies. It has no subject-matter of its own but is a method or type of mental operation which can take as its object any area or subject-matter or type of experience. Major objects of philosophic consideration are metaphysics (theory of the ultimate nature of Being), epistemology (theory of knowledge), philosophy of mind, logic (the study of reasoning and argument), aesthetics (theory of beauty), moral philosophy (theory of conduct), social philosophy, political philosophy, philosophy of law, philosophy of science, and so on. For centuries law and politics had a common philosophic foundation,[50] while economics and sociology emerged later from this same body of thought. Only in the nineteenth century did law tend to be divorced from politics and economics, but a countermovement, starting in the latter half of the nineteenth century, urged the unification of the social sciences, stressing the interrelation and interaction of all and their common background of philosophical thinking. The study

---

[49] See Dewey, "Philosophy" in *Encyc.Soc.Sc.*, XII, 118; Emmet and Hobbs, "Ethics" in *Int.Encyc.Soc.Sc.*; Edwards (ed.), *Encyclopaedia of Philosophy* (8 vols., 1967); Passmore, *A Hundred Years of Philosophy.*

[50] See Cairns, *Legal Philosophy from Plato to Hegel*; Cohen, "Philosophy and Legal Science" (1932) 32 Col.L.R. 1103; Gordley, *Philosophy and the Development of Modern Contract Doctrine.*

of law, as of all the other social sciences, inevitably leads to questions of the rightness or wrongness of conduct, the ends sought to be attained, the justifiability of means and ends, the problem of justice, the validity of reasoning, the meanings of the terms used and the proper use of terminology, and so on, all of which are essentially philosophic problems. The philosophy of law, or the critical examination of the propositions, presuppositions and underlying ideas of legal systems in the light of philosophical ideas and methods is an important part of jurisprudence (in the narrower sense of that word).

Of the recognised branches of philosophy three, logic and scientific method, moral philosophy and political philosophy, are vitally important, because the light they cast on problems of law and the study of law in relation to and in the light of these branches, forms legal philosophy or philosophy of law. Other branches such as epistemology, philosophy of man, philosophy of mind, aesthetics and metaphysics have lesser connection with legal studies.

Logic and scientific method serves an important purpose by clarifying ideas as to thinking and reasoning, and as to the validity of inferences drawn from initial propositions.[51] Law has many logical characteristics; it is a body of propositions, some general, some particular, forming a more or less systematic structure, and legal principles and problems can be classified, defined and distinguished. While logic does assist in legal thinking, it does not by itself ensure legally correct or just answers. At most it tests the correctness of thinking, but the basis for the reasoning may still be legally inaccurate,[52] and the final determination of a legal issue may be a matter of policy or discretion[53] not determined by logic at all. Logic does not provide, or guarantee the correctness of, the bases for reasoning. Thus a judge's finding that one spouse had committed adultery is a basis for logical reasoning to a legal conclusion, but cannot itself be checked or controverted by logic.[54]

Ethics or moral philosophy is the normative science of the conduct of human beings living in societies; it studies human conduct and seeks to determine standards for judging its goodness or badness, rightness or

---

[51] "No science affords more opportunity for exerting the reasoning faculty than that of law": Kames, *Elucidations*, preface.

[52] Thus logically valid conclusions in a particular case could be drawn from an initial general premiss such as: In Scotland a wife can divorce her husband for incompatibility of temperament, though that premiss is legally unsound, and any conclusion therefrom consequently legally unsound also. See, *e.g.* R.H. Thouless, *Straight and Crooked Thinking*; E.R. Emmet, *The Use of Reason*; H.J. Berman, "Legal Reasoning" in *Int.Encyc.Soc.Sc.*, IX, 197.

[53] *e.g.* the appropriate sum to award as damages, the appropriate penalty, whether to give custody of a child to one parent or the other.

[54] On the place of logic in law, see further Cohen, "The Place of Logic in the Law" (1915) 29 H.L.R. 622; Dewey, "Logical Method and Law" (1924) 10 Cornell L.Q. 17; Lloyd, "Reason and Logic in the Common Law" (1948) 64 L.Q.R. 468; Guest, "Logic in the Law" in *Oxford Essays in Jurisprudence*, 176; Castberg, *Problems of Legal Philosophy*, Chap. 3.

wrongness, and accordingly evaluates conduct by reference to some such criterion as whether it promotes the general happiness or could without absurdity be generalised into a universal rule of conduct.[55] It examines the validity of such standards and the meaning of such concepts as "right," "duty," "good," "ought," "liability" and "responsibility." Distinct from but related to moral philosophy is practical morality, the examination of what people in practice regard as right or wrong, which also has great relevance to legal issues. Its overlap with law is obvious; both study and approve or censure human conduct, but using different standards. Acutely difficult but interesting problems arise as to whether, and how far, law should seek to promote and secure ethical values; should it, for example, punish conduct which is morally objectionable but may be harmless to the general community? How far can a child of five be held "responsible" for wrongdoing? How far, again, are a person's motives and intentions relevant to his moral guilt and to his legal guilt? Legal phenomena are also moral phenomena.[56] Moral claims or rights and legal claims or rights may coincide. Thus a person injured by the fault of another has a legal claim against that other for compensation and most people would say that he has a moral claim also, or indeed that he has a legal claim because the law recognises his moral claim. In other cases, the two may diverge; a beggar may have a moral claim to alms, but he has no legal claim. Similarly, moral duties and legal duties may coincide, such as not to kill or to steal, or they may differ. There is no general legal duty to try to rescue a person in danger, but there may be a moral one. To some extent, as society develops there is a constant trend to recognise moral claims and duties as legal ones also.

In some cases, an individual may find a conflict between his or her moral views of right and wrong and his or her legal duty to obey the law. Thus individuals sometimes, for moral reasons, refuse to obey the law, and whether there is justification for this may be an acutely difficult issue.[57] An interesting instance of the intrusion of ethics into law is the City Code on Take-overs and Mergers formulated by a working party to consider good business practice in the conduct of take-overs and mergers of companies. The Code is formulated in writing, is detailed and substantial, but is a code of business ethics, not a code of law, and the main sanctions for contravention are public censure and private reprimand by the Panel on Take-overs and Mergers.

Law has always been connected with the exercise of power in states and political philosophy or the study of how power should be distributed and

---

[55] The literature is enormous; good modern introductions are Lillie, *An Introduction to Ethics*; Hospers, *Human Conduct: An Introduction to the Problems of Ethics*; Williams, *Morality: An Introduction to Ethics.* See also Sidgwick, *History of Ethics.*

[56] Miller, *Lectures on the Philosophy of Law*, 9.

[57] See, *e.g.* K. Greenawalt, *Conflicts of Law and Morality.*

exercised in states is accordingly important for law. The difference between the legal systems of states organised as dictatorships and those organised as liberal democracies is readily apparent. At the theoretical level, politics and law constantly interact and influence each other. Very important is the question whether law should or can check political action; is government subject to law?

In some respects, the law treats of matters ethically neutral, as when it lays down the rule of the road and the rules as to authentication of deeds, where there has to be a rule, though the rule currently adopted in Scotland can hardly be said to be good or bad in comparison with the alternative, but many matters raising legal issues also raise moral issues.[58] The overlap between ethics and law is important in relation to the conduct of individuals practising skilled professions, including law, and may give guidance on what a person may fairly and rightly do or not do in particular circumstances.[59] Thus many professions have formal or informal, written or unwritten, rules of professional ethics or codes of conduct.

Moral or ethical views are particularly important in some areas of medical science and many modern developments in medicine raise acutely difficult moral and ethical issues, such as of the rightness or wrongness, in particular circumstances, of abortion,[60] contraception, euthanasia,[61] artificial insemination, *in vitro* fertilisation,[62] or the like. Some of these techniques may be controlled only by the participant's view of the moral rightness or wrongness of using the relevant technique, some are controlled by law, and some, in the views of certain people, should be controlled by law or banned and made punishable. Much medical ethics involves the application of moral theories and beliefs to medical problems.[63]

The concept of justice and the relations between human law and ideal justice are other topics of common interest to law and ethics.

The examination of moral problems inherent in legal issues leads on in some cases to metaphysical problems such as, for example, the status and

---

[58] See among many books, Pound, *Law and Morals; Introduction to the Philosophy of Law; Jurisprudence*, II, 215; Stone, *Province and Function of Law*, Chap. 16; Friedmann, *Legal Theory*; Cahn, *The Moral Decision*; Goodhart, *English Law and the Moral Law*; Lloyd, *Public Policy*; Hart, *Punishment and Responsibility; Law, Liberty and Morality*; Hacker and Raz (ed.), *Law, Morality and Society*; Feinberg, *The Moral Limits of the Criminal Law* (4 vols.); Greenawalt, *Conflicts of Law and Morality*; Raz, *The Morality of Freedom*; Perry, *Morality, Politics and Law*; see also Ames, "Law and Morals" (1909) 22 H.L.R. 97; Winfield, "Ethics in English Case Law" (1931) 45 H.L.R. 112, and *Select Legal Essays*, 266; Cohen, "Philosophy and Legal Science" (1932) 32 Col.L.R. 1103, and in *Law and the Social Order* (1933), 219; Cohen, "Law and Scientific Method" in the same, 184; Cohen, "Moral Aspects of the Criminal Law" (1940) 49 Yale L.J. 987; Hart, "Positivism and the Separation of Law and Morals" (1958) 71 H.L.R. 593; Fuller, "Positivism and Fidelity to Law," *ibid.*, 630.

[59] *e.g.* Cranston (ed.), *Legal Ethics and Professional Responsibility* (1996); Parker and Sampford (ed.), *Legal Ethics and Legal Practice* (1996).

[60] See Abortion Act 1967.

[61] Keown (ed.), *Euthanasia Examined*.

[62] See Human Fertilisation and Embryology Act 1990.

[63] See further Beauchamp and Childress, *Principles of Biomedical Ethics* (1979).

existence of universal propositions, such as that all persons should obey the law, or what a rule of law, in the most general sense, is, or to the examination of the most abstract general ideas, such as Right, Freedom or Liability. One point at which everyday law touches metaphysics is when we speak of an accident "causing" injuries and are driven to inquire what is really meant by "cause" and "causation."[64] So, too, deep study of legal issues leads on to such questions as human and divine justice, crime and sin, and the legal attitude to life and death.[65] All these and similar problems go to make up that part of jurisprudence known as philosophy of law.

Law and Religion

Religion is not usually regarded as a social science, but it is inseparable from the social sciences.[66] Many of the most critical problems in the social sciences involve a religious factor. The attitudes, beliefs, faiths and practices which constitute religion have important connections with law. In early and primitive societies law is frequently conceived as existing by divine revelation. Much law grew out of religion and priests were commonly repositories of legal knowledge and had wide, or even exclusive, jurisdictional powers. Religion, morals and law were indistinguishably blended.[67] In early Scotland most of the literate men, including those who worked as judges, notaries and in other capacities in the administration of law, were clerics. Like law, religion is a vast subject of study with its own history, philosophy, theology, institutions, variant bodies of doctrines and forms,[68] but in practice in many societies it is a powerful social control which provides ways of life and codes of conduct which are major forces regulating men's actings in many contexts, which impel men to act in certain ways and deter them from acting in others. Religion's systems include moral principles and precepts and a person's views on many legal issues are likely to be influenced by both his moral and his religious views.

---

[64] See Hart and Honoré, *Causation in the Law*; Castberg, *Problems of Legal Philosophy*, Chap. 4.

[65] Books casting interesting light on such problems are Williams, *The Sanctity of Life and the Criminal Law*, and St. John-Stevas, *Life, Death and the Law*. See also Lord Devlin, "The Enforcement of Morals" (British Academy Maccabaean Lecture, 1959), also in *The Enforcement of Morals* (1968); Hart, *Law, Liberty and Morality*.

[66] See generally Bertholet, "Religion" in *Encyc.Soc.Sc.*, XIII, 229; Gertz and others, "Religion" in *Int.Encyc.Soc.Sc.*, XIII, 398; Wilson, *Religion in Secular Society*; Lyall, "Religion and Law" 1976 J.R. 58.

[67] Maine, *Ancient Law*, Chap. 1.

[68] There are many parallels between law and religion, the books of authority, the ritual of courts, the part played by priests and judges, the complicated bodies of dogma, the distinction between crime and sin, and others. See generally Yinger, *The Scientific Study of Religion*; Weber, *The Protestant Ethic and the Spirit of Capitalism*; Tawney, *Religion and the Rise of Capitalism*; Lenski, *The Religious Factor: A Sociological Study of Religion's Impact on Politics, Economics and Family Life*; Hill, *Society and Puritanism in Pre-Revolutionary England*; St. John-Stevas, *Life, Death and the Law*.

Christianity has powerfully influenced all the legal systems of Western Europe, both in general and in particular ways at particular times. The underlying ideas of religion, belief in the value of the human personality, in justice, sympathy, charity, forgiveness, honour and truth have similarly penetrated legal practices and influenced legal rules. The Christian Church itself developed an extensive and refined system of law, the canon law,[69] which had wide influence on many spheres of activity, particularly before the Reformation, and had permanent influence on secular legal systems.

The canon law of the Roman Church not only regulated the church and the clergy but considerable areas of lay life which were deemed to have religious overtones, and courts staffed by clerics applying canon law exercised wide jurisdiction. After the Reformation of 1560 the reformed church and its strict body of religious beliefs strongly influenced the state and its laws; membership of the established Church was a requisite for holding most offices. Much morality was based on the Bible[70] and the Bible was regularly referred to as authority for many matters, such as on marriage and divorce, contract, witchcraft, evidence, and other matters.[71] The Reformed Church, its assemblies and ministers were very powerful influences on parliament and the courts, on public opinion, morality and social conduct, while dispute on matters of religious beliefs and practices, the government of the Church, by episcopacy or presbyterianism, gave rise to many conflicts. Toleration of religious minorities (Episcopalians, Jews, Catholics) has only gradually been accepted, and their churches are voluntary associations whereas the Church of Scotland is legally established. Many legislators and judges have had strong religious convictions which have influenced their views on legal issues, and the development of the hard-working attitude of the Scot has been linked with the acceptance of Calvinism.[72]

In modern Scotland the influence of religion and religious leaders has been less but is not negligible. The law still protects religion against blasphemy. The continuing practice of taking oaths rests on generally accepted beliefs in a God who punishes oath-breaking and that an oath does bind, oblige and constrain the taker not to contravene his oath. Religious views affect views on such topics as adultery, contraception, prostitution, homosexuality, divorce; are they sinful?; should they be criminal,[73] or tolerated but disapproved, or fully accepted?

---

[69] On the canon law see further Chaps. 2 and 3, *infra*.

[70] Kent, *Israel's Laws and Legal Precedents*; Daube, *Studies in Biblical Law*.

[71] H.J. Berman, *The Interaction of Law and Religion*; Bryce, "The Relations of Law and Religion" in *Studies in History and Jurisprudence*, II, 638; Denning, *The Changing Law* (1953), 99 *et seq*.

[72] Max Weber, *The Protestant Ethic and the Spirit of Capitalism*; G. Marshall, *Presbyteries and Profits* (1980).

[73] Adultery was at one time a capital crime by Scots law. On prostitution see Sexual Offences (Scotland) Act 1976. On homosexuality see Sexual Offences Act 1967, s. 1 (England); Crimial Justice (Scotland) Act 1980, s. 80; and *T., Petitioner*, 1996 S.C.L.R. 897.

In some other countries, religion is still a very potent force in government and law. In modern Israel, religion is a strong force regulating state and law.[74] In Islamic countries, religion, the precepts of the Koran and its expositors, strongly influence government and law.[75]

The Theoretical and Practical Sides of Legal Science

Like the other main social sciences, legal science has two sides to its study; there is the theoretical and philosophical study, seeking to classify, rationalise, explain, restate, criticise and evaluate the existing principles of law, to trace their origins, examine their consistency one with another, compare them with those accepted at earlier periods or in other contemporary societies, to relate them to their philosophical bases and evaluate them by ideal standards, and to give consideration to their amendment and reform. This side is concerned with such questions as why the law is what it is, what it has been, what it is elsewhere, how its terms are used, and its rules classified and arranged, whether it is fair or not and whether it should be otherwise. Secondly, there is the study of law as a reasonably coherent and systematic body of principles and rules capable of practical application to the affairs of men in everyday life, to the defining of their claims and liabilities in particular circumstances and to the resolution of their controversies and the decision of disputes. This side is concerned with what the existing law prescribes, permits or forbids, and with its application to specific people in particular circumstances. Sir Frederick Pollock once distinguished between the practice of law as an art, and the study of law as a science. So, too, law has been called "social engineering" by analogy with the way in which principles of physical science can be used by engineers for practical ends. In the university the emphasis is naturally on the study of law as a science, with pure law; in everyday life the emphasis is on law as a practical art, with applied law.

This distinction is sometimes drawn in some other studies by a distinction in names, such as that between economic theory and economic science or applied economics, political philosophy or theory or thought and political science or politics or government, social theory or philosophy or sociology and social science, moral philosophy or ethics and morals or morality, science of religion and religious beliefs and practices, pure (natural) science or natural philosophy and applied science, and so on, though the terminology is not always consistent and there is no clear or sharp line of division between the more theoretical and the more practical or applied aspects of any branch of knowledge. In legal studies, this same

---

[74] Hecht (ed.), *Introduction to the Sources and History of Jewish Law*, Chap. 15.
[75] Schacht, *Introduction to Islamic Law*.

distinction is sometimes drawn between jurisprudence[76] or legal theory and philosophy, and law or legal principles or legal dogmatics or even legal science (in a narrower sense of that phrase), though the term Law is more commonly used for both sides of legal science. In every case, the pure or more theoretical and philosophical study and the applied or more practical overlap and their problems constantly run into one another. A problem of practical application may require for its answer a thorough examination of the theoretical basis of the principle to be applied. But it is important to note that law is not only, or even primarily, a body of rules or formulae for practical application to the solution of concrete problems. This is the obvious, the common, aspect of law but not by any means the whole of law as a science or as a study, since the theory and the abstract principles underlie every particular rule and application.

Legal Science

Legal science is accordingly the systematised body of knowledge concerned with law in the most general sense of that word, the systematic examination and exposition of matters legal, institutions, offices, doctrines, principles and rules, concepts and techniques. What then is law? A full study of the nature of law is an important branch of jurisprudence and legal philosophy and it is a topic of much complexity. But it is desirable at an early stage in legal studies to formulate a provisional idea of the general nature of law which can be corrected and refined in the light of later study. It is necessary at once to put aside such uses of the term "law" as in "law of gravitation" or the other so-called "laws" of the natural sciences, since these physical or scientific "laws" are generalisations explaining various uniformities in the phenomena of nature, *descriptive of what happens* in certain defined circumstances,[77] or similar "laws" in the social sciences, such as the "law of diminishing returns" in economics, and also such uses as "natural" or "moral" law, which expresses an ideal

---

[76] The term jurisprudence may accordingly be used, first, as earlier in this chapter, in its widest and most general sense, as *juris prudentia* or *juris scientia*, for legal science, or the science of law; secondly, for that branch of legal science which deals with general problems of the theory of law, particularly with the examination of the concepts and terminology of law, "the comparative anatomy of developed systems of law", and sometimes including also problems of the philosophy of law (on this sense, see further p. 52, *infra*); and occasionally, thirdly, as a grandiloquent synonym for the dogmatic principles of one legal system or a branch thereof, *e.g.* Scottish jurisprudence, medical jurisprudence. In France *la jurisprudence* means what we call case law (on which see Chap. 10). Jurisprudence in its second sense is an important element in legal studies, just as is law, *i.e.* the dogmatic exposition of accepted principles. The terminology is further complicated by the fact that some writers speak of "the science of jurisprudence" (in the second sense), or call jurisprudence (in the second sense) the "science of law", as distinct from dogmatic exposition of law, which itself is sometimes called "legal science" (in the narrower sense of that phrase). These words and phrases do not have completely fixed or settled usages or meanings. See further Campbell, "A Note on the Word 'Jurisprudence' " (1942) 58 L.Q.R. 334.

[77] Salmond, *Jurisprudence* (12th ed.), 24; Holland, *Jurisprudence* (13th ed.), 17.

standard of conduct to which rules of positive law, *i.e.* the law laid down in particular communities, *ought to* conform so as to make human conduct be in accordance with moral beliefs as to right and wrong. This latter use of the term "law" is, however, nearer to the jural significance in that it has the connotation of a rule for human conduct which is absent from the former, purely descriptive, use.

It is also necessary to distinguish "a law," or a single principle or rule, and the plural "laws," and the phrase "the law," used both of the totality of laws of a country, *e.g.* the law of Scotland, and of a distinct division of such a totality, *e.g.* the law of property, all of which connote bodies of actual principles and rules, from the abstract notion of law itself.

In the sense which is of jural significance, the law consists of a body of rules or precepts or norms for the regulation of social conduct, recognised as obligatory, and enforceable. Rules of law are *prescriptive* of conduct, prescribing what must be done, not merely descriptive of what happens. Different jurists emphasise different aspects of this body of rules. Thus some[78] stress the fact that those rules which are termed "law" are based on the will and force of the organised political community, the state, and define law as the commands of superior authority. This serves to distinguish rules of law from customary practices and rules voluntarily agreed upon and observed by particular groups, from conduct merely habitual or accepted by reason of moral or religious belief.

Others stress the source of the principles of law, calling it "the dictate of reason, determining every rational being to that which is congruous and convenient for the nature and condition thereof."[79]

Others emphasise the end to be attained by those rules of social conduct, defining it, for example, as "the body of principles recognised and applied by the state in the administration of justice"[80] or "the expression of the idea of right involved in the relation of two or more human beings,"[81] or "the sum of the rules of justice administered in a state and by its authority,"[82] and these views reflect the very prevalent belief that law is and should be related to right and justice, that it does not exist merely to regulate life or resolve controversies but exists to do so in a manner consistent with justice.

In recent times law has been regarded and defined largely by reference to its function in society, sometimes with an emphasis on the way in which it is applied by the courts. For example: "The prophecies of what courts will do in fact and nothing more pretentious, are what I mean by the law."[83] "What these officials [judges or sheriffs or clerks or jailers or

---

[78] *e.g.* Hobbes, Bentham, Austin, Amos, Markby, Holland.
[79] Stair, *Inst.,* I, 1, 1.
[80] Salmond, *Jurisprudence*, 41.
[81] Miller, *Philosophy of Law*, 9.
[82] Pollock, *First Book of Jurisprudence*, 17.
[83] Holmes, "The Path of the Law" (1897) 10 H.L.R. 457, 461.

lawyers] do about disputes is, to my mind, the law itself."[84] "A body of social rules prescribing external conduct and considered justiciable."[85] Other definitions emphasise that its function is to resolve conflicts of claims and interests of individuals and groups and to harmonise their differing desires with the minimum of disagreement. Stress is also sometimes laid on the fact that law in the abstract, in the most general sense of the word, or the legal order of society is more than the total of the specific rules.[86] The law is "the body of precepts and received ideals and the technique of using them, established or recognised by organised human society for the delimitation and securing of interests" (an interest being a demand or want or desire which human beings either individually or in groups seek to satisfy and of which the ordering of human relations in civilised society must take account).[87] Or again: "The legal order is a regime of adjusting relations and ordering conduct through the systematic and orderly application of the force of a politically organised society, in order to prevent friction in human use and enjoyment of the goods of existence and eliminate waste of them."[88] Law or the legal order in society is a social force, a complex network which comprises ideals, such as justice, institutions, such as courts, persons, such as judges and policemen, precepts, both general principles and detailed rules, techniques of interpreting and applying them, procedures and practices, which grow up as a society develops, subject to many influences, and existing to regulate the organisation of the society, its relations to other similar societies, to maintain order and decent conditions of life, and to resolve conflicting claims between members of the society. It is more than the total of the principles and rules, and they are not all of the same nature.

Law as Social Control

The legal system of a country is in substance a form of social control; that is, a body of principles and rules regulative of human conduct in society, persuading persons to do some things and constraining them from doing others.[89] It is thus intimately related to the social functions that are the subject-matter of the other social sciences and to the regulative

---

[84] Llewellyn, *The Bramble Bush*, 3.

[85] Kantorowicz, *The Definition of Law*, 79.

[86] If "law" is merely a totality of laws, a computer disk could be the most learned lawyer in the world. But there is more to law than that.

[87] Pound, "Theory of Social Interests," in Hall, *Readings in Jurisprudence*, 238; see also Pound, "A Survey of Social Interests" (1943) 57 H.L.R. 1, reprinted in Vanderbilt, *Studying Law*, 439, and *Jurisprudence*, III, Chaps. 14 and 15.

[88] Pound, "Introduction to American Law," in Vanderbilt, *Studying Law*, 379, and *Justice According to Law*, 48. On the problems of defining law see Hart, *The Concept of Law*, Chap. 1.

[89] On social controls generally, see MacIver and Page, *Society*, 137 *et seq.*; 175–181. The concept is a sociological one and an example of the influence this science has had on the study of law. See further Everett, "Social Control," *Encyc.Soc.Sc.*, IV, 344; Pound, *Social Control through Law*; Bodenheimer, *Jurisprudence*, Chap. 13.

influence of social, religious and moral beliefs. The main bodies of rules which exist and operate as social controls in this way are law, religion, morals, custom, fashion, convention, etiquette, and professional, club, trade or union rules.[90] Each has its distinctive forms of sanction brought to bear on one who transgresses the rules. In many particular sets of circumstances conduct such as stealing may contravene several sets of rules and several of these social controls may all be operating simultaneously on an individual and influencing his conduct. Thus conscience pricks him for doing wrong, religious feeling causes remorse for sin, custom and habit of society frown on his conduct and may result in his being shunned, despised or ostracised, while the legal order may cause him to be fined or imprisoned or forced to pay compensation for what he has done.

State law, however, differs from the other social controls in that it is more widespread, extending to and covering far more activities than does any other form of control, its rules are more fixed and definite, being frequently prescribed in a strict verbal form, its operation extends in general to all persons subject to the state's authority, its authority is greater in that it may override and cancel the prescriptions of other social controls, and, lastly, it alone may be enforced by the whole authority of the state by means of fines, imprisonment or pecuniary compensation. Law is accordingly a very important form of social control, of regulative influence, over practically every form of human conduct.

The concept of law as social control is one which provides a readily comprehensible idea of the notion of law in general, and the other definitions quoted may be treated as simply more particularised statements, emphasising respectively the fact of enforcement by the state, the aim of securing justice, and the mode of functioning of the law.

The Methods of Legal Science

The full understanding of a legal system or any branch of it requires study from four standpoints; these are the analytical, breaking down the problem-situation and ascertaining what elements compose it and what rules are applicable to each part of the subject and its problems; the historical, ascertaining how and why these rules have come to be accepted and to take their modern form; the philosophical, considering whether those rules are consistent with the needs of society, and with accepted ideas of right and justice; and the comparative, seeing how other societies at a similar stage of civilisation face up to the same or corresponding problems. For proper appreciation, that is, one must find out what the rules are here and now, what they once were and how and why they have come to be what they are, whether they are satisfactory judged by an ideal

---

[90] See also Schauer, *Playing by the Rules*.

standard, and how they appear compared with the rules which are accepted elsewhere.[91]

Law and the Legal System

The application of the controlling factor in society which is called "law" to various sets of circumstances requires the existence in each independent society of a legal system, which comprises a complex of legislative organs,[92] executive agencies,[93] an establishment of courts and tribunals,[94] of individuals who act as judges, clerks, prosecutors, gaolers, legal representatives and advisers, and in other capacities,[95] a coherent body of particular principles, doctrines and rules of law,[96] with techniques of handling them[97] and means for amending, restating and adding to them,[98] and an apparatus of procedure whereby individuals may bring controversies and conflicts of claims before the courts for resolution.[99] It is this legal system in any particular country which individualises the general concept of law into specific principles and rules and applies them to the determination of specific controversies.

The Scottish Legal System

Within the territorial limits designated as Scotland, the state has developed an organisation of courts and legal practitioners, a body of principles, rules and precepts, and a body of knowledge and thinking about law which amounts to the Scottish legal system. It is largely indigenous, having grown and developed naturally within the country rather than having been imposed from without, yet it is not narrowly parochial, having shared in drawing something from the legal systems of antiquity, nor yet insular, having strong historical connections and logical affinities with legal systems of and derived from continental Europe. It is unitary in that it has grown as a body rather than been formed by aggregation or merging of substantially different elements; it is reasonably simple in being remarkably free from anomalies, absurdities and historical survivals which have outlived their usefulness and their justification; and it is firmly rooted in general principles, so that much can be explained as deduction from, or detailed working out of, great overriding principles based on reason and justice. Accordingly, the main elements in the

---

[91] Bryce, "The Methods of Legal Science" in *Studies in History and Jurisprudence*, II, 607; Kantorowicz and Patterson, "Legal Science: A Summary of Its Methodology" (1928) 28 Col.L.R. 679.

[92] Chap. 6, *infra*.

[93] Chap. 7, *infra*.

[94] Chap. 8, *infra*.

[95] Chap. 9, *infra*.

[96] Chaps. 10–11, *infra*.

[97] Chap. 14, *infra*.

[98] Chap. 14, *infra.*

[99] Chaps. 12–13, *infra*.

Scottish legal system which will require detailed examination are the history and systematic structure of the law, the organisation of courts and the personnel of the law, and the principles and rules applicable to various sets of circumstances.

Conclusion

Legal science, or jurisprudence (in its broad sense), or the study of law in its most general sense, is a body of knowledge akin to and related to politics, economics, and other studies of human behaviour, activities and relations; like them, it has an historical aspect, a theoretical and philosophic aspect (jurisprudence in the narrow sense),[1] a comparative aspect and a doctrinal aspect, dealing with the actual content of specific legal systems, international, supranational and national, which sets out the currently accepted principles and rules. The present book seeks to deal with some of the main elements in the historical, comparative and theoretical aspects of the law of Scotland and of its most general doctrines and structure as an introduction to the detailed study of its dogmatic content and of the applications thereof to particular problems, and ultimately to the study of the philosophy of law.

FURTHER READING

Law and the Social Sciences
Arnold: *The Folklore of Capitalism.*
Barnes and Becker: *Social Thought from Lore to Science.*
Cairns: *Law and the Social Sciences.*
Carlston: *Law and the Structures of Social Action.*
Cohen: *Law and the Social Order.*
Cohen and Cohen: *Readings in Jurisprudence and Legal Philosophy*, Part 4.
Dicey: *Law and Public Opinion in England in the Nineteenth Century.*
Friedmann: *Law in a Changing Society.*
Ginsberg (ed.): *Law and Opinion in England in the Twentieth Century.*
Gurvitch: *Sociology of Law.*
Hall: *Readings in Jurisprudence*, Part 3.
Hartley and Griffith: *Government and Law.*
Ogburn and Goldenweiser (eds.): *The Social Sciences and their Interrelations.*
Patterson: *Jurisprudence.*
Pound: *Social Control through Law.*
Robson: *Civilisation and the Growth of Law.*
Sawer: *Law in Society.*
Stone: *The Province and Function of Law*, Part 3.
        Social Dimensions of Law and Justice.

---

[1] Some books on jurisprudence are mainly concerned with legal theory (classification, terminology, etc.), others with legal philosophy (ideals, justice, etc.), but the two branches are not separable and the titles of books on jurisprudence frequently use the terms "theory" and "philosophy" indifferently.

Law and History
Bryce: *Studies in History and Jurisprudence.*
Diamond: *Evolution of Law and Order.*
       Primitive Law, Past and Present.
Holdsworth: *Sources and Literature of English Law.*
       History of English Law, 17 vols.
Keir: *Constitutional History of Modern Britain.*
Lupoi: *On the Origins of the European Legal Order.*
Macdonnell and Manson (ed.): *Great Jurists of the World.*
McKechnie (ed.): *Sources and Literature of Scots Law.*
Maine: *Ancient Law.*
Paton (ed.): *Introduction to Scottish Legal History.*
Pollock and Maitland: *History of English Law before Edward I.*
Stein: *Roman Law in European History.*
Ullman: *Principles of Government and Politics in the Middle Ages.*
Vinogradoff: *Historical Jurisprudence*, 2 vols.
Walker: *Legal History of Scotland*, 6 vols.
       The Scottish Jurists.
Winfield: *Chief Sources of English Legal History.*

Law and Philosophy
Barker: *Principles of Social and Political Theory.*
Berolzheimer: *The World's Legal Philosophies.*
Cahn: *The Moral Decision.*
Cairns: *Legal Philosophy from Plato to Hegel.*
       Theory of Legal Science.
Cohen: *Ethical Systems and Legal Ideals.*
Cohen and Cohen: *Readings in Jurisprudence and Legal Philosophy*, Part 3.
D'Entrèves: *Natural Law.*
Duff: *Philosophy and the Criminal Law.*
Friedrich: *Philosophy of Law in Historical Perspective.*
Goodhart: *English Law and the Moral Law.*
Hall: *Readings in Jurisprudence*, Part 1.
Hamburger: *Morals and Law—Aristotle's Legal Theory.*
Hart: *Law, Liberty and Morality.*
       Punishment and Responsibility.
       The Concept of Law.
Hayek: *Law, Legislation and Liberty.*
Jones: *Historical Introduction to the Theory of Law.*
Morris: *The Great Legal Philosophers.*
Patterson: *Jurisprudence.*
Pound: *Law and Morals.*
       Introduction to the Philosophy of Law.
Radin: *Law as Logic and Experience.*
Raz: *The Concept of a Legal System.*
Rubin: *Ethics and Authority in International Law.*
Stone: *The Province and Functions of Law*, Parts 1 and 2.
       Legal System and Lawyer's Reasonings.
       Human Law and Human Justice.

Law and Religion
Daube: *Studies in Biblical Law.*
Fyzee: *Outlines of Muhammadan Law.*
Hecht: *Introduction to the History and Sources of Jewish Law.*
Kagan: *Three Great Systems of Jurisprudence.*
Kent: *Israel's Laws and Legal Precedents.*
Micklem: *Law and the Laws.*

CHAPTER 2

THE DIVISIONS OF LEGAL SCIENCE

IT conduces to completeness of understanding and effective study of legal science to divide up the whole subject-matter of legal science into a number of distinguishable and fairly distinct divisions or subjects.[1] No division of the subject-matter of legal studies is wholly satisfactory[2] and, however it be done, some topics are difficult to classify, while others again fall logically into more than one class. There is necessarily overlapping at the edges in any such classification, but this is no bad thing because it emphasises that the whole of legal knowledge is ultimately a unity which in turn has very indefinite frontiers with other fields of knowledge.[3] Knowledge gained from the study of one division may cast light on a problem within another division. Moreover, legal controversies not infrequently involve issues pertaining to several of the divisions so that the convenience of such a division should not be allowed to lead to mental compartmentation. Proper classification of legal problems may also be of practical importance with regard both to finding the law, and correct application of the rules.

A generally satisfactory fundamental division of legal science is into (1) legal history, or the study of the development of legal institutions, ideas and doctrines in civilised communities, and particularly in our own community; (2) legal theory and philosophy, or jurisprudence, dealing with the most general ideas about law; (3) comparative legal studies, comparing and contrasting the attitudes adopted by different legal systems to particular problems, their different organisations of justice and courts, their different modes of thinking, and so on; (4) international law, or the body of law governing international institutions such as the United Nations and existing as between independent sovereign states and political communities; (5) supranational law, or the law of regional organisations of political communities; and (6) the various bodies of state, national or municipal law operating within these various states and communities and

---

[1] The student should observe that the division into branches does not necessarily correspond in number, name or scope with the subjects of a university degree curriculum.

[2] Stair, I, 1, 3–12, distinguished the law of nature (or equity, or the moral law), the positive law of God, and human law, which is further distinguished into the law of nations (*i.e.* international law) and the law of each society of people, or their civil law. Erskine, I, 1, 7, divides law into the law of nature (*i.e.* roughly jurisprudence), the law of nations, and civil or municipal law. So too Mackenzie, *Inst.*, I, 1, 3. See also Bankt., I, 1, 25.

[3] *cf.* Chap. 1, *supra.*

within the provinces thereof which have distinct legal systems, differing from each other in greater or lesser extent. The first three divisions are studies which contribute to our understanding of the science of law. The latter three are largely bodies of principles and rules for application to particular problems. Each of these divisions may be further subdivided for study under distinct heads and sub-heads.

I.—LEGAL HISTORY

Legal history is of importance as showing how legal institutions (such as courts) legal concepts (such as contract or landownership) and legal principles (such as liability for harm done without justification) have originated and developed, or been imposed by one legal system on another, or been copied or borrowed by one from another. It is also of importance as revealing the original scope of and justification for a particular institution, rule or concept, and in many cases a modern rule can be understood only in the light of its origins and development.

There are two main aspects of legal history; first the development of law in human societies generally, and more particularly in those civilisations which have contributed to the general Western tradition in law, as in general spiritual and intellectual matters; and secondly, the development of legal institutions and law within particular countries, that is the histories of distinct legal systems. These two aspects are interrelated and cannot be divorced.[4]

The more general aspects of legal history are sometimes known as historical jurisprudence. Historical jurisprudence studies the origins and development of legal institutions and ideas of law generally, of law as a factor in human society. In default of evidence from written records as to the administration of justice and law in ancient and primitive societies, jurists draw inferences from the legal practices of primitive peoples living at the present day, whose customs and ways of life are recorded by social anthropologists. Legal history proper differs from historical jurisprudence in that the former seeks simply to follow out, record, explain and understand the changes and developments which have taken place in the evolution of each particular system of law, to discover the causes of the specific changes which have taken place, and to disclose the historical origins, bases and justifications of modern rules. It follows that there is a body of historical knowledge relative to every distinct system of law— though in the earlier periods one system tends to resemble and overlap other related systems[5]—and the influence of, and deliberate borrowing from, other systems are factors always to be kept in mind.

---

[4] The history of law in Scotland is dealt with in Chap. 4.

[5] Thus in the period prior to the War of Independence, Scottish legal development very much resembles that of England. So, too, all the European systems deriving from Roman law have marked affinities in the medieval period.

Legal history necessarily overlaps with constitutional history, though the latter subject is more particularly concerned with tracing the origins and development of governmental institutions, such as the legislative body, the superior executive body, the Council of Ministers or Cabinet, and so on, which are matters of public law, while legal history is concerned only with the development of rules of private law, such as contract and succession. Both legal and constitutional history are concerned with such topics as the development of the courts and the rights of the subject, though even there a difference of emphasis is usually discernible, the former study being more concerned with the legal aspects and the latter with the political aspects. So, too, both legal and constitutional history necessarily overlap with social, political, religious and economic history because these studies relate to and cast light on the background in which the legal system developed, and frequently provide the explanation for purely legal changes. Law does not develop in a vacuum, sealed off from other facets of the development of the society it relates to; it is an integral part of society and changes with it.

The study of legal history necessarily depends on the discovery, examination and interpretation of records and archives, and in most countries legal societies exist for the purpose of bringing to light, editing, and publishing material from public and private historical collections.[6] But diligent search and a discerning eye can find information of legal importance in every kind of historical material, charters, rent-rolls, taxation lists, memoirs, letters, parish registers and similar records. In Scotland, the study of legal history has hitherto been inadequately pursued, and a great deal of research remains to be done.

LAW IN EARLY CIVILISATIONS

All the evidence is that law first emerged as custom becoming obligatory. Extensive remains exist of various bodies of written laws from some of the early civilisations of the Middle East, which evidence not only a high degree of general civilisation but also a degree of legal maturity and sophistication. The earliest fragments date from about 2900 B.C. It is known that in the time of the Third Dynasty in Egypt (2815–2690 B.C.) formal documents were required for important legal transactions, but detailed knowledge of the legal institutions and rules is scanty.[7]

About 2100 B.C. Ur-Nammu of Sumer, or possibly his son Shulgi promulgated laws. The most substantial body of law is the Laws of King

---

[6] In Scotland, the Stair Society exists for this purpose, but much legal material has been published by the Scottish History Society, the Scottish Text Society and the Scottish Burgh Records Society, and by such older clubs as the Maitland, the Bannatyne, and the Spalding Clubs. In England, the great legal-historical society is the Selden Society.

[7] Seidl, "Law" in Glanville (ed.), *The Legacy of Egypt*, 198.

Hammurabi of Babylon,[8] dating from about 1800 B.C., which take the form, not so much of a code or statement of the law, but of a series of amendments to the common law of Babylon, classified under major headings. Though ancient, they are not primitive but evidence considerable legal maturity. Thousands of legal documents containing contracts, conveyances and reported cases have also been recovered from Babylonia, dating down to about 300 B.C. Then there are fragmentary records of Old Assyrian laws and legal documents of about 2300 B.C., and more extensive records of Middle Assyrian enactments dating from between 1450 and 1250 B.C., also modifications of pre-existing customary law.[9]

From Asia Minor have come Hittite treaties and laws from the period 1600–1300 B.C.,[10] and from Palestine some primitive codes of about 750 B.C. and, more importantly, the bodies of rules found in various books of the Old Testament, dating from about 600 B.C.[11] Through the spread of Christianity, the latter have entered into the basic beliefs of much of Western civilisation, though more through religious and moral prescription than by direct legal influence. Some authorities attribute the Law of Moses and the Ten Commandments to about 1235 B.C.

In Greece there are fragmentary records of law-givers and laws (such as Lycurgus at Sparta, *c.* 875 B.C., the possibly mythical Zaleucus of Locri, *c.* 675 B.C., Charondas of Catana, *c.* 675 B.C., Draco at Athens, *c.* 625 B.C., and Solon at Athens, *c.* 595 B.C.) covering roughly from the ninth to the sixth centuries B.C. The Code of Gortyn in Crete probably belongs to the fifth century B.C.[12] Classical Athens had an extensive and developed system of law,[13] but more significant for the ideas of law and justice in later Western civilisation was the contribution of the Greek thinkers, much of whose work, particularly some of the writings of Plato and Aristotle, has had permanent influence on Western thinking, as much about law and justice as about morals or politics.

Historically interesting as these early bodies of law are, they have had little direct or permanent influence on any modern Western European legal system. However, this is not the case with the law of Rome.

---

[8] See Driver and Miles, *The Babylonian Laws*, 2 vols.

[9] See Driver and Miles, *The Assyrian Laws; Camb. Anc. His.*, Vol. II (2), 474; Vol. III, 104.

[10] See Neufeld, *The Hittite Laws*.

[11] These include particularly Exodus, xx–xxiii; Leviticus, xvii–xxvi; Deuteronomy, v–xxvi; and Ezekiel, xl–xlviii. See further *Camb.Anc.Hist.*, Vol. III, 481; Kent, *Israel's Laws and Legal Precedents*; Daube, *Studies in Biblical Law*; Phillips, *Ancient Israel's Criminal Law: A New Approach to the Decalogue*; Hecht, *Introduction to the History and Sources of Jewish Law*; Derrett, *Law in the New Testament*.

[12] Vinogradoff, *Historical Jurisprudence*, Vol. II; Wyse, in *Companion to Greek Studies* (ed. Whibley), 429–490.

[13] Jones, *Law and Legal Theory of the Greeks*; Harrison, *Law of Athens*; McDowell, *The Law in Classical Athens*; McDowell, *Spartan Law*; Saunders, *Plato's Penal Code*; Foxhall (ed.), *Greek Law in its Political Setting*.

CIVIL OR ROMAN LAW

The Civil or Roman law is in the first place the law of the ancient city of Rome and the Roman empire, from the foundation of the city (traditionally 753 B.C.) to the fall of the Western empire in the fifth century A.D., and even thereafter until the fall of the Eastern empire with the capture of Constantinople by the Turks in 1453. The system really begins[14] with the adoption of the Laws of the Twelve Tables in about 450 B.C., which established a system of law for Roman citizens only (*jus civile*), characterised by rigidity and formality.

In 242 B.C. the increase of foreigners in Rome made it necessary to appoint a special judge, the peregrine praetor, to deal with causes in which a foreigner was involved, and he and the urban praetor, who dealt with cases involving only citizens, both issued edicts defining the circumstances in which they would give particular remedies. These edicts became important sources of new and revised law which came to be known as *jus praetorium* or *jus honorarium*. In the late republican period, from about 150 B.C. to 27 B.C., this was the chief reforming factor in Roman law.[15] Also in this period, the *jus gentium* came to be of importance. This was the body of law applicable equally to Roman citizens and to foreigners, a system based on common principles of the Mediterranean peoples, with a strong Roman flavouring but free from formalistic elements; it was later applied to Roman provincials also. It came to be connected with the theoretical idea of a law common to all peoples and dictated by nature, a notion taken over by the Romans from Greek philosophy.

In the early empire (27 B.C. to A.D. 100) legal literature developed[16] and the praetors' edicts tended to become fixed and carried on from year to year, as is evidenced by the growing practice of writing commentaries on the edict. In or about A.D. 131 the emperor Hadrian had the jurist Salvius Julianus revise and settle the edicts, which thereafter became fixed, and alterable only by the emperor. The classical age of the law was reached in the second century and the first half of the third, considerably later than the classical age of Latin literature, and it is marked by extensive juristic writing and the detailed working out of principles. The great age was short and soon over; Papinian was killed in 212, Ulpian in 228, and Ulpian's pupil Modestinus was the last of the great jurists. By A.D. 300 jurisprudence was stricken with sterility; the sole source of law was now the emperor. The most important work surviving in its original form from this

---

[14] For the history, see Muirhead, *Historical Introduction to the Private Law of Rome* (3rd ed.); Jolowicz, *Historical Introduction to the Study of Roman Law* (3rd ed.); Conrat, *Geschichte der Quellen und Literatur des römischen Rechts*. For the law, see Buckland, *Text-book of Roman Law from Augustus to Justinian*; Girard, *Manuel Elémentaire du droit romain* (8th ed.).

[15] Watson, *Law Making in the Later Roman Republic*, Chaps. 3–6; Jolowicz, *op. cit.*, Chap. 23.

[16] On this, see Schulz, *History of Roman Legal Science*.

period is the *Institutes* of Gaius, a student's textbook written about A.D. 161, which is of unique importance as evidence of the state of the law in the classical period, and which subsequently formed the basis of Justinian's *Institutes*.

In 426 Valentinian III issued his Law of Citations giving primary authority to the works of Papinian, Paul, Ulpian, Modestinus and Gaius, laying down that the view of the majority should be accepted, and, if they were equally divided Papinian's view was to rule. Secondary authority attached to any author referred to by one of the five principal authorities. The rule is deplorable because it substitutes counting heads for evaluating reasons.

While the law did not stand still, there was falling off in legal literature after 235; new ideas were introduced, especially from the East, while the law was also influenced by the growing importance of the eastern half of the empire with its capital at Constantinople. More and more, law-making had become the function of the emperor, and in the third and later centuries attempts were made to collect the mass of imperial constitutions. Two unofficial collections are known, the *Codex Gregorianus* (301) containing constitutions from Hadrian (117–138) to Diocletian (284–305), and the *Codex Hermogenianus* (365) containing mainly those of Diocletian's time. Neither has survived, but they are known from quotations. They may have been made in the East, because the tendency was for the imperial centre to shift eastwards; in 326–328 Constantine removed the imperial court to Byzantium, now renamed Constantinople, whilst in the fourth century the seat of the Western government was removed first to Milan and then to Ravenna. The later Roman empire from 285 to 476 was generally ruled by a college of two or more emperors, some in the west, some in the east. In theory they all jointly ruled the whole empire and all laws and official pronouncements were issued in the names of all, but constitutions issued by one emperor were generally promulgated in his part of the empire only. In 438 the *Codex Theodosianus* was promulgated. It was an official collection of imperial statutes beginning with Constantine I; a collection rather than a code. Thereafter, it was enacted that a constitution issued by one emperor was not to apply in the other's dominions unless he accepted and promulgated it. Moreover, by the time it was issued, the barbarians were already striking at the empire.[17]

Fall of the Western Empire

In the fourth and fifth centuries the encroachments of barbarian tribes on the empire increased and the empire was twice divided into East and

---

[17] A valuable summary of the later days of the Roman empire is in A.H.M. Jones, *The Decline of the Ancient World*; see also *The European Inheritance*, I, 222–249. For a fuller account, see *Camb. Med. Hist.*, Vol. IV, esp. Chap. 21. See also Gibbon, *Decline and Fall of the Roman Empire*, Chap. 44; Bryce, *Holy Roman Empire*, Chaps. II and III; Bury, *Invasion of Europe by the Barbarians, passim*.

West portions for ease of administration and defence. The weakness of successive Western emperors culminated in the capture and sack of Rome by the Visigoths under Alaric in 410. The Franks and Burgundians founded kingdoms in northern Gaul, and the Visigoths in southern Gaul, while the Vandals passed through Spain and conquered North Africa. Rome was again sacked in 454, by the Vandals, and the empire in the West came to an end in 476 when the last puppet emperor was deposed. The Eastern half always enjoyed greater political stability and was less beset with civil war; it was socially and economically richer, and was to stand for another thousand years until the Turks captured Constantinople in 1453. The two halves had never become completely unified or integrated, and remained Greek and Latin though united politically. By the end of the fifth century, Germanic kingdoms, superficially romanised, had been established all over Western Europe—Visigoths in south-west Gaul and Spain, Burgundians in south-east Gaul, Ostrogoths in Italy, Vandals in Africa. Rather later, the Franks established themselves between the Rhine and the Somme, the Alamanni on the upper Rhine and Danube, the Lombards in north Italy, the Bavarians on the Danube and in the Alps, the Angles, Jutes and Saxons in South Britain.[18]

Roman Law in the West

The Western provinces of the former Roman Empire adhered to the former law summed up in the *Codex Theodosianus* of A.D. 438.[19] There was legislation by the emperors down to that date, fragments of older legislation contained in the private collections known as the *Codex Gregorianus* and the *Codex Hermogenianus,* numerous *Novellae* of early fifth-century emperors, and a great volume of older jurisprudence laid down in opinions and treatises going back to the classical age. The temporary reconquering of part of Italy by Justinian's armies in the sixth century had no legal or permanent consequences and his legislation was ineffective there. But other law was beginning; the barbarians had been writing down their customs and barbarian kings had begun to issue law books for their Roman subjects, while books of ecclesiastical law were also being compiled.

Roman law in the provinces had become a debased body of rules by the fifth century, when many races of foreigners were within the Empire and occupying posts of authority and importance in the civil and military administration. For such peoples in the provinces, various statements of barbarised Roman law were prepared in the late fifth and early sixth centuries. The principal were the *Edictum Theodorici* for the Ostrogothic kingdom (*c.* A.D. 500), the *Lex Romana Burgundionum* (*c.* A.D. 500) and

---

[18] Wallace-Hadrill, *The Barbarian West, 400–1000, passim.*
[19] Roby, "Roman Law" in *Camb.Med.Hist.*, Vol. III, Chap. 3.

the *Lex Romana Visigothorum*, also known as the *Breviarium Alaricianum* (A.D. 506), of which the last became the standard source of Roman law in Western Europe during the first half of the Middle Ages. It was a more or less complete code for the use of the Roman populace in France and Spain, comprising the enactments of the later Empire with interpretations of the text designed to make the sense of the laws as clear as possible, and consisted of three main portions, an introductory survey for beginners, legal and jurisprudential doctrines laid down by authorities, and a body of enactments by recent emperors.[20] But the most important event for the subsequent history and influence of Roman law happened in the East after the fall of the Western Empire.

Justinian

When Justinian[21] became Eastern emperor at Constantinople in 527, he set out to collect, codify and reform the mass of law which had grown up over the centuries. His efforts resulted in the promulgation of (a) *The Old Codex* (529): a new collection of imperial constitutions superseding the older ones and including later legislation; (b) *The Fifty Decisions*: a collection of 50 constitutions settling matters of dispute and abolishing some institutions and distinctions no longer of practical importance; (c) *The Digest* or *Pandects* (533): a collection of excerpts from the works of jurists, amended and omitting obsolete or superfluous matter, arranged in 50 books according to subject-matter: the *Digest* in some measure preserved some of the writings of the classical jurists who were really responsible for the greatness of the Roman law; (d) *The Institutes* (533): a systematic new book for the elementary instruction of students, based on Gaius's *Institutes* and on other elementary works; (e) *The New Codex* (534): a revision of the Old Codex in the light of *The Fifty Decisions* and other later constitutions; and (f) *The Novels* (*Novellae Constitutiones*) or later legislation. The Institutes, Digest, (new) Codex and Novels together form the *Corpus Juris Civilis*.[22]

After Justinian's time, Greek versions of parts of the *Corpus Juris* were made in the East and selections published modifying some of the enactments, particularly to make the law more consonant with Christian principles. Under Leo the Wise (886–911) was prepared the *Basilica*[23] in

---

[20] For a valuable comparison of the Breviary with Justinian's *Corpus Juris*, see Vinogradoff, *Roman Law in Medieval Europe* (2nd ed.), 18–21, where he shows how much the Breviary evidences intellectual decay. See also King, *Law and Society in the Visigothic Kingdom*.

[21] On Justinian and his work see Diehl, "Justinian", in *Camb.Med.Hist.*, Vol. 2, Chaps. 1–2; Browning, *Justinian and Theodora*; Honoré, *Tribonian*.

[22] The standard edition is the Berlin one edited by Krueger, Mommsen and Schoell in three volumes: The parts are cited by book, title, and paragraph or fragment: thus Inst. I, iii, 3; D. (or Dig.) IX, 2, 7, 1; C.I, xviii, 12; the *Novels* are cited by number, *e.g.* Nov. 118. The compendious title *Corpus Juris Civilis* was not given until much later, being copied from the title *Corpus Juris Canonici*.

[23] See further Lawson, "The Basilica" (1931–32) 46 L.Q.R. 486; 47 L.Q.R. 536; Collinet, "Byzantine Legislation," *Camb.Med.Hist.*, IV, Chap. 20.

which are fused, in 60 books, all the parts of Justinian's compilations, in simplified Greek versions of the sixth and seventh centuries, with some changes. This remained the law of the Eastern Empire until the fall of Constantinople in 1453. There was some revival of legal studies in the eleventh century and later, and about 1345 the *Hexabiblos* was compiled at Thessalonica. This still had a measure of authority in Greece until the promulgation of the modern Civil Code in 1946.

The West after Justinian

Justinian's *Corpus Juris* was long accepted, and even known, only in the East and in parts of Italy. The *Breviarium Alaricianum* still comprised the Roman law for the West, and legal knowledge decayed seriously in the Dark Ages. The *Lex Romana Curiensis* of the late eighth century, a statement of legal custom for the population of Eastern Switzerland, and used also in the Tyrol and Northern Italy, testifies to even greater decadence and is little more than custom flavoured by Roman law.

In the Dark Ages and early Middle Ages, law was essentially personal and local rather than territorial, since no state was strong enough to enforce a legal order or system of its own. Moreover, the entry of Goths, Franks and Lombards into the former Roman provinces had not involved the disappearance of Roman inhabitants, and their special legal status was allowed to continue and relations between them were governed by their own racial law. So, too, men of each nation, such as Burgundians or Bavarians or Salian Franks, lived under their own law, which raised difficulties when members of different nationalities wished to enter into legal transactions. This system of national laws gave rise to problems of conflict of laws.[24]

Moreover, in most districts local customs arose to regulate the ordinary dealings of the people, and these tended to take their colouring from the prevailing national majority and to modify any surviving traces of Roman law. Thus, until the advent of the Saracens and Normans legal customs were built on a basis of Roman law in Southern Italy where the Byzantine Empire still held sway, in the Romagna, and in Southern France and Northern Spain where the *Breviarium Alaricianum* was applied.[25]

In other districts, Northern France, Germany and England, the barbarian laws applied but Roman institutions and legal customs still had influence, particularly since the clergy still followed Roman law. Roman influence was strongest in the case of the Ostrogoths of Northern Italy and Austria and of the Visigoths of Spain and France, who adopted Roman

---

[24] In a famous letter from Bishop Agobard of Lyons to Ludwig the Pious in about 850, it is narrated that "It often occurs that five men walking or sitting together are each of them living under a different law," and it became customary for the parties to a deed or action to make an express declaration of which system they lived by.

[25] Vinogradoff, *op. cit.*, 28.

enactments wholesale, quite apart from Imperial Roman law codified for Roman fellow-citizens.[26]

Legal learning did not, however, entirely disappear in these times and still survived in part and can be found in medieval salvage of the wreckage of antiquity, such as in Bishop Isidore of Seville's *Etymologiae*, and in clerical abstracts and glosses or explanations of older texts.[27]

The Corpus Juris in the West

In the West, Justinian's law was rediscovered in Italy in the eleventh century.[28] The study centred on Bologna[29] where Irnerius[30] began the succession of Glossators,[31] or scholars who wrote glosses on the text, settling its form, explaining it, resolving contradictions, deducing maxims and discussing concrete cases, the glosses becoming in the end a commentary. The men who administered local laws and customs were trained in the *Corpus Juris* and its more civilised rules influenced the natural growth of the law of developing communities. The *Summa* of Azo (*fl. c.* 1190) was an indispensable text, while the Gloss of Accursius (*ob. c.* 1260) was a standard commentary on the text.

About 1300 there arose the school of Commentators,[32] of whom the greatest were Bartolus of Sassoferrato (1314–57) and his pupil, Baldus (1327–1400). They sought to make the Civil Law applicable to the practice of their time, adapting it to living conditions, and to harmonise it with the feudal, Germanic or canon laws then in force. They transformed it and made it living law, but at the cost of false reasoning, pedantry and voluminous confusion. "The great achievement of the Commentators, the Post-Glossators, was in fact the transformation of the Roman law into a medieval Italian law. They created a literature in Romano-Italian law which not only possessed authority in Italy itself, but played a role of great importance in the legal and political life of Europe as a whole. Thus it was the living Romano-Italian law of the Commentators, and not the pure Roman law of Justinian, which crossed the Alps into Germany in the age of the Reception."[33]

---

[26] *Op. cit.*, 30.

[27] *Op. cit.*, 37–41; see also Jenks, *Law and Politics in the Middle Ages*, Chaps. 1, 2.

[28] The great authority on the later Roman law is Savigny's *Geschichte des Römischen Rechts im Mittelalter* (1822); see also *Continental Legal History Series*, Vol. I, for a general survey.

[29] Provence, Pavia and Ravenna were also early centres of the revival.

[30] See Dove Wilson, "Irnerius" (1894) 6 J.R. 304.

[31] See Vinogradoff, *Roman Law in Medieval Europe* (2nd ed.), Chap. 2; Hazeltine, "Roman and Canon Law in the Middle Ages," *Camb.Med.Hist.*, V, 697; Hazeltine, "Glossators," in *Encyc.Soc.Sc.*, VI, 679; Hazeltine, Introd. to Ullman, *Medieval Idea of Law*; Kantorowicz and Buckland, *Studies in the Glossators of the Roman Law*.

[32] See Hazeltine, "Commentators," in *Encyc.Soc.Sc.*, III, 679; Woolf, *Bartolus of Sassoferrato*; Ullman, "Bartolus on Customary Law" (1941) 52 J.R. 263.

[33] Hazeltine, Introd. to Ullman, *Medieval Idea of Law*, xix; see also Hazeltine, *Camb.Med.Hist.*, V, 697, and on the legal and political theories of the Glossators and Commentators, see Carlyle, *History of Medieval Political Theory in the West*, Vols. II and VI.

During this period from 1100 to 1500 the Roman law became the basis for legal science throughout Western Europe and its importance and influence spread rapidly. Moreover, in this period great political and economic changes were taking place, towns were developing, and the laws of commerce, trade, agriculture, fairs, and the older customary law, gradually elaborated to regulate the relations of men living by agriculture, which had become inadequate for a populace depending on industry and commerce. Roman law was looked to for its embodiment of the old Roman cultural ideal and as carrying an aura of the old Roman glory and unity, but particularly since it contained principles capable of solving many of the problems of the more cultivated society which was arising, and of the developing trade and commerce. It made important contributions to the solution of specific problems and became the basis for much development.

The study spread[34] to France where, in the south (the *pays du droit écrit*), it gradually superseded the older Roman law books as the law of the land, modified only by local custom. In northern France (the *pays du droit coûtumier*), it was mingled with the traditional customs in the thirteenth century, and it was freely used in Philippe de Beaumanoir's *Coûtumes de Beauvaisis* (*c.* 1280).

The third great school of Roman law studies is that of the Humanists, which rose following the decline of the Commentators about the beginning of the fifteenth century. They had a historical sense and began to try to reconstruct the classical law from the amended passages found in the *Digest* by detecting the interpolations made in the texts included in the *Corpus Juris* by the compilers. This movement was very strong in France and is represented by such jurists as Cujacius (Jacques Cujas, 1520–90), Donellus (Hugues Doneau, 1527–91) and Faber (Antoine Favre, 1557–1624), while Jacobus Gothefredus (Jacques Godefroy, 1587–1652) published a great edition of the Theodosian Code, with commentary. Rather later, Pothier[35] in France published in 1748 his *Pandectae Justinianae in novum ordinem digestae*, recreating the correct order of the text, and on that foundation wrote a series of treatises on aspects of French law, such as the *Traité des Obligations* (1761).

In Germany, Roman law began to oust the native tribal law in the later Middle Ages, facilitated by the theory of continuity of the Holy Roman Empire with the older Empire of the West,[36] and by the lack of political unity among the Germanic states. About the fourteenth century, there

---

[34] On the extension, see Munroe Smith, *Development of European Law; Continental Legal History Series*, Vol. 1, General Survey; "Law," by Vinogradoff, le Bras and Meynial in *The Legacy of the Middle Ages*; Taylor-Cameron, "Roman Law in the Early Middle Ages" (1895–98) 7 J.R. 241; 8 J.R. 118; 10 J.R. 438.

[35] On Pothier, see Macdonnell (ed.), *Great Jurists of the World*, 447.

[36] For an account of this, see Bryce, *The Holy Roman Empire*.

took place the "Reception" in Germany of civil and canon law, which were widely studied in the universities. While in theory the *Corpus Juris* was accepted only as subsidiary and its rules were only to be applied if Germanic law were silent, in practice Germanic law was to a large extent superseded. In 1495, the central Imperial court adopted Roman law for its guidance as the common law of the Empire and it exercised such a considerable influence on the legal institutions of all the states of the Empire that the "Reception" spread. Roman law remained a main source of Germanic law until the German Civil Code of 1900, and in the nineteenth century Savigny and his successors created an elaborate, highly systematised body of law (*Pandektenrecht*) on the basis of the *Corpus Juris*.[37] So, too, until the promulgation of the Code Napoleon in 1804, the customs, particularly of Paris, influenced and supplemented by Roman law, constituted the law of France.[38] The German and French codes in turn have been copied repeatedly in codes all over the world.

In Holland, resort was had to the Roman law to supplement the inadequacies of general and local customs, and Roman law was "received" in all the provinces, in varying degrees, from the fifteenth to the seventeenth centuries; also in Holland there flourished many great jurists whose writings on law, particularly on Roman law, have been very important and influential.[39] The law of Holland was carried to South Africa by the early Dutch settlers there and although in Holland itself it was superseded by the French civil code during the Napoleonic wars, in South Africa it took root, developed and survived as the Roman-Dutch law.

Roman law probably entered Scotland[40] initially through the church and the canon law, but by the sixteenth century it had come sometimes to be referred to in supplement of native customary or common law. Knowledge of Roman law was increased by the long association of Scotland with France, and the works of the French jurists of the fifteenth and sixteenth centuries were well known to Scottish students who studied at such universities as Bourges. Some doctrines of Roman law were introduced by legislation. In the seventeenth century the writings of French and Dutch civilians were well known, and when Stair wrote his *Institutions* he naturally turned to Roman law, as developed by these civilians, to fill gaps

---

[37] See further Wieacker, *A History of Private Law in Europe*.

[38] On France, see Brissaud, *Manuel d'Histoire du Droit Français*; Esmein, *Histoire du Droit Français*; Olivier-Martin, *Histoire du Droit Français*. On Germany, see Hubner, *Institutionen des deutschen Privatrechts* (trans. in *Continental Legal History Series*); Fehr, *Deutsche Rechtsgeschichte*.

[39] In this connection the long-standing practice of Scottish advocates studying in Holland must be remembered since Holland is the channel through which much Roman law came to Scotland.

[40] See further Baird Smith, "Roman Law," in Stair Society, *Sources and Literature of Scots Law*, and references there; Dove Wilson, "Reception of the Roman Law in Scotland" (1898) 9 J.R. 361; Miller, "Reception of Roman Law in Scotland" (1923) 35 J.R. 362.

and harmonise differences. In the seventeenth and eighteenth centuries Scottish students frequented the Dutch universities, and the citation of the Dutch and German commentators can be traced in the earlier Scottish collected decisions.[41] The Roman law which was adopted and introduced was generally a simplified form, ignoring elaborate refinements, accepted on its merits and for its reason and equity, but not as of binding force. After the Union of 1707 English influence tended to grow and this has been more pronounced with the passage of time. Simultaneously, reliance on Roman law has tended to decline, and in the twentieth century it is seldom referred to except in matters previously adopted from the Roman law; reference to the older French, Dutch and German commentators is rare.

The Roman law never became a constituent element of English law, although it was influential when legal doctrines were being formulated in the twelfth and thirteenth centuries and was continuously studied in the universities,[42] and in particular topics it has been a direct source of English rules. For this reason, Roman law has been less influential in the parts of the world settled from England. Thus, apart from Quebec and Louisiana, North America has taken its law initially and fundamentally from England. But, largely through the French and German codes, principles stemming originally from Roman law have spread all over the world.

Permanent Importance of Roman Law

Roman law is still a material subject of legal study for several reasons. Firstly, the development and working out of their great system of law by the Roman jurists over a thousand years is an excellent example of the modes of growth and development of a legal system. Furthermore, this development was one of the great intellectual achievements of antiquity, and Roman law is entitled to be placed with Greek philosophy and Jewish religious thought as one of the most important and powerful intellectual forces in European civilisation inherited by the modern from the ancient world.[43] "Roman law, next to Christianity, was the greatest factor in the creation of modern civilisation, and it is the greatest intellectual legacy of Rome."[44]

---

[41] Feenstra and Waal, *Seventeenth Century Law Professors and Their Influence on the Development of the Civil Law*, 82.

[42] Vinogradoff, *op. cit.*, 97 *et seq.*; Winfield, *Chief Sources of English Legal History*, Chap. 4; Scrutton, "Influence of Roman Law on the Law of England" in *Essays in Anglo-American Legal History*, I, 208; Potter, *Historical Introduction to English Law* (4th ed.), 631; Plucknett, *Concise History of the Common Law* (5th ed.), 294; Powell, "Roman Law in Common Law Courts" [1958] C.L.P., 19.

[43] This point is well brought out in de Burgh, *Legacy of the Ancient World*, esp. Chaps. 7, 8 and 11. See also Vinogradoff, "The Work of Rome," in *Collected Papers*, Vol. I, 222; Meynial, "Roman Law" in *The Legacy of the Middle Ages*; Bryce, Inaugural Lecture, in *Studies in History and Jurisprudence*, II, 860; Lobingier, "The Value and Place of Roman Law in the Technical Curriculum" (1918) 30 J.R. 136.

[44] Buckland (1931) J.S.P.T.L. 25.

Secondly, the rules, doctrines, concepts and terminology of Roman law were closely studied everywhere in Europe from the end of the Dark Ages until modern times, and have powerfully influenced legal thinking and terminology and the actual content of many modern systems of law. Roman law has unique significance as a common source of legal concepts. "Roman law is still the foundation for the liberal education of a lawyer, the training and the sharpening of his logical equipment. The methods of reasoning of the Roman jurists their way of approaching a legal problem we still follow today."[45] "It may be said that the Romans have fixed for all time the categories of juristic thought."[46]

Thirdly, the rules of Roman law have been a material source of rules accepted and applied in modern systems, and modern systems have frequently turned to Roman law for rules to apply to new sets of circumstances. By acquaintance with Roman law, the English-speaking legal student gains a key to the understanding of the many modern systems of law which derive ultimately from Rome—of French law, German law and the many systems based on these systems, of the Roman-Dutch law of South Africa,[47] international law, and of much of jurisprudence. Roman law is thus fundamental to jurisprudence and comparative legal study. Roman law and English law between them cover a large part of the civilised, and most of the uncivilised world.[48] The reception of Roman law created a great body of continental law which served, along with the feudal law, canon law, and the law merchant, to unify the diverse legal systems of much of Western Europe.[49]

Fourthly, Roman law was taken as the basis of international law by Grotius and his successors. The founders of international law turned unhesitatingly to Roman law for the rules of their system whenever the relations between ruling princes seemed to them to be analogous to those of private persons. The international rules as to territory are still, in essentials, the Roman rules of property.

"From the purely academic point of view we cannot afford to neglect a branch of legal learning which has had so large an historical effect, a branch of learning which is still so necessary to a scientific study of law. From the purely practical point of view we cannot afford to neglect a branch of learning which is necessary to the proper understanding of international law, and of foreign Codes de Commerce."[50]

---

[45] Meynial, in *The Legacy of the Middle Ages*, 399.

[46] Cuq, *Institutions juridiques des Romains* (2nd ed.), I, xxiv.

[47] See generally Hahlo and Kahn, *The South African Legal System and its Background*, Part II; see also Smith, "Scots Law and Roman-Dutch Law: A Shared Tradition," 1961 J.R. 32.

[48] Bryce, *Studies in History and Jurisprudence*, I, 74.

[49] Munroe Smith, *General View of European Legal History*, 3, 28. See also Coing, "The Roman Law as Jus Commune on the Continent" (1973) 89 L.Q.R. 505.

[50] Holdsworth, *Sources and Literature of English Law*, 235. *Cf.* Lobingier, "The Value and Place of Roman Law in the Technical Curriculum" (1918) 30 J.R. 136.

The debt of Scots law to Roman law is substantial, and Roman law still needs to be studied in Scotland as a material source of the living law of Scotland.[51] Scotland, unlike England, to some extent "received" the Roman law and it had considerable influence from the late sixteenth to the mid-eighteenth centuries. Stair, Mackenzie, Bankton and Erskine all consider that in default of native statute or custom great weight attaches to the Roman law, and the courts constantly referred to continental treatises on the Roman and canon law. Since about 1800 this influence has been less, but it remains a fact that Roman law was a factor of major importance in the formative period of modern Scots law, with particular influence on the law of moveable property and obligations, and its influence is not yet wholly spent.[52]

OTHER INDIGENOUS EUROPEAN SYSTEMS

Early Celtic Law

Of the law of the Celtic peoples who early inhabited much of the British Isles we have only limited knowledge. Later, when the Celtic peoples were pushed north and west into Scotland, Wales and Ireland, there are records of law, but at least in Scotland none of this seems to have had any material influence on later law.[53]

Early Teutonic Law

Among the Teutonic tribes described in Tacitus' *Germania* there was little organised law. Early Teutonic law was primarily the unwritten custom of the tribe, but there is evidence of tribal assemblies and allegiance to kings, and traces of courts of the tribe and the county division. The law was mostly concerned with wrongs and there was a recognised system of compensation for injuries or death (wergeld), originally paid in cattle.

Much of Gaul and Germany up to the Rhine-Danube frontier was occupied by the Roman legions for the first four centuries of the Christian era, but in the fifth century most of the Roman provinces in the West fell into the hands of the barbarians, and Germanic kingdoms were founded in the former Roman provinces. Thus, Franks and Burgundians came to hold

---

[51] Baird Smith in Stair Society, *Sources and Literature*, p. 177; Smith, *Short Commentary on the Law of Scotland*, 19–24; Mackintosh, "Our Debt to Roman Law" (1926) 38 J.R. 327. *Cf. Stewart's Executrix v. London, Midland and Scottish Railway Co.*, 1943 S.C.(H.L.) 19, 38.

[52] "The Roman law, though interesting, is only of service as showing the foundation on which the Scots law rests. The real question must always be what is the law of Scotland:" *Cantiere San Rocco v. Clyde Shipbuilding Co.*, 1923 S.C.(H.L.) 105, 123, *per* Lord Dunedin.

[53] See Dillon and Chadwick, *The Celtic Realms*, Chap. 5, Cameron, *Celtic Law*; for Wales, Ellis, *Welsh Tribal Law and Custom in the Middle Ages*; Melville, *The Laws of Hywel Dda*; Owen, *Ancient Laws and Institutes of Wales*; and for Ireland, Thurneysen, *Studies in Early Irish Law*; Macneill, *Early Irish Laws and Institutions*; Hennessey and others (ed.), *Ancient Laws of Ireland*.

Gaul, Visigoths south Gaul and Spain, and Ostrogoths Italy and most of central Europe. Later the Lombards took Italy from the Ostrogoths.

The Leges Barbarorum

From some of these Germanic kingdoms there have survived bodies of law, mainly codifications of criminal law and procedure, partly containing existing customary law and partly new statutory rules. The earliest is the code of the Visigoths, the *Leges Visigothorum*, of the King Euric (*c.* 475) which remained in force among the Visigoths of Spain until replaced by that of Leovigild (*c.* 580), when it was made applicable to all the subjects in the kingdom. A new code, applicable to Visigoths and Romans alike, was made by Recesswinth (*c.* 670) and is known as the *Liber judiciorum*, and a revision made in 681 by King Erwig is known as the *Lex Visigothorum renovata*.

Not much later is the *Lex Salica* of the Salian Franks, a compilation of different dates, originally issued by King Chlodwig in North France about 500, and later amended, added to and corrected. It is pre-eminently a penal code, stating the amounts of fines for various crimes, but containing some civil enactments, notably a chapter on succession to land declaring that daughters cannot inherit land. The *Lex Ripuaria* of the Ripuarian Franks is influenced by, and in part adopts, the Salic law.

Among the Burgundians a code, known as the *Lex Burgundionum*, the *Liber Constitutionum,* or *Lex Gundobada*, was compiled by King Gundobad about 500, and shows strong traces of Roman influence. It applied between Burgundians and also to cases between Romans and Burgundians, and was appealed to as late as the eleventh century. Of the laws of the Alamanni there have survived two texts, the *Pactus Alamannorum* of the seventh century, and the *Lex Alamannorum* of the eighth.

The laws of the Lombards, the *Leges Langobardorum*, are more substantial. The first part, the *Edictus Langobardorum* was promulgated by King Rothari at Pavia in 643. This edict is systematically arranged, clearly compiled by jurists who knew Roman law, but presents Germanic law. It was augmented by later rulers, and after the union of the Lombards to the Frankish Kingdom, the capitularies made for the kingdom were applied to Italy, though there were also special capitularies, *Capitula Italica*, for Italy. Compilations were early made in Italy for the use of lawyers. Thus the contents of the edict with its accretions were arranged into a *Concordia de Singulis Causis* (830). In the tenth century was made the *Capitulare Langobardorum*, a collection of the capitularies in use in Italy, and in the following century, under the influence of the school of law at Pavia, appeared the *Liber legis Langobardorum* (also called *Liber Papiensis* and the *Lombarda*) of which there are two versions, known as the *Lombarda Casinensis* and the *Lombarda Vulgata*.

The law of the Bavarians, the *Lex Baiuvariorum*, was taken partly from the law of Euric and partly from the *Lex Alamannorum* and the *Lex*

Salica and dates from about 745. The *Lex Saxonum* (containing ancient customary enactments of Saxony) dates from about 802, the *Lex Thuringorum* (containing local customs and partly based on the *Capitulare legi Ribuariae additum*) is of about the same date, and there is also a mixed collection of enactments known as the *Lex Frisionum* of about the same date.[54]

Germanic Law in England

As part of the great migrations westwards, Angles, Saxons and Jutes moved into south Britain, and about 600 Aethelbert of Kent began to write the dooms (or judgments) of the people of Kent. Before 700 there appeared the dooms of Ine in Wessex and later Offa of Mercia is known to have published laws. There are many such bodies of law—partly statements of customary law, partly new law—in the centuries before the Norman Conquest, all in the vernacular, uninfluenced by Roman law and little influenced by canon law.[55] After the Conquest, it was one of the achievements of the Angevin kings of England to build up a system and convert the laws of the Mercians, the West Saxons, the Danes and the Normans into the law of England, a task achieved chiefly by the early development of a strong central court from which itinerant justices went out to hear cases in local courts by the law common to all England, the common law of England. By the twelfth century, the king's court had become the most powerful organisation in the kingdom, a highly organised body of officials, with financial, administrative and judicial functions, and Assizes and Ordinances were being promulgated.[56]

CANON LAW

Canon law is the body of laws framed by an ecclesiastical body for its own regulation, and particularly the law of the Roman Church.[57] In the early centuries of the Christian Church there was no general legislation, but the various communities framed rules themselves and in time collections were made in the East of decisions by councils and bishops, and rather later in

---

[54] See generally Canciani, *Barbarorum leges antiquae*; Walter, *Corpus juris germanici antiqui*; *Monumenta Germaniae Historica, Leges*; Brunner, *Deutsche Rechtsgeschichte*.

[55] Brunner, "The Sources of English Law," in *Essays in Anglo-American Legal History*, II, 7; Pollock, "English Law before the Norman Conquest" (1898) 14 L.Q.R. 291; Richardson and Sayles, *Law and Legislation from Aethelberht to Magna Carta*. See also Thorpe, *Ancient Laws and Institutes of England*.

[56] Mrs. Green, "The Centralisation of Norman Justice under Henry II," in *Essays in Anglo-American Legal History*, I, 111. See also Pollock and Maitland, *History of English Law*, Chap. 1; Jenks, *Law and Politics in the Middle Ages*, Chaps. 1 and 2. For development after the Conquest, see Plucknett, *Concise History of the Common Law*, Chap. 2.

[57] For the history, see *Continental Legal History Series*, Vol. I, 705–724; Munroe Smith, *Development of European Law*, 191–212; Tardif, *Histoire des Sources du droit canonique*; Brundage, *Medieval Canon Law*.

the West. From the Council of Nicaea in 325 onwards, general councils of the church frequently promulgated general rules on the government of the church, its organisation, theology and practice. The churches of Britain tended to remain outside the centralising movement. The canon law of the Western (Roman Catholic) and Eastern (Orthodox) churches was much the same until they separated in 1054. In the Middle Ages the canon law was a common law for Europe, sharing in the authority conceded to Roman law on which, along with Holy Scripture, it was based. Roman law was the temporal law of the clergy and the councils and popes drew inspiration therefrom. The canon law, like the Roman, was a principal branch of university study down to the Reformation.

The principal sources of medieval canon law were the New Testament, canons or decrees of councils, ecumenical, national or provincial, and the custom of the Church. Collections of these were made both in the West and in the East, into which forged documents sometimes found their way. Important works were Burchard of Worms's *Decretum* (*c.* 1025) in 20 books, and the *Tripartita*, *Decretum* and *Panormia* of Ivo, Bishop of Chartres (*c.* 1100).

About 1148 Gratian, a monk of Bologna, published the treatise at first called the *Concordia discordantium canonum* and later the *Decretum*, in which he brought together and tried to make into a coherent juridical system the vast body of texts of different periods furnished by earlier collections. Gratian drew on the existing collections, the works of the fathers and the ecclesiastical councils, and the Roman law, as well as later councils, and recent decretals down to the Lateran council of 1139, and fitted the texts into a treatise in three parts.[58] It made canon law into a science. The *Decretum* was a work of only private authority, but it has subsequently been the basis of instruction in canon law in all universities, been commented on by the most illustrious canonists, and having been cited, corrected and edited by the popes, has obtained an authority recognised and accepted by the Roman Church.

The disciples of Gratian collected later papal decretals into five large compilations (*Quinque Compilationes Antiquae* of which the most important is the *Breviarium extravagantium* compiled about 1190 by Bernard of Pavia), and which were condensed into a single collection by Raymond of Pennaforte in 1234, under the orders of Gregory IX, as *Liber Extra* or *Liber Decretalium Gregorii IX*. Two official collections followed, one prepared by a committee of canonists under Boniface VIII and published in 1298. Since it followed the five books of Gregory IX, it was called the *Liber Sextus*. The other collection was called the *Clementinae*, from Pope

---

[58] The first part consists of 101 Distinctions subdivided into Canons, the second of 36 Causes divided into Questions and subdivided into Canons, and the third of five Distinctions divided into Canons.

Clement V, and promulgated in 1317. There are also two later collections of private authority, the *Extravagantes* (*i.e. extra collectiones publicas*) of John XXII, and the *Extravagantes communes* of several popes down to Sixtus IV in 1484. These various collections complete the body of law known as the *Corpus Juris Canonici*.[59] All existed separately until gathered together by order of Pope Gregory XIII and published with official authority in 1580. The documents contained in the *Corpus Juris Canonici* were frequently published with glosses or commentaries in the margins; the common gloss on the *Decretum* is that of Joannes Teutonicus (d. 1245), but there were many other commentators on parts of the *Corpus*, including Raymond of Pennaforte, Hostiensis (Henricus de Segusio, Bishop of Ostia) (d. 1271), and Panormitanus (Niccolo de' Tudeschis, Archbishop of Palermo) (d. 1445).[60] After the Council of Trent (1545–63), pontifical constitutions continued to appear, and a revised Codex of Canon Law was promulgated by Benedict XV in 1917.[61] A further revised Code of Canon Law came into force in 1983.

In addition, the canon law included bodies of local canons, bodies of state law on ecclesiastical matters, and the decisions of the Tribunal of the Rota and of the Congregations of Cardinals, while an enormous and valuable literature of commentaries grew up round the texts and decisions.

The canon law in Scotland[62] prior to the Reformation was generally that of the Continent of Europe and the usages of the Church were similar to those in France, rather than in England. In the twelfth century Robert, Bishop of St. Andrews, with the consent of David I, promulgated to his clergy the *Exceptiones Ecclesiasticarum Regularum,* the lineage of which had been traced to the *Decretum* of Ivo of Chartres. Later Scottish provincial councils promulgated canons in supplement of rules of the general canon law.

In the Middle Ages the Church courts exercised wide civil jurisdiction, including all matters of marriage, legitimacy and succession, with a possible ultimate appeal to Rome. At the Reformation, the canon law of marriage, legitimacy and succession was taken over by the Scottish secular

---

[59] This title is met from the 12th century, but was not officially adopted until 1671. The best edition is by Friedberg (2 vols., Leipzig, 1879–81). See also P. Fournier and G. Le Bras, *Histoire des Collections Canoniques en Occident*, 1931. On the modes of citation see Brundage, *Medieval Canon Law*, App. I.

[60] On these scholars see Brundage, *Medieval Canon Law*, App. II.

[61] On the modern canon law, see Willock, "A Civil Lawyer looks at the Canon Law" (1962) 11 I.C.L.Q. 89.

[62] For Scotland, see Baird Smith, "Canon Law," in *Sources and Literature of Scots Law*, Stair Society; Mylne, *Canon Law; Statuta Ecclesiae Scoticanae* (ed. Robertson); *Statutes of the Scottish Church* (ed. Patrick); Stair, I, 1, 14; Fraser on *Husband and Wife*, Introduction; *Hay's Lectures on Marriage* (Stair Society). See also Mortimer, *Western Canon Law*; Maitland, *Roman Canon Law in the Church of England*; Moore, *Introduction to English Canon Law*; Galante, "The Modern Study of Canon Law," in *Essays in Legal History* (ed. Vinogradoff).

courts and survived almost unimpaired as part of the common law on these subjects.[63]

In Catholic countries, the canon law of the Roman Church has had a continuous influence on the legal and social system, and in practically every system of law stemming from Western Europe it has been influential to some extent. "Decretals and canons of a date earlier than the fifteenth century still govern the administration of the best disciplined and, from the point of view of numbers, the greatest of all monarchies—that of the Sovereign Pontiff—and regulate the religious and social life of the three hundred millions of the faithful of whom it is composed . . . The principles developed by the Church and applied by her during the period when no one disputed her control over all civil matters in which the salvation of souls was concerned, still underlie a considerable portion of the common law of the West, and are predominant in large provinces such as those of marriage or of obligations."[64]

Canon law played an essential role in the transmission of ancient Greek and Roman law and of Justinian's law, to Western Europe in the Middle Ages. From the renaissance of legal studies in the eleventh century, the civil law and canon law were principal subjects of study in the universities of Europe,[65] and the pre-Reformation Scottish universities were founded to study and teach, *inter alia*, civil and canon law.[66] Though since the Reformation the study of canon law has been largely abandoned in Britain, its historical importance was considerable and reference to the canonists as ultimate sources of some of the principles of modern law may still on occasion be required.[67] Public law and the law of nations, criminal law and procedure, civil law and procedure of Western Europe all owe something to canonist principles.

FEUDAL LAW

Feudalism originated in the anarchic kingdom of the Merovingian Franks in the sixth century, where bodies of retainers came to attach themselves to more powerful neighbours for protection, giving some service in return.[68] This protective relationship was constituted by commendation,

---

[63] *Cf.* the list of authorities cited in Fraser on *Husband and Wife*, Vol. II, p. xxxiv; see also *Collins v. Collins* (1884) 11 R.(H.L.) 19, 31, *per* Lord Watson; Brundage, *Law, Sex and Christian Society in Medieval Europe*; Brundage, *Sex, Law and Marriage in the Middle Ages.*

[64] Le Bras, "Canon Law," in *Legacy of the Middle Ages.*

[65] Rashdall, *The Universities of Europe in the Middle Ages, passim*; De Ridder-Symoens (ed.) *A History of the University in Europe*, I, 388; II 455, 509, 599. See further Durkan and Kirk, *The University of Glasgow 1451–1577*, 127–38; Grant, *Story of the University of Edinburgh*, I, 35, 63, 123, 167.

[66] Hence the degree in law (LL.B) is still *baccalaureus utriusque juris* (*i.e.* both civil and canon laws).

[67] See, *e.g. Kerr v. Martin* (1840) 2 D. 752; *Annan v. Annan*, 1948 S.C. 532. Notice, too, the reliance on canonists in Lord Fraser's treatise on *Husband and Wife.*

[68] See generally Vinogradoff, *Camb.Med.Hist.*, Vol. II, Chap. 20; Vol. III, Chap. 18; Ganshof, *Feudalism* (trans. Grierson); Bloch, *Feudal Society* (trans. Manyon), and "Feudalism" in *Encyc.Soc.Sc.*

and gradually each party came to have recognised obligations, the one to serve and respect his superior, the other to aid and support his vassal. It was often convenient to bestow on a person sufficient land to maintain him, which was done by a grant of a tenement or benefice, normally for life.

Later the institutions of vassalage and the benefice coalesced, and by the time of Charlemagne persons of higher social classes had become prepared to become vassals of the king. The tracts of land granted to them enabled them to create vassals for themselves. Throughout the eighth and ninth centuries the practice spread, coupled with a steady rise in the social status of vassals, and they now included the most important persons in the land. The mutual relationship was created by a promise of fealty by the vassal to his lord. In time, the services due from vassal to lord came to be better defined and more specialised, and they might include duties in the lord's household or in the management of his estates; but by the ninth century military services were taking precedence over all others. It was also recognised by then that both parties had interests in the benefice, the lord as owner and the vassal as holder in benefice, and by the ninth century benefices were becoming not personal, but inheritable, if the lord confirmed the benefice to the son of the former vassal.

Charlemagne and his advisers also found vassalage a remedy for the lack of administrators, judges and trained soldiers by attaching duties to a lord in the position of vassal of serving by advice, administering and doing justice among sub-vassals, and of giving military service as a mounted knight. By the classical age of feudalism, the tenth to thirteenth centuries, the relationship was worked out in detail and the vassal's tenement came to be known as his fief or fee.

Feudalism in its French form spread into England in the wake of the Norman Conquest, and into other countries.[69] In Northern Italy, feudalism attained a character rather different from elsewhere and is illustrated by the *Libri Feudorum* or *Consuetudines Feudorum*,[70] a private compilation made in Lombardy about 1100 by, it is thought, a feudal judge of Milan, but this found general acceptance throughout Western Europe. Later Italian jurists wrote on and commented on the law of the feus. Feudal relationships became more universal in England than ever in France or Germany, but in each country the rules of the feudal relationship were largely a matter of local or regional custom, and in each country jurists wrote works expounding the feudal customs of their country. Among such are Glanvill's *De Legibus et Consuetudinibus Angliae* in England (c. 1180)

---

[69] As to England, see Pollock and Maitland, *History of English Law before Edward I*; Round, *Feudal England*; Stenton, *The First Century of English Feudalism*; *Anglo-Saxon England*; Barrow, *Feudal Britain*.

[70] Ed. Lehmann, 1896; translated by Lord Clyde as Appendix to his translation of Craig's *Jus Feudale*.

and Philippe de Beaumanoir's *Coutumier de Beauvaisis* in northern France (*c.* 1280). About 1600 Sir Thomas Craig in Scotland wrote a *Jus Feudale*, which was used as a text in Germany as well as being valuable in Scotland.

THE LAW MERCHANT

The conduct of commerce by itinerant merchants originated far back in history, particularly in Mediterranean lands. In Roman law, trade with foreigners was regulated not by the civil law applicable to citizens, but by the *jus gentium*, which was more liberal and applied uniformly to any part of the world. Much business was done in medieval times at the great fairs and markets of Europe. Peripatetic merchants needed speedy resolution of their disputes, and the gathering of merchants from many countries tended to give an international character to the principles applied. During the Middle Ages the custom of merchants seems to have been developed principally in the Mediterranean cities and in Italy. Bills of exchange were probably invented by a Florentine and were well known in the Middle Ages. Insurance was recognised early in the Middle Ages, chambers of insurance to record contracts of insurance in case of dispute being found in Barcelona in the thirteenth century, in Bruges in 1310 and in London in 1574.[71] Company and banking law, and bankruptcy developed first in medieval times.

By the thirteenth century, it was accepted in England that pleas of merchants were wont to be decided by the law merchant at boroughs and fairs and that this law was different from the common law of England. Markets and fairs had their own machinery for resolving disputes, the most famous being the courts of piepowder, specially concerned with merchants who travelled from market to market, but these were later largely superseded by courts of the staple.

Later, the law merchant was administered in the English common law courts as a body of customs, to be proved as a fact in each individual case of doubt, but during the Chief Justiceship of Lord Mansfield it was incorporated into the common law, and to a substantial extent it is through following the English decisions that it has come to be incorporated in Scots law also.

Important contributions to the development of this branch of law were made by the writings of commercial men in England in the seventeenth and eighteenth centuries. Malynes' *Lex Mercatoria* (1622) treated of commercial and maritime law, money, bills and the courts in which the law merchant was administered, and set down in permanent form many of the mercantile usages and practices now becoming settled. Marius wrote a

---

[71] See generally Bewes, *Romance of the Law Merchant*; Lord Murray, "The Law Merchant" in *Sources and Literature of Scots Law*, (Stair Society) 241.

tract on bills of exchange in 1651, and in 1676 Molloy dealt with similar topics in his *De Jure Maritimo et Navali*. Later works included Beawes's *Lex Mercatoria Rediviva* (1751) which deals with the matters of trade and all the principal topics of commercial and maritime law, and Magens's essay on insurance (1755).

In England and Scotland, from the eighteenth century onwards, commercial litigation fell into the hands of the ordinary courts and the relevant principles became part of the ordinary law,[72] whereas in European countries generally, commercial law remained separate from the ordinary law and, when legal systems came to be codified, separate codes were normally enacted for civil and for commercial law.

MARITIME LAW

The earliest traces of legal rules on maritime matters come from the Mediterranean.[73] Seaborne commerce there developed early and we know of a body of law, the *Lex Rhodia*, which grew up in the maritime centre of Rhodes two or three centuries before Christ. The *Basilica* of the late ninth century contained a collection of maritime rules and there was another, possibly earlier, collection known as the Rhodian Sea Law.[74]

Later, maritime law developed as the custom of various ports and can be found in the custumals of commercial towns, later more widely adopted. Of these, particularly important are: the Laws or Judgments of Oléron, based on decisions of the merchant court of Oléron, probably dating from the twelfth century, which were adopted by the seaports of Normandy and Brittany, transplanted into England and copied in English compilations, such as the Black Book of the Admiralty[75]; the *Consolato del Mare* of about 1340, compiled from the customs of Barcelona and accepted in the Mediterranean; and the codes of Lubeck and Wisby, current in the Baltic and influenced by the Laws of Oléron. The Wisby sea laws are cited in Scotland in Balfour's *Practicks*. There were others too, such as the sea laws of Amalfi and Trani. Welwod, Professor of Law at St. Andrews, published *The Sea Laws of Scotland*[76] in 1590, and in 1613 an *Abridgment of All the Sea Laws*.

In Scotland and England, the maritime law was administered by the local Admiralty courts from early times, and also in Scotland by the Dean

---

[72] In this process of incorporating the principles of the law merchant into the fabric of English law, the work of Chief Justices Coke, Holt and Mansfield was of outstanding importance. For England, see generally Holdsworth, *History of English Law*, V, 60; VIII, 99; XII, 524; *Select Cases concerning the Law Merchant* (Selden Society, 3 vols.).

[73] See Sanborn, *Origins of the Early English Maritime and Commercial Law*; and "Maritime Law" in *Encyc.Soc.Sc.*; Holdsworth, "The Law Merchant" in *Essays in Anglo-American Legal History*, I, 289.

[74] See Ashburner, *The Rhodian Sea Law*.

[75] Ed. Sir Travers Twiss (Rolls Series). This was a collection of documents for the use of the English Court of Admiralty, not earlier than the mid-15th century.

[76] Reprinted in *Scottish Text Society Miscellany*, 1933.

of Guild and the Water Bailie. It continued to partake of an international character and the main forms of maritime legal documents, such as the charterparty, were settled in outline at an early date.

In Scotland, the Court of Admiralty was merged in the Court of Session in 1830, since at least when the maritime law has been administered as part of Scots law. In England, in 1875 the High Court of Admiralty was made part of the Probate, Divorce and Admiralty Division of the High Court. Since 1971 it has been part of the Queen's Bench Division.

ENGLISH LAW

The development of the law of England has been as significant for the law of the modern British Commonwealth, and of English-speaking parts of the world generally, as the Roman law has been for most European countries and the civilisations derived therefrom.[77] The Norman Conquest and the greater power and unifying tendencies of the Norman kings were a decisive influence in creating a common law in place of the pre-existing bodies of local customary law. The kings assumed control of the administration of justice and gradually a system of courts developed out of the Curia Regis. The courts of Exchequer, Common Pleas and King's Bench successively emerged, and the Norman and Angevin kings adopted the system of sending out royal justices throughout the kingdom to hold assizes, at first only for criminal, but later (1285) also for civil cases, and this was a powerful factor in creating a law common to all England. The characteristic of common law procedure was that there was a separate form of initial writ for each cause of action, and the slow development of various forms of action, which went on for some six centuries, had a profound influence on the development and content of the rules of substantive law. The mode of trial depended on the form of action.

The victory of royal justice over local courts and regional customary law was completed by the rise of the Justices of the Peace in the thirteenth and fourteenth centuries. From 1363 they held sessions quarterly, and Parliament regularly added duties, both judicial and administrative, to their original police function.

Equity

The common law thus early became hidebound by formalism, and hence became rigid and inflexible and unable to do justice in cases not covered by an existing form of action. The practice developed of petitioning the

---

[77] On the development of English law generally, see Plucknett, *Concise History of the Common Law*; Baker, *Introduction to English Legal History*; Pollock and Maitland, *History of English Law before the Time of Edward I* (2 vols.); Holdsworth, *History of English Law* (17 vols.). See also Winfield, *Chief Sources of English Legal History*; Holdsworth, *Sources and Literature of English Law*.

king for a remedy. He delegated the disposal of these petitions to the Chancellor (always in medieval times an ecclesiastic) as keeper of the King's conscience. In time, the Chancellor came to sit regularly to dispose of such petitions, thereby creating the Court of Chancery,[78] which tended to develop the rules for dealing consistently with particular petitions. Thus there developed a body of rules of equity, and these were developed particularly by such notable Chancellors as Bacon, Nottingham, Hardwicke and Eldon,[79] though particularly under Eldon Chancery proceedings became intolerably slow and expensive.[80] The principles administered by the Chancellors thus became over the centuries a body of rules mainly concerned to right the injustices and supply the defects of the common law, and its most significant contributions to English law were the rules relating to trusts, many of the rules as to mortgages, and the remedies of injunction, specific performance and rescission. Latterly the rules of equity were as well settled and nearly as rigid as the rules of common law, though not quite so trammelled by procedural formalism, but more bedevilled by prolixity and delay.

Blackstone

Important in the development was the publication of Blackstone's *Commentaries on The Laws of England* (1765–69), the most complete work hitherto written on English law, accurate in statement, lucid and elegant in exposition. "The *Commentaries* summed up, in accurate and readable form, the logical system which, with some help from the Legislature, had been built up by the legal profession throughout many centuries."[81] It summed up the law as it had developed down to the mid-eighteenth century. Though not blind to the defects of the law, Blackstone tended to be satisfied with the law as it was. The book had immense influence in England and in America and remains a legal classic.

Reform in the Nineteenth Century

Extensive reform of the court system was effected in the nineteenth century, culminating in 1875 in the abolition of all the older superior courts and the creation of the modern High Court and Court of Appeal. The High Court was at first divided into five divisions (Exchequer, Common Pleas, Queen's Bench, Chancery, and Probate, Divorce and Admiralty) with jurisdictions corresponding to the separate courts which they replaced, but in 1880 the first three were amalgamated into the

---

[78] On the development of equity, see Plucknett, *Concise History*, Part 5; Holdsworth, *History of English Law*, I, 395; Kerly, *Historical Sketch of the Court of Chancery*.

[79] On Eldon see R. Melikan, *John Scott, Lord Eldon, 1751–1838*.

[80] The case of *Jarndyce v. Jarndyce* in Dickens's *Bleak House* is a not unfair picture of the slow working of the Court of Chancery in its last years.

[81] Holdsworth, *Sources and Literature of English Law*, 158. On Blackstone, see also Hanbury, *The Vinerian Chair and Legal Education*.

Queen's Bench Division. In 1971 the last was renamed the Family Division.

At that time, common law and equity were nominally merged and all courts were empowered to give both legal and equitable remedies, but many traces of the former division still survive. Barristers still tend to practise in common law matters or chancery matters, which are dealt with in the divisions of the court corresponding to the old separate courts.

Local courts of limited jurisdiction had largely disappeared in England in medieval times and the modern system of county courts was created in 1846.

Expansion of the Common Law

The law of England went abroad with the Pilgrim Fathers, with later colonists in America and Canada, and later to South Africa, Australia and New Zealand. Though in time these countries, and other former British colonies, developed their own legal systems, it has generally been on the basis of English common law and equity, and in some cases there have survived abroad elements which have disappeared from the law now known in England. In Quebec, the common law did not displace law based on French (ultimately Roman) law, and in South Africa it influenced, but did not supersede, the Roman-Dutch law imported by the original Dutch settlers, which is the main basis of South African law.[82]

Scots Law

The development of Scots law is considered in Chapter 4.

II.—LEGAL THEORY AND PHILOSOPHY OR JURISPRUDENCE

The topic of jurisprudence[83] is variously defined as the "examination of the precepts, ideals and techniques of the law in the light derived from present knowledge in disciplines other than the law,"[84] "the body of theories of and about law,"[85] "the study and systematic arrangement of the

---

[82] On the expansion of the common law, see Bryce, "The Extension of Roman and English Law Throughout the World" in *Studies in History and Jurisprudence*, I, 72; volumes in the series *The British Commonwealth; The Development of Its Laws and Constitutions,* and since 1965 the *Annual Survey of Commonwealth Law.* On development in America, see Pound, *The Formative Era of American Law*; Wigmore (ed.), *Essays in Anglo-American Legal History* (3 vols.). Kent's *Commentaries on American Law*, founded on Blackstone, were published in 1826–30.

[83] On the meaning of the word itself, see Brown, "Ulpian's Definition of Jurisprudence" (1921) 33 J.R. 128; Campbell, "A Note on The Word Jurisprudence" (1943) 58 L.Q.R. 334. Numerous phrases are used as synonyms of jurisprudence in this sense; they include legal theory or theory of law, legal philosophy or philosophy of law, legal thought, and legal science or science of law.

[84] Stone, *Province and Function of Law*, 25; *Legal Systems and Lawyer's Reasonings*, 16.

[85] Patterson, *Jurisprudence: Men and Ideas of the Law*, 1.

general principles of law in its widest sense,"[86] and "the science of the first principles of the civil law . . . those more fundamental conceptions and principles which serve as the basis of the concrete details of the law."[87]

It is essentially thinking about law in general, as distinct from seeking to know what the law of any system on a particular matter is. It is concerned with such problems as the nature of law; the historical origins and development from primitive times of legal institutions and ideas generally; their relationship with other social phenomena; the relationship of law with theories of morality and of the state; the relation between law and justice and the manner in which law maintains justice; the sources of the law and their interpretation; the examination of the judicial process; and the elucidation of the meaning, significance and use of such fundamental legal conceptions as the terms right, duty, obligation, ownership, possession, malice, intention, motive, liability and so on, but different jurists at different times have approached these and kindred problems from very different angles and have evolved very different and contradictory theories. The one general element in all jurisprudence is the attempt to question presuppositions, to examine critically and analyse and discover the general ideas, principles and theory underlying various sets of actual rules of law.[88]

The literature of jurisprudence is enormous, frequently voluminous and obscure, and in every language, while its pursuit frequently draws heavily on disciplines, such as logic, philosophy and psychology, sociology and political theory, relatively unfamiliar to the legal student but which help to cast light on central problems of legal studies.

Furthermore, the approach of different jurists and different books is very diverse,[89] some dealing in a most abstract way with the most general notions and problems, and having little apparent connection with the legal system actually applied in any country, while others deal almost exclusively with specific systems of law to such an extent as to be in many respects little more than generalised accounts of that legal system, examining general notions entirely in the light of one particular system of law.

Broadly speaking, there are three main schools of jurists, or approaches to jurisprudence.[90] The first, the oldest and most voluminous, is philosophical jurisprudence.[91] It deals with such topics as the concept of justice and

[86] Keeton, *Elementary Principles of Jurisprudence*, 4.

[87] Salmond, *Jurisprudence*, 2. See further Allen, "Jurisprudence—What and Why," in *Legal Duties*, 1; Pound, *Jurisprudence*, I, Chap. 1.

[88] It is sometimes denied that any principles can be discovered at all: see, *e.g.* Harvey, "A Job for Jurisprudence" (1944) 7 M.L.R. 42, and the reply, Kennedy, "Another Job for Jurisprudence" (1945) 8 M.L.R. 21.

[89] See Vinogradoff, "The Study of Jurisprudence," in *Collected Papers*, II, 205, and "Aims and Methods of Jurisprudence," *ibid*. 319; Allen, "Jurisprudence—What and Why," in *Legal Duties*, 1.

[90] Stone, *Province and Function of Law*, Chap. 1, pp. 182–187.

[91] Some leading figures of this school are St. Thomas Aquinas, Grotius, Bentham, Kant, Hegel, Jhering, Lorimer, Stammler, del Vecchio, Geny, Duguit.

its relations with law; the distinction, if any, between the spheres of law, morality and other factors of social control; the ethical significance and validity of fundamental legal conceptions and principles; and the criticism of legal institutions, and problems of legal reform. This approach has been favoured more on the Continent than in Britain and frequently by scholars who were philosophers primarily rather than jurists, and whose theories of law reflect their philosophical positions. This approach comprises many different and even conflicting theories, arrived at from different philosophic standpoints. It includes natural lawyers, who see law as based on a higher law ordained by God, divine or natural reason, positivists, who see law as fundamentally the commands of political superiors to inferiors and distinct from morals, and Marxists; who see law as economically determined and an instrument whereby the economic rulers keep the masses in subjection.

The second school is analytical jurisprudence, which has found greatest favour in the English-speaking countries.[92] It has been profoundly influenced by its founder John Austin,[93] and for long after his time analytical jurisprudence was regarded in English-speaking countries as the main topic of juristic speculation. It proceeds mainly by seeking to resolve a legal system into its fundamental conceptions (such as rights, obligation, possession), and subjecting these to close examination. Accordingly, it relies largely on logic and semantics. But disregard of the moral and social implications of law tends to reduce purely analytical jurisprudence to arid formalism so that it cannot usefully be pursued alone and the later followers of Austin have not avoided all questions of the rightness of law and its relation to justice. A modern development, which is the highest development of analytical positivism, is the Pure Theory of Hans Kelsen.

The third school is sociological jurisprudence, which has been developed very largely in America in the present century.[94] It studies particularly the interaction between social forces and the law, and the ways in which law works and gives effect to the different claims, interests, rights and duties of men interacting in society. This school of jurisprudence has to a large extent superseded the nineteenth-century school of historical

---

[92] In fact Austin owed a great deal to Jeremy Bentham. Leading figures include Austin, Markby, Holland, Salmond.

[93] 1790–1859: Professor of Jurisprudence at University College, London, 1826–32; *The Province of Jurisprudence Determined* was first published in 1832. On Austin, see further the article in D.N.B., Vol. II by Sir John Macdonell; Sarah Austin's Memoir in the 5th edition of his *Lectures on Jurisprudence*, and the Introduction to the 1954 edition of the *Province* (ed. Hart) in the Library of Ideas.

[94] Leading figures are Pound, Frank, Llewellyn and Stone. Sociological jurisprudence is connected with, but distinct from, sociology of law, which is the sociological analysis of the phenomena of law, such as courts and judges, legislators and lawyers, law-abiding and law-breaking, of the relations between law and society, conflict resolution, and the functioning of law. See Ehrlich, *Fundamental Principles of the Sociology of Law*; Timasheff, *Introduction to the Sociology of Law*; Sawer, *Law in Society*; Selznik, "Sociology of Law" in *Int.Encyc.Soc.Sc.*

jurisprudence[95] which was primarily concerned with the manner of growth of legal systems, their evolution and organic development, and the evaluation of the various sources and influences which had contributed to their forms and characteristics.[96] Associated with sociological jurisprudence is American Realism, which stresses what courts do about disputes, and Scandinavian Realism, which sees law as directed not to justice but to social aims and social justice.

The importance of jurisprudence cannot be overestimated. It is a fundamental branch of legal study, though too frequently it receives inadequate attention, and legal study generally pays too much attention to dogmatic rules of law. Law-making and law-enforcing without ideals is worthless. "Philosophy of law lies at the base of all divisions of legal science."[97] "This neglect of legal theory and philosophy, added to a concentration on the substantive rules of law, must inevitably lead to a failure by the general body of lawyers, to appreciate not only the nature and purpose of law but also the place of law among the other social sciences." "We have entered upon a period of profound social and legal adjustments—particularly in the department of social legislation. Yet the general body of English lawyers is wholly untrained in legal science."[98]

It is true that law is a practical matter, but "the law is not identical with the science of the law. Every science is essentially theory; at the very basis of every action, however practical, is always theory, and no science is possible without philosophy."[99]

Jurisprudence, moreover, is not without practical utility and the most fundamentally important cases frequently turn on an essentially jurisprudential point, such as the scope and purpose of the criminal law,[1] or the morality of penalising an attempt at rescue,[2] or the liability to punishment of a person of "diminished responsibility."[3] Similarly the reform of the law of divorce, or abortion, or sexual offences raises jurisprudential and moral problems.

III.—COMPARATIVE LEGAL STUDIES

Despite its name, comparative law is neither a body of law nor a branch or department of the law of any country and it would be better named

---

[95] Some writers treat the historical school as a distinct, fourth, school of jurisprudence.

[96] See further Kantorowicz, "Savigny and the Historical School of Law" (1938) 53 L.Q.R. 326. Leading figures are Savigny, Puchta, Maine, Bryce and Vinogradoff.

[97] Kocourek, *An Introduction to the Science of Law*, 3.

[98] Parry, "Economic Theories in English Case Law," 47 L.Q.R. 183, 186. Note that the terms legal science and science of law are sometimes used, as here, in the narrow sense of legal theory or jurisprudence.

[99] Kunz, "The American Science of International Law," in *Law: A Century of Progress*, II, 166, 182.

[1] *Shaw v. D.P.P.* [1962] A.C. 220.

[2] *Steel v. Glasgow Iron and Steel Co.*, 1944 S.C. 237.

[3] *Kirkwood v. H.M. Advocate*, 1939 J.C. 36.

comparative legal studies.[4] It is, rather, a technique of study and research originating from the facts that different countries have different systems and rules of law, applying different legal solutions to very similar problems, and that it is enlightening and stimulating to see what these other solutions are, so as not to fall into the easy error of thinking that the solution propounded by one's own legal system is the best, or the natural, or the only one.[5] This involves obtaining at least a general acquaintance with the judicial structure and the sources, literature and main principles of some foreign systems of law. There are in the world about 180 recognised states, each of which has at least one legal system. Many have distinct systems in provinces or territories within the state. Not only complete legal systems, but also any major branches of several legal systems, can usefully be compared; thus, study may be directed to comparative constitutions, comparative law of contract, of delict, of matrimonial property, or of criminal procedure.[6]

The function of comparative legal study is variously said to be the ascertainment of principles common to all civilised systems of law, or the discovery of the causes which underlie the development and extinction of legal institutions, or the promotion of unification of legal rules followed in civilised communities, but in fact the comparative method is sufficiently elastic to embrace all activities concerned with the study of foreign law, the resemblances and differences between different legal systems, and the results achieved by different legal methods, techniques and principles applied to fundamentally similar problems.[7] This study may have practical as well as cultural value as the increase in international intercourse today more frequently requires some appreciation of foreign legal doctrines and conceptions, or at least awareness of the salient characteristics of the other systems involved. So, too, comparative study may suggest ways of law reform, or a solution for problems not hitherto determined in the student's own system. Traditionally, Scots law has been developed and studied comparatively, and the institutional writers, particularly Stair and Bankton, have a strongly developed comparative approach.[8]

Many of the world's developed legal systems fall conveniently into two families: those which are derived ultimately from the Civil or Roman law,

---

[4] The best general introduction to the subject is Gutteridge, *Comparative Law* (2nd ed.), 1949. See also Derrett (ed.), *An Introduction to Legal Systems*; David and Brierley, *Major Legal Systems in the World Today*; Buckland and McNair, *Roman Law and Common Law* (2nd ed.), by Lawson; Lawson, *A Common Lawyer looks at the Civil Law*; Schmitthoff, "The Science of Comparative Law" (1939) 7 C.L.J. 95; Lord Cooper, "The Importance of Comparative Law in Scotland," in *Selected Papers*, 142; Lord Macmillan, "Scots Law as a subject of Comparative Study" (1933) 48 L.Q.R. 477.

[5] *cf.* Lepaulle, "The Function of Comparative Law" (1922) 35 H.L.R. 838, 858; Gutteridge, "The Value of Comparative Law" (1931) J.S.P.T.L. 26.

[6] *cf.* Hazeltine, "The Study of Comparative Legal History" (1927) J.S.P.T.L. 27.

[7] *cf.* Walton, "The Study of Foreign Laws" (1934) 46 J.R. 1; Gutteridge, "Comparative Law and the Law of Nations" (1944) 21 B.Y.I.L. 1.

[7] *cf.* Lord Cooper, "The Importance of Comparative Law in Scotland," in *Selected Papers*, 142.

or have absorbed it as a principal ingredient in their modern developed system; and those based on the common law, which, Germanic in origin, was developed from the eleventh century by the English courts and spread over the world with the English people and language.[9] The former is the foundation or a principal element in the law of modern continental European countries, Central and South America, Quebec, Louisiana, South Africa, Ceylon and Scotland,[10] and French, Dutch, Spanish and Portuguese colonies and settlements; the latter is the basis of the law of England and Wales, Ireland, the United States (except Louisiana and Puerto Rico), Canada (except Quebec), Australia and New Zealand, of India (except over Hindus and Mohammedans as to inheritance and family law), and generally in former British colonies. While there is this familial distinction, some systems, basically of the Roman law family, have been and are being much influenced by common law conceptions and methods, as in the cases of Scotland, Louisiana and South Africa,[11] so much so as sometimes to be described as mixed or hybrid systems. The Scandinavian countries have distinct legal systems which embody features characteristic of both civil law and common law countries.[12] After 1945, the system of law developed since 1917 in Russia based on Communist ideology, was extended as a concomitant of military occupation to all the countries of Eastern Europe and transformed their legal systems into systems on the Russian model[13] while Communist China has also radically changed its legal system in the same general direction and made it an agency for changing its society.[14] Islamic law, based on the Koran, is a powerful influence in North Africa and the Middle East,[15] and former colonial territories in Africa, on gaining independence, commonly develop legal systems incorporating elements of Islamic or tribal law, and of civil or common law from the legal system of the former governing European power.

---

[9] See Schlesinger, *Comparative Law; Cases and Materials, passim;* von Mehren, *The Civil Law System*, Chap. 1; Symposium on "The Migration of the Common Law" (1960) 76 L.Q.R. 41. See also Wigmore, *Panorama of the World's Legal Systems*, 3 vols.

[10] René David, *Introduction à l'Etude du Droit privé de l'Angleterre*, 164, characterises Scots law as "très différent du droit anglais," and Levy Ullman, "The Law of Scotland" (1925) 37 J.R. 370, described it as "absolutely Roman in character."

[11] Amos, "The Common Law and the Civil Law in the British Commonwealth of Nations" (1937) 50 H.L.R. 1249, *cf.* Lawson, *Rational Strength of English Law*, 5; Jolowicz, "The Civil Law in Louisiana" [1954] C.L.P., 1; Hahlo and Kahn, *South Africa: the Development of Its Laws.*

[12] Orfield, *The Growth of Scandinavian Law;* Gomard, "Civil Law, Common Law and Scandinavian Law" (1961) 5 *Scand. Studies in Law*, 27.

[13] See further Gsovski and Grzybowski, *Government, Law and Courts in the Soviet Union and Eastern Europe*, 2 vols. For modern law see Butler, *Russian Law.*

[14] Buxbaum, "Preliminary Trends in the Development of the Legal Institutions of Communist China" (1962) 11 I.C.L.Q. 1.

[15] Fyzee, *Outline of Muhammadan Law;* Anderson, *Islamic Law in Africa.*

IV.—PUBLIC INTERNATIONAL LAW

Legal rules regulating international relations and the practices of states *inter se* have existed from a very early period,[16] but modern international law is a product of the turbulent sixteenth and seventeenth centuries, which witnessed the break-up of the medieval community of mankind under the Pope and the Emperor and, as part of the turmoil produced by the Renaissance and the Reformation, the emergence of independent nation-states, each administered by a separate government with its own particular law.[17] Thus there grew up a body of "rules which determine the conduct of the general body of civilised states in their mutual dealings."[18] The name International Law was invented by Jeremy Bentham in 1780.[19] It may now be described as "the body of customary and conventional rules which are considered legally binding by civilised states in their intercourse with each other,"[20] or "the body of rules and usages which among civilised independent states are recognised as binding upon their several governments in their dealings with one another and with each other's subjects,"[21] or "the principles and rules of conduct declaratory thereof which states feel themselves bound to observe, and, therefore, do commonly observe in their relations with each other."[22]

The modern system dates from the publication in 1625 of Hugo Grotius' *De Jure Belli ac Pacis*[23] though the system had been taking shape in the works of such jurists as Vitoria, Suarez, Ayala and Gentilis in the previous century. The immediate source of his work was to be found in the barbarities of the European Wars of Religion, and particularly of the Thirty Years' War (1618–48). The first result of the Peace of Westphalia, which ended that war, was the formal recognition of a society of independent nations occupying defined territory, equal before the law, and transacting with one another as principal parties without reference to Pope or Emperor. Since that time, general congresses of states, the practice of establishing embassies and legations at the courts of other

---

[16] See, *e.g.* I Samuel xv, 18; II Samuel xii, 31; Greek and Roman instances cited in Holland, *Lectures on International Law*, 10–15; Vinogradoff, "Historical Types in International Law," in *Collected Papers*, II, 248; and generally Walker, *History of the Law of Nations*; Nussbaum, *Short History of the Law of Nations*; Butler and Maccoby, *Development of International Law*.

[17] Lawrence, *Principles of International Law*, Chap. 2; Pollock in 12 *Camb.Mod.Hist.*, Chap. 22.

[18] Lawrence, *Principles of International Law* (7th ed.), 1.

[19] Bentham, *Introduction to the Principles of Morals and Legislation*, Chap. xvii, s. xxv.

[20] Oppenheim, *International Law*, I, 4.

[21] Pollock in 12 *Camb.Mod.Hist.*, 703.

[22] Hyde, *International Law*, I, 1; see further Lauterpacht, *The Function of Law in the International Community*; Jenks, "The Scope of International Law" (1954) 31 B.Y.I.L. 1.

[23] Hugo de Groot or Grotius: 1585–1645: scholar and jurist; Grand Pensionary of West Friesland and Holland: Swedish ambassador to France, 1634–44. See Lauterpacht, "The Grotian Tradition in International Law" (1946) 23 B.Y.I.L. 1; and Oppenheim, *International Law*, I, 79 *et seq.* and further A. Nussbaum, *A Concise History of the Law of Nations* (1934).

states, and diplomatic, commercial and legal relations between states have become formalised. International law, accordingly, has come to be the body of rules which regulates the actions of civilised states in their dealings with one another, defining the essentials of state personality, the conditions under which states are recognised as coming into existence or disappearing, their sovereignty, jurisdiction, mutual responsibilities, and their rights, duties and privileges *inter se* in time of peace and war, as amicable partners, as belligerents and as neutrals. It deals also with international organisations and institutions and resolution of international disputes.

This body of law was built up largely from the writings of jurists, such as the followers of Grotius: men such as Pufendorf,[24] Thomasius,[25] Burlamaqui,[26] Wolff,[27] Vattel,[28] Bynkershoek[29] and von Martens.[30] They based their work, originally, largely on Roman law, theology, canon law and the concept of a "law of nature," and, later, on developing usages.[31]

It must be remembered that it is disputable how far international law is properly called law in the strict sense of that word, in respect that it lacks some of the usually accepted criteria of law.[32] Thus there is no legislative body which promulgates rules of law, authoritatively declaring the true rule and altering previous rules; there is only a rudimentary and frequently ineffective system of sanction or compulsion in case of disobedience; and the jurisdiction of international tribunals is limited, their decisions are frequently flouted or ignored, and are not enforceable with the same certainty as those of domestic tribunals.[33] To a large extent international law is still the custom and practice of nations, a body of rules binding so far as accepted, and for that reason it is still commonly defined in terms of rules and standards of conduct rather than of law.

Thus, Hall[34] defined international law as consisting in "certain rules of conduct which modern civilised states regard as being binding on them in their relations with one another with a force comparable in nature and

---

[24] 1632–94; Professor of the Law of Nature at Heidelberg, 1661; Professor of Jurisprudence at Lund, 1670; *De jure naturae et gentium*, 1672; historiographer at Stockholm, 1677, and at Berlin, 1688.

[25] 1655–1728; Professor at Leipzig and later at Halle; *Fundamenta juris naturae et gentium*, 1705.

[26] 1694–1748; *Principes du droit naturel*, 1747.

[27] 1679–1754; *Institutiones juris naturae et gentium*, Halle, 1750.

[28] 1714–67; *Le droit des gens*, 1758.

[29] 1673–1743; *De dominio maris*, 1702; *De foro legatorum*, 1721; *Quaestiones juris publici libri duo*, 1737.

[30] 1756–1821; *Précis du droit des gens modernes de l'Europe*, 1788.

[31] McNair, "The Debt of International Law in Britain to the Civil Law and Civilians" (1953) 39 *Trans.Grotius.Soc.* 183; Johnson, "The Scottish Tradition in International Law" (1978) 9 *Can.Y.B.I.L.* 3.

[32] See also Ago, "Positive Law and International Law" (1957) 51 A.J.I.L. 691.

[33] Collier and Lowe, *The Settlement of Disputes in International Law*.

[34] *Treatise on International Law* (8th ed.), I.

degree to that binding the conscientious person to obey the laws of his country, and which they also regard as being enforceable by appropriate means in case of infringement." In fact, however, this controversy is academic and international law is increasingly, and now usually, regarded as law, though still underdeveloped in comparison with state law in respect of definiteness and enforcement, and it is being increasingly accepted expressly as binding on states. "The best evidence for the existence of international law is that every actual state recognises that it does exist and that it is itself under an obligation to observe it. States may often violate international law just as individuals often violate municipal law; but no more than individuals do states defend their violations by claiming that they are above the law."[35]

The subjects of international law are states—their existence, recognition, jurisdiction, and responsibility—transactions between states, agreements and disputes. The sources of modern international law are: international conventions establishing rules expressly recognised by the contracting states; international custom as evidence of a general practice recognised as law; the general principles of law recognised by civilised nations; judicial decisions; and the teachings of the most highly qualified publicists of the various nations, as subsidiary means for the determination of rules of law.[36] In modern times, treaties, alliances and conventions, ordinances of particular states, the practice and custom of states, decisions of international tribunals and courts, and opinions of jurists to their governments have added substantially to the volume of law recognised, while more recently the growth and development of international institutions and agencies has also contributed a large volume of new law.[37] The Hague Conferences of 1899 and 1907 reduced to written form many of the rules hitherto unwritten, such as the rights and duties of neutral states. Later international conferences have reached agreements on many disputable issues. The League of Nations and the United Nations Organisation, and their respective subsidiary organs, including the Permanent Court of International Justice (1921) and the International Court of Justice (1946), have made much new law,[38] while increasing international intercourse has continually raised fresh problems. National legislation is frequently passed to incorporate international conventions into domestic law.

International administrative, social and economic organisations have developed enormously in the past century and such bodies as the

---

[35] Brierley, *Outlook for International Law*, 5; see also Fitzmaurice, "Foundations of the Authority of International Law and the Problem of Enforcement" (1956) 19 M.L.R. 1; McNair, "General Principles of Law Recognised by Civilised Nations" (1957) 33 B.Y.I.L. 1.

[36] Statute of the International Court of Justice, 1945, Art. 38.

[37] See Lauterpacht, *The Development of International Law by the International Court*; McNair, "International Law in Great Britain, 1920–70" (1971) 87 L.Q.R. 173.

[38] See also Lauterpacht, *Private Law Sources and Analogies of International Law*; "Decisions of Municipal Courts as a Source of International Law" (1939) 16 B.Y.I.L. 65; *Development of International Law by the International Court, passim.*

Universal Postal Union (1878) and the International Labour Organisation (1919) have added great volumes to the body of international agreement, while the growth of population, science, industry, commerce, foreign trade and investment in recent times have made international relations even more complex and more in need of legal regulation.[39] The conduct of foreign relations of every kind requires regard to relevant principles of international law. The body of law relating to international organisations and peaceful relations now greatly outweighs the subjects of war and neutrality which bulk so largely in the older books. But international law is still a long way short of the developed state attained by the municipal law of the more advanced countries.

It is uncertain whether international law is deemed incorporated as a whole into Scots law or is part of Scots law only in so far as accepted and recognised by the courts and thereby transformed into rules of Scots law.[39a] If a statute conflicts with a rule of customary international law, the statute must be applied.[40]

The United Nations operates through the Security Council of 15 members, which is concerned with the peaceful settlement of disputes likely to endanger the maintenance of international peace and security, and it may take action including the use of the armed force of members states. A notable example of such action was the expulsion of Iraq from Kuwait in 1991 (the "Gulf War") by a multinational force. Its other organs are the General Assembly, which discusses and recommends, the International Court of Justice, which adjudicates on disputes between states only, the Economic and Social Council, the Trusteeship Council, and the secretariat. There are also a large number of specialised agencies, including the International Labour Organisation, the World Health Organisation and the International Monetary Fund.

Moreover, in modern times international law is ceasing to be primarily a body of law between states, but "increasingly includes cross-frontier relationships of individual organisations and corporate bodies which call for appropriate legal regulation on an international basis,[41] problems of economic and technological interdependence requiring the regulation on the basis of common rules of matters which do not *per se* involve inter-state relations in any real sense, and rights designed to provide the individual, and in some cases organisations, with a measure of protection against the individual member states of the international community."[42] Most modern international law is treaty law, indeed international legislation, and increasingly it deals with trade, commerce, finance and trans-

---

[39] See generally Ball and Killough, *International Relations*.
[39a] See *Kaur v. Lord Advocate*, 1980 S.C. 319.
[40] *Mortensen v. Peters* (1906) 8 F. (J.) 93.
[41] *e.g.* the International Civil Aviation Organisation.
[42] Jenks, "The Scope of International Law" (1954) 31 B.Y.I.L. 1.

frontier aspects of topics of private law,[43] while the influence of juristic writing in developing international law is diminishing.

One purpose of the United Nations is to promote international co-operation for the protection of human rights. In 1948 it adopted a Universal Declaration of Human Rights and in 1966 International Covenants on Economic, Social and Cultural Rights and on Civil and Political Rights, but none of these is directly enforceable by aggrieved persons.

The relations between international law and state law are unsettled. British practice is to regard customary international law as part of British law (though in case of conflict a British statute must receive effect),[44] and Acts of Parliament have normally to be interpreted so as not to conflict with international law. But treaties have generally to be incorporated in British law by Act of Parliament before they are recognised in state law.[45]

V.—SUPRANATIONAL LAW

Supranational law arises where a group of states, without entering into any kind of federation or union, have created new institutions and transferred part of their national sovereign powers thereto. These institutions are not properly international, but only regional and limited in membership, yet their organisations and its law are above and wider than national law; it is intermediate in generality between international and national law.[46]

Since 1945, particularly in the face of the Russian threat to the independence of Western European countries, there has been a developing movement for the integration of these countries, towards a goal described by Sir Winston Churchill in 1946 as a "United States of Europe." The first European organisation was created by the Brussels Treaty of 1948 between Britain, France and the Benelux countries, followed closely by the Organisation for European Economic Co-operation in response to the American Marshall Plan to aid the recovery of Europe. In 1949 the Council of Europe was set up by these five countries along with Italy, Ireland and the three Scandinavian countries, with a Committee of Ministers and Consultative Assembly which can, however, only recommend to member governments.[47] In 1954 the Brussels Treaty Organisation was enlarged and converted into Western European

---

[43] Jennings, "The State of International Law Today" (1957) 4 J.S.P.T.L.(N.S.) 95; see also Jennings, "The Progressive Development of International Law" (1947) 24 B.Y.I.L. 301; McNair, "International Law in Great Britain, 1920–70" (1971) 87 L.Q.R. 173.

[44] *Mortensen v. Peters*, (1906) 8 F.(J) 93.

[45] *Walker v. Baird* [1892] A.C. 491, 497.

[46] For the meaning of the term "supranational" see Robertson, *European Institutions*, pp. 105–108. See also Efron and Nanes, "The Common Market and Euratom Treaties: Supranationality and the Integration of Europe" (1957) 6 I.C.L.Q. 670; Warner, "The Relationship between EEC Law and the National Laws of Member-States" (1977) 93 L.Q.R. 349.

[47] See generally Robertson, *The Council of Europe* (1961).

Union, a defence organisation, itself largely superseded since 1955 by NATO.[48] NATO is an association of European countries together with the United States of America and Canada, for co-operation particularly in defence. In 1960 a convention for the formation of the Organisation for Economic Co-operation and Development was signed; this included the United States of America and Canada and converted OEEC into an Atlantic Organisation (OECD).

The European Convention on Human Rights

In 1948 the United Nations adopted a Universal Declaration of Human Rights as a common standard of achievement. This was not legally binding, but some of its statements may have become customary international law. The rights stated were more precisely defined in 1976 by the International Covenant on Civil and Political Rights and the International Covenant on Economic, Social and Cultural Rights. Under the auspices of the Council of Europe, its member states concluded in 1950 a Convention for the Protection of Human Rights and Fundamental Freedoms, with later protocols.[49] What basis there is for alleging the existence of any such rights, what they may be, and how they are defined or qualified has given, and gives, rise to much jurisprudential dispute.[50] The Convention sets out in general terms certain substantive rights which states which are parties to the Convention are bound to accord to anyone within their jurisdiction, regardless of nationality. It created also a European Commission on Human Rights consisting of one member from each state, elected for six years, which decides issues by a majority of those present and voting, and a European Court of Human Rights, sitting in Strasbourg, consisting of one judge from each member state, elected by the Consultative Committee from a list submitted by members of the Council of Europe.[51] In 1998 the Commission and the Court were merged, with 40 judges sitting in panels of seven; cases may be referred to a grand chamber of 17, which, in some cases, might also hear appeals from panels. Though persons in Britain, once they had exhausted remedies available to them under Scots or English law, might complain to the Commission and, if it allowed it, to the Court, the rights set out in the Convention were not until 1998 part of

---

[48] France left NATO in 1967 and in consequence NATO headquarters were moved to Brussels which is the seat of the North Atlantic Council composed of the permanent representatives of the member states to the Organisation.

[49] See Jacobs and White, *The European Convention on Human Rights* (1996); Waldock, "The European Convention for the Protection of Human Rights and Fundamental Freedoms" (1958) 34 B.Y.I.L. 356; Robertson, "The European Court of Human Rights" (1959) 9 A.J.C.L. 1.

[50] See *e.g.* Shestack, "The Jurisprudence of Human Rights" in Meron (ed.) *Human Rights in International Law* (1984); Donnelly, *The Concept of Human Rights* (1985).

[51] For each case the court consists of a chamber of seven. The Commission was abolished in 1999.

nor directly enforceable in United Kingdom courts.[52] Persons cannot appeal to this Court from any United Kingdom court; if they wish to raise the matter they must do so separately.

The Court has no power to strike down national laws which it has held have infringed a person's human rights, but contracting states generally act to comply with the Court's decisions.

There is much criticism of the Convention and the Court's wide interpretations of it.

Judgments are binding in international law.[53] States against which a case is brought successfully are expected to alter their domestic laws to comply with Convention obligations. The main difficulty is to ensure compliance with the court's judgments.

In 1998, by the Human Rights Act 1998, Parliament laid down that a court or tribunal determining a question which had arisen in connection with a right set out in most of the Articles of the Convention, must take into account any judgment, decision, declaration or advisory opinion of the European Court of Human Rights, opinion of the Commission on Human Rights given in a report adopted under the Convention, decision of the Commission, or decision of the Committee of Ministers under Art. 46 of the Convention, so far as, in the opinion of the court or tribunal, it is relevant to the proceedings in which that question has arisen. Legislation must be read and given effect in a way which is compatible with Convention Rights. A court may make a declaration that a legislative decision is incompatible with a Convention Right. If a Minister of the Crown considers that there are compelling reasons to do so, he may by order make such amendments to the legislation as he considers necessary to remove the incompatibility.

The European Social Charter

This was intended to be complementary to the Human Rights Convention and guarantees a number of economic and social rights, such as the right to just conditions of employment. There is no machinery for direct enforcement of its provisions. In 1952 the Assembly of the Council of Europe adopted a recommendation for the establishment of a European Court of Justice and a European Act for the peaceful settlement of disputes, but later the International Court was put in place of the proposed European Court. The Assembly has also worked on a number of other Conventions of legal importance.[54]

---

[52] *Kaur v. Lord Advocate*, 1980 S.C. 319, 324, 328, 329, 332; *Malone v. Commissioner of Police of the Metropolis (No. 2)* [1979] Ch. 344; *Mutasa v. Att-Gen.* [1980] Q.B. 114; *Moore v. Secretary of State for Scotland*, 1985, S.L.T. 38, 41.

[53] Decisions are reported in European Human Rights Reports (Sweet & Maxwell) and Butterworths Human Rights Cases.

[54] See further Robertson, "The Legal Work of the Council of Europe" (1961) 10 I.C.L.Q. 143.

The European Communities

In 1951 France, Germany, Italy, Belgium, Holland and Luxembourg by a Treaty of Paris successfully formed the European Coal and Steel Community (ECSC) to pool their resources of iron, steel and coal in a single market without frontier barriers, and in 1957 they signed two Treaties of Rome[55] and thereby established the European Atomic Energy Community (Euratom), and the European Economic Community (EEC), (the Common Market), planning an area in which goods, persons, services and capital could move freely without hindrance at national frontiers by tariffs or import restrictions.

These three communities had each a High Authority (ECSC) or Executive Commission (EEC and Euratom) as executive, and a Council. In 1967 by a "Merger Treaty" the executives were merged into a single European Commission, and they have a single Council of Ministers, one European Parliamentary Assembly and one Court of Justice for all three. Though commonly referred to as the EC or European Community, the three communities continue to exist separately, regulated by the distinct treaties. All, like some other international organisations, report to the Assembly of the Council of Europe. Outside the Common Market, the United Kingdom took the lead in forming the European Free Trade Association (EFTA), to establish a free market between its members.[56] Greece and Turkey subsequently sought to be associated with EEC, and in 1961 the United Kingdom announced its intention to seek to join EEC and, in 1962, also to join ECSC and Euratom. These approaches were rejected by the European Community at the instance of France; a further application to join in 1967 was similarly rejected, but in 1973 the United Kingdom, Ireland and Denmark joined the three communities.[57] Greece joined in 1981, Spain and Portugal in 1986 and Austria, Finland and Sweden in 1995. Other countries are seeking membership, while others again, such as Malta, have sought association with the European Communities.

Agreement was reached in 1991 between the EC and the countries of EFTA to create a European Economic Area giving the latter countries entry to the EC's internal market, with free movement of goods, people, capital and services, but without subjection to the EC authorities or

---

[55] The text of the Paris and Rome Treaties is printed in Sweet & Maxwell's *European Community Treaties.*

[56] See European Free Trade Association Convention (Cmnd. 906, 1960) and European Free Trade Association Act 1960 (c. 19).

[57] European Communities Act 1972 (c. 8). Subsequent Orders made under the Act define what are the "Community Treaties" for the purposes of that Act. The terms on which the U.K. joined were "renegotiated" in 1974 and in a national referendum in June 1975 under the Referendum Act 1975 the people of the U.K. voted for continued membership; the voting was: To stay in—17·3m (43·2 per cent.); To withdraw—8·4m (21 per cent.); Abstained 14·3m (35·8 per cent.). Accordingly, only a minority of the electorate positively supported continued membership.

participation in EC decision-making.[58] This became effective 1994. There is nothing to prevent a state leaving the EC.

The Single European Act of 1986[59] made changes in the way the Communities work. The Treaty on European Union signed at Maastricht in 1992[60] brought into being the European Union, increased the powers of the European Parliament, sought to create a common foreign and security policy, and made provision for a move to a single currency with the creation of a European Central Bank having financial and legal powers. There is an agreement on social policy outside the direct ambit of the EC Treaty.

The European Communities thus set up are supranational entities and have legal personality under international law; each has legal personality in the law of each member state, but their constitutions do not. They are the product of continental political and legal philosophy and this influences their nature, legal structure and attitude to application and interpretation of law. There are five Community institutions: the Council of the EU, formerly called the Council of Ministers, which acts as principal legislative organ, consists of appropriate representatives of the governments of the member states, takes the policy decisions and seeks to co-ordinate the policies of the national governments and those of the Communities as a whole; the Commission, consisting of 20 members, two from each of the five major states and one from each of the others, which has functions of initiative, preparation, decision and execution; the Assembly or, now, European Parliament, which meets at Strasbourg,[61] to which the European Commission reports; and the Court of Justice of the Community, sitting at Luxembourg, which has to decide whether decisions of the executives and of the Council of the EU should be annulled, and other problems of the legal interpretation of the various treaties.[62] The judgments of the court have the force of law in community countries and are directly enforceable on individuals, firms, governments and the European Commission.[63] The Court of Auditors seeks to keep track of money. Since 1979 the members of the Parliament have been directly elected by the voters in the Member States. It elects its own President and vice-presidents, and members sit not as national blocs but in political groups. It operates largely through standing committees concerned with particular topics, *e.g.* agriculture. It does not legislate, but may discuss the

---

[58] The European Economic Area is judicially supervised by an EFTA Court and a joint committee to ensure harmony between the EEA Agreement and provisions of EU law: [1992] C.L.Y. 4735.

[59] Made effective in the U.K. by the European Communities (Amendment) Act 1986 (c. 58).

[60] Made effective in the U.K. by the European Communities (Amendment) Act 1993 (c. 32).

[61] Most committee meetings are held in Brussels.

[62] See further Arnull, *The European Union and its Court of Justice.*

[63] They are reported in Britain in the *Recueil de la Jurisprudence de la Cour* (1954–) in the *Common Market Law Reports* (1962–) and sometimes elsewhere.

Commission's annual report and debate the Commission's annual legislative programme. It must be consulted about certain legislative proposals and may put questions to the Council and the Commission. Its most important power (exercised in 1998) is to pass a motion of censure on the Commission, which causes the resignation of the whole Commission. But the Parliament is a very weak body compared with the UK and other national parliaments.

Since 1991 there has been a Community Ombudsman, appointed by the Parliament after each quinquennial election, to whom persons can complain of maladministration in the activities of the Commission institutions or bodies. Since 1974 there have also been regular meetings of heads of state and government, known as meetings of the European Council,[64] which has increasingly assumed overall authority in policy-making, though this body had no existence under the treaties and no power to make binding decisions. By resolution of 1978, it set up the European Monetary System. The Single European Act of 1986 recognised the European Council but gave it no powers or functions. It was to bring together the Heads of State of Governments and the President of the Commission of the Communities, with their foreign ministers, and to meet twice a year. There are also the body known as COREPER, the permanent representatives at Brussels of the member states, which is responsible for preparing the work of the EC Council and carrying out tasks assigned to it by the Council; and various consultative committees, *e.g.* on transport or monetary problems. The Maastricht Treaty created a Committee of the Regions consisting of representatives of regional and local bodies with advisory status.

Since 1974 a series of conferences have developed the organisation, increasingly in the direction of political union. The Single European Act 1986[65] declared it an object of the European Communities to make progress towards European unity. In some areas, it also replaced the requirement for unanimity in Council with qualified majority voting, which disabled any single state or a small minority of states from blocking certain initiatives. It renamed the Assembly as the European Parliament. A summit conference at Maastricht in 1991 gave rise to the Treaty on European Union, which sought to hasten progress of the internal market towards further European unity by political union and economic and monetary union. It also adopted the title European Union instead of European Community. It agreed that by 1999 all Member States which met the economic criteria would irrevocably fix exchange rates and automatically join a single currency, but a protocol to the Treaty secured for the United Kingdom an "opt out" from the single currency, and the

---

[64] Note that this body is distinct from both the Council of Europe and the EU Council or Council of Ministers under the EC Treaties. It first met in 1975.

[65] Given effect to by the European Communities (Amendment) Act 1986.

Social Chapter was excluded from the formal Treaty but made in an agreement signed by all the other (eleven) Member States. The Treaty also kept foreign, security and defence policy in the hands of national governments. The term "subsidiarity", the principle whereby decisions are taken at national level wherever possible, was adopted in the Treaty, rather than federalism, but subsidiarity never seems to be applied in practice. It was only with difficulty that the Treaty was ratified by parliament.[66]

Successive summit meetings[67] of the Member States have resulted in more and more powers being demanded by the leaders of the EU.

As a body which is a distinct legal entity, the Communities (taken together) have from their foundation been creating a body of law regulating their own organisation and those aspects of the life and work of the member states controlled by the Communities. It is an autonomous legal system independent of the systems of all member states.

Sources of EC now EU Law

The sources of Community law are (1) the founding treaties, accession treaties providing for the accession of new member states, ancillary protocols and conventions, treaties amplifying or amending the founding treaties, conventions between member states concluded within the ambit of the founding treaties, such as the Convention on Jurisdiction and the Enforcement of Judgments in Civil and Commercial Matters of 1968,[68] agreements with non-member states and associations of such states, and other international agreements; (2) legislation and decisions of Community institutions; (3) case-law of the Court of Justice of the Communities; (4) general principles of law drawn from the constitutions and legal systems of member states or international agreements to which the member states are parties; and (5) the opinions of jurists, academic writings, influential reports, answers to questions raised in the European Parliament, and statements issued by the Commission.

Among the "general principles", the Court of Justice has recognised (1) the principle of respect for fundamental human rights, such as the principles that a defender is entitled to know the claim made against him and to be heard in his own defence, that a person should not be tried twice for one offence or punished twice, that a person cannot be compelled to make admissions of wrongful conduct, to his own prejudice, and that a person charged is entitled to legal assistance in his defence; (2) the principle of certainty, that the application of the law to a particular set

---

[66] Given effect to by the European Communities (Amendment) Act 1993. See also *R. v. Secretary of State for Foreign and Commonwealth Affairs, ex p. Lord Rees-Mogg* [1994] Q.B. 552; *Monckton v. Lord Advocate*, 1995. S.L.T. 1201.

[67] In the European Communities (Amendment) Act, 1998.

[68] Given effect to in Britain by the Civil Jurisdiction and Judgments Act 1982.

of facts must be reasonably predictable; (3) the principle of proportionality, that means must be proportional to the end sought, and (4) the principle of equality of treatment and non-discrimination, so that persons similarly situated should be treated in the same way.

Language

The EU is a multi-lingual organisation, a fact which adds greatly to the problems of communication and of interpretation of law made by it. The Council determined that the official and working languages of the Community institutions are Danish, Dutch, English, Finnish, French, German, Greek, Italian, Portuguese, Spanish and Swedish. The *Official Journal*, and regulations and documents of general application, appear in all these 11 languages. Different language versions are equally authentic and interpretation of legislation involves comparison of different language versions. Legal concepts do not, however, necessarily have the same meaning as their nearest translation in another language, nor the same meaning in Community law as in the domestic law of member states. This leads the European Court sometimes to resort to consideration of the spirit of the text rather than literal interpretation of legislation. Proceedings before the European Court may be carried on in any of the languages, but the members of the Court in practice use French among themselves and most judgments are drafted and agreed in French. The language problem will become worse as the EU further enlarges, and it will be necessary to work in a few major languages only.[69]

The Subject-Matter of Community Law

Community law deals with topics of law connected with the furtherance of the purposes of the treaties, the co-ordination of national economic policies on agriculture, transport, steel, coal and atomic energy, the abolition of state restrictions on the free movement of goods, persons, services and capital, promotion of a common commercial policy, prevention of unfair trading practices, and harmonisation of national laws where their divergence impedes the creation or operation of the common market.

The Effect of Joining on Scots and English Law

The consequences of joining the EU for Scots and English law are profound. In the first place, joining involved the surrender by Parliament to EU institutions of some of its sovereign powers: certain powers were reserved to Community institutions and Parliament had to repeal inconsistent laws and refrain from encroaching on areas of Community

---

[69] Until at least the 17th century learned men all over Europe wrote and communicated in Latin and the Vatican still issues formal writs in that language. To adopt Latin would be a sensible compromise between national languages.

competence; in cases of conflict between Community law and municipal law, the former must prevail; and neither the British Parliament nor the courts could legislate or decide on any matter in a manner contrary to the EU rule.[70] This partial surrender of sovereignty was attacked by some individuals as illegally signing away some of the constitutional powers of the Crown[71] and as contravening the Treaty of Union of 1707.[72] In the second place, it involved accepting the primacy of Community law as rules having, in their various spheres, higher authority than any rules of national law. In cases of conflict, national rules must give way to Community rules.[73] Even an Act of Parliament can be struck down by the European Court as contrary to EU law.[74] Increasingly the EU (particularly the Commission) is becoming a dictator. In the third place, EU law does not merely affect governments and confer rights or impose duties on them, but provisions of EU law have direct applicability and, in some cases, direct effect. Direct application means that EU regulations become law in each member state when adopted by the relevant Community institution, without need for national re-enactment or ratification, so that they have simultaneous and uniform application throughout the Community. Direct effect is a concept developed by the European Court and means that some provisions of Community law may create rights and obligations enforceable by individuals in Community countries through their national courts, notwithstanding any contrary rule of the national law, or the absence of any rule at all.[75] This is done by the individual seeking the remedy appropriate under national law, but claiming it by virtue of EU law.[76] The test whether a provision of Community law has direct effect is whether (1) it imposes a clear and precise obligation on member states; (2) it is unconditional and subject to no limitation, or only limitations exactly defined as to nature and extent; and (3) the member state is left with no real discretion as to the application of the rule in question.[77] Thus, it has been held that Community rules requiring that men and women receive equal pay for equal work, gave rise to rights enforceable by individuals in

---

[70] A national court has no power to decide that measures taken by EC institutions are invalid: *Firma Foto-Frost v. Hauptzollamt Lubeck-Ost* (314/85) [1987] E.C.R. 4199.

[71] *Blackburn v. Attorney General* [1971] 1 W.L.R. 1037; *McWhirter v. Attorney General* [1972] C.M.L.R. 882.

[72] *Gibson v. Lord Advocate*, 1975 S.C. 136.

[73] *Macarthys v. Smith* [1979] 3 All E.R. 325, 329; *Garland v. B.R. Engineering* [1983] 2 A.C. 751, 771; *Litster v. Forth Dry Dock Co.* [1990] A.C. 546, 1989 S.L.T. 540.

[74] *R. v. Secretary of State for Transport, ex p. Factortame Ltd* [1990] 2 A.C. 85 [1991] 1 A.C. 603; and see H.W.R. Wade "What has Happened to the Sovereignty of Parliament" (1991) 107 L.Q.R. 1; and *R. v. Secretary of State for Employment, ex p. Equal Opportunities Commission* [1994] 1 A.C. 1.

[75] *Van Gend en Loos v. Nederlandse Tariefcommissie* [1963] E.C.R. 3; *Costa v. ENEL* [1964] E.C.R. 585.

[76] *Argyll Group plc v. Distillers Co. plc*, 1987 S.L.T. 514; *Brown v. Secretary of State for Scotland*, 1989 S.L.T. 402.

[77] *Van Duyn v. Home Office* [1975] Ch.D. 358.

national courts against private employers.[78] Where provisions of Community law do not have direct effect, it is for member states to incorporate them in their legal systems in whatever way they think appropriate. It is also noteworthy that questions of Community law and its application may arise not only in the superior courts, but also in any court or tribunal in the United Kingdom. It is all-pervasive and not a matter only for government or courts of ultimate appeal.

The political implications of these developments indicate that the developing economic unification of Europe is only a stage towards greater political unification or federation. The Single European Act 1986 cleared the way for demands that a single market required further social, political, financial and legal integration. Thus, there is clearly developing a body of law within the European Union distinct both from international law and from the national systems of the constituent states. It has come and will come increasingly, to affect the legal relations of individuals and the legal systems of the countries, and to supersede national laws. A declared object, as well as a practical necessity, of the developing European Union is the approximation of national systems of law, starting with the protection of industrial property and the development of a European law of patents, trade-marks, designs and models, and the development of a common law on bankruptcy, companies, the enforcement of judgments, and so on. In 1987 a working group of experts appointed by the Commission started work on the approximation of the civil procedural law in Europe; it reported in 1993. Projects for common criminal law, at least in some respects, have been floated. British membership also has constitutional significance in involving constitutional limitations on the sovereign powers of Parliament. The increasing economic relations between the countries will also give rise to a sharply increased number of problems of international private law, while domestic courts also have to apply Community law in certain circumstances, since the treaties make Community law a part of the municipal law of each member state. An understanding of the salient principles and general structure of the domestic legal systems of other EU countries will, similarly, become of increasing importance.

The real question in the 1990s is whether the EU is becoming a dictatorship dominated by Germany, created by a few politicians for their own greater glory, crushing all independent action by member states and reducing them to provinces of a super-state, or whether it should revert to an association of states for co-operation.

---

[78] *Defrenne v. Sabena* [1976] E.C.R. 455; *Marshall v. Southampton and South West Hampshire AHA (No. 1) (C152/84)* [1986] Q.B. 401; [1981] 1 All E.R. 122.

VI.—STATE OR MUNICIPAL LAW

The bodies of state, national, domestic, civil or municipal law[79] comprise the whole body of doctrines, principles and rules accepted, applied and enforced in a particular state or political community. They are what are commonly called the law of the particular country.[80] Every state and territory recognised as a political entity possesses a whole apparatus of state law which may differ very substantially from that in an adjacent state; indeed many states, such as the United Kingdom and the United States, have several distinct bodies of municipal law in force in different parts of the one state. There are therefore several hundred bodies of municipal law in the world. In practice, the similarities and differences were formerly dictated by the origins, sources and historical borrowings of the legal system in the state in question and by the existence in many cases of federal or common legislative bodies and final courts of appeal. In modern times, differences are dictated more by different social and economic conditions and the different policies pursued by the political superiors in the state in question.

Since there are numerous distinct and independent political communities in the world, each having and enforcing its own legal system or systems, it is unfortunately true that legal science is not a unified body of knowledge like medical or engineering science which, learned in one country, is valid everywhere. While there are affinities between certain legal systems, there is a greater or lesser measure of distinctness, so that one state's legal system differs from every other at least in details, and sometimes in fundamentals too. Accordingly, for practical purposes students of law must confine themselves to an intimate knowledge of one or two systems of law with, at most, a general knowledge of some others, and an understanding of those elements of legal thought common to many, if not all, actual systems of law, and of the international and supranational law which holds as between the distinct political communities themselves.

The Subject-Matter of Municipal Law

The subject-matter of these doctrines, principles and rules is rights and duties, that is, those claims, powers, privileges, immunities and other advantages conferred on persons over and against other persons, and those burdens, liabilities and disabilities which are imposed and incumbent on persons in relation to other persons. Those rules of law are binding on all persons in the country under the common authority of the state and are

---

[79] State law is sometimes called civil, as being enacted by a *civitas* or state, or municipal, which originally connoted laws binding *municipia*, or dependent states, but was later extended also to laws enacted by sovereign states: Ersk., I, 1, 18.

[80] *cf.* Mackenzie, *Inst.* I, 1, 6; "Civil or Municipal Laws are the particular Laws and Customs of every Nation, or People, who are under one Sovereign Power."

administered by the courts, being invoked as need arises, sometimes by a public official, sometimes by an aggrieved individual seeking redress. Thus, if A enters a shop and buys a book, the law confers on him a right to obtain delivery of the book, which right it will enforce at his instance, if need be; imposes on him a duty to pay the agreed price, which duty it will enforce at the instance of the bookseller, if need be; and imposes on the bookseller a duty to hand over the book with a corresponding right to recover the price.[81] In the majority of cases, of course, people implement their legal rights and duties without compulsion or resort to the courts. The classification, analysis and examination of these concepts of rights and duties is an important element of jurisprudence, but cannot be pursued further here.[82]

It is important to discover the scientific, analytical arrangement of the legal principles in force in one community. It reveals that the body of law is an ordered system with a coherent, logical structure. Without arrangement, the rules of any system would be a jumble, and it is one of the jobs of jurists to put principles into some order. The mass of legal principles may be classified in various ways.[83] Classification is important as facilitating study, as showing the logical structure of the legal system and permitting scientific examination of its doctrines and principles, and is especially important where legal problems involving a foreign element are present.[84] The method and accuracy of classification of the principles, and the cases to which they apply, may be of great practical importance. The choice of remedy, or of which court should be approached to grant it may depend on whether a claim is classified as of one kind or another. The same classification is not applicable to all systems of municipal law, because the way a given system groups and classifies its doctrines and rules is usually affected by its history. But certain broad divisions are so commonly found as to deserve mention.

Public Law and Private Law

State law is usually divided first into public law and private law.[85] While the distinction has been current since the time of the Greeks and of the Roman law at least, and is commonly accepted and generally understood, its basis is difficult to define and different jurists distinguish

---

[81] Pollock, *First Book of Jurisprudence*, Chap. 4.

[82] See further Holland, *Jurisprudence* (13th ed.), Chap. 7; Salmond, *Jurisprudence* (12th ed.), Chaps. 10–11; Dias, *Jurisprudence*, Chap. 8.

[83] See Markby, *Elements of Law*, Chap. 7; Holland, *Jurisprudence*, Chap. 9; Salmond, *Jurisprudence*, Appx. III; Jolowicz, *Lectures on Jurisprudence*, Part III; Paton, *Textbook of Jurisprudence* (4th ed.), Chap. 11; Pound, "Classification of Law" (1934) 11 N.Y.U.L.Q.R. 319.

[84] Hence in international private law (conflict of laws) careful classification of the problem-situation is essential.

[85] On this, see further Jones, *Historical Introduction to the Theory of Law*, 139–163; Jolowicz, *Roman Foundations of Modern Law*, Chap. 7; and *Lectures on Jurisprudence*, Chap. 21; Mitchell, "Public law and private law" (1905) 17 J.R. 30.

the two bodies of law in different ways, while there is not complete agreement as to whether certain topics should be placed under the one head or the other. One explanation is that public law regulates relations between superior and inferior, and private law relations between equal persons. Again, it is said that the division corresponds to the two-fold activity of the state, in providing an organisation of government and means for the maintenance of order and the repression of disorder, and on the other hand providing machinery for the settlement of disputes and the resolution of conflicts of interest between private persons.[86] Questions between the state and the individual, however, give rise to some difficulty of classification.

Again it is generally true that a mark of public law is that the state or a state department is a party to the legal relationship or controversy, while private law applies as between private individuals.[87] But this test is not by any means invariable, since in many legal relationships the state and its agencies are subject to the ordinary principles of private law, as in owning property and making commercial contracts. Hence, "public law comprises the rules which specially relate to the structure, powers, rights and activities of the state. Private law includes all the residue of legal principles. It comprises all those rules which specially concern the subjects of the state in their relations to each other together with those rules which are common to the state and its subjects."[88] Markby,[89] in explanation of the distinction drawn in Justinian's *Institutes*,[90] wrote: "Public law is that portion of law in which our attention is directed mainly to the state; private law is that in which it is mainly directed to the individual. I do not think that it means that these topics are capable of exact separation; but that our attitude changes in regard to them. And, according as we assume one attitude or the other, we call law public or private." Pollock[91] expressed the view: "No rule of law can be said, in the last resort, to exist merely for the benefit of the state or merely for the benefit of the individual. But some departments of legal rules have regard in the first instance to the protection and interests of the commonwealth, others to those of its individual members . . . The topics of public and private law are by no means mutually exclusive."

Accordingly, this division is not wholly clear-cut and there is no essential or inherent difference in nature between the two kinds of law; both may be relevant in particular cases, and both come before the same courts. Some would deny the existence of the division, though its general convenience causes it usually to be retained.

---

[86] Keeton, *Elementary Principles of Jurisprudence* (2nd ed.), 227–228.
[87] This was the view of Holland, *Jurisprudence* (13th ed.), 128–129.
[88] Salmond, *Jurisprudence*, 506.
[89] *Elements of Law*, 151.
[90] Inst. I, 1, 4. *Jus publicum est quod ad statum rei Romanae spectat, jus privatum quod ad singulorum utilitatem pertinet.*
[91] *First Book of Jurisprudence*, Chap. 4, reprinted in *Jurisprudence and Legal Essays.*

This division is more sharply drawn in some continental systems of law, which sometimes have distinct courts for public and private issues. In the United Kingdom this is not so, and the distinction is less important in practice than in theory.

Civil and Criminal Law

Another fundamental division is that into civil[92] and criminal law,[93] or into civil, administrative and criminal law. This is a cross-division which sub-divides each of public and private law. This distinction is fundamentally one of procedure, since the classification of any subject depends mainly on whether infringements and infractions of the rules are pursued in civil courts by civil procedure for the purpose of obtaining a remedy—such as payment of a debt, an award of damages, a divorce, the stopping of a wrong, or the like—or in criminal courts by criminal procedure for the purpose of punishing the wrongdoer, deterring him and others from offending similarly, and maintaining peace, order and the safety of person and property. In fact, most legal relationships give rise to remedies in the civil courts only. In the sphere of wrongs, there is no universal touchstone by which one can classify some wrongs and injuries as essentially offences against the state or the community at large, or merely against private persons, dealt with respectively in criminal courts by criminal procedure and by civil courts under civil procedure. Some wrongful acts may be either, and pursued in either or even in both ways; many others are one or other only, but the only guidance which can be given as to whether or not a particular course of conduct is a crime, and therefore of concern to the criminal law, is to discover whether or not it is conduct which the state power on behalf of the community has determined to repress and punish by fine and imprisonment.[94] If not, if it is left to the individual to work out a remedy himself by action in the civil courts, the conduct is not criminal nor of concern to the criminal law.

In most developed states today, this procedural division is incomplete, in that many rights such as to social security benefits are conferred by administrative law, and disputes relative thereto determined neither by

---

[92] The uses of the term "civil law" are numerous and confusing. The main ones are (i) the civil law of Rome, as opposed to the canon law—*Corpus Juris Civilis* and *Corpus Juris Canonici*, the twin subjects of legal study in the Middle Ages; (ii) the civil law of Rome, as opposed to the praetorian law—*jus civile* and *jus praetorium*; (iii) civil law, as opposed to common law, with reference to the main families of legal systems; (iv) civil (or municipal or state) law, as opposed to international law; (v) civil law, as opposed to martial or military law (on this see *Green v. Lord Advocate*, 1918 S.C. 667); (vi) civil law, as opposed to criminal law; (vii) civil law, as opposed to ecclesiastical law.

[93] See further on this distinction Salmond, *Jurisprudence*, 507.

[94] Kenny, "The Nature of a Crime," in his *Outlines of Criminal Law*, 16th ed., Appendix I; Allen, "The Nature of Crime" in *Legal Duties*, 220; Hall, *General Principles of Criminal Law*, Chaps. 5–7; Winfield, *Province of the Law of Tort*, Chap. 8; Williams, "The Definition of Crime" [1955] *Curr.Leg. Problems*, 107; Smith and Hogan, *Criminal Law*, Chap. 2. *cf. Pty. Articles Trade Assoc. v. Att.-Gen. for Canada* [1931] A.C. 310 at p. 324.

civil nor by criminal courts but by administrative tribunals.[95] In nature and content, administrative law is like civil rather than criminal law but is distinct in respect of administration and adjudication. This division might, therefore, be regarded as tripartite rather than bipartite.

The volume of civil law is enormously greater and more heterogeneous than the criminal law, and for this reason this division is not very helpful since it merely segregates the criminal law from the whole mass. Of greater interest is the issue whether the body of criminal law should be grouped with the public or private spheres of law. It may be classified with private law[96] on the basis that most criminal wrongs are done to individuals (albeit pursued and punished by the state), or with public law[97] on the basis that criminal wrongs, even though done directly to individuals, are indirectly detrimental to the peace and order of the community. Moreover, they are dealt with by state agencies on behalf of the community, and today an increasing number of crimes and petty offences are not done against any individual at all, but are declared criminal and repressed simply because of their injurious tendency to the communal interest, to the national economy, or to people generally. Also, many fundamental public rights are frequently in issue in criminal cases.

Law and Equity

English private law down to 1875 drew a fairly clear distinction between rules of law, or of common law, which were those developed by the King's courts, and equity, which were the rules developed by the Chancellors in the Courts of Chancery or of Equity. Thus there came to be legal rights and equitable rights, legal remedies and equitable remedies, and so on, which sometimes overlapped and sometimes conflicted.[98] In 1875 the Judicature Acts abolished the dualism of courts and merged the administration of common law and equity, but did not merge the substantive rules or the rights and remedies, though providing that in cases of conflict the rules of equity should prevail.

This distinction between law and equity was carried over into most of the systems of law founded on English law and still survives in some of them to a greater extent than it does in England. The distinction has, however, never been known in Scots law nor any system based on Roman law.

Civil and Commercial Law

Systems of law, such as the French and the German, which have been strongly influenced by the Roman civil law, commonly divide private law

---

[95] Thus France has a highly developed system of administrative courts. See Hamson, *Executive Discretion and Judicial Control*; Brown and Garner, *French Administrative Law*.

[96] This view is taken by Salmond, *Jurisprudence*, 507.

[97] As by Holland, Markby and Pollock.

[98] On its origins and development, see p. 50, *supra*.

into separate bodies of civil and commercial laws representing fundamental rules derived from the (Roman) civil law, applicable to ordinary persons, and rules derived from the laws merchant and maritime, applicable to persons engaged in business. Thus, the French and German systems have separate Civil and Commercial Codes. This distinction has little significance in Scots or English law.[99]

Substantive and Adjective Law

Another distinction of great materiality which subdivides each of the major divisions of state law, civil, administrative and criminal, is that between substantive law and adjective law, although at many points the dividing line is difficult to draw. Adjective law is sometimes equated with procedure or procedural law,[1] but properly it covers more than procedure. Broadly speaking, substantive law defines the rights and claims, liberties and privileges, duties and liabilities of persons, while adjective law defines the means whereby, the circumstances in which, the qualifications under which, and the legal procedure whereby, those rights can be vindicated or those duties enforced.[2] Adjective law covers evidence, procedure and pleading, matters of practice, the enforcement of decrees and related topics. There is accordingly a body of adjective law attaching to each of civil and criminal law and their respective sets of courts, while a rather less definite body of adjective law also attaches to administrative law and its tribunals. The distinction is sometimes put briefly as being that between "right" and "remedy", but this is inaccurate in that substantive rights and duties and remedial rights and duties all equally exist by rules of law, and are distinct from the means whereby remedies are sought and enforced when a substantive right is infringed. A contracting party has a right to have the contract performed and, failing performance, a right to a remedy for breach of contract. The method by which a right can be enforced, sometimes determines to some extent the nature or content of the right. On the other hand, the distinction is at some points quite clear, and accurate delimitation of the two areas may be of crucial importance, as in some problems of conflict of laws.[3] It is a distinction not without practical importance,[4] because unless adjective and procedural law works quickly, cheaply and efficiently, substantive law is deprived of much of its value.[5]

---

[99] The Civil Jurisdiction and Judgments Act 1982, implementing the provision of the EEC Treaty, dealt with "civil and commercial matters", but with exceptions.

[1] *e.g.* Holland, *Jurisprudence*, 358.

[2] Procedure has been described as: "The mode of proceeding by which a legal right is enforced, as distinguished from the law which gives or defines the right, and which by means of the proceeding the court is to administer—the machinery as distinguished from its products": *Poyser v. Minors* (1881) L.R. 7 Q.B.D. 329, 333.

[3] See, *e.g. McElroy v. McAllister*, 1949 S.C. 110.

[4] Thus, *e.g.* in Scots law it is a rule that loan of money may be proved by writ only. If I lend money and seek to recover it, but have lost the debtor's written acknowledgment, is my right gone, or only my remedy barred? What happens if I later find the debtor's writ?

[5] *cf.* Harvey, "A Job for Jurisprudence" (1944) 7 M.L.R. 42, 49; Lord Cooper, "Defects in the British Judicial Machinery" in (1953) 2 J.S.P.T.L.(N.S.) 91 and *Selected Papers*, 244.

FURTHER READING

Arrangement and Classification
Hall: *Readings in Jurisprudence*, Chap. 14.
Holland: *Jurisprudence*, Chap. 9.
Paton: *Jurisprudence*, Chap. 11.
Pound: *Jurisprudence*, Vol. V.

Legal History
Continental Legal History Series: Vol. I—*General Survey.*
  Vol. II—*Great Jurists of the World.*
  Vol. X—*Progress in the Nineteenth Century.*
Diamond: *Evolution of Law and Order.*
Gilissen: *Introduction historique au droit.*
Monier, Cardascia et Imbert: *Histoire des Institutions et des Faits Sociaux.*
Van Caenegan: *Historical Introduction to Private Law.*
  Historical Introduction to Western Constitutional Law.

Early Law
Fleming: *Domesday Book and the Law.*
Jones: *Law and Legal Theory of the Greeks.*
Maine: *Ancient Law.*
Munroe Smith: *Development of European Law.*
Vinogradoff: *Historical Jurisprudence*, 2 vols.

Roman Law
Bryce: "Extension of Roman and English Law throughout the World," in *Studies in History and Jurisprudence*, I, 72.
Buckland: *Textbook of Roman Law.*
Buckland and McNair: *Roman Law and Common Law.*
Carey-Miller and Zimmermann (eds): *The Civil Law Tradition and Scots Law.*
Evans-Jones (ed.): *The Civil Law Tradition in Scotland.*
Jolowicz: *Historical Introduction to the study of Roman Law.*
  Roman Foundations of Modern Law.
Koschaker: *Europa und die römische Recht.*
Lawson: *A Common Lawyer looks at the Civil Law.*
Lewis and Ibbetson: *The Roman Law Tradition.*
Lupoi: *On the Origins of the European Legal Order.*
Mackintosh: *Roman Law in Modern Practice.*
Schulz: *Classical Roman Law.*
  Roman Legal Science.
Stein: *Roman Law in European History.*
Ullman: *The Medieval Idea of Law.*
Vinogradoff: *Roman Law in Mediaeval Europe.*

Canon Law
Brundage: *Medieval Canon Law.*
Maitland: *Roman Canon Law in the Church of England.*
Mortimer: *Western Canon Law.*
Mylne: *Canon Law.*

Feudal Law
Bloch: *Feudal Society.*
Ganshof: *Feudalism.*
Herlihy: *History of Feudalism.*
Reynolds: *Fiefs and Vassals.*

Law Merchant
Carter: "Early History of the Law Merchant in England" (1901) 17 L.Q.R. 232.
Holdsworth: *History of English Law*, Vol. 5.
Mitchell: *The Law Merchant.*
Sanborn: *Origins of the Early English Maritime and Commercial Law.*

Maritime Law
Ashburner: *The Rhodian Sea Law.*
Holdsworth: *History of English Law*, Vol. 5.
Senior: "Early Writers on Maritime Law" (1921) 37 L.Q.R. 323.

English Law
Holdsworth: *Sources and Literature of English Law.*
James: *Introduction to English Law.*
Plucknett: *Concise History of the Common Law.*

Jurisprudence
Allen: *Law in the Making.*
Cairns: *Legal Philosophy from Plato to Hegel.*
Cohen and Cohen: *Readings in Jurisprudence and Legal Philosophy.*
Duff: *Philosophy and the Criminal Law.*
Friedmann: *Legal Theory.*
Friedrich: *Philosophy of Law in Historical Perspective.*
Hall: *Readings in Jurisprudence.*
Hart: *The Concept of Law.*
Jones: *Historical Introduction to the Theory of Law.*
Kelly: *Short History of Western Legal Theory.*
Lloyd: *Introduction to Jurisprudence.*
Morris: *The Great Legal Philosophers.*
Paton: *Jurisprudence.*
Pound: *Jurisprudence*, 5 vols.
    Introduction to the Philosophy of Law.
Simpson and Stone: *Cases and Readings on Law and Society*, 3 vols.
Stone: *Legal System and Lawyer's Reasonings.*
    Human Law and Human Justice.
    Social Dimension of Law and Justice.

Comparative Legal Studies
Arminjon, Nolde and Wolff: *Traité de Droit Comparé.*
Bell and others: *Principles of French Law.*
David: *Traité Elémentaire de Droit Civil Comparé.*
Finer and others: *Comparing Constitutions.*
Gutteridge: *Comparative Law.*
Horn and others: *German Private and Commercial Law.*
James: *Introduction to English Law.*
Lee: *Introduction to Roman Dutch Law.*

Roberts-Wray: *Commonwealth Law.*
Schlesinger: *Comparative Law.*
Van Mehren: *The Civil Law System.*
Watkin: *An Historical Introduction to Modern Civil Law.*
Yntema: *"Roman Law as the Basis of Comparative Law" in Law: A Century of Progress, II*, 346.
Zweigert and Kotz: *Introduction to Comparative Law.*

Public International Law
Bowett: *Law of International Institutions.*
Brownlie: *Principles of Public International Law.*
Butler and Maccoby: *The Development of International Law.*
Lauterpacht: *Function of Law in the International Community.*
            International Law and Human Rights.
            Development of International Law by the International Court.
Merills: *International Dispute Settlement.*
Starke: *Introduction to International Law.*
Wright: *The Role of International Law in the Elimination of War.*

Supranational Law
Collins: *European Community Law in the United Kingdom.*
Craig and de Burca: *EU Law.*
Hartley: *Foundations of European Community Law.*
Jacobs and White: *The European Convention on Human Rights.*
Mackenzie Stuart: *The European Communities and the Rule of Law.*
Pinder: *The Building of the European Union.*
Robertson: *European Institutions.*
            The Council of Europe.
            Law of International Institutions in Europe.

State or Municipal Law
Dunedin: *Divergencies and Convergencies of English and Scots Law,* Glasgow Univ. Publications, 1935.
Fisher: "Scotland and the Roman Law" (1947) 22 Tulane L.R. 13.
Gibb: "Interrelation of the Legal Systems of Scotland and England" (1937) 53 L.Q.R. 61.
Goudy: *Fate of Roman Law North and South of the Tweed,* 1894.
Keith: *The Spirit of the Law of Scotland* (Holdsworth Club, Birmingham, 1957).
Levy-Ullman: "The Law of Scotland" (1925) 37 J.R. 370.
            The English Legal Tradition
Lovat-Fraser: "Some Points of Difference between English and Scottish Law" (1895) 10 L.Q.R. 340; 11 L.Q.R. 1.
Macmillan: "Two Ways of Thinking" in *Law and Other Things.*
Normand: *Scottish Judicature and Legal Procedure* (Holdsworth Club, 1941).
Radbruch: "Anglo-American Jurisprudence through Continental Eyes" (1937) 52 L.Q.R. 530.
Smith: *British Justice: The Scottish Contribution.*
            "English Influence on the Law of Scotland" (1954) 3 Am.Jo.Compar. L. 522.
            "The Common Law Cuckoo," 1956 *Butterworth's South African Law Review,* 147.
            "Strange Gods: The Crisis of Scots Law as a Civilian System," 1959 J.R. 119.
            "Scots Law and Roman-Dutch Law," 1961 J.R. 32.

Stein: "Influence of Roman Law on the Law of Scotland" (1957) 23 *Studia et Documenta Historiae et Juris*, 149 and 1963 J.R. 205.

"Roman Law in Medieval Scotland" in *The Character and Influence of the Roman   Civil Law*, 269.

Walker: "Some Characteristics of Scots Law" (1955) 18 M.L.R. 321.

CHAPTER 3

FUNDAMENTAL IDEAS

IN modern times, the existence of legal systems and bodies of law is essentially connected not so much with racial groups or the adherents of particular religions as with states.

The State

The State is the name usually given to associations of individuals living in a determinate tract of land and organised as a political community with a head of state and a structure of government. In earlier times, cities and their inhabitants might be separate states, but today states are commonly based on nations, peoples living in demarcated areas of the world who accept a common political and legal organisation. The concept of the State is a major subject of study in political thought or theory (dealing with what the structure of the state should be)[1] and in political science (dealing with the structure of the different states in the world).[2] States may unite, or fragment into lesser independent states; some are unitary, *e.g.* France, but others are federal, *e.g.* Canada and Germany, being made up of smaller units—called provinces (in Canada), states (in the United States and Australia), Länder (in Germany)—which each have some independence and distinctive characteristics.

Accordingly, states are the entities which are the subjects of international law. It is states which own territory and claim territorial waters, cede territory, make treaties and conventions, have disputes and make war, are members of the UN and other international organisations, and litigate in the international court. Similarly, it is states which are members of the EU and represented in its institutions. The major characteristic of a state is that it is independent and not subject to the legal control of another state, though it may be subject to the political domination or economic influence of another. Also it is sovereign over all its own constituent parts or territories and those living and working therein. Individuals living there are normally and predominantly citizens of that state and owe it allegiance and, if called on, must pay for, work for and fight for that state.[3]

---

[1] *e.g.* R. MacIver, *The State*; Barker, *Principles of Social and Political Theory*; A. P. D'Entrèves, *The Notion of the State*; N. Barry, *Introduction to Modern Political Theory*.

[2] *e.g.* S. E. Finer, *Comparative Government*.

[3] See further Green, *The Authority of the State*.

In Britain the state evolved from the personal primacy of kings, and the term "sovereign" is used of the king or queen and persons owe allegiance to the sovereign, currently the Queen. State officials are still nominally the Queen's servants and the armed forces are Her Majesty's forces, the Queen's navy, army and air force. So, too, the term "the Crown" has been transferred from the royal ceremonial headgear to a term for the Head of State, or to the government, and a representation of the crown is commonly used as a symbol of State or government ownership or control. The State is distinct from the person who is Head of State, from the Government, and from Parliament, though any one of these may speak for or represent the State on particular occasions.

A primary purpose of the association of people in a territory as a State is the preservation of their own safety and independence against external aggression and the defence of the way of life which they regard as desirable. This way of life may include preservation of their religion, language, customs and other distinctive characteristics. Another major purpose is the securing and maintenance of internal peace and order. In modern times, the State is increasingly expected to manage the national economy to secure economic prosperity. Persons living in a country also increasingly look to the State to provide and secure, directly or through organisations established for the purpose, the conditions of an agreeable life, a health service, an education service, a social security system, protection of the environment, water supply, housing, a transport system, a postal system and many other services. If anything goes wrong, *e.g.* an earthquake, the State or government is expected to come to the rescue. The State itself has no resources, but only what it takes from its citizens, and hence there is need for an elaborate taxing system. As nation-states have grown in importance and power, the tendency has been to personify them and attribute to a State a will and exercises of that will, *e.g.* by saying that Britain proposes, France objects, Germany wants, and so on, as if these states were intelligent beings. This has led in some political philosophies to the glorification, even deification, of States as entities and ends in themselves[4], and to the view that the lives and property of all within its frontiers are at the service of the State.

Nations
Nowadays a State is frequently a national state, in that the people, who reside within the territorial boundaries of the state consider themselves to have an identity as a nation or a people. But this is not necessarily so. A nation or a people is a large community with a large measure of ethnic similarity, a common history, common traditions, language, culture, religion and consciousness of its distinctness—though there are always

---

[4] Hegel, *Philosophy of Right* (trs. Knox).

some persons who differ in some respects and who may be resident
minorities and never become fully integrated into the nation.[5] The identity
that many states and nations have achieved has led to state and nation
becoming equated and confused. But they are distinct and different forms
of communities. The state is a political organisation; the nation is a
community of persons having a consciousness of solidarity. The boundaries of states and nations do not always coincide; a state may encompass
more than one nation,[6] or a nation may be spread over two or more
states.[7] A powerful force since 1914 has been that of nations seeking to
assert their distinctness and independence and to break out of states and
form states of their own.[8]

In the sixteenth and seventeenth centuries the Welsh, a Celtic people,
came to be largely assimilated to the Anglo-Saxon-Norman culture of
England, and this was aided by the incorporation of Wales into the
English state, though it has never been complete. In 1707 Scotland had
long been a free, independent kingdom, a national and sovereign state.
The Union of 1707 created a united state of Great Britain but it did not
create a united British nation, in that in law, church, public administration
and many aspects of culture, feelings and customs, Scots and English were,
and have remained, distinct.[9] Accordingly, the United Kingdom is not a
unitary but a pluralistic state. Scotland has been said to be a stateless
nation. The concepts of British nationality and British citizenship are
modern, artificial and purely legal ones.

Sovereignty

Closely associated with the concept of the State is the concept of
sovereignty. Sovereignty means the ultimate legal authority or right of
superiority in a State, which can in the last resort overrule any other
authority. The concept of sovereignty is at least as much a political one as
a legal one. It has been developed mainly since the seventeenth century,[10]
and is examined at length in many works on political thought.[11] It is
important in public international and public law. It is plain that in every

---

[5] See B. Askin, *State and Nation*; H. Seton-Watson, *Nations and States*; Tivey, *The Nation-State*.

[6] *e.g.* the former Czechoslovakia, Yugoslavia. Consequently the terminology of "international law" and "supranational law" are misleading because both operate between or over states and not nations, but the terminology is too well-settled to be disturbed.

[7] *e.g.* Germans in Austria and in Germany.

[8] *e.g.* the break-up of India in 1947 into India, Pakistan and Bangladesh.

[9] It is significant that in many games "internationals" are played between Scots and English, Welsh and Irish, as well as between Scots and French. See further W. Ferguson, *The Identity of the Scottish Nation;* H. Kearney, *The British Isles;* N. Davies, *The Isles: A History.*

[10] F.H. Hinsley, *Sovereignty*; C. E. Merriam, *History of the Theory of Sovereignty since Rousseau*; Jones, *Historical Introduction to the Theory of Law.*

[11] *e.g.* Laski, *Grammar of Politics*; Laski, *The Foundations of Sovereignty*; Bryce, *Studies in History and Jurisprudence*; Lucas, *Legal Status of Sovereignty*; H. E. Cohen, *Recent Theories of Sovereignty.*

State, as in every association or organisation, some person or body of persons must have the ultimate power. Indeed, in international law one of the attributes of being a State recognised in the international community is that it is sovereign over its territory and all persons within its territory and not subject legally to any external higher authority, though it may for political or economic reasons defer to another state. When Scotland entered into the Treaty of Union with England in 1707, it surrendered all its sovereignty to the institutions of the new State of Great Britain; so did England. It is by virtue of sovereignty that States make treaties, cede territory, exclude aliens, exercise jurisdiction over all within their frontiers, and make or change internal law.

Wherein Sovereignty Resides

A question of importance is in whom this power of sovereignty is vested in a particular State. In a country having a written Constitution, sovereignty resides in the Constitution, and no person, legislature, court or other body can lawfully act save as the Constitution has authorised him or it to act. Frequently, there is a Constitutional Court with power to determine whether a particular act (legislative, executive or judicial) is *ultra vires* (beyond the powers).[12] In such a case, it is arguable that, apart from the theoretical possibility of a revolution which overthrows the Constitution, sovereignty resides in the persons or bodies which can lawfully amend the Constitution, or in the court which can declare particular acts as authorised or unauthorised. In the United Kingdom it is now settled that sovereignty is vested in the Queen-in-Parliament, because that composite body can lawfully effect anything, take away any person's property in whole or in part (or even his life), alter or abolish any person's legal rights of any kind (even retrospectively),[13] change the constitution of the country in any way (as by abolishing the House of Lords), or change any institutions, such as the Court of Session, in any way. It cannot be controlled by appeal to any court inside[14] or outside the country, or by appeal to any principle of justice, morality, human rights or the like. Sovereignty does not reside in the Queen, because by convention she must act on ministers' advice and cannot now withhold assent from a Bill passed by the Lords and Commons, nor in the Lords, because the Commons can after a year's delay override the Lords' refusal to pass a

---

[12] In the U.S.A. the Supreme Court is guardian of the Constitution and can strike down even an Act of Congress which is contrary to the Constitution.

[13] *e.g.* War Damage Act 1965, overruling decision in *Burmah Oil Co. (Burma Trading) Ltd v. Lord Advocate*, 1964 S.C. (H.L.) 117.

[14] In *McCormick v. Lord Advocate*, 1953 S.C. 396, the Court of Session held that an individual could not challenge the style and title adopted by Queen Elizabeth II on her accession, but Lord President Cooper reserved his opinion on whether post-1707 parliaments had unlimited sovereignty in alteration of the Treaty of Union. (The Union agreement was an international treaty, approved by the two parliaments, not an Act.)

Bill,[15] nor in the Commons, because a Bill passed by them must be put to the Lords and to the Queen for Royal Assent. Furthermore, the accepted view now is that Parliament cannot bind itself for the future, nor bind any future parliament. Any parliament can alter or reverse any legislation enacted by itself or by any previous parliament, and this has very frequently been done. All legislation is temporary. But Parliament in 1972 accepted existing and future EC law and disabled itself from making contrary legislation. It thereby gave away its sovereignty over large, and growing areas of policy affected by the successive treaties defining the powers of EU institutions.

Delegation of Sovereignty

Sovereignty can be delegated, in whole or in part. A dictator commonly gets the persons who have sovereignty in the state in question to delegate all powers to him. If, as has occasionally been suggested, Parliament were to empower certain ministers to do whatever they thought fit without further reference to Parliament, it would be a competent delegation of sovereign powers, and in wartime Parliament has sometimes come near to doing this.

Division of Sovereignty

Sovereignty may be divided. In the United Kingdom, legislative sovereignty is in the composite Queen-in-Parliament, but executive sovereignty is in the Queen, acting on the advice of ministers, though in practice the Queen's ministers are responsible to the House of Commons and cannot do anything for which they cannot, if need be, win a vote of confidence in the House. Until the Parliament Acts of 1911 and 1949, the House of Lords, as ultimate court of appeal, was the sovereign judicature and could not have its decisions overruled save by legislation made with its own consent; since those Acts, the last qualification has gone and sovereignty in judicature has passed to the Queen-in-Parliament,[16] or in cases under the Parliament Acts, to the Queen and the Commons. The Court of Session and the High Court of Justiciary have never been sovereign in their spheres.

Limitations on Sovereignty

It further follows from the concept of sovereignty that it is unlimited; if there is any legal limitation, internal or external to the State, no person or body therein is fully sovereign. In fact sovereign power is frequently limited by political, moral or practical considerations. When the United

---

[15] Under the provisions of the Parliament Acts 1911 and 1949.
[16] War Damage Act 1965, overruling *Burmah Oil Co. (Burma Trading) v. Lord Advocate, supra.*

Kingdom transferred the sovereignty of British India to newly created governments there in 1947, it did so partly because continued enforcement of British sovereignty was becoming increasingly resented and might have become impossible to enforce in the event of widespread and determined resistance.

Surrender of Sovereignty

As an important consequence of acceding to the Treaties establishing the European Communities and becoming a member of them, the United Kingdom has surrendered sovereignty in certain matters to the unelected bureaucrats of the Commission.[17] What they lay down by regulation or directive must be accepted as law and given effect to in the United Kingdom, and United Kingdom courts must accept the meanings given to the Treaties and EU legislation by the European Court. It is indeed a striking illustration of the sovereignty of Parliament that it could by ordinary Acts[18] give away some of its own sovereignty, possibly beyond recall. As the European Union enlarges and develops, many of the most heated arguments will be directed to whether the United Kingdom should or should not transfer further elements of sovereignty to the Community institutions. It is one thing to co-operate with an organisation but another to surrender to it even the power to cease co-operation. It follows that the EU has in certain respects acquired sovereignty over the member states.

It is otherwise with international organisations and the International Court of Justice. The United Kingdom has not transferred any sovereignty to them, even if it has accepted legal obligations to conform to their decisions and give effect to them. As a matter of law, it could withdraw from the organisations, though that would be politically, morally and, frequently, economically dangerous and detrimental. Similarly with supranational organisations other than the EU, such as NATO; as a matter of law, the United Kingdom could denounce the relevant treaty and leave the organisation; it has not surrendered any sovereignty, though it has limited its freedom of action by agreeing to participate in the organisations for the furtherance of their purposes. The European Court has ruled that the sovereignty of member states is restricted by Communities membership, and that to the extent of this restriction, the Community institutions exercise sovereign rights.[19] For practical purposes, this sovereignty is vested in the Commission, but in the last resort the European Parliament can dismiss the Commission as a whole and, accordingly, legal sovereignty can be said to be vested in the Parliament.

---

[17] The power of Parliament to make this surrender was unsuccessfully challenged in *Blackburn v. Att.-Gen.* [1971] 2 All E.R. 1380.

[18] European Communities Act 1972, the European Communities (Amendment) Act 1986 and the European Communities (Amendment) Act 1993.

[19] *Van Gend en Loos v. Nederlandse Tarief Commissie* (26/62) [1963] E.C.R. 3, 12; [1963] C.M.L.R. 105, 129.

The State and Law

The relationships of states and law are complex. A State is a legal person in international and supranational law, by recognition and acceptance by other states, and it may be a person in its own system of law.

Each State necessarily has a legal structure and organisation, defined by its own constitution and practices, just as a company or a club has a legal structure and organisation, with a titular head (Queen, President), executive body, and machinery for making, applying and enforcing the internal law of the state.

Another characteristic of a State is that it establishes and maintains a legal system for the individuals living within its boundaries—what is known as the law of the state, *e.g.* law of France—and sometimes also permits constituent provinces or states, though not themselves States, to maintain in certain respects their own systems of law—*e.g.* law of Scotland, law of Quebec. This constitutes the administrative, criminal and civil law of the particular territory. Generally, residents in a state are compulsorily subject to that law by residence. To a small extent, residents who belong to another state may still claim subjection to the law of their state of permanent home.[20]

Every independent state has, of necessity, one or more systems of law for its subjects. Each is a controlling force in society, comprising ideals, persons, institutions, techniques and practices, doctrines, principles and rules, procedures and means of applying and enforcing the rules, enabling the state to regulate the relations in life of its citizens. A fundamental distinction is between the abstract and general concepts designated Law, and the concrete and particular instances designated "a law", or "laws" or "the law" (such as "the law of property" or "the law of Scotland"), which comprise the specific doctrines, principles and rules utilised by the particular legal system to achieve its ends. Law as a study is much more than the aggregate of the doctrines, principles and rules in force, and their observance, in a particular state or province; what use would they be without courts, judges, techniques of finding, interpreting and applying law, practices of pleading, and much more? But to those involved in the system, as judges, legal advisers and others concerned with applying the law, the doctrines, principles and rules, and the machinery for applying them, are more important.

The State has legal rights against its citizens—to obedience to its commands, the payment of taxes imposed, sometimes to military service— and citizens owe duties to the State. A duty imposed by statute is primarily a duty owed to the State with a penalty for non-compliance,[21] though some

---

[20] A person domiciled, *i.e.* having his permanent home in Scotland, but resident in England or France, will have his intestate estate divided by the law of his permanent home country.
[21] *East Suffolk Rivers Catchment Board v. Kent* [1941] A.C. 74, 88.

such duties are interpreted as also implying a duty to compensate a person harmed by non-implement.[22]

A question of much interest is whether and to what extent a State is itself subject to law. It is subject to international law, both general and the particular elements created by conventions to which that state is a party, and to the rules of any supranational body, such as the EU, of which it has agreed to become a member. But is a State subject to any, more fundamental body of law which has higher authority than it, or that of any international or supranational organisation which it has joined? Some theorists in the past contended that a sovereign person or State was subject to the law of God or the law of nature.[23] But even if one can define the content in a particular case of either of these alleged bodies of law of higher authority, they are unenforceable against a State.

Another question of interest and importance is the nature and extent of any rights the individual has against the State in which he lives. The practical answer is that if a state is sovereign, individuals have against it only those kinds of claims which it has conceded, and that it can withdraw these or repudiate them at any time. Thus a claim for compensation for private property justifiably destroyed by state forces in wartime, to prevent it falling into enemy hands, was upheld by the court[24] but then repudiated by the State by retrospective legislation.[25] But in practice, modern democratic states give, or allow to individuals very substantial sets of claims against their State and allow judgments to go against the State and its departments and agencies in the state courts, and the State satisfies those judgments.[26]

The difficulty of enforcing rights against an omnipotent state has in some cases led politicians to try to define some rights in Declarations or Bills of Rights, and to try to put them beyond the power of the State to abridge or abolish save by special procedure or by special majorities. But a determined State can always get round even such expedients.[27] In Scotland in the late seventeenth century, there were appeals to the "fundamental laws of the nation" or of the kingdom, and in the Claim of Right of 1689, the Estates asserted that James VII had invaded the fundamental constitution of the kingdom. But there was no statement of what those were or how they were protected. So, too, it can be argued that the framers of the

---

[22] *Galashiels Gas Co. Ltd v. Millar*, 1949 S.C.(H.L.) 31; *Matuszczyk v. National Coal Board*, 1953 S.C. 8, 18.

[23] Gough, *Fundamental Law in English Constitutional History, passim.*

[24] *Burmah Oil Co. (Burma Trading) Ltd v. Lord Advocate*, 1964 S.C.(H.L.) 117.

[25] War Damage Act 1965. Similarly Education (Scotland) Act 1973, overruling *Malloch v. Aberdeen Corporation*, 1974 S.L.T. 253.

[26] Crown Proceedings Act 1947.

[27] This is well illustrated in South Africa: see *Harris v. Minister of the Interior*, 1952 (2) S.A. 428; *Collins v. Minister of the Interior*, 1957 (1) S.A. 552.

Treaty of Union of 1707 sought to establish its provisions as fundamental and beyond Parliament's power to alter.[28]

The Rule of Law

This doctrine is to the effect that the actions of all persons in the State, not only ordinary individuals, but also the Crown, ministers, civil servants, the army, the police, local authorities, and every other body or person having any power, must exercise his authority and power within the limits law has prescribed for him, and under and in accordance with the relevant rules of law, and must, if challenged, be able to justify his action by pointing to the rule which authorised it and empowered him. It is the opposite of unfettered or uncontrolled or despotic power.

The efficacy of the doctrine of the rule of law requires, firstly, that there be means for checking the grant of, and, if necessary, for withdrawing authority or powers, and secondly, means of securing decisions on whether particular exercises of power were or were not authorised. There is no value in constitutions or Declarations or Bills of Rights, international or national, unless these conditions of efficacy are satisfied. The first condition of efficacy can be satisfied by an elected assembly which scrutinises grants of powers and is able and willing, in appropriate cases, to refuse them. But such an elected assembly, if weak, overawed or evilly intentioned, can easily grant powers too readily or too widely. Thus, if, as has sometimes been suggested, Parliament were to pass an Enabling Act empowering ministers by statutory instrument to do whatever they thought right in the national interest, Parliament would have abdicated its function and law would not rule. Sometimes, particularly during war, Parliament has come dangerously close to doing this. How well Parliament performs this function depends on how ready members are to regulate the grant of powers. The rule of law is not guaranteed merely by the existence of an elected assembly.

The second condition of efficacy is satisfied only if: there is procedural machinery for bringing cases of alleged excess of power before courts and allowing them to be challenged and examined; lawyers who will fearlessly challenge them and advance arguments against their validity; and honest and upright judges who will examine cases of exercise of power brought before them and decide by their consciences and without regard to consequences. For this purpose, the process of judicial review is important.

The vital importance of judges and lawyers in preserving the rule of law is clear, and it is also obvious that there may be a constant struggle between high politicians and administrators seeking to promote their

---

[28] T.B. Smith, "The Union of 1707 as Fundamental Law," in *Studies Critical and Comparative*, 1; R. King Murray, "The Anglo-Scottish Union," 1961 S.L.T. (News) 161.

policies (or possibly chancing their arms on exercising a power,)[29] and lawyers seeking to keep them within bounds. This struggle is more obvious in issues of public and criminal law than in matters of private law. The struggle may extend to the further problem: is a minister or other authority successfully challenged, going to accept the decision or can he, and will he seek to, ignore or override that decision? In Britain the answer is that, because of the doctrine of parliamentary sovereignty, Parliament can always, and can frequently be persuaded to, overrule an inconvenient decision, and even retrospectively authorise some act or indemnify the party from the consequences of having overstepped the legal limits.

THE EXPRESSION OF LEGAL PRECEPTS

The precepts of the law which have to be applied to different sets of facts are not all of the same form, and the form they take in particular cases does not depend on their source, that is, on whether the precepts in question are laid down by statute or have been developed by judges in cases. Doctrines, principles and rules have to be distinguished, and it has to be said that these three types of precept have no fixed or settled definitions and are not sharply or clearly distinguished from one another. What one judge or jurist may call a doctrine, another may call a principle, and similarly with principle and rule. Nevertheless, an attempt must be made to explain what are frequently meant by these terms.

Doctrines

The term doctrine is usually applied to a very broad category of precept which can comprehend a number of more particular principles and even more specific rules. Thus, one comes across the doctrine of public policy,[30] the doctrine of undue influence,[31] the doctrine of prescription (comprising various principles and rules extinguishing rights of various kinds after the lapse of various periods of time), the doctrine of fault-liability (that liability in damages arises from harm caused by fault of commission or omission, not merely from its occurrence), the doctrine of "direct effect" of EU legislation,[32] and many more.

Principles

Principles are the broad formulations or generalisations which underlie and comprehend particular rules. They are broader than rules, and justify

---

[29] This is not always reprehensible. A procurator-fiscal may prosecute certain conduct which he honestly believes is or should be criminal, to test whether it is criminal or falls through a gap in the law.

[30] *Mullan v. Anderson (No. 2)*, 1997 S.L.T. 93.

[31] *National Westminster Bank v. Morgan* [1985] 1 All E.R. 830, 831.

[32] *e.g. Smith v. Watson* 1982 J.C. 34.

and explain various particular rules. Principles may be so broad as to be indefinite and uncertain, yet they can frequently be expressed concisely and accurately, embracing within them numerous particular rules and yet harmonising them. They are the authoritative starting-point or basis for legal reasoning wherever legal provision must be made for a situation not governed by a strict or precise rule of law. Principles are not commonly laid down by statute or case, but are commonly arrived at inductively by jurists from consideration of the particular decisions of various cases, and then set out in textbooks; they are sometimes hinted at or even tentatively formulated by judges in particular cases,[33] though such formulations may subsequently be found, in the light of criticism and other cases, to be too wide or too narrow, or otherwise to require correction or reformulation.

Thus, it is a principle that a person should not be allowed to profit from another's loss when there was no intention to gift or otherwise to confer benefit. This principle explains, connects into a coherent body, and justifies such specific rules as that a payment made when it was not due may be recovered, that payment made on the faith of an agreement which later fails is recoverable, and that work done voluntarily in an emergency on behalf of an absent person should be recompensed. It is a principle that a contract between two persons does not confer rights or duties on any third party—though to this there are various exceptions. It is a principle that no valid right in security can be created over corporeal things without transferring them to the security-holder—though again there are import-ant execeptions. It is a principle that an employer must take reasonable care for the safety of his employees. This last principle justifies numerous particular rules worked out in particular cases, such as that in this case the employer should have given a warning, in that case put up protective fencing, in another case should have ensured that a ladder was safe, and so on. From a principle it is possible to deduce other particular rules applicable to circumstances hitherto unrecognised, so that one great merit of a legal principle is that it has not been exhausted by the deduction of the recognised specific rules from it but remains a reservoir of future rules. It is largely through principles that the law grows and develops and keeps in touch with the feelings and beliefs of the community; principles need to be elastic and flexible, yet not wholly formless.

Sometimes a judge has to choose between two competing principles,[34] and frequently he has to choose between different verbal formulations of a principle.

It is sometimes difficult to say whether a statement of law is a distinct principle or a qualification of, or exception to another principle.

---

[33] *e.g. Hadley v. Baxendale* (1854) 9 Ex. 341, restated in *Victoria Laundry v. Newman* [1949] 2 K.B. 528; *Rylands v. Fletcher* (1868) L.R. 3 H.L. 330, restated in *Read v. Lyons* [1947] A.C. 156; *Donoghue v. Stevenson* 1932 S.C.(H.L.) 31.

[34] *e.g. Allcard v. Skinner* [1887] 36 Ch.D. 145, 182.

Rules

Rules are categorical precepts attaching a distinct, definite and detailed legal effect or consequence to definite and prescribed facts. They are more specific and detailed than principles. For example, it is a legal rule that a person convicted of murder must be sentenced to life imprisonment, that to be self-proving a formal deed for the sale of land must be signed by the granter and attested by one witness, that the driver of a goods vehicle may not drive for more than a prescribed number of hours, that a person cannot marry until 16 years of age and so on. Rules may be laid down by statute, by the decision of a court, or set out in an authoritative book. Such rules may be rigid, or may be flexible, as where they confer a measure of discretion; so the rule is that if a person has been injured by the negligence of another, the other must pay such damages in compensation as the court may think reasonable to award. A common advantage of a rule is that it is definite and certain, but it may on that account be unadaptable to new conditions or changing circumstances[35]; it may become out of date and obsolete, though this is less likely if the rule contains a standard or confers a discretion.

THE CONSTITUENT ELEMENTS OF DOCTRINES, PRINCIPLES AND RULES

Doctrines, principles and rules of law are embodied in statements formulated in terms of legal concepts, legal standards and grants of discretion.

Concepts

A legal concept is an abstract general notion or idea which serves as a category of legal thought or classification, the title given to a set of facts and circumstances which satisfies certain legal requirements and has certain legal consequences. It is a generally understood category into which facts may be put in order that definite principles or rules may be applicable thereto. Thus marriage, contract, negligence, culpable homicide, partnership, duty, tenure, and many more terms are legal concepts. These and other similar concepts are the terms of legal thought and expression, in that doctrines, principles and rules are built up of them and legal consequences attach to them. So, if a court holds that the relationship between two persons was a "marriage," there immediately attach to them all the legal consequences which many statutes, cases and authoritative books have prescribed as the legal consequences of marriage, such as the duty to adhere and to aliment, the inability of either to marry another, and so on. If the court holds that the relationship in the circumstances was

---

[35] *e.g.* a rule formulated in the days of horse-drawn traffic may be unsuitable for mechanised traffic. See, *e.g. Crawford v. Lumsden*, 1951 S.L.T. (Notes) 62.

merely cohabitation, different legal consequences attach.[36] The connotations of concepts frequently convey complex and abstract legal ideas, and one task of jurisprudence is to analyse the constituents and requisites of particular legal concepts, to see how the words are used and what they mean in different contexts and different branches of the law. Endless controversy, for example, has raged over the concept of "possession."[37] British law is in some ways deficient in legal concepts, in that some ideas are not clearly formulated in a legal concept and statutes frequently establish their own definitions of words for the purpose of that statute only, rather than generally. Some legal concepts, such as those of corporate personality, property and future interests in land, are highly abstract and not always easy to explain or to comprehend. The definition of a "crime," for example, has given rise to much thought, discussion and writing, and probably no concise yet comprehensive description of the indicia and characteristics of a crime has yet been made.

Legal concepts do not always coincide in connotation with the everyday uses of the same verbal form. So not everything which in common speech is called "negligence" truly amounts to negligence in law, nor is every "contract" or "crime" truly such in law. In each department of the law, considerable attention must be paid to discovering the constituent elements of the concepts used so that legally accurate uses of the word may be distinguished from instances which have apparent similarities. Statutes frequently contain long interpretation sections defining particular terms in special, frequently very extended, ways. As a result everyday words such as "factory," "development" and "family" may become legal concepts with meanings in the context of statute and cases thereon, materially different from their everyday meaning, with important legal consequences. So, too, in decided cases concepts may be explained, and in the course of time, refined and modified.[38]

The Concept of Law

An absolutely fundamental concept is the concept of law itself.[39] Is law something divinely ordained and disclosed by divine revelation, is it something deduced from the nature of man, is it the command of a political superior, or is it something else? None of these answers is adequate. The discussion of this question is a major subject of jurisprudence.

---

[36] *e.g. Walker v. Roberts* 1998 S.L.T. 1133.

[37] *c.f. Kaur v. Singh* 1998 S.C. 180.

[38] Fletcher, *The Basic Concepts of Legal Thought.* For discussions of various concepts and legal words see the list of "Words and Phrases" in the *Current Law Yearbooks* referring to cases in which the concepts and words have been discussed.

[39] Among very many books, see Thomas Aquinas, *Summa Theologiae*; Finnis, *Natural Law and Natural Rights*; Austin, *The Province of Jurisprudence Determined*; Hart, *The Concept of Law*; Morton, *An Institutional Theory of Law.*

The Concept of Justice

Another concept, central to thinking about society and government as well as thinking about law, is justice, which similarly provokes endless discussion. What is the essential element of the general notion of justice, as distinct from particular instances which individuals for one reason or another regard, and label, as instances of justice or injustice? What should be, or is, the relationship between justice and law?

Every state professes to seek to secure justice by its system of law. We speak of "courts of justice", "the administration of justice", a "miscarriage of justice". The word sometimes occurs in judicial titles.[40] Classical Greek thinkers considered justice one of the cardinal virtues natural to all men. Cicero contended that in the definition of law there inhered the idea and principle of choosing what was just and true.[41] Roman law called it the set and constant purpose which gives to every man his due.[42] The medieval Church distinguished the seven virtues[43] and the seven deadly sins.[44] Justice is frequently symbolised on seals, at coronations and in other contexts by a sword or a pair of scales for weighing. Since then, philosophers have debated the nature and requisites of justice, and scholars in many fields discussed what it means in social, political, economic, legal and other contexts.[45] Justice is usually thought to involve certain elements—equality, fairness, respect for persons—but there seems no finite list of criteria.

It is perfectly possible for justice to be administered without law, by honourable, thoughtful persons hearing disputes and saying what they think right and fair. But such a system, feasible in simple conditions or among undeveloped people, would not work in a developed society. Without guidelines or rules there would be too many variant decisions and people could have no advance knowledge of what might be held right or wrong, valid or void. Accordingly, attempts have always been made to achieve justice by having law. In legal contexts, justice must generally include acting to conform to the relevant rules of law, being those which the state has established or recognised to achieve justice. But occasionally a judge finds himself bound to obey a law which he believes not to confer justice in the circumstances; he cannot be faulted for applying it because it is, on the whole, better that there should be a rule and eveyone conform to it than that everyone apply their own rule.

---

[40] In England judges of the High Court are designated "Mr (or Mrs) Justice X", and of the Court of Appeal "Lord Justice".

[41] *De Legibus*, II, 11.

[42] Justinian, *Inst.*, I, 1, 1.

[43] Faith, hope, love, prudence, temperance, courage and justice.

[44] Pride, envy, anger, sloth, avarice, gluttony and lechery.

[45] See, *e.g.* R. Pound, *Justice According to Law*; J. Rawls, *A Theory of Justice*; B. M. Barry, *The Liberal Theory of Justice*; J. R. Lucas, *On Justice*; H. Kelsen, *What is Justice?*; N. M. Nathan, *The Concept of Justice*; K. D. Moore, *Pardons: Justice, Mercy and the Public Interest*; E. Rakowski, *Equal Justice*; W. Godwin, *Enquiry concerning Political Justice*; D. Miller, *Social Justice*.

One respect in which justice is frequently expressly invoked is where it is needed for adjudication to conform to the principles of natural justice. These include at least two principles: that the person judging should hear both or all parties equally before deciding; and that a person judging should have no personal interest in the outcome of the dispute, nor stand to gain or lose by the decision.

Also, there are instances where a rule of law expressly refers the decision of a point to what is "fair and just", or in other similar terms. This is truly a reference to the judge's moral sense, to his own feeling of what is in the circumstances "fair and just" or right.

Rights and Duties

The two most frequently occurring legal concepts are "rights" and "duties" and both terms are frequently abused or misused. Many of the "rights" and "duties" asserted by politicians are not rights or duties at all, but merely aspirations or hopes or demands.[46] Properly speaking, a "right" is confined to a claim which is a kind of advantage recognised by the legal system and enforceable against another person, such as the right (claim) to receive payment of a debt. Conversely, a "duty" is a kind of burden recognised by the legal system, which should have been, or should now be, discharged and which can be enforced, such as the duty to pay a debt. A distinction falls to be drawn between legal rights and duties and merely social or moral rights and duties. The distinction depends on the source of the right or duty in question; whether is created or recognised by a rule of law, or is merely a precept of social or moral behaviour. The duty to pay tax is a legal duty. The duty to help one's neighbour, or to give to charity, is normally a social or moral one only. Similarly, acute problems arise as to alleged "natural rights"[47] or "human rights."[48] A legal right or duty moreover, is not necessarily one which is morally right. Some taxes may be condemned as morally wrong, but if they are imposed by law the legal right to exact and the legal duty to pay exist.[49]

Scholars have pointed out that even in legal discourse the word "right" is used in four main distinguishable senses: (a) a claim enforceable by law, what one can exact from another; (b) a liberty or privilege, what one may legally do; what is allowed by law such as to wear a beard, make a will, walk along a right of way, or join a trade union—but which is not

---

[46] Is abortion a "woman's right"? Other words similarly abused and misused are "justice," "democracy," "freedom," "fair."

[47] cf. J. Finnis, *Natural Law and Natural Rights*.

[48] cf. C.S. Nino, *The Ethics of Human Rights*; J. Waldron, *The Right of Private Property*; S. Buckle, *Natural Law and Theory of Property*.

[49] cf. J. Raz, *The Morality of Freedom*; L. W. Sumner, *The Moral Foundation of Rights*.

enforceable against anyone;[50] (c) a power, what the law assists, what one can do and another cannot—such as to rescind a contract—for fraud, by licence sell excisable liquor or exercise a monopoly by patent, and (d) an immunity, what law grants to one but denies to others, what one can do free from certain liabilities—such as the "right" of a charity to receive money free of tax. A right (claim) is what I can enforce and others ought to do for me; a liberty is what I may do with impunity; a power is what I can do effectively; an immunity is what others cannot do in relation to me.

Similarly, the word "duty" is used in four main distinguishable senses (a) a burden on one to do something to or for another, such as to pay a debt, (b) an inability, such as to prevent or object to the action of another, (c) a liability or subjection, such as to have to put up with certain conduct of another, and (d) a disability, what one cannot do, such as to sell property one does not own. These represent respectively what I must do, what I cannot do, what I must accept or put up with, and what I am disabled from doing.[51]

Furthermore, the four senses of right and the four senses of duty correspond with each other, so that each one of each pair can be said to be correlative of the other.[52] This implies that in a relationship, such as of buyer and seller, the one has a right against the other and the other a duty to the one, *e.g.* the right to receive delivery in exchange for payment and the duty to make delivery.[53] There are other rights and duties arising from the same relationship, such as the right to receive, and the duty to make, delivery of goods answering the contract description and of merchantable quality.[54] Similar examples can be worked out for the liberty-inability, power-liability and immunity-disability relationships, and more complicated logical relationships have also been worked out. Accordingly, every time a lawyer comes across the word "right" or "duty" he should consider in which of the four senses the particular word is being used. Which one of the eight could be substituted for the word "right" or "duty," as the case may be, without altering the real meaning and possibly, rather, clarifying the real meaning? It does not matter whether the precise terms of this analysis are followed provided the lawyer utilises the analysis to clarify his thinking and arguing.

---

[50] "The 'right' to legal representation at a trial is not a right (claim) but a privilege or liberty, or power to engage counsel, and if a person chooses not to engage counsel his constitutional rights have not been infringed": *Robinson v. R.* [1985] 2 All E.R. 594, 600. Similarly if an accused dismisses his counsel. So, too, the "right" of free speech is a liberty or privilege; see C.E. Baker, *Human Liberty and Freedom of Speech*; K. Greenawalt, *Speech, Crime and the Uses of Language*.

[51] Salmond, *Jurisprudence*, Chap. 7, and earlier authorities cited there. Some other writers have suggested variations on the terms used for some of the senses of rights and duties. See Hall, *Readings in Jurisprudence*, Chap. 11.

[52] See, *e.g.* Prescription and Limitation (Scotland) Act 1973, ss. 8(2), 15(2).

[53] Sale of Goods Act 1979, ss. 27–28.

[54] *Ibid.* ss. 13–14.

Rights and duties can be further distinguished and classified, into positive and negative, rights *in rem* and *in personam*, and in other ways.

Civil Rights and Liberties

This label is frequently given to the rights and liberties which individuals enjoy against authorities and each other, and in some states they are declared in constitutions, Bills of Rights or other special enactments, but in others, notably the United Kingdom, must be found in common law and ordinary legislation. Whether civil rights and liberties really exist in a state depends not on whether there is an enactment on paper conferring or guaranteeing them, but on whether individuals can actually enforce them. They include freedom of expression, of religion and belief, the right to privacy, the right of public meeting, and various other rights and liberties. The extent of the powers of the police frequently raises issues of civil liberties.

It is often a matter of dispute whether a particular civil right or liberty exists, or whether it exists in particular circumstances, and precisely what it covers. In most cases, civil rights and liberties are necessarily qualified in the interests of others. So, freedom of expression is qualified by rules penalising seditious, blasphemous and slanderous expressions. There cannot be an unqualified freedom from being arrested by the police. Unqualified liberty is anarchy.[55]

Human or Fundamental Rights

Human rights are those rights alleged to belong to human beings by natural law as an attribute of their being human. The idea was known to the philosophers and poets of the ancient world, to early Christianity, St. Thomas Aquinas, the Spanish jurist-theologians of the sixteenth century, Grotius, Locke and other thinkers of the seventeenth century. Assertions of such rights received verbal formulation in the Scottish Claim of Right and the English Bill of Rights (1689), the Virginia Declaration of Rights (1776), the American Declaration of Independence (1776), the French Declaration of the Rights of Man (1789) and the American Bill of Rights (the first 10 amendments to the Federal Constitution) (1791). Some such rights were treated as matters of international concern in some international treaties from the seventeenth century onwards which sought to ensure religious freedom. From 1814 the suppression of slavery became an international concern as did, later, the securing of reasonable standards in social and labour relations. The Charter of the United Nations of 1945 reaffirmed faith in "fundamental human rights, the dignity and worth of

---

[55] See generally works on Constitutional Law; Ewing and Finnie: *Civil Liberties in Scotland: Cases and Materials*; Bailey, Harris and Jones: *Civil Liberties; Cases and Materials*; Zander, *A Bill of Rights?*; Baker, *Human Liberty and Freedom of Speech*; Greenawalt, *Speech, Crime and the Uses of Language*.

the human person, in the equal rights of men and women and of nations large and small," and in 1948 the UN adopted a Universal Declaration of Human Rights, later supplemented by additional treaties. The Council of Europe agreed in 1950 to a European Convention on Human Rights, with a European Commission on Human Rights and a European Court of Human Rights.[56] The United Kingdom did not make the Convention a part of United Kingdom law, though it accepted the compulsory jurisdiction of the Court. It incorporated most of it in 1998.[57] All these "rights" are truly rights only so far as they are accepted and recognised by the appropriate authority. To call them "human" or "natural" confers no status or validity on them. The great problem of all such declarations is that they are framed in broad and general terms,[58] that disputes on interpretation can and do easily arise and require to be solved by litigation, disputes over whether particular conduct is or is not protected or outlawed, and that many people think that some of the kinds of conduct alleged to be, or held to be, infringements are not infringments of human rights at all but reasonable restrictions on undesirable conduct. Interpretation of the Constitution of the United States shows how rights conferred in general terms gradually became extended by decisions, to cover cases never contemplated when they were enacted.

Other Concepts

The law utilises numerous other concepts, many of which require elucidation and careful examination. Other important concepts are jurisdiction, persons, things, property, ownership, possession, crime, attempt, intention, malice, negligence, recklessness, responsibility, liability, and many more terms regularly used in statements of and about the law and rules thereof.[59] Good textbooks about any branch of law devote considerable attention to elucidation of the concepts utilised in statements of and about that branch of law.

Standards

Sometimes principles and rules do not prescribe specific or definite legal consequences but prescribe standards of conduct or evaluation. A legal standard is a measure for conduct, to be applied according to the circumstances of each individual case. The standard is the main means

---

[56] Ritchie, *Natural Rights*; Lauterpacht, *International Law and Human Rights*; Fawcett, *Application of the European Convention on Human Rights*; Weil, *The European Convention on Human Rights*.

[57] Human Rights Act 1998.

[58] *e.g.* what is "respect for his private and family life" guaranteed by Convention, Art. 8? Is three strokes of a birch on a youth, as a punishment for assault on another causing bodily harm, a "degrading" punishment? What makes a trial not a "fair trial"?

[59] For a philosopher's view that mistaken views about the meanings of words embodying key legal concepts have sometimes led to bad decisions, see White, *Misleading Cases*.

whereby both legal principles and rules maintain flexibility. Where the standard is employed, principles and rules are usually expressed not in absolute but in relative terms, and this enables the court in a particular case to consider the precise circumstances of that case and to determine whether the conduct falls short of or comes up to the desired level. The law is full of expressions of such standards as "the reasonable man," "the prudent trustee," "the *bonus paterfamilias*," "fair rent," "reasonable precautions," "the reasonably competent practitioner." The use of such standards enables account to be taken of individual circumstances; consider how much more flexible is the rule "unsatisfactory goods must be returned within a reasonable time" than such a rigid rule as " . . . within seven days." The former gives room for discretion and allows account to be taken of difficulties; the latter might be very unfair in particular cases. Sometimes the law does impose fixed rather than relative standards, as where it prescribes a speed limit of 30 miles per hour in built-up areas, or the amount of alcohol in the blood which renders a driver unfit to drive.

Discretion

Discretion is a person's ability or entitlement to choose and exercise his own judgment as to what is appropriate, or right, or best in the circumstances, as opposed to his being subject to a rule compelling him or dictating what must be done in such a case. It involves consideration of what is fair, reasonable, proper, just or right and the decision to adopt the course which he thinks most likely to promote the end prescribed or desired. It is essentially a reference to the moral judgment of the person.[60]

Judicial discretion is the power, frequently conferred on judges by doctrines, principles or rules of law, to do in some respect what seems to the judge to be right and just in the circumstances. In some cases, judges have unfettered discretion, in others their discretion can be exercised only within limits fixed, or guidelines laid down, by statute or previous cases. Accordingly, judges have discretion as to how much damages to award to an injured person, but the discretion must be exercised in accordance with guidelines laid down by superior courts in previous cases. So, too, judges usually have considerable discretion as to the penalty to impose for particular crimes, but again only within limits prescribed by statutes and previous authoritative rulings of higher courts.[61]

An important consequence of a power being discretionary is that a judge's exercise of that power can be challenged on appeal, only if it can be shown that it has contravened the guidelines or was plainly unreasonable or ridiculous. Similarly, persons who administer or execute the law,

---

[60] *Glasgow West Housing Association Ltd v. Siddique,* 1998 S.C. 375. See generally, Galligan, *Discretionary Powers.*

[61] R. Pattenden, *Judicial Discretion and Criminal Litigation.* Robertson, *Judicial Discretion in the House of Lords. cf.* also *McRae v. McRae,* 1979 S.C. 15.

such as tax inspectors or procurators-fiscal or policemen, can sometimes exercise a measure of discretion whether, in particular circumstances to prosecute, or merely to warn or take some other action.

The total exclusion of discretion by law is probably impossible and would certainly frequently produce inconvenience or even injustice. Conversely, unfettered discretion by judges and administrators might produce fair results in many cases, but is liable to be unequal in operation and totally negatives the principle that law should be reasonably predictable in operation; it might be justice, but it would cease to be justice according to law.

In many cases, persons other than judges (*e.g.* trustees) are given considerable discretion to act as they think best.

How these Elements are Used

In practice the formulation of statements of law on any topic may utilise all the elements just discussed. Thus it is a common law *principle*, deduced from the *doctrine* of fault liability for harm, that a person physically injured on the road by the *fault* (concept) of another has a *right* (concept) to recover compensation from him, and one *rule* derived from this is that a person who by driving *without reasonable care* (standard) causes injury to another is deemed legally *negligent* (concept) and is therefore under a *duty* (concept) to pay to the injured person such *damages* (concept) as the court *in its discretion* thinks *fair and appropriate* (standard). Again, a statute[62] lays down the *principle* that every *employee to whom the Act applies* (concept) has the *right* (concept) not to be *unfairly dismissed* (concept); the statute goes on to define these concepts in considerable detail.

THE VOCABULARY OF LAW

Language and Words

Since the legal order consists of the regulation of conduct by the application of various kinds of principles and rules to various sets of factual circumstances, the enormous importance in legal connections of language and words must not be overlooked. The principles and rules and other precepts of law are formulated verbally in statutes and orders, in judicial and administrative decisions, and in books of authority, and the circumstances of fact to which rules of law are to be applied are frequently expressed in verbal form in contracts, agreements, wills, deeds, dispositions and other writings, and are brought before courts by way of written pleadings, indictments or complaints, while oral evidence of facts is given in verbal form. It is apparent that an important part of both the study and the application of law consists of the correct appreciation and understanding of the uses and meanings of words, the accurate formulation of

---

[62] Employment Protection (Consolidation) Act 1978 (c. 44), ss. 57 *et seq.*

thought in words so as to convey precisely the meaning intended, and the careful analysis of language used so as to extract from its precise connotations and implications.[63] Attention to word-meaning and usage is of practical importance in legal study, and good textbooks devote considerable attention to the analysis of the legal terms and words relevant to their subject-matter. The same techniques of analysis are also used in jurisprudence.[64]

Unfortunately, law does not have such a large, highly technical vocabulary as medicine and engineering. Legal thinking and writing would be much more accurate and clearer if it did, but in fact law for the most part utilises everyday words of the English language.

It has to be admitted that many terms used in legal connections, and many more in social, ethical and political studies, are vague and do not necessarily cause the hearer immediately to have in mind the same thing as the speaker. Such phrases as "reasonable care", "unreasonable restraint of trade", "satisfied beyond reasonable doubt", leave room for differences of opinion and do not refer to a concrete measurable criterion. It is the vagueness which can easily permit judges to differ in opinion as to the decision of a case even though the facts may be established and the law well settled. So, if the law is that rejected goods must be returned to the seller "within a reasonable time" and they have in fact been returned in 10 days, one judge may consider that 10 days was reasonable in the circumstances of the case; another that it was not reasonable, but unduly delayed. This is even more so in the case of such words as "just", "wrong", and "unconstitutional" which are sometimes used emotionally and with no clear significance.

Many words have several senses or meanings which require to be carefully distinguished, since the word is not always used with the same connotation in all legal discourse. "Malice" may mean simply the deliberate doing of a legally wrongful act, or it may mean malevolence, spite or ill-will; "property" may mean the legal rights of proprietorship[65], or may mean the actual object to which these legal rights relate.[66]

There are numerous words which have two or more distinct senses— one or more in ordinary everyday speech and one with a particular and

---

[63] See Sapir, "Language," in *Encyc.Soc.Sc.*, IX, 158.

[64] A valuable discussion of this topic in legal connections is Williams, "Language and the Law" (1945) 61 L.Q.R. 71, 179, 293 and 384; (1946) 62 L.Q.R. 387. See also Corbin, "Legal Analysis and Terminology" (1919) 29 Yale L.J. 163; Chafee, "The Disorderly Conduct of Words" (1941) 41 Col.L.R. 381. The student interested in pursuing this topic should make the acquaintance of such works as Fowler's *Modern English Usage* and *The King's English* and make frequent reference to both legal and standard English dictionaries. See also B. A. Garner, *A Dictionary of Modern Legal Usage*. The study of literature and other languages does much to develop the sensitive weighing and handling of words.

[65] In the Sale of Goods Act 1979 there are rules for the passing or transference of the "property," which means the right of property or ownership and is quite a distinct matter from the transfer of the goods sold.

[66] As in the estate agent's phrase "a desirable property."

rather different meaning in legal discourse. "Negligence" in ordinary speech means carelessness, whereas in law it means a failure to fulfil the duty of care imposed in the circumstances by the law, whether or not that be carelessness in the common sense. "Charity" in everyday speech means helping the needy, but it has a wider meaning in law and the interpretation of the word "charity" in legal contexts has given rise to immense controversy. Particular statutes sometimes define particular words for the purposes of that statute, sometimes more narrowly, sometimes more broadly than the everyday meaning of the word.

This category of words is further distinct from the category of words which have definite legal meanings only and which are seldom, if ever, used in everyday discourse, words such as "vitious intromitter", "eik", "purging an irritancy", "bailee." English law was formerly rich in words peculiarly legal, but many have now disappeared. Scots law has not so many peculiarly legal terms, but all British law is weak in accurate technical terminology as compared with medicine or engineering.

This close attention to words and the verbal form of statutes, deeds and other legal expressions must extend to the commonest and most ordinary parts of speech, since it may be of crucial importance whether "or" or "and" be used, "may" or "shall", "among" or "between". For example, the precise position of the word "only" in a sentence may be crucial. Every indication of meaning which can be gathered from a grammatical shift may be important.

Closely connected with this topic is the body of guiding principles and presumptions which have been developed by the courts to assist them in the difficult task of statutory interpretation,[67] a problem which perplexes courts and legal advisers precisely because the communication of ideas by words can never be achieved with complete accuracy and perfect freedom from ambiguity.

LAW AND FACT

Elements in a Legal Situation
The situations which the judge or lawyer has to deal with are seldom exclusively matters of pure law and may indeed involve law only incidentally. In every such situation there are four elements: the relevant principles and rules of law, which are abstract and general; facts, which are concrete and specific; persons, who are complex, possibly irrational and unpredictable; and the physical, social, intellectual, economic, political and other environments which form the background to the acts and events under inquiry. Of these elements, two require special attention, though the others remain factors which cannot be ignored: those two are fact and law.

---

[67] These principles are discussed in Chap. 10, *infra*.

Fact and Law

In all legal discussion the distinction between fact and law has to be kept in mind, for it is a distinction of fundamental importance in many connections.[68] A question of fact concerns the existence in past or present time of some act or event or state of things, cognisable or ascertainable by the senses; a question of law concerns the existence, or content, or applicability, of some doctrine, principle or rule of the legal system. Thus, for example, what A said, what B heard, whether C's car was going fast at the moment of impact, whether D intended to kill E, whether F warned G of his danger, questions of time, place, speed, direction, colour, temperature, lighting, weather, visibility, mental state, identity, and generally anything cognisable by the senses, or by inference from sense-data, are questions of fact. Facts include information discovered by measurements, scientific tests, post-mortem examinations and the like, the causes of injury or death, of mechanical failures, of economic losses and other events. Facts also include opinions offered by experts, based on their tests, examinations and other investigations.[69] On the other hand, whether J's conduct was legally reckless, whether K's departure from his wife amounted in law to desertion, whether L's killing amounted legally to murder or not, whether M's vehicle was a "trailer" within the meaning of the Act, and so on, are questions of law, which cannot be decided by the senses but only by determination of whether or not the fact in issue falls within the verbally defined limits of some doctrine, principle or rule of law, from which certain legal consequences will follow, such as entitlement to remedy or liability to some penalty. A question of law concerns the existence, or content, or applicability of a precept of law to certain circumstances. Thus, whether S is liable in damages for defamation depends on (a) what he said, and the circumstances in which he said it (fact), and (b) whether these words in these circumstances legally amount to defamation (law). So, too, other legal controversies and problems can be resolved into factual and legal elements.[70]

It should be remembered that either the factual or legal element may be admitted on all sides, or be so clear as to be beyond argument. Therefore, it may be admitted that X struck the blow, but be argued that in the circumstances it was not murder but culpable homicide; or it may be admitted that the killing of Y was murder, but be disputed whether X was the person who did it. The proper meaning or interpretation of statutes and documents, or statements made, are always questions of law.

This distinction between questions of fact and questions of law arises in many contexts and is of great practical importance. When drafting

---

[68] See further Corbin, "Legal Analysis and Terminology" (1919) 29 Yale L.J. 163 and in Hall, *Readings in Jurisprudence*, 471; Wilson, "A Note on Fact and Law" (1963) 26 M.L.R. 609.

[69] Even where the result of an examination is stated by an expert as his opinion, that he expressed that opinion is a fact, and what the opinion is, is a fact.

[70] *e.g. McLennan v. McLennan*, 1958 S.C. 105.

pleadings for an action in court, a lawyer seeks to state the facts, as he understands them and as his client has put them before him, not to state how he proposes to prove these facts if they are denied, nor to argue the point of law involved, though the facts alleged must be sufficient, if admitted or proved, to justify the grant of the remedy he has claimed.[71] Again, whether a party alleging his error as a ground for repudiating liability under a contract alleges an error in fact or an error in law is very important.[72] A sheriff when deciding a civil case, must make findings in fact and in law separately.[73] In many circumstances, an appeal may be taken on questions of law only, but not on questions of fact.[74]

Certain consequences of this distinction must also be borne in mind. A question of fact has to be determined, if disputed, by proof, by adducing evidence of what happened, what was said, or seen, or heard, or done, and so on. Questions of law, on the other hand, are determined not by evidence[75] but by legal argument, by adducing to the judges or other persons concerned with making the decision, statements in statutes, cases and books of authority which persuade them to the view that the appropriate rule of the legal system is one to a particular effect—*e.g.* that a mistake by a man as to his wife's previous chastity does not give him ground for having the marriage annulled.[76] A court or other tribunal is presumed to know the law of its own country; accordingly, one need not, and must not, seek to prove the law to it, but must simply seek to persuade it by legal argument as to which particular rule or exception, or what formulation of the rule should be applied in the circumstances. But one must enlighten a court as to the facts in issue by leading evidence of them, unless those facts are admitted or are not in dispute.

The whole body of principles and rules of law relative to evidence regulates how facts may or must be proved, by what evidence—*e.g.* by writing only—and the practices and methods of eliciting evidence. Some facts, such as a person's knowledge or intention or state of mind at a material time—*e.g.* prior animosity, or indifference to possible consequences of his actions—cannot be proved directly but only by proving other conduct or surrounding circumstances from which a judge or jury can draw the inference that the person must have known or intended or had the requisite state of mind at the material time.[77]

---

[71] See further, Chap. 12, *infra*.

[72] Walker on *Contracts and Related Obligations* (3rd ed.), paras. 14.4 *et seq.*

[73] Chap. 12, *infra*.

[74] Chaps. 12 and 13, *infra*. *Rae v. Criminal Injuries Compensation Board* 1997 S.L.T. 291.

[75] An exception to this principle arises in the cases where the law of *another* country is in issue, *e.g.* a matter of English law in a Scottish court, and vice versa. In such cases the foreign law is treated as a question of fact (since the court does not have judicial knowledge of a foreign system) and its rules must be proved by evidence, as by producing as witnesses practitioners of the other systems involved, *e.g.* English barristers, as in *Rosses v. Bhagvat Sinhjee* (1891) 19 R. 31, or by remitting to the courts of the other system for a statement on their law.

[76] *Lang v. Lang*, 1921 S.C. 44, overruling *Stein v. Stein*, 1914 S.C. 903.

[77] *e.g. R. v. Hancock* [1986] A.C. 455.

When investigating questions of fact which arise in a legal context and leading evidence of them, lawyers often have to use the knowledge developed by practitioners in other very different branches of study and used by other professionals as part of their background knowledge. For example, to investigate whether a bus crash, which caused deaths, was a pure accident or imported legal liability to the bus company or its insurers to pay compensation, involves inquiry into the factual cause of the crash, which may involve the driver's immediate pre-accident health or state of mind (a medical problem), the state of the road at the time and place (a civil engineering problem), and the state of the vehicle and whether, *e.g.* brake failure caused it to crash (a mechanical engineering problem).[78] Accordingly, whether a pursuer can receive damages or not will depend not only on the relevant rules of law, but, on what experts in these other disciplines report as the result of their investigations into the circumstances and whether they convince the court or jury of the probable correctness of their explanation.

As persons, their intentions and states of mind, their behaviour, their bodily states and the effect thereon of events are constantly arising in legal contexts, the lawyer has frequently to bring in medical evidence.

Consequently, there is no science or body of practical knowledge outside the law which may not in some circumstances have to be invoked to help to explain some question of fact which is in issue. Aeronautics, architecture, ballistics, building, engineering, navigation and many more may enter into a case, and the lawyer has to rely on the skills of experts in other subjects of which he himself has little knowledge.

These bodies of knowledge and the opinions of persons skilled in them do not themselves decide the questions of fact or the matters in dispute. They provide information and evidence on questions of fact to which principles of law can be applied. If an architect's evidence is that he and, he believes, most other architects would have deemed certain foundations inadequate for a particular site, the court may reach the conclusion in fact that they were inadequate, and the conclusion in law that a builder who put down those foundations was lacking in due care in doing so.

While these are the fundamental distinctions between questions of fact and questions of law, subsidiary meanings of the terms are also found. In the determination of certain litigated controversies, a jury has a part to play and matters which are for the decision of the jury are rather arbitrarily called questions of fact, and matters reserved for the decision of the presiding judge are called questions of law; this nomenclature persists notwithstanding that certain of the matters which are committed to the judge may be in their nature questions of fact.[79] This difficulty is not so

---

[78] *e.g. Dingwall v. Walter Alexander & Sons (Midland) Ltd*, 1982 S.C.(H.L.) 179.

[79] In a case of damages for malicious prosecution, the pursuer must prove that the defender initiated the prosecution maliciously and without probable cause. It is a question for the judge whether facts have been proved which suffice to imply malice and lack of probable cause, even though this is factual in nature.

apparent in cases decided by a judge sitting alone, since he has to decide issues both of fact and law.

Also, any question which is determined by some rule of law, such as the punishment for treason, may be called a question of law, even although it depends on the facts and circumstances of the case,[80] or is determined by the exercise of the judge's discretion.[81]

Lastly, a question of law may be a question as to what the true rule of law is, applicable to a particular matter. So, in special cases and stated cases[82] certain admitted or proved facts are set before the court and a question of law formulated, raising a problem of the applicability or otherwise of some rule or principle of law, whether a statutory provision applies, whether a particular doctrine deduced from case law governs the case thus presented, or what effect a particular rule has in the circumstances.

The differences are also relevant to explaining the outcome of a dispute or prosecution. A person may escape liability for breach of contract because his act or omission did not amount to breach (fact), or because his act or omission was excused by a provision in the contract (law). If a person accused of crime is discharged, it may be because he was not proved to have done the act charged (fact), or because the act did not in the circumstances amount to the crime charged (law).

Transformation of Fact into Law

As the law develops and grows in complexity, there is in some circumstances a tendency for matters which in their nature are truly matters of fact, to be treated as matters of law and determined by rules of law accordingly. In some cases, legal presumptions arise by virtue of which the law deems some state of fact to exist, whether in truth it exists or not. For example, there is a legal presumption that children under eight years of age are incapable of committing crime, which applies despite any indications of capacity or intention in fact; no contrary proof can countervail. Also, certain conduct may by a legal fiction be "deemed to be" fraudulent or criminal, with the result that it will be so in law, whatever it may have been in fact. A further class of presumptions exists whereby certain factual circumstances have certain legal validity and consequences, unless the presumption is rebutted (that is, unless it can be shown that in fact and in truth the circumstances were otherwise), *e.g.* every man is presumed sane, every man is presumed innocent, and so on.

---

[80] Under the Sale of Goods Act 1979, unsatisfactory goods must be returned "within a reasonable time," and what is a reasonable time is a question of fact, *i.e.* it has to be decided in the circumstances of each case. There is no rule laid down as to what is a reasonable time, no rule that a week or a month is reasonable.

[81] In a divorce case the judge has a discretion as to which parent to give custody of the children and he is not bound by law to give to one rather than the other.

[82] As to these, see Chap. 12, *infra*.

Further, once it has been decided in one case that certain kinds of facts amount to cruelty, or adultery, or culpable homicide, or such other legal category, similar facts arising subsequently will have the same effect as a matter of law, by the operation of the doctrine of judicial precedent.[83]

In all these cases, the circumstances of fact have ceased to be purely factual in that certain legal force and effect necessarily attaches to them by operation of law from their mere existence.

Mixed Questions of Fact and Law

Questions frequently arise in which elements of both fact and of law are present and intermixed. These arise in two forms. First, the problem may be really a composite one depending both on the existence of facts and also on the sufficiency of these facts for some legal purpose. Therefore, the question whether partnership exists between two persons depends both on the terms of the agreement entered into by them (fact) and on the sufficiency of an agreement in those terms to constitute what the law will recognise as a partnership (law). Very many questions which arise are of this type—*e.g.* whether A had murdered B, whether C had slandered D, whether E had married F, whether G had wrongfully imprisoned H, and so on—and a very common fault in pleading before a court is to make statements of this composite kind which beg the question whether the facts are truly legally sufficient to justify the use of the term having a legal connotation. So, to state that "by letters of 1st and 2nd May the pursuer and the defender *contracted* to . . . " begs the question whether the letters (the existence and terms of which are facts) did, as interpreted by the court, truly constitute a contract, which is a matter of law.

Secondly, mixed questions of fact and law may arise where a judicial discretion may be exercised only within legally determined limits. Many powers of imposing fines and imprisonment are of this kind, and in such cases the question for the court is one of fact, so far as concerns the appropriate measure of punishment to be imposed in any particular case in the exercise of its discretion, and one of law so far as concerns the limits within which the discretion may operate.[84]

The questions set to juries and answered by their general verdicts are frequently problems of mixed fact and law. When a jury returns a verdict that the prisoner is guilty of culpable homicide, they are truly reporting two things: that in their view the prisoner had done certain things (fact), *and* that these happenings amounted in the circumstances to culpable homicide, as that legal category has been explained to the jury by the presiding judge in his charge to the jury (law).

---

[83] On judicial precedent, see further, Chap. 10, *infra*.

[84] In such a case there is, of course, frequently a prior mixed question of fact and law on the matter of liability—*e.g.* was the accused guilty of reckless driving?—before the question as to punishment arises. The latter question alone would arise if the accused pleaded guilty or were convicted.

Difficulties as to Facts or Law

The preceding discussion must not obscure the difficulty that in many cases matters of fact or of law, or of both, remain doubtful or disputed until the final decision in a litigation reaches a conclusion which binds the parties. Facts in a textbook problem or a reported case are set down as matters fixed and established, but in practice matters of fact may remain in doubt. The judge or jury, in hearing evidence, is trying to reconstruct what really happened, as in a detective novel, from fragmentary, misleading and inaccurate clues. What emerges may be not a finding of what happened, but of what the judge or jury *think* must have happened, as being the sequence of happenings most consistent, in their view, with the bulk of the testimony.[85] The facts finally held to have been "proved" are at the mercy of witnesses who did not notice, who cannot remember, of parties who have failed to keep letters, who cannot recall where or when, who did not think something was worth mentioning to the lawyer, or who could not be found or have died, of cars which did not stop, workmen who have left no address, bystanders who did not give their names, and so on. Accordingly, the facts disclosed by a client to his legal adviser frequently contain gaps and uncertainties, and they invariably conflict with some of the evidence adduced by the opposing party. Frequently, much of this arises from the fact that something happens quickly and suddenly and is all over before anyone has had a chance to observe what was happening. The human senses are fallible recorders of events, and honest testimony may be very inaccurate. Difficulties as to facts and discrepancies in evidence arise far more from faulty observation, or inattention, or forgetfulness, or the unavailability of witnesses or of corroborative evidence than from dishonesty by witnesses, though there is a great deal of lying, in criminal cases particularly. What a court holds happened in fact depends on interpretation of evidence given of facts, inferences from those facts, and experience of what normally happens.

Similarly, even if and when some state of facts is "found" by the court to have "happened," it may still be uncertain precisely which principle or rule of law, or what precise verbal formulation of it, falls to be applied. It may not be at all clear what rule applies, nor whether any existing rule can be applied, nor whether resort must be had to analogy or formulation of a new rule or modification of an old one to cover the case, because principles and rules of law are frequently much vaguer and less precise than the exact and categorical prescriptions which laymen think of as rules of law.

Even then, much may depend on the temperament of the judge. Where he has to apply a flexible standard of law, such as "reasonable care," the

---

[85] On the uncertainty of judicial fact-finding, see Frank, *Courts on Trial* (1949), and "What Courts do in Fact" in Hall, *Readings in Jurisprudence*, 1103.

answer to the problem whether reasonable care was in fact taken in the circumstances held to have happened depends not on any fixed touch-stone, but on whether that judge *thinks* that reasonable care was taken. Another judge might think differently.

Acts and Events

Facts can also be distinguished into acts and events. An act is a happening brought about by human activity, positive (by acting) or negative (by abstaining or refraining from acting); an event is a happening which occurs independently of human intervention. The difference may be important in relation to moral responsibility and legal liability. Death caused by being shot by another, and caused by being struck by a falling tree, have different legal consequences. But it may be difficult to say whether a happening was an act or its immediate consequence, or an event. When a driver died at the wheel and his vehicle injured a pedestrian, was this the result of his act, or failure to act, or was it an accident (an event)?[86] When a man drove his car off a ferry and into the sea and died, was this an act (suicide) or an event (accident)?[87] An act or forbearance has usually to be taken along with its immediate and necessary consequences. Pulling the trigger of a pistol is the act, but the immediate and almost inevitable consequence (the firing, the flight of the bullet) cannot be severed from the act for the purposes of determining responsibility and legal liability; they are treated as inseparable parts of the act.

Acts require close examination. An act is generally thought to require, as well as a muscular movement, some exercise of the human will (consciously doing or abstaining), with a particular state of knowledge and intention, and sometimes also with a particular motive. Importance attaches to whether a person acting was bound or required to have acted (or on the other hand was forbidden to have acted), and to whether a person abstaining was bound or required to have abstained, or should have acted rather than abstained. The will to act or abstain may be overridden by force or illness. An omission (or not doing) is not an act; but may be significant where the person should by law have acted and his failure or forgetfulness is culpable, *e.g.* forgetting to exhibit warning lights. Some other omissions, *e.g.* to carry an umbrella today, may be of no significance.

Fact and Opinion

A distinction has sometimes to be drawn, particularly in the context of expert evidence, between fact and opinion. What a person has seen, heard

---

[86] *Waugh v. Allan*, 1964 S.C.(H.L.) 102.
[87] *Glenlight Shipping Co. v. Excess Insurance Co.*, 1983 S.L.T. 241.

or otherwise observed are facts, and that, guided by his professional knowledge, he has formed an opinion on the basis of these facts is itself a fact, but the substance or content of the opinion itself—*e.g.* that the death was caused by poison, that the accident was caused by a particular mechanical failure—is not a fact but a view reached by him, a conclusion or deduction or inference from observed facts, based on his knowledge, training, experience, possibly on tests done, and other expertise concerned with the particular subject-matter and expressed in his opinion. The fact that the person, however eminent, honestly reached the opinion does not imply that the opinion cannot be mistaken.[88] Another expert might reach a different opinion. Both opinions are facts and the court or jury has to determine which it accepts as accurate. If a person says that a vehicle is in sound condition, he may be asserting a fact, or expressing an opinion. A competent mechanic might be held to be asserting a fact, an unskilled layman to be merely stating an opinion.[89]

Persons

The personality, qualities and other attributes of the persons involved in a dispute may also be material. People are not standard, uniform objects. They will have likes and dislikes, intentions, motives, reasons; they may be intelligent, simple or senile; all these may be relevant as background material and cast light on, or even be essential, facts in the issue under consideration.[90]

Environment

The social, economic, political and other environment in which a dispute or prosecution arises may also be relevant. What is done in conditions of political or religious strife, in the heat of a trade dispute,[91] or the like, may be highly relevant to the proper interpretation and understanding of what persons involved said and did.

FURTHER READING

The State
Barker: *Principles of Social and Political Theory.*
Lindsay: *The Modern Democratic State.*
Mabbott: *The State and the Citizen.*

Sovereignty
Cohen: *Recent Theories of Sovereignty.*

---

[88] *e.g. Lothian Assessor v. Wilson*, 1979 S.C. 341
[89] *e.g. Flynn v. Scott*, 1949 S.C. 442.
[90] *e.g. Mackay v. Campbell*, 1966 S.C. 237; 1967 S.C. (H.L.) 53, at p. 61; *Honeyman's Exrs. v. Sharp*, 1978 S.C. 223.
[91] *e.g. R. v. Hancock* [1986] A.C. 455.

Hinsley: *Sovereignty.*
McCormick: *Questioning Sovereignty.*

The Expression of Legal Precepts
Hohfeld: *Fundamental Legal Conceptions.*
Kocourek: *Jural Relations.*
Schauer: *Playing by the Rules.*

The Vocabulary of Law
Bell: *Dictionary and Digest of the Law of Scotland.*
Broom: *Legal Maxims.*
Chase: *The Tyranny of Words.*
Garner: *Dictionary of Modern Legal Usage.*
Hexner: *Studies in Legal Terminology.*
Jowitt: *Dictionary of English Law.*
Lloyd: *Introduction to Jurisprudence.*
Philbrick: *Language and the Law.*
Trayner: *Latin Maxims and Phrases.*
Walker: *Oxford Companion to Law.*
Wharton: *Law Lexicon.*
Williams: "Language and the Law" (1945) 61 L.Q.R. 71, 179, 293, 384; (1946) 62
        L.Q.R. 387.

Law and Fact
Cardozo: *Nature of the Judicial Process.*
Frank: *Courts on Trial*
Salmond: *Jurisprudence.*

CHAPTER 4

THE DEVELOPMENT OF SCOTS LAW

THE modern Scottish legal system, and the complex body of doctrines, principles and rules which it utilises, have not been the creation of a single edict, but represent the present state of a long and slow process of development and evolution, in which numerous factors have played a part; political and governmental changes, social and economic developments, borrowing from other systems, the effects of war, religious upheaval, constitutional moves, and other factors. At different times different influences have been predominant. Not only does an outline of the historical development of the Scottish legal system show how that system has come to take its present shape, but also it helps to explain numerous practices and rules which survived long after the conditions which gave rise to them had passed away, and some of which still survive to upset the simplicity and symmetry of the law, and sometimes to cause confusion and even injustice.

Early Times

Very little is known of legal institutions or rules of law in Scotland prior to the year A.D. 1000, and nothing from any earlier period can be shown to have exercised any material or permanent influence on the development of the modern law.[1] For ordinary purposes, the story starts after that date. It should be noted that the influence of Roman law on Scots law was not effected by the Roman occupation of the South of Scotland in the second century.

I.—THE FEUDAL PERIOD

Introduction of Feudalism

After the victory at Carham over the Northumbrians in 1018, the Scottish kingdom reached its present boundaries by the incorporation of Lothian, the northern part of Northumbria.[2] Northumbrian influence had

---

[1] Rait and Pryde, *Scotland*, 13; Ritchie, *Normans in Scotland*, xiii. Traces of Celtic law are discussed in Cameron, *Celtic Law*. See also Levie, "Celtic Tribal Law and Custom in Scotland" (1927) 39 J.R. 191; Cameron, "Gaelic Notitiae in the Book of Deer" (1939) 51 J.R. 150; Jackson, *The Gaelic Notes in the Book of Deer*; Chadwick, *Celtic Britain*, 80; Dillon and Chadwick, *The Celtic Realms*, Chap. 5; Chadwick, *Early Scotland*.
[2] On the formation of the kingdom, see also Dickinson, *Scotland to 1603*, Chap. 6; Duncan, *Scotland: The Making of the Kingdom*.

penetrated into Lothian prior to then, though it was long before the more outlying parts of the kingdom were assimilated and lost their previous characteristics. Civilisation was confined to the Lothians and the coastal plain round to the Moray Firth, and particularly the districts near the burghs and baronial and ecclesiastical centres.

In the Gaelic Highlands the populace probably lived under the influence of Celtic customs, traces of which are found in the Senchus Mor and the Book of Aicill. Argyll had been settled from Ireland and the incomers had probably brought customs similar to those known in Ireland. In the Britons of Strathclyde[3] there was a point of contact with the traditions of early Welsh law, while in Galloway traces of customary law persisted as late as 1384. Orkney, Shetland, the Western Isles and large tracts of land north of Dingwall had been occupied by Scandinavians and long remained independent, while Orkney and Shetland were governed by Norse law down to 1468.

An important factor in the assimilation of Anglo-Saxon influences was the marriage of Malcolm III (Canmore) (1057–93) to the Saxon princess Margaret about 1070. The queen had great influence on her husband and used it to strengthen the Anglo-Saxon influences on Church and state. In the course of the next two centuries the population of the Lowlands became converted into an English-speaking community, with life organised on the model of the Anglo-Saxon-Norman Kingdom of England, and spiritually more akin to England than to Gaelic Scotland.[4]

The Norman Conquest of England in and after 1066 influenced Scotland less immediately and directly than it did England, but gradually it permeated and influenced Lowland Scottish society and institutions, and southern influences were potent in Scotland for many years. Normans began to come to Scotland from about 1080, and by 1150 "Scotland was Normanised beyond recall. Normans held the chief offices in Church and State. Land and power had largely passed into Norman hands. The old feudal system had been changed to Norman-feudal. A French aristocracy had been established, a French civilisation implanted."[5]

Prior to 1124, Norman feudalism[6] had probably made some headway in the south of Scotland but was not generally accepted.[7] The process of

---

[3] MacQuarrie, "The Kings of Strathclyde, c. 400–1018" in Grant and Stringer (ed.), *Medieval Scotland*, 1. The so-called *Leges inter Brettos et Scotos* may come from Celtic origins.

[4] Rait and Pryde, *Scotland*, 13; Ritchie, *op. cit.*, xiii. The text in A.P.S. I entitled the "Laws of Malcolm MacKenneth" is not truly of this period but of the later 14th century; Duncan, "The 'Laws of Malcolm MacKenneth'", in Grant and Stringer (ed.) *Medieval Scotland*, 239.

[5] Ritchie, *Normans in Scotland*, xv. For Celtic opposition to Anglo-Norman feudalism, see Dickinson, *op. cit.* 60. See further, Barrow, *The Anglo-Norman Era in Scottish History*; Gardner, "Historical Survey of the Law of Scotland prior to the reign of David I" (1945) 57 J.R. 34, 65; Levie, "Anglian Influence on Early Scottish Law" (1940) 52 J.R. 95.

[6] On feudalism in general, see Ganshof, *Feudalism* (trs. Grierson); Barrow, *Feudal Britain, 1066–1314, passim*; Vinogradoff, "Origins of Feudalism," 2 Camb.Med.Hist., Chap. 20; *idem.*, "Feudalism," 3 Camb.Med.Hist., Chap. 18.

[7] Hume Brown, *History of Scotland*, I, 73; Ritchie, *op. cit.* 67–83, 160–175; Barrow, "Beginnings of Feudalism in Scotland," *The Kingdom of the Scots*, Chap. 10.

Anglicisation or Anglo-Normanisation was definitely accepted in the reign of David I (1124–53)[8] and the law, as much as the court and the Church, was subjected to English influence. David, trained as a knight under Henry I of England, did much to reproduce in his own realm the pattern of feudal government and institutions prevailing in Norman England, at least in the southern third of the kingdom.[9] The features of this system (at once a social, military and legal one) were church-building and monastic development, the grant of land in knights' fees to be held in knight-service for the provision of one or more knights,[10] castle-building, the use of professional cavalry, and the requirement of homage and fealty from tenants. Under Malcolm (1153–65) and William the Lion (1165–1214) military feudalism became more intensive.

The feudal system of land tenure whereby land was held by a "vassal" from a lord in return for certain services, the grant being confirmed by written Latin charter, was introduced into Scotland by the twelfth century. The system was by this time well developed in England and on the Continent. After 1153 the practice seems to have been to grant tracts of land in return for the service of a knight or even of a part of a knight, for the Scottish barons were men of lesser substance than their English counterparts.[11] There were, however, large estates held by military service, and within them a fairly systematic process of subinfeudation, that is, of giving smaller areas of land to a sub-vassal to be held by him of his lord by the performance of feudal duties.

The characteristics of the system were that it was at once a decentralised method of government and administration, a social and economic system, and a system of land tenure. In all these aspects its introduction had lasting importance and influence in Scotland, and the land law is still fundamentally feudal. Moreover, a grant of land to be held in feudal tenure naturally conveyed with it the right to hold a court for the feudal tenants and civil and criminal jurisdiction over them, the extent of jurisdiction varying with the rank of the grantee.[12]

Land and the accompanying jurisdiction over the population were conferred by royal charter both upon the king's Anglo-Norman friends and on some native Scottish chiefs, who had their customary rights confirmed and enlarged by the grant of feudal jurisdiction.[13] This system

---

[8] On his reign, see generally, Innes, *Scotland in the Middle Ages*, Chap. 4; Dickinson, *op. cit.*, Chap. 8; and generally, Cooper in *Introduction to Scottish Legal History* (Stair Society), Chap. 1. His surviving charters are printed in Barrow (ed.) *The Charters of David I* (1999).

[9] Ritchie, *op. cit.* 179–190.

[10] Neilson, "Tenure by Knight-Service in Scotland" (1899) 11 J.R. 71, 173; see also Neilson, "Scottish Serjeanties" (1899) 15 L.Q.R. 405.

[11] Barrow, *op. cit.* 293; *Charters of David I* (ed. Barrow), *op. cit.*; *Acts of Malcolm IV* (ed. Barrow); *Acts of William I* (ed. Barrow), *passim*.

[12] Dickinson, *op. cit.* 84–93; Milne, in *Introduction* (Stair Society), Chap. 13; see specimen charter in Dickinson and others, *Source Book of Scottish History*, I, 90–94.

[13] *Ibid.* 20; Ritchie, *op. cit.* 237–242.

seems to have fitted quite well into the previously existing Celtic method of land tenure under which land was held by the chief and his near kindred, and there seems to have been little racial displacement or dispossession of existing holders of land.[14] By the end of the thirteenth century, old Celtic institutions had been feudalised as far as the Moray Firth and in some more remote areas where, however, Celtic custom in the main lasted for several more centuries.[15]

The institution of this land system was the basis of the family in Anglicised Lowland Scotland as much as was the clan system in the Celtic Highlands, and extensive grants of land were made in David's lifetime to men of Saxon, Norman or Danish extraction. Particularly in Strathclyde, Lothian and Fife, castles were planted and feudal communities developed, with land held by vassals and sub-vassals of the king, which greatly strengthened the royal authority.[16] The majority of those who farmed the land were tenants, usually from year to year, and only gradually did it become common to hold lands for a lifetime, or perpetually, for a fixed money rent. Tenure in feu-farm developed gradually from the twelfth century. Below the free tenants were a great number, the majority of the whole people, who had neither secure tenure nor complete personal freedom; they varied from husbandmen to people tied to the soil (*adscripti glebae*) and even to outright slaves. Servile status was, however, tending to disappear.

One of the incidents of feudalism was the establishment of areas as forests or hunting reserves, which gave rise to a body of forest law under which hunting in the forests was reserved to the grantees of hunting rights, foresters were appointed, and the rules were enforced.[17] This developed in time into the modern game laws.

Feudal Administration

Feudalism introduced the idea that the king was lord of the whole land and the fountain of all justice. From the time of David I we know of a court presided over by the king. The king's court could hear appeals from lower courts and cases relating to important persons or matters. The king sat with the officers of his household and such great men as were with him at the time. Later he began to summon other tenants-in-chief, and those regularly called to give the king counsel became his council. In time this council began to sit in various capacities—for finance, for justice, for affairs of state. By the end of the thirteenth century, a sitting for discussion, a *parliamentum*, had become primarily a sitting of the council

---

[14] Rait and Pryde, *op. cit.* 19.
[15] Skene, *Celtic Scotland*, III, 287 *et seq.*
[16] Hume Brown, I, 89–90.
[17] See Gilbert, *Hunting and Hunting Reserves in Medieval Scotland* (including text of the Leges Forestarum); Dickinson, "Forest Courts," in *Introduction to Scottish Legal History*, 402.

as supreme court which laid down the law or changed it. Parliament was primarily a court of law, while a council, strengthened by summoning additional persons and called a general council, was primarily a deliberative body.[18]

A great council of the realm, or *Curia Regis*, was established on the English model. In theory it consisted of all tenants-in-chief and the chief ecclesiastical dignitaries.[19] The burgesses did not appear until later.

David I also introduced the political officers and institutions of the feudal monarchy, such as the chancellor, chamberlain, justiciar, constable and steward.[20] A royal officer, the *iudex*, was important from the eleventh to the thirteenth century. *Iudices* were attached to a province and their commonest function seems to have been perambulating marches, to determine the lawful boundaries of estates.[21] A network of sheriffdoms began to spread over the whole country, under sheriffs who were the king's representatives, charged with the maintenance of order and the collection of the revenue in the king's name.[22] A court was held in the burghs fortnightly, presided over by the king's bailie. Periodically, the chamberlain held an ayre, or court, in each royal burgh, at which all the burgesses had to be present, to ensure that the king had his dues from trade and that there were no breaches of trading or commercial relations.

The performance of important services to the king passed into office by invisible steps. A man of importance[23] had rights and privileges and land to support him: he tended to acquire powers (military, administrative, or judicial) in a definite area so that his service came to be in effect an office under the Crown, and both office and district came to be called a barony, and both passed to his heir after confirmation by the king.[24]

The Justice-Ayres

Under David, the justiciars appear as important officials.[25] This office is also of Norman origin. The justiciar, or justice-general, was originally the

---

[18] Dickinson, *op. cit.* 98–100; Duncan, "The Early Parliaments of Scotland" (1966) 45 S.H.R. 36.

[19] Dickinson, *op. cit.* 99; Rait and Pryde, *op. cit.* 21; Ritchie, *op. cit.* 208–209; Rait, *Parliaments of Scotland*, 1.

[20] Dickinson, *op. cit.* 96–98; Ritchie, *op. cit.* 184; Innes, *Scotch Legal Antiquities*, 74–85; Duncan, in *Introduction to Scottish Legal History* (Stair Society), Chap. 23; Bateson, "The Scottish King's Household" (1901) 13 J.R. 405; (1902) 14 J.R. 35; and Scottish History Society, *Miscellany*, II, 3.

[21] Barrow, *The Kingdom of the Scots*, Chap. 2.

[22] Rait and Pryde, *op. cit.* 21; Hume Brown, *op. cit.* I, 88, Dickinson, *op. cit.* 95; see also Vary Campbell, "The Sheriff in Scotland" (1900) 12 J.R. 15; Ferguson, "The Sheriff in Scotland" (1910) 22 J.R. 105. See also *Sheriff Court Book of Fife*, ed. Dickinson (Scottish History Society), Appx. D.

[23] In Norman-French "baron" was simply a man, later a man of importance in battle or council.

[24] Ritchie, 222–223. In this way primogeniture became accepted as the rule of succession in heritage.

[25] See generally, Dickinson, in *Introduction to Scottish Legal History* (Stair Society), Chap. 31, and on procedure, *ibid.*, Chap. 33; Barrow, *The Kingdom of the Scots*, Chap. 3 (also in (1971) J.R. 97).

king's delegate for administration and the administration of justice. He originally had supreme jurisdiction both in civil and criminal matters, and the general administration of justice seems to have been entrusted at an early date to two justiciars, one for the north and one for the south of the kingdom, under whom various inferior judges exercised subordinate and delegated jurisdiction. Later, a third justiciar is also known of.[26] Their office was to dispense justice in civil and criminal cases not dealt with by the king's court, and they had to hold justice-ayres or circuit-courts in spring and autumn for that purpose, though in times of trouble the ayres were irregular. They also had a prominent role in the processes of perambulation and measurement of lands, and in the related act of giving sasine which often followed perambulation. They had further to supervise the sheriffs. At this time the office was not hereditary.[27]

While Edward I had Scotland temporarily subjugated, he appointed eight justiciars, and Robert Bruce seems to have maintained five.[28] The justiciars were commonly high nobles and had wide competence, political and governmental as well as legal. The justiciar's court seems to have evolved considerably in the thirteenth century. The office of justice-general, however, later became hereditary and remained so till 1836 when on the death of the Duke of Montrose, the then holder of the office, it was united with that of Lord President of the Court of Session. After the institution of the College of Justice in 1532, the justiciar never judged in civil matters. In 1672[29] the supreme criminal court was reformed and constituted the High Court of Justiciary.

The limited power of the Crown at this time and the inadequate central machinery of government, combined with feudal theory to effect a wide dispersion of judicial functions and powers among men and families of importance all over the country, which powers were linked to landholding and readily became not merely territorial but hereditary.[30]

Rise of the Burghs

About the time of David I there began to develop the burghs, which were inhabited places (usually adjacent to a royal castle), latterly, if not originally, possessing charters which granted the burgesses privileges, such as of holding a fair, or freedom from tolls.[31] Burghs were fundamentally

---

[26] See list in Cooper, *Select Scots Cases of the Thirteenth Century.*
[27] Mackinnon, *Constitutional History of Scotland*, 128.
[28] Tytler, I, 248; Dickinson, 161.
[29] Courts Act 1672, c. 16.
[30] Hill Burton, II, 54 *et seq.*
[31] The model was Norman, as with most of David's introductions: Dickinson, *op. cit.* 104; Ritchie, *Normans in Scotland*, 323. See also Pryde, "Origin of the Burgh in Scotland" (1935) 47 J.R. 271; "Burghal Administration," in *Source Book of Administrative Law*, 1–11; "The Scottish Burghs" (1949) 28 S.H.R. 155, and *The Burghs of Scotland*; Neilson, "On Some Scottish Burghal Origins" (1902) 14 J.R. 129; Innes, *Scotland in the Middle Ages*, Chap. 5; and specimen burgh charters in *Source Book of Scottish History*, I, 102–105.

economic organisations acting as market-centres for the sheriffdoms, and they tended to attract foreigners and merchants to settle there, but they also served as colonies, outposts of political control.[32] The weekly market in the burgh was the regular occasion for local trade and burghs were frequently granted the monopoly of trade in a particular area, which was known as its "liberty."[33] So, too, burghs were the exclusive centres of foreign trade and the trades of the burgh had an exclusive right in craft work. The burgesses soon acquired the right to elect their own provost, bailies and other officers.

From the deliberations of the Four Burghs, originally Berwick, Roxburgh, Edinburgh and Stirling, there emerged the *Leges Quatuor Burgorum*, a code of municipal regulations, partly copied and adapted from rules accepted in English boroughs.

Burghal privileges were granted in consideration of liability to provide a share in any grant of money to the king, at first one-fifth and, later one-sixth of the total. The apportionment of this among the individual burghs was the work of the Convention of Royal Burghs, a body which comes into the limelight in the sixteenth century.[34]

Apart from these royal burghs with royal charters, there were established from early times burghs dependent on ecclesiastical magnates or lay barons, burghs of barony, and burghs of regality which were erected by lords of regalities. Burghs of barony were founded as early as royal burghs, with similar commercial privileges, and were frequently ecclesiastical foundations. They were always erected by a subject-superior under licence from the king.[35] Many such burghs were erected in the fifteenth, sixteenth and seventeenth centuries. The administration of burghs of barony depended on the superior, or on agreement with him, and consequently varied from one town to another.

A lord of regality frequently had within his lands a jurisdiction as wide as that of the king, including jurisdiction in the crimes normally reserved to the royal courts—the pleas of the Crown—and such a lord might create a burgh, though his exceptional jurisdiction did not make a corresponding extension of the burgh's commercial powers. That might, however, be done by special arrangement.[36] Burghs of barony or of regality might be raised to royal rank.

Guild Merchants and Burgh Courts

In many burghs, a merchant guild was formed. Later craftsmen were sometimes admitted to it, and this was probably the first official recognition of self-control, as against control by the superior of the burgh. An Act

---

[32] Mackenzie, *The Scottish Burghs*, 1–50.

[33] *Ibid.* 66.

[34] *Ibid.* 76; Ritchie, *op. cit.* 327–330. See also Pagan, *The Convention of the Royal Burghs of Scotland*, 53.

[35] *Ibid.* 79–80; Dickinson, *op. cit.* 84; see also Ferguson, "The Barony in Scotland" (1912) 24 J.R. 99.

[36] *Ibid.* 78.

of Parliament in 1593 approved the power and jurisdiction of the Dean of
Guild and his council in burghs to deal with actions between merchants, or
between merchant and mariner.[37] This gradually fell into desuetude, but
from about the sixteenth century the Dean of Guild was recognised as
having a common law jurisdiction over buildings, nuisances and questions
of neighbourhood, and this long survived in the form of jurisdiction to
regulate streets and buildings.[38]

Apart from the guild, every burgh tended to develop a court to enforce
its regulations and settle disputes, which tended in turn to assume powers
of administration. All burgesses, unless excused, had to attend the three
head courts of the year (Yule, Easter and Michaelmas). The burgh bailies
may have had power to try all crimes except the four pleas of the Crown,
but this was early attenuated to dealing with boundary disputes, failure to
use proper weights and measures or observe the market rules, and various
offences such as encroaching on another's land or allowing animals to
trespass on another's fields.[39] The competence of the burgh courts was cut
down by the rise of the Court of Session and the justices of the peace, so
that the bailies came to be limited to trivial cases and petty disputes.[40]

The chamberlain had some supervisory functions over burghs. In his
annual ayre or circuit he dealt with appeals from the burgh court, decided
disputes between burghs, and investigated the mode in which the bailies
had been discharging their functions. From 1292 the *Curia Quatuor
Burgorum* met under the presidency of the chamberlain to hear appeals
from the burgh courts and from the ayre,[41] and to lay down the law of the
burghs which may have been influenced by the *Leges Quatuor Burgorum*[42]
borrowed from Newcastle. The chamberlain's power disappeared in the
fifteenth century and the *Curia* vanished about 1500.

Only in the fourteenth century, under the necessity of financial strin-
gency, did the great burghs obtain representation in Parliament, and from
the informal discussions of the burgh commissioners to Parliament there
arose the Convention of Royal Burghs (1552) with legislative, executive
and financial jurisdiction.[43]

Barony and Regality Courts

The term baron in early feudal law included any considerable tenant but
later came to be restricted, for the most part, to those who held lands

---

[37] Mackenzie, *op. cit.* 100–105; McKechnie, in *Source Book of Administrative Law*, 95–104;
Pryde in *Introduction to Scottish Legal History* (Stair Society), Chap. 29.
[38] McKechnie, *loc. cit.* 100–101; Pryde, in *Introduction* (Stair Society), Chap. 29.
[39] Pryde, in *Source Book of Administrative Law*, 4; Dickinson, *op. cit.* 114–115.
[40] Pryde, in *Source Book*, 8.
[41] Pryde, in *Source Book*, 5; Dickinson, *op. cit.* 97; *Source Book of Scottish History*, I, 228–230.
[42] Printed in A.P.S. I. 329. The four burghs were at first Berwick, Edinburgh, Roxburgh, and
Stirling, and later Edinburgh, Stirling, Lanark and Linlithgow.
[43] Dickinson, *op. cit.* 283–84.

direct of the king, which had been erected by the grant *in liberam baroniam*.[44] Barony tenure was characterised by being a unity—a unit for administration and law, and possessing its own offices and baron-bailie—and when lands were granted *in liberam baroniam*, the charters included a clause granting certain rights of public justice. The barony always had a legal *caput* which was inseparable from it and wherein was centred the jurisdiction. The baron by accepting the barony, accepted responsibility to the king for ordinary public justice within the lands included in the barony; he had power of pit and gallows, *fossa et furca*.[45] Hence a grant of barony excluded to that extent the king's officers, and in time this exclusion grew greater so that certain barons received all rights of public justice including even the four pleas of the Crown[46] and other royal rights so that they became holders *in regalitatem*. A regality was a barony with fuller jurisdictional and administrative rights, the precise rights depending on the charter of erection.[47] The only right excluded was the right to try treason. Regalities were in fact so much petty kingdoms that the realm was divided into royalty and regality.[48]

Barony jurisdiction appears to have been granted from the twelfth century and such grants were common in the later Middle Ages.[49] The baron usually held court at the *caput baroniae* at various intervals as need arose.[50] For most of the people, the baron court of their lord was the one which affected them. It might be presided over by the baron or by his bailie, or by both, or by two bailies, and the judges of the court were the suitors, that is, those tenants who held land by suit of court, for whom attendance at court was a feudal burden attached to the holding of their land.[51] The sentence, or doom, was pronounced by the dempster, or doomsman.[52] The court had civil jurisdiction in matters of debt, possession, lawburrows,[53] breach of arrestment, bloodwite[54] and deforcement,[55] and criminal jurisdiction in theft and slaughter.[56]

In time these jurisdictions tended to fall into disuse with the development of centralised institutions and courts. By the seventeenth century,

---

[44] Dickinson, *op. cit.* 84–85, *Barony Court Book of Carnwath* (ed. Dickinson), xiv. See also Ferguson, "The Barony in Scotland" (1912) 24 J.R. 99.

[45] *Ibid.* xx–xxvi.

[46] Murder, arson, rape and robbery.

[47] *Ibid.* xxxix–xl.

[48] Prior to the Reformation there were over 50 regalities in Scotland: Pryde, *Kirkintilloch Burgh Court Book*, xlii.

[49] On the details of barony jurisdiction, see Innes, *Scotch Legal Antiquities*, 54–60; McIntyre, in *Introduction to Scottish Legal History* (Stair Society), Chap. 28.

[50] *cf.* Ritchie, *Normans in Scotland*, 311.

[51] On the suitors of the court, see also Hamilton-Grierson in (1917) 14 S.H.R. 1 and Dickinson in *Sheriff Court Book of Fife*, Introd., lxxii.

[52] *Barony Court Book of Carnwath*, lxxx.

[53] Surety for keeping the peace.

[54] Fines for bloodshed.

[55] *Ibid.* civ.

[56] *Ibid.* cvii.

only regalities or earldoms might still punish capitally and baron courts
had given up this jurisdiction. They disappeared with the abolition of the
heritable jurisdictions in 1747.

The Sheriff Courts

The establishment of the office of sheriff in Scotland is probably to be
attributed to David I[57] and many areas in the south and east were erected
into sheriffdoms in the twelfth and thirteenth centuries.[58] England supplied the model, where the Norman kings had introduced their own
officer, the *vicecomes* or shirereeve. The Scottish sheriffdom seems to
have been an artificial unit which did not coincide with previous divisions
of the land or natural boundaries, and was frequently dependent on a
castle.[59] The sheriffs were appointed from among the Scoto-Norman
barons and gradually royal sheriffs were established over the whole
kingdom, showing the power of the central government. The sheriff was
the king's judicial, financial, administrative and military officer and
gradually the office became almost uniformly heritable.[60] The office had to
be fitted into the existing system and it is uncertain how the office
compared with that of the mair, who continued to sit as an assessor in the
sheriff's court.[61]

The sheriff court was originally held at the castle and was the king's
court of the sheriffdom, which consisted of the lands which owed court
duty and military service to the castle.[62] Head courts were held thrice a
year and lesser courts at intermediate times at irregular intervals, which
probably averaged six weeks. Head courts were courts held at the seat of
the sheriffdom, attended by the full complement of those who owed the
duty of suit of court[63] and presided over by the sheriff in person; at them,
all the more important business was transacted. The lesser courts might be
held at different places in the sheriffdom. As burghs tended to grow up
beneath the walls of the castle, the burgh became the *caput* of the
sheriffdom, and by the sixteenth century all courts were held in the
tolbooth of the head burgh of the sheriffdom.[64]

The sheriff court was the king's baron court and within the sheriffdom
the sheriff administered both civil and criminal justice. He might not deal

---

[57] Dickinson, *op. cit.* 101; *Sheriff Court Book of Fife* (ed. Dickinson, Scottish History Society),
347. See also Philip in *Source Book of Administrative Law*, 74–80; Malcolm, "The Office of
Sheriff in Scotland" (1923) 20 S.H.R. 129, 222, 290; Milne, *Introduction to Scottish Legal History*
(Stair Society), Chap. 25.

[58] *Ibid.* 347–368. On sheriffs in the 12th century see Barrow, *Regesta Regum Scottorum*, I, 35;
II, 28. Some sheriffs probably replaced earlier thanes who were the links between the king and
local communities north of the Forth.

[59] *Ibid.* 384; Ritchie, 319.

[60] *Ibid.* xxxi–xxxiii. See specimen sheriff's account in *Source Book of Scottish History*, I, 96–99.

[61] Ritchie, *op. cit.* 321.

[62] *Ibid.* 372. *cf. ibid.* 311.

[63] See *Source Book of Scottish History*, I, 101.

[64] *Sheriff Court Book of Fife*, xi–xx.

with cases involving the four pleas of the Crown, nor exercise jurisdiction over any ecclesiastical person. Nor, of course, had he jurisdiction within stewartries, where the king's steward was the sole competent judge, nor within regalities, nor within burghs, since burgesses claimed to be heard only before their own courts or the chamberlain's ayre. Personal exemptions were also sometimes granted.[65] In civil matters, the sheriff could deal with actions of molestation, removing, ejection, spuilzie, and all kinds of personal actions.[66] Many civil actions could begin only when a complainer presented a brieve bought from the king's chancery, addressed to the sheriff, stating a grievance and ordering investigation by a sworn inquest. The sheriff was the presiding officer in the court, controlling procedure, and instructing the suitors in the law, but the judgment was that of the suitors.[67]

The sheriff had also an oversight of the proper administration of justice in inferior courts within the sheriffdom, and his court was the court of appeal against decisions of baron courts within the sheriffdom.[68] He had to uphold the Church courts, search for and pursue rebels put to the horn, guard prisoners, arrest idle men, issue tokens to beg, keep the castles in repair, supervise the efficiency of the arms and the holding of the wappinschaw, execute royal writs and letters, and carry out many more administrative duties.[69]

Ecclesiastical Courts

In the medieval kingdom, the clergy and the religious houses were of great importance.[70] From 1192 the ten dioceses of the Scottish Kingdom (other than Galloway) were recognised by the papacy as the special daughter of Rome and exempt from metropolitan authority, even though not (until 1472) having an archbishop, and they held provincial councils.[71] These exercised judicial functions and made collections of ecclesiastical statutes for use at both provincial and diocesan level. Bishops and abbots were among the kings' chief advisers and played an important part in government. They were favoured by David I and grew rich and powerful under him. Not least, the Church imported into the kingdom an element of scholarship and of the canon law of the Roman Church, and it was probably through this infusion of canon law that Roman law came first to

---

[65] *Ibid.* xxvii.
[66] *Ibid.* xxxviii and Appx. B.
[67] Appeal lay to the court of the justiciar, when he visited the *caput* of the sheriffdom.
[68] *Ibid.* xxxix.
[69] *Ibid.* xl–xlv.
[70] See generally, Dickinson, *op. cit.* 117–124; Easson, *Scottish Religious Houses*; Dowden, *Medieval Church in Scotland*; Innes, *Scotch Legal Antiquities*, 161–208; and on the Church courts, Donaldson in *Introduction* (Stair Society), Chap. 27.
[71] Watt, "The Provincial Council of the Scottish Church, 1215–1472" in Grant and Stringer (ed.), *Medieval Scotland*, 140.

influence Scottish procedure. The ecclesiastical foundations were frequently given grants of jurisdiction and the right to hold courts, criminal as well as civil.

A great volume of the litigation in the thirteenth century, even involving laymen, took place before ecclesiastical tribunals, particularly before judges-delegate; these were prelates, usually three in number, constituting an *ad hoc* tribunal by mandate from the Pope or papal legate, with instructions to carry out specified procedure. These mandates were obtained by the prospective pursuer in the action.[72] The judges-delegate might carry the case to conclusion without further reference to Rome, or refer back for instructions and guidance in case of difficulty, or even report the facts to Rome for final hearing and decision there. Appeals might be made to Rome at any stage. The judges-delegate dealt with a great variety of cases, claims to money, lands, for damages or specific implement, for reduction of a decree arbitral, or even for an award of sequestration.[73]

As the thirteenth century proceeded, there was increasing resort to lay tribunals,[74] and cases were heard before the king in Council or in Parliament, the justiciar, and the sheriff. The justiciars numbered usually two and never more than four, and the sheriffs numbered from 20 to 30, so the judicial establishment of the country was inadequate. The system of papal judges-delegate lost some of its importance by the time of the War of Independence, but the Courts Christian remained.[75]

Procedure

In the period before the foundation of the College of Justice, the primary procedural writ was the brieve, a short writ issued from the Chancery, in the form of a command in the king's name, requiring an official, a commissioner or a party to take some action which it was thought justice required.[76] Sometimes the brieve had to be "retoured", in which case the verdict was returned to the Chancery. The system contributed greatly to the development of a uniform system of law, common to most of the country. This system was in operation in the thirteenth century, though not fully developed, and was extended in 1424 by James I after his return from captivity.[77]

---

[72] Cooper, *Select Scottish Cases*, xxvii; see also Stein, "Roman Law in Scotland," *Ius Romanum Medii Aevi*, v. 13b, 23.

[73] *Ibid.* xxxi–xxxii.

[74] *Ibid.* xxxvii.

[75] Donaldson, "Church Courts" in *Introduction to Scottish Legal History* (Stair Society), Chap. 27.

[76] Dickinson, *op. cit.* 101. See generally, McKechnie, *Judicial Process upon Brieves* 1219–1532; Lord Cooper, Introd. to *Register of Brieves* (Stair Society); Innes, *Scotch Legal Antiquities*, 220–240; Hamilton-Grierson (ed.), Bisset's *Rolment of Courtis*, III, 41; Maxwell, in *Introduction to Scottish Legal History*, Chap. 32; MacQueen, *Common Law and Feudal Society in Medieval Scotland*, 105 *et seq.*

[77] For specimens and the procedure thereunder, see Innes, *op. cit.* 233–237, and *Source Book of Scottish History*, I, 95–98.

Scottish brieves were undoubtedly founded on English models though papal practice probably also had some influence. English forms were, however, often discarded or modified and Scotland had fewer and more adaptable basic writs than the great multiplication of writs in the English register.[78] After 1532, brieves tended to give way to other forms of initial writs in litigation; the brieve passed into the summons under the signet and fell into desuetude as a means of initiating litigation.

The brieve also had other uses. In its widest sense, a brieve covered any kind of formal writ, administrative or judicial, issued by the king. Other brieves were used as a means of obtaining the factual answer to problems. Such were the brieves of succession, terce and tutory. Very important was the brieve *de recto* by which the title to heritage could be determined.[79]

Modes of Trial—the Jury

The common modes of trial in early times were battle, compurgation— whereby a man could clear himself by the oath of a prescribed number of oath-helpers or compurgators that they believed his oath to be true—or the ordeal by water or by hot iron.[80] The fourth Lateran Council of 1215 prohibited clerical assistance at ordeals and the withdrawal of religious sanction contributed to its disappearance; it seems to have vanished by 1230. Proof by writ or by witnesses is little heard of in the twelfth and thirteenth centuries and seems to have developed first in the burgh courts.

The jury system came to Scotland in the wake of feudalism, and by 1230 it is possible that the jury had definitely superseded the ordeal, but at first it was difficult to distinguish the jury from sworn witnesses or from compurgators. The jury was frequently chosen by the pursuer in conjunction with the officers of court. For long there was no settled number for a jury, and the rule that the number should be odd was arrived at only gradually and later.[81]

The jury disappeared in nearly all civil cases after 1532 though retained for some special kinds of cases, but remained in criminal cases, though latterly a greatly increased number of criminal cases have been allowed to be heard summarily. In 1815 the jury was imported afresh for some civil cases.

Private Law in the Feudal Period

It is difficult to obtain or to present in brief compass a general picture of private law at this early period. Much early law was local and

---

[78] On the English register, see Pollock and Maitland's *History of English Law*, I, 150, 195; Plucknett, *Concise History*, 276–277.

[79] MacQueen, *Common Law and Feudal Society in Medieval Scotland*, 105 *et seq.*

[80] Innes, *Scotch Legal Antiquities*, 209–222; *idem, Scotland in the Middle Ages*, 182–189; Neilson, *Trial by Combat*. Bartlett, *Trial by Fire and Water*. As late as 1567 Bothwell, when suspected of Darnley's death, offered to prove his innocence by battle. Compurgation is last mentioned in 1622.

[81] Dickinson, *op. cit.* 100; Dickinson, *Sheriff Court Book of Fife*, Introd. lxxxvi. See also, Willock, *The Jury in Scotland*, 20–37.

customary.[82] Predominantly it was concerned with complaints against violence and wrongdoing and included much which in later times would have been classed as criminal. The oldest laws describe a system of combined fines and compensation for murder and personal injuries, which represents the beginnings of the commutation of the blood-feud into judicial remedy. There were elaborate tariffs of fines and compensation varying with the status of the injured man and the gravity of his injuries. Wrongs predominate and there is little of contract, while testamentary law was within the jurisdiction of the Church. Marriage and family relations were regulated by canon law.

Accordingly, in the period immediately before the War of Independence, Scots law appears to have closely resembled Anglo-Norman law but even then to have had distinct differences. There had been borrowing, not wholesale nor indiscriminate, but critical, with adaptations and simplifications. Scots law and English law were recognisably different, though bearing many marks of close relationship.[83] Canon law had also established itself in many spheres. "Development as compared with England proceeded not on parallel, but on gradually diverging, lines—the divergence being due in part to the inability of Scotland to keep abreast with the rapid progress made in England from Glanvill, through Bracton, to the Edwardian law, and in part to Scotland's deliberate refusal, under the influence of the Romano-canonical tradition, to absorb the more technical and artificial features of the Bractonian law. By the end of the [thirteenth] century the divergence was already marked, not only in the rejection of much that England had introduced, and in the adoption of ideas and expedients which Scotland did not owe to England but in a general effort towards greater simplicity, flexibility and directness."[84] Law and custom, moreover, varied from one area to another depending on the extent of Celtic or Norman tradition. There were still places for Brehon law, the laws of Galloway, the laws of the forest, the laws of the burghs and even the law of clan MacDuff.[85] Disputes on the Anglo-Scottish border seem to have been regulated by a body of March laws.[86] Knowledge and study of Roman law only began to revive in the twelfth century and it was not an important influence.

This early period of Scottish legal development was abruptly terminated by the death of Alexander III in 1286, followed by that of the heiress to the throne, the Maid of Norway, in 1290. In 1291 Edward I of England

---

[82] See *Source Book of Scottish History*, I, 114–118; Miller, "The Reception of Roman Civil Law and Roman Canon Law in Scotland in the Reign of David I" (1923) 35 J.R. 362.

[83] Cooper, "Scottish Legal Tradition," in *Selected Papers*, 175. See also Cooper, "A Scottish Law Student at Oxford in 1250" (1944) 56 J.R. 57.

[84] Cooper, Introd. to *Register of Brieves*, 25.

[85] Bannerman, "MacDuff of Fife" in Grant and Stringer (ed.), *Medieval Scotland*, 20.

[86] Stones and Rae, "George Neilson: The March Laws" in *Stair Society Miscellany I*, 1. Scott, "The March Laws Reconsidered" in Grant and Stringer, *op. cit.* 114.

intervened, and there ensued The Great Cause, in which Edward adjudged the Crown of Scotland to John Balliol.[87] Edward's subsequent attempt to incorporate Scotland into England[88] provoked the War of Independence, not ended till 1329, and inaugurated a period of frequent warfare which lasted until nearly 1603. From 1290 the two countries' legal systems pursued increasingly divergent lines, though some of the customary and feudal and canon law survived to a later period.

II.—FOURTEENTH TO SIXTEENTH CENTURIES

The War of Independence and After

During the English occupation of Scotland after 1296 Edward I appointed eight justiciars in 1305 and he took action with a view to establishing an Exchequer on the English model, and possibly also a Chancery, at Berwick.[89] He increased the number of sheriffs, while 20 commissioners drew up an Ordinance for the Government of Scotland,[90] but in a few months this existed on paper only.

The period from 1329 to about 1600[91] is a period of political strife and economic troubles, of weak kings and frequent royal minorities, which was an unkindly background for the development of law. Yet even in this period there were enacted a few statutes which are even yet of fundamental importance. If satisfactory judicial machinery had been established, the Scoto-Norman law which had already been developed might have continued to evolve steadily as did English law. But by reason of the absence of a powerful central court and settled government, no such development could take place and despite many attempts it was not until 1532 that the requisite court was created.[92] This was the period when Scots law as a science and a philosophy reached its nadir, yet even so, the evidence is that there was plenty of law and plenty of lawyers.

---

[87] This period is examined in detail in Stones and Simpson, *Edward I and the Throne of Scotland, 1290–1296.*

[88] Edward removed the records of Scotland to London, where many of them were lost, and the Stone of Destiny, which was built into the Coronation Chair, but returned to Scotland in 1996.

[89] Cooper, *Select Scottish Cases of the Thirteenth Century,* xlv. See also 25 S.H.R. 27.

[90] A.P.S. I, 119; Stones, *Anglo-Scottish Relations, 1174–1328,* pp. 120–129. It was sometimes thought that *Regiam Majestatem* was a product of this commission. See also, Barrow, *Robert Bruce,* 133.

[91] On this see generally, Cooper, "The Dark Age of Scottish Legal History," in *Selected Papers,* 219; Paton, in *Introduction to Scottish Legal History,* Chap. 2; Levie, "Place of the War of Independence in Scottish Legal History" (1943) 55 J.R. 121; and Nicholson, *Scotland: The Later Middle Ages.* The label "Dark Age" is mistaken. We know a good deal about the legal system and it was not primitive.

[92] *Ibid.* 226–227.

Law Books—Regiam Majestatem and Quoniam Attachiamenta

The principal source of knowledge of Scoto-Norman law in later times is the book called, from its opening words, *Regiam Majestatem*.[93] It describes law and practice as they were under Alexander III or even later, rather than under David I, and was probably privately and unofficially compiled, possibly about 1285; maybe even as late as about 1320. It is not original or distinctively Scottish but is based on Glanvill's[94] *De Legibus et Consuetudinibus Angliae* (1187), but with amendments, adaptations to Scottish conditions, and variations on the original, since by its time Scots law had progressed beyond the stage described by Glanvill. But Glanvill was the basis because it provided an account of the main features of the system which Scotland was developing. There is also some reliance on the early Scots statutes and the primitive laws of the Brets and Scots, which probably survived in Galloway into the fourteenth century, and on Roman and canon law,[95] particularly the *Corpus Juris*, the *Decretum* and *Decretales*, the *Summa* of Azo, Tancred's *Ordo Judiciarius,* Raymond of Penaforte's *Summa de Casibus*, Goffredo of Trani's *Summa* and other canonists. It attempts to cover the whole field of civil and criminal law and procedure from the standpoint of the royal courts. The arrangement, following Justinian's *Institutes*, is in four books.

The subsequent history of the *Regiam* has been chequered. It was repeatedly chosen as part of the basis for intended revisions of the laws,[96] was condemned by Stair as "no part of our law," accepted by others, and yet was still being cited in court in the twentieth century. The modern view is that it is quite authentic; an attempt, founded on Glanvill, probably made by an unknown cleric in the late thirteenth or early fourteenth century, to set out the existing law of Scotland. Some of the modification, to adapt the text to Scottish conditions, is either inadequately done or unfinished.

The *Quoniam Attachiamenta* (usually printed along with the *Regiam*), belongs to the fourteenth century and is exclusively Scottish. It is essentially a systematic manual of instruction dealing with feudal courts, based on experience gained in practice. It includes styles and forms and

---

[93] Edited with a valuable introduction by Lord Cooper for the Stair Society. See also Buchanan, "The MSS of Regiam Majestatem" (1937) 49 J.R. 217; Richardson, "Roman Law in the Regiam Majestatem" (1955) 67 J.R. 155; Duncan, "Regiam Majestatem: A Reconsideration," 1961 J.R. 199; Harding, "Regiam Majestatem amongst Medieval Law Books", 1984 J.R. 97; MacQueen, *Common Law and Feudal Society in Medieval Scotland*, 89–98.

[94] While this book is called Glanvill, it was probably written not by Glanvill (Henry II of England's Justiciar) but by his nephew, Hubert Walter: see further, Plucknett, *Concise History of the Common Law*, 5th ed., 256–257.

[95] Richardson, "Roman Law in *Regiam Majestatem*" (1955) 67 J.R. 155; Stein, "Source of the Romano-canonical part of *Regiam Majestatem*" (1969) 48 S.H.R. 107; Stein, "Roman Law in Scotland" in *Ius Romanum Medii Aevi*, V, part 13b, 23.

[96] In 1425, 1469, 1566 and 1649. See Mackay, *Memoir of Stair*, 42–43. Projects of 1574 and 1628 did not expressly refer to *Regiam Majestatem*.

even practical hints, and utilises a new technical vocabulary. Nothing is known of its author. It may fairly be described as the earliest purely Scottish legal work.[97]

Developments after 1329 generally

After Bannockburn, there followed a period of reconstruction; some reform and consolidation of the system of land tenure was carried through, probably devised by Bernard, Abbot of Arbroath and Chancellor of the kingdom. Under it the basic unit of land held from the Crown was the barony, usually held by knight service or archer service, but sometimes for payment of money or in frankalmoign. The reorganisation was designed to strengthen both defence and the administration of justice.[98]

Many of the provisions of the reforming measures passed at this time assume the existence and use of Anglo-Norman forms of procedure, and amend them to an extent which shows that Scotland had progressed considerably towards the construction of an independent legal system.[99]

The feudal pattern of society steadily tended to dissolve and effective power tended to become concentrated in fewer and larger units, though the judicial power continued dispersed, and consequently inefficient, for too long. Yet the period does not lack legal interest. In 1326 there was convoked at Cambuskenneth the first Parliament, so far as known, at which burghal representatives were present.

After Bruce's death in 1329, Edward III of England revived the attempt to subjugate Scotland and warfare ensued. Edward Balliol was crowned King as vassal of Edward III in 1332 and in 1334 ceded much of the Lowlands to Edward, but most of the ceded territory was recovered by 1341. At about this time, common enmity towards England gave France and Scotland a common interest, and in 1346 David II was captured while invading England and remained a prisoner till 1357. Part of the exorbitant ransom was never paid, but the extraordinary efforts required of an impoverished kingdom to meet the ransom resulted in important constitutional developments.[1] Meetings of Parliament and of the general council became frequent; burgesses came to attend the former certainly from 1366 and the latter from 1357, since their concurrence in the levying of taxation and the quadrupling of the great custom was thought essential. But the economic drain also militated against the enforcement of law and order.[2]

The fifteenth and sixteenth centuries witnessed the passing of much statute law of great immediate and permanent importance. Among the

---

[97] Cooper, Introd. to *Regiam Majestatem*, 47–50; Fergus, *Quoniam Attachiamenta* (Stair Society).

[98] Rait and Pryde, *op. cit.* 33–34; Dickinson, *op. cit.* 172; Barrow, *Robert Bruce*, 416–421.

[99] Cooper, *Select Cases*, xlii.

[1] Nicholson, *Scotland: The Later Middle Ages*, Chap. 7.

[2] Dickinson, *op. cit.* 187, see also, *Source Book*, I, 184–188; 194–203.

most notable of these statutes are: the Leases Act 1449, which gave a
tenant a continuing right against a purchaser of the land from the
landlord; the Prescription Act 1469 and later Acts establishing the long
negative prescription; and the Act 1573, c. 55, which long regulated
divorce for desertion. A number of the statutes of this period are still in
force.[3] "Had it not been for these statutes, modern Scots law would have
been an entirely different thing in many respects, and their enactment is
proof positive of the existence of legal statesmanship of a high order at
the time when they were passed."[4]

The Beginnings of Parliament

Parliament is first referred to in Scotland in the latter years of the
thirteenth century[5] and seems to have originated earlier in that century,
springing from a reinforced meeting of the King's Council. Two forms of
this larger body are distinguishable, namely, Parliament and General
Council. The distinction lay in that Parliament was the supreme court of
law and, unlike General Council, it was summoned publicly and in
accordance with judicial procedure.[6] Both bodies were competent in
legislation and finance, but Parliament alone had jurisdiction in cases of
treason and appeals from subordinate courts, the latter by the process of
"falsing of dooms". About 1530 the term "Convention of Estates" seems
to have superseded that of General Council, though Conventions do not
seem at first to have claimed parliamentary powers.[7]

From the mid-fourteenth century the presence of burgesses was normal
and, following French practice, Parliament came to be referred to as the
assembly of the three Estates, or the Estates.[8] The three Estates were
clergy, tenants-in-chief, and burgesses, though at a late date tenants-in-
chief were superseded by Lords of Parliament and commissioners of shires
(who were representatives of tenants-in-chief of lower rank than Lords of
Parliament), while in its last years, apart from some Officers of State, it
was composed of two groups which represented the original estate of
tenants-in-chief and of one group which represented the original estate of
burgesses.[9] The three Estates met separately for deliberation and discussion, as well as in a single chamber for the disposal of legislative and
judicial business.

Also about this time, there was adopted the practice of delegating
parliamentary powers to committees, which became in time a salient, but

---

[3] See Statute Law Revision (Scotland) Act 1964, Sched. 2.
[4] Cooper, *Selected Papers*, 227.
[5] On earlier assemblies, see Innes, *Scotch Legal Antiquities*, 99–103.
[6] Rait, *Parliaments of Scotland*, 128.
[7] *Ibid.* 130–164.
[8] Dickinson, *op. cit.* 189–190.
[9] *Ibid.* 188–189. The Franchise Act of 1587, largely re-enacting an Act of 1428, regulated the
county franchise until 1832: Dickinson, *op. cit.* 213, 381.

regrettable, feature of the Scottish Parliament.[10] One was the Committee of Articles. Out of another, the Committee for Causes, and similar judicial committees, there eventually evolved the Court of Session.[11] Parliament alone was competent to deal with some matters, in particular "falsed dooms" which were brought up from court to court, possibly originating in a baron court and advancing through the court of a sheriff or lord of regality and coming up to Parliament via the justice-ayre. Resort to the King's Council could not be had unless due order had been infringed at some stage or the form of law not observed. But questions of unusual character or importance might be remitted to Parliament by the royal ministers.[12]

Parliament as Supreme Court

It is quite apparent that, from the first, Parliament was a meeting of the Estates exercising judicial functions. In 1370 the Estates elected a committee to deal with matters of justice and delegation of judicial functions can be traced from at least 1341. In 1384 the Estates nominated the king's eldest son "to administer the common law throughout the kingdom."[13] In 1398 the regular holding of Parliaments was ordained so that the king's subjects might be "servit of the law."[14] It was both a court of first instance and a court of appeal and had jurisdiction in both civil and criminal causes.

As a court of first instance, it was specially concerned with cases of treason, most other criminal matters falling to the justiciars and the sheriffs. In civil matters, there were constant efforts made to limit the judicial functions of the Estates, but even after the establishment of the Court of Session, special circumstances or private influence might bring cases directly to Parliament.[15]

As a court of appeal, the most important jurisdiction was the "falsing of dooms" in civil cases.[16] Appeals were allowed from baronial courts to the sheriff, from burgh courts to the court of the Four Burghs, and from the sheriff court to the justiciar.

Judicial authority in Parliament belonged to the whole Parliament and to every Estate thereof, but very early came to be exercised by committees. Committees of the Great Council had been appointed to discharge judicial functions even before the War of Independence. In 1341

---

[10] Hume Brown, I, 181; *Source Book*, I, 204.
[11] On the judicial committees, see *Acta Dominorum Concilii*, II (ed. Neilson and Paton), Introd.; Rait, *Parliaments of Scotland*, 458 *et seq.*; Hamilton-Grierson, "Judicial Committees of the Scottish Parliament, 1369–70 to 1544" (1924) 22 S.H.R. 1.
[12] Hannay, *College of Justice*, 2–3.
[13] A.P.S. I, 550.
[14] A.P.S. I, 573.
[15] Rait, *Parliaments of Scotland*, 456.
[16] A.P.S. II, 246, 254.

two auditors were appointed *ad audiendum et terminandum supplicationes et querelas* after the end of the Parliamentary session, and judicial commissions were again appointed in 1369 and 1370. These auditors had to hear the cases and probably suggest suitable disposal for them, the final decision being pronounced in Parliament. Thereafter, the practice of appointing Lords Auditors was regular.[17]

Ecclesiastical Courts

Before the Reformation, the bishop of each diocese had his own consistorial court, presided over by a judge known as the Official, who was skilled in the canon and frequently also in the civil law. From his decisions there was normally no appeal to the bishop.[18]

The ecclesiastical courts were chiefly occupied with matrimonial cases, questions of legitimacy and illegitimacy, and of dowry, with causes relating to testacy and intestacy, with the interpretation of wills, and with cases of slander. The canon lawyers also tried to extend the jurisdiction of the Church courts to all cases of contract which had been fortified by the oaths of the parties. They also had to deal with disputes as to patronage, or tithes, or concerning Church property, and petty cases of assaults on ecclesiastics or brawling in sacred places. In addition, much business came before the bishop's court by consent of parties.[19]

The majority of the matrimonial causes were instituted with a view to obtaining a declaration of the nullity of a pretended marriage. Marriage was considered indissoluble so long as the spouses lived, and the only divorce granted was a separation *a mensa et thoro*, which did not permit remarriage of the parties.[20]

Apart from the body of ecclesiastical legislation which formed the canon law and was the general law of the Church throughout Western Christendom, there was a substantial amount of legislation by provincial synods peculiar to Scotland.[21] Much of this was drawn from the statutes of English councils. Some dealt with clerical duties and conduct but a great deal concerned the laity also.

The Auld Alliance

The period from 1329 to the death of James II in 1460 was also the really significant period of the alliance with France. By 1460 the English

---

[17] Rait, *op. cit.* 459–460.

[18] Dowden, *Medieval Church in Scotland*, 288; Donaldson, in *Introduction to Scottish Legal History*, Chap. 27. Ollivant, *The Court of the Official in Pre-Reformation Scotland* (Stair Society).

[19] *Ibid.* 287. For specimens of the work of the courts, see *Liber Officialis Sancti Andree* (ed. Innes, 1844), and Dowden, 295–298. See also Hannay, "Scotland and the Canon Law" (1937) 49 J.R. 25; Anton, "Medieval Scottish Executors and the Courts Spiritual" (1955) 67 J.R. 129.

[20] *Ibid.* 290.

[21] *Ibid.* 224–239. They may be found in *Statutes of the Scottish Church* (ed. Patrick, Scottish History Society).

had been finally expelled from both Scotland and France and France was now on the threshold of developing into a great European power. Neither any longer needed the alliance but its tradition persisted long after 1460 and led Scotland into disastrous adventures.[22]

The influence of France on Scottish civilisation in these and later years was considerable and it replaced that of England in the legal and administrative, as in most other, spheres.[23] A number of Scottish practices appear to owe their origin to French influence: the sitting of the king *pro tribunali*, analogous to the *Lit de Justice* of the French kings; the institution of the Scottish parliamentary auditors, analogous to the *maitres de requêtes*, about 1341, shortly after David II returned from France; the provision of counsel for the poor, found in France in 1400 and 1414 and instituted in Scotland in 1424; and the development of a body of practitioners inferior to counsel, *les solliciteurs*.[24] Apart from direct influence, both countries were influenced by feudalism. Scottish students resorted regularly to Orleans, Bourges and Louvain prior to the Reformation, and the French connection was the channel through which, particularly in the medieval period, the Roman and feudal laws were received into Scotland.[25]

The Origins of the Session

Warfare, invasion and rebellion continued to be the rule until about 1424 when James I (1406–37), who had been captured at sea in 1405 on his way to refuge in France, was ransomed and released. He returned to Scotland determined to introduce law and order, "to make the key keep the castle and the bracken bush the cow" and set about repressing disorder. He tried to apply to Scotland many ideas learned during his captivity in England. Serious attempts were made to establish Parliament as an effective legislature. Parliament was summoned frequently and many measures taken to improve the machinery of government.[26]

James early tried to reform the ordinary courts, which were always giving cause for complaint, by an Act ordaining that there be made officers and ministers of law through all the realm to give law to the king's commons. The attempt failed and the king tried another method. An Act

---

[22] Rait and Pryde, *op. cit.* 40.

[23] *Ibid.* See also Smith, "Influence of the Auld Alliance on the Law of Scotland," 1961 S.L.T.(News) 125.

[24] Neilson and Paton, Introduction to *Acta Dominorum Concilii*, II. See also Gardner, "French and Dutch Influence," in *Sources and Literature* (Stair Society), 226; Walton, "Relationship of the Law of France to the Law of Scotland" (1902) 14 J.R. 19; "Influence of France on Scots Law" (1895) 3 S.L.T. 189; Ross, *Lectures on Conveyancing and Diligence*, I, 180, 235, 414, 420.

[25] Cameron, "Scottish Students at Paris University, 1466–92" (1936) 48 J.R. 228; see also Mitchell, "Scottish Law Students in Italy in the Later Middle Ages" (1937) 49 J.R. 19.

[26] *Source Book*, II, 10, 13. See also Hannay, "Observations on the Officers of the Scottish Parliament" (1932) 44 J.R. 125.

of 1426[27] decreed that the chancellor and certain discreet persons chosen from each Estate should sit three times a year and determine complaints and causes.[28] Nine members were usually chosen, three from each Estate, with the Clerk Register in attendance. This was modelled on the auditorial committee of Parliament, but, distinct therefrom and was intended to relieve the council of business and administer justice more regularly than could be done in connection with Parliament. There is little information on the working of the new institution, but it flourished sufficiently to acquire the name of "the session" and survived to about 1468 or 1470, when this model of session seems to have been abandoned.[29]

Another Act of 1426 directed all freeholders of the Crown, both great and small, to attend Parliament and General Council in person, but in 1428 it was laid down that only the greater tenants-in-chief would be summoned by writ; the other freeholders need not attend but might be represented by two commissioners from each shire and these were to elect a speaker on the English model. Neither Act seems to have been operative.[30]

Yet another facet of the urge to establish settled government and to enforce law and order was the appointment of a commission in 1425 to examine the books of law, that is, *Regiam Majestatem* and *Quoniam Attachiamenta*, and amend the laws that needed amending. Nothing seems to have come of this.[31] An Act of 1426 provided that all the king's subjects were to be governed by the king's laws, not by particular laws or privileges. Thus there was to be a common law of the realm.[32]

There was also a considerable volume of well-intentioned social and economic regulation, such as the regulation of dress and prices, the prohibition of football and poaching, and the exhortation to hunt wolves and sow peas and beans.[33] It is clear that the executive was inadequate to enforce these Acts.

In 1450 the king was to choose certain discreet persons of the three Estates who were to hold three sessions a year along with the chancellor. In 1456 the Estates themselves chose nine judges, three from each Estate, to sit in three sections after the General Council which appointed them had dispersed, to hear and decide cases. In 1458 the Estates provided that the Session was to be continued until the next Parliament and the Lords of

---

[27] A.P.S. II, 11.

[28] Rait and Pryde, 37; Hannay, *College of Justice*, 5–7; and generally, Balfour-Melville, *James I*; Brown, *James I*. See also Duncan, in *Introduction to Scottish Legal History*, Chap. 23; *Source Book*, II, 45–46.

[29] Hannay, *op. cit.* 8; Dickinson, *op. cit.* 210.

[30] Rait and Pryde, *op. cit.* 38; Hume Brown, *op. cit.* I, 218–219; Dickinson, *op. cit.* 213–214.

[31] Cooper, *Regiam Majestatem* (Stair Society), 1.

[32] Dickinson, *op. cit.* 209; Nicholson, *op. cit.* 309.

[33] Rait and Pryde, *op. cit.*, 38; Nicholson, *op. cit.*, 309; Menzies, "The Social Legislation of James I, 1424–37" (1927) 39 J.R. 262.

Session were to hold three sittings of 40 days each at Edinburgh, Perth and Aberdeen. Three of each Estate were appointed for each sitting. This was supplementary both to the local courts and the parliamentary auditors. Further Sessions seem to have been appointed in 1460, 1464–65 and 1468, but the Parliament of 1467 appointed auditors in two divisions, *ad querelas* and *ad judicia contradicta*, with the provision that causes undecided during the parliamentary session should be decided by the Lords of Council.[34] This "continuing" of cases from Parliament to council became regular after this time.

While Parliament continued to meet regularly during the reign of James III (1460–88), the Lords of the Articles were the virtual masters of the country and their existence was detrimental to the development of a strong and effective Parliament.[35] A committee for causes and complaints, usually of three members from each Estate, was appointed at least 14 times during the reign. The committee for falsed dooms was appointed less frequently.

In 1469 there was a revival of the project of revising the law, the king's laws, *Regiam Majestatem*, Acts, statutes and other books, but again nothing came of it and the administration of justice languished during the reign.[36] Sessions of the council for civil causes, as distinct from sessions of the Lords Auditors, began at least as early as 1478,[37] and the council found itself increasingly committed to dealing with civil causes.

In 1471 it was made possible to make direct complaint to the council in respect of an error at the trial, and in 1487 a summons of reduction was recognised as a mode of appeal as an alternative to falsing a doom. Falsing survived for the better part of another century but the tendency was to facilitate access to the council.[38] In the late fifteenth century it was apparent that the council could not avoid responsibility for civil justice, though it was frequently interrupted by affairs of state.

In 1488 the king was slain in the course of a rebellion and it is significant of the increased prestige of the monarchy that the rebels deemed it necessary to obtain parliamentary approval of their conduct and sought to explain to the people and to foreign countries that they had not been guilty of rebellion.[39]

Under James IV (1488–1513) there was material improvement in the administration of justice and the king personally took an active part in holding the justice-ayres all over the kingdom.[40]

---

[34] A.P.S. II, 88. For a collection of materials showing the evolution of the central court, see Neilson and Paton (ed.), *Acta Dominorum Concilii*, 1496–1501, pp. x–xxviii.

[35] Hume Brown, I, 289; Nicholson, Chap. 15.

[36] A.P.S. II, 97, c.20.

[37] Hannay, *College of Justice*, 22.

[38] Hannay, *op. cit.* 10–11.

[39] Rait and Pryde, *op. cit.* 41.

[40] Hume Brown, I, 340–341; Hannay, *op. cit.* 15–16; Mackie, *King James IV of Scotland*, 57–58, 192–193.

In 1491 the Chancellor was ordained to sit with certain lords of council, or else the lords of session, for the disposal of civil causes, three times a year, during the terms which James I had fixed for the auditorial sessions.[41] At first there was no clear distinction between judicial business and General Council business and the personnel were always mixed, partly officers of state, partly members of the privy council and partly others brought in to be lords of session.

In 1495 an attempt was made to settle a "table" or distribution of summonses, in fact, a court roll, and the experiment was tried of disposing of session business in conjunction with that of the justice-ayres. This was unsuccessful, as was an attempt in 1503 to group the shires so that cases might come up in order and litigants be aware of approximate dates.[42]

In 1504 the privy council proposed the institution of a council to sit continually in Edinburgh and decide all civil matters, apparently to fill the gaps between sessions but not to supersede the customary sittings of council. This body was set up, but was to be itinerant and to have the same power as the lords of session, and it came to be known as the "daily council" and in 1505 the lords of session and the King's Council sat concurrently on civil business. The term "session" was applied indiscriminately to both, but the association of the lords of session with the Chancellor, and the fact that they sat in Edinburgh, warrants the conclusion that the Court of Session had now evolved.[43] The whole of the fifteenth century is therefore a period of experiment, false starts and struggle against arrears of judicial business, and the detail of the story is not clear. The burgh courts continued to exercise both civil and criminal jurisdiction in their own spheres and to deal with much legal work of everyday concern.[44]

Similarly, in the fifteenth century there was much legislation concerned with procedure, summonses, exceptions and appeals, the holding of justice—ayres for administration of criminal justice, and sheriff court procedure.

The College of Justice

The foundation of the College of Justice is legally the most important event in the reign of James V (1513–42).[45] In the early years of the reign there was a growing tendency for the session to become a specialised branch of council's work. Thus, in 1526 eight persons were added to the lords of secret council to sit on the next session, and nearly all seem to

---

[41] A.P.S. II, 226.
[42] Hannay, *op. cit.* 16–18.
[43] *Ibid.* 19–21.
[44] Dickinson, *op. cit.* 284–85.
[45] See generally, Irvine Smith, "The Transition to the Modern Law," in *Introduction to Scottish Legal History* (Stair Society), Chap. 3.

have been experienced in law.[46] By 1527, 11 of those subsequently appointed senators of the College of Justice in 1532 were already acting.[47] But some settled remuneration was needed if judges were to be permanent, and this was still lacking. The king badly needed money and approached the Pope, who in July 1531 imposed a tithe on the Scottish Church for three years as a subsidy for the defence of the realm. It probably owed something to pressure on the Pope by the Emperor, arising from enmity towards Henry VIII of England. In September, a further bull was issued, narrating the king's desire to establish a college of judges,[48] and requiring the prelates to contribute a large sum annually for this purpose. The project of the College of Justice seems to have been extemporised as a pretext for obtaining the subsidy.[49] The prelates sought to offer a composition for the perpetual tax and, pending settlement of this issue, a President and 14 others were named to sit in the interval until the college might be established. No scheme had really been thought out and it was difficult to fit the contemplated college of judges into the pattern of lords of council and session.

It was provided that the Chancellor, if present, might occupy the presidential chair, and that the king might nominate three or four lords of his great council to take part in the judicial business as extra-ordinary lords. The president and half the the 14 judges were to be clerics.[50] Negotiations over the ecclesiastical subsidy and preoccupation with defence caused delay and it was not until 1535 that the Pope granted the bull creating the College of Justice.[51] In 1541 Parliament confirmed the first institution of the college in 1532, ratified the papal bull and ordained that the college should remain perpetually for the administration of justice to the lieges of the realm.[52] It also gave the senators power to make Acts for the ordering of process and the expedition of justice, which became known as Acts of Sederunt. The importance for the development of the law and the proper administration of justice of having a permanent supreme court was immense.

At first, the court sat as a collegiate body, but by about 1554 there is evidence of lords proceeding to the outer tolbooth to hear witnesses, and

---

[46] Hannay, *op. cit.* 29–30.

[47] *Ibid.* 35.

[48] The view that the College was founded on the model of the Parlement of Paris is a mistake. If it had any model it was the Collegio dei Giudici of Pavia: Hannay, *op. cit.* 49; Stein, "The College of Judges of Pavia" (1952) 64 J.R. 204; McKechnie in *Common Errors in Scottish History* (Historical Assoc. 1956). See also Thomson, "The Old Fifteen" (1921) 33 J.R. 225; J.S. H(enderson), "The Scottish College of Justice in the 16th century" (1934) 50 L.Q.R. 120; "Connection between the Parlement of Paris and the Court of Session" (1897) 5 S.L.T. 72, 74.

[49] Hannay, *op. cit.* 50–54; Dickinson, *op. cit.* 305.

[50] McNeill, "Senators of the College of Justice, 1532–69" (1978) J.R. 209; *idem*, "Senators of the College of Justice, 1569–78" (1960) J.R. 120.

[51] Hannay, *op. cit.* 56–61.

[52] A.P.S. II, 371; *Source Book*, II, 48–52.

before 1600 it seems to have become settled practice to have two or three ordinary lords sitting in the outer house dealing with bills and witnesses.[53] From its foundation, the court exercised a supervisory jurisdiction over lower courts and arrogated to itself jurisdiction in heritage, formerly reserved to feudal courts.[54]

Legal Consequences of the Reformation

Anti-Catholic religious doctrines had been making headway in Scotland for some time before 1546 when the Reformation flared into life with the murder of Cardinal Beaton in St. Andrews castle. The new religious opinions made steady progress despite attempts at repression.[55] In 1559 direct action was resorted to and much ecclesiastical property was damaged.[56]

When the Estates met in 1560, Knox's Confession of Faith[57] was ratified and the papal authority abolished, the mass forbidden, and all practices contrary to the new creed condemned. The first General Assembly of the Reformed Kirk met in 1560. An Act of that year also abolished all papal jurisdictions and brought to an end the courts of the Officials in the dioceses and appeals therefrom to Rome.

Consistorial cases and all matters formerly competent in the ecclesiastical tribunals were determined by the Court of Session from 1560 to 1563, though the kirk sessions in various parts of the country constituted themselves consistorial courts. In 1563, however, there was established the Commissary Court of Edinburgh, with four judges authorised to determine all causes formerly competent in the courts of the Roman Officials, and jurisdiction over all Scotland in matters of marriage, divorce and bastardy.[58] The office of Commissary was held by some learned lawyers, but the slowness of the court's proceedings gave rise to general dissatisfaction. Appeal lay to the Court of Session. Despite the change, the consistorial law of the old courts, based on the canon law of the pre-Reformation provincial councils of the Scottish Church, continued to be observed, except in so far as expressly altered by the reformers.[59] Thus, marriage by consent and marriage by promise followed by coitus continued to be law till 1940.

The previous marriage law was defective in having excessively extended the forbidden degrees of relationship for marriage[60] which resulted in

---

[53] Hannay, 91–98. See also Cooper, "The King versus the Court of Session" (1946) 58 J.R. 83, and *Selected Papers*, 116; and Cooper, "The Central Courts after 1532" in *Introduction* (Stair Society), Chap. 24.

[54] MacQueen, *Common Law and Feudal Society*, 215.

[55] The Reformation began in Germany in 1517; there are instances of reformed opinions in Scotland from about 1528 and in 1531 Henry VIII in England got Parliament to make him Supreme Head of the Church in England.

[56] Hume Brown, II, 20–70; Dickinson, *op. cit.* 339–40.

[57] Printed in his *History of the Reformation in Scotland* (ed. Dickinson), II, 257.

[58] This court was created by royal charter and ratified by Parliament in 1592.

[59] See further, *Introduction to Scottish Legal History* (Stair Society), Chaps. 6, 7 and 8.

[60] Hay Fleming, *Reformation in Scotland*, 477–502; Dowden, *Medieval Church in Scotland*, 251. See also Fraser on *Husband and Wife* (2nd ed.), 104–134; Hay's *Lectures on Marriage*, 185 *et seq.*

much uncertainty whether persons were married or not and much ingenuity in finding grounds on which marriages might be declared null.

Mary, Queen of Scots, who had been brought up in France since 1548, returned to Scotland in 1561, but tolerated the establishment of a Protestant Church though she herself remained a Catholic, an attitude tolerated by her subjects. In 1565 she married Darnley, son of the Earl of Lennox, and proclaimed that he be named and styled King. But in 1567 his lodging was blown up and he was found strangled in the garden. Early in 1567 Mary was forced to abdicate in favour of her son, who was crowned as James VI.

In 1567 Parliament annulled all laws, acts and constitutions, canon, civil or municipal, contrary to the reformed religion, and later provided that marriage should be open to all related in the second degree or more remotely.[61]

The most material change was, however, in the introduction of judicial divorce. Prior to the Reformation, separation only was recognised in accordance with the general canon law of the West.[62] Immediately after the Reformation, however, the courts held that divorce for adultery was competent at common law.[63] In 1573 divorce for malicious desertion, persisted in for four years,[64] was introduced by statute, although the statute narrates that since 1560 it had been the law that divorce was allowed for desertion, and divorces on both grounds were regularly granted from that time onward.[65]

Canon and Roman Law

The Reformation put an end to the study of canon law in Scotland, though the branches of law founded on canon law continued to be based on it for centuries longer. In the sixteenth century there are more references to Roman law, but its influence was not great.

Medieval Legal Literature—Practicks

The establishment of the Court of Session gave rise to a new kind of legal literature; notes of judgments made privately by judges for their own use, passed from hand to hand and frequently copied. The collections came to be known by the names of their compilers. Two kinds of

---

[61] Hay Fleming, *op. cit.* 503; Fraser, *op. cit.* 112.

[62] *cf.* Hay's *Lectures on Marriage*, 59.

[63] Fraser, *op. cit.* 1141.

[64] Reduced to three years in 1938, two years in 1976; the other grounds of divorce are modern.

[65] Judicial divorce, as distinct from divorce by Act of Parliament, was not permitted in England until 1857.

practicks[66] developed: those which contained only notes of decisions, usually in chronological order, which are the forerunners of the later law reports; and those which included abstracts of statutes and other materials, such as passages from *Regiam Majestatem*, as well as notes of cases and practical observations, and which were usually digested under alphabetical subject-headings. The best-known examples of the latter kind are the *Practicks* of Balfour,[67] Spotiswoode[68] and Hope,[69] and this kind of *Practicks* is the forerunner of the modern textbook or encyclopaedia. Balfour's *Practicks* in particular is regarded as authoritative and is of the greatest importance for the law of Scotland down to 1579 because it preserves matter from earlier collections now lost and covers the whole field of Scots law. Collections of *Practicks* continued to be made well into the seventeenth century, until the decision-Practicks were superseded by the early published reports and the digest-Practicks by the treatises of Craig and Stair.[70]

Criminal Law, 1328–1600

Repeated attempts were made in those centuries to have justice-ayres held, but most criminal cases were dealt with fairly summarily in sheriff and baron courts. From 1587 the Lord Advocate emerged as the chief public prosecutor. Homicide, assaults and theft were the common crimes and hanging the penalty in most cases. But too many crimes went unpunished.

Private Law, 1328–1600

If informality and lack of precision characterised procedure at this time, the substantive law was in no better state. The records contain specimens of many kinds of actions, usually exhibiting the common tendency of undeveloped law "to conceive of any legal question as one of wrongdoing and its suppression."[71] "With insignificant exceptions one and all of them are envisaged simply as the infliction of a wrong by the defender upon the pursuer, as if the only chapter in the law of Scotland were one devoted to delicts or torts. Irrespective of whether the action is one for breach of contract, or for payment of a debt or the price of goods sold, or for damages, or for specific implement, or for delivery, or for warrandice of title, or for reduction of a challenged transaction, or for half a hundred

---

[66] See McKechnie, "Practicks" in *Sources and Literature* (Stair Society), 25. "Practick" means a decision or precedent, and hence in the plural a collection of decisions.

[67] Published in 1754; reprinted by the Stair Society, 1962–63; see McKechnie, "Balfour's Practicks" (1931) 43 J.R. 179; McNeill, "Sir James Balfour of Pittendreich" (1960) J.R. 1, 120.

[68] Published 1706.

[69] Published by the Stair Society in 1937–38 in two volumes as Hope's *Major Practicks*. A slighter collection by the same Hope was published in 1726 as Hope's *Minor Practicks*.

[70] See also Donaldson, "The Legal Profession in Scottish Society in the Sixteenth and Seventeenth centuries" (1976) J.R. 1.

[71] Daube, "The Scales of Justice" (1951) 63 J.R. 124.

other things, the pursuer simply takes objection to the 'wrangous' detention and withholding of something, or the 'wrangous' occupation and
labouring of certain lands, and so on; and the common form of judgment
is one which simply finds that the defender did 'wrang' or did 'na wrang,'
as the case may be. It is hardly an exaggeration to say that each pursuer
eventually presented himself before the tribunal in the guise of 'an infant
crying in the night, and with no language but a cry' and that the whole of
Scots law had been compressed into a single commandment: 'Thou shalt
do na wrang'."[72] Spuilzie (spoliation) is the commonest ground of action.
There is disappointingly little evidence of cases of contract, though
agreements must have been common in trade.

While this was the case with litigation, in this same period land law was
being developed to a high degree and charters evidence a considerable
measure of skill in conveyancing.[73] Much land was conveyed from the
Crown and the Church to laymen, to be held in feu-ferm. There were
significant reforms in leases, giving tenants a real right to their lands
notwithstanding a change of landowner[74] while an Act of 1469 introduced
the long prescription.[75]

Moreover there is distinct evidence in this period of the emergence of a
class of professional lawyers; notaries public became common and notarial
instruments, particularly instruments of sasine, were in common use after
1430.[76] There is also evidence of a professional body of pleaders before
the courts.

III.—THE UNION OF THE CROWNS AND AFTER

The Union of the Crowns[77] brought many changes; it greatly increased the
prestige of the monarch, who was now King of England also, but it
removed the king from personal participation in the government of
Scotland. James utilised in Scotland the Tudor device of government by
council, and the Privy Council became the main executive and, to some
extent, the legislative body. He also managed Parliament by utilising the
committee of the Lords of the Articles, whose composition was not unlike
that of the Privy Council. Even the General Assemblies were convened by
him and their work prearranged. The business of government was mainly
effected by the great officers of state who were the leading members of

---

[72] Cooper, "Dark Age," in *Selected Papers*, 219.
[73] Conacher, "Feudal Tenures in Scotland in the 15th and 16th Centuries" (1936) 48 J.R.
189; Nicholson, "Feudal Developments in Late Mediaeval Scotland" (1973) J.R. 1.
[74] Leases Act 1449 (A.P.S. II, 35).
[75] Prescription Act 1469 (A.P.S. II, 95).
[76] Robertson "The Development of the Law" in Brown (ed.), *Scottish Society in the Fifteenth
Century*, 148.
[77] This is inaccurately named. The crowns were not united but the same person was both
King of Scots and King of England.

the Privy Council, and their supervision extended to every branch of the national administration.

In 1604 a project for the complete union of Scotland and England, a matter urged by the king in his first speech to the English Parliament, resulted in the appointment of commissioners to discuss the issue. The project broke down on account of the English refusal to concede parity to the Scots on account of the latter's lesser wealth and resources.[78] The furthest James was able to go was to obtain from the English Parliament the repeal of the Acts which treated Scotland as a hostile country, and the decision[79] that Scots born after his accession to the English throne were not aliens in England. A similar concession was made by the Scottish Parliament for the king's English subjects.[80] Beyond that, his scheme for an incorporating union failed. James also assumed by proclamation the title of King of Great Britain,[81] while he also gave Scottish trade a measure of commercial freedom in England.

James had ordained (1587) that justice-ayres should be held twice a year in every shire, with eight persons specially commissioned to conduct them.[82] In 1609 he enlarged the duties of the office of justice of the peace so as to comprise the functions of a local magistracy. A sufficient number was to be appointed for every shire, those of lesser rank to be paid for their services, and they were endowed with all the duties of magistracy, save that capital offenders and those of high rank were to be referred to the Council, and the powers of provosts and bailies of burghs were also saved.[83] In 1611 Norse law and customs were abolished in Orkney and Shetland, and the isles were annexed to the Crown in 1612.[84]

James meanwhile steadily pursued his ecclesiastical policy, directed towards the full restoration of episcopacy in Scotland. Bishops had been restored and their powers extended, while in 1610 the king imposed on the country two Courts of High Commission (united in 1615) for the punishment of ecclesiastical offences.[85] Each was under an Archbishop and had authority over the whole populace in life or religion, and they came to be a byword for wide and indefinite powers, arbitrary action, unreasonable severity and tyranny.[86]

---

[78] Hume Brown, II, 246; Hill Burton, V, 401–408; Rait and Pryde, 60–61. Sir Thomas Craig was one of the Scottish Commissioners and his arguments are printed in *De Unione Regnorum Britanniae Tractatus* (ed. Sanford Terry, S.H.S.). See also *Source Book*, III, 456–461. See also Levack, "The Proposed Union of English Law and Scots Law in the Seventeenth Century" (1975) J.R. 97.

[79] *Calvin's Case*, or the case of the *post-nati*: (1608) 2 St.Tr. 459; 7 Co.Rep. 6a.

[80] Hill Burton, V, 409–410; Pryde, *op. cit.* 3.

[81] Rymer, XVI, 603.

[82] A.P.S. III, 458; *Source Book*, III, 283–285.

[83] Hume Brown, II, 277–278; Pryde, *Scotland from 1603*, 5; *Source Book*, III, 278–282. For the history of the office see *Wright v. Bell* (1905) 8 F. 291, 306.

[84] Pryde, *op. cit.* 5.

[85] Hume Brown, II, 249; *Source Book*, III, 58–60.

[86] *Ibid.* 250.

Mounting Opposition under Charles I

The reign of Charles I opened with trouble. He secured the passage in October 1625 of a very comprehensive Act of Revocation which threatened the resumption by the Crown of all grants of land made by it since 1542, including most of the gifts of old Church lands.[87] This attempt to take back the bulk of property of the pre-Reformation Church alienated most of the nobles, since most of them had acquired some of the former Church lands, and they tended to ally with the Presbyterians against the king. Charles, however, pushed through his policy in the face of opposition.

In the following year the king initiated legal proceedings for annulling many titles to ecclesiastical lands and teinds or tithes, which had come to be largely in the hands of lay owners, other than the heritors or owners of the lands, and known as titulars, since he planned the provision of a reasonable maintenance for the clergy from the teinds.[88] Only in 1633 was he able to pronounce a final deliverance settling the composition for which the heritors were entitled to purchase their teinds from the titulars. While the plan was sensible and put ministerial stipends on a sure basis, the king's actions antagonised many of the nobles and lords.

Charles even sought to revive one of his father's institutions, known as the Commission for Grievances, with enlarged powers which would have virtually made it a Scottish Star Chamber, but strenuous opposition made him desist.[89]

Through control of the Lords of the Articles, Charles secured much legislation of the kind he desired, including Acts relative to religion which made clear his intention to make the Church of Scotland conform to the Laudian pattern of the Church of England. This body of legislation excited both attention and hostility and in 1635 a new Book of Canons was imposed, while a new Court of High Commission with more extensive powers was established to secure the operation of the new canons.[90] In 1637 the attempt to impose Laud's Liturgy led to riots, the National Covenant, and the Glasgow Assembly in 1638 which swept away all the traces of episcopacy and abolished the Court of High Commission.[91] Then followed the Bishops' Wars and the quarrels between king and Parliament in England which resulted in the Civil War. The struggle between king and Parliament took place mainly in England, but not without intervention by the Scottish army. The last stages of Charles's reign and his execution were, however, wholly the acts of his English subjects. During the years

---

[87] Rait and Pryde, *op. cit.* 63; Hume Brown, II, 286–289. See also Macmillan, "The Court of Session in 1629" (1900) 12 J.R. 137.

[88] Rait and Pryde, *op. cit.* 62; Hume Brown, II, 286–289; *Source Book*, III, 66–67.

[89] Hume Brown, II, 285.

[90] *Ibid.* 298–299.

[91] See *Source Book*, III, 90–115.

1638–49 the Parliament and the General Assembly had played a larger part than ever before in the affairs of the country, and had made real advances in the government of the country.[92] At the same time the parishes and burghs advanced in importance and the system of shires was extended and completed.[93]

Commonwealth and Protectorate

Scotland espoused the cause of Charles II and came to blows with the English in consequence. Cromwell defeated the Scottish royalist forces at Dunbar (1650) and Worcester (1651) and proceeded to the subjugation of the country. The Estates were captured at Alyth, the royal robes and public records sent from Stirling to London, and arrangements made for the government of the country. Eight commissioners were entrusted with the task. The first idea had been to convert Scotland into a province of England, but more generous conditions were proposed later. Scotland and England were to be made into one Commonwealth with all convenient speed, liberty of worship secured, and compensation paid for damage caused to England by the resistance on Charles's behalf.[94] The representatives of the shires and burghs had no option but to acquiesce. Deputies had further to be chosen to go to London, not so much to discuss the proposed union as to supply information for the Bill to effect it. Scotland sent 30 members to the Commonwealth and Protectorate Parliaments, 20 representing the 33 shires and 10 representing 57 of the burghs; some of the features of this system of representation, such as double-county seats and districts of burghs, appeared in much later schemes of parliamentary representation.[95] The representation allotted in 1651 was in fact ridiculously inadequate and many of the members were English officers, mere ciphers of the government.[96]

The Privy Council and Court of Session ceased to function on Cromwell's invasion in 1650 and the Commonwealth appointed seven Commissioners, of whom four were English, to administer justice.[97] Their efficiency and impartiality contrasted favourably with their dilatory predecessors. The court sat as a body, each judge acting as president for a week in rotation. The heritable jurisdictions were abolished and the judges went

---

[92] See Young, *The Scottish Parliament, 1639–1661*.

[93] Pryde, *op. cit.* 10–12.

[94] Hume Brown, II, 365–366. The detailed story is traced in *The Cromwellian Union* (ed. Terry, Scottish History Society). See also *Source Book*, III, 146–151.

[95] Pryde, *op. cit.* 14–15.

[96] Rait and Pryde, *op. cit.* 67–68; *Source Book*, III, 248–251; 462–468; F.C. Dow, *Cromwellian Scotland, passim*.

[97] Mackay, *Memoir of Stair*, 58–59. The Scots were Sir John Hope of Craighall, Colonel William Lockhart and John Swinton of Swinton. See also McMillan, "Judicial System of the Commonwealth in Scotland" (1937) 49 J.R. 232; Cooper, "Cromwell's Judges and their Influence on Scots Law" (1946) 58 J.R. 20 and in *Selected Papers*, 111; Dow, *Cromwellian Scotland*, 176, 221.

on circuit. The Outer House was abolished but restored in 1655.[98] Scotland benefited on the whole from the firm rule of the Protectorate in matters of administration and justice.

Consideration of union was still proceeding when Cromwell dissolved Parliament and was appointed Protector by the Instrument of Government (1654). Later in that year the Council produced the Ordinance of Union which provided that Scotland was henceforth to make one Commonwealth with England and to send 30 members to the Union Parliament. The Protectorate Parliament was, however, dissolved before it could confirm the Ordinance of Union.

In 1656 the Commissioners for the government of Scotland were replaced by a Council of State of eight, while seven were appointed to supervise the administration of justice, and in the following year the Ordinance of Union was approved by the second Protectorate Parliament; but within a year the Long Parliament of England was restored and the whole question of union reopened.[99] The restoration of the Stuarts in 1660 put an end to hopes of union and to the English domination, yet it has to be conceded that peace and order had been better maintained under the Protectorate than ever before.

The Restoration

The Scottish Parliament met again in 1661, but it was a carefully selected body of members and passed a large volume of subservient legislation, ending the union of 1651–60 and restoring the nearly absolute monarchy of the days of James VI.[1] A general Rescissory Act declared null and void the proceedings of every Parliament since 1633. The Privy Council now proceeded to restore episcopacy and from 1662 onwards the Privy Council was the effective government of the country. The Court of High Commission was even revived in 1664 to enforce royal ecclesiastical policy, but was so detested that it fell into abeyance within a couple of years.[2]

The Court of Session was restored, Stair being one of the judges, and from 1661 he was named Vice-President.[3] In 1664 he resigned, having refused to take the Declaration that it was unlawful for subjects to enter into Leagues and Covenants, but was then readmitted by the king's personal intervention.[4]

Free trade with England came to an end at the Restoration and Scottish trade began again to suffer from the English Navigation Acts. Charles II

---

[98] Mackay, 60–62. Stair was raised to the bench in 1657, but the courts were closed from Cromwell's death in 1658 till the Restoration.

[99] Hume Brown, II, 374–375.

[1] Gray, "Judicial Proceedings of the Parliaments of Scotland, 1660–88" (1924) 36 J.R. 135.

[2] Hume Brown, II, 385–393; *Source Book*, III, 152–160.

[3] Mackay, *Memoir of Stair*, 70–71.

[4] *Ibid.* 74–79.

was unable to secure for Scotland the privileges obtained by James VI and I. Negotiations in 1667 for a commercial treaty came to naught, but consequent on that failure Commissioners were again appointed by both Parliaments to treat of union.[5] The Commissioners met at Westminster for two months in 1670 and adjourned but did not reassemble. The conference failed on the refusal of the English to accept the Scottish demand that the existing numbers of members of the Scottish Parliament should sit in a Parliament of Great Britain, and over the difficulty of appeals to Parliament, the Scottish Commissioners being insistent that no appeals could lie from Council and Session to the proposed Parliament of Great Britain.[6] Four years later this problem gave rise to the secession of the Bar.

In a litigation between Lords Dunfermline and Callendar in the Court of Session, the defeated party sought to appeal to the Estates of Parliament and the counsel for the appellants were suspended from their profession. This was taken as an insult to the whole Bar and some 50 members of the Faculty of Advocates seceded and remained out for two years until the matter was compromised in 1676.[2]

The Privy Council continued to govern Scotland, in a bitter atmosphere of religious antagonism and repression of Presbyterianism, until 1679 when the Duke of York (later James VII) became Royal Commissioner. In 1681 he convened a Parliament which passed a Test Act, prescribing a test to be taken henceforth by all holding offices of trust in Church and State.[8] Stair, Lord President of the Court of Session, and others resigned rather than take the Test. The Privy Council governed for the rest of the reign and persisted in seeking the repression of Covenanters, a task in which Sir George Mackenzie, the Lord Advocate, distinguished himself as a fanatic for the prerogative.[9]

In 1685 James VII succeeded his brother; tyranny and persecution continued. His attempts to grant indulgence to Catholics further roused opposition and by 1688 Scotland as much as England was looking to William of Orange (James' Protestant son-in-law) for deliverance. He gathered a force, landed at Torbay, and James fled to France. A Convention Parliament assembled and in April 1689 made a declaration that James had forfeited the Crown and that the throne was now vacant. They offered the Crown to William and Mary, bringing to an end the period from 1603 during most of which Scotland had been governed autocratically and repressively. The Claim of Right detailed James's misdeeds and asserted various claims to liberties.

---

[5] Lord Stair was one of the Commissioners. For the negotiations, see *The Cromwellian Union* (ed. Terry, S.H.S.), Appx.

[6] Rait and Pryde, 75–76; Mackay, *Memoir of Stair*, 90.

[7] See further Mackay, *op. cit.* 113–116; Hill Burton, VII, 194–195; Sir George Mackenzie's *Memoirs*, 267 *et seq.*

[8] *Source Book*, III, 185–189.

[9] Hume Brown, II, 141–221.

Despite being after 1660 excluded from English markets, Scottish manufacturers and traders developed trade with the American colonies and elsewhere. A substantial number of joint-stock enterprises were started and in 1695 the Bank of Scotland was established. But the project for a Scottish trading colony at Darien was a disastrous failure. Many more burghs of barony were erected to serve districts, and annual fairs and weekly markets were allowed without need for being held in burghs.

The High Court of Justiciary[10]

From the feudal period there had existed the institution of justiciars for Scotland, and by the middle of James V's reign the office of justice-general was apparently exercised by one individual with various deputes. In 1587 Parliament had again to enact that justice-ayres should be held by the justice-general and his deputes commissioned for the purpose. Down to the sixteenth century the office was not hereditary but it then became hereditary in the family of Argyll. Argyll in 1628 resigned the office into the hands of Charles I but reserved his rights as justice-general for Argyll, Tarbet and the Isles.

In 1672 the office of justice-depute was abolished and the High Court of Justiciary created, consisting of the Justice-General, Justice-Clerk[11] and five[12] judges of the Court of Session as Commissioners of Justiciary, for the trial of criminal causes in Edinburgh.[13] The office of Lord Justice-General became a sinecure post, and not till 1808 was it provided that on the death of the existing holder (the Duke of Montrose), which happened in 1837, the office should be held by the Lord President. The same Act divided the kingdom into three districts and appointed circuit courts to be held each spring, a system which with modifications still survives. An Act of 1701 sought to prevent wrongous imprisonment and delays in trials.

The Public Registers of Deeds

The Scottish registers are, in some cases, of great antiquity, that of the Great Seal being extant since 1306; but of greatest importance for the land law was the institution in 1617 of the General Register of Sasines, which maintains from henceforth a continuous record of all transactions relating to or affecting landed property, the existence and accuracy of which has been of the greatest value in ensuring the validity and security of such

---

[10] See further Dickinson in *Introduction* (Stair Society), Chap. 31; Scott, "Archives of the High Court of Justiciary" (1891) 3 J.R. 197; 4 J.R. 32, 105, 293.

[11] He was originally clerk of the justiciar's court, later acted as assessor, and did not become a judge until the seventeenth century: see Ersk., I, 3, 26; Hannay, "Office of Justice Clerk" (1935) 47 J.R. 311.

[12] Only in 1887 by the Criminal Procedure Act did all judges of the Court of Session become Lords Commissioners of Justiciary also.

[13] Mackinnon, *Constitutional History of Scotland*, 260–261; Ersk., I, 3, 26; *Source Book*, III, 283–287.

transactions, since search of the Sasine register for the appropriate county will reveal previous transactions with the land and many of the burdens affecting it.[14] In 1672 the system was developed by the requirement of keeping a minute-book recording those in whose favour charters and writs were granted, while permission was given for writs and charters to be written book-wise.

Development of Private Law in the Seventeenth Century

Despite civil war and religious persecution, private law was greatly developed and improved in the seventeenth century.[15] Much legislation of fundamental and permanent importance was passed, such as the statutes of prescription,[16] the regulation of the law of entail,[17] new regulations for the conduct of business in the Court of Session,[18] an Act nullifying alienations in defraud of creditors,[19] regulating the execution of deeds,[20] settlement of the law of tithes, rules for the division of commonties and runrig lands, which were complementary to the statutes for the encouragement of agriculture, the statutory recognition of the fundamental principles of bankruptcy, and many other important pieces of legislation. Trading enterprise flourished and many joint-stock companies were established.[21]

It is remarkable that at this time, despite (apart from the disturbances), the extent of royal and other authority and the weakness of Parliament, so many measures of such importance and beneficial character were passed. It is apparent that the leading lawyers and statesmen must have had profound knowledge of the law and also a strong desire to develop and improve the legal system and the judicial institutions.[22]

---

[14] Registration Act 1617, c. 16; *Source Book*, III, 565. There had been earlier attempts in 1425, 1469, 1555 and 1587. Registration is now governed by the Land Registers (Scotland) Act 1868. Other registers include the Register of Deeds (since 1554) in which, *inter alia*, wills are now registered, the Registers of Inhibitions and Adjudications, of Hornings, of Service of Heirs and others. There are now 16 registers in all, mostly of considerable antiquity and all of great legal and historical value. See further, Milne, *The Scottish Office*, 190–192; *Edinburgh* (Third Statistical Account), pp. 226–229.
[15] See further, Irvine Smith, "The Rise of Modern Scots Law, 1660–1707," in *Introduction to Scottish Legal History*, Chap. 4.
[16] Prescription Acts 1617, c. 12; and 1669, c. 9.
[17] Entail Act 1685, c. 22.
[18] Courts Act 1672, c 16.
[19] Bankruptcy Act 1621, c. 18.
[20] Subscription of Deeds Act 1681, c. 5.
[21] Pryde, *op. cit.* 31. See also Conacher, "Land Tenure in the Seventeenth Century" (1938) 50 J.R. 18.
[22] See also Gibb, "International Private Law in Scotland in the 16th and 17th Centuries" (1927) 39 J.R. 369.

The Seventeenth-Century Jurists

In the seventeenth century flourished a considerable number of jurists of great importance for the development of the law, whose works are still of value and authority.[23]

Sir Thomas Craig of Riccarton (1540–1607), justice-depute in 1564, was the first Scottish systematic writer on law, as distinct from a collector of decisions and statutes.[24] His *Jus Feudale* (1603, pub. 1654) deals with the origin of law and traces the progress of the civil, canon and feudal laws. His exposition of the feudal law makes the work the first Scottish institutional text though there is only a modest amount of reference to specifically Scottish conditions. He also wrote on the succession to the English throne, a treatise on the Union of the Kingdoms of Scotland and England[25] and much Latin verse.

Sir John Skene (?1549–1611), Lord Advocate and later Lord Clerk Register, was the first great legal antiquary, somewhat erratic and inaccurate, but deserving of great credit for his work. He produced an edition of the statutes in 1597, first edited the *Regiam Majestatem* and *Quoniam Attachiamenta* in 1609 and produced in *De Verborum Significatione*, an invaluable glossary of ancient legal terms.

Sir Thomas Hope of Craighall (?1580–1646), Lord Advocate and father of three judges, is said to have been the most eminent advocate of his time. He compiled the *Major Practicks*[26] and the *Minor Practicks*.[27] He acted for Charles I in the famous revocation of grants of Church lands in 1625, which led to the law of teinds being put on a satisfactory footing. He was a partisan of the Solemn League and Covenant and responsible for the legal side of much of the Covenanters' activities.

Other notables of the Bar about this time were Sir Robert Spotiswoode, author of a *Practicks*,[28] Sir Thomas Nicolson, Sir John Gilmour, who defended Montrose in 1641 and held office as Lord President from 1660 to 1670, and Sir John Nisbet who was the last to combine the offices of Lord Advocate and Lord of Session, which he did in 1664. He wrote *Doubts and Questions in the Law*[29] which were answered many years later by Sir John Steuart, Lord Advocate under Queen Anne.[30]

---

[23] See generally, Cooper, "The Scottish Lawyer's Library in the Seventeenth Century," in *Selected Papers*, 276, and *Introduction* (Stair Society), Chap. 3; Donaldson, "The Legal Profession in Scottish Society in the Sixteenth and Seventeenth Centuries" 1976 J.R. 1.

[24] See Fraser Tytler's *Life of Sir Thomas Craig of Riccarton, passim*, and Law, "Cragii Jus Feudale" (1898) 10 J.R. 177.

[25] Published by the Scottish History Society, 1909.

[26] Edited by Lord Clyde, Stair Society, Vols. 3 and 4, 1937–38.

[27] Published 1726 and 1734.

[28] Published in 1706.

[29] Known as Dirleton's *Doubts*. (His judicial title was Lord Dirleton.) See Young, "Sir John Nisbet of Dirleton" (1909) 21 J.R. 170.

[30] Published as *Dirleton's Doubts and Questions in The Law of Scotland Resolved and Answered* in 1715 and 1762.

Sir John Lauder of Fountainhall (1646–1722)[31] was concerned in most of the great causes of the time. He left voluminous manuscripts and two volumes of printed decisions, too infrequently referred to, since they contain much interesting and entertaining matter about the law, the courts and the personalities of the times, and cast much light on the history and state of Scotland in the middle of the century.

Stair

Born in Ayrshire in 1619, James Dalrymple, later (1664) baronet and (1690) first Viscount Stair, graduated at Glasgow, served with Glencairn's Regiment in the Bishops' War and was a regent in philosophy in Glasgow University (1641–47) before passing advocate in 1648. In 1649 he was secretary of the commission sent to The Hague to treat with Charles II and was one of those who met Charles when he landed in Scotland in 1650. In 1657 he became a judge under the Protectorate, being continued in office at the Restoration, but retired from office in 1663 to avoid taking the "declaration" abjuring the right to take up arms against the king. In the following year he resumed office, having made a modified declaration. In 1670 he was one of the Scottish commissioners to London to treat of a Union with England.

In 1671 he was appointed Lord President of the Court of Session and was sworn of the Privy Council. In 1672 he was largely responsible for a series of revised regulations governing jurisdiction and procedure,[32] while in the following year he advocated a more clement policy towards the Covenanters.

In 1681 he was ejected from his post for failure to take the Test, and retired to his wife's estate in Galloway, where he occupied himself with completing his *Institutions*, and later withdrew to Leyden, whence he published his *Decisions* (two vols. 1684 and 1687), the first series of reports published in Scotland.[33] In 1688 he returned with William of Orange, and in the following year was readmitted as President, which office he held until his death in 1695.[34]

The publication of Stair's *Institutions* in 1681 (2nd ed., revised and enlarged, 1693) marked the creation of modern Scots law. It is "an original amalgam of Roman law, feudal law and native customary law,

---

[31] G. Law, "Fountainhall" (1897) 11 J.R. 59, 173.
[32] Mackay, *Memoir of Stair*, 94–100.
[33] Durie's *Decisions* relate to an earlier period but were not published till 1690.
[34] See generally Stair's *Institutions* (Tercentenary ed., ed. Walker), Introd.; *Stair Tercentenary Studies* (Stair Society), *passim*. See also Graham, *Annals of the Viscount and First and Second Earls of Stair*; Thomson, "The First Viscount Stair" (1924) 36 J.R. 33; Duncan, "Viscount Stair" (1934) 46 J.R. 103; Cooper, "Stair the Scientist" (1955) 67 J.R. 23; J.W. Lewis, "The Moral Character of Positive Law in Stair's Institutions" 1976 J.R. 127; Campbell, "Stair's Scotland: The Social and Economic Background" 1981 J.R. 110; Donaldson, "Stair's Scotland: The Intellectual Inheritance" 1981 J.R. 128.

systematised by resort to the law of nature and the Bible, and illuminated by many flashes of ideal metaphysic."[35] It is not merely a compendium of municipal law, but is also an essay in historical and comparative jurisprudence. Rules are classed analytically and deduced from principles, with frequent reference to the philosophic bases of the positive law.[36] Though he drew on civil, canon and feudal law, his principal sources are Scottish customs, decisions and statutes. "Its outstanding feature is the emphasis consistently laid upon first principles, and the systematic development of these principles in harmony with the most enlarged and comprehensive views of comparative jurisprudence. The *Institutions* are no mere compendium of Scots Law; for Stair made the whole science of jurisprudence his province."[37]

Mackenzie

Sir George Mackenzie of Rosehaugh,[38] born in 1636, came to the Bar in 1659 and early distinguished himself. In 1677 he became King's Advocate and won his sobriquet of "Bloody" Mackenzie by relentless persecution of the Covenanters. In 1686 he was removed from office for refusal to concur in the exercise of the dispensing power in favour of Catholics, was restored briefly in 1688 and retired to Oxford in 1689, where he pursued literary work till his death in 1691. Mackenzie was a good scholar, with an extensive knowledge of legal literature.

His writings include *Aretina* (an early specimen of prose fiction), moral essays, political writings in support of the prerogative,[39] and many legal works, particularly an important treatise on criminal law,[40] one on actions, observations on the statutes, commentaries on the Bankruptcy Act and the Entail Act, a *Science of Heraldry* (1680) and an *Institutions of the Law of Scotland* (1684). This, however, though well regarded, is a slight work and quite overshadowed by Stair's *Institutions*.[41] As much as anything he will be remembered for the foundation of the Advocates' Library, now the National Library of Scotland, which he inaugurated with a notable oration.[42]

---

[35] Cooper, "Scottish Legal Tradition," in *Selected Papers*, 177; Walker, "The Importance of Stair's Work for the Modern Lawyer" 1981 J.R. 161.

[36] See further, Campbell, *The Structure of Stair's Institutions*.

[37] Cooper, "Some Classics of Scottish Legal Literature," in *Selected Papers*, 39, 43.

[38] See Lang, *Sir George Mackenzie of Rosehaugh*; article in D.N.B.; Brown, "Sir George Mackenzie" (1901) 13 J.R. 261; Brown, "Sir George Mackenzie of Rosehaugh" (1902) 9 S.L.T. 1, and "Mackenzie's Institutions" (1901) 8 S.L.T. 105, 113, 130, 138, 145, 154, 157; 9 S.L.T. 9. Young, "Sir George Mackenzie of Rosehaugh" (1907) 19 J.R. 266; Most of Mackenzie's writings are collected in his *Works* (2 vols., 1716–22).

[39] *Jus Regium, or the Just and Solid Foundations of Monarchy in General* (1684).

[40] *The Laws and Customs of Scotland in Matters Criminal* (1674).

[41] MacQueen, "Mackenzie's *Institutions* in Scottish legal history" (1984) 29 J.L.S. 498.

[42] Dickson, "The Advocates' Library" (1902) 14 J.R. 1, 113, 214; "The National Library of Scotland" (1928) 40 J.R. 172; "David Hume and the Advocates' Library" (1932) 44 J.R. 1; Cadell and Matheson, *For the Encouragement of Learning*; Brown, *Building for Books*; St. Clair and Craik, *The Advocate's Library*. Mackenzie's oration, translated by J. H. Loudon, is in the *Transactions of the Edinburgh Bibliographical Society* (1946) II, p. 273.

Private Law

Private law was steadily becoming more developed. Many of the problems of contracts—such as formalities, risk, error—were debated in reported cases. In delict, cases of spuilzie, ejection and intrusion were common, as were assythment (compensation) for slaughter, liability for escape of cattle, and other harms. The obligation to make restitution, based on Roman law principles, was recognised. There were important statutes on bankruptcy.

The Movement towards Union

In 1689 yet another attempt was made to effect a union of the Parliaments.[43] The Scottish Convention appointed commissioners to treat of complete union, except in Church government, and offered to accept King William as arbiter in any dispute about the terms of union. The English Parliament refused, however, to appoint commissioners though William was himself favourable. No further progress could be made during William's reign since he had become personally unpopular and anti-English feelings had been aroused by the massacre of Glencoe and the failure of the Darien Scheme.[44]

In 1700 at the height of the Darien controversy, William again recommended to the English Parliament the appointment of commissioners to discuss union, but while the Lords agreed, the Commons declined the royal recommendation. The Lords discussed the matter again in 1701, and in 1702 William renewed his request and it was endorsed by Anne on her accession later in the year. Accordingly, a commission sat from October 1702 until February 1703 but again proved fruitless, the insuperable objection being that of the English to free trade between the two countries.[45]

Further consideration of union between the two countries was provoked by the question of the succession to the throne which arose sharply after the death of all Queen Anne's children. The English Parliament in 1701, by the Act of Settlement, limited the succession to the English Crown on the House of Hanover, but the Scottish Parliament had taken no action and English statesmen feared the possibility of a restoration of the Stuarts, which might endanger the Protestant succession in England and the system of limited constitutional monarchy established in 1688. Hence union became politically desirable for England, though there was still great unwillingness to concede the equal privileges of trade with England and the English colonies.[46] The Scottish Parliament sought to take

---

[43] Stewart, "The Scottish Parliament, 1690–1702" (1927) 39 J.R. 10, 169, 291, 408.
[44] Rait and Pryde, *op. cit.* 76–77; Pryde, *op. cit.* 48. See also, *Source Book*, III, 337–344; Pratt Insh, *The Company of Scotland trading to Africa and the Indies;* Prebble, *The Darien Disaster.*
[45] Rait and Pryde, *op. cit.* 79; Hume Brown, III, 83–84.
[46] Rait and Pryde, *op. cit.* 79–80.

advantage of the Queen's difficult situation and her entanglement in the war of the Spanish Succession against Louis XIV. In 1703 an Act was passed to the effect that no future sovereign should have power to make war or peace without the consent of the Scottish Parliament.[47] Anne consented to this but refused assent to the Bill entitled the Act of Security, under which, on the death of Anne without issue, the Scottish Estates were to name a successor from the Protestant descendants of the old royal line of Scotland; but this was not to be the same person as the designated successor to the throne of England unless there were such conditions of government settled and enacted as might secure the honour and sovereignty of the kingdom, the freedom and power of Parliament, the religion, freedom and trade of the nation from English or foreign influence.[48] The Act was passed the following year by dint of Parliament refusing supply for the first time in its history.[49] This and other measures were not designed to force a union, since the Country Party had in mind complete separation from England and in this had the support of the Jacobites who wished to avoid the recognition of the Electress of Hanover and her line as heirs to the Scottish Crown.[50]

The English Parliament recognised the danger of allowing a settlement to wait until Anne's death. By the Aliens Act of 1705[51] they again authorised the Queen to negotiate with any commissioners who might be appointed by the Scots, and provided further, as a counterweight to the Act of Security, that from Christmas 1705 until the Scottish Parliament should have passed an Act settling the Crown of Scotland upon the designated successor to the Crown of England, every native of Scotland, with a few exceptions, should be an alien in England and that, apart from a few exceptions, trade between England and Scotland should be prohibited.[52]

The debates of the Scottish Parliament that summer were heated and of crucial importance for the future; they took place in an atmosphere of confused excitement and amid popular agitation against union. In September, however, Parliament resolved that commissioners should be nominated, not by itself but by the Queen, to treat of union, a resolution with the practical consequence that the Scottish commissioners would be selected from advocates of union. In November the English Parliament repealed the threatening clauses of the Aliens Act.[53]

The joint commission met in London in April 1706 and early agreed on three main points, an incorporating, rather than a federal, union, guarantees by the English of complete freedom of trade, and an undertaking by

---

[47] *Source Book*, III, 472.
[48] *Source Book*, III, 473–477.
[49] Clark, *Later Stuarts*, 275–276; Hume Brown, III, 88–94.
[50] Rait and Pryde, *op. cit.* 81.
[51] *Source Book*, III, 477–478.
[52] Clark, *op. cit.* 276; Hume Brown, III, 94.
[53] *Source Book*, III, 480.

the Scots to recognise the Electress of Hanover and the heirs of her body being Protestants, as successors to Anne as Queen of Scotland. Agreement was also reached on taxation and the jurisdiction of the Scottish courts, but the sharpest difference arose over the number of Scottish representatives in the new Parliament of Great Britain. The Scots asked for 50 members in the House of Commons but the English suggested 38, and later proposed 45 with 16 representative peers in the House of Lords,[54] and agreement was reached on this basis. These numbers were unsatisfactory and inadequate on the basis of population, though they were liable to produce great unsettlement of the balance of political forces in the new chambers and they did result during Anne's later years in policy being influenced by the Scottish members. Each country ceased to have exclusive control of its own political affairs, a state which has, however, resulted in the long run in far more English influence on Scotland than the other way.

The English gave up their exclusive commercial privileges, a great sacrifice according to the economic notions of the times which did not foresee the ultimate advantages of an extension of the free-trade area, and paid a sum of £398,085 to the Scottish exchequer as an "Equivalent" for the share of the national debt which Scotland was to assume. The Scots accepted the principle that taxation and trade regulation should be uniform in the two countries in future, though this was made acceptable by substantial tax concessions.[55]

The commissioners completed their work in three months and the articles of union were ratified by the Scottish Estates in January 1707[56] in the face of many protests and indications of popular disapproval, rioting in Edinburgh and accusations of bribery. The Estates at the same time passed an Act for the Security of the Church of Scotland as an essential part of the union settlement.[57] They were ratified by the English Parliament in March[58] and came into force on May 1, 1707; in October of that year the first Parliament of Great Britain met at Westminster.[59]

It is noteworthy that the agreement was, and is, not an Act of either Parliament, still less of the new Parliament of Great Britain, but a Treaty between two states, ratified by the parliaments of each.[60] Under the Treaty, the two Kingdoms were "forever after" united into one Kingdom,

---

[54] On these, see Fergusson, *The Sixteen Peers of Scotland*. By the Peerage Act 1963, all Scottish peers became entitled to sit and vote in the House of Lords.

[55] Hume Brown, III, 100–110; Pryde, *The Treaty of Union*, 20–24; *Source Book*, III, 480–489.

[56] A.P.S. XI, 406, c. 7.

[57] *Source Book*, III, 489–492.

[58] 6 Anne (c. 11).

[59] Rait and Pryde, *op. cit.* 82–83; Clark, *op. cit.* 276–278; Hume Brown, III, 110. See also Smith, "The Union of 1707 as Fundamental Law" [1957] Pub.L. 99.

[60] The agreement was a treaty made by the signatories of the Commissioners and regulated by international law, not made but merely ratified and approved by the separate Parliaments.

by the name of Great Britain; the succession to the monarchy was settled in the way fixed by the English Act of Settlement of 1700; and each Parliament extinguished itself and created a new parliament. The view that the Scottish Parliament was merely adjourned is a mistake; it was dissolved.[61]

The Preservation of Scots Law by the Union

The continuance of Scots law and the Scottish courts was provided for in the Treaty of Union by provisions (Art. XIX) that the Court of Session and Court of Justiciary should continue in all time coming, that the Court of Admiralty should always be continued in Scotland, that no causes in Scotland should be "cognoscible by the Courts of Chancery, Queen's Bench, Common Pleas or any other court in Westminster Hall", and that there should be a Court of Exchequer in Scotland after the union for deciding questions concerning the revenues of customs and excises. Heritable offices, superiorities and jurisdictions were preserved (Art. XX) and also the rights and privileges of the royal burghs (Art. XXI). Laws concerning regulation of trade, customs and excises were to be the same in both countries after the union, but all other laws in use in Scotland were, after the union and notwithstanding it, to remain in force as before "but alterable by the Parliament of Great Britain, with this difference betwixt the laws concerning publick right policy and civil government and those which concern private right, that the laws which concern publick right policy and civil government may be made the same throughout the whole United Kingdom; But that no alteration be made in laws which concern private right except for evident utility of the subjects within Scotland" (Art. XVIII). The right of the House of Lords to continue to hear appeals from England and to hear appeals from Scotland was simply evaded by the Treaty, since the House of Lords was not another "court in Westminster Hall."

Nevertheless, among the first measures of the new Parliament of Great Britain were the abolition of the Scottish Privy Council,[62] the regulation of the system of Justices of the Peace, and the establishment of a new Court of Exchequer in Scotland. A year later, in defiance of the Treaty, the Government put through an Act applying one law of treason, the ancient English one, to both countries,[63] and a commission of Oyer and Terminer superseded the High Court of Justiciary in this field of law.[64]

IV.—THE EIGHTEENTH CENTURY

In the early years of the eighteenth century there was much dissatisfaction with the union.

---

[61] Fountainhall, *Decisions* II, 366.
[62] *Source Book*, III, 495; McNeill, "The Passing of the Scottish Privy Council" (1965) J.R. 263.
[63] Dickson, "The Scots Law of Treason" (1899) 10 J.R. 243.
[64] Hume Brown, III, 143–144; Hill Burton, VIII, 210–216.

Serious grievances appeared during 1707–08 during the passage of the Act for abolishing the Scottish Privy Council and increasing the powers of the justices of the peace, though the objections must be discounted at least in part as those of parties interested in maintaining the instrument for controlling elections.[65]

Again in 1708 Parliament, following a threatened Jacobite landing in the Forth, substituted the English law of treason for that of Scotland and united all the Scottish parties into an unsuccessful opposition, though the motives of some of the peers for the opposition were rather mixed. In 1711 the House of Lords ruled in the case of the Duke of Hamilton and Brandon that no British title could confer on a Scottish noble the right to a seat in the House of Lords, and this was deeply resented as a national insult and proof of England's twisting of the Union to its own advantage.[66] In the following year a Toleration Act which permitted episcopalian modes of worship, and a Patronage Act which restored lay patronage of ecclesiastical livings, both aroused fear and anti-union feeling among the Presbyterians. The latter Act[67] was a clear breach of the Treaty, both in letter and in spirit.[68]

Dissatisfaction arose particularly over questions of taxation, especially the malt tax of 1713, which was inequitable and technically contrary to the Treaty.[69] In that year, a motion for the repeal of the union was lost in the House of Lords by only four votes.[70] The growing practice of taking appeals from the Court of Session to the House of Lords seems to have excited little popular discontent or excitement, though ecclesiastical feeling was offended by the decision in *Greenshields'* case which tolerated the Episcopal Church of Scotland, and more so by the Act of Toleration in 1712 which sanctioned episcopacy and prescribed unacceptable oaths for the clergy, both Presbyterian and Episcopalian.[71] It appears that initially union was in one way or another distasteful to a majority of both peoples and was only made acceptable by the pressure of events.[72]

In 1715 the first Jacobite rebellion broke out. The government sought to preserve the loyalty of Scotland by an Act commonly known as the Clan Act, by which every Crown vassal was to forfeit his lands if found guilty of treasonable correspondence with the Pretender, while entails and settlements in favour of children or other heirs were made void from August 1,

---

[65] Rait and Pryde, *op. cit.* 86. See further, Riley, *The English Ministers and Scotland, 1707–1727*; McNeill, "The passing of the Scottish Privy Council" (1965) J.R. 263.

[66] Rait and Pryde, *op. cit.* 87. See also Yeaman, "Edinburgh before the Fifteen" (1937) 49 J.R. 152.

[67] 10 Anne, c. 12.

[68] Rait and Pryde, *op. cit.* 87; Hume Brown, III, 143–144.

[69] Clark, *op. cit.* 280–281.

[70] Hume Brown, III, 152–153. Whether the union could have been "repealed" is a different question.

[71] Stephen, *History of the Scottish Church*, II, 468; Grub, *Ecclesiastical History of Scotland*, III, 361–367; Pryde, *op. cit.* 94–95.

[72] Rait and Pryde, *op. cit.* 86.

1715, in all time coming. This threat hung over the heads of all lords who might think of departing from allegiance to the Hanoverian dynasty.[73]

The rebellion was a military failure and two Acts followed, one appointing a Commission to deal with estates forfeited during the rebellion, and the other for disarming the Highlands as a means of securing the peace of the country.[74] In breach of the Treaty of Union, many prisoners were removed from Scotland to Carlisle for trial under the treason law. This caused much bad feeling among all classes in Scotland. Though attempts were made to enforce the new treason law, it is questionable if any instances occurred of punishment by the courts of criminal justice for concern in the insurrection. The penal retributions were inflicted through English tribunals, and were thus treasured in the Scots mind as a national aggression and injury.[75] The proceedings of the Forfeited Estates Commissioners[76] were equally loathed; their actings were hindered by the Scottish Court of Exchequer and the Court of Session and few would buy the forfeited estates until the York Buildings Company, which had been founded to supply London with water from the Thames, came forward as chief purchaser.[77] Further resentment attended the proceedings of a commission of Oyer and Terminer sent to Scotland to take proceedings in absence against Jacobites who had fled. Its failure was proof not of Jacobite sympathies but of Scottish resentment and bitterness at English interference.

Dissatisfaction with the government was also shown in the resistance of the Faculty of Advocates in 1722 to the Crown's appointment of Patrick Haldane, one of the commissioners on the forfeited estates, as a Lord of Session. The court held that Haldane had not made out his qualification to be received as a judge, but this decision was, it need hardly be said, reversed by the House of Lords. The government, however, withdrew the nomination but by statute abolished the court's veto on nominees, leaving the privilege of subjecting the presentee to an examination, and abolished also the extraordinary Lords of Session.[78]

In 1725 an Act for Disarming the Highlands was passed and a serious attempt made to bring the country within civilisation. General Wade began to erect barracks and forts, and made roads throughout the Highlands to check cattle-lifting and the gathering of troops,[79] while a little later the Highland regiments began to be raised.

---

[73] Hume Brown, III, 162–163.
[74] *Ibid.* 189.
[75] Hill Burton, VIII, 331–338.
[76] Hill Burton, VIII, 348–350.
[77] Hume Brown, III, 190–193.
[78] Hill Burton, VIII, 352. See also Parker, "A Rejected Judge" (1929) 41 J.R. 193.
[79] Hill Burton, VIII, 368–378; Hume Brown, III, 211–212. On the roads, see further, Salmond, *Wade in Scotland*.

House of Lords Appeals

There was no express provision in the Treaty as to whether any appeal was to be permitted to the House of Lords of the Parliament of Great Britain. In England appeal to the House of Lords by writ of error had become established by the seventeenth century. In Scotland it was an uncertain question how far any appeal lay from the Scottish courts to the Scottish Parliament. In so far as it did, it did not lie to the House of Lords, because there was no distinct House of Lords in the Scottish Parliament. The Treaty avoided the difficulty but its silence on the matter left open the possibility of appeal.

In 1707–08 the Earl of Rosebery tried an appeal to the House of Lords and the jurisdiction was accepted by the House. In 1711 an Episcopalian clergyman, James Greenshields, was imprisoned in Edinburgh for openly using the Anglican form of service, and the Court of Session upheld the action of the presbytery and the magistrates. Appeal was taken to the House of Lords and the Lords reversed the Court of Session and ordered Greenshields' release.[80] The decision caused great alarm in Scotland, but thereafter Scottish appeals multiplied and were very numerous in the eighteenth century.[81] Since then the House of Lords has continued to entertain appeals from Scotland and the practice, however erroneous, is now settled.

Central Government

After the abolition of the Scottish Privy Council in 1708, the government of Scotland was, until 1746, sometimes in the hands of a third Secretary of State but was frequently entrusted to one or other of the joint Secretaries of State.[82] Responsibility fell to the northern Secretary of State until 1782, and thereafter to the Home Secretary assisted by the Lord Advocate. In the intervals, Scottish affairs were managed by a Scottish noble or by the Lord Advocate. The management consisted largely of control of elections and the dispensing of patronage. The most successful manager was Henry Dundas, later Viscount Melville, during the years 1783 to 1806.[83]

Local Government

At the time of the Union the functions of local government were distributed among six agencies which had developed with little reference to each other and at different periods. The sheriffs and the burghs had

---

[80] There were earlier appeals in 1708, but *Greenshields'* case attracted more attention. See also Malcolm, "The House of Lords and Appeals from Scotland" (1910) 22 J.R. 295.

[81] Turberville, *The House of Lords in the Eighteenth Century*, 140.

[82] Lovat Fraser, "Scottish Administration in the Eighteenth Century" (1912) 24 J.R. 122.

[83] Lovat Fraser, "A Famous Lord Advocate" (1902) 14 J.R. 350; "The Impeachment of Lord Melville" (1912) 24 J.R. 235. See also M. Fry, *The Dundas Despotism*.

arisen in the twelfth century, baronies and regalities in the fourteenth, kirk sessions in the sixteenth, and justices of the peace and commissioners of supply in the seventeenth.

The administrative functions of the sheriff had formerly been the collection of Crown dues, execution of royal writs, publication of statutes, and latterly making the return of the shire members. These functions were, however, restricted as the sheriffships became heritable in the hands of the great families, and administrative power was curtailed while legal jurisdiction increased.[84]

The royal burghs had each a constitution or "sett" which entrusted power to a provost, bailies and self-elective town councils, and they remained into the nineteenth century self-contained agencies of local government, frequently enjoying substantial revenues. The merchant guilds and crafts in the burghs had numerous exclusive privileges which legally survived until 1846 though they had been largely abandoned by then. Measures for the control of the burghs were enacted from time to time, notably in 1822, but this was too late and the courts refused to enforce them.[85]

The baronies and regalities had formerly enjoyed substantial jurisdictional rights, but by 1707 these had very largely fallen into abeyance. Their executive duties, however, continued; these were to preserve common lands, pastures, woods and mosses, dykes and ditches and to keep the assizes of bread and ale. After the abolition of heritable jurisdictions in 1747, even their administrative functions fell into desuetude though particular instances survived until much later.[86]

The kirk sessions established at the Reformation acted under the general guidance of the commissioners of supply and, in burghs, in co-operation with the town council. Expenditure required the sanction of the heritors of the parish, *i.e.* the heritable proprietors appearing on the valuation roll of the parish.[87] The kirk session managed the parish schools, paid small allowances to the poor, aged and indigent and distributed charitable relief in case of need. It was permissible to lay assessments on the parish after 1663, half on owners, half on occupiers, but these were unpopular and infrequently resorted to, and most funds came from church collections and mortifications for the poor. The poor law system was, however, disintegrating and badly needed reform by the nineteenth century.[88]

In Scotland the justices of the peace, introduced in 1609, never enjoyed either the powers or the prestige of their English counterparts. After 1708,

---

[84] Rait and Pryde, *op. cit.* 177–178.
[85] *ibid.* 178.
[86] Hill Burton, VIII, 517–518; Rait and Pryde, 178.
[87] The meaning of the term is discussed at length in Black's *Parochial Ecclesiastical Law of Scotland* (4th ed.), p. 44.
[88] Rait and Pryde, *op. cit.* 179; Ferguson, *Dawn of Scottish Social Welfare*, Chap. 7.

however, they did enjoy considerable administrative powers, having jurisdiction over the settlement of disputes as to work and wages, weights and
measures; they had to suppress riots, support customs officers and
supervise prisons and almshouses and, from 1718, in conjunction with the
commissioners of supply, to see to the maintenance of country roads and
bridges.[89] From 1756 they had to grant or renew liquor licences, and from
1795 they could handle small debt cases. But from about 1820 the powers
and functions of the justices diminished.

The commissioners of supply were recognised by statute in 1667 but had
existed on a customary basis before then. They were a county committee
of wealthy landowners appointed to allocate the monthly cess or land tax,
and their organisation made it convenient to entrust them with other
duties such as the enforcement of the Education Act of 1696 and, with the
justices, the control of vagabonds and the upkeep of roads.[90] For practical
purposes, the commissioners ceased to be important after county councils
were established in 1889.

Break-up of the Clan System and the Heritable Jurisdictions

The measures adopted to restore and ensure internal peace after the
defeat of the second Jacobite rebellion at Culloden provoked considerable
dissatisfaction. The chief constitutional change was the abolition in 1748
of heritable jurisdictions, in breach of the Treaty of Union.[91] Compensation amounting to £152,000 was paid, of which £21,000 went to the Duke
of Argyll in compensation for his right of justiciary over Argyll and the
Western Isles. Thereafter, the power and prestige of the sheriff courts
advanced steadily and in 1787 the office of sheriff-substitute was recognised and made a salaried office. So, too, the holding of land in return for
military service was abolished and lands thus held converted to ordinary
feudal tenure.[92]

After Culloden the Highlands were treated with unforgiveable savagery
and the measures for disarming the Highlands and breaking up the clan
system were unnecessarily severe.[93] The tartan and the pipes were
proscribed as military and as badges of sedition, and were not legalised
again till 1782, while suppression and persecution contributed materially
to the great emigration to North America about the middle of the
century.[94]

An Act of 1752 disposed of the estates which had been forfeited after
the rebellion and devoted their revenues to the improvement of Highland

---

[89] Hill Burton, VIII, 210; Rait and Pryde, *op. cit.* 179.
[90] Rait and Pryde, *op. cit.* 180.
[91] Pryde, *op. cit.* 65; Omond, *Lord Advocates of Scotland*, II, 32–38, 41–42; Dickson,
"Heritable Jurisdictions" (1897) 9 J.R. 428.
[92] Hill Burton, VIII, 503–504; Hume Brown, III, 330.
[93] See Prebble, *Culloden*; Watt, "The Treason Trials at Carlisle after the '45" (1911) 23 J.R.
124; Bartholomew, "The Highland Clans in the Law of Scotland" (1901) 13 J.R. 205, 307.
[94] Hume Brown, III, 328–329.

farms, the establishment of schools and the planting of forests.[95] The Act had beneficial results and many areas were greatly improved. A few years later followed another beneficial measure in the Act for the better preservation of turnpike road, under which dues were levied from vehicles and spent on the maintenance of the public roads, while in 1770 Montgomery's Entail Act empowered heirs of entail in possession to grant leases for substantial periods on certain conditions, a provision which greatly tended towards the agricultural improvement of the country.[96]

In 1782–84 the Act prohibiting the wearing of the Highland dress was repealed, and the forfeited estates restored to the legal heirs but on condition that debts charged on them were to go to the public benefit and particularly towards the expense of completing the Forth and Clyde canal and of making roads in the Highlands.[97]

Heritable Jurisdictions and the Inferior Courts

The abolition of the heritable jurisdictions affected not only rights of jurisdiction held by virtue of grants of barony or regality but also the office of sheriff all over the country.

The office of sheriff had early tended to become hereditary in the line of a powerful Crown vassal and by 1747 23 out of 33 sheriffs held thus. But since about 1357 there had been a growing practice for the sheriff to appoint a qualified depute to perform the judicial work. In 1747 the qualified depute everywhere replaced the hereditary officer and became the sheriff of the county.[98] In 1828 the name Depute was dropped and he became the modern Sheriff, since 1971 called Sheriff-Principal. The Sheriff-Depute in turn appointed sheriffs-substitute who held office during his pleasure and were paid by him. In 1787 it was provided that the sheriff-substitute should be paid by the Crown, and from 1825 it was provided that the sheriff-substitute should be a trained lawyer, while in 1877 that office became a distinct Crown appointment.

Legal Literature—Bankton, Erskine, Millar and Kames

The eighteenth century saw some very distinguished lawyers and judges.[99] On the bench the work of Forbes, Dundas and Ilay Campbell was outstanding.[1] But now, among the jurists the academic was becoming

---

[95] Rait and Pryde, *op. cit.* 97; Hume Brown, III, 337–338; Pryde, *op. cit.* 153.

[96] Hume Brown, III, 345.

[97] *Ibid.* 352–353; Pryde, *op. cit.* 155.

[98] For list of the first sheriffs, see Omond, *Lord Advocates*, II, 43–44. See also Malcolm, in *Introduction* (Stair Society), Chap. 26.

[99] See also Ramsay, "Eighteenth Century Advocates and Their Study of Literature" (1939) 51 J.R. 23; Stein, "Legal Thought in Eighteenth Century Scotland" (1957) J.R. 3.

[1] Some impression of practice at the Bar in the 1770s can be gained from Wimsatt and Pottle (ed.), *Boswell for the Defence*; see also Henderson, "James Boswell and his Practice at the Bar" (1905) 17 J.R. 105; Simpson, "Boswell as an Advocate" (1922) 34 J.R. 201; Duke, "Boswell Among the Lawyers" (1926) 38 J.R. 341; Roughead, "The Wandering Jurist" (1931) 43 J.R. 30, 138; Ramsay, "Boswell's First Criminal Case" (1938) 50 J.R. 315; Murray, "Some Civil Cases of James Boswell" (1940) 52 J.R. 222.

prominent for the first time. William Forbes, Professor of Law at Glasgow (1714–46), wrote books on *Bills of Exchange, Tithes* and *Justices of the Peace*, as well as a small *Institutes of the Law of Scotland*.[2]

In 1751 there appeared the *Institutes* of Andrew McDouall, Lord Bankton, a work still of considerable authority and value and notable for its extensive comparisons with the law of England, but overshadowed by the work of Erskine.

John Erskine of Carnock[3] was born in 1695 and passed advocate in 1719. In 1737 he became professor of Scots law at Edinburgh, which chair he held until he retired in 1765. In 1754 he published his *Principles of the Law of Scotland* for use as the textbook of the class, a function which it performed in repeated editions until well into the twentieth century. He died in 1768. His larger work, the *Institute of the Law of Scotland*, was not published in his lifetime but appeared posthumously in 1773, and soon achieved a place in juristic regard second only to Stair's *Institutions*. Erskine displays classical Scots law, deduced from principle and considered in leisurely prose, not yet overwhelmed by the citation of difficult or even contradictory decisions or by masses of barely comprehensible statutory amendment. It is as the final and authoritative exponent of the older law of Scotland, resting on the Roman law and the feudal customs, that Erskine stands supreme. His work lacks the philosophic breadth of Stair and the bold insight of Bell, and he probably failed to appreciate that, even when he wrote, the centre of interest in legal studies was shifting from the law of property to commercial law. His treatment is academic, cautious, exact and workmanlike rather than inspired, but yet worthy of the highest admiration and respect.

John Millar, professor of law at Glasgow from 1761 to 1801,[4] was the most celebrated and successful law teacher of his time; his writings included *The Origin of the Distinction of Ranks*, an interesting early sociological study, and *An Historical View of the English Government*, the first constitutional history of Britain. He was a notable supporter of the liberties of the subject and an outspoken advocate of parliamentary reform. Also in the eighteenth century appeared some of the collections of styles of deeds, which are the beginning of modern conveyancing practice.[5]

Of the judiciary, Henry Home, Lord Kames (1696–1782), was among the most notable. He passed advocate in 1723 and was raised to the Bench in 1752. His literary output was considerable and diverse—collections of decisions,[6] essays on legal subjects, antiquities, on morality and natural

---

[2] Forbes' major work, *The Great Body of the Law of Scotland*, has never been published but remains in manuscript in Glasgow University Library.

[3] See Grant, *Story of the University of Edinburgh*, II, 372, and D.N.B.

[4] See further, Lehmann, *John Millar of Glasgow*; and "John Millar" (1961) J.R. 218; K. Haakonssen, "John Millar and the Science of a Legislator" 1985 J.R. 41.

[5] See Macmillan, "The Old Scots Conveyancers" (1898–99) 10 J.R. 425; 11 J.R. 41.

[6] *Remarkable Decisions*, 1716–28, continued later, 1730–52; *Select Decisions*, 1752–68 (pub. 1780); *Dictionary of the Decisions of the Court of Session* (completed by Woodhouselee, 4 vols., 1741).

religion, literary criticism, farming and education. The works still of most interest and value are the *Historical Law Tracts* (1757) and the *Principles of Equity* (1760), the latter of which examined, with much comparative reference to English law, the principles on which rules of law might be modified in application by an overriding equitable discretion. In this connection he conducted extensive correspondence with Lord Hardwicke and Lord Mansfield in England. "We moderns are hardly enough aware of how much the Scotch lawyer is indebted to Henry Home, Lord Kames. His versatile and truly philosophical mind neglected nothing. He enriched the law of Scotland by his collections of remarkable decisions, by his abridgment of the Statutes, and by a large body of ingenious speculations and criticisms upon law and legal decisions."[7]

Another distinguished judge was David Dalrymple, Lord Hailes (1726–92) a great-grandson of Viscount Stair.[8] He was a fine scholar, a man of letters, friend of James Boswell and Dr Johnson and of most of the literary figures of his time, and a humane judge. Among his numerous publications are *A Catalogue of the Lords of Session to 1752, An Examination of Some of the Arguments for the High Antiquity of Regiam Majestatem, The Annals of Scotland* and two volumes of *Decisions of the Lords of Council and Session*, 1766–1791.

The eighteenth century practically saw the end of the old intimacy between Scotland and the Continent and of the practice of young men resorting, formerly to France and later to Holland, for study of the Roman law as expounded by the commentators and the great civilians. Craig, Mackenzie, Spotiswoode and Fountainhall had studied at Orleans, Poitiers, Bourges or Paris. In the seventeenth and eighteenth centuries it is known that numerous Scottish lawyers studied at Leyden alone. Stair was there in exile from 1682 to 1688[9]; Lord President Forbes studied there, and Lord President Dundas at Utrecht. Most cogent evidence of the link can be seen in the older books of the Advocates' Library, founded in 1681, of which the great majority are Continental treatises, mostly from France, Holland and Northern Germany, but some drawn from further away. "From their sojourn in Holland the aspirants to practice in the

---

[7] Innes, *Scotch Legal Antiquities*, 10. On Kames, see also Fraser Tytler's *Memoirs of the Life and Writing of Henry Home of Kames*; Ross, *Lord Kames and the Scotland of his Day*; Lehmann, *Henry Home, Lord Kames and the Scottish Enlightenment*; Brown, "Kames's Principles of Equity" (1903) 10 S.L.T.(News) 94, 111, 127, 159, 173, 181; Brown, "A Master of Equity" (1904) 20 L.Q.R. 308; Brown, "Lord Kames: A Judicial Historian" (1911) 23 J.R. 180; Brown, "Equity" (1914) 26 J.R. 338; Lehmann, "The Historical Approach in the Juridical Writings of Lord Kames" (1964) J.R. 17. On other judges see Cloyd, *Lord Monboddo*; Walton, "Lord Monboddo" (1896) 8 J.R. 360; Brown, "Lord Monboddo: A Judicial Metaphysician" (1905) 17 J.R. 167; Lyell, "The Real Weir of Hermiston" (1904) 16 J.R. 115.

[8] F.P. Walton, "The Humours of Hailes" (1894) 8 J.R. 233. In 1997 the National Trust for Scotland acquired Hailes' house, Newhailes near Musselburgh.

[9] Feenstra and Waal, *Seventeenth Century Leiden Law Professors and Their Influence on the Development of the Civil Law*, 82. On Stair's familiarity with Continental jurists, see Campbell, *The Structure of Stair's Institutions*.

Parliament House brought back with them not only the principles which they had imbibed from the masters of the Roman-Dutch law but also the treatises with which the law schools of the Dutch Universities were so prolific. No Scots lawyer's library was complete in those days which did not contain the works of Grotius, Vinnius, the Voets, Heineccius and other learned civilians. Collections of decisions of the Scottish judges were few and inaccessible, and the Court of Session, with its predilection for principle rather than precedent, heard many arguments, adorned with citations of the Roman law and its Dutch commentators."[10] Scots law has still, for this reason, an affinity with the Roman-Dutch law of South Africa.

The Scottish Enlightenment

In the latter part of the eighteenth century there arose the brilliant flourishing of ideas which has been called the Scottish Enlightenment, a period outstanding for innovative thinking and writing, in philosophy (Francis Hutcheson, Thomas Reid and Adam Smith), history (Hume and Robertson, Wodrow and Keith), economics (Adam Smith again), science (Black, James Watt), literature (Smollett, Thomson, Allan Ramsay) and in law. The *Encyclopaedia Britannica* first appeared, at Edinburgh, in 1771.[11]

Criminal Law

Criminal law continued little altered, though significant developments were the recognition of insanity at the time as a defence and, from 1867, of diminished responsibility as reducing murder to culpable homicide. Criminal procedure was characterised by frequent long arguments on the relevancy of charges, but by short trials.

Private Law in the Eighteenth Century

The later eighteenth century was the classical age of the Scottish common law, developed and brought to maturity by Erskine and not yet debased or defiled by inconsidered statutes, uncritical following of English principles or ignorant interference by an English House of Lords.[12] It largely coincided with the great days, the golden age, of Edinburgh and the efflorescence of the arts and letters, and of the Scottish School of

---

[10] *Stewart v. L.M.S. Ry.*, 1943 S.C.(H.L.) 19, 38 *per* Lord Macmillan.

[11] Campbell and Skinner (ed.), *The Origins and Nature of the Scottish Enlightenment*; Daiches (ed.) *A Hotbed of Genius*.

[12] See further, Paton, "The Eighteenth Century and Later," in *Introduction to Scottish Legal History*, Chap. 5; Inglis, "Eighteenth Century Pleading" (1907) 19 J.R. 42; Waugh, "Gleanings from the 18th Century Law Reports" (1903) 15 J.R. 164; Ramsay, "Eighteenth Century Advocates and their Study of Legal and General Literature" (1931) 43 J.R. 23; Stein, "General Notions of Contract and Property in Eighteenth Century Scottish Thought" 1963 J.R. 1; Walker, "Lawyers of the Scottish Enlightment and their Influence on the American Constitution" 1988 J.R. 4.

philosophy. Material prosperity advanced and the law had to take account of more settled conditions, developing agriculture, industry and commerce, and a more complicated social and economic order.[13] But there was not much alteration of private law by statute.

Agriculture, industry and commerce

Before the agricultural improvements of the eighteenth century, three forms of landholding were important: steelbow, where the landlord provided some of the working, as well as fixed, capital; tacksmen's holdings, whereby tacksmen held leases and sublet the land at higher rents and exacted military obligations from their sub-tenants; and runrig, where farms were let to joint tenants, who farmed strips of it. The control after the Jacobite rebellions destroyed the second, and agricultural improvements changed the first and third, consolidating land into bigger farms and introducing better methods of farming. Acts of 1695 authorised the division of commonties and of lands held in runrig, and other Acts authorised the straightening of boundaries and the fencing of holdings. These facilitated the introduction of new methods of agricultural production, changes in crops, rotation and farm implements.

The Union gave a stimulus to industry and trade, notably the tobacco trade with America; the Forth and Clyde Canal was cut to improve communications and a start was made with improvements to the roads; ironworks were established, notably at Carron in 1759; and finance was improved as the banking system developed.[14]

V.—THE MODERN PERIOD

The keynotes of the period since the Napoleonic wars have been reform, the increasing volume and importance of public and especially administrative law, the growing bulk and complexity of statutory law, and the increase of English influence and the tendency to assimilate Scots law to English. Constitutionally it has been a period of constant reform and movement towards democracy.

The Movement for Reform

In 1792 the Society of Friends of the People was formed and branches spread over Scotland and England. The doctrines of liberty found ready acceptance. The government became alarmed and prosecutions were initiated. The first in Scotland was of Thomas Muir of Huntershill, a young advocate and champion of reform, who was unfairly tried and

---

[13] See generally Lenman, *Economic History of Modern Scotland*, 67 *et seq.*
[14] Hamilton, *An Economic History of Scotland in the Eighteenth Century, passim.*

sentenced to transportation.[15] Further trials, public excitement and government fears continued, but calm was restored by 1795. However, the movement for reform continued and grew in strength.

After Waterloo there was a severe economic depression which gave rise to a spirit of unrest and the founding of revolutionary societies. Sedition was feared, especially in Glasgow, and a number of weavers were tried in 1818, but general opinion had changed since Muir's trial and the prosecutions mostly failed.[16]

Discontent and agitation for reform continued throughout the 1820s; fruits of the movement were found in the reforms of the Court of Session in 1808 and 1825 and a measure of 1822 giving jurisdiction over burgh accounts to the Court of Exchequer.

The Scottish Reform Bill was passed in 1832, raising Scottish representation from 45 to 53, redistributing seats and extending the franchise, and the following year saw the reform of the burghs, putting an end to the self-election of the magistrates.[17]

Central Government

In the second half of the nineteenth century, criticism began to be directed against the system whereby the Lord Advocate administered Scotland, under the loose control of the Home Secretary. This administration consisted very largely in the management of elections and the dispensing of patronage. It was brought to its peak of perfection by Henry Dundas (later Viscount Melville) between 1783 and 1806.[18] From 1827 until the creation of the Secretaryship for Scotland in 1885, the Home Secretary was the Minister nominally responsible, though *ad hoc* bodies tended to be set up to exercise some administrative functions. Such were the Board of Supervision (for Poor Law) in 1845 and the Prison Commissioners in 1877.[19]

Under the third Reform Act (1884–85) Scotland for the first time was given her proper share of representatives according to population, with 72 members, while the grievance over the maladministration of Scottish affairs was to a small extent remedied by the creation of an under-secretaryship of Home Affairs, with Scotland as his special charge, and only a year later the office of Secretary for Scotland was created.[20] About

---

[15] Hume Brown, III, 381–382; Craik, *Century of Scottish History*, II, 149–154; Meikle, *Scotland and the French Revolution, passim*; Roughead, "An Advocate of Reform" (1938) 50 J.R. 231; Bewley, *Thomas Muir of Huntershill*. See also Cockburn, *An examination of the Trials for Sedition in Scotland*.

[16] Craik, II, 284–291.

[17] *Ibid.* II, 365–371; Pryde, *op. cit.* 192–196.

[18] See Matheson, *Life of Henry Dundas, Viscount Melville*. Fry, *The Dundas Despotism*.

[19] See the tracing of the development of the office of Secretary of State for Scotland in Milne, *The Scottish Office*, Chap. 2.

[20] On this, see further, Mure Mackenzie, *Scotland in Modern Times*, 267–269; Hanham, "The Creation of the Scottish Office, 1881–87," 1965 J.R. 205. A list of the holders of the office can be found in Milne, *The Scottish Office*, 216.

this time too the troubles in Ireland caused many of the Scottish Liberal members[21] to speculate on the need to review the terms of the Union and speak of devolution within the United Kingdom.[22] In 1894 a concession was made to the demand for devolution which from 1889 to 1895 underlay a perennial motion in favour of a separate parliament for Scotland, by the establishment of the procedure whereby all Scottish members were included in a Scottish Grand Committee for the consideration of a Bill.[23] It was revived in 1907 as a concession to nationalist sentiment and became a standing committee, while in 1912 the House of Commons approved a resolution to grant equal treatment in the matter of devolution to Scotland and Ireland. Irish affairs, however, were more pressing.[24]

The tendency of the twentieth century has been to increase the direct responsibility of the Secretary of State for Scottish administration and to bring under his control matters formerly entrusted to distinct Boards and Commissions. There has also been an increasing and salutary tendency to assign to the Scottish Secretary matters on which there is a distinctive tradition or body of law or pattern of administration, or where Scottish conditions are notably different from those in England and Wales.

The Reorganisation of Offices (Scotland) Act 1939 brought together the several Scottish Departments which had formerly existed under the control of the Secretary of State for Scotland, and these now became branches of the Scottish Office, having their principal home in Edinburgh and a liaison office in London.

In 1951 the group of Ministers responsible for Scottish affairs was increased by the appointment of a Minister of State, Scottish Office, and a third Under-Secretary of State, which, with the Lord Advocate and Solicitor-General, brought up to seven the group in the government available for the direction of Scottish affairs.

The Select Committee on Scottish Affairs is appointed by the House of Commons as one of the select committees which examine the policy, administration and expenditure of the major government departments.

Local Government

The reform of local government[25] began with the Acts of 1833 whereby the magistrates and town councils of the 66 royal and 13 parliamentary burghs were to be elected by the £10 householders.

A whole series of statutes authorised royal burghs and burghs of barony (1833), parliamentary burghs (1847), and other populous places (1850,

---

[21] The Liberals consistently held most of the Scottish seats from 1833 to 1900.

[22] Rait and Pryde, *op. cit.* 121; Mure Mackenzie, *op. cit.* 270.

[23] *Ibid.* 124; Mure Mackenzie, 273–275.

[24] *Ibid.* 127, and see p. 128 as to the Government of Scotland Bill sought to be introduced in 1913 and 1914, and p. 133 as to Home Rule Bills between 1919 and 1927. See also Mure Mackenzie, 392–398.

[25] See generally Pryde, *op. cit.* 188–190, and "Burghal Administration," in McLarty (ed.), *Source Book of Administrative Law*, Chap. 1.

1862) to adopt a uniform code of "police," covering watching, lighting, paving, cleansing and water supply, and thereby to become "police burghs." In the police burgh, authority was entrusted to police magistrates and police commissioners, who might or might not be the same as the bailies and councillors, and this dual administration lasted to the end of the nineteenth century. Minor reforms included the abrogation of the exclusive rights of guildry and craft and burgess-ship, the abolition of petty customs, transfer to the county council of the duty of maintaining a police force, and authority to appoint a stipendiary magistrate.

This trend culminated in the Burgh Police (Scotland) Acts 1892 and 1903, and the Town Councils (Scotland) Act 1900, under which over 200 towns administered their own machinery for preserving order, health and good government.

In the counties[26] a regular, paid police force made its appearance under Acts of 1839 and 1857, its administration being entrusted to the commissioners of supply.[27] The justices of the peace also had administrative functions, particularly in connection with roads and bridges.

In 1845 parochial boards were established to take over administration of the poor law; they were composed of elected members, kirk session delegates, heritors and burgh magistrates. The whole of Scotland was supervised by a Board of Supervision of nine members. These parochial boards were given further duties later, in connection with registration (1854) and public health and water supply (1867).[28]

In 1853 the Forbes Mackenzie Act commenced the system of licensing of public-houses, while 1854 saw the introduction of compulsory registration of births, deaths and marriages, and in 1872 popularly elected school boards were set up in each burgh and parish with power to levy a local rate for education and to compel attendance up to the age of 13.[29]

In 1877 prisons were transferred from local control to the Home Secretary, assisted by a Prisons Commission. In 1878 county road trustees assumed responsibility for all roads and bridges, superseding the older statute-labour roads and turnpike trusts.[30]

In 1889 a substantial reform of local government was effected by the establishment of comprehensive authorities in the shape of popularly elected county councils.[31] They took over the functions of commissioners of supply, justices of the peace and county road trustees, administered the police in smaller burghs, and public health services. They were authorised

---

[26] On the counties, see Slevin, "Rural Administration," in McLarty (ed.), *Source Book of Administrative Law*, Chap. 2.

[27] Rait and Pryde, *op. cit.* 180.

[28] Slevin, "Rural Administration," in McLarty (ed.), *Source Book of Administrative Law*, Chap. 2; Ferguson, *Dawn of Scottish Social Welfare*, Chap. 8.

[29] Rait and Pryde, *op. cit.* 181.

[30] *ibid.*; Pryde, *op. cit.* 207.

[31] Rait and Pryde, *op. cit.* 123–124.

to levy a consolidated rate in place of the former separate assessments. In the larger shires, district committees were to act as their agents in matters of roads and public health. As regards police and capital works, the final say was given to the standing joint committee composed of seven county councillors and seven commissioners of supply, with the sheriff as chairman.[32]

In 1894 popularly elected parish councils were set up in lieu of the old parochial boards and charged with the administration of poor relief and all local matters, with a Local Government Board to co-ordinate their activities.[33] District committees composed of county councillors for the district, and one parish councillor from each parish and from any burgh within the district, formed a link between county and parish.[34] In 1900 the term "commissioners of police" was abolished and burghs reverted to the historic titles of provost, bailies and councillors.

The Local Government (Scotland) Act 1929 recast the whole system, sweeping away the older and *ad hoc* authorities, and substituting county, town and district councils to which all powers and functions were entrusted. This pattern was amended only in detail in 1947. Burghs were divided into three categories, counties of cities, a small number of large burghs and a large number of small burghs. The Act provided an admirable scheme, but it was found in practice to remove most power to the larger authorities and to increase reliance on the central government, a tendency visible in other fields of administration also.

A fresh structure came into force in 1975.[35] Counties and burghs ceased to have functions in local government and all such powers were assigned to three all-purpose islands authorities, and elsewhere divided between nine regional and 53 district councils. Most of the country, accordingly, had a two-tier system of local government, with some functions exercised by Regions and some by Districts within Regions. This proved disastrous, an expensive proliferation of spendthrift bureaucracies, while Regions and Districts were frequently at loggerheads. A further new structure was established in 1996; it comprised 32 all-purpose authorities, four for cities, 25 for counties, parts of counties and groups of counties, and three for groups of islands. Elections were to be held every three years. Serious defects of local government are the low intellectual quality of many councillors, frequent suspicions of nepotism, and regular financial profligacy.

Various functions have since 1945 been transferred from local to national organisations and dependence on the Exchequer for money is

---

[32] *Ibid.* 181; Slevin, *loc. cit.* 17–19.
[33] Rait and Pryde, 124.
[34] *Ibid.* 181; Slevin, *loc. cit.* 17–19; Whetstone, *Scottish County Government in the 18th and 19th Centuries*.
[35] Local Government (Scotland) Act 1973.

heavy, which tends also to effect a transfer of control. There has also since 1945 been widespread dissatisfaction with the way in which everything of consequence is managed from, or its decisions reached in, London and with remote control which frequently reveals ignorance of local conditions and disregard of local sentiment.

Special Authorities

In the Highlands, high rents and ejections among the crofters produced much bad feeling and hardship and some outbursts of violence when in 1886 the Crofters' Holdings Act sought to fix fair rents, guarantee security of tenure, enlarge existing holdings and allow compensation for improvements. The Crofters Commission was appointed with executive and judicial functions, and toured the northern counties seeking to settle disputes and alleviate difficulties.[36] In 1897 a Congested Districts Board was set up for the settlement of land scheduled as suitable for new holdings and small farms. In 1911 its work was passed to the Board of Agriculture and in 1912 the Crofters Commission gave place to the Scottish Land Court.[37] In 1955, however, a new Crofters Commission was appointed, charged with the reorganisation, development and regulation of crofting in the crofting counties.[38]

Conflict between Church and State and the Disruption

The courts and the General Assembly of the Church came into sharp conflict in the 1830s. In 1834 the Assembly passed the Veto Act whereby the dissent of a majority of male heads of families was to prevent the presentation of a minister to a charge by the patron of the living. In 1835 the Presbytery rejected a presentee to the church of Auchterarder under the Veto Act. The Court of Session held[39] that the Veto Act (of Assembly) was contrary to the Patronage Act (of Parliament) of 1711 and this view was upheld by the House of Lords. The difficulties were also apparent in the Lethendy case,[40] and the Strathbogie[41] and other cases, which resulted in the Assembly defying the court and the court interdicting the Assembly. The controversy continued; appeals to Parliament failed of effect, and in 1843 a large body of ministers and laity seceded from the Church and formed the Free Church of Scotland.[42] Patronage was abolished in 1874

---

[36] Rait and Pryde, *op. cit.* 124; Mure Mackenzie, 294.

[37] Mure Mackenzie, 294–295.

[38] Laird, in *Source Book of Administrative Law*, 90–91.

[39] *Earl of Kinnoull v. Fergusson* (1841) 3 D. 778; (1842) 1 Bell 662; (1843) 5 D. 1010.

[40] *Clark v. Stirling* (1839) 1 D. 955.

[41] *Presbytery of Strathbogie* (1839) 2 D. 258, 585, 1047, 1380; *Edwards v. Cruickshank* (1840) 3 D. 283; *Presbytery of Strathbogie* (1842) 4 D. 1298; *Cruickshank v. Gordon* (1843) 5 D. 909, *Edwards v. Leith* (1843) 15 Sc.Jur. 375.

[42] Hume Brown, III, 423–431; Pryde, 184–186; Taylor, "Church and State in Scotland" (1957) 2 J.R.(N.S.) 121, 125 *et seq.* See also Crabb Watt, *John Inglis*, 60–73; Craik, *Century of Scottish History*, Chap. 22; Grub, *Ecclesiastical History of Scotland*, IV, 203–235; Cunningham, *Church History of Scotland*, II, 450 *et seq.*: Burleigh, *Church History of Scotland*, 334; Lyall, *Of Presbyters and Kings*, 23–53.

but the breach between the Church and the Free Church was healed only in 1929, and then not completely.

The House of Lords and Scots Appeals

In the first half of the nineteenth century the reputation of the House of Lords as an appeal court from Scotland, never high, touched its nadir.[43] Yet appeals from Scotland were numerous.[44] Appeals were regularly taken to the Lords, frequently merely to waste time. Many appeals were heard by the Lord Chancellor or a single Law Lord sitting with two lay peers to make up a quorum. Some Lord Chancellors frankly confessed their ignorance of Scots law on the matter under appeal, others merely showed it in their judgments, which frequently reversed the Court of Session, while judgments were regularly and normally thought, and sometimes spoken, in terms of English law and not even translated into the terms of art of Scots law. It is not surprising that decisions of the Lords continued to be worthless as statements of Scots law and, so far as influential, to be seriously detrimental to the principles of Scots law. Repeatedly Lords, in complete ignorance of the principles, asserted that the law of Scotland *must* be the same as the law of England.[45] An infamous example, which fastened on Scots law the wickedly unjust rule of common employment,[46] is *Bartonshill Coal Co. v. Reid*[47] where Lord Cranworth, having discussed the English cases, said: "But if such be the law of England, on what ground can it be argued not to be the law of Scotland?" In cases of doubt, moreover, the Lords sometimes consulted the judges, but the *English* judges,[48] and this practice persisted in isolated cases as late as 1904.[49]

By 1866 the position had become intolerable. "For at least a century there had been intense dissatisfaction in Scotland with the constitution of the House of Lords as Court of Appeal. Scottish lawyers in particular felt aggrieved because they had to plead before a foreign tribunal which had to be instructed in the elements of their system . . . the House of Lords, as a bench of competent judges, had thus to a great degree lost the confidence of the profession in Scotland. Lawyers naturally thought the administration of Scots law in the court of last resort could not be entrusted to men who were conversant only with a foreign system, and who showed little or no consideration for the opinions of Scotch judges— at least not that deference accorded to them in the days of Mansfield and Erskine. There were other reasons for the discontent. In many cases—for

---

[43] See Gibb, *Law from Over the Border*, Chap. 3.
[44] Stevens, *Law and Politics*, 15.
[45] Gibb, *op. cit.* 57.
[46] Abolished by statute in 1948; the rule was *not* part of Scots law prior to 1858.
[47] (1858) 3 Macq. 266, 285.
[48] *e.g. Baillie v. Grant*, (1832) 6 W. & S. 40.
[49] In *Free Church of Scotland v. Overtoun* (1904) 7 F.(H.L.) 1: this appears from the *Memoirs of Lord Salvesen* (ed. Andorsen, 1949), pp. 66–67. Salvesen was one of the counsel in the case.

example, the *Douglas*, the *Roxburghe* and the *Queensberry* cases—property to the value of half a million had been involved. These were great causes and attracted wide notice. But hundreds of others had stood in the same position as far as the feebleness of the House of Lords as the ultimate judicature, constituted without a Scotch judge, was concerned. It was esteemed a radical defect, as indefensible as absurd, that the judges knew little or nothing about the law they had to administer. Even the English members of the bench from time to time kicked against the pricks. Some of them, like Lord Redesdale, who officiated in the *Queensberry* cases (1819) openly confessed that they had to divest themselves of English prejudice before studying a Scotch case. . . . Scotch lawyers have resented the interposition of an English mixture into the solid body of their Roman system."[50] "The general sentiment of the Scottish people was that the House of Lords was not a tribunal which could be trusted, and for a long time it had been felt in the Parliament House, and also among English lawyers, that the court of final appeal would be strengthened by the presence of a judge who was thoroughly acquainted from practical experience, with the law of Scotland."[51]

Accordingly, so as to have someone in the House who knew something about Scots law, and to be a counterpart in the Upper House as expositor of Scottish measures to the Lord Advocate in the Commons, in 1866 Lord President McNeill was raised to the peerage as Lord Colonsay.[52] He did not, however, make any great mark there and died in 1874.

In 1873 the Judicature Act abolished the jurisdiction of the House of Lords, but this provision never came into force and in 1876 the Appellate Jurisdiction Act provided for salaried Lords of Appeal in Ordinary with life peerages.[53] While this jurisdiction is still doubtfully satisfactory, it is at least less objectionable than before 1867.[54] At least since 1876 the House has never lacked at least one Scottish Law Lord,[55] though it is still the case that Scottish appeals are decided by a tribunal all of whom may be, and the majority of whom almost invariably are, English lawyers.

The consequence of this strange jurisdiction has been the introduction of much English law into Scotland, much of it then or subsequently misunderstood, and the assimilation of much Scots law to English, usually

---

[50] Crabb Watt, *John Inglis*, 256–257.

[51] Omond, *Lord Advocates of Scotland, 1834–80,* 146.

[52] Mackenzie, "Lord Colonsay and his Island" (1931) 43 J.R. 1.

[53] See Stevens, "Final Appeal: Reform of the House of Lords and Privy Council, 1867–76" (1964) 80 L.Q.R. 343.

[54] See modern cases discussed by Gibb, *op. cit.*, Chap. 4.

[55] The succession has been Lords Gordon, Watson, Robertson, Shaw of Dunfermline, Dunedin, Macmillan, Thankerton, Normand, Reid, Keith of Avonholm, Guest, Kilbrandon, Fraser of Tullybelton, Keith of Kinkel, Mackay of Clashfern, Jauncey of Tulliechettle, Hope of Craighead and Clyde, while other Scottish judges who were peers, such as Lords Kinnear and Shand have also sat occasionally. See Macnaghten, Stormonth-Darling and Haldane, "Lord Watson" (1899) 13 J.R. 269; Paterson, "Scottish Lords of Appeal, 1876–1988" 1988 J.R. 235.

to the detriment of the native rule. Opinions still differ as to the merits of the practice of an appeal to Westminster, and it is significant that the Scottish criminal law, where no such appeal has ever been permitted, has developed on quite satisfactory lines without the influence of appeal to the Lords. Since 1876, however, Scots law has at least been represented by distinguished jurists in the House and contributed something to its judgments. Lords Watson and Reid in particular have been highly esteemed as much in English as in Scottish appeals.[56]

The Superior Courts

The pattern of the Court of Session remained substantially unchanged from its foundation until after 1800.[57] It remained a unitary court, sitting and deliberating as a whole, though two or three judges might at any time be on duty in rotation in the Outer House acting as Lord Ordinary, dealing with witnesses, oaths and the preliminary stages of actions, or in the Bill Chamber authorising the initiation of exceptional forms of actions, but such judges were delegates of the whole court rather than independent judges. The system had, however, ceased to be satisfactory by the early nineteenth century and the first third of that century saw a flood of reports of commissions and committees, pamphlets and memoranda urging change.

In 1808 the Inner House was divided into the First and Second Divisions, consisting respectively of the Lord President and seven ordinary Lords, and the Lord Justice-Clerk and six ordinary Lords; all the Lords Ordinary sat in rotation in the Outer House preparing cases for hearing in the Inner House. In 1810 the four junior judges of the First Division and the three junior judges of the Second Division became permanent Lords Ordinary sitting only in the Outer House. Further adjustment seemed necessary and in 1825 the court was settled on the basis of an Inner House of two Divisions, each of four judges (including the Lord President and Lord Justice-Clerk in the First and Second Divisions respectively) and an Outer House of seven Lords Ordinary.[58] In 1830 the Outer House was allowed to diminish to five and the total to 13, but in 1948 the traditional number of 15 was again authorised[59] and later statutes[60] raised the authorised number to 32. But all decrees, though issued by a single judge, are decrees of the Court of Session.

An important change in procedure was made in 1850 by the Court of Session Act of that year.[61] Hitherto, litigation had been conducted largely

---

[56] See Blom-Cooper and Drewry, *Final Appeal*, 156–157; Stevens, *Law and Politics*.

[57] See generally, Cooper, "The Central Courts after 1532," in *Introduction to Scottish Legal History*, Chap. 24.

[58] See *Purves v. Carswell* (1905) 8 F. 351, 354. The Divisions were enlarged to five each in 2001.

[59] Administration of Justice (Scotland) Act 1948, s. 1.

[60] Restrictive Trade Practices Act 1956, s. 32; Criminal Justice (Scotland) Act 1963, s. 49; Resale Prices Act 1964, s. 9; Administration of Justice Act 1968, s. 1; now Court of Session Act 1988, s. 1, and orders made thereunder.

[61] See further, Maxwell, in *Introduction* (Stair Society), Chap. 32.

by written pleadings, learned and voluminous,[62] but thereafter it was incompetent to order "cases or minutes of debate or other written argument to be prepared by the parties." "These minutes of debate gave employment to scores of men who could not address a judge without blushing or stammering—honest, able worms that burrowed away their lives amid the parchment, the print, and the moths of Voet and Heineccius, of Stair and Erskine, of the Jus Feudale and the Pandects . . . from 1850 forward Vinnius and the Corpus Juris vanished into obscurity."[63] Written pleadings became much briefer and oral argument thereon became normal.

Even after the Act of 1850, reform of procedure was sadly required, because the mills of justice ground slowly. The Distribution of Business Act of 1857 gave some relief and the Court of Session Act of 1868, though attacked as anglicising, instituted an improved and expeditious procedure.

A factor which made for expedition was the change in the method of taking proofs. Down to the beginning of the century the depositions of witnesses were taken by the Lord Ordinary in his week of duty in the Outer House. They then resorted to the device of appointing commissioners to hear witnesses, write down the gist of their testimony and report, but neither commissioner nor judge reported on the import of the evidence or the credibility of the witnesses. This continued until 1866 when it was provided that in all ordinary cases proof should be led before the Lord Ordinary, but the success of the change was due largely to the adoption of the practice of having shorthand notes taken, which was first sanctioned by the Conjugal Rights Act of 1861. At first the judges dictated the evidence to the shorthand writer but this was later given over and in 1866 shorthand notes became competent in all civil cases. Some judges, however, such as Inglis, always took the notes themselves.

In 1913 much of the mass of Acts of Sederunt regulating practice was consolidated into the Consolidating Act of Sederunt and this in turn was superseded in 1936 by Rules of Court made under the authority of the Administration of Justice (Scotland) Act 1933. The principal excrescence on a reasonably simple and direct system of procedure was, and is, the persistence of civil jury trial, an expensive time-wasting alien imposition and an unsuitable mode of trial to boot, which was nevertheless recommended for retention, in a restricted sphere, by a departmental committee in 1959.[64]

---

[62] A specimen of this style at its best is Thomas Thomson's Memorial on Old Extent, written for the case of *Cranstoun v. Gibson*, May 16, 1818, F.C., and printed by the Stair Society in 1946.

[63] Crabb Watt, *John Inglis*, 54–55.

[64] *Report of the Committee on Civil Jury Trial in Scotland* (Cmnd. 851, 1959).

The Admiralty Court

In the sixteenth century[65] the Court of Admiralty sat to exercise the judicial functions of the Admiral of Scotland and, but for the opposition of the other courts, would probably have captured most of the commercial litigation by reason of the suitability of its jurisdiction and procedure. It had jurisdiction in maritime causes, civil and criminal, over the whole of Scotland. It administered the customary law of the sea, particularly the Laws of Oleron. But the Court of Session and the Court of Justiciary were jealous of this rival and stole business from it despite attempts at parliamentary protection.[66] In 1825 the jurisdiction in prize was transferred to the English Court of Admiralty,[67] and in 1828 a jurisdiction in criminal causes, cumulative with that of the Admiralty Court, was conferred on the Court of Justiciary. Finally in 1830 the civil jurisdiction of the Admiralty Court was transferred to the Court of Session and to the sheriffs, and thereafter the criminal jurisdiction was merged in that of the Justiciary Court and of the sheriffs.

The Jury Court

The jury as a tribunal for determining disputed issues of fact in civil matters had vanished by the sixteenth century. In 1810, however, a Royal Commission suggested the introduction of civil juries on the English model and in 1815 this was put into effect by the creation of a separate tribunal, first of three and later of five judges, entitled the "Lords Commissioners of the Jury Court in Civil Causes."[68] The Chief Commissioner was William Adam who, though a Scot, had practised only in England. This court had no original jurisdiction but acted only on remit from the Court of Session or Admiralty Court. The experiment never seems to have been much of a success and subsequent statutes limited the causes in which jury trial was requisite.

In 1830 the powers and duties of the Jury Court were transferred to the Court of Session and the court abolished. The Royal Commission of 1868 reported that the institution of civil jury trial had not given general satisfaction, but it has nevertheless survived, despite constant criticism and the withering away in England of civil jury trial on the model of which it was established.[69]

---

[65] See further, *Acta Curiae Admirallatus Scotiae*, ed. Wade (Stair Society), Vol. 2; Baty, "The Judge Admiral of Scotland" (1916) 28 J.R. 144; McMillan, "The Scottish Court of Admiralty" (1922) 34 J.R. 38, 164.

[66] Acts 1609, c. 22, and 1681, c. 82.

[67] A violation of Art. XIX of the Treaty of Union.

[68] For the reasons underlying the introduction of jury trial, see Gibb, *Law from Over the Border*, 45 *et seq.*; Phillipson, The *Scottish Whigs and the Reform of the Court of Session.*

[69] See *Report of the Committee on Civil Jury Trial* (Cmnd. 851, 1959). For criticisms, see Sidgwick, *Elements of Politics*, 491 *et seq.*; Lord Cooper, "Trial by Jury in Scotland," in *Selected Papers*, pp. 58–70, and "The Scottish Legal Tradition," *ibid.* pp. 172–200. As to England, see Jackson, "Incidence of Jury Trial during the past Century" (1937) 1 M.L.R. 132, and "Jury Trial Today" (1938) 6 Camb.L.J. 367; Glanville Williams, *The Proof of Guilt*, Chap. 10.

The Court of Exchequer

This court was created in 1708 pursuant to the Treaty of Union and consisted of the High Treasurer of Great Britain,[70] a Chief Baron,[71] and four ordinary Barons[71] of Exchequer. The court sat in Edinburgh and was concerned mainly with questions of customs, excise, revenue and Crown debts. During the nineteenth century the functions of the court were curtailed by various statutes and in 1856 it was merged in the Court of Session. Revenue cases coming before the Court of Session continue, however, to be designated Exchequer causes.

The Commissary Courts

The Reformation left undischarged the functions formerly attaching to the courts of the Officials in each diocese by abolishing all jurisdiction depending on papal authority. In 1563 a new Commissary Court was created for Edinburgh and commissaries named for each diocese.[72] The chief court consisted of four with a jurisdiction over the bishopric of Edinburgh and a general jurisdiction over the whole of Scotland in matters of marriage, divorce, legitimacy, status and the moveable succession of Scottish subjects dying abroad or not subject to another jurisdiction. Down to the nineteenth century the commissaries nearly monopolised jurisdiction in actions affecting status and succession, both at first instance and on intermediate appeal, and despite the Reformation continued to develop the law largely in reliance on Continental jurists, canonists and civilians.[73]

In 1823 the inferior commissaries became merged in the sheriff courts, though they were not formally abolished until 1876 and the name still survives in the designation of executry business as "commissary business", just as matrimonial causes are still designated "consistorial causes". The Commissary Court of Edinburgh was suppressed as supreme consistorial court in 1830 and wholly abolished in 1836, since when its functions have been performed by the common law courts.

The Teind Court

An Act of 1708 transferred to the Court of Session in the capacity of Commission for the Plantation of Kirks and Valuation of Teinds, work relating to parish churches and manses, stipends and teinds previously

---

[70] The office of Treasurer has been entrusted since 1714 to a commission consisting of the First Lord of the Treasury, the Chancellor of the Exchequer and the junior Lords of the Treasury. See also, Clerk and Scrope, *Historical View of the Court of Exchequer in Scotland* (1820); *Inland Revenue v. Barrs*, 1959 S.C. 273; affd. 1961 S.C.(H.L.) 22.

[71] From Norman-French *baron*, a man; they were not in any sense peers.

[72] Donaldson, "The Church Courts," in *Introduction to Scottish Legal History*, Chap. 27.

[73] Walton (ed.), *Lord Hermand's Consistorial Decisions 1684–1777* (Stair Society). The work of the court is examined in Leneman, *Alienated Affections: The Scottish Experience of Divorce and Separation. 1684–1830.*

entrusted to various *ad hoc* commissions. The court in this capacity continued to perform numerous administrative and judicial functions, both those of the older commissions and further duties imposed by later legislation. From 1839 the Lords Commissioners of Teinds comprised the judges of the Inner House together with the second junior Lord Ordinary, any five of whom, it was provided in 1868, should form a quorum. Most of the now much diminished work is today done by the second junior Lord Ordinary as Lord Ordinary on Teinds.

The Bill Chamber

The Bill Chamber originated in an Act of Sederunt of 1532 as a Vacation Court, but in addition acquired a special jurisdiction, granting leave to issue certain kinds of privileged summonses and to use certain kinds of diligence. Down to 1933 it retained control of the processes of suspension or suspension and interdict, and in the nineteenth century statute conferred on the Bill Chamber miscellaneous special jurisdictions, particularly in relation to bankruptcy, entails and judicial factories. The Bill Chamber was, during session, under the junior Lord Ordinary and had its own office and staff and a great deal of peculiar and detailed procedure. In 1933 it was merged with the Court of Session and its jurisdiction became ordinary Outer House jurisdiction.

The Legal Profession

The Faculty of Advocates maintained its position as a learned and influential society as well as one of the most honourable professional bodies; its ranks included not only the most distinguished lawyers but also wits, scholars, politicians and men of letters.

The Faculty for long differed from the English Bar in having no formal differentiation between senior and junior[74]; a man "gave up writing" (pleadings) when of sufficient age and experience, but the absence of a distinct status placed the senior advocate in an invidious position when appearing before the House of Lords or meeting English counsel. In 1857–58 the problem of precedence was much discussed and was settled by according ex-law officers precedence postponed only to the Lord Advocate, the Dean of Faculty[75] and the Solicitor-General. In 1892 a petition craving Her Majesty to create a roll of Queen's Counsel in Scotland was granted, since when a formal distinction between senior and junior counsel has subsisted.

The status of the solicitor's profession was immensely promoted by the Law Agents Act of 1873 which for the first time demanded the passing of

---

[74] King's Counsel are known in English law from the 16th century; Bacon did much to define their position and secure their privileges.

[75] A list of the Deans of Faculty in the 19th century will be found in Crabb Watt, *John Inglis*, 111, and lists of Deans since 1698 and Vice-Deans since 1754 in 1972 S.L.T.(News) 217.

examinations as a requirement for admission to practice. The former requirement of apprenticeship continued, and continues as traineeship, but since 1873 a significant feature has been the steadily increasing number of trainees who have graduated in one of the universities. Equally significant has been the increasing number of solicitors employed in local government and in industry.

In 1949 the Law Society of Scotland was established by statute, so that the profession had for the first time a national body including all solicitors. The former societies and the local bodies, however, continued. It acquired further statutory powers in 1958 and exercises a wide authority over the qualification and professional conduct of solicitors. It was set up partly to administer the legal aid scheme introduced in 1949, but this was later transferred to the Scottish Legal Aid Board.

Legal Literature—Hume and Bell

Since the early nineteenth century the greatest contributions to the literature of the law have come from the academic lawyers. David Hume (1756–1838), a nephew of the philosopher of the same name, was Professor of Scots Law at Edinburgh from 1786 to 1822, and published the *Commentaries on the Law of Scotland respecting Crimes* in 1797, a book which has always been accepted as of the highest authority on the subject. He also published a valuable volume of *Decisions* and his academic lectures were highly regarded and frequently cited.[76] They have subsequently been published by the Stair Society.[77] Hume had also been a Principal Clerk of Session contemporaneously with Sir Walter Scott and was promoted a Baron of Exchequer in 1822.[78]

George Joseph Bell (1770–1843), his successor as Professor of Scots Law (1822–43), took an active part in promoting improvements in Court of Session procedure but made his name as a jurist with his *Commentaries on the Law of Scotland and on the Principles of Mercantile Jurisprudence* (1810, based on an earlier book of 1800 on bankruptcy), which set out to systematise the principles of the law merchant and to reconcile them with the fundamental principles of Scots law, and the *Principles of the Law of Scotland*, published originally as a textbook for students (1829) and later revised and enlarged.[79] He published also *Illustrations from Adjudged Cases of the Law of Scotland* (3 vols., 1836–38) as a companion work for students and an early specimen of the students' case-book, and other legal textbooks. He contributed immensely not only to the exposition but also to the creation of mercantile law and to the harmonisation of Scots law on

---

[76] See, *e.g. Biggart v. City of Glasgow Bank* (1879) 6 R. 470, 475–476, *per* Lord Deas.
[77] Ed. Paton, 6 vols. 1939–57 (Stair Society).
[78] See further Paton's *Life of Hume*, in Vol. 6 of the Stair Society edition of the *Lectures*.
[79] Nadelmann, "Joseph Story and George Joseph Bell", 1959 J.R. 31; Gorla, "Bell, one of the Founding Fathers . . .", 1982 J.R. 121.

the topic with the decisions of English and other courts. Bell became a Principal Clerk of Session in 1832 and Lord Advocate Jeffrey would have made him a judge had there been a vacancy. He was also chairman of a royal commission with a wide remit, which produced three important reports. Bell's successor, John Schank More (1784–1861), Professor 1843–61, published a modern, annotated edition of Stair in 1832. His *Lectures* were posthumously published.[80]

Walter Ross, W.S., published in 1792 his *Lectures on the History and Practice of the Law of Scotland relative to Conveyancing and Legal Diligence* which are still valuable and which influenced the Society of Writers to the Signet to institute a lectureship in conveyancing in Edinburgh University, which was promoted to a chair in 1825. The Juridical Society of Edinburgh first published its *Collection of Styles or Complete System of Conveyancing* in 1787–94, a work of great utility to practitioners. In the sphere of jurisprudence some mark was made by James Lorimer of Edinburgh[81] and Galbraith Miller of Glasgow.[82] Archibald Alison, later Sheriff of Lanarkshire, published in 1832–33 his *Principles* and *Practice of the Criminal Law of Scotland,* works which rank second to Hume in that field.[83]

The Bench and Bar in the early nineteenth century continued the tradition of scholarship not confined to the law.[84] Francis Jeffrey was among the brilliant group who founded the *Edinburgh Review,* Henry Cockburn wrote those *Memorials* which are still the finest evocation of the Edinburgh of his young days, while Walter Scott wrote the *Waverley Novels* in the intervals of duty as Principal Clerk of Session and Sheriff-Depute of Selkirk.[85] Thomas Thomson, as depute Clerk Register, laboured to organise and publish many of the invaluable public records, and through the Bannatyne Club published many more volumes of immense historical interest and value.

Later in the century many judges made important contributions to the development of the law. Over the years 1858–91 Lord President Inglis[86] set out in classic judgments many principles of the steadily developing law while Lord McLaren[87] wrote the standard book on *Wills and Succession*

---

[80] Edited by McLaren, 2 vols., 1864.

[81] *Institutes of Law* (1872); *Institutes of the Law of Nations* (1883). On him see Flint, "Professor Lorimer" (1890) 2 J.R. 113; Thomson, "Lorimer's Juristic Theory" (1896) 8 J.R. 242.

[82] *Lectures on the Philosophy of Law* (1884); *Law of Nature and Nations in Scotland* (1896); *The Data of Jurisprudence* (1903).

[83] Michie, *An Enlightenment Tory in Victorian Scotland.*

[84] It is noteworthy that the two greatest biographies in the English language, Boswell's *Life of Johnson* and Lockhart's *Life of Scott,* were written by advocates. At the end of the century R. L. Stevenson was an advocate but did not practise. On him see Guthrie, "R. L. Stevenson" (1919) 31 J.R. 161; (1920) 32 J.R. 71, 129.

[85] McDonald, "Sir Walter Scott's Fee Book" (1950) 62 J.R. 288; Dobie, "Law and Lawyers in the Waverley Novels" (1920) 32 J.R. 244, 317; Marshall, *Sir Walter Scott and Scots Law.*

[86] Crabb Watt, *John Inglis*; McLaren, "Lord President Inglis" (1893) 4 J.R. 14.

[87] Kennedy, "Lord McLaren" (1910) 22 J.R. 181.

and Lord Fraser[88] authoritative books on *Husband and Wife, Parent and Child* and *Master and Servant*. In the House of Lords Lord Watson[89] and, later, Lord Reid[90] were outstanding judges both in Scottish and English cases.

In the twentieth century Lord Dunedin[91] and Lord Cooper[92] were outstanding on the Bench while Professor Sir John Rankine wrote still valuable books on *Land Ownership* and *Leases* and Professor Gloag's book on *Contract* won a high reputation for its breadth and grasp of principle. The foundation of the Stair Society in 1934 showed a quickening interest in Scottish legal history, while the Law Faculties of the universities began to concern themselves as much with the theory, history, philosophy, analysis and criticism of law, and with its wider implications, as with its dogmatic exposition and practical applications, and the foundation of the Scottish Universities Law Institute in 1960 marked the beginning of a major undertaking in restating Scots law in modern form.[93] Since about 1975 there has been also a great proliferation of modern textbooks on many branches of law.

Developments in Public Law

Since 1830 and particularly since 1900 there has been an enormous growth in the bulk and importance of public, particularly administrative, law, in such matters as public health, housing, town and country planning, social security, taxation and the regulation of industry and trade.

Developments in Private Law

The two factors which most influenced the development of Scots law since 1800 have been increasing statutory modification of common law doctrines and increasing reliance on English rather than Roman law as a source for borrowing.[94] Hardly any branch of common law has escaped statutory modification, while many topics of entirely statutory creation have developed. Most of these changes reflect changes in public opinion, in prevailing social, political and economic philosophy, and in conceptions of the functions and responsibilities of the state, or the changes wrought by two world wars, which necessitated an unparalleled amount of state control and interference with matters of private concern.[95] Industrial law

---

[88] Goudy, "Lord Fraser" (1889) 1 J.R. 178.

[89] McNaghten, "Lord Watson" (1899) 11 J.R. 269; Stormonth-Darling, *op. cit.* 272; Haldane, *op. cit.* 278.

[90] Blom-Cooper and Drewry, *Final Appeal*, 156.

[91] "Dunedin, the greatest master of the principles of Scots Law in our time": *per* Lord Macmillan, *Stewart v. L.M.S. Ry.*, 1943 S.C.(H.L.) 19, 38.

[92] See Smith, "The Contribution of Lord Cooper of Culross to the Law of Scotland" (1955) 67 J.R. 249 and in Lord Cooper's *Selected Papers*, xxix.

[93] See 1961 S.L.T.(News) 97.

[94] See also *Introduction to Scottish Legal History*, 53–63.

[95] See generally Dicey, *Lectures on the Relation between Law and Public Opinion in England in the Nineteenth Century*; Ginsberg (ed.), *Law and Opinion in England in the Twentieth Century*; Friedmann, *Law in a Changing Society*; Smith, "Scots Law in the Victorian Era" (1901) 13 J.R. 152; Walker, "Law and Opinion in Britain since 1900" (1956) J.R. 117, 213.

and social welfare legislation[96] are both almost entirely modern statutory creations.

Since about 1800 the central, heavily populated, belt of Scotland has been a largely commercial and industrial area.[97] From 1840 railways became the predominant form of transport. These developments produced great changes in the kinds of legal claims and disputes; industrial accidents and railway accidents gave rise to many cases.[98]

The nineteenth century was a great period for the formulation and working out of legal principles in cases and judicial decisions, and in many branches of the law the basic modern formulation of the principles is still to be found in nineteenth-century cases. In contrast, the twentieth century since 1914 has been concerned increasingly with the interpretation of statutory provisions, and comparatively few common law decisions of really outstanding significance have been pronounced. *Donoghue v. Stevenson*[99] is undoubtedly the principal decision of the century, with the most profound influence on the development of the law.

In nearly all branches of law references to the *Digest* and the civilians have come to be replaced by reference (usually uncritical and too frequently mistaken) to English law and English books.[1] Much unsuitable or misunderstood law has thereby infiltrated into Scotland, and warnings have been uttered from the Bench as to the dangers of ignorant use of non-native sources of law. Students, practitioners, judges and the House of Lords have all on various occasions been decoyed by the similarity of result attained by the two systems into saying that the principle is the same in both countries, or into relying on English authorities or more up-to-date English textbooks.

Statute has effected numerous and far-reaching reforms, especially in property law. The fetters which bound entailed property and rendered it unsaleable and unburdenable with debt had subsisted since Sir George Mackenzie's Act of 1685, relieved only by the Act of 1746, which authorised the sale of entailed hands to the Crown for public purposes, and the Montgomery Act of 1770, which further authorised leasing, powers extended by the Rosebery Act of 1836. The Aberdeen Act of 1824 and the Rutherford Act of 1840 conferred wider powers on the heir of entail, the latter legalising under certain conditions the alienation of the

---

[96] See generally Ferguson, *Dawn of Scottish Social Welfare; Scottish Social Welfare*, 1864–1914; Marwick, *Economic Developments in Victorian Scotland*; Mackinnon, *Social and Industrial History of Scotland*; Hutchins and Harrison, *History of the Factory Acts*.

[97] Lenman, *Economic History of Modern Scotland*, 101 *et seq.*

[98] For early cases arising out of railway accidents see *Morton v. Edinburgh & Glasgow Ry.* (1845) 8 D. 288; *McGlashan v. Dundee & Perth Ry.* (1848) 10 D. 1397; *Cargill v. Dundee & Perth Ry.* (1848) 11 D. 216.

[99] 1932 S.C.(H.L.) 31.

[1] See Henderson, "English Cases as Scots Authorities" (1900) 12 J.R. 304; Burn-Murdoch, "English Law in Scots Practice" (1908–09) 20 J.R. 346; 21 J.R. 59, 148.

estate. Acts of 1875 and 1882 led up to the Act of 1914 which prohibited the creation of future entails.

The feudal system of landholding was simplified and conveyancing shortened by a series of Acts leading up to the Consolidation Act of 1868 while Gordon's Act of 1874 made further sweeping changes in the direction of simplifying land transfer, a process continued in the present century in 1924 and 1938,[2] and carried further by Acts of 1970 and 1974. An Act of 1979 provided for the introduction, in stages, of registration of title to land, which will ultimately greatly simplify conveyancing.

In the Highlands, the proprietors in the late eighteenth and early nineteenth centuries transformed much of the interior of the West and North Highland counties into large sheep-farms, clearing out the crofters and settling them in crofting townships on patches of ground near the coast. When sheep-farming became less profitable owing to wool and mutton coming from Australia and New Zealand, large sheep-farms were turned into deer forests. Population had increased despite emigration, but migration and depopulation followed the clearances and the ruin of the kelp industry.[3] The middle years of the nineteenth century were years of great hardship and destitution. The government remedy was emigration, suggested by a commission in 1841: friction and unrest resulted, evictions for non-payment of rent were common and there were instances in the 1880s of violence, resistance to ejection measures and clashes with the police and the military. A Commission of Enquiry was set up in 1883 which resulted in the Crofters' Holdings Act of 1886, which conferred security of tenure on certain conditions, fixed fair rent, compensation for improvements and gave facilities for the enlargement of holdings. It set up the Crofters' Commission which performed executive and judicial functions until superseded by the Land Court under the Small Landholders Act of 1911.[4] A new Crofters' Commission was set up in 1955 to reorganise and develop crofting in the crofting counties.

The place of agriculture in the Scottish economy has declined steadily since about 1825, though in the nineteenth century the farmers had a secure home market and were aided by flexible rents and a lighter burden of poor law than in England. Moreover, landlords were generally willing to devote resources to agricultural development.

In the law of persons, Brougham's Act of 1856 killed runaway marriages at Gretna Green by requiring three weeks' residence in Scotland for the validity of the marriage; two of the common law forms of irregular marriage were abolished in 1939 and civil marriage introduced, while the grounds of divorce were widened in 1938 and this, combined with the

---

[2] See further Monteath, in *Introduction* (Stair Society), Chap. 14.
[3] See Campbell, *Scotland since 1707*; Mackenzie, *The Highland Clearances*; Prebble, *The Highland Clearances*.
SUP}4 Mackinnon, *Social and Industrial History of Scotland from the Union*, 74.

disturbance to family life effected by the War and a changed social attitude to divorce, made divorce a common form of litigation. From 1861 there was steady progress towards recognising the independent capacity of the married woman and the equality of the spouses. Many statutory changes ameliorated the position of the illegitimate child, while changes in guardianship made the welfare of the child the paramount consideration.[5]

In the nineteenth century, industry and commerce flourished and Scotland exported goods all over the world. Railways were built and roads improved. The coal, iron and steel industries developed rapidly but have declined steadily in the twentieth century. Moreover, rapid industrialisation gave rise to poor housing, drunkenness, pawn shops, payment of wages by the truck system and arrestment of wages for debt, all social problems with legal consequences.[6]

During the nineteenth century, contract increased in importance as commerce flourished. In the second half of the century there were passed the Mercantile Law Amendment Act of 1856, designed to assimilate in large measure the laws of Scotland and of England in business matters and the forerunner of the Sale of Goods Act 1893; the Bills of Exchange Act 1882, and other pieces of partial codification; the Bankruptcy Act of 1856, later superseded by Act of 1913 and then of 1985, and the Merchant Shipping Act 1894 replaced in 1995. In the twentieth century much legislation was directed to the protection of the consumer, for example, the Consumer Credit Act 1974.

Conditions contributed very much to the development of the law of reparation. More settled conditions and greater willingness to abide by the law reduced the number of cases of spuilzie and deliberate wrong-doing. At the same time, increasing use of machinery and the coming of railways and later of road traffic brought more into prominence wrongs of negligence, particularly personal injuries, arising out of travel and industrial accidents. The increasing congestion of the roads similarly gave rise to the large number of traffic offences dealt with in the summary criminal courts.[7] In the twentieth century the decision in *Donoghue v. Stevenson*[8] and the general doctrine there stated of persons owing duties to their neighbour not to harm him by conduct foreseeably liable to do so, gave rise to a flood of claims founded on alleged negligence, such that by the end of the century every person thinking himself damnified in any way, sought damages from someone for some alleged, frequently very far-fetched, breach of duty.

---

[5] See further *Introduction* (Stair Society), Chaps. 8–11.
[6] See further Campbell, *Scotland since 1707*; Idem, *The Rise and Fall of Scottish Industry, 1707–1939*; Marwick, *Economic Developments in Victorian Scotland*; Slaven, *The Development of the West of Scotland, 1750–1960*.
[7] *Ibid.* Chap. 20.
[8] 1932 S.C.(H.L.) 31.

From early in the nineteenth century, legislation strove to improve the position of factory workers and, increasingly, to make provision for their safety, health and welfare. The common law claim of an injured employee for damages for injury was reinforced by recognition of his claim for breach of statutory duty, and by his claims, independently of proof of fault on the employer's part, under the Employers' Liability Act 1880, and subsequently to workmen's compensation (1897) and then to industrial injuries benefit (1946). Trade unions held illegal at common law from 1766 were recognised from 1871 as lawful institutions, and collective bargaining, and conditions of work fixed by statute, arbitration or independent bodies largely replaced individual contracts of employment.[9]

The great extension, enlargement and development of industrial enterprises in the nineteenth century made for conditions with which the private individual and the partnership could not cope. "After 1720, the foundation of joint-stock companies was controlled by the so-called 'Bubble Act' of that year, a panic measure passed by Parliament as a direct consequence of the public scandal caused by the collapse of the South Sea Company. This law prohibited the formation of new joint-stock companies unless sanctioned by private Act of Parliament or Crown charter. The law stood unrepealed until 1825. It never affected the continuance of those aristocrats among the older public companies, the East India Company (founded in 1600) or the Hudson's Bay Company (founded in 1670), or the Bank of England. Long before it was repealed as the need for collective capital increased, the ingenuity of lawyers and business men got round the Act by promoting the formation of unincorporate joint-stock associations."[10] This expedient allowed a considerable growth of company enterprise in certain fields, such as insurance. But the old law of partnerships in an age of business instability and enterprise on larger scales frequently brought ruin because of the absence of limitation on liability.[11] Partnership or unincorporated enterprise was manifestly unsuitable for the great investment in railways after 1840[12]; it had the economic advantages of combined capital but the members' liability for the debts of the concern was unlimited as in partnership, and legal

---

[9] See further, Smith, in *Introduction* (Stair Society), Chap. 12, and "Master and Servant: Further Historical Outlines" (1958) 3 J.R.(N.S.) 215.

[10] Court, *Concise Economic History of Britain from 1750*, 84; see also Brown, "The Genesis of Company Law in England and Scotland" (1901) 13 J.R. 185; Roberton Christie, "Company Law: Joint Stock Enterprise in Scotland before the Companies Acts" (1909) 21 J.R. 128; Holdsworth, "The Early History of Commercial Societies" (1916) 28 J.R. 305; Campbell, "The Law and the Joint Stock Company in Scotland," in Payne (ed.), *Studies in Scottish Business History*, 136.

[11] *cf.* the ruin of Sir Walter Scott in the failure of Ballantyne's in 1825, and the cases arising out of the failure of the City of Glasgow Bank in 1878.

[12] On the development of Scottish railways, see Mackinnon, *Social and Industrial History of Scotland from the Union*, 131–143; Pryde, *op. cit.* 239–240; Robertson, *The Origins of the Scottish Railway System*; Thomas, *Regional History of the Railways of Great Britain*, Vols. 6 and 15.

proceedings by or against the concern were apt to be intricate and laborious. In 1837 it was provided that the privilege of incorporation might be obtained not only by private Act or Crown charter but also by letters patent, and by the Registration Act of 1844 any company might register by a simple process and thereby become incorporated as a single entity in law. In 1856 limited liability was extended to all registered companies. A consolidating Act in 1862 extended the new facilities to insurance companies, and codified the law. Banks were for long excluded from limited liability and for long were also reluctant to take advantage of the privilege, and in consequence the failure of the joint-stock but unlimited City of Glasgow Bank in 1878 caused widespread ruin.[13] In 1879 the legal difficulties in the way of adoption by the banks of limited liability were removed. The law of companies has several times subsequently been consolidated afresh, each time incorporating new provisions designed to protect the investor from fraud, duplicity or misrepresentation.

Criminal law continued to develop with only small statutory interference, but methods of treatment and reformation of criminals were very largely altered in the twentieth century and the rules affecting punishment and treatment have become much more complicated as attempts have been made to humanise and individualise penalties. Procedure was greatly rationalised by the Criminal Procedure Act of 1887 which greatly simplified indictments, a development extended to the summary criminal courts by the Summary Jurisdiction Act 1907 (both replaced in 1975).

In the civil courts, procedure was simplified by the Consolidating Act of Sederunt of 1913, itself superseded by the Rules of Court of 1936 (now 1994), while the Sheriff Courts Acts of 1907 and 1971 continued the same process for the sheriff court.

A tendency of great importance, particularly under social welfare legislation, has been to remove controversies from the courts altogether and to commit them to a great variety of *ad hoc* tribunals.

Overall, the tendency of the years since 1914 has been to interfere more and more with the liberty of the subject, to regulate his actings in more and more ways, and to produce a patchwork of *ad hoc* amendments and alterations of the common law to meet particular difficulties. The tendency towards legal chaos has been strong. Parliament has steadily been working, partly by ignorance, partly by the lack of interest of the majority of members, partly by the desire to unify conditions throughout the United Kingdom, and partly by declining to legislate separately for

---

[13] The directors were tried for fraud in the High Court and received various terms of imprisonment. See Wallace, *Trial of the City of Glasgow Bank Directors* (Notable Scottish Trials Series). The call on the shareholders of the bank was very heavy and this gave rise to much litigation in the next few years, mainly by shareholders seeking to have their names removed from the list of shareholders, and thereby to escape contribution. See also Kerr, *History of Banking in Scotland*; Mackinnon, *Social and Industrial History*, 154.

Scotland, for the destruction of Scots law. Occasionally a feature of Scots law has been adopted for England, but more usually the assumption has been that what will do for England is good for Scotland and Scottish members have too often aided and abetted this process, or at least acquiesced in it.

The Resurgence of National Spirit

Over the years since 1707, despite government or misgovernment from remote London, despite harshness, ignorance, apathy and neglect which treated Scotland sometimes as a rather laughable backwood, sometimes as a conquered, sometimes merely as a forgotten, province, there have never been lacking Scots who preserved the idea of Scotland as a nation, though others sought to ape the English in all things, English speech, English-type education, and English-type law.[14] The struggle for home rule for Ireland in the latter part of the nineteenth century evoked sympathy from the Scottish Liberals, many of whom favoured devolution to local Parliaments, and the Scottish Home Rule Association was instituted, with Liberal support, in 1886 and some propaganda for Scottish self-government thereafter continued. But in 1913 and 1914 the Liberal Government refused to consider a Government of Scotland Bill which would have set up a Scottish Parliament similar to what should, but for the war, have come into being in Ireland.

The issue of home rule reasserted itself in the inter-war years. Bills were put before Parliament between 1918 and 1927 and were shelved, though the Scottish Liberals adopted from 1924 a plan for federal government. Governmental indifference and the troubles of the inter-war years secured that nothing happened.

The wider powers granted to the Scottish Standing Committee in 1948 were a concession to nationalist sentiment, which was further evidenced by local plebiscites and strong approval from the General Assembly of the Church of Scotland for a separate Scottish Parliament. In 1949 nationalist sympathisers organised the Scottish Covenant movement which obtained some two million signatures from persons supporting the principle of a Scottish Parliament. In 1950 a small group removed the Stone of Destiny from Westminster Abbey and transported it to Scotland. It was returned, draped in a saltire flag, to Arbroath Abbey[15] in April 1951, and the incident was dismissed by some as an idiotic prank, an outrage and sacrilege, and viewed by others as a possibly mistaken but sincere

---

[14] See generally, Coupland, *Welsh and Scottish Nationalism*; Paton, *The Claim of Scotland*; Hanham, *Scottish Nationalism*.

[15] An action doubtless intended to, and certainly evoking, memories of the Declaration of Arbroath of 1320, in which the barons of Scotland asserted the liberty of Scotland and declined ever to consent to subject themselves to the dominion of the English. See the text in *Source Book*, I, 151.

expression of indignation at the perpetuation of an ancient wrong, dissatisfaction with alien rule and a blow for their country. In 1996 the Stone was returned to Scotland. In 1952 on the accession of Queen Elizabeth there were protests against the ill-warranted assumption of the title Queen Elizabeth the Second.[16]

Scottish Affairs in Parliament

In Parliament itself some concessions have been made; since 1948 a public Bill certified by the Speaker as relating only to Scotland is referred for consideration in principle to the Scottish Grand Committee, which comprises all the 72 members for Scottish constituencies plus 10 to 15 others so as to maintain the balance of parties in the committee the same as in the House of Commons as a whole. After this the Bill is formally read a second time on the floor of the House and referred for detailed clause-by-clause examination to the Scottish Standing Committee which, set up in 1894 and 1895 and regularly since 1907, comprises 30 members for Scottish constituencies, plus up to 20 more to maintain the balance of parties. Scottish provisions in a United Kingdom Bill may also be referred to the Scottish Standing Committee. The Scottish Grand Committee also since 1948 spends up to six days in any parliamentary session considering the Scottish estimates, as well as two days given to Scottish estimates debates in the full House, and not more than two days in considering specified matters relating exclusively to Scotland which may have been referred for discussion. One of the new Select Committees established in 1979 deals with Scottish affairs and it may question the ministers and senior officials of the Scottish Office on matters for which they are responsible. Since 1899 there has also been the distinctive system of considering private legislation, now regulated by the Private Legislation Procedure (Scotland) Act 1936, whereby a body desiring parliamentary powers applies to the Secretary of State for Scotland for a provisional order granting the desired powers. If the request is opposed, or if an inquiry seems necessary, an inquiry is held in Scotland before four commissioners drawn from panels of members of both Houses of Parliament. If the Secretary of State is satisfied, he makes the order as requested and submits it to Parliament for ratification scheduled to a provisional order confirmation Act, which is dealt with under an expedited procedure. This has almost completely superseded private Bill procedure in Scotland.

Scottish Administration

Prior to 1885 Scottish administration was handled nominally by the Home Secretary and in practice by the Lord Advocate. In that year was

---

[16] See *MacCormick v. Lord Advocate*, 1953 S.C. 396. It seems that the question of the Queen's title was just assumed, the Scottish part in forming the United Kingdom and possible Scottish feeling being forgotten. The form of proclamation used in all Commonwealth countries also, equally wrongly, used the number.

created the office of Secretary for Scotland and there were transferred to him the functions of the Home Secretary relative to Scotland, and certain others discharged by the Privy Council, the Treasury and the Local Government Board. He also became responsible to Parliament for the independent Scottish boards by that time established in Edinburgh, namely, the Board of Supervision (later the Local Government Board for Scotland), the Fishery Board, the Prison Commission, and the General Board of Commissioners in Lunacy (later the General Board of Control for Scotland). Further boards were created later, notably the Congested Districts (Scotland) Commissioners (1897), the Scottish Insurance Commissioners (1911), the Board of Agriculture for Scotland (1912) and the Highlands and Islands (Medical Services) Board (1913). The Scottish Board of Health on its creation in 1919 took over the functions of the Local Government Board for Scotland, the Scottish Insurance Commissioners and the Highlands and Islands (Medical Services) Board.

In 1926 the office of Secretary for Scotland was promoted to that of one of His Majesty's Principal Secretaries of State, and the holder then became Secretary of State for Scotland. In 1928 the Scottish Board of Agriculture, the Scottish Board of Health and the Scottish Prison Commissioners were replaced by the Department of Agriculture for Scotland, the Department of Health for Scotland and the Prisons Department for Scotland, each a statutory body independent of the Secretary of State, but under his control and direction. In the 1930s there was a substantial movement of offices and staff from London to Edinburgh; in 1939 St. Andrew's House, Edinburgh, was opened as the Secretary of State's headquarters, the London office remaining mainly for liaison purposes with Parliament and with departments based in London. Also in 1939 the Reorganisation of Offices (Scotland) Act abolished the independent departments and vested their functions in the Secretary of State, which he accordingly exercised through several departments. In addition many Great Britain Departments of State, such as the Ministry of Social Security, have regional offices in Scotland.

The ministerial staff responsible for Scottish affairs has also increased; a Parliamentary Under-Secretary of State was appointed in 1919, a second in 1940 and a third in 1951; in that year also a Minister of State, Scottish Office, was appointed as the Secretary of State's principal deputy; the Lord Advocate and Solicitor-General for Scotland are also available for assistance, though they may not be Members of Parliament.

Since 1945 the Secretary of State's responsibilities have several times been extended. Thus in 1954 he became responsible for Scottish roads, and for the appointment of Justices of the Peace in Scotland. In addition numerous independent bodies, such as the Crofters' Commission (1955), the Red Deer Commission (1959), the Highlands and Islands Development Board (1965) (now Scottish Enterprise and Highlands and Islands

Enterprise (1990)), Scottish Homes (1988) and the like, have close contact with the Secretary of State's Department.[17]

There have accordingly been material moves towards transferring authority from London to Edinburgh. But Parliament, eager to thrust self-government on many underdeveloped and politically immature parts of the Commonwealth—some trivial in size, importance and capacity, and many with no native tradition of law and government—stubbornly refused to consider any real devolution of power, despite growing evidence of pressure of business on Parliament and constant pleas of lack of time to legislate for Scotland.

Inadequacies of the System

These steps have not satisfied many people. The Scottish Standing and Scottish Grand Committees have no powers of legislative initiative, nor of veto. They can consider a Bill affecting Scotland at certain stages, but only if and when the Cabinet has decided to legislate for Scotland, and in the terms thus decided. Even the unanimous wish of all the Scottish M.P.s for a Bill could not cause such a Bill to be introduced, and a power of amendment in committee (subject to being wiped out at a later stage) is no equivalent for a power to decide when and whether and in what terms to legislate. Conversely, if the Cabinet resolved to bring in a Bill, say, to abolish Scots law or the Presbyterian Church, the unanimous opposition of the Scottish M.P.s would not necessarily be able to secure its rejection. Also many fundamental matters of principle are decided for the United Kingdom and it is then a matter of enacting the principle in the terms of the two legal systems. Many fundamental issues are contained in United Kingdom Acts which could not be considered by the Scottish Committee in either of its forms. Scots law is made and unmade, and commonly mangled and ruined, in a legislative assembly in which the Scottish members are outnumbered by eight to one, a body the great majority of whose members have no interest or need to know or to care about the law or government of Scotland. The people of Scotland are not masters of their own fate in law or government. Their strong desire may be ignored, or outvoted in a House of Commons two-thirds empty, and they cannot lawfully resist the most outrageous destruction of their institutions.

These matters have become important only over the past 100 years or so because of, on the one hand, the extensions of the franchise and, on the other, the enormous growth in governmental control and interference with the life of the individual, with liberty of action, with freedom of contract, and with law generally. A basic trouble has been that power and patronage

---

[17] Report of the Royal Commission on Scottish Affairs, 1953–54 (Cmd. 9219, 1954), Appx. 2—Summary of the History of Scottish Administration; Milne, *The Scottish Office*; *Handbook on Scottish Administration* (1967 ed.).

have always lain in London and a Member of Parliament must be an obedient and diligent servant of the London-based and London-centred parties. There is no room in modern British politics for the non-conformist or for independence of mind or thought. It is alleged that Scotland has full control of its affairs by having their administration in Scotland, but the administration merely executes the policy and gives effect to the ideas of others elsewhere. St. Andrew's House has freedom of action only within limits and only to execute what has been enacted in London.

The Balfour Commission to inquire into Scottish Affairs, set up in 1951 was precluded from considering Home Rule and the Labour Party rejected it in 1958 in favour of more central direction.

In the late 1960s the feeling grew stronger. In 1967 the Scottish Nationalist candidate won a parliamentary seat at Hamilton and candidates of that party made extensive gains all over the country in local authority elections. The Liberal Party in 1966 and 1968 introduced Bills to give Scotland and Wales separate Parliaments on lines generally similar to that created for Northern Ireland in 1920.

In May 1968 the Leader of the Opposition, Mr Heath, proposed the creation of an elected Scottish Assembly to take part in legislation in conjunction with Parliament, the details to be worked out by a constitutional committee. The precise constitution, powers and functions of this body were left very vague. Later in the same month, the General Assembly of the Church of Scotland overwhelmingly approved a recommendation whereby it, "convinced of the need for an effective form of self-government in Scotland within the framework of the United Kingdom, [asked] Her Majesty's Government for the early appointment of a royal commission, consisting of Scots widely representative of Scottish interests, to meet in Scotland with powers to call for evidence, to make recommendations which may enable the people of Scotland to choose the form and extent of self-government best suited to the nation's well-being, and to treat the matter with the utmost urgency." A few months later the government announced the setting up of a Royal Commission on the constitutional structure of the United Kingdom and the question of devolution.

A report on Scotland's government[18] by a committee appointed by the Conservative party proposed the creation of a Scottish Assembly with power to co-ordinate regional views, meet and question Scottish ministers, discuss government proposals and debate matters of concern to Scotland, and power to participate in the framing and passage of Scottish legislation.

The Royal Commission on the Constitution[19] rejected both the separation of Scotland from the United Kingdom and the creation of a federal

---

[18] *Scotland's Government* (Scottish Constitutional Committee, 1970).
[19] Report, Cmnd. 5460, 1973.

structure, but recommended a measure of devolution, in the form of the creation of an elected regional assembly.

In 1974 the number of Scottish Nationalist M.P.s rose to 11, and the Labour government then elected had included in its manifesto a pledge to create a directly-elected Scottish Assembly. Parliament eventually passed the Scotland Act 1978 which provided for an elected Scottish Assembly with power to pass Scottish Assembly Acts on a wide range of subjects, including courts and civil and criminal law generally, and for a Scottish Executive. Section 85 provided that the Act could be brought into force only if in a referendum in Scotland a majority, and at least 40 per cent of the persons entitled to vote, voted yes on the question whether it should be brought into force.[20] This condition not having been satisfied, the Act was repealed. But further measures were introduced to devolve administration to Scotland and allow special treatment of Scottish business in Parliament. Agitation, however, continued for changes, varying from devolution to full independence. Many bodies of opinion came together in what became the Scottish Constitutional Convention. It published in 1989 a *Claim for Right for Scotland*[21] as a declaration of policy, which included a claim for "the constitutional rights Scotland expects within the United Kingdom", a request for a Scottish Parliament with legislative powers, and in 1995, *Scotland's Parliament, Scotland's Right*, which contained proposals for a scheme of devolution.

The government elected in 1997 promised to hold a referendum in Scotland to ascertain whether people in Scotland wanted a Scottish Parliament and for it to have tax-varying powers. The Referendum (Scotland and Wales) Act 1997 authorised this and a referendum was held in September 1997; votes on both heads were in favour[22] and effect was given to the vote by the Scotland Act 1998; though it was little scrutinised in the Commons debates, the Lords highlighted many difficulties. Following the vote in the referendum the Secretary of State for Scotland appointed a Consultative Steering Group which produced a report in January 1999, *Shaping Scotland's Parliament*, which served as a model for the Scottish Parliament's first Standing Orders.

The Scottish Parliament

It is important to observe some fundamental points. The Scottish Parliament created was not a revival or recreation of the parliament

---

[20] The electorate was estimated to number 3.74 million and the voting was: Yes—1.23m (33 per cent.); No—1.15m (31 per cent.); Abstained—1.36m (36 per cent.).

[21] There had been at least two previous Claims of Right, that issued by the Scottish Convention in 1689 as a prelude to offering the crown of Scotland to William and Mary, and that of 1842 passed by the General Assembly of the Church of Scotland stating its case for legislation abolishing lay patronage in the Kirk.

[22] Of those who voted: 74.3 per cent voted for a Scottish parliament (composition and power not yet disclosed) and 25.7 per cent against; and 63.5 per cent voted for tax-varying powers and 36.5 per cent against. The percentages of the electorate were: for a parliament, 41.5 per cent; for no parliament, 13.8 per cent; did not vote 44 per cent. The Yes vote accordingly did not secure a majority of the electorate. The strongest voice was that of the abstainers.

dissolved in 1707, which was differently constituted; nor was it, like the 1707 parliament, a sovereign parliament with powers legally unrestrained; nor was it part of a federal structure in which powers are divided between a central (federal) parliament and the state or provincial parliaments, the division being defined by a constitution, as in the U.S. or Germany. It is a subordinate body to which certain powers have been devolved or handed down by the Westminster Parliament. Section 28 of the 1998 Act provides that it may make laws within its field of competence, but (ss.7) "this section does not affect the power of the Parliament of the United Kingdom to make laws for Scotland". Accordingly, Westminster still has full power to legislate even in an area, *e.g.* criminal law, devolved to Holyrood and can at any time legislate if it chooses to do so or if Holyrood failed to do so, or overrule anything in Holyrood legislation, or repeal anything Holyrood did. Westminster moreover retains power to extend or restrict the powers of Holyrood or even to abolish it. Devolution, accordingly, has not affected the existence of the United Kingdom as the state recognised in international law, and by the other nation-states, nor conferred on Holyrood absolute power to legislate in any field or any topic. The unity of the United Kingdom and the supremacy of the Westminster Parliament continue unqualified. Many enactments are protected from modification by Act of the Scottish Parliament[23] and the law on reserved matters cannot be modified[24] nor can the Scotland Act itself be modified, save for exceptions.[25]

Structure of the Scottish Parliament

The Act provided for a Scottish Parliament of 129 members, 73 elected on the simple majority, *i.e.* first past the post, system by the 72 constituencies which return members to Westminster, but with Orkney and Shetland divided into two constituencies,[26] plus 56 regional members elected on the additional member system of proportional representation, seven from each of the eight regional constituencies used until 1999 for elections to the European Parliament. Each political party prepared a list, in its order of preference, of persons who would take places. These are sometimes distinguished as "constituency" members and "list" members, but all have equal status and powers and are designated M.S.P. Every part of the country is represented by a constituency and a share of the seven list members of the old European constituency. The complicated system goes far, however, to secure that the composition of the parliament agrees fairly closely with the votes cast for the different parties, assuming, which

---

[23] Sched. 4, Pt I, para. 1.
[24] Sched. 4, Pt I, para. 2. On reserved matters see Sched. 5 (which extends to 18 pages).
[25] Sched. 4, Pt I, para. 4.
[26] This involves that some constituencies, notably Orkney, Shetland and the Western Isles, contain quite modest electorates, very much smaller that those of many on the mainland.

is generally the case, that the voters vote for the persons of the same party in both their constituency and list votes. The system, however, stresses party affiliation of candidates and play down voters' personal regard for candidates.[27] Definition of the membership of the Scottish Parliament by reference in part to the constituencies in use for Westminster implies that if the number of these is changed for any reason the size of the Scottish Parliament will automatically be changed.

The Scottish Parliament is unicameral and not divided into Lords and Commons. Accordingly, members of the Lords in Westminster can both vote for and be elected to the Scottish Parliament.[28] So can clergy. An M.S.P. can also be an M.P. Parliaments are elected for a fixed term of four years,[29] but may be dissolved at any time if a two-thirds majority of the Parliament as a whole votes for dissolution, or it is unable to nominate a First Minister within 28 days.

Presiding Officer and administration

At its first meeting after a General Election, the parliament elects from its members a Presiding Officer and two deputies.[30] There is a Scottish Parliamentary Corporate Body to provide the parliament with property, staff and services. It appoints a Clerk of the Parliament and Assistant Clerks.

VI.—SOME FACTORS IN SCOTTISH LEGAL HISTORY

It is desirable, finally, to abstract some elements which have been powerful factors at different times in shaping Scottish legal history.

Christianity

Christianity and the Bible were influential in the formative years of the common law, both directly, influencing legislation, such as the Incest Act and the Marriage Act of 1567, and indirectly, promoting regard for honour, fairness, honourable conduct and regard for women and children. Much older legislation was based on general acceptance of Christianity and its moral values. For centuries judges were influenced by Christian faith.

---

[27] In the first election (May 1999) there was an electoral turnout of only 58%. Seats and shares of the vote were divided as follows: Constituency votes— Con–0 (16%), Lab–53 (39%), Lib-Dem–12 (14%), S.N.P. 7 (20%), Other–1 (3%); Party Lists— Con–18 (15%), Lab–3 (35%), Lib-Dem–5 (13%), S.N.P. 28 (28%), Other–2 (3%); Total seats— Con–18, Lab–56, Lib-Dem–17, S.N.P. 35, Other–3. As no party secured an absolute majority (65 seats) an Executive was formed by Labour-Lib.Dem. coalition. The low turnout seems to indicate lack of enthusiasm for the existence of the parliament.

[28] In the May 1999 election three Lords were elected: Lord Selkirk of Douglas (Con.), Lord Watson of Invergowrie (Lab.) and Lord Steel of Aikwood (Lib.Dem.).

[29] Hence elections are due in 2003, 2007, etc.

[30] The first Presiding Officer elected was Lord Steel of Aikwood (Lib.Dem) who as David Steel had been leader of the Lib.Dems. at Westminster.

Roman Law

Roman law was profoundly influential in the times of the earlier institutional writers and its force is not yet exhausted.[31] It has been the traditional fundamental training in legal science, a quarry of principles, terminology and examples, was accepted as influential in many cases, and was a constant subject of study and source for principles to supplement indigenous doctrines. It was never "received" or adopted entire in Scotland as it was in Germany, but various principles were woven into the texture of the native law, and no statement of the law of Scotland can avoid reference to it. It was the basis of Scots law on pupils and minors, tutors and curators, moveable property, securities, servitudes, succession to moveables, and parts of contract, quasi-contract and delict.[32] Since 1800, however, it has declined in importance and is not now a major force in the development of the law. "Roman law then, is probably spent as a source of new law in Scotland; it is rare for the *Corpus Juris* to be cited in the Court of Session. But the Roman notions which were introduced into Scots law during its formative period were embedded so firmly in its structure that many parts still bear an unmistakably Roman stamp; they cannot be fully comprehended without a knowledge of the Roman institutions from which they derive."[33] It would, however, be advantageous if there were more tendency today, in default of immediate authority, to look to the Roman law and systems founded thereon such as the Roman-Dutch law of South Africa than to the English common law for guidance.

Canon Law

The pre-Reformation canon law of the Roman Church, in Scotland as elsewhere, has had a lasting influence on the law of the personal and domestic relations, marriage, separation and divorce, wills and succession. But the canon law has also had its influence on contract and on the form

---

[31] See Goudy, *The Fate of Roman Law North and South of the Tweed*, 1894; Dove Wilson, "Historical Development of Scots Law" (1896) 8 J.R. 217; *idem*, "The Reception of Roman Law in Scotland" (1897) 9 J.R. 361; Miller, "Reception of Roman Law in Scotland" (1923) 35 J.R. 362; Baird Smith in *Sources and Literature of Scots Law* (Stair Society) 171; Mackintosh, *Roman Law in Modern Practice*; Campbell, "The Romanisation of Scottish Law" (1942) 22 Bost. U.L.R. 581; Fisher, "Scotland and the Roman Law" (1947) 22 Tulane L.R. 13; Stein, "Influence of Roman Law on the Law of Scotland" (1957) 23 *Studia et Documenta Historiae et Juris*, 149, and (1963) J.R. 205; Smith, "Strange Gods: The Crisis of Scots Law as a Civilian System" (1959) 4 J.R.(N.S.) 119; Campbell, "Diritto scozzese e diritto romano," in *Bartolo Sassoferrato, Studi e Documenti per il VI centenario*. I, 75 (1962); Stein, "Roman Law in Scotland" in *Jus Romanum Medii Aevi*, V, part. 13b; Evans-Jones (ed.) *The Civil Law Tradition in Scotland* (Stair Society) (1995); Carey-Miller and Zimmermann (eds) *The Civilian Tradition and Scots Law* (1997).

[32] For modern examples of the acceptance of Roman law principles in Scotland see *Central Motors v. Cessnock Garage Co.*, 1925 S.C. 796; *Wills' Trs. v. Cairngorm School Ltd.*, 1976 S.C.(H.L.) 30; *Sloan's Dairies v. Glasgow Corp.*, 1977 S.C. 223.

[33] Stein, "The Influence of Roman Law on the Law of Scotland" (1963) J.R. 205, 245.

of deeds and writs.[34] In most branches, however, its influence is largely spent and the canonical principles have been overlaid by legislation and a native tradition of decisions. Nevertheless, even in the twentieth century its force cannot be ignored and resort may still have to be had to the texts and commentaries thereon.

Feudal Law

The medieval feudal law which came from Normandy through England has been the source, and is still the basis, of the land law and of heritable property.[35] In Scotland, particularly since the War of Independence, it has developed on its own lines and Scotland at once preserved a feudal system simpler and closer to the original than did England, and also avoided the complications imported into England by the premature rigidity of the common law, the consequent rise of equity and the growth of a dual system of legal and equitable interests in property.[36]

The Law Merchant

The law merchant was the embodiment of customs and usages established by general convenience and a common sense of justice for the carrying on of trade, gradually and continuously recognised, first locally and eventually internationally. The principles of mercantile law have always been to some extent international, having been developed by the trading intercourse of mercantile communities largely independently of their national systems of law. The trading relations of Scotland with the Continent necessitated and stimulated the adoption of customary rules widely accepted abroad, and strengthened the legal connections with these principles common to Western Europe, to the countries of which, in consequence, Scots law in these branches shows close affinities.

The writings of Bell[37] and adoption of principles already accepted by English courts were material factors in introducing principles from the law merchant.

The development of commercial law in the last two centuries has been greatly stimulated by the industrial revolution and the development of Britain as a great commercial and trading community with commercial interests and connections all over the world. The courts steadily developed mercantile customs and incorporated them into the general body of law,

---

[34] In 1775 Lord Hailes said (*Maxwell v. Gordon*, Hailes' Decisions, 624): "The Canon Law is not the Law of Scotland, but the Law of Scotland contains much of the Canon Law. This is so certain that, in many cases, we determine according to the Canon Law, without knowing it." On canon law influence, see further, Baird Smith, "Canon Law," in *Sources and Literature of Scots Law* (Stair Society), 183; Hermand's *Consistorial Decisions*, ed. Walton (Stair Society), *passim*.

[35] *cf.* Farran, *Principles of Scots and English Land Law*.

[36] See further, Girvan, "Feudal Law" in *Sources and Literature of Scots Law* (Stair Society), 193.

[37] See Bell, *Comm.*, Preface.

but there was and is no distinct and self-contained body of commercial rules, as in some foreign codes and legal systems.

The Maritime Law

The general maritime law of Europe was also of a largely international character in the Middle Ages and was administered in local courts like the law merchant. Gradually the great maritime codes were recognised as authoritative and much Roman principle came to be incorporated. Later the Court of Admiralty developed the principles as does its successor, the Court of Session. From the seventeenth century, maritime law in Scotland and England developed on similar lines and in both it was absorbed into the general body of the common law and it is now common to the United Kingdom.

English Law

From early times there has been some borrowing from England. Since 1800 English law has been a most powerful factor, not so often imported on its merits as taken over and applied by mistake, in ignorance, through reliance on English books or cases, frequently without appreciation of the subtle differences between the two systems of law, and by subordination to a single Parliament often ignorant and careless of Scottish conditions, traditions and sentiment, composed of men sometimes more concerned with party than with country, and by the existence of an ultimate appeal in civil causes to a court composed as to a majority of English lawyers with no necessary knowledge of, qualification in, or sympathy with, the principles of Scots law. In most branches of public law, mercantile and industrial law, contract and delict, English influence has been powerful; its influence has been least in land law and succession. The much greater number of reported cases has led to English cases being cited and followed too often without regard to their consistency with Scottish principles. No branch of law has escaped the influence of legislation, frequently imbued with an English spirit and cast in English models of terminology and procedure, albeit sometimes "translated" for Scotland, while too often Scottish appeals to the House of Lords have been judged from the standpoint of what English law would sanction. The warnings of Bell and some of the greatest Scottish judges against the promiscuous citation, acceptance and following of English authorities have constantly to be borne in mind, of the danger of spoiling Scots law by misunderstanding and misapplying English law.[38]

European Law

The rapidly increasing volume of regulation emanating from the European Communities and pursuance of the policy of imposition of

---

[38] See Brodie-Innes, "Some Outstanding Differences between English and Scots Law" (1914–16) 26 J.R. 396; 27 J.R. 28, 175, 312; 28 J.R. 62; Smith, "English Influences on the Law of Scotland," in *Studies Critical and Comparative*, 116.

common rules is steadily assimilating parts of Scots law (particularly in commercial matters) to that being imposed on the member states.

The Threat to the Scottish Legal Tradition

The greatest threat today to the Scottish legal tradition lies in Scotland, in the apathy and ignorance of Scotsmen, in their failure to study, cherish, conserve, restate and develop their traditional principles. Facile acceptance of English books and judgments, acceptance of English legal training as of value in Scotland, ignorance of everything but narrow practicalities, unwillingness and inability to search far back for a true principle consistent with the traditional development of the native law, have all militated against the vigorous survival of Scots law. So, too, the growth in parliamentary powers and the ubiquity of legislation have accompanied a decline in the quality of Parliament and an interest in power, and in party and class advantage, rather than in good legislation and government.

Beyond that, the Scottish legal tradition is in danger, like so many other national and traditional institutions, from the modern tendency to amalgamate the smaller into, and identify it with, the larger, to prescribe from the centre a dead uniformity and to obliterate individual characteristics, to abolish the well-settled and replace by untried new, and from modern ignorance of the value of the native law. The growing dominance of Europe is a major threat to Scots law. Such tendencies spell the end of what is left of Scotland's independent life and culture, her law included. But Scots law is part of Scotland's heritage. "The Scottish legal tradition is a thing to be prized both in Scotland and beyond its borders, and the public of Scotland should be more conscious of the fact. It is in a very real sense a typical product of the Scottish ethos, and has attracted to its enthusiastic service some of the greatest figures in our country's history. . . . The truth is that law is the reflection of the spirit of a people, and so long as the Scots are conscious that they are a people, they must preserve their law."[39]

FURTHER READING

The general histories of Hume Brown, Dickinson and Pryde, Lynch, the Edinburgh History of Scotland (4 vols.) and the New History of Scotland (8 vols.) give the background. More specifically legal are:

Barrow: *The Anglo-Norman Era in Scottish History.*
Brunton and Haig: *Historical Account of the Senators of the College of Justice.*
Campbell: *Lives of the Lord Chancellors,* 10 vols.
Cockburn: *Life of Lord Jeffrey.*
　　　　　Memorials of his Time.
　　　　　Journal.
　　　　　Circuit Journeys.

---

[39] Cooper, "Scottish Legal Tradition," in *Selected Papers*, 197–198, 199.

Cooper (Lord): *Selected Papers.*
Cowan: *The Lord Chancellors of Scotland,* 2 vols.
Dicey and Rait: *Thoughts on the Union between England and Scotland.*
Fergusson: *The Sixteen Peers of Scotland.*
Fraser Tytler: *Memoirs of the Life and Writings of Henry Home of Kames,* 2 vols.
Fry: *The Dundas Despotism.*
Grant: *The Faculty of Advocates in Scotland, 1532–1943* (Scottish Record Society).
Hannay: *The College of Justice,* reprinted in *The College of Justice* (Stair Society).
           Early History of the Scottish Signet, in revised *History of the Society of Writers to H.M. Signet,* reprinted in *The College of Justice* (Stair Society).
Heuston: *Lives of the Lord Chancellors,* I 1885–1940 and II 1940–70.
Howden: "History of the Scottish Constitution" (1898–99) 10 J.R. 64; 11 J.R. 209.
Hume Brown: *Union of England and Scotland.*
Innes: *Scotch Legal Antiquities.*
        Scotland in the Middle Ages.
        Sketches of Early Scotch History.
Kames: *Historical Law Tracts.*
Keir: *Constitutional History of Modern Britain since 1485.*
Lang: *Sir George Mackenzie of Rosehaugh.*
Lehmann: *Henry Home, Lord Kames, and the Scottish Enlightenment.*
Mackay: *Memoir of Sir James Dalrymple, First Viscount Stair.*
Mackinnon: *Union of England and Scotland.*
            Constitutional History of Scotland.
McLarty (ed.): *Source-book and History of Administrative Law in Scotland.*
Marshall: *Sir Walter Scott and Scots Law.*
Menary: *Life and Letters of Duncan Forbes of Culloden.*
Milne: *The Scottish Office.*
Murray: *Early Burgh Organisation in Scotland,* 2 vols.
         Legal Practice in Ayr and the West of Scotland.
Omond: *Arniston Memoirs.*
        The Lord Advocates of Scotland, 3 vols.
Paton: *The Claim of Scotland.*
Phillipson: *The Scottish Whigs and the Reform of the Court of Session, 1785–1830* (Stair Society).
Pryde: *The Treaty of Union.*
Rait: *The Parliaments of Scotland.*
Rait and Pryde: *Scotland.*
Ross: *Lord Kames and the Scotland of his Day.*
Speirs: "Catalogue of Senators of the College of Justice, 1834–1972," in 1972 S.L.T. (News) 233; sequel 1979 S.L.T. (News) 323.
Stair Society: *Sources and Literature of Scots Law.*
                Introduction to Scottish Legal History.
Terry: *The Scottish Parliament, 1603–1707.*
Walker: *Legal History of Scotland,* 6 vols. (to 1900).
         The Scottish Jurists.
W.S. Society: *History of the Society of Writers to Her Majesty's Signet.*
Wight: *Inquiry into the Rise and Progress of Parliament, chiefly in Scotland.*
    See also publications of the Stair Society, Scottish History Society, Scottish Burgh Records Society, Scottish Record Society, Scottish Text Society, Maitland, Bannatyne and Spalding Clubs, Proceedings of the Society of Antiquaries in Scotland, and of local antiquarian and historical societies, and articles in periodicals, particularly the *Juridical Review* and *Scottish Historical Review.*

CHAPTER 5

THE STRUCTURE OF SCOTS LAW

THE great body of doctrines, principles and rules which comprise Scots law
can be grouped so as to form a logical structure with major divisions, subdivisions, branches, headings and sub-headings, and an understanding of
this logical structure is an aid to study and understanding of the principles
and rules and important in the practical task of finding and applying the
law.[1] It is important to understand the whole structure so as to see the
relations of different divisions to one another, or, to put it metaphorically,
to have a bird's eye view of the whole territory, to know where the
different areas lie in relation to one another, before exploring any one.
There are various possible bases of division,[2] but the most generally
valuable one is based on classification of the principles and rules according
to the concepts used; concepts are ideas of classes of objects of thought,
general notions or ideas, and on the basis of certain legal concepts one can
bring together legal principles and rules which have something in common. For example, the concept of "contract" embraces many general
principles and many more detailed rules all applicable to certain facts with
a common element, namely, involving an agreement of two people to do
something to or for each other. Hence, "contract" is a major sub-division
of the whole body of the law and a pigeon-hole in which one can classify
many rules about transactions between people. Within this, one may
classify in more detail under various headings and sub-headings, such as
contracts of sale, of hiring, of employment, of insurance, and so on. In its
structure Scots law accords generally with the common pattern of modern
Western legal systems,[3] though differing in details and having its own
nomenclature for many of the categories. In codified systems the chapter
headings of the Code provide a structure; in an uncodified system it is for
the jurists to develop a structure.

---

[1] In essence this is the application of classification theory to the body of norms which
constitutes Scots law.

[2] One could group rules according to the function of the rules, or their consequences or the
kind of rights involved, or the sets of facts to which they apply, and some books do deal with
rules on the basis of facts, *e.g.* the law as to animals, or road traffic, or industrial relations. Even
an alphabetical classification, as in encyclopaedias or the *Index to the Statutes* or *Current Law*,
requires selection of concepts, *e.g.* contract, housing, negligence, as headings under which
particular rules may be grouped.

[3] Chap. 2, Branch 6, *supra.*

Public and Private Law

The fundamental division between public and private law, recognised in Roman law and in Continental legal systems, is recognised in Scotland. According to Stair[4]: "Rights . . . are divided into public and private rights. Public rights are those which concern the state of the commonwealth. Private rights are the rights of persons and particular incorporations . . . " Similarly, Erskine[5] wrote: "The public law is that which hath more immediately in view the public weal and the preservation and good order of society; as laws concerning the constitution of the State, the administration of the government, the police of the country, public revenue, trade and manufactures, the punishment of crimes, etc. Private law is that which is chiefly intended for ascertaining the civil rights of individuals." The distinction accordingly is generally one of whether the interests of the state, its departments or agencies are involved or not. It may be important for the purposes of choice of remedy and of procedure. Thus, judicial review is appropriate only in cases raising issues of public law, not private law disputes.[6]

In Scotland, and in England, no clear or rigid division can be drawn between those two major bodies of law, largely because of the absence of any written constitution and of special courts or procedure for dealing with issues of public law generally. Only to a limited extent are there special courts charged with matters of public law, in that some controversies of specified kinds are determined not by ordinary civil courts but by statutory tribunals, and even then appeal sometimes lies to the superior civil courts.[7] Public law issues may arise in the context of purely private law disputes in the civil courts[8] as much as in administrative tribunals or criminal courts, and government departments and public bodies commonly sue and are sued in the civil courts like private persons.[9] Moreover, the growth of governmental interference with many kinds of private law relationships, such as employment and leases, commercial and industrial enterprises, and the all-pervading effect of taxation, make it impossible to regard the two bodies as self-contained or clearly distinguished.

---

[4] I, 1, 23. Similarly Bankton, I, 1, 53.

[5] I, 1, 29. The distinction is also found in Art. 18 of the Articles of Union of 1707, and is used by William Forbes in his *Institutes* (1722) and Gilbert Stuart's *Observations concerning the Public Law of Scotland* (1779). See also *Gibson v. Lord Advocate*, 1975 S.C. 136, 141; *O'Reilly v. Mackman* [1982] 3 All. E.R. 680, 692; *Mercury Communications v. Director General of Telecommunications* [1996] 1 W.L.R. 48.

[6] *Connor v. Strathclyde R.C.*, 1986 S.L.T. 530; *Bank of Scotland v. IMRO*, 1989 S.L.T. 432; *Tehrani v. Argyll & Clyde Health Board*, 1990 S.L.T. 118; *Criper v. Edinburgh University*, 1991 S.L.T. 129.

[7] Chap. 8, *infra*.

[8] *e.g. McKie v. Western S.M.T. Co.*, 1952 S.C. 206; *Whitehall v. Whitehall*, 1957 S.C. 30; *Gibson, supra*.

[9] *e.g. Palmer v. Inverness Hospitals Board*, 1963 S.C. 311; *Peter Holmes & Son v. Secretary of State for Scotland*, 1965 S.C. 1; *Bulkeley-Gavin v. Inland Revenue*, 1965 S.C. 232; *Ayr Magistrates v. Secretary of State for Scotland*, 1965 S.C. 394.

Social security and tax law seem to belong more appropriately to public than to private law though they have substantial impacts on private law issues. Criminal law is particularly appropriately classified as public rather than private law in Scotland because the prosecution of criminal charges is almost invariably carried through in Scotland by officials acting in the public interest, and not by wronged individuals.[10] But the sources and literature of criminal law are distinct from those of the rest of public law and criminal law is usually regarded as a separate branch of public law.

Administrative, Criminal and Civil Law

The divisions between administrative, criminal and civil law are also well recognised in Scots law but are hard to define. They depend fundamentally on the purpose and methods of application of the particular rules, administrative law existing to define and apply principles of public policy, *e.g.* in relation to taxation, housing, planning or social security, in particular cases, criminal existing to define what kinds of conduct are deemed objectionable or harmful to the community as a whole and to repress infringements thereof by the punishment of the offenders, and civil existing to define the mutual rights and duties of persons and to provide remedies where one has failed to implement his legal duties to or has had his legal rights breached by the other. There are distinct sets of administrative, criminal and civil courts and tribunals with their separate bodies of procedure.[11] Though the line of division is frequently clear, being determined by the purpose of the proceedings, the courts in which and the procedure by which matters fall to be decided, there are difficult cases,[12] and anomalies such as the rule that children's hearings, dealing largely with children who have committed offences, are deemed to be civil, not criminal.[13]

In general, much of the public law is administrative or civil in character and only some of the public law is criminal; all of the private law is civil. In so far as this distinction depends on the courts and procedure whereby cases are decided, it is confused because today many issues of a civil character are decided by courts of special jurisdiction, and by special tribunals, and issues of administrative character sometimes decided by, or by appeal to, civil courts, so that one must think, at least procedurally, of administrative and civil, as opposed to criminal law.

Civil and Commercial Law

No sharp distinction exists or has ever existed in Scots law between bodies of civil and of commercial law, in that there are no distinct codes

---

[10] *cf.* Bankt., I, 1, 53; Ersk., I, 1, 29 " . . . that part of the public law that relates to crimes. . . . "

[11] See Chap. 8, *infra*.

[12] *e.g. Wright v. Kennedy*, 1946 J.C. 142; *Berkeley v. Finnie*, 1949 J.C. 118; *Haldane v. Allan*, 1956 J.C. 41. Many questions of administrative law arise in civil courts. See, *e.g. Hamilton v. Roxburghshire C.C.*, 1970 S.C. 248.

[13] *cf. McGregor v. D.*, 1977 S.C. 330.

or statutes dealing with the one as distinct from the other, and, in general, the same rules apply to a transaction such as sale or carriage whether the parties are private citizens or merchants or traders, and whether it is a private transaction or one done in the course of trade or business.[14] As in England, doctrines which originated in the laws merchant and maritime have long since been absorbed into the general body of the private law rather than being kept apart in a separate body of law.[15] "This general law merchant is in England said to form part of the common law; and it is so much a part of that law that it requires not to be proved by witnesses, like matter of foreign regulation, but is noted judicially by the court . . . the same principle operates as in England; and our courts are daily in the habit of proceeding on this law merchant as fully authoritative in Scotland, and of allowing the decisions of courts and the writings of lawyers to be cited in illustration of it."[16] In Continental systems on the other hand, civil and commercial law are frequently distinct bodies of law, regulated by distinct codes and statutes, with distinct courts.[17] In the United Kingdom, "commercial law" or "mercantile law" are only labels for those sets of principles and rules of civil law which frequently arise in commercial relations.

The important Civil Jurisdiction and Judgments Act 1982, implementing the Convention between Member States of the EC on Jurisdiction and the Enforcement of Judgments in Civil and Commercial Matters of 1968,[18] lays down a common code for the EC countries in "civil and commercial matters," defined, very imprecisely only, as excluding revenue, customs and administrative matters, natural persons, matrimonial property, wills and succession, bankruptcy, social security and arbitration.[19]

Common Law and Equity

The distinction drawn in English law and systems in the English-speaking world based thereon, between courts and principles of common law, and courts and doctrines of equity, has never existed in Scotland. But it does not follow either that doctrines and principles founded on the idea of equity, of natural justice, reason and fairness are absent from Scots law, or that the doctrines which were and are the subject-matter of Chancery or equity proceedings in England are without their Scottish counterparts.

---

[14] Some modern statutes draw distinctions for certain purposes between "consumer" transactions and "commercial" transactions.

[15] For the meaningful use of the term "commercial law," see p. 233, *infra*. The Scottish Court of Admiralty was absorbed in the Court of Session in 1830.

[16] Bell, *Commentaries*, Preface, xi.

[17] It is noteworthy that in Scotland and England "commercial law" or "mercantile law" are not used as subject headings in the *Laws of Scotland* or *Halsbury's Laws of England*, the *Index to the Statutes,* or the *Digests* or *Current Law*.

[18] Later amended.

[19] See further *Re State of Norway* [1989] 1 All E.R. 716, 723 (H.L.).

The Court of Session has always been a court of both law and equity and the law of Scotland a mixed body of rules of strict law and of principles founded on equity.[20] It was observed by Lord Kames, and it is still true, that pleas and defences and remedies founded on equity, and in many cases closely comparable to those developed by the Chancery in England, have long been administered by the Scottish courts as part of their ordinary jurisdiction and so are interwoven into the fabric of the ordinary Scots law. "In England, where the courts of equity and common law are different, the boundary between equity and common law, where the legislature doth not interpose, will remain always the same. But in Scotland and other countries where equity and common law are united in one court, the boundary varies imperceptibly; for what originally is a rule in equity, loses its character when it is fully established in practice; and then it is considered as common law: thus the *actio negotiorum gestio*, retention, salvage, etc., are in Scotland scarce now considered as depending on principles of equity."[21]

The ordinary equitable jurisdiction of the Court of Session includes, in the sphere of contract, application of the principles of retention, compensation, rescission and rectification of contracts, relief against penalty and irritancy clauses, the insistence on fiduciary duties in many relationships, the obligations of restitution, various principles in the law of succession, many doctrines of the law of trusts, and, in the sphere of remedies, specific implement and interdict, and the defences of personal bar. This ordinary equitable jurisdiction, being treated as part of the common law, is not exclusive to the Court of Session but may be exercised by all courts.[22]

In addition to its ordinary equitable jurisdiction, the Court of Session has a *nobile officium*, or extraordinary equitable power to do justice in case of necessity or strong expediency, where ordinary procedure would provide no remedy.[23] The chief categories of cases where this power is now exercised are where there are omissions or defects in statutes or statutory procedure, particularly in bankruptcy, or omissions or defects in deeds or writings which frustrate their true purpose, particularly in the sphere of trusts, and the grant of remedies on petition to the Inner House in cases not competent to the Outer House or the sheriff court.[24] The court is slow to exercise this power unless there is exact or closely analogous precedent for its exercise.

The High Court of Justiciary has a similar, though more restricted, *nobile officium*, exercised by three or more of the Lords Commissioners of

---

[20] Bankton IV, 7, 19 and 23.
[21] Kames, *Principles of Equity*, 17.
[22] Walker, "Equity in Scots Law" (1954) 66 J.R. 103.
[23] Stair, IV, 3, 1; Bankton IV, 7, 24; Ersk. I, 3, 22; Kames, *Historical Law Tracts*, 231. See also *Gibson's Trustees*, 1933 S.C. 190, 198, *per* L. P. Clyde.
[24] Mackay, *Practice of the Court of Session*, 1209; MacLaren, *Court of Session Practice*, 100, 828; *London and Clydeside Estates v. Aberdeen*, 1980 S.C.(H.L.) 1, 36; *Humphries v. X and Y*, 1982 S.C. 79, 82.

Justiciary, and an inherent jurisdiction to prevent injustice and provide a remedy for all extraordinary occurrences in criminal business not otherwise provided for.[25] The Court of Teinds has a similar power.[26]

Common Law and Statute Law

The distinction between common law[27] and statute law depends on the source of the particular rules in question, and this distinction is met with in public and private, administrative, criminal and civil law. Common law was originally the body of law common to the whole country, based on ancient customs, practices, moral standards and beliefs and worked out and built up in the courts by the process of authoritative declaration of the rules and their application in specific cases. It is judge-made law. Statute law or legislation enacted by Parliaments, was long thought of as an alien source of rules breaking in upon the established doctrines of the law. In consequence, rules and principles tend to be distinguished according as their source is in case law worked out and declared by the courts on the basis of ancient custom and practice, or in the statutes of the legislative bodies. This distinction corresponds to that mentioned in older books between consuetudinary and statutory, or unwritten and written law.[28] A common law right of action is not lost by desuetude[29] but may be abolished by statute.[30]

In consequence of this distinction, mention will be found in the books of common law crimes and statutory crimes or offences, common law rights and statutory rights, and so on.[31] The difference is not merely in the origin and source of the crime or right in question but in that in the former case

---

[25] Hume, II, 59; Alison, II, 23; see also, *e.g. Sweeney* (1894) 1 Adam 392; *Graham Hunter* (1904) 4 Adam 523; *Lamond Lawson* (1909) 6 Adam 118; *Wylie v. H.M.A.*, 1966 S.L.T. 149; *Wang Ping Nam v. Federal German Republic Minister of Justice*, 1972 J.C. 43; *Lloyd's & Scottish Finance v. H.M.A.*, 1974 S.L.T. 3; *Ferguson v. H.M.A.*, 1980 J.C. 27. See also "Nobile Officium of the High Court of Justiciary," 1974 S.L.T.(News) 37.

[26] *Cumbernauld Minister v. Dumbartonshire Heritors*, 1920 S.C. 625.

[27] The term "common law" is used in various senses with different counterparts. Of these the principal are (i) the common law or Anglo-American system of law as contrasted with civil law systems, deriving from the law of Rome; (ii) common law (in England) as distinct from equity; (iii) common law of the realm as distinct from particular local or customary law; (iv) common law as contrasted with statute law, as here discussed. See further Salmond, *Jurisprudence*, 81–99; Ersk., I, 1, 28. In old Scottish books and statutes the term "common law" is occasionally used as meaning the civil, or civil and canon, law of Rome, as being the basic common rules of Scotland, distinct from the statutory law.

[28] Ersk., I, 1, 30 and 43. *Cf.* Mackenzie, *Inst.* I, 1, 9–10.

[29] *McKendrick v. Sinclair*, 1972 S.C.(H.L.) 25.

[30] Damages (Scotland) Act 1976, s. 8.

[31] Thus the claim of one person to damages for the loss caused by the death of a spouse, parent or child, is a common law claim, in that it has no other origin than ancient custom, recognised and defined in authoritative decisions of which the leading case is *Eisten v. N.B. Ry.* (1870) 8 M. 980. The claim of a person to Industrial Injury Benefit is statutory in that it was conferred by and is obtainable only under conditions specified in what is now the Social Security Contributions and Benefits Act 1992, as amended by later Acts and amplified by subordinate legislation made thereunder. Again, murder is a common law crime; to be in charge of a vehicle while under the influence of drink is a statutory crime.

the definition and conditions attaching to the right or claim or power in question have to be gathered mainly from the decisions in which the courts recognised, defined and restated the right or claim in question, while in the latter the definition and conditions are laid down in authoritative form in the statute, though subsequent decisions may be of value in showing the interpretation put by the courts on the verbal formulation adopted in the statute.

Substantive and Adjective Law

In both public (including constitutional, administrative and criminal) and private or civil law the distinction between substantive and adjective law is material. The substantive law of each branch sets out the principles and rules defining, in administrative law the rights and duties of persons and authorities, in criminal law the kinds of conduct which are punishable, and in private law what rights, powers and privileges attach to legal persons in various circumstances and what duties, liabilities and disabilities are incumbent on them in other circumstances—such as the mutual rights and duties of husbands and wives, buyers and sellers, landlords and tenants, employers and employees, careless drivers and their victims, and so on—and also what secondary or remedial rights and duties come into being on a primary right being violated or a primary duty not being implemented—such as the right to recover damages when a contract is not properly performed. The adjective law of each branch comprises the rules as to how rights are vindicated and duties enforced. In administrative law the adjective law deals with the constitution and powers of administrative bodies and tribunals, the mode of proceedings, and the awards they may make. In criminal law it deals with the jurisdiction of the various criminal courts, their procedure, the evidence competent in them, the punishments they may award and the rights of appeal therefrom. In private law the adjective law comprises the rules as to the modes of effectuating rights, the rules as to the jurisdiction of the courts, the rules of evidence, the rules as to the machinery of procedure and diligence whereby claims may be brought before courts for determination and the decrees of those courts enforced. Remedies and procedure are separate though closely connected; not every civil remedy requires that any formal legal step or approach to the court be made, and the recognised classes of legal remedies do not correspond exactly with the recognised categories of legal action. Adjective law is not synonymous with, but wider than, law of procedure.

Similarly, the antithesis sometimes referred to between "right" and "remedy" is a false one; substantive rights, such as not to be injured, and remedial rights, such as to be compensated if one has in fact been injured by another's fault, are both equally legal rights, but the former is logically prior to the latter, and the latter right is contingent, and comes into existence only if the former right has been infringed. The distinction does not correspond to that between substantive and adjective law. Actions and procedure come into play if need be to declare a claimant's entitlement to a remedy and to enforce his claim. Substantive and adjective law are constantly overlapping and interacting and no study or statement of either can avoid consideration of the other.

PUBLIC LAW

The public law of Scotland comprises all the bodies of principles and rules dealing with the legal organisation of the community and its control and direction of the affairs of individuals. These bodies of rules have greatly increased in bulk, scope and importance in the last century on account of the increased and still increasing power of the state and the greater extent to which it controls, supervises and interferes in matters with which it previously had little or no concern. State regulation, initiative, control and management, state or public enterprises and agencies abound in modern Britain and all tend to increase the importance of public law.[32]

The General Part

The term "General Part" is better known in continental codes than in uncodified British law. The General Part deals with those matters common to the whole of the Public Law, such as the authoritative literature, the sources of the principles, their authority and interpretation, and the most fundamental and general concepts and ideas which run through all the specific and particular branches and rules. Salmond[33] called it the Introductory Portion—"all those rules which by their preliminary character or of the generality of their application cannot be appropriately relegated to any special department."

Constitutional Law

The body of legal principles which determines the constitution or legal structure of a state, the essential and fundamental elements of its organisation, make up its constitutional law.[34] It deals with the structure, powers and functions of the supreme power in the state, together with those of all the more important of the subordinate departments of government.[35] More specifically it deals with the head of the state and his powers; the composition and powers of the legislative bodies; the status and powers of Ministers, the executive and of the civil service; the courts and their judges; the armed forces; the relations of Church and state and the legal position and powers of the established Church; the relations

---

[32] *Town Investments v. Dept. of the Environment* [1977] 1 All E.R. 813, 817.
[33] *Jurisprudence*, App. III.
[34] Salmond, *Jurisprudence*, 138; *cf.* Dicey, *Law of the Constitution* (10th ed.), Chap. 1.
[35] *Ibid.* 506.

between central government and local or subordinate authorities; relations with foreign countries, the Commonwealth and the colonies; the public revenue and the law of taxation; citizenship and its rights, such as those to personal liberty, freedom of speech and of association, and public duties, such as of jury service and assistance in the maintenance of order.[36]

Constitutional law is made up of two main elements, rules of law derived from statute, decided cases and custom, and a body of rules, understandings, habits or practices which are not in strictness rules of law (in the sense that they will not be enforced by the courts), commonly termed conventions of the constitution.[37] Yet these conventional rules and practices, while of very particular interest to the historian and political scientist, cannot be ignored by the lawyer because they complete the structure, the bare bones of which are supplied by the law. Without the conventions, the constitutional machinery would probably be unworkable, while many of the conventions could be ignored or flouted only at the expense of causing sooner or later a breach of the law or the breakdown of the machinery of government. Hence constitutional law has been defined as the rules of law, including binding conventions, "which regulate the structure of the principal organs of government and their relationship to each other, and determine their principal functions."[38]

Constitutional law, possibly more than any other branch of law, requires to be studied with constant reference to its history and development. Many of its institutions and fundamental rules can be explained only by reference to the past circumstances which gave rise to them or caused the evolution to take a particular course. In consequence constitutional, legal and political history must regularly be prayed in aid for explanation, while many of the problems of the constitutional lawyer are equally pressing problems of the political scientist, because the organisation of the state is both a legal and a political conception and form of association or institution. The very haphazard historical development of the British Constitution, coupled with the fact that it has never been reduced as a whole to writing in the form of a single comprehensive legal document, as is customary in other countries, is one reason for the tangled and illogical nature of many of the rules of constitutional law. The close connection between law and politics in the sphere of constitutional law may be seen from the fact that the working of the British Constitution must be explained not merely in terms of rules of law but also of practices or conventions of political origin.

---

[36] Hood Phillips, *Constitutional and Administrative Law*, 12. The whole of Chaps. 1 and 2 are enlightening.

[37] The term was invented by A.V. Dicey in his *Law of the Constitution* (1885; 10th ed., 1960) and has been generally accepted since. See his discussion of the distinction at pp. 24–30.

[38] Wade and Phillips, *Constitutional Law*, 3.

Administrative Law

Administrative law has been recognised as a distinct branch of law and topic of legal study in Britain only in the last 80 years or so, owing to the enormous growth of its manifestations during that period, though the subject is really much older. There is no rigid line between it and constitutional law because the difference is mainly one of convenience and degree, constitutional law dealing with structure and with the broader rules which regulate function, while the details of function are left to administrative law.[39]

It is the law of public administration, that part of public law which prescribes the nature of the activities of the executive and administrative portions of government, the powers and duties of executive departments, agencies and officials and their relations with individuals, the forms and instruments in and through which the lower ranges of government operate.[40]

Thus, it deals with the organisation and functions of the various departments of the central government, such as the Treasury and the Scotland Office, the various authorities of local government, such as the councils, which exercise functions within particular limited areas only, and of the agencies and statutory bodies set up by the state yet not departments thereof, for the exercise of various specific social or economic functions, such as the Benefits Agency, Health and Safety Commission, Highlands and Islands Enterprise, Scottish Health Boards, the British Broadcasting Corporation. The first execute the policy of Parliament, under the directions of the Ministers of the Crown, the second the policy of representatives elected by local government electors within the framework set by Parliament, but the third are neither government departments under the control of Ministers of State nor are they elected by the electorate.[41] The functions of central departments, agencies and local authorities are very numerous and the law is bulky and complicated: it covers such matters as police and fire services, public utilities, roads and bridges, public education, housing, social services, public health, licensing, town and country planning, the regulation of industry, trade and agriculture, supervision of factories and mines, valuation and rating, compulsory purchase of land and compensation therefor, and all the great variety of circumstances in which the state exercises control or guidance over

---

[39] Maitland, *Constitutional History*, 526–539.

[40] Salmond, *Jurisprudence*, 506–507; *cf.* Jennings, *The Law and the Constitution* (3rd ed.), 194. See also Chap. 11, *infra*.

[41] See generally Campion (ed.), *British Government since 1918*; Greaves, "Public Service Boards" (1944) 7 M.L.R. 25; Friedmann, "The New Public Corporations and the Law" (1947) 10 M.L.R. 233, 377; Wade, "The Constitutional Aspect of the Public Corporation" (1949) *Current Legal Problems*, 172; Robson, "The Public Corporations in Britain To-day" (1950) 63 H.L.R. 1321; Robson, *Nationalised Industry and Public Ownership*; Friedmann, *Law and Social Change*, Chap. 9.

people's lives in the general interest, or directly or indirectly, provides some benefit or service for them.

Departments and local authorities, moreover, have had delegated to them by Parliament certain limited legislative powers, of making rules binding within limited spheres only, in the form of rules, orders, by-laws, and so on, and the scope of and limitations on these powers also fall to be studied.

While administrative agencies and officials work to some extent through the ordinary civil and criminal courts and processes, of great importance are the special administrative courts, tribunals and procedures frequently set up to determine matters of controversy arising in the course of administering some particular service or body of administrative controls, so that to some extent along with each branch of the public administration, one must study the particular machinery provided for enforcement or the resolution of disputes in connection therewith. Thus the system of National Insurance set up in 1946 brought into existence not only a new Ministry[42] and a mass of new legal rights and duties, but also a special system of tribunals for determining disputes concerning entitlement to payment of benefits.

The problems of administrative law are amongst the most interesting of the present day, not least because they are frequently politico-economic-legal and not purely legal, in that they raise fundamental problems of social policy and of government as well as of pure law. The salient problems of administrative law can probably be said to be:

(1) The extent to which and the powers under which Ministers and departments of state enjoy authority delegated by Parliament to make rules, regulations and orders, filling in with details the gaps left by skeleton legislation, and the control of this delegated legislative power by the courts.[43]

(2) The extent to which and the ways in which the individual may, either through the ordinary civil courts or by administrative means, inquire into, question and challenge the exercise of administrative powers and in some cases check and limit such executive action.[44]

(3) The extent to which the ordinary courts can review and control the proceedings of administrative tribunals and officials exercising a judicial power or right to determine disputes.[45]

---

[42] Now the Ministry of Social Security: Ministry of Social Security Act 1966.

[43] See generally Carr, *Delegated Legislation*; *Concerning English Administrative Law*; Allen, *Law and Orders*; *Law in the Making*; Sieghart, *Government by Decree*; Kersell, *Parliamentary Supervision of Delegated Legislation*; Report of the Committee on Ministers' Powers (Cmd. 4060, 1932).

[44] The above books and Report of the Committee on Administrative Tribunals and Enquiries (Cmnd. 218, 1957).

[45] See Griffith and Street, *Administrative Law*; Allen, *Law and Orders*; de Smith, *Judicial Review of Administrative Action*.

```
                              ┌─General Part
                              │    Sources and literature
                              │    Authority and interpretation of sources
                              │    Fundamental concepts—the rule of law, separation
                              │        of powers
                              ├─Constitutional law
                              │    The Crown
                              │    The executive—Privy Council Cabinet, Scottish Executive
                              │    The legislature—Parliament; Scottish Parliament
                              │    The judicial system, courts of general and special
                              │        jurisdiction
                              │    The civil service
                              │    The police
                              │    The armed forces; courts-martial
                              │    Established churches; ecclesiastical law
                              │    Public revenue and taxation
                              │    Nationality and citizenship
                              │    Rights and liberties of citizens
                              │    Commonwealth, colonial and foreign relations
                              ├─Administrative law
                              │    Powers and functions of central departments
                              │    Powers and functions of local authorities
                   ┌─PUBLIC─  │    Powers and functions of public agencies
                   │  LAW     │    Delegated legislative powers
                   │          │    Delegated judicial powers—statutory
                   │          │        tribunals
                   │          │    Control of powers by Parliament and courts
                   │          │    Regulation of industry and trade
                   │          │    Social security system
                   │          ├─Adjective administrative law: tribunals
                   │          ├─Substantive criminal law
                   │          │    Sources and literature
                   │          │    Investigation and prosecution of crime
                   │          │    Nature of crime generally
                   │          │    Principles of liability in general
                   │          │    Liability in special cases
                   │          │    Constituent elements of various specific crimes
                   │          ├─Adjective criminal law
                   │          │    Jurisdiction of criminal courts
                   │          │    Criminal procedure
                   │          │    Evidence in criminal cases
                   │          │    Punishment and treatment
                   │          │    Appeal, commutation of sentence and pardon
                   │          ├─General Part
                   │          │    Sources and literature
                   │          │    Authority and interpretation of sources
                   │          │    Fundamental concepts—personality, rights, duties
                   │          │    General principles—good faith, public policy
                   │          │    Effect of time on rights
                   │          ├─International Private Law
                   │          │    Preliminary concepts and classification
                   │          │    Jurisdiction of Scottish or foreign court
                   │          │    Choice of law
                   │          │    Effect of foreign judgments
                   │          ├─Law of persons
       LAW OF      │          │    Legal personality and its attributes
       SCOTLAND─   │          │    Natural persons—status and capacity
                   │          │        in domestic relations—husband and wife
                   │          │                              parent and child
                   │          │                              guardian and ward
                   ▼          ▼    Unincorporated associations
                                       unestablished churches, clubs and societies
```

partnerships
trade unions and employers' associations
friendly societies
Juristic persons or corporations
  public corporations and boards
  local authorities
  chartered and incorporated institutions
  companies
  building societies
  industrial, provident and co-operative societies
—Law of obligations
  Natural obligations
  Voluntary and contractual obligations
    General principles
    Particular contracts; commercial contracts
  Quasi-contractual obligations
    General principles
    Particular cases
  Delictual obligations
    General principles
    Particular delicts
  Obligations arising from trust, statute, decree or
    other source
—Law of property
  Divisions of property—conversion; fixtures
  Rights in objects of property—ownership,
    possession
  Corporeal heritable property
    subjects thereof and rights therein
  Incorporeal heritable property
    subjects thereof and rights therein
  Corporeal moveable property
    subjects thereof and rights therein
  Incorporeal moveable and intellectual property
    subjects thereof and rights therein
  Trusts, public and private, and trustees
  Judicial factors
  Succession on death
    Legal rights
    Intestacy—devolution of property by law
    Testacy—making and interpretation of wills
    Other modes of transfer of property on death
    Powers and duties of executors
  Bankruptcy, trust deeds and arrangements with
    creditors
—Law of civil remedies
—Adjective law
  Conveyancing
    Authentication of deeds
    Requisites of various kinds of deeds
    Examination and completion of title
    Registration of deeds
  Jurisdiction of civil courts
  Civil procedure
  Pleading and practice
  Evidence in civil cases
  Diligence and enforcement of decrees
  Appeal
  Legal profession, representation
  Expenses and Legal Aid
  Arbitration

PRIVATE
LAW

(4) The way in which adequate supervision and control of public corporations may be exercised by Parliament in the interests of the consumer and taxpayer, while allowing the authority freedom from detailed control and avoiding excessive centralisation.[46]

(5) Special rules relative to litigation against executive officials and departments, a topic sometimes conveniently entitled Crown Proceedings.[47]

Administrative law exhibits equally with constitutional law the defects of unplanned historical development, lack of coherent system, and a welter of individual cases, each facet of public administration having a system of its own.[48] The law is developing rapidly and is constantly undergoing change, though much remains to be done to fashion it into a coherent body of doctrine. Public dissatisfaction with aspects of it has twice given rise to investigations of aspects of the subject by strong committees[49] which recommended many changes, not all of which have been carried into effect.[50] It is in the sphere of administrative law more than any other that the rights and liberties of the subject are involved in modern times, and most of the important cases illustrate one facet or another of the constant struggle between the state and the individual, between government and freedom.

Adjective Administrative Law

This is concerned with the machinery of claims, decisions, tribunals and their procedures whereby disputes are decided, very largely by tribunals other than the ordinary courts, and appeals.

Substantive Criminal Law

While constitutional and administrative law overlap and run into one another, criminal law stands rather apart from the rest of public law, with a considerable literature of its own. The criminal law consists of the body of rules relative to crimes and offences, that is, to such human acts and omissions as the supreme authority in the state wishes to prevent and suppress, and consequently declares illegal, deserving to be repressed, and punishable. The distinction between wrongs which are criminal and those

---

[46] See Morrison, *Government and Parliament*, Chap. 12; Friedmann, *Law and Social Change in Contemporary Britain*, Chap. 9.

[47] See Bickford Smith and Middleton, *The Crown Proceedings Act 1947;* Glanville Williams, *Crown Proceedings*.

[48] The principal discussions, analyses and criticisms are Allen, *Law and Orders*; Robson, *Justice and Administrative Law*; Schwartz, *Law and the Executive in Britain*; Carr, *Concerning English Administrative Law*.

[49] Committee on Ministers' Powers (Donoughmore Committee), 1931–32 (Report—Cmd. 4060), and Committee on Administrative Tribunals and Enquiries (Franks Committee), 1955–57 (Report—Cmnd. 218).

[50] See Tribunals and Inquiries Acts 1958, 1966 and 1971, now Tribunals and Inquiries Act 1992.

which are rated by the legal system as merely civil wrongs or delicts giving a civil remedy in damages only, depends not on the essential nature of the act or omission in question but simply on whether the government policy of the time deems the activity to deserve repression by punishment on the ground that its doing or repetition would be harmful to the community. Some wrongful conduct, such as assault, may be both a crime and a delict; conversely, adultery was once a crime and is now only a delict[51], while modern social policy requires many kinds of conduct to be made criminal and repressed though they were previously innocent. Accordingly, the main distinguishing mark of criminal law is that the state rather than an individual initiates proceedings, the law having as its object the punishment of the wrongdoer and the repression of such conduct, rather than compensation for a person harmed.

So, too, classification as criminal does not necessarily follow from the inherent wrongness or wickedness or immorality of an act; thus it is no crime to commit fornication, nor, in general, to let a person drown. In some cases abortion is criminal; in some cases it is innocent. Unless the activity has been condemned by common law or statute as criminal, it may be done with impunity so far as the criminal law is concerned, however immoral or potentially harmful it may be.

A distinctive characteristic of those activities declared criminal is that they are dealt with by legal proceedings of a special kind, in distinct courts and by distinct procedure, and for practical purposes an important classification of crimes is into those triable by a judge and jury in the superior criminal courts, carrying a heavy penalty, and those triable by a sheriff or magistrate, without a jury, in the inferior criminal courts and carrying only a limited penalty. There is also a substantial area of overlap between the two in that some crimes may, according to circumstances, be dealt with either in the superior or inferior courts.

In the study of substantive criminal law there are three main topics for consideration: there is the general problem of criminal liability, that is, the question of what physical acts or omissions and what concomitant mental states will import criminal liability[52]; there is the problem of variations in liability, that is, of what differences from the normal rules of liability exist in the case of individuals who are in some respect abnormal, either temporarily or permanently, as by reason of youth, insanity, intoxication, pregnancy or amnesia; and lastly, there is the problem of what factual and

---

[51] The confusion between criminal wrongs and civil wrongs (delicts) is very marked in early systems of law; see, *e.g.* Maine's *Ancient Law*, Chap. 1; Walker, "The Development of Reparation" (1952) 64 J.R. 101; Robson, *Civilisation and the Growth of Law*, Chap. 8.

[52] See further Allen, "The Nature of a Crime," in *Legal Duties*, 221; Kenny, "The Nature of a Crime," in his *Outlines of Criminal Law* (16th ed.), Appx. I; Hall, *General Principles of Criminal Law, passim*; Williams, *The Criminal Law—The General Part*; Brett, *Inquiry into Criminal Guilt*, Chap. 2. Gordon, *Criminal Law of Scotland* Chaps. 1–3. *cf.* also Hall Williams, "The Proper Scope and Function of the Criminal Law" (1958) 74 L.Q.R. 76.

mental elements are required to constitute various specific and individual types of crimes, this being the application in detail of the general conditions of criminal liability to particular crimes. When dealing with these specific crimes, they are often conveniently grouped into crimes against the state (such as treason and breach of the peace) which are harmful to the peace and order of the community, crimes against the person (such as murder, rape, and assault) which are infringements of some individual's personal integrity, and crimes against persons in their property (such as fire-raising, malicious damage, theft and reset).[53]

Adjective Criminal Law

In adjective criminal law the main topics are the constitution and competence or jurisdiction of the different courts dealing with criminal cases, the means of investigating crimes, of apprehension of suspects, and of initiating criminal proceedings, the steps which have to be gone through before, at and after trial, the course of procedure at trial, specialities of the rules of evidence in criminal cases, the protection of the accused, the provision for appeal and the modes of punishment or treatment of the convicted which may be ordered in different circumstances.[54] The discussion of the purposes of punishment and treatment and of the most appropriate methods for various kinds of criminals and crimes is so important as to be a subject in itself, and one nowadays attracting greater attention more commensurate with its importance.

Criminology and Penology

The body of criminal law and procedure is necessarily closely connected with those other branches of social studies which are concerned with the nature and volume of socially harmful conduct in the community.[55] The criminal law and its procedure is the instrument of the criminal policy of the state in its task of repressing and punishing socially harmful conduct. That policy leans heavily on criminology, the study of the causes of crime and criminality, both those causes which may be traced to the mental and physical constitution or abnormalities of the delinquent, such as his heredity and innate defects of character, and those which may be ascribed to the effects of social environment, such as bad housing, evil companions, poverty or unemployment, poor conditions of work and so on. "Criminology is the body of knowledge regarding crime as a social phenomenon . . . The objective of criminology is the development of a body of general and verified principles and of other types of knowledge regarding this process of law, crime, and treatment or prevention."[56]

---

[53] Crimes against property are by far the most numerous.
[54] See further Chap. 14, *infra.*
[55] See Radzinowicz and Turner, "The Meaning and Scope of Criminal Science," in *Modern Approach to Criminal Law* (1948), 12 *et seq.*
[56] Sutherland and Cressey, *Principles of Criminology* (6th ed.), 3 see also Maguire (ed.), *Oxford Handbook of Criminology.*

Further knowledge of the causes of crime naturally leads to the study of suitable measures to remove or neutralise them and also, so long as criminal conduct continues to take place, study must similarly be devoted to methods of education, deterrence, repression and punishment, the suitability of particular sanctions for particular individuals, the institutions in which offenders should be treated and the methods of training and reformation which can best be employed to bring home to the offender the wrongness of his conduct and lead him on release to live an honest life.[57] This is the science of penology, which increasingly influences state criminal policy.

While neither criminology nor penology is a branch of law in the strict sense, both are so bound up with criminal law that the study of the latter inevitably leads to the former, and it is from the criminal policy of the country, informed by the discoveries of criminology and penology, that guidance can be found for the reform and development of criminal law.[58] These sciences in turn lean heavily on sociology, statistics, psychology and psychiatry.

PRIVATE LAW

Private law is the other major branch of Scots law, dealing in the main with legal relations of individuals with other individuals or with state departments and agencies in matters wherein the latter have no special privileges, but only the rights and powers, duties and liabilities of private individuals. It defines what interests, claims or demands are recognised and protected by rules of law and how they may be vindicated against other individuals. Despite the growth of state intervention it is the private law which is of greatest concern to the layman and his legal adviser and most of the personal and economic relationships a man has with other men are regulated by private law.

The fundamental and best-known division of private law is still that of the Roman lawyers,[59] into law of persons, law of things, and law of actions, and this, with its subdivisions, is the basis for most later classifications. Another classification formerly employed was into personal rights, that is, claims against another individual only, and real rights, that is, claims enforceable against some object of property such as a man's house.[60] The

---

[57] See further Morris (ed.), *The Oxford History of the Prison*; Fox, *English Prison and Borstal System*; Walker, *Crime and Punishment in Britain*.

[58] A good general introduction to this subject are the volumes of the *English Studies in Criminal Science* (now *Cambridge Criminology*) *Series*, especially Vol. I: *Penal Reform in England*; Vol. II: *Mental Abnormality and Crime*; and Vol. IV: *Modern Approach to Criminal Law*.

[59] Gaius, I, 8, *Inst.*, I, iii, 12. *Omne autem jus quo utimur, vel ad personas pertinet, vel ad res vel ad actiones. Cf.* Ersk., I, 2, 1.

[60] See, *e.g.* Ersk., IV, 1, 10.

division here adopted, based on the Roman one, is convenient for study and understanding as well as for practical purposes.

The General Part

For academic purposes it is again useful to segregate for separate study the most general ideas which apply throughout the whole of private law, such topics as the recognised sources of law,[61] their respective authority and the accepted principles for their interpretation, the most fundamental concepts, such as legal personality, status, rights and duties, obligations, property and so on, principles of wide general application such as good faith, public policy and personal bar, and the effect of lapse of time on rights, as by cutting them off, altering the rules of proof, or limiting the right to sue on those rights. These general ideas have to be gathered from their piecemeal examination in books on diverse specific topics and in Scots and common law systems are largely relegated to books on Jurisprudence, whereas in civil law systems they belong to the General or Introductory Part of the Civil Code.[62]

International Private Law

It has been pointed out already that in general every state or national territory has a distinct system of law, and the courts and other agencies for enforcing that law. It follows that a group of facts raising a legal problem may involve a foreign element, in that one of the parties may live under another legal regime, or that some material fact, such as the performance of a contract, may take place in a foreign country. In recent years the extension of business and commercial relations throughout the world, of foreign travel and service abroad, of intermarriage and migration, have increased this tendency and swelled the number of cases in which a foreign element arises. Accordingly, in every case involving any non-Scottish element three preliminary problems fall to be determined, namely, what country's courts have jurisdiction, or the legal power of determining this controversy; secondly, once that has been decided, what system of law falls to be applied to determine the controversy; and, thirdly, what effect is to be given to any foreign judgment in existence on the matter in issue.[63]

The rules which exist for resolving these preliminary problems are the rules of international private law, conflict of laws, or private international

---

[61] For the term "sources of law," see Chap. 10, *infra.*

[62] These topics are to some extent dealt with in the opening sections of the works of the institutional writers: see *e.g.* Stair, I, 1; Ersk., I 1. The German Civil Code has a General Part, and a Special Part divided into Obligations, Things, Family Law, Inheritance.

[63] While logically the possibility that a problem raises an issue of International Private Law has in every case to be considered first, it is in fact convenient to postpone the study of the principles of International Private Law to a late stage in legal studies, dealing with cases having a foreign element only after the principles applicable to cases not thus complicated have been studied.

law. All three names have found support, yet none is specially felicitous.[64] The first is probably best as indicating what the topic truly covers, namely, private law so far as it has an international or extra-national character or has to take account of extra-national factors.[65]

It is to be noted that, despite the similarity of names, these rules have no connection with, or even similarity to, Public International Law,[66] and that unlike that body of law, the rules of international private law are not common to all or many legal systems, but are bodies of rules which are part of each particular legal system and vary from one state to another as do the other parts of the several legal systems. International private law or private international law is therefore that part of the private law of a particular state which determines, in a case involving a foreign element, whether the courts of that state have jurisdiction to determine the issue and, if so, what system of law falls to be applied, and what effect given to any foreign judgment there may be. It is in a sense a series of appendices to the main branches of private law, in that a question of conflict of laws may arise in any and every branch of private law.[67] Thus marriage is a matter of private law: if it involves a foreign element, *e.g.* if one of the parties is a foreigner, or it was celebrated abroad, the international private law rules relative to marriage come into play. So, too, there are conflict of laws rules applicable to contracts, property, and so on. Moreover, it is noteworthy that the rules of international private law do not solve the actual problems which arise, but simply answer the preliminary questions which will enable the Scottish courts to decide whether it is their duty or not to decide the case, by directing them to deal with or to decline to handle the controversy, and in the former case, to apply Scots law or another system, as may be required in the circumstances. It is then for the rules of the Scots law or other system chosen to determine the rights and duties of the parties.

It further follows that in some cases the appropriate answer given by this country's rules of international private law will be that this country's courts have no jurisdiction to deal with the case, or that they have jurisdiction but must apply another country's rules of private law to the matter in issue; it is therefore not in every case that a country's courts will adjudicate upon a case brought before them, or will apply their own

---

[64] The name "conflict of laws" is supported by the Bills of Exchange Act 1882, s. 72; see also *Ewing* v. *Orr-Ewing* (1885) 13 R.(H.L.) 1.

[65] Notice that for the purposes of the Scottish rules of International Private Law, England is a foreign country as much as France or Texas. The converse is equally true.

[66] See further Stevenson, "Relationship of Private International Law to Public International Laws" (1952) 52 Col.L.R. 561; Gutteridge, "Comparative Law and the Conflict of Laws" (1944) Trans. Grotius Society, 119; Schmitthoff, "The Science of Comparative Law" (1939) 7 Camb.L.J. 107; Starke, "The Relation between Private and Public International Law" (1937) 52 L.Q.R. 395; Beckett, "What is Private International Law?" (1926) 7 B.Y.I.L. 73.

[67] Such questions do not arise in public law since it is concerned only with transactions within the frontiers of the country in question.

system of private law to that case. The justification for this possible declinature of jurisdiction, or application of another country's rules of law, by a court is fundamentally the interests of justice, and the general practice of civilised countries in recognising by the comity of nations, and giving effect to, rights acquired under another legal system or properly enforceable by other courts. Difficulties may arise, however, as to the determination of what foreign rules may be applied by a state, because the domestic private law of some states might be unsuitable for application or recognition by another state. The tendency is to recognise all rights acquired under the law of another country unless their recognition is flatly contradictory to fundamental principles of British law.[68]

In modern times many changes have been made in rules of international private law to give effect to international conventions or European conventions so as to minimise differences between particular legal systems.[69]

Law of Persons

Law deals with the rights and duties of legal persons, and duties and rights attach to legal persons. But there are "persons" in law who are not individual human beings, who are groups of individuals collectively personified by law as artificial or juristic persons, and also groups which are treated as entities for some purposes yet not fully recognised as legal persons. Personality is in law the attribution by the legal system of legal existence, of the ability to have legal rights and to be subject to legal duties, and it is for the law itself to lay down what kinds of human beings, of groups of beings and of institutions, have legal personality.[70]

The law of natural persons deals with all the rights, privileges and powers which attach by law to an individual as such, independently of rights acquired by contract or rights arising from the possession of property. It relates first to the recognition of an individual's legal personality, or his existence in the eyes of the law, and of his legal status and capacity, as being a minor or a person of full age or an incapax, and as having various rights, powers and immunities, and being subject to various duties, liabilities and disabilities.[71]

Secondly, the law of persons deals with the law of domestic relations, those legal rules which affect an individual by reason of his membership of

---

[68] On the history of the subject, see Yntema, "The Historic Bases of Private International Law" (1953) 2 A.J.C.L. 297; Sack, "Conflict of Laws in the History of English Law," in *Law, A Century of Progress*, III, 342.

[69] *e.g.* the important Civil Jurisdiction and Judgments Act 1982.

[70] On the concept of personality see further Salmond, *Jurisprudence*, Chap. 15.

[71] Much of the detail of this branch of the law of persons is, for reasons of convenience, discussed also in connection with constitutional law (*e.g.* the right to become an M.P. or a naturalised subject), or contract (*e.g.* power to make a contract), or reparation (*e.g.* rights to liberty, reputation and freedom from harm), or property (*e.g.* right of landowner to cut timber).

a family group and govern his interactions with others of that group. This branch falls into three main divisions, concerned respectively with relations flowing from marriage, parenthood, and guardianship, frequently called the law of husband and wife, parent and child, and guardian and ward, respectively.[72] In each of these spheres one is concerned with the constitution and termination of the relationship, the mutual rights and duties which flow from it during its subsistence, and the regulation of the matrimonial or family property rights of the parties.

At the centre of all these relationships lies the cardinal social, moral and religious institution of marriage of which the root conception is a lasting and permanent, though possibly not lifelong, union of one male and one female for cohabitation, as distinct from a merely temporary association.[73] This idea of lasting union has been recognised by every legal system in varying degrees; in Christian countries monogamous marriage alone is fully recognised, though polygamous or potentially polygamous marriages contracted under other legal and religious regimes are not necessarily wholly devoid of recognition and effect.

The nature of marriage and the conditions under which it may be contracted and under which, if indeed at all, it may be dissolved, is a difficult modern social, moral and religious as well as legal problem.[74] The rules of law on the subject at any time can only be those which commend themselves as a compromise solution to a large proportion of the community. The legal rules, it should be noted, are those of the state and not of the individual's Church, so that the state law may permit a person to do what his religious beliefs and his Church will not permit him to do, and conversely. The legal rules are those which seem best, having regard to marriage primarily as a social institution, though they naturally tend to correspond fairly closely with the general view of the principal Churches. But there are many matters on which the law is silent and the Churches may exert their influence on their own members unhindered.

It follows that there are bodies of legal rules regulating the contracting of marriage and the dissolution of marriage and the consequences which result in various departments of law from the fact that two individuals are husband and wife. Formerly, the fact that a woman was married placed her under numerous and serious legal disabilities, but over the last 150 years the movement has been towards the emancipation of women and these disabilities are now greatly diminished.[75]

In the same way legal consequences, mutual rights and duties, follow from the birth of children, and these differ according as the children are

---

[72] The name "Family Law" is being increasingly given to this branch of the subject, as a convenient compendious term for its main topics.

[73] On marriage generally see Westermarcks's *History of Human Marriage*; James, *Marriage and Society*; Lecky, *History of European Morals*.

[74] See Report of the Royal Commission on Marriage and Divorce (Cmd. 9678, 1956).

[75] See *A Century of Family Law, 1857–1957* (ed. Graveson and Crane). The details belong to English law only, but the general parts apply substantially to Scotland also.

legitimate or illegitimate, while there must also be considered the intermediate categories of those who are born illegitimate but later legitimated, or who are adopted by individuals as their children though not born as such.

The last division of family law, guardianship, arises from the natural incapacity of young persons and persons of defective mental capacity to look after themselves or exercise the judgment required in legal transactions. Accordingly, there is a body of rules laying down the extent of legal incapacity of various categories of persons too young or mentally too weak to be allowed to act on their own behalf, prescribing what persons may act on their behalf and by what means the appropriate person may be selected, appointed and authorised to act on behalf of the ward, and what the mutual rights and duties of guardian and ward shall be.

Guardianship, it should not be overlooked, is not merely a matter between the parties, but is today of increased social importance as part of the complex legal machinery for the care and protection of children and others unable to look after themselves, and it is now regarded as increasingly important that these persons should have as good opportunities as other individuals for growing up and developing their potentialities.

The law of natural persons also covers the capacities and powers of individuals in extra-domestic relations, that is, *vis-à-vis* persons outside the family, the status, capacity and powers of exceptional persons such as aliens, bankrupts, convicts, and persons of unsound mind, in their relations with other persons, and the special capacities and powers attaching to persons by virtue of professional qualifications.

It has been pointed out that legal persons include not only human beings or natural persons; there are also groups of persons who come together for particular purposes and form voluntary associations. These associations are, to some extent and for limited purposes, treated by the law as legal entities, but are unincorporated, *i.e.* not fully recognised as legal persons in themselves.[76] The device of association is, rather, a collective name for the group of members, though in some cases such associations come very close to being legal persons or corporations. Of this kind are churches other than the legally established Church, friendly societies, trade unions, partnerships, and many clubs, societies and professional bodies.

Thirdly, however, there are those other cases where the groups formed by the association of individuals for specific purposes are treated by the law as themselves legal entities or juristic persons, with legal powers and capacities, liabilities and duties, quite independent and separate from those attaching to the persons who form the group. This arises only where

---

[76] See generally Lloyd, *Unincorporated Associations*.

the group is incorporated in a manner recognised by law; the corporation, not the members, owns the property, sues and is sued, can contract, do wrong, and even commit crime, and it will still exist if all the members die.[77] The main examples of juristic persons are public corporations incorporated by charter or statute, such as the British Broadcasting Corporation, and municipal corporations, both considered in their private capacities, *e.g.* as employers or buyers of goods, chartered bodies such as Universities, Royal Colleges and professional institutions, companies incorporated under the Companies Acts, building societies, and industrial and provident societies.

In the cases of voluntary associations and of corporations, the law of persons defines the way in which the association or corporation comes into being, its powers and capacities, its duties and liabilities, the relations between the body and its members and outsiders, the position of the representatives who act in its name, and the way in which the association or corporation may be ended and dissolved. While in many respects associations and corporations can act like natural persons, in other respects they cannot, nor are the different kinds of associations and of corporations all alike. The powers of each depend on the kind of corporation it belongs to and the powers given to that kind by the relevant Acts.

Law of Obligations

The law of obligations covers all those sets of circumstances when two persons come to be so placed that the law imposes a legal link or bond of obligation between them, from which flows rights, duties, liabilities, privileges, disabilities and powers as between one and another.[78] This department of law falls into eight branches.

The first branch deals with natural obligations arising by force of law from the natural relations of spouses, parents and children.

The second is the law of voluntary obligations, which deals with the rules whereby individuals may voluntarily bind themselves by promises to do something to or for another, such as to pay money annually to a charity.

The third deals with the rules whereby persons may contract or agree in legal and binding form to create certain rights and duties, claims and liabilities between themselves and exigible from each other only. Thus where A and B agree, the one to buy and the other to sell, there is a legal

---

[77] See further Geldart, "Legal Personality" (1911) 27 L.Q.R. 90; Wolff, "On the Nature of Legal Persons" (1938) 54 L.Q.R. 494; Gray, *Nature and Sources of the Law*, Chap. 2; Hallis, *Corporate Personality*; Salmond, *Jurisprudence*, Chap. 15; Maitland, "Trust and Corporation" in *Collected Papers*, III, 321, and *Selected Essays*, 141. See also Gower, *Modern Company Law* (6th ed.), Chaps. 1–4 and 11.

[78] *cf. Inst.* III, 13, *pr. Obligatio est juris vinculum, quo necessitate adstringimur alicuius solvendae rei, secundum nostrae civitatis jura.*

contract of sale, and the law imposes duties on one to deliver the goods and on the other to pay the price, or grants remedies for defective performance or non-performance. The general principles of the law of contract deal with the capacity of individuals to contract, the illegality of some contracts, the form requisite for some contracts, the effect of such factors as error or fraud on the making of a valid contract, performance, and remedies for breach of contract. These general principles of the law of contract have been deduced inductively by jurists from the examination of many particular cases. The law of contract also includes the particular and specific kinds of contracts such as sale, hiring, carriage, lease and others, which, as well as being regulated by the general principles applicable to all or at least most kinds of contracts, frequently have specialities and peculiarities applicable only to contracts of those particular kinds. In many cases, too, there are statutory provisions applicable to particular kinds of contracts only. The particular kinds of contracts fall into two groups, those which create a personal relationship, such as agency, banking contracts, employment or partnership, and those which are intended to transfer, temporarily or permanently, outright or in security, interests in various kinds of property, such as carriage by land, sea and air, custody, deposit, hire, hire-purchase, lease, loan and sale.

The fourth branch of obligations, usually known as quasi-contract or restitution, covers various miscellaneous cases of obligation which are neither truly contractual, despite the name, nor truly delictual, but which resemble contract in that they might have arisen from contract and may even fictionally be supposed to have done so, and resemble reparation or delict in that the obligation is imposed by force of the general law rather than undertaken by agreement of the parties. The circumstances giving rise to a quasi-contractual obligation all have the common element that, if the law did not impose in these circumstances an obligation to make restitution, one party would benefit unjustifiably and the other would lose. Thus quasi-contractual obligations of restitution are imposed by law where one man pays by mistake money which he did not owe, or where one comes into possession of another's property not intended for him.

The fifth branch of obligations is the law of delict or reparation, concerned with circumstances where the law by its own force and independently of any agreement imposes on one individual a legal obligation to make compensation for, or otherwise to remedy, a legal wrong he has done to another, which has constituted an infringement of a legal right vested in that other person by a general principle of law. Thus the law invests individuals generally with a right to freedom from bodily harm; if X injures Y unjustifiably, that is a delict and the law creates an obligation of reparation, imposing on X the duty to compensate Y, and giving Y a right of legal action to recover reasonable reparation from X for his injuries. The law of delict defines the circumstances in which, and conditions under which, such a claim to reparation arises. There is again a body of general principles applicable generally to all or at least most delicts, dealing with such matters as title to sue, the liability of one person for another, the general grounds of liability, defences and exemptions from liability, the effect of insurance and contributory negligence, the remedies, and so on. In addition there are principles applicable to specific delicts, to harm done in particular ways. The main specific delicts are harms to a person in his body or mind, in his domestic relationships, in his liberty, his reputation, his property, his economic relationships with others, but the list of ways in which a person may be harmed is not closed and new kinds of wrongs may yet be recognised as actionable and justifying remedy.

The sixth branch of obligations is the relationship of trust, whereby one person transfers property to another to manage and apply as he has directed, frequently for the benefit of others after his death, or for charitable purposes.

The seventh branch of obligations deals with obligations imposed on parties by statute, such as some duties on employers to have care for the safety of employees, and the eighth with obligations imposed by decree of court, such as to pay another money or refrain from conduct injurious to him.

These bodies of law are of enormous practical importance. Contract is obviously of great importance in business and trade, and commercial undertakings engage every day in numerous contracts, of employment of men, of hiring of plant, of purchase of material, of sale of finished products, of carriage of goods to consignees, and so on. The individual likewise enters into and performs contracts every time he buys a newspaper, travels on public transport, orders shoes, instructs the plumber to repair his water-taps, and so on. Quasi-contract or restitution is much less common or important yet arises not infrequently. Delict or reparation is similarly of widespread and everyday importance. Every accident in the street or at work may give rise to a claim of damages in reparation for the breach of duty, *i.e.* the legal duty or obligation, imposed on each of us by the legal system, not unjustifiably to injure or do harm to our neighbour.

The law of obligations in one branch or another accordingly regulates a great deal of our relations with one another in the normal life of society and it covers a very extensive body of principles and rules of law. It is important to remember that the number of cases of breach of contract or cases where contracts fail of their intended effect are enormously outnumbered by the cases where legally valid contracts are made, duly performed on both sides, and terminated to the complete satisfaction of both parties, all in accordance with the rules of the law of contract, but without the legal system being formally invoked at all. So, too, in the great majority of cases persons avoid doing unjustifiable harm to others and avoid coming under the duty to pay damages in compensation for wrong, that is, they manage to observe the legal obligation not to do wrong to others.

Law of Property

The law of property[79] consists of all the rules conferring, defining and regulating legal rights vested in individuals over material and immaterial things, rights of ownership, possession, use, alienation and disposal. It is a large and important subject of law because of the great number, importance, utility and value of the kinds of objects of property recognised, and of the number and variety of the kinds of legal rights which may be exercised in relation thereto. For various reasons, partly historical, partly rational, various kinds of objects of rights of property have special sets of rules applicable to them. Moreover, in modern times legislative intervention in property law has been common, the underlying notion being to limit or prevent the use of property for personal or selfish ends and to encourage and even require its use in the interest of the general welfare. Thus, disposal on death is limited by taxation and the rules of succession, and use during life is regulated by requirements of licences, planning permission, requisition or compulsory purchase by public authorities, and so on.

Objects of property, accordingly, take many forms and a distinction must be drawn at once between *heritable* and *moveable* objects of property,[80] which, in general, comprise land and buildings on the one hand and goods, such as clothes, furniture and vehicles, on the other hand. This is not a distinction drawn entirely on logical grounds but stems from the dualism of rules of succession on death whereby, for reasons explicable only by legal history, some property (heritable property) formerly descended to the person designated by the law as heir, and some (moveable property) descended to the persons designated by the law as next-of-kin. Difficult questions sometimes arise as to whether some thing is in the circumstances heritable or moveable, and it must be noted that a thing may shift from one category to the other: thus trees are heritable, but when cut the timber is moveable. This distinction, moreover, is similar to but does not quite coincide with the physical distinction between immoveable and moveable property, which is a distinction important where problems of conflict of laws arise.

Cutting across this division into heritable and moveable objects of property is the distinction of *corporeal* and *incorporeal* objects of property,

---

[79] Note that the word "property" may mean either the legal rights of property, of owning, holding, using and disposing of a thing, or the thing itself over which legal rights subsist (*e.g.* "desirable property situated at . . . "). The former is the more correct legal meaning of the word. The latter is properly an object of rights of property or a piece of property.

[80] This corresponds, in general though *not* exactly, to the distinction in English law between real and personal property; land is real property, books, money and shares personal property. In neither system does the distinction correspond *exactly* to that between moveables and immoveables. Note also that "moveable" in this connotation is spelled with an "e." On the distinction between heritable and moveable property, see further Erskine, *Inst.*, II, 2; Bell's *Commentaries*, II, 1–10.

according as there is a corporeal, visible and tangible object over which the property-rights subsist, such as land, buildings or goods, or only an incorporeal right, such as patent rights and copyrights, shares in companies, leases or servitudes. In the latter case, all that exists is the legal right, which may, however, be represented by some tangible object such as a deed, certificate or other piece of paper; but in such a case the paper is only evidence of the right, and is not itself the object of the proprietary right.

A further distinction of importance applicable to all kinds of objects of property is that between *jura in re propria*, or the rights which an individual may exercise over or in relation to objects of his own property, whether material or immaterial, and *jura in re aliena*, or those rights which an individual may possess and exercise in or over objects of the property of another, whether material or immaterial.

The rights, *jura in re propria* or proprietary rights, which a man has over his own property are those of ownership and possession. The full rights of ownership include the power to use the property, deal with its fruits or produce or earnings, and to use up or consume or destroy; the power to possess in person or by another; the power to sell or to give or burden as security for debt; and the power to bequeath or give by will. These rights are not by any means unqualified; thus the common law rules of nuisance limit the uses to which land may be put, while statutory regulations restrict building or development, and the power of bequest is restricted by the doctrine of legal rights.[81] The modern tendency is to limit very much by statute the exercise of the rights of ownership in the general interest of the community. Social and political theory and the economic exigencies of modern times have played havoc with property rights and there is as much law, and more complicated law, dealing with what one is not now allowed to do than with what one may do at common law.

Jura in re aliena, on the other hand, are created by the transfer by an owner to another of certain of the mass of rights which he enjoys by virtue of his ownership; in consequence the other party comes to have certain defined and limited rights in property which he does not himself own. *Jura in re aliena* are always incorporeal. The commonest forms of such rights are, first, the taking of a lease of land or buildings, whereby a tenant acquires the right to possess and occupy certain property for a defined period and on conditions defined partly by the general law (both of statute and of common law) and partly by the terms of the lease or tenancy agreement. The comparable transaction in moveable property is that of letting on hire. The second important kind of *jus in re aliena* consists of the transfer of property, heritable or moveable, to another in security for the repayment of money borrowed by the owner from that other. This has

---

[81] See under Succession, *infra*.

various forms, some applicable to heritable property[82] and some to moveable property[83]; in some the title is transferred to the lender[84] but in others, particularly of moveable property, only possession and not full title of ownership is transferred.[85] The third main item under this heading is the servitude, or right of another to put an owner's property to a certain class of definitely limited uses[86] or to prevent the owner from putting it to a certain class of determined uses.[87] A servitude right is normally real, *i.e.* attaching to and exercisable over a piece of land, but there is a small class of personal servitudes, of which the only important example is liferent, or the right of one person to occupy or use certain property during his lifetime only, and not as absolute owner, and for that period to be a burden or encumbrance on the rights of the owner. The last kind of *jus in re aliena* is the trust, where the holder of property as trustee has his rights, *ex facie* as owner, qualified by the claims of the beneficiary, for whose benefit he holds the property.[88]

These distinctions may be summed up in tabular form.[89]

PROPERTY

		Heritable	*Moveable*	
Jura in re propria	over material things	land, buildings, woods,	goods, vehicles, furniture	Corporeal property
	over immaterial rights	arms, dignities, titles of honour	patents, trade-marks, debts, claims for damages	
Jura in re aliena	over material things	leases, servitudes, some dispositions in security	trusts, liens, some dispositions in security	Incorporeal property
	over immaterial rights	reversionary rights under entail	assignations in security	

Accordingly, the law of property falls naturally into a preliminary part and four main branches. The preliminary part deals with the classification of things and rights as heritable or moveable, corporeal or incorporeal;

---

[82] *e.g.* standard security; floating charge.

[83] *e.g.* pawn or pledge; floating charge; assignation in security (for incorporeals).

[84] *e.g.* in disposition or assignation in security.

[85] *e.g.* in pledge.

[86] *e.g.* right of way, *i.e.* right to pass over X's land by a determined path.

[87] *e.g.* right *altius non tollendi*, to prevent X raising his building higher and thereby cutting off light and air.

[88] On trusts, see further, p. 227, *infra.*

[89] The items of property listed in the two columns are examples of each class only, not a complete enumeration.

with "fixtures," that is, with the circumstances in which a thing moveable by nature may be treated in law as so affixed to heritage as to be heritable; and with the doctrines of conversion and reconversion, that is, with the circumstances in which a claim to heritable property may be changed in law to a claim to moveable property and vice versa, as where for example, land bequeathed by will has been converted into money before the will takes effect. The four branches are (i) corporeal heritable property, such as land, buildings, growing timber and crops; (ii) incorporeal heritable property, such as titles and rights to arms, leases of land, servitudes over land and some security rights secured over land; (iii) corporeal moveable property, such as vehicles, furniture, books, animals, trading stock and machinery; and (iv) incorporeal moveable property, such as claims of debt or for damages, patents and trade-marks, commercial goodwill, shares in companies and some security rights. Those kinds of rights in incorporeal moveables which in most cases are recognised by statutes for the protection of men's intellectual creations such as patents and copyrights, are frequently called "intellectual property." The rules of law are not always the same for the four branches; thus, sale of land differs in certain respects from sale of goods, such as vehicles, and the mode of taking security over land for the repayment of money differs from the mode of taking security over trading stock or company shares. Under each of the branches have to be considered the kinds of property covered, the rights (*jura in re propria*) conferred by ownership and possession of that kind of property, the rights (*jura in re aliena*) which others may enjoy in that kind of property, and the circumstances in which and the legal modes by which the various rights in that kind of property can come into being, can be transferred voluntarily or by operation of law, outright or in security for debt, and can be extinguished.

Trusts

A further branch of the law is the law of trusts. Though the existence of a trust creates many kinds of obligations, the law of trusts is usually discussed along with the law of property. A trust is the legal relationship which arises when property is transferred by one person (the truster) to another or others (the trustee(s)) to hold and administer for a third (the beneficiary), or for stated purposes, the trustee having legal title to the property and formal ownership, but being under an obligation to use his ownership for the benefit of the other, the beneficiary, who is entitled to the benefit of the trust property. "When a person has rights which he is bound to exercise on behalf of another or for the accomplishment of some particular purpose he is said to have those rights in trust for that other or for that purpose and he is called a trustee."[90] The purposes of the trust

---

[90] Maitland, *Lectures on Equity*, 44.

operate as limitations on the trustee's ownership and powers of disposal and are commonly declared in a deed or will under which the truster creates the trust.[91]

The trust concept has many and varied uses; it has been and is of social importance in protecting inexperienced, absent or incapable owners whose property is held and managed by trustees on their behalf. It is the normal way in which endowments for charitable, religious and educational purposes are held and administered. Again, the property of unincorporated groups and communities such as some clubs, churches, trade unions, is commonly held by trustees on behalf of their body of members. In the international sphere the concept has been applied to the protection and supervision of less developed communities by more advanced ones.[92]

Private law trusts are classified as private or public, private where the property is held for individuals, public where it is held for charitable, educational or other public purposes. There is a great mass of law dealing with trustees' powers and duties in different circumstances, the most striking feature of which is the strict insistence by the court that the trustee must always take care, be diligent in his duties, and never make any personal profit from his trusteeship or otherwise permit a conflict to arise between his personal interests and those of the funds under his care. Trusteeship is an onerous responsibility, but the high standards exacted have played a considerable part in the maintenance of public morality, probity and honour, while the courts have extended this by treating company directors and others having charge of property not their own as trustees, and thus enforced a generally high standard of commercial morality.

The Judicial Factor is a kind of trustee; he is a person appointed by the court and answerable thereto, but his functions are similar to those of the trustee in that they normally consist in holding, administering or otherwise dealing with property on behalf of another, who is absent, or incapax, or bankrupt or otherwise cannot be allowed to handle it himself. While he is an officer appointed by the court, he is usually an accountant or other man of business and is not a permanent court official.

Succession

An important branch of the law of property, both in heritable and moveable objects, consists of the rules of succession, which determine the way in which property devolves on other persons on the death of its owner. It falls into three sections. In the first place, there are certain

---

[91] Bell, *Prin.*, para. 1991. The trust has been greatly developed in English law: a classic passage is Maitland's *Lectures on Equity*, lects III–IV. But history and practice in Scotland have not followed English models entirely.

[92] The Trusteeship Council of the United Nations operating under the United Nations Charter, Chaps. 11–13.

claims existing at common law in Scotland known as "legal rights," conferring on certain relatives of a deceased rights to succeed to specified proportions of the moveable property of the deceased. These claims are of the nature of debts against the estate and may be claimed whatever the deceased may have wanted or prescribed by his will and even against his wishes. Accordingly, it is not possible in Scotland completely to disinherit the relatives protected by these provisions.

Secondly, there is the body of rules of intestate succession, which apply in the cases where there is no will, or no will which is valid and effectual, or where any will left has failed in part or has left part of the estate undisposed of; these rules prescribe to what persons and in what proportions the estate should be distributed. There are also certain statutory preferences under which in particular cases certain relatives have preferential claims on the property of the deceased. Until 1964, separate sets of rules existed for heritable property and for moveable property and further rules dealt with the interaction of the two sets of rules where the deceased left both kinds of property. Since 1964 a common set of rules deals with both heritable and moveable property, save in certain special cases.

Thirdly, there are the rules of testate succession, covering the case where the deceased leaves a will. These rules prescribe the requirements for the form and validity of a will or testamentary declaration by the owner on how he wishes his property to devolve or be distributed on his death, and there are various principles of construction and presumptions which have been developed to assist the courts in interpreting the various forms of written expressions which are found in wills.

A pendant to the law of succession is the body of rules governing the rights and duties of executors, who are the individuals appointed by the deceased, or by the court, to ingather the deceased's estate, pay his debts, and distribute it according to his will or the rules of succession.

Succession is in practice materially affected by the incidence of inheritance tax, prescribing what percentage of a deceased person's estate falls to the government on his death. This is itself a substantial body of statutory law and of the interpretations placed on the various statutory provisions in particular circumstances, and the effect of taxation has always to be considered in framing wills and settlements of property.

Bankruptcy

Insolvency or bankruptcy is the state of a person who cannot pay his debts. The court may in appropriate circumstances sequestrate the estates of an insolvent person and appoint a trustee in bankruptcy[93] to take his

---

[93] The person appointed must possess the statutory qualifications to act as an insolvency practitioner.

property, heritable and moveable, out of his hands and administer it for the benefit of his creditors, distributing it rateably among them. The debtor is bound to assist in the realisation and distribution of his estates and, when he is discharged, he is freed from liability for his debts. As an alternative to going through the procedure of bankruptcy, an insolvent person may voluntarily sign a trust deed, making over his property to a trustee who administers it for behoof of the creditors, or make an arrangement with his creditors, called a composition contract, whereby he agrees to pay each so much in the pound of his debt.

Law of Civil Remedies

The law of civil remedies defines what remedial rights may be claimed by a person aggrieved by an infringement of his rights, and in what circumstances one remedy or another is competent or appropriate. Remedies include judicial declarator of rights, interdict against infringement of rights, claims for payment of money owed, damages in compensation for harm done, divorce, and many others.

Adjective Private Law

This is a compendious term for the bodies of law governing the means of giving effect to rights, and the rules governing civil actions to obtain these remedies. The older books, following the Roman law, call it the law of actions, but this is too limited.

Conveyancing

The topic of conveyancing is an adjunct to the law of property. "Conveyancing is the art which deals with the transfer of property by writing . . . transfer includes every kind of right in and over property which can be originated, conveyed, or extinguished by writing."[94] It accordingly covers the requisites of deeds in general and the form of the particular deeds appropriate to create, transfer or extinguish all the different kinds of rights which may subsist in and over the various kinds of property, in particular their transfer on sale or by succession from one person to another. Rules of the law of property define what rights may subsist in various kinds of property, who may hold them and what the incidents of his enjoyment of those rights are: conveyancing law and practice prescribe how the rights may be created, transferred or extinguished. Hence, conveyancing covers the examination of the written title-deeds to land to ascertain a person's rights therein, and the framing of the deeds requisite to convey those rights to a buyer, the preparation of dispositions in security, wills, leases and similar documents affecting property rights.

---

[94] Wood, *Lectures on Conveyancing*, 1; *cf.* Halliday, *Conveyancing Law and Practice*, I, 4; Bell's *Law Dictionary, s.v.*; Jowitt's *Dictionary of English Law, s.v.*

The handling of conveyancing occupies a large part of the time and attention of many solicitors, and it involves drafting and practical techniques and rules of professional practice as well as law, and requires practical instruction as much as study.

Jurisdiction, Procedure and Practice of Courts

Other branches of adjective law prescribe the circumstances in which and the manner in which actions to obtain remedies may be brought and carried through in the various civil courts. It is plain that it is of no advantage to a man to have a legal right or claim against another if he cannot in case of necessity vindicate that right speedily and cheaply, and the importance of a simple and inexpensive method of bringing disputes before a court and having them determined and enforced can hardly be stressed too much. It is equally true that for the legal practitioner knowledge of procedure is important so that he will know in what way best to obtain the remedy required by his client.

First, there are rules prescribing the structure and the competence or jurisdiction[95] of the various civil courts in different kinds of civil cases, the kinds of claims which may be made in different circumstances, and rules governing procedure or the steps to be taken to initiate the claim and the stages it must or may go through before hearing, the course of events at the hearing, and the rules regulating appeals. Procedure is constantly in danger of being treated as an end in itself rather than as merely a means to facilitate the ascertainment of rights and the adjudication of disputes. It is today less possible than it formerly was to lose a good case through mistakes in procedure, but mistaken procedure may still waste much time and money.

An adjunct of civil procedure is the art of pleading,[96] of framing properly and accurately the written statements which are necessary steps in litigation. This is something of an art in itself, requiring an extensive knowledge of law and of procedure, a ready pen, and a subtle and even crafty insight into the strategy and tactics of litigation. In the past, pleading has sometimes been practised rather as an intellectual exercise for its own sake than for its proper function, which is to bring before the court as shortly and accurately as possible the litigant's version of what

---

[95] Notice that jurisdiction means (1) the *power* of issuing an enforceable decree or order, and also (2) the *area* within which a particular court may issue valid and enforceable decrees or orders. Thus the Court of Session has jurisdiction in cases of reduction (sense 1) but actions for debt may be brought in Edinburgh Sheriff Court only against individuals residing within the jurisdiction thereof (sense 2).

[96] The art of advocacy or oral pleading and argument is a further more remote adjunct, which is, however, almost completely unrestrained by rules of law, depending almost entirely on the arts of rhetoric and logic, yet requiring an extensive underlying knowledge of procedure and evidence as well as of law. It is a subject by itself, best learned by experience and following good exemplars. See further, Munkman, *The Technique of Advocacy*.

events happened, his contentions as to what legal result should follow, and to afford his opponent fair notice of the case the latter has to meet.

The law of evidence is likewise intimately connected with procedure and pleading. Evidence comprises the facts, documents and testimony which may legally be adduced at a judicial inquiry to prove or disprove the existence or happening of some matter in dispute. The principles of the law of evidence define, first, what matters the judge is expected, as an intelligent and educated man, to know,[97] and in what cases the judge must[98] or may[99] presume some fact. Then there are principles regulating the admissibility or competency of particular kinds of evidence, such as whether certain persons may give evidence, whether oral evidence may be given or only written, whether evidence of what the witness was told by another may be given, and so on; there are other principles relating to the relevancy of evidence, or its pertinency to the matter under inquiry, such as whether previous incidents similar to that under investigation may be adduced as evidence, or whether actings or statements should be proved as tending to establish intention or other state of mind, and principles regulating the mode of proof of particular kinds of facts, such as that a trust may be proved only by writing or the defender's admission on oath.

There are numerous other topics important to evidence, such as oaths and affirmations, questions of onus of proof, identification of persons, authentication of documents, sufficiency of evidence and corroboration, and the weight of evidence and its evaluation.

While pleading and procedure may tend to be technical and somewhat arid, the study of evidence is valuable for developing the logical and reasoning faculties, and is of great importance in legal practice because points of evidence frequently crop up and if objection is not taken instantly, some damaging statement may be made.

Diligence deals with the various ways of enforcing a decree obtained against a defender and is a topic of some size and complexity.

Closely connected with procedure are the rules regulating the representation of litigants and prescribing which litigants may be granted legal aid, *i.e.* financial assistance from public funds to litigate, and the principles of expenses, defining who must bear the cost of particular steps of litigation.

Arbitration is the determination of a dispute not by resort to the courts, but by an arbiter or arbiters. Any matter, except an issue relating to the status of an individual or of a criminal nature, may be referred to arbitration. In many cases contracts provide that disputes arising in the

---

[97] *e.g.* the main facts of geography, history, physical science, social and commercial life, etc.

[98] *e.g.* that a child under eight is incapable of committing crime; in such cases no evidence to the contrary is allowed.

[99] *e.g.* that a person confined in a mental hospital for five years is incurably insane; presumptions of this latter kind may be rebutted by evidence to the contrary.

performance of the contract are to be determined by arbitration. In some cases, statute directs that certain disputes are to be referred to arbitration. Arbitration may be preferable to litigation in some circumstances, as being quicker, less formal and more private, and permitting the parties to choose an arbiter familiar with the technicalities of the subject in dispute. It is not necessarily cheaper. Commercial contracts frequently provide for the settlement of disputes by arbitration in accordance with rules framed by a trade association. The London Chamber of Commerce maintains a Court of Arbitration which has great experience in settling commercial disputes.[1]

Mercantile, Commercial or Business Law; Industrial or Labour or Employment Law; Agricultural Law

In Scots law, as in Anglo-American legal systems generally, mercantile or commercial or business law is not a distinct branch of law or body of legal rules applicable to a particular class of persons or transaction,[2] but is only a convenient name for a group of topics of the general law of the land.[3] Any special rules applicable to merchants or traders under the law merchant or the general maritime law have long since been absorbed into the general body of the law,[4] and the legal principles applicable to sale, insurance, cheques, patents, insolvency and so on apply equally to all persons, whether merchants or not, whether in any particular kind of business or not, whose activities or transactions fall under that legal heading.

These names therefore do not denote distinct branches of law or logical divisions of the legal system, but are at most cross-divisions, merely convenient compendious names for groups of specific topics selected from all the recognised branches of law and brought together because of common relevance to particular professions and aspects of business life. Books bearing these titles are manuals only, usually for persons whose

---

[1] See further, bibliography, in Chap. 11, *infra.*

[2] Pound, *Jurisprudence*, V, 73; Keeton and Lloyd, *The British Commonwealth—England*, 232, 347; Paton, *Jurisprudence*, 216–217; Keeton, *Jurisprudence*, 228, 416. It is otherwise in French, German and some other systems of law founded closely on the Roman law, which have separate commercial codes, the rules based on the law merchant not having been absorbed into the general law. Hence French private law is divisible into *droit civil* and *droit commercial*, but there is a movement to integrate commercial law with *droit civil*. See further, Schlesinger, *Comparative law*, 186; Van Mehren, *The Civil Law System*, 43–54.

[3] The same is also true of banking law, engineering law, medical, dental, veterinary and nursing law (commonly miscalled "medical jurisprudence," etc.), and any other similar collection of legal principles relevant to the work of a particular profession.

[4] For England, see Holdsworth, *History of English Law*, V, 60; VII, 99; Plucknett, *Concise History of the Common Law*, 657. For Scotland, see Bell's *Commentaries*, Preface, where he says: "The same principle operates as in England; and our courts are daily in the habit of proceeding on this law-merchant as fully authoritative in Scotland, and of allowing the decisions of courts and the writings of lawyers to be cited in illustration of it. . . . The English books afford valuable aid in cultivating the subject of Mercantile Law." But Bell's *Commentaries* was not meant to be, and is not, a treatise on mercantile law alone.

concern is only with the topics of law relevant in their particular business or profession; the lawyer finds his law applicable to commercial or industrial relations under the general branches and analytic headings of the law and in the detailed treatises on particular heads thereof.[5] In consequence the scope and boundaries of these groups are very vague and indefinite.

Books on mercantile law usually deal with partnerships and companies (from the law of persons), contract generally and the specific contracts of sale, carriage and insurance (from the law of obligations), moveable property, including bills and cheques, securities and bankruptcy (from the law of property), and arbitration (from the law of actions).

In modern times the law on certain mercantile topics has been restated and modified by statute, but the statutes have been more concerned to achieve a settled formulation of the rules than to innovate so that reference is still frequently, necessarily made to older cases and practice.[6] The law of companies is, however, entirely a modern statutory creation. Prior to the nineteenth century trading enterprises were either partnerships or set up by Royal Charter,[7] private Act of Parliament[8] or by contract between the members.[9] Private Act became common but was expensive and inconvenient and the principle of limited liability, that each shareholder was to be liable to the amount of the nominal value of his shares and no more, was conceded in 1862. The law has been periodically restated and modified since then, with increased stress on the disclosure of information to the public and the present or prospective shareholder.

Characteristics of topics included in mercantile law have been relative informality, a large degree of freedom to the parties to make what bargains they chose, and steady change and development. Thus in recent years the law on both carriage by air and on the financing of transactions by commercial credits has developed very much. The volume of commercial transactions taking place in the United Kingdom and with persons abroad is large and the problems which arise are numerous and interesting, frequently involving large sums of money and great commercial

---

[5] Such headings as mercantile law, industrial law and so on are not found in encyclopedias, digests of cases, or other reference books; the particular branch of law in question, such as carriage, employment, insurance, etc., must be looked for.

[6] Some of the principal statutes are the Bills of Exchange Act 1882; the Partnership Act 1890; the Sale of Goods Act 1893 (now 1979); the Merchant Shipping Acts 1894–1995; the Marine Insurance Act 1906; the Bankruptcy (Scotland) Act 1985; the Carriage of Goods by Sea Act 1971; the Carriage by Air Act 1961.

[7] *e.g.* The Bank of Scotland, the East India Company.

[8] *e.g.* The Royal Bank of Scotland, early railway companies.

[9] The standard work is W. R. Scott, *Constitution and Finance of English, Scottish and Irish Joint Stock Companies to 1720* (3 vols., 1910–12); see also Carr, *Select Charters of Trading Companies* (Selden Society); Causton and Keane, *Early Chartered Companies, 1296–1858*; Davis, *Corporations* (2 vols.); Formoy, *Historical Foundations of Modern Company Law*; Hunt, *Development of Business Corporation in England, 1800–67*.

reputations, while every change in commercial practice or technique is liable to react on the law.[10]

The study of industrial (or labour or employment law) commonly covers trade unions and industrial associations (from the law of persons), contract generally and the specific contract of employment (traditionally known as the law of master and servant), and the employer's delictual liability for wrongs by or to the employee (from the law of obligations), industrial property, such as patents and trade-marks (from the law of property), and arbitration and the settlement of industrial disputes (from the law of actions). The fundamental topic is the contractual relationship of master and servant,[11] employer and employee, a relationship which gives rise to numerous contractual and delictual rights between the parties and between them and third parties. On this stem there has been grafted since 1800 an enormous growth of statute law and subordinate legislation regulating wages and holidays, hours and conditions of work, and providing in great detail for the safety, health and welfare of the employee. The complexity of modern industry requires separate provisions for many particular kinds of industrial enterprises. In modern times, as part of the national system of social security,[12] there have developed provisions for unemployment insurance[13] and for insurance against the loss caused by industrial injuries.[14] Again, one of the significant modern social and economic developments has been the development of freedom to associate in trade unions for the purpose of collective bargaining[15] and the legal aspects of trade union activity, industrial disputes and their settlement are of profound importance. Elements of public law, such as the control of monopolies may also be considered in the context of industrial law, and some relevant elements in the total situation, such as collective bargaining between employers and trade unions, are very little regulated by law at all.

Agricultural law deals with contract generally, the particular contracts of sale, hiring and employment, delictual liability to and for employees and for animals, the law of landownership, leases and smallholdings, compensation and arbitration. It may include partnerships and even companies and many topics of public law such as farm subsidies, and taxation.

---

[10] See Lord Devlin, "Commercial Law and Commercial Practice," in *Samples of Lawmaking*, 28.

[11] In the older books the law of master and servant was usually dealt with as part of the law of persons, or of domestic relations, but this treatment is appropriate only to domestic servants now.

[12] The history, background and development of this may be studied in the (Beveridge) Report on Social Insurance and Allied Services, 1942 (Cmd. 6404), App. B.

[13] Social Security Contributions and Benefits Act 1992, as amended, superseding legislation which originated with the National Insurance Act 1911.

[14] Social Security Contributions and Benefits Act 1992, Pt V, as amended, replacing the Workmen's Compensation Acts 1897–1943.

[15] This can be studied in such books as Cole's *Short History of the British Working Class Movement, 1789–1947*, and in books on social and economic history such as Gregg's *Social and Economic History of Britain, 1760–1965*.

These titles accordingly connote functional selections of topics which are useful for particular groups of students and particular professions, but the student of the law and of the legal system as a whole must regard them as divisions cutting across the logical and analytical classification of the law and not as distinct branches of law. In the same way, books can bring together all the principles of law relevant to the theatre, or engineering operations, or any other species of activity.[16]

Forensic Science, Medicine and Psychiatry

These subjects are not branches of the law at all, but are applications of science, medicine and psychiatry to the purposes of the law and the ends of justice. In many sets of circumstances, both in civil but even more so in criminal law, the lawyer has to call on the scientist, doctor[17] or psychiatrist for assistance in the elucidation or interpretation of facts, particularly where difficult issues as to the state of mind or body of some person arise for determination. Thus, scientific knowledge is called on in questions involving forgery, poisons and weapons, medical knowledge in cases of wounding, homicide, sexual offences and the like, and psychiatric knowledge in regard to cases of mental deficiency or abnormality, diminished responsibility and other difficult mental states. There is no good reason why there should not equally be subjects of forensic engineering or forensic architecture where the knowledge of experts in other branches of learning must be called on to assist legal purposes, but the three branches referred to have legal importance with particular frequency because the law is always dealing with human beings and their actings, and has so often to answer the questions Who, When, How and Why, about these human beings before it can seek to apply a legal rule. These branches of knowledge, and indeed all expert testimony from persons skilled in sciences other than law, supply evidence of states of fact and the bases for inference of fact, so that they are adjuncts of the law of evidence. They do not themselves answer problems of law. Much of the confusion and dispute between legal and medical approaches to insanity

---

[16] It is noteworthy also that the institutional writers and main text-writers deal with the topics sometimes brought under the headings of mercantile, industrial or agricultural law in the context of their general expositions of the private law as a whole. Thus, *e.g.* Bell's *Principles* deals with all the different kinds of commercial contracts in Book First, with industrial property in Book Second, and with bankruptcy in Book Fifth. So, too, do Erskine's *Principles*, Hume's *Lectures* and More's *Lectures*. Furthermore, the study of law under such titles as commercial and industrial law is overlapping and very repetitive, and it is not possible on any such basis to construct a convenient or satisfactory classification of the whole legal system, because much of the law would have to be restated for each of the types of human relations. Similarly, the grouping of cases or rules under topic-headings arranged alphabetically, as in legal encyclopedias and other reference works, is useful only to the person who understands the analytical arrangement. For purposes of exposition, study and understanding, analytical classification remains the only satisfactory basis.

[17] Forensic medicine is sometimes called Medical Jurisprudence but, despite the name, it has no connection at all with Jurisprudence in the sense of legal theory.

would be avoided if it were remembered that the function of the forensic physician or psychiatrist is to supply expert evidence from which a judge or jury may, as tribunal of fact, determine whether or not the person under examination is insane within the legal definition thereof, which is concerned with responsibility for conduct and liability to the legal consequences thereof, rather than with insanity in a medical sense.

Scots Law and English

Having now surveyed the main departments of the law, it may be of value, in view of the proximity of English law and of its constant tendency to encroach on Scots law, to consider the points of contact and distinctness between the two systems. It is too often assumed that Scots law is much the same as English, or a pale reflection, or substantially the same with different terminology, or with a few minor variations.[18] In fact it is radically different,[19] has developed differently under the influence of different agencies, and frequently arrives at results not dissimilar to those of English law but from very different premises and by a very different train of reasoning.[20] It is all too common to find in judgments, even of the highest courts,[21] statements or assumptions that the laws of Scotland and of England are the same on the matter in issue; these are frequently unjustified and frequently made by persons with no real qualification to say so.

Quite apart from terminology and procedure of enforcement, the principles and content of the rules of Scots law are different from English. This is most noticeable in property law where the two systems are poles apart in their land law.[22] The differences are lesser in family law, in reparation and in contract, and least in mercantile and industrial topics. In public law, the difference is quite substantial in constitutional and administrative law, very material in criminal law, and at its least in taxation. Pleading and procedure are quite different in both civil and criminal matters, but evidence rather less so, though not by any means the same in the two systems.

In its reliance on broad principles the Scots law shows affinity with civil law systems of the Continent rather than with the Anglo-American common law. "The civilian naturally reasons from principles to instances, the common lawyer from instances to principles. The civilian puts his faith

---

[18] Lawson, *The Rational Strength of English Law*, persistently underestimates the differences.

[19] René David, *Introduction à l'Etude du Droit Privé de l'Angleterre*, 164, considers Scots law as "très different du droit anglais."

[20] Untold harm has been done to Scots law by lawyers and judges, even of the House of Lords, who have assumed that because Scots and English law both give a remedy for the same wrong, they do so for the same reasons. See further, Walker, "Some Characteristics of Scots Law" (1955) 18 M.L.R. 321.

[21] Gibb, *Law from Over the Border, passim.*

[22] See Farran, *Principles of Scots and English Land Law.*

in syllogisms,[23] the common lawyer in precedents. . . . The civilian thinks in terms of rights and duties, the common lawyer in terms of remedies. The civilian is chiefly concerned with the policy and rationale of a rule of law, the common lawyer with its pedigree. The instinct of the civilian is to systematise. The working rule of the common lawyer is *solvitur ambulando.* . . . The differences in methods are fundamental and far more significant than the apparent similarity of the end products of widely different processes of thought."[24]

Accordingly, while Scots law operates in an environment very similar to that of English law and is subject to a common court of final appeal[25] and a common legislative body and higher executive, it is, in varying degrees in different topics, a distinct system with principles and methods of legal thought of its own which are not necessarily inferior to English. It can never safely, and should never, be assumed that any principle or rule of English law either is or should be the law of Scotland, and the Scottish rule should always be sought independently.

FURTHER READING

Hall: *Readings in Jurisprudence,* Chap. 14—Classification.
Cooper: *The Scottish Legal Tradition.*
Gibb: *Preface to Scots Law.*
Jolowicz, *Lectures in Jurisprudence,* Part III.
Markby, *Elements of Law,* Chap. VIII.
Mitchell: *Constitutional Law.*
Paton, *Textbook of Jurisprudence,* Books IV–VI.
Smith: *British Justice—The Scottish Contribution.*
     Studies Critical and Comparative.
     Short Commentary on the Law of Scotland.

---

[23] On this mode of legal reasoning in Scotland, see Walker, "The Theory of Relevancy" (1951) 63 J.R. 1.

[24] Cooper, "The Common and the Civil Law—A Scot's View" (1950) 63 H.L.R. 468, 471.

[25] Except that no Scottish criminal appeals go to the House of Lords.

CHAPTER 6

THE LEGISLATIVE ORGANS OF SCOTS LAW

AMONG the important institutions of the Scottish legal system are the bodies and persons having legislative power, that is power to lay down general rules, or new rules, and to abrogate or alter old rules and to make authoritative declarations of what the law on some matter is, or is to be. They are distinguishable into (a) the treaties establishing the European Communities, the Council of the EU and the Commission of the Communities; (b) the Council of the EU and the Commission, which have powers to make rules in furtherance of their policies in implement of the Treaties; (c) the United Kingdom Parliament having supreme legislative power in all other respects throughout the United Kingdom; (d) the Scottish Parliament having delegated power to legislate for Scotland in certain fields; and (e) numerous persons and bodies having legislative powers delegated by the United Kingdom Parliament or the Scottish Parliament to legislate within limited spheres.

EUROPEAN UNION

On matters to which it applies, EU law is superior to United Kingdom law.[1] The treaties establishing the three European Communities (Coal and Steel Community, Economic Community and Atomic Energy Community) operate by virtue of statutory incorporation in all Member States[2] and accordingly have force equivalent to legislation therein,[3] and have also created law-making organs (namely the Council of the EU and the Commission of the European Communities) and empowered them to make secondary or more detailed legislation. The European Council and the European Parliament have no delegated legislative powers.

---

[1] *Costa v. Ente Nazionale per l'Energia Elettrica (ENEL) (C6/64)* [1964] E.C.R. 1141; *R. v. Secretary of State for Transport, ex p. Factortame* [1990] 2 A.C. 85, [1991] A.C. 603.

[2] It was effected in the UK by the European Communities Act 1972, and the European Communities (Amendment) Acts 1986, 1993 and 1998. From 1999, Articles of the treaties are cited by arabic numbers followed by two letters indicating the treaty concerned, *viz.* EC for the EC Treaty as renumbered by the Treaty of Amsterdam 1997, CS for the ECSC Treaty, EA for the Euratom Treaty, and EU for the European Union Treaty (Maastricht) 1992. There are provisions for citation of Articles as formerly numbered and for those replaced en bloc by the Treaty of Amsterdam, see *Practice Notes—Treaty Citation* [1999] All E.R. (E.C.) 481 and 646.

[3] Breach by the Government of an article of a Treaty may give rise to a claim for breach of statutory duty: *Bourgoin SA v. Ministry of Agriculture, Fisheries and Food* [1986] Q.B. 716.

The European Council is not, strictly speaking, an E.U. institution. It consists of national presidents, prime ministers and foreign ministers, and meets at least every six months, to decide the overall direction of the EU on difficult issues. These representatives speak for their national interests.

The Council of the EU consists of one representative of ministerial rank from each Member State. It is a distinct institution and may sue and be sued before the European Court. The Presidency is held by the Member States in rotation for six months at a time[4] and decisions may be taken in a few cases by simple majority, but in most cases a qualified majority is required under which the votes are weighted by reference to the population size of the Member States;[5] and some treaty provisions, including constitutional measures and approximation of laws, require unanimity. It has its own Secretariat-General and Legal Services. The work of the Council is prepared by COREPER, the committee of permanent ambassadors of Member States to the Communities, permanently based at Brussels, and by working parties of national civil servants.

The Council is the principal legislative organ of the Communities; in general the Council must act on a proposal from the Commission, with a text prepared by it and formally submitted as a Commission proposal. It may amend a Commission proposal unanimously only. In certain cases it must consult the European Parliament. It may also confer on the Commission substantial powers for the implementing of acts of Council.

The Commission is the main initiator and co-ordinator of policy, and the executive agency; at present it consists of 20 members, two nominated by each of the five larger states[6] and one by each of the others, for five-year renewable terms. The President and two Vice-Presidents are appointed from the members for two and a half year renewable terms. Each Commissioner is assisted by a small *cabinet* or private office, and has responsibility for one or more portfolios or fields of activity, and all are assisted by European civil servants organised in Directorates-General, Directorates and Divisions, each dealing with particular areas of policy. There is also a Secretariat General and a Legal Service. The Commission acts as a unit with a quorum of eight and reaches decisions by simple majority. It is the function of the Commission to make proposals for legislation, usually after consultation with the interests likely to be affected in the Member States; it cannot itself legislate but may be empowered by Council regulations to make delegated legislation in implement of a legislative programme, *e.g.* on agriculture,[7] and has powers to ensure that

---

[4] Merger Treaty 1965, Art. 2.

[5] The total weight is 87 votes and 62 are required for a qualified majority; the UK has 10 votes.

[6] By convention since 1973 one of the UK Commissioners has been drawn from the Conservative party and one from the Labour party; they are normally experienced politicians.

[7] See *France, Italy and UK v. EC Commission* [1982] E.C.R. 2545; [1982] 3 C.M.L.R. 144.

the provisions of the treaties and the measures taken by the institutions thereunder are applied. Hence it may bring actions against Member States in the European Court for failure to implement obligations under EC law.

The European Parliament is the least powerful institution, originally consisting of delegates from Member States' national parliaments but now consisting of 626 members (MEPs) directly elected by the adults of the Member States for five-year terms.[8] Peers, clergy and M.P.s may be elected, but officers of the EU and members of national governments may not. It holds its plenary sessions at Strasbourg.

It elects its own President and 14 Vice-Presidents for $2^{1}/_{2}$ years and has adopted its own rules of procedure. It is assisted by five Questors with special responsibility for administrative and financial matters concerning members, a Secretary-General and secretariat. Unlike the House of Commons there is no Government and no Opposition and the Chamber is semi-circular, like a continental-country chamber and wholly unlike the House of Commons where Government and Opposition face each other. The members do not sit as national delegations but in political groups of like-minded members from different countries. The Parliament operates through numerous standing committees, each dealing with an area of Community policy, and they prepare reports which form the basis of debates in the full Parliament.

The Parliament has no legislative power, though it can recommend to the Council and the Commission and it has to be consulted by the Council in cases specified in the treaties; even then its view is not binding. It has some weak political control through supervision of the Council and Commission and can discuss the Commission's annual general report. It can put questions to the Commission to which the latter must reply, or to the Council but to which the Council need not reply. It may also censure the Commission and cause it to resign as a body, and it has several times rejected the draft Community budget.

The Court of Auditors, established in 1977, has the function of examining the accounts of all Community institutions, to ensure that all revenue has been received, that all expenditure is lawful, and that financial management is effective. It consists of one representative from each Member State, appointed by the Council.

The Council of the EU and the Commission may both[9] make *regulations*, which have general application, bind the Member States in their entirety and are directly applicable, having the force of law in Member

---

[8] The UK elects 87 MEPs, 72 from England, eight from Scotland, four from Wales and three from Northern Ireland. Elections have been held every five years from 1979. See European Assembly Elections Acts 1978 and 1981; European Assembly Elections Regs. 1986 (S.I. 1986 No. 2209).

[9] It was effected in the UK by the European Communities Act 1972, and the European Communities (Amendment) Act 1986. ECSC Treaty, Art. 14; EEC Treaty, Art. 189; Euratom Treaty, Art. 161.

States' territories without need for confirmation or other action by their national legislatures. They may each also issue *directives* addressed to Member States binding as to the result to be achieved, but having to be implemented by the states in whatever manner they deem appropriate,[10] and *decisions* addressed either to Member States or to corporations or individuals therein, binding on the addressee only, but binding completely and leaving no discretion in the manner in which they are carried out. There is a confusing variety of legislative procedures in the EU. Whether an act of the organs of the Communities is a regulation, directive or decision is determined by its content and object, not by its form. *Recommendations* made under the ECSC Treaty can have, but other recommendations, and *opinions*, issued by Community organs, have no binding force and cannot be regarded as legislative. The legality of acts, including binding regulations, directives and decisions, of the Council and the Commission, is controlled by the Court of the European Communities, which can invalidate any act contravening the Treaties.

There are also two consultative bodies, appointed by the Council, the Economic and Social Committee and the Committee of the Regions, to give a voice to local authorities, and a number of organisations and other bodies, including the European Monetary Institute and the European Police Office (Europol).

Publication

The treaties and other primary sources of EU law are published by the Office for Official Publications of the EU, by The Stationery Office and, unofficially, by commercial publishers.

The *Official Journal* of the EU, cited as O.J., is published in all the Community languages,[11] in two series, "L" (Legislation) and "C" (Information and notices, and proceedings in the European Parliament). Community acts are cited by their classification, number and year, with the number, date and page reference of the *Official Journal*[12] or by the letters O.J. with the year, series letter, number and page.[13] Directives and decisions are cited by the year and number.[14] The text of most EU law is also available in the *Encyclopaedia of European Community Law*,[15] which consists of three series, *viz.* A: United Kingdom sources; B: EC Treaties; and C: Community secondary legislation.

Information on new EU legislation is given in *Current Law* and indexes are published periodically by the EU as *Directory of Community Legislation*

---

[10] This is frequently effected in the United Kingdom by amendment of relevant legislation.

[11] Prior to British admission in 1973 English was not an official language and references are to the *Journal Officiel*.

[12] *e.g.* Reg. 1234/92 (O.J. L 123, 9.4.92, p. 3).

[13] *e.g.* O.J. 1992, L 123/3.

[14] *e.g.* O.J. 92/567.

[15] Ed. K. R. Simmonds, published by Sweet and Maxwell Ltd.

in Force, by Butterworths as *European Communities Legislation: Current Status*, and by other commercial publishers.

The Legal Service of the Commission has established CELEX, an automated documentation system covering the treaties, Community legislation, working documents and parliamentary questions and answers, to serve the institutions and in due course national bodies and interested persons.

Prospective and Retrospective Application

EU legislation is normally prospective but it has been held that Community rules applied to practices established before the coming into force of the relevant treaty if their effect continued thereafter. Legislation is presumed prospective only and not retrospective unless there is clear provision to that effect. Regulations come into force on the date specified in them, or if no date is specified, on the twentieth day following publication. Directives and decisions have to be notified to those to whom they are addressed and take effect on such notification.

Implementing EC Legislation in the United Kingdom

Certain legislation of EU institutions becomes law in the United Kingdom when adopted by the relevant institution, *viz.* decisions under the ECSC Treaty,[16] regulations under the EEC and Euratom Treaties and decisions under the EEC and Euratom treaties in so far as they are legislative rather than mere application of the law.[17] Though a directive *ex facie* binds Member States, it may have direct effect[18] and be directly enforceable in national courts by persons affected.[19] In cases where EU legislation requires to be implemented by the United Kingdom the European Communities Act 1972 enables the making of Orders in Council and enables designated ministers and departments to make regulations: for implementing any Community obligation of the United Kingdom; or enabling it to be implemented; or enabling any rights enjoyed or to be enjoyed by the United Kingdom under or by virtue of the treaties to be exercised; or for the purpose of dealing with matters arising out of or related to any such obligation or rights; or the coming into force or the operation from time to time of the provisions giving legal force to Community rights.

---

[16] ECSC Treaty, Art. 14.

[17] EEC Treaty, Art., 189; Euratom Treaty, Art. 161. Indeed the European Court has said that these should not be re-enacted: *Variola SpA v. Amministrazione Italiana delle Finanze* [1973] E.C.R. 981.

[18] On "direct effect" see p. 701, *supra*.

[19] *Marshall v. Southampton and South West Hampshire AHA (No. 1)* (C152/84) [1986] Q.B. 401; *Litster v. Forth Dry Dock and Engineering Co. Ltd*, 1989 S.L.T. 540.

Scrutiny of Proposed EU Legislation in the United Kingdom

Both Houses of the United Kingdom Parliament have established Select Committees to scrutinise proposed EU legislation.[20] The House of Commons committee has to consider draft proposals, report if they raise issues of legal or political importance and to make recommendations to the House, and in 1980 the House of Commons resolved that no minister should agree in the Council of the EU to proposed EU legislation unless the committee had indicated that agreement need not be withheld, or the minister decided that it should not be withheld, in which latter case he was to explain his reasons to the House. The House of Lords Committee has wider terms of reference and has also produced reports of its own on approximation of laws and other matters. It operates through sub-committees, one of which includes a number of Lords of Appeal in Ordinary and considers any EC proposal which would lead to significant changes in United Kingdom law or have far-reaching implications for areas of United Kingdom law.

The European Communities Act 1972, in so far as purporting to enact certain regulations of the EEC Council, is not contrary to Article XVIII of the Treaty of Union 1707.[21]

Proof

All European Communities legislation which is published in the *Official Journal* is judicially noticed and proved by production of the text in the *Journal*.[22]

UNITED KINGDOM LEGISLATION

Within the United Kingdom, supreme legislative power is vested in the United Kingdom Parliament sitting at Westminster and is exercised by considering Bills and, if thought fit, by passing them into law as statutes or Acts of Parliament.[23] A statute or Act of Parliament is a pronouncement by the Queen by and with the advice of both Houses of Parliament, the effect of which is to declare the law or change the law, or both.

Legislative Drafting

The first appearance of official draftsmen of Bills was about 1800, but until 1869 each department of state made its own arrangements for

---

[20] Lord Fraser of Tullybelton, "Scrutiny of Community Legislation in the UK Parliament," *In Memoriam J. D. B. Mitchell*, 29.

[21] *Gibson v. Lord Advocate*, 1975 S.C. 136.

[22] European Communities Act 1972, s. 3(2).

[23] The structure, composition and legislative procedures of Parliament belong to constitutional law and are dealt with in books on that subject and in Erskine May's *Parliamentary Practice*. Parliament also has other functions than legislation, but legislation occupies much of its time.

drafting with consequent inconsistency of language, style and arrangement. In 1869 there was established the office of Parliamentary Counsel to the Treasury (consisting of two barristers, with a small office staff), to draft legislation for all Government Bills, except Scottish and Irish ones.[24] Scottish Bills were drafted in the Lord Advocate's office. A private member had to, and has to, get his Bill drafted himself, though if the Government supports his proposals, it may give him the assistance of a parliamentary draftsman. Since it was established, the office of Parliamentary Counsel has greatly expanded.[25] The Scotland Office is responsible for drafting legislation so far as affecting Scotland. This latter office is also responsible for the drafting and presentation to Parliament of subordinate legislation affecting Scotland. The draftsmen also draft amendments moved during the passage of the legislation and frequently redraft amendments proposed by backbenchers which the Government is prepared to accept in principle. There has been much criticism of the structure, language and form of Bills and Acts.[26]

Bills

At the present time a projected piece of legislation during its passage through Parliament is called a Bill,[27] and these may be of three kinds, each being subject to different procedure in Parliament. These are (*a*) public Bills which relate to matters of public policy generally, alter the general law, and apply generally to the members of the public who fall within their scope; most of these are Government Bills introduced by Ministers on behalf of the Government in pursuance of the Government's policy and thereby assured of the general support in Parliament of the supporters of the Government.[28] Every such Bill must be approved by the Cabinet, which must approve the main points of the proposed Bill and authorise its being drafted. It may be considered by an *ad hoc* committee of the Cabinet at which the views of other Departments are considered and legal, financial, economic and other implications are considered.[28] Some public Bills are, however, introduced by private members in the limited time made available to them. These private members' Bills are not sponsored

---

[24] Mr. (later Lord) Thring, then Parliamentary Counsel to the Home Office, was the first holder of the office, and was responsible for considerable improvements in the style and arrangement of statutes. The Interpretation Act 1889 assisted the process by generalising the definitions of common terms in statutes. On the history, see Ilbert, *Legislative Methods and Forms*, 77–85, and for practical guidance on drafting, pp. 237–334 thereof. See also Ilbert, *Mechanics of Law Making*, 56 *et seq*. On drafting and the early stages of a Bill, see Ram, "Improvement of the Statute Book," 1951 J.S.P.T.L. 442. On the modern position, see Mackenzie and Grove, *Central Administration in Britain*.

[25] On the drafting process see Sir Harold Kent, *In on the Act*, 43 *et seq*.

[26] Statute Law Society reports: *Statute Law Deficiencies* (1970); *Statute Law—the Key to Clarity* (1972); Report of the Renton Committee on *The Preparation of Legislation*, Cmnd. 6053 (1975); Dale, *Legislative Drafting—a New Approach* (1977), 331.

[27] For procedure see Erskine May, *Parliamentary Practice*, Chap. 21.

[28] Butler, "The Birth of a Bill—The Education Act," 1949, *Parliamentary Affairs* 210.

or supported by the Government and may even be contrary to its policy, though they may on the other hand be adopted later by the Government and their passage facilitated.[29]

(b) Private Bills, which are for the particular interest or benefit of any person or body and are solicited by the parties concerned, and deal with local or personal matters such as giving special power to a local authority, or dealing with private estates, names, peerage or status. Private Bills are brought in on petition and are usually referred to private Bill committees, before whom the promoters have to establish their case for obtaining the parliamentary powers they seek.[30]

(c) Hybrid Bills, which are introduced as public Bills but affect private interests in much the same way as private Bills, and have a special procedure.[31]

There should also be noted Provisional Order Confirmation Bills which were Bills introduced to have confirmed by Parliament orders and schemes made by Ministers.[32] Local authorities and private bodies requiring statutory powers, frequently obtained them in this way. This avoided the expense of private Bills. Their proposals were made to the Secretary of State for Scotland who, if satisfied as to their desirability, and if necessary after a public inquiry, issued a provisional order confirming the scheme, and later introduced (as a public Bill) a Bill confirming the provisional order and giving it statutory effect. Since 1999, the confirmation is made by Act of the Scottish Parliament.[33] The resulting Act is classified as a local Act.

Acts

When Bills have passed through all their stages and received the Royal Assent, they become Acts of Parliament or Statutes. Acts are now[34] classified as public or private[35] and as general, local or personal. A public Act is one which is judicially noticed by the courts and the terms of which

---

[29] Notice that private members' Bills and private Bills are completely different things; the one is introduced by a private member, rather than a Minister, but is a public Bill; the other is sponsored to affect private interests, not general to the whole country.

[30] See Erskine May, *Parliamentary Practice, op. cit.*, Chap. 35.

[31] Erskine May, *op. cit.*, Chap. 21.

[32] The procedure is regulated by the Private Legislation Procedure (Scotland) Act 1936. See also Constable, Beveridge and Macmillan, *Provisional Orders*. For examples, see Dunoon Burgh Order Confirmation Act 1954 (2 & 3 Eliz. 2, c. xxiii); Writers to the Signet Widows' Fund Order Confirmation Act 1965 (1965, c. xii); Glasgow Corporation (Carnoustie Street) Bridge Order Confirmation Act 1966 (1966, c. ii). In England procedure by provisional order has been largely superseded by procedure under the Statutory Orders (Special Procedure) Acts 1945 and 1965 (also applicable to Scotland), on which see Molson in (1950) 3 *Parliamentary Affairs* 458 and Erskine May, *op. cit.*, Chap. 40.

[33] Scotland Act 1998 (c. 46), s. 94.

[34] There were formerly other classifications at different times, for which see Ilbert, *Legislative Methods and Forms*, 26, 49; Craies' *Statute Law* (7th ed.), 56–57; Erskine May, *op. cit.*, Chaps. 21, 39.

[35] This classification, it should be noted, is entirely different from the classification of Bills before Parliament into public and private.

accordingly need not be proved, whereas a private Act is one the existence and terms of which have to be proved by the party founding on it in any court in which it is founded on. Every Act passed since 1850 is now deemed public in this sense, and to be judicially taken notice of as such, unless the contrary is expressly provided and declared by the Act.[36] An Act is general, local or personal according to the extent of its operation, applying to the whole community, or to a locality, or to a particular individual. A public Bill may be general, local or personal in nature, but always emerges as a public Act; a private Bill may be local or personal in nature, but emerges as a public Act in the former case and a private Act in the latter because all personal Acts contain a provision that "this Act shall not be deemed to be a public Act."[37] The main distinction is accordingly between public and general Acts on the one hand and public and local and personal on the other. This distinction had been described[38] as follows: "A general Act prima facie is that which applies to the whole community. In the natural meaning of the term it means an Act of Parliament which is unlimited both in its area and as regards the individual in its effects. And as opposed to that you get statutes which may well be public because of the importance of the subjects with which they deal and their general interest to the community, but which are limited in respect of area—a limitation which makes them local—or limited in respect of individuals or persons—a limitation which makes them personal."

Publication of Legislation

When a Bill has been presented to Parliament by a Minister or private member, it is printed on blue paper and can be purchased by the public from The Stationery Office. A Bill amended in committee is usually reprinted as amended before report to the House and again when transmitted to the other House.

Once a Bill has received Royal Assent and become an Act, it is assigned a chapter number and copies are printed by the Queen's Printer on white paper and may be purchased by the public from The Stationery Office. All the statutes so printed for one year are bound up in one or more volumes and published by The Stationery Office as the *Public General Statutes* for the calendar year. They are also reprinted in various editions by various commercial publishers.

Nearly all private Acts are printed by the Queen's Printer but are not now published as bound volumes. An annual list of titles is issued by The Stationery Office[39] in which private Acts are classified as (1) (a) ordinary private Acts; (b) public Acts of a local character including Provisional

---

[36] Interpretation Act 1978, s. 3.
[37] See, *e.g.* Arundel Estate Act 1957 (5 & 6 Eliz. 2, c. *1*), s. 8.
[38] *R. v. London County Council* [1893] 2 Q.B. 454, 462, *per* Bowen L.J.
[39] Table of the Local and Personal Acts (including the Public Acts of a local character).

Order Confirmation Acts,[40] and (2) personal Acts. A few personal Acts are not printed; this category is now almost obsolete.

The classification adopted in Queen's Printer's editions of the statutes is now:

(1) Public General Statutes, *i.e.* judicially noticed and also of general application or importance. These have chapter numbers in arabic characters.

(2) Local (formerly local and personal), either

    (*a*) public, *i.e.* to be judicially noticed, but of a local character,[41] or

    (*b*) not public, *i.e.* declared "not to be deemed a public Act."

These have chapter numbers in small Roman numerals.

(3) Personal, *i.e.* relating to individuals' personal affairs, either

    (*a*) printed by the Queen's Printer, or

    (*b*) not so printed (now almost obsolete).

Those in group (*a*) are numbered in italicised arabic figures.[42]

Other Descriptions of Statutes

Some other terms applied to Acts are merely descriptive and not strictly classificatory. Thus an Act may be called *declaratory* if passed to explain and declare the pre-existing law on some particular subject to remove doubts thereon, and frequently to set aside what Parliament believes to have been an erroneous interpretation or judicial mistake.[43] A *codifying Act* is passed to reduce to the form of a code the whole of the existing statute law and case law on a given subject,[44] and thus to state the whole law on that topic in codified form, and a *consolidating Act* to bring together into one Act provisions previously contained in a number of statutes,[45] usually with corrections and minor improvements, but not effecting major changes of substance. Consolidating Acts may, exceptionally, profess to consolidate with amendments, but these are comparatively rare. Consolidating Acts are presumed not to change the law

---

[40] These are numbered indiscriminately in the order of passing and assigned chapter numbers in small Roman type.

[41] Including Provisional Order Confirmation Acts.

[42] Examples, taken from the 1893 statutes, are: The Rules Publication Act 1893 (56 & 57 Vict. c. 66) (Public general); East Fife Central Railway Act 1893 (56 & 57 Vict. c. cxcvi) (Local); Ryland's Estate Act 1893 (56 & 57 Vict. c. *1*) (Private—printed by the Queen's Printer); and Fleming's Divorce Act 1893 (Private—not printed). Unprinted personal Acts are not numbered and are now almost obsolete. The last private Act dealing with divorce is said to have been passed in 1923.

[43] *e.g.* Territorial Waters Jurisdiction Act 1878, passed to overrule the decision in *R. v. Keyn* (1876) 2 Ex.D. 63.

[44] *e.g.* Bills of Exchange Act 1882; Partnership Act 1890; Sale of Goods Act 1893 (now 1979); Marine Insurance Act 1906.

[45] *e.g.* Titles to Land Consolidation Act 1868; Companies Act 1985; Sale of Goods Act 1979; Employment Protection Consolidation Act 1978. Consolidating Acts do *not* seek to incorporate the substance of case law as do codifying Acts. But it must be noted that the terms "codifying" and "consolidating" are sometimes used carelessly and incorrectly, rather than with their strict connotation.

but simply to re-enact it in convenient consolidated form.[46] *Statute Law Revision Acts* and *Statute Law (Repeals) Acts* are passed periodically to repeal and remove from the Statute Book spent, obsolete, superseded and unnecessary enactments.[47] *Clauses Acts*, common in the mid-nineteenth century, contained "common form" clauses and provisions intended to be incorporated by reference in common kinds of private Bills, so as to promote uniformity and reduce the length of such Bills.[48]

Long Title and Short Title

Most statutes have a formal long title which appears at the commencement and indicates the scope and purpose of the Act. Thus, *e.g.* "An Act to consolidate the law relating to the Sale of Goods." Old Acts have in many cases a very full and cumbrous long title setting out the purpose of the Act at some length.

It has also long been the practice to provide in a section of each Act, now usually near the end, for a short title, by which name the Act is usually known and cited. Thus section 64 of the above-mentioned Act provides: "This Act may be cited as 'The Sale of Goods Act 1979.' " In 1896 the Short Titles Act was passed, which thus christened a large number of older Acts to facilitate their citation, and the Statute Law Revision Act 1948 continued the process. The 1896 Act also gives collective titles to many groups of statutes relating to the same subject-matter.[49] The Statute Law Revision (Scotland) Act 1964 by Schedule 2 confers short titles on most of the Acts of the pre-1707 Parliament of Scotland,[50] which were previously cited by year and chapter number only.

In the case of amending Acts or further Acts on a topic already dealt with by legislation, it is commonly provided that the Act and the prior Acts may be cited together by a collective title, *e.g.* the Merchant Shipping Acts 1894 to 1995. Parts of an amending Act may be cited with certain earlier legislation by one collective title, and other parts with other earlier legislation by a different collective title.[51]

Apart from these official titles many Acts have acquired popular titles by which, though entirely unofficially, they are commonly known in the

---

[46] Much consolidation of statute law has been done since 1945, mostly under the authority of the Consolidation of Enactments (Procedure) Act 1949.

[47] *e.g.* Statute Law Revision (Scotland) Act 1964.

[48] *e.g.* Railways Clauses Consolidation Act 1845; Lands Clauses Consolidation (Scotland) Act 1845.

[49] The current *Index to the Statutes in Force* tells what Acts are comprehended under collective titles.

[50] This christening omits Acts prior to 1424, Acts not of general application and the Acts of 1633–61, which were repealed at the Restoration. These short titles are also listed in the *Chronological Table of the Acts of the Parliaments of Scotland, 1424–1707* in the *Chronological Table of the Statutes*, Vol. II.

[51] Thus parts of the Companies Act 1967 might be cited with earlier Acts as the Companies Acts 1948 to 1980, other parts may be cited with the Insurance Companies Act 1958 as the Insurance Companies Acts 1958 to 1967.

profession and often cited in books, such as the Montgomery and Rutherford Entail Acts, so called from the Lord Advocates who sponsored them.[52]

Date of Royal Assent

Immediately after the title is stated the day, month and year on which the Royal Assent was given to the Act.[53] This is the date of "the passing of the Act."[54]

Preamble

Statutes sometimes have a preamble setting out the facts or state of the law for which Parliament is proposing to legislate.[55] In modern times the preamble is often superseded in the case of public Bills by a memorandum or White Paper explaining the object of the Bill. Most modern statutes have a brief preamble or none at all. Some modern statutes have preambles to particular sections or groups of sections.[56]

Words of Enactment

After the title or after the preamble, if any, there appears the enacting formula, namely: "Be it enacted by the Queen's Most Excellent Majesty, by and with the advice and consent of the Lords Spiritual and Temporal, and Commons, in this present Parliament assembled, and by the authority of the same, as follows."[57]

Words of Grant

In statutes which originated in Bills introduced in pursuance of financial resolutions, the words of enactment are preceded by words narrating the resolution.

Divisions of Statutes

Statutes are divided into sections, subsections and paragraphs; thus the Companies Act 1985, s. 30(3)(*b*)(ii), means subparagraph (ii) of paragraph (*b*) of subsection (3) of section 30 of the Act. Lengthy Acts or Acts dealing with distinct topics are frequently divided into numbered parts, and occasionally the parts are divided into numbered chapters which themselves may be subdivided by italicised cross-headings.[58] The numbering of

---

[52] A list of such popular titles is printed in Craies on *Statute Law* (6th ed.), App. A.

[53] Acts of Parliament (Commencement) Act 1793.

[54] *Tomlinson v. Bullock* (1879) 4 Q.B.D. 230.

[55] A famous modern preamble is that to the [English] Matrimonial Causes Act 1937.

[56] The preamble is not part of the Act; *Renfrew C.C. v. Orphan Homes of Scotland* (1898) 1 F. 186.

[57] A modified formula is used in the case of statutes enacted in accordance with the provisions of the Parliament Acts 1911 and 1949.

[58] The lengthy Income and Corporation Taxes Act 1988 is divided into 19 parts, each containing several chapters. This is analogous to the division of a textbook into parts and chapters and is a different and modern use of the term "chapter" in the statutory connection.

the sections runs consecutively through the whole Act. The subject-matter of groups of sections is indicated by brief headings, and the subject-matter of each section is indicated by a brief marginal note. The correct mode of citing the various divisions and subdivisions of legislative instruments should also be noticed. It is as follows:

Bill (before Parliament); clause; subsection; paragraph.

Act of Parliament; section; subsection; paragraph; sub-paragraph.

Schedule to Act; paragraph; sub-paragraph.

Order in Council; article; paragraph; sub-paragraph.

Regulations; regulation; paragraph; sub-paragraph.

Rules; rule; paragraph; sub-paragraph.

Marginal Notes

The subject-matter of each section is indicated by brief marginal or side notes.

Schedules

Schedules are sometimes appended to Acts, containing matter which cannot conveniently be put into the body of the text, such as forms, lists of previous Acts repealed or affected, and matters of detail. The Schedule is part of the enactment and effect may have to be given to something in a Schedule as against an earlier provision in the body of the Act, but the enactment cannot be restrained or limited by the terms of a mere form inserted for convenience in a Schedule. Schedules are numbered and divided into paragraphs and sub-paragraphs, not sections. They may also be divided into parts consisting of groups of paragraphs.

Citation of Statutes

The Acts of the pre-Union Scottish Parliament were formerly cited by the calendar year and chapter number of the Act as printed in Glendook's edition of 1681, *e.g.* Act 1449 c. 17, or by the volume, page and chapter number of the Record edition,[59] *e.g.* A.P.S. II, 127 c. 3. The latter is more common in historical than in legal texts, and the same Act does not always bear the same number in both the Record and the Glendook duodecimo editions.[60] Either of these modes of citation is found in older books and still applies to Scots Acts which have been repealed. The Statute Law Revision (Scotland) Act 1964, Sched. 2, gives short titles to all surviving Acts of the Parliaments of Scotland, and the proper mode of citing such

---

[59] *i.e.* the *Acts of the Parliaments of Scotland*, edited by Thomas Thomson and Cosmo Innes, published by the Record Commission in 12 very large volumes in 1814–75.

[60] See McN[eill], "Citation of Scots Statutes," 1959 S.L.T. (News) 112. The *Acts of the Parliament of Scotland* (revised edition, HMSO, 1966) which reprints all the Acts then surviving and as amended gives both the Record edition and the Glendook edition chapter number. Both are also given in the Statute Law Revision (Scotland) Act 1964, Scheds. 1 and 2.

Acts thereafter is by the short title, *e.g.* The Royal Mines Act 1424, or by the calendar year and chapter number, or by the volume, page and chapter number of the Record edition.

Statutes of the British and United Kingdom Parliaments prior to 1963 are cited by an antiquated and clumsy method which must, however, be understood. Each Act when it received the Royal Assent was given a number whereby it became a chapter of the session's legislation; the numbers ran consecutively within each session of Parliament; each session of Parliament was numbered according to the regnal year or years of the sovereign during which it sat. Confusion arose from the fact that the sovereign's regnal years did not coincide with calendar years, and sessions of Parliament did not coincide with either.[61]

It may be explained as follows: George VI came to the throne on December 11, 1936, so that the year until December 10, 1937, was I Geo. 6, and so on. The period from December 11, 1951, until his death on February 6, 1952, was therefore 16 Geo. 6. On his death Elizabeth II succeeded and the year to February 5, 1953, was accordingly 1 Eliz. 2, and so on.[62] Each of these regnal years, it will be noted, covers parts of two calendar years.[63] Now the session of Parliament[64] normally commences with the state opening by the sovereign about November each year, and continues with occasional adjournments until prorogation the following autumn, but sessions may be longer or shorter than this and so may fall into one, or be spread over two, or even run into a third, regnal year.[65] A new session also starts when Parliament assembles after a General Election.

When any session started it bore the number of the sovereign's regnal year in which the opening took place, say, 3 Eliz. 2, and this continued till the anniversary of her accession when the session became 3 & 4 Eliz. 2; if the same session should have run past the next anniversary of the

---

[61] See further, Plucknett, "Legal Chronology," in *Handbook of Dates for Students of English History* (ed. Cheney: Royal Hist. Socy. 1945).

[62] A table of regnal years is printed in the *Parliament House Book* and in Sweet & Maxwell's *Guide to Law Reports and Statutes*.

[63] Hence a statute of a particular calendar year, *e.g.* 1950, might belong to either the session 12, 13 & 14 Geo. 6 or the session 14 Geo. 6. or the session 14 & 15 Geo. 6.

[64] A session is the period between the opening of Parliament by the Queen and its prorogation (which ends the session, but not the Parliament) or dissolution (which ends the life of that Parliament and requires a General Election). During a session Parliament may adjourn, and normally does so over Christmas, Easter and the summer: adjournment does not end the session. On prorogation and dissolution (but not on adjournment) all Bills in progress lapse and must be reintroduced in the next session and debated afresh.

[65] Thus the parliamentary session 1948–49 extended into three regnal years and the citation is 12, 13 & 14 Geo. 6, though prints of Acts issued at the start, when it was not certain that the session would extend into the second regnal year, would originally be numbered 12 Geo. 6, and later, but before it was known that the session would extend into the third regnal year, would be renumbered 12 & 13 Geo. 6, and only finally get their definitive numbering. This was followed by a shorter session in 1950 which all fell within one regnal year and is consequently cited as 14 Geo. 6. The next session (1950–51) was 14 & 15 Geo. 6.

accession, it would have become 3, 4 & 5 Eliz. 2. The statutes numbered within that session accordingly started as, *e.g.* 3 Eliz. 2 (c. 15), and after the anniversary of the accession, became renumbered retrospectively as, *e.g.* 3 & 4 Eliz. 2 (c. 15). It was, however, possible, if a parliamentary session was held wholly within one regnal year (as in 1950) and another session started in the same regnal year and carried on into the next, to have two *different* statutes of the same calendar year (1950), which are cited, *e.g.* 14 Geo. 6 (c. 3), and 14 & 15 Geo. 6 (c. 3).[66] It also follows from this system that the attribution to a statute of a short title, *e.g.* the—Act 1938, does not give a certain indication which volume of statutes the particular Act may be found in; it might be in the 1937–38 volume or the 1938–39 volume.[67] Until 1940, volumes contained the Acts of the parliamentary session, but since 1939 they contain those of the calendar year.

The numbering of statutes as chapters arose, at least in England, from the fact that at one time all the Acts passed in one session were called a "statute," and the chapters were on distinct topics, but the word "statute" has now for long been used to denote a separate Act and not a collection of Acts, but it is still technically called a chapter.

By the Interpretation Act 1978, s. 19, an Act may be cited in any Act, instrument or document either by its short title with or without a reference to the chapter, or by reference to the regnal year (and session if more than one), and chapter. By the Acts of Parliament Numbering and Citation Act 1962, s. 1, Acts passed in 1963 and later years may be cited by short title or by the calendar year and chapter number, *e.g.* 1978 (c. 30), and this latter mode has now been adopted for the marginal references in post-1962 Acts to pre-1963 legislation.[68]

It should also be noted that public general statutes are numbered in arabic numbers, *e.g.* (c. 19), local Acts in small Roman numbers, *e.g.* (c. xxvi), and personal Acts by italicised arabic numbers, *e.g.* (c. *53*). Accordingly there may in one year be two or even three statutes bearing the same number, but printed in different ways.[69]

Promulgation of Legislation

No form of public announcement, in the Press or on radio or TV or otherwise, need be made to acquaint the public with the fact that any Act has been passed. The serious newspapers and professional journals

---

[66] See further, Carr, "Citation of Statutes," in *Cambridge Legal Essays*, 72, and (1940) 56 L.Q.R. 460.

[67] Take the case of the Finance Act 1955 (3 & 4 Eliz. 2, c. 15); the Finance (No. 2) Act 1955 (4 Eliz. 2, c. 17); and the Finance Act 1956 (4 & 5 Eliz. 2, c. 54). Despite the dates, the latter two belong to the same parliamentary session and the former of them was later renumbered as 4 & 5 Eliz. 2, c. 17.

[68] See, *e.g.* marginal references in Queen's Printer's editions of the Law Reform (Miscellaneous Provisions) (Scotland) Act 1966, especially s. 8.

[69] For examples, see p. 248, *supra*, notes.

normally report that certain Bills have been passed, and the journals also frequently report and comment on the substance of the changes made by new Acts. But the public, lay and professional, are themselves responsible for keeping up with new legislation. Ignorance of the law is no excuse for failure to perform a statutory obligation.[70]

Proof

Every Act passed after 1850 is a public Act to be judicially noticed as such, unless the contrary is expressly provided by the Act.[71] Private Acts of before 1851 require to be proved unless the Act provides that it is to be judicially noticed as a public Act. Accordingly, normally an Act can be cited to a court from a Queen's Printer's edition without need to prove the accuracy of the text.

Commencement

The "commencement" of an Act means the time at which the Act comes into operation. Since 1793 it has been the rule that an Act prima facie comes into force at the beginning of the day on which it receives the Royal Assent[72] and this date is stated on printed copies on the first page, immediately below the long title. Hence the phrase "the passing of this Act" means the date of the Royal Assent and not any date fixed by the Act as that on which it or parts of it are to come into operation.[73] But modern Acts commonly provide for the Act or parts of it coming into force on a specified later date,[74] or provide that a particular Minister of the Crown or other person may, by statutory instrument, bring the Act into force on a date selected by him, usually called "the appointed day," and may provide for his bringing different parts of the Act into force on different dates.[75] Hence a statute may have been passed and yet not be, or be only in part, in force, and further research is frequently necessary to discover whether, and what parts of, an Act have been brought into force.[76] Some statutes, or parts of statutes, are not brought into force for years; some are never brought into force. A statute, or part thereof, brought into effect is effective from the first moment of the day on which it is brought into effect.[77] Once passed, however, it stands on the Statute Book, whether or not it has been brought into operation in whole or in part, until repealed.

---

[70] *Carter v. McLaren* (1871) L.R. 2 Sc. & D. 120, 125.

[71] Interpretation Act 1978, s. 3.

[72] Interpretation Act 1978, s. 4.

[73] *Tomlinson v. Bullock* (1878) 4 Q.B.D. 230; *R. v. Smith; R. v. Weston* [1910] 1 K.B. 17.

[74] *e.g.* the Succession (Scotland) Act 1964, s. 38(3), provides that it is to come into operation on the expiry of three months beginning with the date on which it was passed.

[75] These are called "Commencement Orders."

[76] Reference needs to be made to the book *Is It in Force?* published annually by Butterworths, and to the monthly parts of *Current Law* thereafter.

[77] *R. v. Logan* [1957] 2 Q.B. 589; Interpretation Act 1978, s. 4.

Where an Act does not come into force on its passing but contains powers to make subordinate legislation, give notices, prescribe forms or do anything else for the purposes of the Act, then that power may be exercised at any time after its passing so as to give full effect to it when it is brought into force.[78]

Application

A statute passed by the United Kingdom Parliament prima facie applies to the whole of the United Kingdom.[79] If it is intended not to apply to Scotland this is normally expressly stated, usually at the end of the Act. If it is intended to apply to Scotland only, this is stated in the Act and the word "(Scotland)" is included in the title.[80] If parts only of an Act are intended to apply to Scotland this may be stated expressly, by making part of the Act apply expressly to Scotland,[81] by stating in certain sections that they do not apply to Scotland,[82] or by stating what provisions apply to Scotland in an "application to Scotland" section.[83] But too frequently the application is left in doubt, and an Act may be held not to be applicable to Scotland if it is expressed as an amendment of a statute from which Scotland was expressly excluded,[84] or if expressed in technical terms of English law without any mention of their Scottish counterparts.[85] An inference that an Act applies to Scotland may be drawn from the fact that Northern Ireland is clearly included[86] or from the fact that Northern Ireland is expressly excluded.[87] Statutes applicable to the United Kingdom as a whole are usually drafted with English conditions in view and in the terminology of English law, but with an "application to Scotland" section which provides that, in the application of the Act to Scotland, particular Scottish terms are to be read for the English terms used in the body of the Act. This is a clumsy expedient because one legal system can never be translated to suit other conditions in this way and the technical terms of one system are never the exact equivalents of those of the other. The only justification is that it saves parliamentary time, but it is productive of

---

[78] Interpretation Act 1978, ss. 13, 22.

[79] *Murray v. Comptroller-General of Patents,* 1932 S.C. 726; *Att.-Gen. for Alberta v. Huggard Assets* [1953] A.C. 420. See further Anton, *Private International Law* (2nd ed.), 90–97.

[80] *cf.* the National Health Service Act 1946 [England and Wales] and the National Health Service (Scotland) Act 1947.

[81] *e.g.* Unfair Contract Terms Act 1977; Part I applies to England and Wales and Northern Ireland, Part II to Scotland; Part III to the United Kingdom.

[82] *e.g.* Sale of Goods Act 1979, ss. 11(1), 22(2).

[83] *e.g.* Criminal Law Act 1977, s. 63 (2).

[84] *Westminster Fire Office v. Glasgow Provident Investment Socy.* (1888) 15 R.(H.L.) 89, 94; *Levy v. Jackson* (1903) 5 F. 1170; *Bell v. Mitchell* (1905) 8 F.(J.) 15. But see *Bridges v. Fordyce* (1847) 6 Bell 1.

[85] *Scottish Drug Depot v. Fraser* (1905) 7 F. 646. But see *Perth Water Commrs. v. McDonald* (1879) 6 R. 1050; *Dunlop v. Goudie* (1895) 22 R.(J.) 34.

[86] *e.g.* Parliamentary Commissioner Act 1967.

[87] *Scottish Drug Depot v. Fraser* (1905) 7 F. 646, 648.

much inconvenience when seeking to read and understand the Act under Scottish conditions.

Similarly, the presumption is that a statute applies to all persons and all conduct within the country or area for which Parliament has legislated, but it may appear from the wording of a provision that only certain persons, *e.g.* British subjects, or certain conduct is affected.

Amendment

Any statute, once passed by Parliament, may be amended or altered in any respect and to any extent by any later statute, and the amendments may in turn be amended or repealed. Hence some Acts have accumulated a great accretion of subsequent changes, the tracing of which may be a matter of difficulty. Amendment may be express, as where a later statute provides that some section or passage or word of a prior Act is to be extended or limited or modified in a stated respect, or that some new words or sections are to be added, or to be substituted for something in the original Act; or amendment may be implied from the occurrence in later legislation of a provision which is in some respect inconsistent with an existing statutory provision and which must take effect instead, as it has to be presumed to represent the later view of the legislature on the matter in issue.[88] All statutory provisions on one topic must be considered together and read as one so that in case of inconsistency the later must have effect and the earlier must give way: *Leges posteriores priores contrarias abrogant*. The repeal of an amendment does not restore the previous wording unless an intention to do so is apparent.

Repeal

A statute, or any part thereof, may be repealed by any subsequent statute.[89] The effect of repeal is complete obliteration of the statute or part affected and it must be considered as if it had never been, except so far as concerns proceedings begun and carried through while it was the existing law.[90] A statute may be repealed as regards England and Wales, and remain in force as regards Scotland, or conversely.[91]

Express repeal is effected by a definite statement in a statute that particular prior statutory provisions, frequently listed in a Schedule, are repealed. To ascertain whether any statute or section has been expressly repealed reference must be made to the *Chronological Table to the Statutes*, the *Index to the Statutes in Force*, to the Table showing the Effect

---

[88] *Mount v. Taylor* (1868) L.R. 3 C.P. 645.

[89] Interpretation Act 1978, s. 2.

[90] *Kay v. Goodwin* (1830) 6 Bing. 576, 582; Interpretation Act 1978, ss. 15–16; *Moray CC v. Maclean*, 1962 S.C. 601.

[91] Thus the Sexual Offences Act 1956 (applicable to England only) repealed the Criminal Law Amendment Act 1885, but left it in force in Scotland.

of the Year's Legislation appended to each annual volume of statutes, and to the Statute Citator in *Current Law*. The *Statutes Revised* prints statutes with the omission of sections repealed by later legislation down to the end of 1948 and the *Statutes in Force* prints statutes as amended and with repealed portions omitted. A great deal of obsolete law is also periodically expunged by Statute Law Revision Acts which effect wholesale repeal of spent and obsolete legislation which has hitherto escaped express repeal.

Implied repeal is effected when a later Act is so plainly repugnant to and contradictory of an earlier one that the two cannot stand together, in which case the earlier gives way and the later rules.[92] It may be difficult in particular cases to say whether a later provision is consistent with an earlier, or so inconsistent as to take precedence over the earlier. The court is, however, loth to imply a repeal in this way.[93] So, too, a special Act is not repealed by a general Act unless there is some express reference to the previous legislation or unless there is a necessary inconsistency in the two Acts standing together.[94]

A statute or part of a statute may be repealed, expressly or impliedly, by subordinate legislation, but only if power to effect such a repeal is conferred by the statute enabling the making of the subordinate legislation.

The repeal of an enactment wholly obliterates what has been repealed, as if it had never been, but, unless the contrary intention appears, does not revive anything not in force or existing at the time when the repeal takes effect.[95] Repeal does not, however, affect the validity of anything done or rights acquired under the repealed Act while it was in force.[96] If a repealing Act or section is itself later repealed the previously repealed statute or section is not thereby revived unless there are express words reviving it.[97] Where an Act altering a rule of common law is repealed, the repeal may revive the common law rule unless a contrary intention appears.[98] In some cases the effect of a repeal is consequently to produce some doubt as to what the surviving law really is. Unrepealed statute law and case law is, of course, not affected by the subsequent repeal of a statute which had itself repealed only other parts of the statute law.

---

[92] *Kutner v. Phillips* [1891] 2 Q.B. 267, 272; *Lang v. Munro* (1892) 19 R.(J.) 53; *Ross v. Ross* (1894) 22 R. 174; *Randall v. Renton* (1902) 5 F.(J.) 16; *Ellen Street Estates Ltd. v. Minister of Health* [1934] 1 K.B. 590; *Moncrieff (Duncan) v. Tayside R.C.*, 1987 S.L.T. 374.

[93] *Bain v. Mackay* (1875) 2 R.(J.) 32; *Dobbs v. Grand Junction Waterworks Co.* (1882) 9 Q.B.D. 151.

[94] *Aberdeen Suburban Tramways Co. v. Aberdeen Magistrates*, 1927 S.C. 683, 689.

[95] Interpretation Act 1978, s. 15.

[96] *Ibid*. s. 16(1)(*b*).

[97] *Ibid*. s. 16(1)(*a*). For an example of revival, see Trade Disputes and Trade Unions Act 1946, s. 1, repealing Trade Disputes and Trade Unions Act 1927, reviving "every enactment and rule of law amended or otherwise affected by that Act . . . as if the Act of 1927 had not been passed." For a more complicated example, see Iron and Steel Act 1967.

[98] *Ibid*. s. 16(1).

Desuetude

In Scotland prior to 1707 the doctrine of desuetude was accepted, whereby non-use or contrary usage for a substantial time was held to cancel an Act and imply repeal thereof. It applies now only to pre-1707 Scots Acts. The doctrine required not merely antiquity of the Act, but that there should be no recent instance known in which the Act had been given effect to, that it should have been long disregarded in practice, or that its provisions were out of line with modern conditions.[99] A large number of obsolete Scots Acts were repealed in 1906 and 1964[1] and there is a presumption, which is, however, rebuttable, that any Scots Act left in force thereby is still in observance and not in desuetude.[2]

The modern rule is that post-1707 legislation cannot be abrogated by non-use or even practice to the contrary and there is probably no authority for the application of desuetude to English or United Kingdom statutes of any period.[3]

Duration

Apart from the few cases to which desuetude applies the rule is accordingly that a statute endures, even though it be not brought into force, or applied or enforced, until it is repealed. Some statutes, however, are passed for a limited period only and lapse automatically at the end of that period, though each year some such Acts are continued in life for a further period by an Expiring Laws Continuance Act. Some Acts again may be expressed to lapse on a specified future date unless previously renewed, while others may be expressed to continue in force until the occasion which has given rise to them is declared to be at an end by Order in Council. Even of the permanent Acts some, such as those conferring some privilege or immunity, can be repealed subsequently by a Statute Law Revision Act as having served their purpose and being "spent."

The Validity of Statutes

If an Act has been agreed to by both Houses of Parliament and received the Royal Assent, it cannot be challenged in or be disregarded by any court on the ground of irregularity in its introduction or passage through Parliament[4] nor even on the ground that it was procured by fraud.[5] The

---

[99] *McAra v. Magistrates of Edinburgh*, 1913 S.C. 1059; *Brown v. Magistrates of Edinburgh*, 1931 S.L.T. 456.

[1] Statute Law Revision (Scotland) Acts 1906 and 1964.

[2] See generally, Smith, "Desuetude" (1895) 7 J.R. 173; Philip, "Some Reflections on Desuetude" (1931) 43 J.R. 260. For the text of Scots Acts still unrepealed, and probably not in desuetude, see *Acts of the Parliaments of Scotland* (revised edition, HMSO, 1966). See also *Britton v. Britton's Curator Bonis*, 1996 S.C. 178.

[3] See Winfield, *Chief Sources of English Legal History*, 78–81.

[4] *Edinburgh and Dalkeith Ry. v. Wauchope* (1842) 1 Bell 252.

[5] *Lee v. Bude and Torrington Junction Ry. Co.* (1871) L.R. 6 C.P. 576; *Labrador Company v. R.* [1893] A.C. 103; *British Railways Board v. Pickin* [1974] A.C. 765; *Sillars v. Smith*, 1982 S.L.T. 539.

courts might have to consider whether a document had received the approval necessary to make it an Act of Parliament. In all genuine statutes this is recited in the enacting formula and the sufficiency of consent could only arise in the absence of such a recital.

It is questionable whether any court can entertain a challenge to the validity of a statute alleged to be in breach of the Treaty of Union of 1707.[6]

The Authority of Statutes

The legislative authority of the Queen in Parliament is supreme, so that whatever a statute may enact is absolutely binding on and must be accepted by all courts and citizens. It follows that Parliament cannot bind its successors, nor protect any provision from subsequent repeal.[7] Any statement of law in an Act of Parliament is authoritative above and notwithstanding any inconsistent rule of common law, custom, under-standing or statement in legal literature. But in doubtful cases the courts presume that Parliament did not intend to interfere with established principles of common law.

PREROGATIVE LEGISLATION

Apart from legislation passed by Parliament with the Royal Assent, the Crown still retains a residual power of legislating in a limited class of cases by issuing Orders in Council, Letters Patent or Proclamations in the exercise of the royal prerogative.[8] Orders in Council are orders expressed to be made by and with the advice of the Privy Council. At least in peacetime these powers are not of great importance, since they relate chiefly to the constitutions of overseas territories of the British Common-wealth, appeals to the Judicial Committee of the Privy Council, regulation of the armed forces and the civil service.[9] The power is also used in wartime to regulate trade, commerce, reprisals and contraband. Such orders are not numerous, nor are they an important source of law within the United Kingdom, but their existence remains possible. A royal proclamation is valid as law if published in the London, Edinburgh or

---

[6] *MacCormick v. Lord Advocate*, 1953 S.C. 396, 412; *Gibson v. L.A.*, 1975 S.C. 136, 144.

[7] *Godden v. Hales* (1686) 11 St.Tr. 1165, 1197. This principle has developed since the eighteenth century. See *City of London v. Wood* (1711) 12 Mod. 687; *Lee, supra.* Previously there were some expressions of view that Parliament could not enact what was contrary to reason or morality. See *Bonham's Case* (1610) 8 Co.Rep. 114, 118; *Day v. Savadge* (1615) Hob. 85, 97; Blackstone, *Commentaries*, I, 41. It is open to argument whether by approving the Treaty of Union of 1707 the two Parliaments did not seek to bind their successors in perpetuity.

[8] For procedure, see Morrison, "The Privy Council Today" (1948) 2 *Parliamentary Affairs* 10. Such prerogative Orders in Council must be distinguished from Orders in Council which are used under the delegated legislative power and contained in a statute, as a means of delegated legislation. These latter are discussed in later paragraphs.

[9] *Council of Civil Service Unions v. Minister for the Civil Service* [1985] A.C. 374.

Belfast Gazette.[10] An Act of Parliament may preserve or supersede a prerogative power to legislate.[11]

LEGISLATION OF THE SCOTTISH PARLIAMENT

The Scottish Parliament, established in 1999,[12] may make laws, known as Acts of the Scottish Parliament,[13] but the empowering section does not affect the power of the United Kingdom Parliament to make laws for Scotland,[14] so that the United Kingdom Parliament can still legislate for Scotland on all matters, including topics delegated to the Scottish Parliament, and its legislation can override any Act of the Scottish Parliament.

Legislative competence

An Act of the Scottish Parliament is not law if any provision of it is outside the legislative competence of the Parliament. This covers provisions which (a) would be law outside Scotland; (b) is related to reserved matters;[15] (c) is in breach of the restrictions in Sched. 4 of the Scotland Act 1998;[16] (d) is incompatible with any of the rights in the European Convention on Human Rights or with EU law; or (e) would remove the Lord Advocate from his position as head of the system of criminal prosecution and investigation of deaths in Scotland.[17]
Legislative competence extends to Scottish private law[18] and Scottish criminal law.[19]

Bills

Proposed Acts are called Bills. All Bills must have a written statement by the Presiding Officer stating whether or not the provisions are within the legislative competence of the Parliament, a Financial Memorandum estimating the cost of proposed changes, and an Auditor-General's report on whether any proposed charge on the Scottish Consolidated Fund is appropriate. Bills may be proposed by the Scottish Executive, or a committee of the Parliament, or an individual member. A member of the Scottish Executive in charge of a Bill has, on or before introduction of the

---

[10] Crown Office Act 1877, s. 3.
[11] *Att.-Gen. v. De Keyser's Royal Hotel Ltd* [1920] A.C. 508, 526.
[12] Scotland Act 1998, s. 28.
[13] Legislation of the pre-1707 Parliaments is known as Acts of the Parliaments of Scotland; that of the new Parliament as Acts of the Scottish Parliament.
[14] Section 28(7).
[15] Schedule 5, *e.g.* defence, foreign affairs. Schedule 5 extends to 18 pages.
[16] Dealing with matters protected from modification by the Scottish Parliament. *e.g.* the Human Rights Act 1998.
[17] Schedules 4 and 5 may be modified by Order in Council.
[18] Section 126(4).
[19] Section 126(5).

Bill, to state in writing that, in his view, the provisions of the Bill would be within legislative competence (s. 31(1)). The Presiding Officer has to decide whether or not, in his view, the Bill would be within legislative competence and must state his decision (s. 31(2)). There must also be Explanatory Notes summarising objectively each provision of the Bill, a Policy Memorandum setting out the Bill's policy objectives, consideration of any alternative approaches, details of consultation exercises and their outcome, and assessments of the effects, if any, of the Bill on equal opportunities, human rights, islands communities, local government, sustainable development and any other matters which the Executive considers relevant.

Drafting

Scottish Executive Bills will be drafted by the Lord Advocate's Department. Private members must draft their own Bills.

Debate

Standing orders of the Parliament have to make provision for (a) general debate on a Bill with opportunity for members to vote on its general principles; (b) the consideration of, and an opportunity for members to vote on, the details of a Bill; and (c) for a final stage at which a Bill can be passed or rejected (s. 36(1)). A Bill is first referred to the relevant subject committee and, if necessary, also to the Subordinate Legislation Committee for consideration. Evidence may be taken. Other committees may be involved, and feedback is given to the lead committee. Once the lead committee has reported to the Parliament, the Parliament itself considers the general principles and decides in the light of the lead committee's report whether these are agreed. The Bill may be referred back to the lead committee for further report and further evidence may be taken. At the second stage, the Bill is given line by line consideration and amendments may be proposed and made. At the third stage, the Bill as amended is considered by the Parliament, which can make further amendments. The Parliament then debates and decides whether the Bill in its final form should be passed. At least a quarter of the M.S.P.'s must vote, either For, Against or Abstain. At this point, up to half the sections of the Bill may be referred back for further second stage discussion by the relevant committee, and thereafter further amendment may be made only to provisions referred back. The Parliament then decides finally whether to approve the Bill or not. It is then submitted for Royal Assent.

Different procedure may be provided for (a) Bills which restate the law; (b) Bills which repeal spent enactments; and (c) Private Bills (s. 36(2)). Provision can be made for reconsideration of a Bill after its passing if and only if the Judicial Committee decides that the Bill or any provision of it is beyond the legislative competence of the Parliament, or a reference in relation to a Bill is withdrawn or an order is made in relation to the Bill by the Secretary of State under s. 35 (s. 36(3) and (4)).

Ultra vires

The Advocate General,[20] the Lord Advocate,[21] or the Attorney General[22] may within four weeks of the passing of a Bill refer to the Judicial Committee of the Privy Council the question of whether the Bill or any provision of it would be within the legislative competence of the Parliament (s. 33).[23] The Judicial Committee may feel obliged to seek a preliminary ruling from the European Court on the compatibility of the Bill with European law, and the Parliament may wish to reconsider the Bill (s. 34).

Royal Assent

A Bill becomes an Act of the Scottish Parliament when it has been passed and receives Royal Assent (s. 28(2)). It is for the Presiding Officer to submit Bills for Royal Assent (s. 32(1)). The Secretary of State may in certain circumstances make an order prohibiting the Presiding Officer from submitting the Bill for Royal Assent (s. 35).

A Bill receives Royal Assent at the beginning of the day on which Letters Patent under the Scottish Seal, signed by Her Majesty's own hand as signifying Her Assent, are recorded in the Register of the Great Seal (s. 28(3)). The date of Royal Assent shall be written on the Act of the Scottish Parliament by the Clerk and shall form part of the Act (s. 28(4)). The Keeper of the Registers of Scotland shall record in the Register of the Great Seal (a) all Letters Patent signed by Her Majesty, and (b) all Royal Proclamations under sections 2(5) and 3(2) which have passed under the Scottish Seal (s. 38(1)).

Validity and judicial notice

The validity of an Act of the Scottish Parliament is not affected by any invalidity in the proceedings of the Parliament leading to its enactment (s. 28(5)). Every Act of the Scottish Parliament shall be judicially noticed (s. 28(6)).

Publication

Acts of the Scottish Parliament are published by The Stationery Office and included in *Current Law Statutes*, in print and on CD ROM.[24]

---

[20] The Scottish legal adviser of the government in London and of the United Kingdom Parliament.

[21] The legal adviser of the Scottish Executive and the Scottish Parliament. He may be of the view that the Parliament is overstepping its competence, or be doubtful and wish to have a ruling.

[22] The chief English legal adviser of the government in London and of the United Kingdom Parliament but not on matters of Scots Law.

[23] The Act does not specify the form in which a reference should be made, nor the procedure thereon. Much would depend on who initiated the challenge.

[24] See also *Scottish Parliament Law Review*, published by W Green, a current awareness service covering Parliamentary Law and Practice, Consultation Process and Committees, Judicial Review and *Ultra Vires*.

Interpretation of Acts of the Scottish Parliament

Any provision of an Act or Bill or subordinate legislation of the Scottish Parliament is to be read as narrowly as is required for it to be within legislative competence, if such a reading is possible, and is to have effect accordingly (s. 101).

SUBORDINATE OR DELEGATED LEGISLATION

Subordinate legislation[25] consists of the body of legislation, usually entitled rules, orders, regulations or by-laws proceeding from any person or body other than, and necessarily lower than, Parliament, such as a Minister of the Crown or a Government Department, to whom or which Parliament has delegated power to make such subordinate legislation, and which in the exercise of this power remains subject to the control of Parliament. It must be apparent from some Act that Parliament did delegate power, and if an enabling Act is repealed, subordinate legislation authorised by it becomes ineffective unless a saving provision preserves its force.[26] Difficult questions may arise as to whether certain instructions issued by a Minister or Department of State are truly legislative, *i.e.* laying down general rules, or executive, *i.e.* dealing with a particular case, applying law rather than making it. The purpose of subordinate legislation is to amplify parliamentary legislation, to provide for matters of detail, to bring particular provisions into force, and to give effect in particular matters to the general purpose and policy of the Act. The majority of the items of delegated legislation are required to be registered, numbered and published, formerly under the Rules Publication Act 1893 and now under the Statutory Instruments Act 1946. Power conferred on a Department is deemed to have been conferred on the Minister of the Crown in charge of the Department. Delegated legislation, if validly made and within the powers of the delegating Act, has the same force and effect as it it were contained in the Act itself. The chief forms of subordinate legislation are:

(1) *Orders in Council.* Some Orders in Council, as has been mentioned, are issued by the Queen in Council in the exercise of the prerogative power, but Parliament also frequently by statute authorises Her Majesty in Council to make Orders in Council and Orders of this class are properly subordinate legislation. Orders of this latter class are usually drafted in one or other of the Government Departments and while the Order in Council is usually reserved for the most important and national purposes,

---

[25] On the development of the practice of delegating a rule-making power, see Report of the Committee on Ministers' Powers (Cmd. 4060), 13–15; Allen, *Law and Orders*, Chap. 2; Sieghart, *Government by Decree*, Part I; Craies, *Statute Law* (7th ed.), 268.

[26] *Inglis's Trs v. Macpherson*, 1910 S.C. 46.

there is no strict rule as to whether the subordinate rule-making function is to be exercised by Order in Council or by other means.[27] It depends on how the empowering provision in the parent Act directs that the delegated legislative power is to be exercised.

(2) *Orders of Council.* Legislation, particularly relating to the oversight of certain professions and professional bodies, sometimes authorises the Privy Council (not the Queen in Council) to make orders for specified purposes.[28]

(3) *Ministerial or Departmental Rules, Orders and Instruments.* This is the most numerous and common kind of delegated legislation, and power to make rules, orders and instruments is regularly conferred by statute on Ministers or Departments of the Crown. Prior to 1948 instances of such legislation were variously called rules, regulations and orders, but by virtue of the Statutory Instruments Act 1946 power conferred on a Minister or Department is now exercisable by statutory instrument and such departmental legislation after 1947 is accordingly called Statutory Instruments.[29] Statutory instruments may relate to any topic at all, as may be authorised by the Act which delegates the legislative power, but subjects commonly covered by statutory instruments are matters of detail, specific requirements for certain purposes of the Act, and lists of items, goods or commodities affected for the time being by statutory provisions.[30] Thus a Minister may be empowered to prescribe by statutory instrument which places or categories of items are affected by some requirement or prohibition in the Act, and he may by further statutory instrument add to or reduce the list of places or categories, or substitute a new list, without the need for further legislation by Parliament. A statutory instrument considered by Parliament can only be held to be *ultra vires* on the ground of illegality if not authorised by the enabling Act or if the procedure followed departed from the requirements of the enabling Act.[31]

---

[27] Thus the power of making Defence Regulations under the Emergency Powers (Defence) Acts of 1939 and 1940 was to be exercised by Order in Council.

[28] See, *e.g.* Medical Act 1983, s. 28.

[29] Statutory instruments are defined by the Statutory Instruments Regulations 1947 in a very clumsy and obscure fashion.

[30] The *Index to the Statutes* lists rule-making powers contained in the legislation on various subjects. The Statute Citator of *Current Law* also indicates whether regulations have been made under any statutory powers.

[31] *Edinburgh D.C. v. Secretary of State for Scotland,* 1985 S.L.T. 551.

(4) *Local Authority By-laws.* Power to make by-laws for their own particular area is conferred on local authorities by general legislation, such as the Local Government (Scotland) Act 1973[32] and the Public Health and other Acts, and also by special private Acts obtained by particular local authorities. A municipal by-law has been defined judicially[33] as "an ordinance affecting the public or some portion of the public imposed by some authority clothed with statutory powers ordering something to be done or not to be done and accompanied by some sanction or penalty for its non-observance. Further, it involves this consequence, that if validly made it has the force of law within the sphere of its legitimate operation." Such general legislation usually designates a "confirming authority," usually a Minister, and provides that by-laws are not to have effect until confirmed. The confirming authority may consider the policy and expediency of by-laws submitted, and may confirm with or without modification or refuse to confirm.[34] By-laws can have force only within the area of the local authority in question and different local authorities may have different powers and may make different by-laws in the exercise thereof. Even though confirmed, a by-law may be challenged in court as *ultra vires* of the authority making it, but if confirmed, the court is hesitant to substitute its view for that of the confirming authority.[35] There is a presumption in favour of the validity of a by-law, particularly if confirmed.[36]

(5) *Public Corporations' Regulations.* Public corporations, such as the British Airports Authority, are empowered by the Acts constituting them to make by-laws and other regulations regulating the performance of their functions and the rights and duties of the public when dealing with the corporation, and these by-laws, if validly made, similarly have the force of law in the places and circumstances and over the persons to which they apply.

(6) *Acts of Sederunt, Acts of Adjournal and Rules Committees' Rules.* Power is conferred by various statutes on various judicial committees to make rules for procedure in court. This power is exercised for the Court of Session and sheriff court by the passing

---

[32] s. 201 gives a general power to local authorities to make by-laws for the good rule and government of the council's area of authority. This is amended by the Local Government etc. (Scotland) Act 1994, Sched. 13 and para. 92. Ss. 202–204 provide a code of procedure for making by-laws, and authorise penalties for infringement of them.

[33] *Kruse v. Johnson* [1898] 2 Q.B. 91, 94.

[34] *Glasgow Corpn. v. Glasgow Churches Council*, 1944 S.C. 97.

[35] *Glasgow Corp., supra*, 125, *Baird v. Glasgow Corp.*, 1935 S.C.(H.L.) 21; see also *Dunmore v. Lindsay* (1903) 5 F.(J.) 14; *Da Prato v. Partick Mags*, 1907 S.C.(H.L.) 5; *Aldred v. Miller*, 1925 J.C. 21; *Freight Transport Association v. Lothian R.C.*, 1977 S.C. 324; *Gordon D.C. v. Hay*, 1978 S.C. 327; *Baker v Glasgow D.C.*, 1981 S.C. 258.

[36] *McCallum v. Brown*, 2000 J.C. 6.

of an Act of Sederunt,[37] which is an ordinance made by the Court of Session for the regulation of judicial procedure under powers conferred on the court at its foundation and repeatedly recognised by statutes since. The High Court of Justiciary similarly has powers conferred on it by various statutes to make by Act of Adjournal rules regulating procedure in that and the inferior criminal courts. Unless the Act conferring the power otherwise provides, any document by which a power conferred in an Act passed after the commencement of the Statutory Instruments Act 1946 to make Acts of Sederunt or Acts of Adjournal is exercised is a statutory instrument, and the provisions of the 1946 Act apply to it.[38] Similarly in England procedure is regulated by the Rules of the Supreme Court made under the authority of the Judicature Acts. These rules again have the force of law in the circumstances to which they apply. Their practical importance is great, since the details of litigation and court procedure are regulated by them more than by Acts of Parliament.

(7) *Acts of Court.* An Act of Court is an administrative or procedural by-law issued by a sheriff principal for the orderly handling of cases in his sheriffdom.[39] It may not conflict with common law, statute or statutory instrument.[40]

(8) *Practice Notes.* Practice notes are instructions or announcements or guidance issued by courts for the guidance of practitioners in dealing with stated kinds of business.[41]

(9) *Autonomous Bodies' Rules.* Autonomous bodies such as professional associations, trade unions, societies and clubs may issue rules which bind their members, but these rules are binding on the individual only by agreement and by reason of his contractual membership of the body in question. A person who joins submits himself to the rules of that body by the contract of membership. Such rules are accordingly not legislation at all and have no force or effect on individuals who are not members. Some such bodies sometimes have powers under statutory authority to make rules binding on their members, such as, *e.g.* the Solicitors Accounts Rules made under the Solicitors (Scotland) Act 1980.

---

[37] The Rules Council (Court of Session) is authorised by the Administration of Justice (Scotland) Act 1933, s. 18, and it recommends to the court changes in the Rules of Court. The power of the court to make Acts of Sederunt was conferred at the foundation of the court (Act 1532, c. 36) but modern Acts of Sederunt are usually passed under specific authority of some particular statute.

[38] Law Reform (Miscellaneous Provisions) (Scotland) Act 1966, s. 10.

[39] Those in force are printed in the *Parliament House Book*.

[40] *U.D.T. v. Stark*, 1981 S.L.T.(Sh.Ct.) 58.

[41] Printed in *Parliament House Book*.

Drafting of Subordinate Legislation

Statutory instruments implementing Acts of Parliament are drafted in the relevant department of government.

Parliamentary Scrutiny

What scrutiny is required depends on the requirements of the Act authorising the making of Orders; it may require affirmative approval by resolution of one or both Houses, or may provide that Orders shall be law unless within a limited period a resolution is passed to annul them, but frequently the only requirement is that the Orders be laid before Parliament. Since 1973 there has been a Joint Select Committee of both Houses on Statutory Instruments to review them from a technical rather than a policy standpoint, and a Commons Select Committee on Statutory Instruments.

Publication of Subordinate Legislation

The law on this matter is in a confused and unsatisfactory state. The substance of it can now[42] be stated as follows:

(1) If in an Act passed *before* 1948 (1) power to *make* subordinate legislation is conferred on a rule-making authority,[43] or (b) power to *confirm or approve* subordinate legislation is conferred on a rule-making authority and expressed to be exercised by Order in Council or Order, or (c) power to *confirm or approve* subordinate legislation is conferred on a rule-making authority, and that legislation has to be laid before Parliament or the House of Commons, *and* the power is exercised *after* 1947 in a document which is legislative rather than executive in character, then the document is a statutory instrument.[44]

(2) If in an Act passed *after* 1947, power to *make*, confirm or approve subordinate legislation is conferred on a rule-making authority, which is expressed to be exercisable by Order in Council, statutory instrument, Act of Sederunt or Act of Adjournal, and the document is either legislative or executive in character, then the document is a statutory instrument.[45]

---

[42] Prior to 1948 the law depended on the now repealed Rules Publication Act 1893.

[43] Defined by s. 4 of the Rules Publication Act 1893 as including every authority authorised to make statutory rules.

[44] Statutory Instruments Act 1946, s. 1(2), as amplified by Statutory Instruments Regulations 1947, reg. 2 (1), and Statutory Instruments (Confirmatory Powers) Order 1947.

[45] Statutory Instruments Act 1946, s. 1(1); Law Reform (Miscellaneous Provisions) (Scotland) Act 1966, s. 10.

Statutory instruments as so defined[46] must be sent to the Queen's Printer, numbered, and, unless otherwise provided by statute or regulations made under the Act of 1946, copies must be printed and put on sale to the public. The statutory instruments of each year are bound up in volumes and issued as the *Statutory Instruments*. But, however legislative in character a document issued under authority of a post-1947 Act may be, if the power of issue is not expressed to be exercisable by Order in Council, statutory instrument, Act of Sederunt or Act of Adjournal, the document is not a statutory instrument within the meaning of the Act or liable to be published as such.[47]

Publication of other Subordinate Legislation

The foregoing arrangements for publication of statutory instruments clearly do not cover all categories of subordinate legislation. Many schemes and orders emanating from Ministers or other authorities are executive rather than legislative and many circulars and instructions issued are intended as guidance and not as binding or laying down general rules of law. Such subordinate legislation other than statutory instruments may be published under particular statutory requirements or by custom and practice, but it may not, and in at least some cases ministerial circulars or letters may have legislative force yet need not be published.[48]

Citation

Statutory instruments normally contain provision for their own citation by short titles, *e.g.* The Students' Allowances (Scotland) Amendment Regulations 1989.

Most statutory instruments are numbered within the calendar year by the Queen's Printer and may accordingly be cited by year and number, *e.g.* S.I. 1989 No. 1112.[49]

Proof

Statutory instruments do not require to be proved,[50] save possibly if there is doubt as to their terms, when production of The Stationery Office copy is at least prima facie proof, or doubt as to issue, which could be established by a list issued by The Stationary Office. In the absence of

---

[46] The definitions are constructed from the Statutory Instruments Act 1946 and the Statutory Instruments Regulations 1947 made thereunder. They came into force on January 1, 1948. See further, Griffith and Street, *Principles of Administrative Law* (4th ed.), 44–60; Allen, *Law and Orders* (2nd ed.), 118–137; Craies, *Statute Law* (7th ed.), 317–319.

[47] *Current Law Yearbooks* contain tables under alphabetical headings showing what statutory instruments were issued in the year.

[48] *Blackpool Corporation v. Locker* [1948] 1 K.B. 349; *Patchett v. Leathem* (1948) 65 T.L.R. 69. See de Smith, "Subdelegation and Circulars" (1949) 12 M.L.R. 37.

[49] Statutory Instruments Act 1946, s. 2.

[50] *Macmillan v. McConnell*, 1917 J.C. 43.

provision requiring judicial notice to be taken of it, other subordinate legislation must be pleaded and proved by the party relying on it. The method of proof depends on any special provision made as to legislation made in exercise of the particular power[51] and, failing such provision, on the general law of evidence.

Applicability

As with statutes, statutory instruments are presumed applicable to all parts of the United Kingdom but they may be expressed to be, or indicate by their terms that they are, applicable to Scotland only.

Amendment and Repeal of Subordinate Legislation

A power in a statute to make subordinate legislation includes, unless the contrary intention is apparent in the Act, a power to rescind, revoke, amend or vary the subordinate legislation, and the latter power is exercisable in the same manner as the original power.[52] A specific power of revocation or amendment is usually conferred by empowering statutes.[53]

Subordinate legislation normally remains in force indefinitely until revoked or superseded. If the empowering Act is repealed the delegated legislation will fall with it, but rules may be expressly saved by the repealing Act and continued in force under it, with the same force and effect as under the former Act.

Subordinate legislation under the Scotland Act 1998

Under the Scotland Act 1998 power to make subordinate legislation conferred by that Act is prima facie exercisable by the Queen by Order in Council, or by a minister of the Crown by order (s. 112(1) and (2)). A power to make subordinate legislation conferred by the Act in relation to its exercise by a Minister of the Crown or a member of the Scottish Executive is exercisable by statutory instrument (s. 112(5)). Powers to make subordinate legislation are conferred by s. 113, and Sched. 7 determines the procedure to apply to subordinate legislation under the Act in relation to each House of Parliament and the Scottish Parliament, particularly in relation to mode of approval by Parliament or the Scottish Executive. The Scottish Parliament is required to have a Committee on Subordinate Legislation, which must be consulted when a Bill proposes to confer power on someone to make subordinate legislation thereunder.

Validity of Subordinate Legislation

Subordinate legislation is valid only if the maker is duly authorised and exercises the authority within the limits authorised and not *ultra vires*.[54] It

---

[51] *e.g.* by certificate: Agricultural Wages (Scotland) Act 1949, s. 15.

[52] Interpretation Act 1978, s. 14.

[53] *Current Law* contains a Table of S.R. & O.s and S.I.s affected by more recent statutory instruments, showing which have been revoked or amended.

[54] *e.g. Att.-Gen. v. Brown* [1920] 1 K.B. 773; *Chester v. Bateson* [1920] 1 K.B. 829; *Drummond v. Pendreich*, 1972 J.C. 2; *Malloch v. Aberdeen Corp.*, 1973 S.C. 227.

may be challenged in the courts and held invalid on such grounds as that the power to legislate was not operative, or the exercise of the power was formally defective, or the legislation was defective in substance. But modern statutes frequently contain provisions purporting to limit the jurisdiction of the courts to challenge the validity of subordinate legislation and acts done thereunder.

Authority of Subordinate Legislation

If validly made, subordinate legislation has the full force and effect of statute, whether or not the authorising statute provides expressly that it is to have effect as if enacted therein.[55]

Sub-delegated Legislation

In the normal case, legislation effected by Parliament authorises subordinate legislation by its delegate only. But in some cases sub-delegation arises where the "parent" Act is very general, giving rise to general delegated legislation and more specific sub-delegated legislation. Thus under the Emergency Powers (Defence) Act 1939, passed at the outbreak of war, Defence Regulations were made; under these Regulations orders were issued; under the orders directions appeared and these in turn authorised the issue of licences in particular and specific cases, so that there were five levels in the hierarchy of legislation. In consequence, while the immediate authority for a piece of subordinate legislation is normally an Act of Parliament, it may be found in something which is itself an exercise of delegated power, such as the Regulations made under an Act.

It is a disputed question whether documents containing sub-delegated legislation are statutory instruments or not. The practice seems to have been to publish some sub-delegated legislation as statutory instruments,[56] though the view has been expressed that the 1946 Act does not apply to sub-delegated legislation.[57]

A question which may also arise in a particular case is whether the delegate of Parliament has been authorised to sub-delegate all or any part of his subordinate legislative powers. It probably depends in each case on the generality of the main statute and the terms in which the delegate's powers are defined, as against which may be adduced the fundamental common-law maxim *delegatus non potest delegare*.[58] The presumption is

---

[55] *Institute of Patent Agents v. Lockwood* (1894) 21 R.(H.L.) 61; *Kruse v. Johnson* [1898] 2 Q.B. 91; *Willingale v. Norris* [1909] 1 K.B. 57.

[56] The orders made under the Defence Regulations, which were made under the Emergency Powers (Defence) Act 1939, were so published.

[57] *Blackpool Corporation v. Locker* [1948] 1 K.B. 349, 369, *per* Scott L.J. Contrary views have been expressed: *Lewisham B.C. v. Roberts* [1949] 2 K.B. 608; see also *Falmouth Boat Construction Co. v. Howell* [1950] 2 K.B. 16, 25; *Simms Motor Units Ltd. v. Minister of Labour* [1946] 2 All E.R. 201, 204.

[58] See further, Griffith and Street, *Principles of Administrative Law*, 63–69; Willis, "Delegatus non potest delegare" (1943) 21 Can. Bar Rev. 257; Garner, "Delegation of Administrative Discretion" (1949) 27 *Public Administration*, 115.

accordingly against any power to delegate further a delegated legislative power.

Codes of Practice

Some statutes require Ministers to issue Codes of Practice or Codes of Conduct for particular circumstances. It is questionable if they should be classified as legislation, because they do not have the force of law, but they give guidance as to conduct, and the fact that a Code was or was not complied with may be given in evidence and has persuasive influence on a court or tribunal. Important examples are the Highway Code,[59] Codes of Practice issued by the Health and Safety Commission,[60] and the Codes issued by the Advisory, Conciliation and Arbitration Service for the improvement of industrial relations.[61] The Commissioner for Public Appointments has published a Code of Practice for Public Appointments Procedures.[62]

Administrative Quasi-legislation

In addition to these recognised forms of legislation and subordinate legislation, various administrative departments sometimes issue notices, circulars, practice notes and other literature which sometimes state the way in which the department concerned proposes to apply or interpret certain statutes or orders, or as to certain arrangements made as to the operation of various matters of law. Some such statements may be of general application and affect in material degree the working of the law,[63] but they are not strictly legislative at all and would be unenforceable in the courts.[64] The legality of guidance given by a circular may be challenged in court.[65] Yet, without any legal force, these modifications may in practice have an important effect, an effect not really distinguishable from that of delegated legislation.

FURTHER READING

European Community Law
Halsbury's *Laws of England*, Vols. 51–52.
Collins: *European Community Law in the United Kingdom.*

---

[59] Road Traffic Act 1972, s. 37.

[60] Health and Safety at Work Act 1974, s. 17.

[61] Employment Protection Act 1975, s. 6. See, *e.g. W. Devis & Son Ltd v. Atkins* [1977] A.C. 931.

[62] [1996] C.L.Y. 117.

[63] Thus the Inland Revenue periodically announce "concessions" that some item or other will not be counted or valued at its full value for taxation purposes. Some of these concessions are published, some not.

[64] See further, Megarry, "Administrative Quasi-Legislation" (1944) 60 L.Q.R. 125, 218; Allen, *Law and Orders* (2nd ed.), 221.

[65] *Gillick v. West Norfolk and Wisbech AHA* [1986] A.C. 112.

Jacobs and Andenas: *European Community Law in the English Courts.*
Lasok: *Law and Institutions of the European Union.*
Mathijsen: *Guide to European Union Law.*
Weatherill and Beaumont: *EU Law.*

United Kingdom Law
Craies: *Statute Law.*
Erskine May: *Parliamentary Practice.*
Griffith and Ryle: *Parliament: Functions, Practices and Procedures.*
Hood Phillips: *Constitutional and Administrative Law.*
Ilbert: *Legislative Methods and Forms.*
     Mechanics of Law Making.
Miers and Page: *Legislation.*
Wade and Phillips: *Constitutional Law.*

CHAPTER 7

THE EXECUTIVE AGENCIES OF SCOTS LAW

THE chief executive of the United Kingdom and of Scotland is the Queen , who exercises executive powers through Ministers of the Crown appointed by her on the advice of the Prime Minister, large bodies of civil servants of various grades appointed to different ministries to apply the department's policies and powers in particular cases, and the staffs of the various executive agencies. The departments or ministries in Whitehall owe their existence and organisation partly to exercises of the Royal prerogative and partly to many statutes. The older departments of state, such as the Treasury, the Home Office and the Foreign Office, originally formed parts of the Royal household and were staffed by personal servants of the monarch, such as the Lord High Treasurer and the King's Secretary. In time, the latter's office came to be divided into a number of distinct fields of responsibility. In modern practice a large number of executive agencies have been created to perform functions deemed less appropriate for civil servants, but reporting to a department of state. The legal sources of executive power are the royal prerogative, common law powers derived from the legal personality and attributes of the Crown, and, particularly today, numerous statutes passed to impose duties on and to empower ministries and their departments to do certain things.

Until the creation of the Scottish Office in 1885, the Lord Advocate was the only Minister of the Crown with special responsibility for Scottish affairs. In 1885 the post of Secretary for Scotland was created, which brought with it responsibility for various Scottish boards.[1] From 1892 the post was held to have a seat in the Cabinet, in 1926 it was promoted to the rank of one of His Majesty's Principal Secretaries of State,[2] and in 1939 the holder was given responsibility for all the Scottish departments of central government, apart from the Lord Advocate's Department and the Crown Office.[3] In addition to his specific responsibilities, the holder was expected to represent the interests of Scotland in the Cabinet in relation to any matter affecting the United Kingdom and *vis-à-vis* departments in Whitehall, and to have an interest in any matter affecting Scotland. He came to be supported by a substantial team of junior ministers.

---

[1] Milne, *The Scottish Office* (1957); Hanham "The Creation of the Scottish Office 1881–87", 1965 J.R. 205; Hanham "The Development of the Scottish Office" in Wolfe (ed.) *Government and Nationalism in Scotland*; J.S. Gibson, *The Thistle and the Crown* (1985).

[2] Secretaries of State Act 1926, s. 1.

[3] For diagram of distribution of functions as at 1987; see Hennessy, *Whitehall*, 461.

This situation was fundamentally altered by the creation of the Scottish Parliament by the Scotland Act 1998.

The Scottish Administration

Under the 1998 Act, Part II, there is a Scottish Executive comprising (a) the First Minister, (b) such Ministers as the First Minister may appoint, and (c) the Lord Advocate and the Solicitor-General for Scotland. A person who holds ministerial office in the United Kingdom government may not be appointed a member of the Scottish Executive, and vice versa.

The First Minister is appointed by the Queen from the members of the Parliament and holds office at her pleasure,[4] but may resign, and ceases to hold office if replaced or if the Parliament resolves that the Executive no longer enjoys the confidence of the Parliament. If he is unable to act, his functions are exercisable by a person designated by the Presiding Officer. He is Keeper of the Scottish Seal. The parliament nominates one of its members for appointment as First Minister after a general election, the First Minister resigning, or the office otherwise becoming vacant (*e.g.* through illness), and the Presiding Officer recommends that person to the Queen for appointment.

The First Minister may, with the agreement of the Parliament and the Queen's approval, appoint ministers from members of the Parliament.[5] Such a minister holds office during the Queen's pleasure, may be removed by the First Minister, and may resign. The First Minister may also, with the Queen's approval, appoint persons from among members of the Scottish Parliament as "junior Scottish Ministers", on the same terms. The First Minister has, with the agreement of the Parliament, to recommend to the Queen the appointment or removal of persons as Lord Advocate or Solicitor-General. Such a person is not necessarily an MSP but, even if not, participates in meetings of the Scottish Executive and may attend and speak in the Parliament, but may not vote.

The Lord Advocate

The modern functions of the Lord Advocate include advising and representing the Crown and departments of state in all civil proceedings

---

[4] In May 1999, Donald Dewar, MP, MSP, hitherto Secretary of State for Scotland, leader of the largest (Labour) party in the Parliament , was appointed First Minister. He then resigned the office of Secretary of State for Scotland.

[5] In May 1999, the First Minister appointed ten Ministers with the following portfolios: (1) Deputy First Minister and Minister for Justice; (2) Enterprise and Lifelong Learning; (3) Children and Education; (4) Health and Community Care; (5) Finance; (6) Social Inclusion, Local Government and Housing; (7) Transport and the Environment; (8) Rural Affairs; (9) Lord Advocate; and (10) the Minister for Parliament and Chief Whip. He also appointed 11 junior Ministers with remits which did not in all respects coincide with the foregoing offices (two Ministers had no junior, three had two juniors). These juniors are not members of the Scottish Executive. Among these, the Solicitor-General ranked as junior minister to the Lord Advocate. There were also a Chief of Staff to the First Minister and a Government official spokesman, and a large number of "special advisers" and "political advisers". The Scottish Office, down to 1999, managed with seven Ministers; the work now required 22!

by or against the Crown in the Scottish Courts and generally protecting the Crown's interests in Scotland, responsibility for law reform, drafting government legislation affecting Scotland, advising on judicial appointments and appointing to some posts, and directing the prosecution in the public interest of all crimes, in which latter task he is assisted by the Solicitor-General for Scotland and a team of advocates-depute, and by the staff of the procurator-fiscal service. Though the Lord Advocate is a political appointment, the prosecution of crime is conducted strictly on a non-political basis.[6]

Prior to 1999 the Lord Advocate or the Solicitor-General for Scotland, or both, might be members of the House of Commons or the House of Lords and might participate in answering for the government and carrying legislation. Since 1999 the responsibilities of both are to the Scottish Parliament.

The Advocate-General

Under the Scotland Act 1998 the function of advising the United Kingdom government and the Westminster Parliament on legal matters affecting Scotland is discharged by a new law officer, the Advocate-General for Scotland,[7] whose duties are not fully specified in the Act.[8] The Advocate-General's Office provides legal services to the United Kingdom departments in Scotland.

Other officers

There are an Auditor-General for Scotland and a Queen's Printer for Scotland.

Ministerial functions

Statutory functions may be conferred on the Scottish Ministers by that name; those of the Scottish Ministers , the First Minister or the Lord Advocate shall be exercisable on behalf of Her Majesty; those of the Scottish Ministers are exercisable by any member of the Scottish Executive. Certain functions are, so far as exercisable within devolved competence, exercisable by the Scottish Ministers instead of by a Minister of the Crown. These include those of Her Majesty's prerogative and other executive functions which are exercisable on behalf of Her Majesty by a Minister of the Crown, other functions conferred upon a Minister of the

---

[6] O'Neill, "The Constitutional Position of the Lord Advocate", 2000 J.L.S.S. 22.

[7] The first Advocate-General was Ms Lynda Clark Q.C., MP. The title Advocate-General is in fact an old one and was sometimes used for the Lord Advocate. It was used in the old Court of Exchequer; see, *e.g. Walker v. Advocate-General* (1813) 1 Dow 111; *Advocate-General v. Sinclair's Trs* (1855) 17 D. 290; *Advocate-General v. Inverness Magistrates* (1856) 18 D. 366; *Advocate-General v. Beattie* (1856) 18 D. 378. The title is also used for a different kind of officer in the Court of Justice of the European Communities.

[8] 1998 Act, ss 32(1), 33(1) and Sched. 6, paras 4, 33 and 34, and Sched. 8, para. 32.

Crown by a prerogative instrument, and functions conferred upon a Minister of the Crown by any pre-commencement enactment, but do not include any retained functions of the Lord Advocate. This section is modified by succeeding sections.

Committees

The Parliament's Standing Orders require it to appoint a Procedure Committee, a Standards Committee, a Finance Committee, an Audit Committee, a European Committee, a Public Petitions Committee, an Equal Opportunities Committee and a Subordinate Legislation Committee, and it may also establish "subject committees" to deal with particular subjects or areas of public policy. Committees comprise between five and 15 M.S.P.'s. Meetings are held in public, usually in Edinburgh, but can be held anywhere in Scotland.

A committee can enquire, as required by Parliament or on its own initiative, into matters competent to it, including policy, administrative and financial arrangements of the Scottish administration, proposals for legislation, European legislation, and international conventions and agreements. Committees can also initiate legislation.

The Secretary of State for Scotland

The office of Secretary of State for Scotland in the United Kingdom government continues to exist with a reduced number of junior ministers and a much reduced permanent staff. It retains its London office at Dover House, Whitehall. Its importance and status have, however, been greatly diminished.[9] It is now called the Scotland Office. The great majority of the functions of the pre-1999 Secretary of State for Scotland have passed to the Scottish Parliament and its Ministers, and the function of the Secretary of State for Scotland and his staff are accordingly now mainly concerned with representing Scotland in relation to matters reserved by the 1998 Act to the Westminster Parliament and matters administered in Scotland by United Kingdom departments, though in many cases these are of great importance because they include the constitution, Europe, defence, finance, social security and other topics. He may also make an order under s. 35 prohibiting the Presiding Officer from submitting a Scottish Bill for Royal Assent.

The Civil Service

The Scottish Ministers are empowered to appoint persons to be members of the staff of the Scottish Administration. These become

---

[9] It would be very retrograde and regrettable if the post of Secretary of State for Scotland disappeared or ceased to be a Cabinet post. The Cabinet would then appear to be an English body only and would not get a Scottish view on reserved matters and would be likely to act in forgetfulness or disregard of the impact on Scotland of action it took.

members of the Home Civil Service. For the most part the staff of the old Scottish Office became the staff of the Scottish Administration. The former Permanent Under-Secretary at the Scottish Office attends meetings of the Scottish Executive in the same way as the Secretary of the Cabinet attends Cabinet meetings in London. The old Scottish Office ceased to exist from July 1, 1999 and became the Scottish Executive, reorganised into (1) the Scottish Executive Corporate Services; (2) the Scottish Executive Finance Department (formerly the Finance Group); (3) the Scottish Executive Secretariat (including the Solicitor's Office); (4) the Scottish Executive Development Department; (5) the Scottish Executive Education Department; (6) the Scottish Executive Enterprise and Lifelong Learning Department (formerly part of the Education and Industry Department; (7) the Scottish Executive Health Department (formerly the Department of Health); (8) the Scottish Executive Justice Department (formerly the Home Department), including the Scottish Courts Administration; and (9) the Scottish Executive Rural Affairs Department (formerly the Agriculture, Environment and Fisheries Department). There are a number of Boards and Agencies under most of the Departments.

There remain a small permanent staff based in Dover House, Whitehall, for liaison with Westminster, and Whitehall departments concerned with reserved matters. This office has been re-titled the Scotland Office.

Public Law

Some departments of state operate on a United Kingdom basis , usually having one or more offices in Scotland. Among such are the Department of Social Security, the Department of Employment and the Department of Trade and Industry. Others are concerned with Scotland only and are departments of the Scottish Executive. All are staffed by Ministers and civil servants, and develop policies in their fields of responsibility, apply the existing law in their work, and regularly seek changes in the law. In recent years some functions have been taken away from the departments of state and passed to new agencies. Thus the Commissioners of Inland Revenue administer income tax and related taxes and are accountable to the Treasury, the Benefits Agency administers social security benefits and is accountable to the Department of Social Security, Companies House (Scotland) is an agency of the Department of Trade and Industry and registers companies in Scotland, Historic Scotland maintains historic buildings and is accountable to the Scottish Executive Education Department, and the Registers of Scotland maintains the public registers, such as the Land Register , and is accountable to the Scottish Executive Justice Department. But although the Scottish Executive Education Department controls and inspects schools in Scotland, the elected local authorities provide and operate the state schools.

There were formerly some public corporations, such as British Gas, operating nationalised industries, but these have mostly disappeared as the relative industries were privatised. In 1994, three public water authorities were created, responsible for water supply and sewerage.

There are also many non-departmental public bodies, which comprise at least three groups of bodies. There are executive bodies, such as the United Kingdom Energy Authority, the Commission for Racial Equality, and the Northern Lighthouse Board, which exercise executive, administrative, regulatory or commercial functions on behalf of the government; these are usually set up by statute, have statutory powers and duties, and employ their own staffs. Then there are advisory bodies set up to advise Ministers and Departments on specific fields of expertise, such as the Medical Research Council, the Industrial Injuries Advisory Council, and the Mental Welfare Commission for Scotland; often these are composed largely of experts serving part-time. Lastly, there are numerous tribunals and quasi-judicial bodies with powers to deal with disputes in specialised fields of law.[10]

Local authorities are directly elected and staffed by local government officers and apply the policies and law laid down by the Parliaments for their responsibilities and also the policies determined by the leaders of the particular local authority, so far as they have been given discretion to determine policy by the relevant legislation. In some cases, notably school education, policy is determined by the Department but administered by local authorities.

Executive departments and local authorities have very wide legal powers, including delegated legislative powers to make rules of law and, in certain spheres, quasi-judicial powers to decide disputes. But their major functions are to implement national Government policy and, in the case of elected local authorities, also the policy of the local authority within the limits within which Parliament has allowed local authorities to form their own policies. The other group of bodies have much more restricted powers but are allowed some measure of freedom to act like large commercial and industrial undertakings, while the last groups have very varied powers and duties.

Thus officials of the Benefits Agency administer the national insurance and other social security schemes, officials of the Department of Trade and Industry exercise oversight of companies, administer the patents, design and trade-marks legislation and have numerous functions in relation to shipping, exports and industrial development, officials of the Board of Inland Revenue assess individuals and companies to tax[11] and officials of Customs and Excise demand VAT. Similarly local authority officers grant or refuse planning permission for development of land, regulate the erection or alteration of buildings, issue compulsory purchase

---

[10] These are examined in Chap. 8.
[11] *e.g. Royal Bank v. L.A.*, 1977 S.C. 116.

orders,[12] enforcement notices under various statutes, and notices for payment of rates, manage as landlords large numbers of rented houses,[13] promote public health and perform a great variety of other functions.[14] Increasingly local authorities are being involved in the protection of consumers against unfair trading practices. Other important executive agencies are the Director-General of Fair Trading, the Equal Opportunities Commission, the Commission for Racial Equality,[15] the Securities and Investment Board, and many more. The exercise of many of these functions falls within and is governed by rules of branches of public law. They may raise problems of the control by Parliament, the courts or the general body of citizens of the exercise of particular powers, and problems of the means of obtaining redress of grievances against public authorities.

Sometimes Parliament creates a new authority and delegates to it statutory powers of direction and control. Thus under the Human Fertilisation and Embryology Act 1990 there has been established a Human Fertilisation and Embryology Authority with powers to license, supervise standards in and guide clinics providing services in the matters regulated by the Act.

Under the Fair Trading Act 1973 a Director General of Fair Trading was appointed, with a Consumer Protection Advisory Committee, to keep under review the carrying on of commercial activities in the United Kingdom and report thereon, with wide powers of enforcement.[16]

The Competition (formerly Monopolies and Mergers) Commission exists to investigate monopolies, mergers, takeovers and similar anti-competitive practices referred to it.[17]

Various non-ministerial government departments have been established to regulate public utility industries and represent consumer interests. These include the Office of Electricity Regulation (OFFER), the Office of Gas and Electricity Markets (Scotland), (OFGAS), Office of the National Lottery (OFLOT), the Occupational Pensions Regulatory Authority (OPRA), the Office of Passenger Rail Franchising (OPRAF), the Office of the Rail Regulator, and the Office of Telecommunications (OFTEL). They have dictatorial powers of enforcement.

The Data Protection Commissioner (formerly Registrar) must maintain a register of data users who hold personal data and of computer bureaux which provide services in respect of personal data, ensure compliance with data registration principles, and consider complaints that any provision of the Act[18] is being contravened. Appeal lies to the Data Protection Tribunal.

---

[12] *e.g. Hoey Ltd. v. Glasgow Corpn.*, 1972 S.C. 200.
[13] *e.g. Dalgleish v. Glasgow Corpn.*, 1976 S.C. 32.
[14] *e.g. Lanarkshire C.C. v. Vincent*, 1976 J.C. 5.
[15] *e.g. Commission for Racial Equality v. Dutton* [1989] 2 W.L.R. 17.
[16] Pensions Act 1995, s. 1.
[17] Competition Act 1998.
[18] Data Protection Acts 1984 and 1998.

But apart from executing the policy of Parliament and, in some cases, of local authorities, the numerous bodies also become legally involved in countless ways with private individuals, firms and companies. They employ staff, buy and sell property, contract with private persons and contractors, do them legal wrongs and in numerous ways get involved with them in legal disputes raising problems of private law. Thus an action arising from an accident on the railway or in a Scottish hospital has to be decided by the same rules of private law as an acts arising from an accident involving a private car.

Criminal Law

The application and execution of the criminal law is mainly effected by the police, by traffic wardens, health and safety inspectors, inspectors of trading standards and many other officials,[19] who may frequently in trivial cases deal with the case by issuing a warning themselves or, in some cases, by fixed penalties, but in all serious cases by report to the procurator-fiscal for prosecution.[20] In all cases of any materiality, the execution of the criminal law is effected by the Crown Office and locally by the procurators-fiscal, acting on information from the police, public officials and private persons.

Private Law

Officers of central and local government,[21] public boards[22] and public corporations[23] invoke and apply private law extensively in their work, and it is also extensively used by managers, administrators and secretaries of commercial and industrial organisations. Buying and selling, employing, securing payment and the like, are their work and all these are effected in legal modes and according to legal rules. Similarly, private law is extensively applied by solicitors, bankers, insurance officials and similar persons in effecting transactions which are governed by rules of law. But a very great deal of the application and utilisation of private law in particular circumstances is in fact done by private persons themselves, by acting in conformity with principles and rules of law, as when individuals marry and support their spouses and children, do work, make and duly perform contracts, send for the plumber, lodge money in the bank, hold, use and transfer property, make wills, administer estates and so on. Sometimes in doing so they require to take, and take, or sometimes fail to take, legal advice and assistance, but in many cases they need not and do

---

[19] *e.g. Porteous v. McNaughton*, 1971 J.C. 12; *Lanarkshire C.C., supra.*

[20] *e.g. Smith v. W. & J. R. Watson Ltd.,* 1977 J.C. 52; *Dean v. Scottish & Newcastle Breweries,* 1977 J.C. 90.

[21] *e.g. Cheetham v. Glasgow Corp.,* 1972 S.C. 243; *Clydebank District Council v. Clink,* 1977 S.C. 147; *Sloan's Dairies Ltd. v. Glasgow Corp.,* 1977 S.C. 223.

[22] *e.g. Crown Estate Commrs. v. Fairlie Yacht Slip Ltd.,* 1976 S.C. 161.

[23] *e.g. Hill v. N.C.B.,* 1976 S.C. 137.

not do so. The vast majority of such applications of law, as in the case of sales in a shop, do not give rise to any difficulty or dispute or controversy, or any dispute which arises is resolved by agreement or compromise. Thus in most cases contracts are duly performed, parties pay their debts and otherwise act in conformity with precepts and standards of law. But in a minority of such relationships there is a dispute or difficulty which cannot be settled without litigation or other application to a court, as where a debtor delays or refuses to pay. Such cases accordingly require the application to, and the decision of the dispute by, one or other of the judicial organs of the community.

INQUIRIES

In exercising executive functions, Ministers and departments rely extensively on inquiries. These are sometimes held to ascertain facts and recommend, but sometimes more to allay public disquiet. They are of various kinds.

Royal Commissions

A Royal Commission is a body of about 12–15 persons appointed by the Crown at the instance of the Government to investigate some matter and report. The chairman is a person of high standing and experience and the Commission and its Report are frequently colloquially known by his name. The members usually include some with experience of the subject being investigated and some who are inexperienced; they are unpaid. The investigation is usually prolonged (usually two or three years), detailed and thorough. The Commission receives written evidence, hears oral evidence, makes visits and may commission research. The Report is presented to Parliament by command of Her Majesty and published as a Blue Book.[24] The recommendations usually include proposals for some, frequently many and radical, changes in the law. Some members may write a Minority Report or indicate dissent or reservations on particular points. Reports frequently also contain valuable statistics, tables and other information. It is for the Government to decide whether to give effect to any, and if so which, of the recommendations. It may adopt any or none of them.[25]

A few Royal Commissions, notably the Royal Commission on the Ancient and Historical Monuments of Scotland, established in 1908 to provide for the survey and recording of ancient and historical monuments, are very long-term and report annually.

---

[24] *e.g.* Report of the (Wheatley) Royal Commission on Local Government in Scotland, 1966–69 (Cmnd. 4150); Report of the (Hughes) Royal Commission on Legal Services in Scotland 1976–80 (Cmnd. 7846).

[25] Very little of the Report of the (Pearson) Royal Commission on Civil Liability, 1976–78 (Cmnd. 7054) has been enacted.

Departmental Committees

A Minister may set up a Departmental Committee to investigate some matter of lesser general and public importance than would justify a Royal Commission. It usually comprises about 12 members, frequently with a judge as chairman, hears evidence and reports to the Minister. Its Report is published as a Blue Book and frequently leads to legislation.[26]

Select Parliamentary Committees of Inquiry

These consisted of small groups of M.P.s and were extensively used in the nineteenth century to investigate problems of current concern. Their reports frequently supported pleas for reforms of various kinds. They are now little used for that purpose and select committees are now concerned to examine the expenditure, administration and policy of the main departments of government.

Tribunals of Inquiry

Under the Tribunals of Inquiry (Evidence) Act 1921, where both Houses of Parliament have resolved that it is expedient that a tribunal be established to inquire into a matter of urgent public importance, there is appointed either by the Crown or by a Secretary of State a small tribunal, usually presided over by a judge, and it is given the powers in the Act. The subject is usually a small but important one. It reports to Parliament. The report may disclose misconduct by individuals or defects in the law on some matter.[27]

Public Local Inquiries

Public local inquiries require to be, or may be, held under various statutes[28] to inform the Minister of certain facts or the state of local public opinion on a matter, but the report is only one of the factors which the Minister must consider in reaching his decision and he is entitled to give greater weight to Government policy or other considerations.[29] These are

---

[26] *e.g.* Franks Committee on Administrative Tribunals and Enquiries, 1957 (Cmnd. 218) resulting in Tribunals and Inquiries Act 1957, now 1971; Mackintosh Committee on the Law of Succession in Scotland, 1951 (Cmnd. 8144) resulting in Succession (Scotland) Act 1964; Grant Committee on the Sheriff Court, 1967 (Cmnd. 3248) resulting in the Sheriff Courts (Scotland) Act, 1971; Thomson Committee on Criminal Procedure, 1972 (Cmnd. 8144) resulting in Criminal Procedure Act 1975.

[27] See also the Report of the Royal Commission on the Tribunals of Inquiry (Evidence) Act 1921, 1966 (Cmnd. 3121). Examples of this kind include the "Lynskey" tribunal in 1948 to investigate alleged bribery of Ministers and civil servants (Cmnd. 7616); the "Parker" inquiry into premature disclosure of information relating to the raising of interest rates (Cmnd. 350); the "Waters" tribunal in 1957 to investigate an allegation that a youth had been assaulted by the police in Thurso (Cmnd. 718); and the "Vassall" inquiry into offences under the Official Secrets Act (Cmnd. 2009). See also Keeton, *Trial by Tribunal.* As to power to punish witnesses for contempt of court, see *Att.-Gen.* v. *Clough* [1963] 1 Q.B. 773; *Att.-Gen.* v. *Mulholland* [1963] 2 Q.B. 477.

[28] Notably Local Government (Scotland) Act 1973, ss. 202–210.

[29] *General Poster Co.* v. *Secretary of State for Scotland*, 1960 S.C. 266, 275; see also Robson, "Public Inquiries as an Instrument of Government" (1954) 1 B.J.A.L. 71.

held by officials of the Department called Reporters and they report to the Minister. Procedural guidelines for town and country planning inquiries, appeals against planning decisions, and the like, have been laid down. Inquiries not governed by these rules usually follow generally similar procedure.[30] Appeal is competent to the courts on limited grounds of law.[31]

Other Statutory Inquiries

The First Minister is empowered to institute inquiries to ascertain whether various statutory bodies are or are not exercising their functions under the National Health Service and whether he needs to exercise his default powers or emergency powers.[32]

Ad Hoc Inquiries

The First Minister may appoint a person, such as a judge, to conduct an inquiry into allegations of miscarriage of justice[33] or probably any other matter, such as a disaster[34] or the cause of riots in a prison.

Inquiry under Police (Scotland) Act

Under the Police (Scotland) Act 1967, s. 29, as amended, the Secretary of State may order an inquiry into alleged misconduct by police officers, such as assaulting a suspect, fabricating evidence or giving false evidence.[35]

Inquiry under the Health and Safety at Work Act

The Health and Safety Commission may direct an investigation or inquiry into any accident, occurrence or other matter which it thinks should be investigated for any of the general purposes of the Health and Safety at Work Act 1974.

Fatal Accidents Inquiries

One of the commonest inquiries is the Fatal Accidents Inquiry held to inquire into the causes of death of a person engaged in any industrial employment or occupation due, or reasonably believed to be due, to

---

[30] *e.g.* inquiry under Local Government (Scotland) Act 1973, s. 210; Education (Scotland) Act 1980, s. 67.

[31] *Wordie Property Co. v. Secretary of State for Scotland,* 1984 S.L.T. 345, 347; *MacPherson v. Secretary of State for Scotland*, 1985 S.L.T. 134; *Glasgow District Council v. Secretary of State for Scotland*, 1989 S.L.T. 256.

[32] National Health Service (Scotland) Act 1978, ss. 76–78 and Sched. 12.

[33] *e.g.* Report by Lord Hunter of Inquiry into the murder of Mrs. Rachel Ross in 1969 (H.C. Papers, 1981–82, No. 444).

[34] *e.g.* Wheatley Report on *Inquiry into Crowd Safety at Sports Grounds*, Cmnd. 4952 (1972); Lord Cullen's Report on the Piper Alpha disaster (HMSO, Cm. 1310, 1991) was held under powers in the Mineral Working (Offshore Installations) Act 1971 and the Offshore Installations (Public Inquiries) Regs. 1974 (S.I. 1974 No. 338).

[35] *cf.* Lord Scarman's Report under the corresponding English Act into the Brixton disorders, 1981. Report, 1981 (Cmnd. 8427).

accident occurring in the course of the employment or occupation, or while in legal custody, and into cases of sudden or suspicious death.[36] The inquiry is held before a sheriff principal or sheriff, and the evidence is collected and presented by the procurator-fiscal. Persons interested may appear personally or by counsel or solicitor, take part in and lead evidence at the inquiry. These include the deceased's relatives, employer, fellow-employees, trade union representatives, and inspectors of mines or of factories. The inquiry is held in public and conducted on the lines of a civil trial, the evidence being recorded. Parties may address the sheriff who thereafter makes a determination setting out the circumstances found by him affecting the death, including precautions which would have avoided the death and any defects in the system of working which contributed to the death. The determination may not be used in evidence or founded upon in subsequent civil or criminal proceedings arising out of the same accident[37] and no witness may be required to answer questions tending to show him guilty of any crime or offence. Determinations are usually in fairly formal terms and seldom include any finding pointing to fault against anyone. They may include recommendations as to the adoption of safety measures in future.

Department of Trade Shipping Inquiries

A sheriff may also have to hold an inquiry into the circumstances attending a shipping casualty,[38] to answer questions raised by the Department of Trade. The sheriff sits with one or more nautical assessors, and parties may appear by counsel or solicitor. The judgment of the court is given in the form of answers to questions proposed by the Department of Trade. Ship's officers, if at fault, may be penalised by having their certificates cancelled or suspended, and the sheriff reports his findings to the Department of Trade, with a confidential annexation setting out the circumstances, the court's opinion of the cause of the casualty and of the conduct of persons involved. A party found to be at fault may appeal to either Division of the Court of Session, which hears the appeal with nautical assessors, in the same way as an ordinary appeal from the sheriff court, and in certain circumstances the Department of Trade may direct a rehearing before the same court, or before a wreck commissioner or a judge of the Court of Session.

Inquiry may also be ordered by the Department of Trade into the conduct of ship's officers, their incompetence, misconduct or failure in

---

[36] Fatal Accidents and Sudden Deaths Inquiry (Scotland) Act 1976. See further Carmichael, *Sudden Deaths and Fatal Accident Inquiries* (1986). A noteworthy instance was the Inquiry conducted by Sheriff Principal Mowat in 1990 into the deaths of persons by blowing up of an aircraft over Lockerbie.

[37] As to disqualification of a sheriff, see *Black v. Scott Lithgow*, 1990 S.L.T. 612.

[38] Merchant Shipping Act 1970, s. 55(1) and Merchant Shipping Act 1979, s. 32; Merchant Shipping (Formal Investigations) Rules 1985.

duties, and this may be held by a sheriff, or a person designated, or the local Marine Board.[39] The procedure is as in the case of an inquiry into a shipping casualty, and there is a report to the Department of Trade.

An analogous inquiry may be held by the sheriff with two assessors, sitting as a Court of Survey, in a dispute between a Department of Trade surveyor and a shipowner as to whether a ship is unsafe, unseaworthy or undermanned, or a passenger vessel so constructed as to be entitled to a passenger certificate.[40] The court may uphold or refuse the appeal and in either case reports to the Department of Trade.

Railway Accidents

The Secretary of State for Transport may on the occurrence of a notifiable accident direct an inquiry by an inspector into the cause thereof, or order a formal investigation of the accident, its causes and the surrounding circumstances by a person with the assistance of a lawyer, or by a sheriff with the assistance of an inspector or assessor.[41] The latter kind of investigation is held in open court.[42]

Civil Aviation Investigations

The Secretary of State for Transport appoints a chief inspector and other inspectors of accidents to make investigations of the cause of aircraft accidents, to determine the causes rather than to allocate blame to anyone. It is conducted in private.[43] A person whose reputation is likely to be affected may after the inspector has reported seek to have findings blaming him reviewed by a review board, consisting of a person appointed by the Lord President, sitting with technical advisers. This board hears evidence and reports. The inspector's report and any review board's report are published.

The Secretary of State may also direct that a public inquiry be held by an experienced lawyer assisted by two assessors having aeronautical experience. It reports to the Secretary of State.

FURTHER READING

Dynes and Walker: *Times Guide to the New British State.*
Hennessy: *Whitehall.*
     : *The Hidden Writing.*
Mackenzie and Grove: *Central Administration in Britain.*
Whitaker's Scottish Almanack (annual).

---

[39] Merchant Shipping Act 1970, s. 52. See *Dept of Transport*, 1989 S.C.L.R. 142.
[40] Merchant Shipping Act 1894, s. 488.
[41] Regulation of Railways Act 1871, ss. 3–7; Transport Act 1968, s. 125.
[42] *Ibid.*, s. 7
[43] Civil Aviation Act 1982, s. 16; Civil Aviation (Investigation of Accidents) Rules 1989 (S.I. 1989 No. 2062).

Chapter 8

THE MODERN JUDICIAL SYSTEM

THE judicial system consists of all the agencies which exist to adjudicate on disputes, to resolve controversies as to legal rights and conflicts of interests and claims, and to enforce legally recognised claims in case of recalcitrance or refusal to conform to law.

The salient features of the modern administration of the law are the existence of separate sets of courts and tribunals for civil, administrative and criminal business, though in fact all Scottish judges may at different times sit in either civil or criminal courts and many English judges may do so too. The civil and criminal courts are mainly of considerable antiquity, but many of the special courts and statutory tribunals are much more modern and they have not yet attained anything like the settled nature, composition or system exhibited by the civil and criminal courts.

A further distinction of courts is into superior and inferior; the former have jurisdiction over the whole country, the latter over only a district; thus the House of Lords, the Court of Session, the High Court of Justiciary and, in England, the Supreme Court of Judicature (comprising the Court of Appeal, the High Court and the Crown Court) are superior courts. The sheriff court and the district court and, in England, the county court and magistrates' courts are inferior courts. Another distinction is into courts and tribunals having original jurisdiction, hearing disputes for the first time, or appellate jurisdiction, hearing disputes appealed from some other individual or court. Some courts at different times exercise both original and appellate jurisdiction. In England a distinction is also drawn between "courts of record" and "courts not of record," depending historically on whether or not the court, superior or inferior, maintained a record of its proceedings, and now on whether it has power to punish for contempt.

It is impossible in modern times to confine the judicial system, the organs for the decision of disputes and the resolution of controversies, to the traditional courts of law. In modern Britain many kinds of issues are justiciable, and by many different kinds of persons and bodies. It is accordingly necessary to consider individually the various civil, administrative, criminal and other tribunals which exist, and to ascertain generally their spheres of competence and the limitations on their powers. In respect of the administrative tribunals, it is difficult, if not impossible, to enumerate or describe them all, since they are constantly changing and developing.

The Judicial Function

A notable characteristic of litigation in Scotland is that it is contentious rather than inquisitorial. The function of the judge is not to act as inquisitor and himself to make an investigation, or even to inquire into a claim or complaint initiated by a party, but is to preside at a forensic contest between two parties, to ensure that the rules of law are applied and followed and to arbitrate between the contending cases. The contentious nature of proceedings is further indicated by the fact that in criminal proceedings the Crown may drop a charge at any stage and that the judge may not pronounce sentence on a finding of guilt unless the prosecutor moves him to do so, and that in civil proceedings it is for the aggrieved party to determine whom to pursue and on what ground of law, on what issues of fact the action is to be fought, whether the action is to be compromised or settled, and whether any of the rules of evidence or of procedure are to be waived. Above all, in both civil and criminal proceedings, the overriding rule is that it is for the parties to determine what evidence they will produce and elicit from witnesses; the judge will not summon other or fresh witnesses or examine them himself, apart from sometimes putting a few supplementary questions to clear up a matter on which he is still in doubt. But his task is to supervise the contending parties and to arrive at a decision on the facts submitted to him, not to engage himself in the search for evidence or information.

The judicial function is not, however, by any means wholly passive, since the judge may take notice of principles of law even though they are not brought to his notice by the parties. He can, for example, dismiss an action founded on an illegal contract even where the parties take no notice of the fact. "In the system of trial which we have evolved in this country, the judge sits to hear and determine the issues raised by the parties, not to conduct an investigation or examination on behalf of society at large, as happens, we believe, in some foreign countries. Even in England, however, a judge is not a mere umpire to answer the question 'How's that?' His object, above all, is to find out the truth, and to do justice according to law."[1]

The existence of the jury system is another element indicating the contentious character of litigation. Where there is a jury,[2] the parties set out to convince the jury, and the judge has merely to explain the relevant law to the jury, take their answer to the questions of fact and law raised by the case, and give effect to their verdict.

In a criminal case it has been pointed out that it is the function of the court to declare what the law is and, if necessary, clarify it, but not to reform the law, which should be done by Parliament[3]

---

[1] *Jones v. N.C.B.* [1957] 2 W.L.R. 760.
[2] Jury trial is confined to criminal trials on indictment and certain kinds of civil claims, so that 98 per cent of cases are tried without a jury.
[3] *Lindsay v. H.M. Advocate*, 1997 J.C. 19.

I.—SCOTLAND

CIVIL COURTS

The Sheriff Court

The inferior, but very useful and important, civil court is the sheriff court.[4] Scotland is divided into six sheriffdoms based on groupings of the local government areas.[5] Each has a sheriff principal usually appointed from senior members of the Bar; the appointment is a full-time one.[6] The office is one of great antiquity and prestige. The modern sheriff principal is the successor of the sheriff-depute, who was the qualified deputy appointed by the former hereditary sheriffs and who became the permanent functionary when the hereditary and titular sheriffs were replaced in 1747.[7] The sheriff-depute formerly appointed sheriffs-substitute at his own hand but since 1825 the sheriff-substitute has had to be a lawyer and since 1877 the office has been a separate Crown appointment. The sheriff-substitute was renamed sheriff in 1971.[8] The sheriff principal still retains, in addition to judicial functions, considerable administrative powers and duties.[9]

The Scottish Ministers are responsible for the organisation and administration of the sheriff courts, a function discharged since 1971 by the Scottish Courts Administration, a body which is also responsible for a variety of other functions in the field of law, and by the Scottish Court Service, which is responsible for staff, court buildings and services.

The sheriff principal has the general responsibility of securing the speedy and efficient disposal of business in the courts of his sheriffdom. Each sheriffdom is divided into several sheriff court districts centred on a town where the sheriff court is held, there being 49 districts in all. In most cases the sheriff court district comprises one or more local government areas, but in some local government areas there are two or more sheriff court districts and sheriff court towns.[10]

---

[4] Sheriff court, *not* sheriff's court. An idea of the amount of business can be gathered from the annual *Civil Judicial Statistics*.

[5] The number, names and sizes of the sheriffdoms have varied at different times. The present Sheriffdoms are: (1) Lothian and Borders; (2) South Strathclyde, Dumfries and Galloway; (3) Glasgow and Strathkelvin; (4) North Strathclyde; (5) Tayside, Central and Fife; and (6) Grampian, Highlands and Islands. For areas, see Sheriffdoms (Alteration of Boundaries) Order 1996 (S.I. 1996 No. 1006).

[6] Until 1975 there were 12 sheriffdoms but only two of the sheriffs principal (Edinburgh and Glasgow) were full-time judges; the others continued in practice at the Bar, visiting the sheriffdoms as required to hear appeals and deal with other business.

[7] See further, *Glasgow Corp. v. Glasgow Churches Council*, 1944 S.C. 97, 126; Philip, in *Source Book of Administrative Law*, 74–76; McDonald, "The Sheriff Court and its Judges," 1952 S.L.T. (News) 121; Malcolm, in *Introduction to Scottish Legal History*, Chap. 26.

[8] Sheriff Courts (Scotland) Act 1971, s. 4.

[9] *Ibid.* 76–78; Dobie, *Sheriff Court Practice*, Chap. 25; Grant Committee Report, Chap. 8.

[10] Sheriff Court Districts (Alteration of Boundaries) Order 1996 (S.I. 1996 No. 1005). See McCaffray, *Index to Sheriff Court Districts in Scotland* (1980); Paton, *Map of Sheriffdoms and Sheriff Court Districts in Scotland* (1980); *Scottish Law Directory* (annual); *Whitaker's Scottish Almanack* (annual); McCaffrey, *Greens Guide to Sheriff Court Districts* (2nd ed.).

Each sheriffdom similarly has a force of several sheriffs who are qualified lawyers of experience permanently resident in the principal towns of the sheriffdom, the number varying according to the place and the amount of business.[11] As a rule they hold courts only in one place but in some cases they hold courts in more than one town.[12] In addition there are several "floating" sheriffs who may be sent to any court if the regular sheriff is ill, or the post vacant. All these persons are salaried. The Scottish Courts Administration also appointed a number of legally qualified persons as temporary sheriffs, who were called on to sit as and when necessary to assist with pressure of work. They received a daily fee when employed.[13] Legally qualified honorary sheriffs are appointed partly as an honour and partly to assist when there is pressure of court business; they may deal with any kind of case. The sheriff principal may also, however, appoint a few honorary sheriffs, either laymen or lawyers. Unqualified honorary sheriffs are appointed mainly as an honour and sit only exceptionally for formal business. Apart from the civil appellate jurisdiction and certain administrative powers of the sheriff principal, the powers of sheriff principal and sheriff are the same. Honorary sheriffs have the same powers.

In civil business the sheriff court is both a court of first instance and a court of appeal, in that cases heard first by a sheriff may be appealed to the sheriff principal. This provision for appeal from a single judge to another single judge is anomalous but it does provide for an appeal being heard locally without undue expense and, though sometimes abused by being used merely for delay, the system gives general satisfaction.

Jurisdiction

The civil jurisdiction of the sheriff court is wide. It extends to actions of debt or damages *without any pecuniary limit whatever* so that cases involving thousands of pounds may be and sometimes are dealt with by the sheriff.[14] Some kinds of cases may be remitted to the Court of Session. Proceedings against the Crown must be remitted if the Lord Advocate produces a certificate that the case may involve an important question of

---

[11] Thus in 2000 Glasgow had 25 (with assistance from Lanark); Edinburgh 14 (several being "floating" and one sitting also at Haddington); Hamilton ten; Dumbarton three and Ayr three each, while such places as Lanark, Banff, Falkirk, Inverness, Greenock and Dumfries have one or two each. Sheriffs principal and sheriffs are addressed as "My Lord" or "My Lady" in court and "sheriff" when off the bench. No judicial robes have ever been prescribed for sheriffs principal or sheriffs, and they wear counsel's robes.

[12] *e.g.* Duns, Selkirk and Jedburgh. For a full list, see the *Parliament House Book.* The Grant Committee Report, Chap. 10, discussed the possibility of closing some courts and opening new courts in areas of increasing population. Thus courts have been authorised at Livingston and Lochgilphead.

[13] Temporary sheriffs were abolished by the Bail, Judicial Appointments etc. (Scotland) Act 2000, as a consquence of *Starrs v. Ruxton,* 2000 J.C. 208.

[14] But most pecuniary claims are for modest sums. See also Grant Committee Report, Chap. 4

law, or be decisive of other cases, or is more fit for trial in the Court of Session.[15] A declarator of presumed death may be remitted.[16] Actions of divorce or for regulating the custody or adoption of children may be remitted at any stage to the Court of Session on the sheriff's own motion.[17] A party may move to have the case remitted to the Court of Session on account of its importance or difficulty.[18] Conversely the Court of Session may remit an action to the sheriff court.[19] The sheriff court also deals with many other kinds of cases, such as contract, delict, heritable rights, landlord and tenant, separation, affiliation and aliment, succession and so on.

At the other end of the scale the sheriff's jurisdiction is exclusive and his decision final in cases where the value of the cause does not exceed £5000.[20] Special procedure applies to claims not exceeding £5000 brought under the Summary Cause Rules[21] or the Small Claims Rules.

The subjects excepted from the sheriff's jurisdiction and reserved to the Court of Session are actions involving status (marriage, nullity of marriage), save that divorce is now competent,[22] inhibitions, actions of adjudication, reductions, petitions for the winding up of companies whose paid-up capital exceeds £120,000, and actions for proving the tenor of a lost document. In certain circumstances the Court of Session may order a case to be transmitted to it, or remit a case from it to the appropriate sheriff court. Various other kinds of causes are excepted and reserved to courts of special jurisdiction or statutory tribunals.

Trial is by the sheriff alone; actions of damages brought by workmen against employers for personal injuries claiming more than £250 might formerly have been tried by a jury of seven.[23]

In certain cases appeal lies to the sheriff principal or sheriff from decisions of other tribunals and authorities,[24] such as children's hearings. Such are usually made by summary application.

---

[15] Crown Proceedings Act 1947, s. 44.

[16] Presumption of Death (Scotland) Act 1977, s. 1.

[17] Sheriff Courts (Scotland) Act 1971, s. 37(2A) as amended.

[18] Sheriff Courts (Scotland) Act, 1971, s. 37: *Butler v. Thom*, 1982 S.L.T. (Sh.Ct.) 57; *Shaw v. Lanarkshire Health Board*, 1988 S.C.L.R. 13; *Data Controls (Middlesborough) v. B.R. Board*, 1990 S.C.L.R. 367.

[19] *Watson v. Babcock Power Ltd*, 1987 S.C.L.R. 624.

[20] *Ibid.* s. 7, amended by 1971 Act, s. 31.

[21] Sheriff Courts (Scotland) Act 1971, ss. 35–38. Down to 1971 a "summary cause" was a simpler form of procedure applicable to cases of lesser value and there was a Sheriff's Small Debt Court with a special procedure for cases not over £50. Down to 1975 there was also a separate Justice of the Peace Small Debt Court with a very limited jurisdiction. It was abolished by the District Courts (Scotland) Act 1975.

[22] Divorce Jurisdiction Court Fees and Legal Aid (Scotland) Act 1983, s. 1.

[23] Sheriff Courts (Scotland) Act 1907, s. 31, amended by 1971 Act, s. 40. For criticism of this, see 1954 S.L.T.(News) 25, 57. The Grant Committee Report recommended the abolition of civil jury trial in the sheriff court and this was done in 1980.

[24] *e.g. Moore v. Clyde Pilotage Authority*, 1943 S.C. 30; *Arcari v. Dunbartonshire County Council*, 1948 S.C. 62.

The sheriff court also exercises important administrative functions, such as dealing with petitions for adoption of children and bankruptcy proceedings. The commissary offices are departments of the sheriff-clerk's offices which deal with the inventories of the estates of deceased persons and issue confirmation of appointments of executors. The office of commissary clerk, formerly separate, is now merged in that of sheriff-clerk, except in Edinburgh, though even there they are held by the same person. The Sheriff Court of Chancery has functions in respect of the completion of title to land by the heirs of deceased persons. The office of Sheriff of Chancery is now held by the sheriff of the Lothians.

Appeals

In civil matters, appeal lies by note of appeal, without leave against final judgments and with leave against interlocutory judgments, from the sheriff to the sheriff principal, or to the Inner House of the Court of Session, or to the sheriff principal and then from his decision to the Inner House of the Court of Session.[25] In summary causes it lies to the sheriff principal by stated case raising questions of law, and no other matters may be raised,[26] and to the Court of Session on a point of law from the final judgment of the sheriff principal if he certifies the cause as suitable for such an appeal.[27] In small claims, appeal does not lie beyond the sheriff principal.[28] This multiplicity of possible appeals is theoretically undesirable, though the system works satisfactorily in practice. The tendency is for defenders to take the long course where delay is of value, as in the case of a tenant's appeal from an order for possession under the Rent Acts. The appeal does not involve a rehearing of the evidence, but only argument on the sheriff's findings as to the facts on the basis of the evidence already heard and on the relevant law. The sheriff principal may affirm, vary or reverse the decision of the sheriff.

The Court of Session

The Court of Session, the superior civil court, is likewise both a court of first instance and a court of appeal. It is, however, notionally still a unitary collegiate court; all judges, other than the Lord President and the Lord Justice-Clerk, have the same rank and title.[29] It sits only in Edinburgh, in the Parliament House,[30] and judges do not take civil business when on

---

[25] Sheriff Courts (Scotland) Act 1907, ss. 27–29: *e.g. Glynwed v. Koronka*, 1977 S.C. 1.

[26] *McFall v. Lochgorm Warehouses*, 1978 S.L.T. (Sh.Ct.) 67; *Hart v. Kitchen*, 1990 S.L.T. 54; *Kostric v. O'Hara*, 1990 S.C.L.R. 129.

[27] Sheriff Courts (Scotland) Act 1971, s. 38: *e.g. Verrico v. Hughes*, 1980 S.C. 179; *Hart v. Kitchen*, 1989 S.C. 391.

[28] Law Reform (Miscellaneous Provisions) (Scotland) Act 1985, s. 18.

[29] The judges are designated Senators of the College of Justice and sometimes Lords of Council and Session, titles reflecting the origin of the court. They wear dark blue worsted robes with maroon facings and scarlet crosses on the facings.

[30] Interesting illustrated accounts of the Parliament House are in *The Pictorial History of Parliament House, Edinburgh* (Pitkin, "Pride of Britain" Books); and Lord Cullen, *Parliament House: A Short History and Guide* (1992). See also Malcolm, in *Introduction to Scottish Legal History*, Chap. 34.

circuit.[31] From 1532 to 1808 the court sat as a group—the "haill fifteen"—but one or two of the judges went out in turn, a week at a time, to hear the preliminary stages of cases in the Outer House. In 1808 the court was divided into two Divisions, presided over by the Lord President and the Lord Justice-Clerk respectively, and in 1825 the First and Second Divisions were reduced to four judges each (including the Lord President and Lord Justice-Clerk), the remaining seven judges becoming permanent Lords Ordinary sitting only in the Outer House. The maximum number of judges is now 32.[32] The Lord President, with the consent of the Secretary of State, may appoint a retired Court of Session judge or Lord of Appeal who is not yet 75 to be a temporary judge.[33] Any person eligible for appointment as a judge of the Court of Session may be appointed a temporary judge for as long as the Secretary of State may determine, but not beyond his 75th birthday. Such a person has all the powers of a Court of Session judge while sitting and is paid as such when sitting, but is not treated as such for the purposes of tenure, retirement, remuneration or pension.[34] The Court has extensive powers by Act of Sederunt to regulate procedure and practice.[35]

Apart from the cases in which the Court of Session has exclusive jurisdiction, such as actions of reduction, the pursuer has the choice of initiating his claim in the appropriate sheriff court or in the Court of Session, and the choice may be determined by such factors as the value or importance of the cause, the availability of jury trial, or the desire to obtain a more authoritative ruling on the issue in dispute than that of a sheriff.

The Outer House—The Lords Ordinary

The Outer House consists of the 24[36] junior Lords of Session who sit singly,[37] sometimes with, usually without, a jury of 12, to determine cases at first instance. The jurisdiction is extensive and extends to all kinds of civil claims unless jurisdiction is expressly excluded by statute. In particular it extends to actions of contract and commercial cases, reparation,

---

[31] For circuits, see p. 325, *infra*.

[32] Court of Session Act 1988, s. 1. Maximum Number of Judges (Scotland) Order 1999 (S.S.I. 1999 No. 158). Appointments had to be made in 2000 because four judges were absent at the Lockerbie trial in the Netherlands.

[33] Law Reform (Miscellaneous Provisions) (Scotland) Act 1985, s. 22.

[34] Law Reform (Miscellaneous Provisions) (Scotland) Act 1990, s. 35(3) and Sched. 4. Thus in 1991 two senior sheriffs and two senior Q.C.s were appointed temporary judges. On temporary judges see *Clancy v. Caird*, 2000 S.L.T. 546.

[35] 1988 Act, s. 5.

[36] One judge is at present (2000) seconded as part-time chairman of the Scottish Law Commission.

[37] Until the Administration of Justice Act 1933, a pursuer might choose his judge and his Division for appeal, which produced some remarkable inequalities between the rolls of different judges, as can be traced in the periodical reports in the *Scots Law Times* (News) prior to that Act.

property and personal status (such as divorce), various kinds of petitions, the appointment of trustees, judicial factors and curators, many matters of succession and trusts, and judicial review of the actings of many authorities.[38]

The Outer House is exclusively a court of first instance in which most Court of Session business is initiated and adjudicated on for the first time. Much of the business does not proceed any further in that the parties rest content with an Outer House judgment; this is particularly so in the case of uncontested actions. The Outer House judges also deal with many petitions of an administrative nature, such as for the appointment of new trustees, or a judicial factor, for sequestration or for the winding up of a company.

Jury trial,[39] despite extensive criticism, is still utilised in certain classes of cases, namely claims of damages for personal injuries, libel or defamation, delinquency or quasi-delinquency, and reduction on the ground of incapacity, essential error or force and fear, but even in these cases a case may be tried by a Lord Ordinary alone by consent or if special cause is shown.[40] While favoured by speculative litigants, it is an uncertain and doubtfully just mode of trial, and many jury verdicts seem questionably satisfactory. In certain cases, actions of damages commenced in the sheriff court may be remitted to the Court of Session for jury trial in the Outer House.

One of the Lords Ordinary is appointed to act as Lord Ordinary in Exchequer causes.[41] Various judges are nominated to deal with commercial cases, intellectual property cases, judicial review cases and optional procedure cases.

The Inner House

Any party to a cause initiated in the Outer House who is dissatisfied with the interlocutor of the Lord Ordinary may, in general, reclaim against that interlocutor to the Inner House.[42] The Inner House consists now of two Divisions, the First and the Second Division, of equal authority, importance and jurisdiction. The Lord President and four senior Lords of Session comprise the First Division, while the Lord Justice-Clerk and four senior Lords sit in the Second Division.[43] Decisions are by a majority and

---

[38] *McDonald v. Secretary of State for Scotland,* 1996 S.L.T. 575.

[39] A committee set up in 1957 under the the the chairmanship of Lord Strachan to examine the question of the retention or abolition of jury trial recommended, by a majority, that it be retained in a limited sphere.

[40] Court of Session Act 1988, s. 9.

[41] Court of Session Act 1988, s. 3; Law Reform (Miscellaneous Provisions) (Scotland) Act 1990, Sched. 4.

[42] *Ibid.* s. 28.

[43] Number of Inner House Judges (Variation) Order, 2001 (S.S.I. 2001 No. 41). Usually only three judges sit, and not five.

the presiding judges have one vote only and no casting vote, so that in the event of equal division, a rehearing is necessary before a larger court.[44] In each Division three judges are a quorum.[45] Either Division may call in a judge from the Outer House or from the other Division to make up a quorum. A vacancy arising in either Division is filled by the appointment, formerly of the senior Lord Ordinary, and now by a Lord Ordinary appointed by the Lord President and Lord Justice-Clerk with the consent of the First Minister and after such consultation as appears appropriate.[46] Any three judges may be constituted by the Lord President as an Extra Division to assist in dealing with Inner House business; he directs a senior judge of the Extra Division to preside. In cases of importance and difficulty the two Divisions may sit together as a Court of Seven Judges, or may even summon additional judges to make a fuller court.[47]

While in practice certain kinds of cases are sometimes appropriated to one Division rather than the other, the two are of co-ordinate authority and there is no formal distinction between the sphere of the one and that of the other. Nor can the litigant now[48] choose to which Division to carry his case.

The Inner House is a court of first instance in respect of special cases,[49] certain petitions, and revenue stated cases, but it is also and mainly a court of appeal, reviewing judgments of the sheriff court and of the Lords Ordinary in the Outer House and hearing various particular appeals against decisions of tribunals and committees. In cases tried by jury, a party dissatisfied may apply to the Inner House for a new trial on limited grounds.[50]

Only exceptionally is evidence heard in a case before the Inner House, in which case it is heard before one judge of the Division who reports thereon to the Division;[51] normally, Inner House business is disposed of by consideration of the transcript of evidence heard in a lower court and by hearing argument thereon, while much of the business involves only argument on law applicable to proved or admitted or undisputed facts and no question of hearing evidence arises.

An Inner House judgment is final in the Court of Session.[52] Exchequer causes at all times take precedence over all other causes in the court. In

---

[44] *Ibid.* s. 36.

[45] Hence when there is pressure of business one judge of the Division can, and frequently does, sit in the Outer House to deal with business there. Similarly, the absence of one judge on criminal circuit does not upset the working of the Division.

[46] Law Reform (Miscellaneous Provisions) (Scotland) Act 1990, Sched. 4.

[47] Court of Session Act 1988, s. 36. Thus in *Wright v. Bell*, (1905) 8 F. 291, all the judges (then 13 in number) sat.

[48] He could prior to 1933.

[49] A special case is a written case setting forth certain facts as admitted and not in controversy and seeking a decision of the legal difficulty raised by those facts. It is frequently adopted in cases of disputes on the interpretation of a will or trust instrument.

[50] Court of Session Act 1988, s. 29.

[51] *Ibid.* s. 37; *e.g. Pirie v. Leask*, 1964 S.L.T. 107.

[52] *Ibid.* s. 39.

these the Lord Advocate, on behalf of the Crown, has the privilege of being heard last.[53]

The House of Lords

The House of Lords has original jurisdiction only in cases of impeachment, breach of privilege and, acting on the recommendation of its Committee of Privileges, in relation to disputed claims to a peerage.[54]

The House of Lords as an appellate body exercises the jurisdiction to deal with appeals to the Queen in Parliament, and in theory appeals are heard by the whole House.[55] In modern practice, however, appeals are heard only by the legally qualified members of the House, namely, the Lord Chancellor, the Lords of Appeal in Ordinary[56] and peers who hold or have held high judicial office, sitting as an appellate Committee of the House. There is a convention that peers who are not legally qualified should not sit at the hearing of appeals.[57] The quorum is three[58] but appeals are frequently heard by five and sometimes, in cases of importance, by seven Law Lords[59]; decision is by a majority.[60] In modern times it has been customary to have at any time two Law Lords of Scottish origin,[61]

---

[53] *Ibid.* s. 21–24.

[54] See, *e.g. Earldom of Annandale and Hartfell*, [1986] A.C. 319.

[55] The Judicature Act 1873 abolished the House of Lords as final court of appeal. The operation of the Act was suspended until 1875 and this provision was repealed before it took effect. See Stevens, "The Final Appeal: Reform of the House of Lords and Privy Council, 1867–76" (1964) 80 L.Q.R. 343; Stevens, "The Role of the Final Appeal Court in a Democracy: The House of Lords Today" (1965) 28 M.L.R. 509; Bevan, "The Appellate Jurisdiction of The House of Lords" (1901) 17 L.Q.R. 155, 357; Blom-Cooper and Drewry, "House of Lords: Reflections on the Social Utility of Final Appellate Courts" (1969) 32 M.L.R. 262. For detailed studies of the working of the House see Blom-Cooper and Drewry, *Final Appeal*; Stevens, *Law and Politics.*

[56] The Appellate Jurisdiction Acts 1876–1947 authorise the appointment of at first, two, later, four, later (1929) seven, then (1947) nine, (1968) 11 and from 1995 12 Lords of Appeal in Ordinary. They are Life Peers and are entitled to sit in the House of Lords, at first during their tenure of office, and since 1887 for life and have the same rights as other peers, but in practice sit on the cross-benches and participate in political debates only on matters concerning law and the administration of justice. They must be barristers or advocates of 15 years' standing or persons who have for two years held high judicial office. For personal information about Law Lords since 1876 see Blom-Cooper and Drewry, pp. 152–183; Stevens, *Law and Politics, passim.*

[57] *O'Connell v. The Queen*, (1844) 11 Cl. & Fin. 155; see also Lord Du Parcq in (1949) *Current Legal Problems* 5, and Megarry, *Miscellany-at-Law*, 11–13.

[58] In *Rylands v. Fletcher* (1868) L.R. 3 H.L. 330 only two Law Lords are reported as being present: see [1945] K.B. 242 and 86 L.Q.R. 160. Since 1960 two Committees of Law Lords may sit simultaneously to hear appeals, and this happened in the autumn of 1962.

[59] *e.g. Murphy v. Brentwood*, [1990] 2 All E.R. 908.

[60] In consequence, the unanimous judgments of a Lord Ordinary and of four (or more) Lords in the Inner House may be reversed by a majority of one in the House of Lords. There are instances, *e.g. Commercial Union Assurance v. Waddell*, 1919 S.C.(H.L.) 38, where the House has been equally divided in which case the appeal has failed. See also *Kennedy v. Spratt*, [1972] A.C. 99.

[61] The Scottish Law Lords since 1876 have been Lords Gordon, Watson, Robertson, Shaw of Dunfermline, Dunedin, Macmillan, Thankerton, Normand, Reid, Keith of Avonholm, Guest, Kilbrandon, Fraser, Keith of Kinkel, Mackay of Clashfern (later Lord Chancellor) Jauncey of Tullichettle, Hope of Craighead, and Clyde. See Paterson, *The Law Lords* (1982); Paterson, "Scottish Lords of Appeal, 1876–1988", 1988 J.R. 235.

while other Scottish judges who were peers have from time to time assisted with the hearing of appeals.[62] There is, however, no rule that a Scottish Law Lord must be present to hear a Scottish appeal, still less that a majority of those sitting should be Scottish Law Lords, so that in the last resort Scottish appeals may be decided by judges a majority (or even all) of whom have no training in, or experience of, Scots law.[63]

Sittings for hearing appeals take place when the House is not sitting for public business. Appeals were formerly heard in the House of Lords chamber, but are now heard in one of the committee rooms. The Lords do not wear wig or gown, but counsel are robed.[64] The Lords sit in the chamber when they vote on the motion put by the Lord Chancellor or senior Law Lord that the appeal be allowed or dismissed. Their judgments are technically speeches in support of or against the motion and were formerly delivered orally. They are now, as a rule, not delivered orally but are issued in typescript and the Lords merely announce that the appeal will be allowed or dismissed for the reasons stated separately.[65] Dissenting opinions have always been allowed and are frequently uttered. If the House should be equally divided the appeal fails. In such a case, or where there is special difficulty, the House may order a case to be reargued.[66] The view of the House is not an operative judgment, but the case is returned to the Court of Session with the House's opinion, which must be translated into an operative decree by a petition to the Court of Session to apply the judgment of the House.

Appeal to the House of Lords is competent both on fact and on law though appeals on fact are not regarded favourably and great weight is attached by the House to the views on the evidence of the trial judge who saw and heard the witnesses.[67] The House is very slow to alter concurring findings of fact by Outer House and Inner House judges.[68] If the case originated in the sheriff court the right of appeal is limited to questions of law.[69] It is incompetent to appeal against an interlocutor of a Lord Ordinary unless it has been reviewed in the Inner House.[70] Appeal may be

---

[62] *e.g.* Lords Shand, Kinnear, Alness and Wheatley. Lords cease to be eligible to hear appeals when they attain 75; Judicial Pensions and Retirement Act 1993.

[63] Thus *A/B Karlshamns Oljefabriker v. Monarch S.S. Co.*, 1949 S.C.(H.L.) 1, was heard by five English Law Lords, and *Grant v. Sun Shipping Co. Ltd.*, 1948 S.C.(H.L.) 73 by four. Conversely *Arenson v. Casson Beckman Rutley & Co.*, [1975] 3 All E.R. 901, an English appeal, was heard by five Law Lords, three of whom were Scottish.

[64] Since 1965 senior counsel wear full-bottomed wigs only when the House is sitting in the Lords chamber for the hearing of appeals or for the delivery of judgments: see [1965] C.L.Y. 3063.

[65] [1963] C.L.Y. 2777.

[66] *Ruabon S.S. Co. v. London Assurance* [1900] A.C. 6; *Bannatyne v. Lord Overtoun* (1904) 7 F.(H.L.) 1; *Jones v. Secretary of State for Social Services* [1972] A.C. 944.

[67] *Thomas v. Thomas*, 1947 S.C.(H.L.) 45.

[68] *Higgins v. Smith*, 1990 S.C.(H.L.) 63.

[69] Court of Session Act 1988, s. 32 (5).

[70] Court of Session Act 1988, s. 40.

taken without leave of the Inner House, against final judgments of the Inner House, which dispose of the action (including judgments in Exchequer cases), or against interlocutory judgments, which dispose of some part or stage of the action, if the judges were not unanimous, or where the interlocutory judgment sustained a dilatory defence and dismissed the action, or, with the leave of the Inner House,[71] against any other interlocutory judgment. An interlocutor granting or refusing a new jury trial is appealable without leave. No appeal is allowed to the House of Lords against a decision of the Court of Session on an appeal relating to estate duty except with the leave of the court.[72] In view of the delay and expense of an appeal to the House of Lords, such appeals are usually taken only where a large sum or an important issue is at stake, or where an important or difficult point of law is in issue. Only half a dozen or so cases are appealed from Scotland to the House of Lords in a year, and the majority of Scottish cases do not go beyond the Inner House.

By a legal fiction, the House of Lords, as the final Court of Appeal from England, Scotland and Northern Ireland, has judicial knowledge of all the legal systems involved, so that it can take cognisance of points of the law of each of these systems even though they have not been pleaded or established by evidence before it.[73] This is, however, the sheerest fiction to ascribe to members of the English Bar and Bench, on their promotion to be Lords of Appeal, a sufficient knowledge of Scots law to correct the judges of the Court of Session.[74] In the past there have been some remarkable confessions of ignorance in the House and some scandalous impositions of foreign law on Scotland.[75] The House of Lords has been responsible for some of the worst misunderstandings and confused law in the Scottish books; over and over again English doctrines have been forced into Scots law by English Law Lords who did not know or realise the fundamental differences of principle and reason which frequently underlie apparent similarities of result, as where remedies are granted in circumstances similar to those justifying the corresponding remedy in English law.

Courts of Special Jurisdiction

Courts of special jurisdiction are courts of law as much as are the ordinary civil and criminal courts, but differ in that they have jurisdiction in particular kinds of claims only.

---

[71] *McIntosh v. B.R. Board*, 1990 S.L.T. 641; *Ferguson v. Maclennan Salmon Co.*, 1990 S.L.T. 658.

[72] *Ibid.* s. 52(3).

[73] *Cooper v. Cooper*, (1888) 15 R.(H.L.) 21; *Elliott v. Joicey*, 1935 S.C.(H.L.) 57.

[74] The converse is, of course, true in the case of Scottish Law Lords sitting in English appeals with the difference that the Scots are most unlikely to be in a majority, if indeed they sit at all. It is fair, however, to add that Lord Watson and Lord Reid won golden opinions for their judgments in English cases while Lord Birkenhead delivered some outstanding judgments in Scottish cases. See also (1956) 19 M.L.R. 95.

[75] Gibb, *Law from Over the Border, passim.*

The Court of the Lord Lyon

The Lord Lyon King of Arms is one of the Officers of State of the Kingdom of Scotland, and the Queen's counsellor in matters armorial, genealogical and ceremonial. The office is very ancient but appeared in its modern form in 1318. He exercises the whole Crown jurisdiction in armorial matters, enforces the laws of arms, and adjudicates in questions of name, family representation and chiefship. He is official adviser to the First Minister in matters relating to the Scottish Honours and ceremonial and, as controller of messengers-at-arms, is head of the department of Scots law relative to execution and diligence.[76]

The Court of the Lord Lyon[77] exercises both a civil and criminal jurisdiction, both at common law and under statute, and almost all heraldic business is conducted therein on judicial lines, legal representation being allowed though not usually necessary. The court is concerned with the establishment of rights to arms and pedigrees which when established are recorded in the Public Register of all Arms and Bearings in Scotland or in the Public Register of all Genealogies and Birthbrieves in Scotland,[78] and with protecting the rights of individuals and of the Crown in Scottish armorial bearings, and over messengers-at-arms. Lyon has, however, no jurisdiction to determine rights of precedence,[79] nor a disputed question of chieftainship.[80] The Lyon Court has a procurator-fiscal who acts as public prosecutor,[81] and has powers of fine and imprisonment,[82] power to erase unwarrantable arms, to break unwarrantable seals and to seize goods on which arms are unwarrantably represented. It may also interdict usurpers of arms.[83] Appeal lies to the Court of Session and to the House of Lords,[84] since arms are incorporeal heritable property.

Lyon also enforces Royal Warrants of Precedency in Scotland, makes Royal Proclamations and acts as Secretary of the Order of the Thistle. He is assisted by Lyon Clerk, three heralds and three pursuivants.

---

[76] Innes of Learney, *Scots Heraldry*, revised ed., Chap. 2, and references therein; Innes, "The Style and Title of Lord Lyon King of Arms" (1932) 44 J.R. 197.

[77] It sits in H.M. Register House, Edinburgh. See also *Introduction to Scottish Legal History*, pp. 397–398.

[78] *Viscountcy of Dudhope*, 1986 S.L.T. (Lyon Ct.) 2; *Viscountcy of Oxfuird*, 1986 S.L.T. (Lyon Ct.) 8; *Cowan of Blackburn*, 1996 S.L.T. (Lyon Ct.) 2; *Gunn*, 1996 S.L.T. (Lyon Ct.) 3; *Douglas-Hamilton*, 1996 S.L.T. (Lyon Ct.) 8.

[79] *Royal College of Surgeons v. Royal College of Physicians*, 1911 S.C. 1054.

[80] *Maclean of Ardgour v. Maclean*, 1938 S.L.T. 49; 1941 S.C. 613.

[81] On his powers see *MacDonald of Keppoch*, 1989 S.L.T. (Lyon Ct.) 2.

[82] *P.F. in Lyon Court v. Baird* [1992] S.L.T. (Lyon Ct.) 2.

[83] Innes of Learney, *supra*. See also Adam, *Clans, Septs and Regiments of the Scottish Highlands* (ed. Innes), *passim*; Milne, *The Scottish Office*, 189–190. Reports of selected cases in Lyon Court are published in the *Scots Law Times*.

[84] *e.g. Stewart Mackenzie v. Fraser Mackenzie*, 1922 S.C.(H.L.) 39; *Dunbar of Kilconzie, Petr.*, 1986 S.L.T. 463.

Court of Teinds

The Court of Teinds is in fact merely a function of the Court of Session, because in statutes the judges have been nominated as Lords Commissioners of Teinds, but has distinct procedure and a separate Teind Clerk. The court now consists of the eight Inner House judges along with the second junior Lord Ordinary, five, including the last-named, to be a quorum. Teinds were originally the tenth part of the fruits of the land and labour assigned for the maintenance of church and clergy.[85] In recent years the whole basis and substance of teind law has been much changed and the business of the court is almost entirely formal and carried through by the Lord Ordinary and the Teind Clerk, without opposition. An appeal lies to the House of Lords.[86]

Lands Valuation Appeal Court

This is a court consisting formerly of three judges of the Court of Session but now of one judge or, where he directs or where the appeal is against a determination of the Lands Tribunal for Scotland in a valuation case, three judges of the Court of Session,[87] which is constituted as and when necessary to dispose of appeals against the determination of the local Valuation Appeal Committees (which are established in each local authority district) or the Lands Tribunal as to the value to be set on heritable property for the purposes of the raising of local rates.[88] The appeal is taken by way of a stated case setting out the facts held by the Committee to be established and the questions of law in issue, and argument is heard on the principle of law in issue.[89] The actual monetary valuation set on a building or set of premises by the assessor is not usually challenged, but problems of statutory interpretation frequently arise, such as questions of whether certain subjects should be entered in the valuation roll or not,[90] whether certain premises are a "retail shop" and entitled to be treated as such,[91] and problems of the proper principle which is to be applied in arriving at a valuation.[92] This court is final and there is no appeal to the House of Lords.

---

[85] See further, Bell's *Law Dictionary*; Black and Christie, *Parochial Ecclesiastical Law*, 395–446, 523–534; Church of Scotland (Property and Endowments) Act 1925. The development of the law is traced in *Galloway v. Earl of Minto*, 1920 S.C. 354; 1922 S.C.(H.L.) 24.

[86] *Galloway, supra.*

[87] Rating and Valuation (Amendment) (Scotland) Act 1984, s. 13.

[88] Decisions are reported in *Session Cases* and *Scots Law Times* and there is a considerable volume of case law. Some of the older authorities are superseded by the Valuation and Rating (Scotland) Act 1956, which made revolutionary changes in the system. On older bases of valuation, see McKechnie, in *Source Book of Administrative Law*, 213–219.

[89] The Court of Session can order a valuation appeal committee to state a case: *Lugano v. Ayrshire Valuation Appeal Committee*, 1972 S.C. 314.

[90] *Grampian Assessor v. Union Grain Storage Aberdeen*, 1989 S.L.T. 361; *Lothian Assessor v. Lowland Leisure*, 1990 S.L.T. 353.

[91] *Perth Assessor v. Shields Motor Car Co.*, 1956 S.C. 186.

[92] e.g. *I.C.I. v. Central Region Assessor*, 1989 S.L.T. (Lands Tr.) 44; *Fife Assessor v. Distillers Co.*, 1989 S.L.T. 770; *Lothian Assessor v. B.P. Petroleum Development*, 1990 S.L.T. 59.

Court of Exchequer

The jurisdiction of the Court of Exchequer in Scotland, remodelled in 1708,[93] was in 1856 transferred to the Court of Session, and that court sits as Court of Exchequer in Scotland when dealing with revenue cases;[94] for long, exchequer causes were subject to procedural specialties.[95] The business consists chiefly of appeals on law by way of stated case from the determination of the Special Commissioners of Income Tax on issues of liability to tax. A further appeal lies to the House of Lords.[96]

Registration of Voters Appeal Court

An appeal on a matter of registration as a parliamentary elector lies from the registration officer to the sheriff and from him to a court of three judges of the Court of Session, whose decision is final. Business only occasionally arises for this court.[97]

Election Petition Court

Petitions presented against the election of Members of Parliament on the ground of illegality or improper practices at the election are heard by a court of two judges of the Court of Session whose decision is final.[98] This court also rarely requires to be constituted.

The Scottish Land Court

The Land Court was established in 1911 in succession to the Crofters Commission set up in 1886.[99] Its work is entirely linked with agriculture and the four members of the court, other than the chairman, are practical agriculturists. The chairman is an experienced lawyer, and has the status and tenure of a judge of the Court of Session.[1] The court makes an annual report which is laid before Parliament.

Its jurisdiction is entirely statutory[2] and has been greatly extended by the increased modern statutory control of agriculture, so that it has to

---

[93] See further, Clerk and Scrope's *Historical View of the Court of Exchequer in Scotland* (1820).

[94] *Lord Advocate v. Tursi,* 1997 S.C.L.R. 264.

[95] See *Inland Revenue v. Hood Barrs*, 1959 S.C. 273; and Bennett Miller, "Certiorari and the Scottish Courts" (1962) 25 M.L.R. 423.

[96] For an example, see *Inland Revenue v. Glasgow Police Athletic Association*, 1952 S.C. 102, reversed by H.L., 1953 S.C.(H.L.) 13.

[97] Representation of the People Act 1949, s. 45. See, *e.g. Edinburgh Electoral Registration Officer v. Robertson*, 1965 S.L.T. 14; *MacCorquodale v. Bovack*, 1984 S.L.T. 328.

[98] Representation of the People Act 1949, s. 107. See, *e.g. Grieve v. Douglas-Home*, 1965 S.C. 313, 315.

[99] A new Crofters Commission was set up in 1955 with duties of reorganising and developing crofting in the crofting counties. The judicial functions of the old Commission (1886–1911) were transferred to the Land Court.

[1] He is not a judge of the Court of Session, but in 1996 Lord Philip, chairman of the Scottish Land Court, transferred and became a judge of the Court of Session.

[2] Small Landholders (Scotland) Act 1911; Agricultural Holdings (Scotland) Act 1949, as amended; Scottish Land Court Act 1993. See further, Lamb: "The Scottish Land Court," 1958 S.L.T. (News) 129. Cases are reported in S.L.T. (Land Ct.)

decide a great variety of questions of considerable scope and value relative to agriculture. Its consent is required to most notices to quit agricultural holdings and it hears appeals from rent review arbitrations. It has extensive powers under the Acts governing crofting and small landholding. It does not have power to decide questions of bequests, relationship or succession, even in relation to land.[3]

A party to a dispute decided by the Land Court may require a case to be stated on a point of law to one of the divisions of the Inner House of the Court of Session.[4]

Restrictive Practices Court

This court was established by the Restrictive Trade Practices Act 1956. It consists of five judges, three English and one a judge of the Court of Session nominated by the Lord President,[5] and not more than 10 other persons (laymen) holding office for not less than three years. It may sit as a single court or in two or more divisions, in Scotland, England or Northern Ireland. The quorum is three, including at least one judicial member. Proceedings may be taken in this court by the Director General of Fair Trading to have certain restrictions, which have been disclosed to and registered with him, found to be contrary to the public interest and the relevant agreement held void to that extent.[6] Restrictions are presumed to be contrary to the public interest unless the court is satisfied that certain general conditions are satisfied. Under the Resale Prices Act 1964 this court also considers claims for exemption of goods from the rule abolishing resale price maintenance. An appeal from the decision of this court lies, in Scotland, to the Court of Session.[7]

STATUTORY TRIBUNALS

Within the last century a large number of statutes have established many bodies, usually called tribunals, with the function of determining issues and disputes arising under these statutes. Many of the disputes arise from the administration of government or certain public services[8] and these

---

[3] *Garvie's Trs. v. Still*, 1972 S.L.T. 29; *MacLennan's Exrx. v. MacLennan*, 1974 S.L.T. (Land Ct.) 3; *Eagle Star Ins. Co. v. Simpson*, 1984 S.L.T.(Land Ct.) 37.

[4] Crofters (Scotland) Act 1961, s. 4.

[5] The other judicial members are three judges of the High Court of England, nominated by the Lord Chancellor, and one judge of the Supreme Court of Northern Ireland nominated by the Lord Chief Justice of Northern Ireland. The Lord Chancellor nominates one of the judicial members to be President of the court. See further, Grunfeld and Yamey, "The Restrictive Trade Practices Act 1956" [1956] 1 P.L. 313; Korah, "The Restrictive Practices Court" (1959) 12 C.L.P. 76; Stevens and Yamey, *The Restrictive Practices Court.*

[6] *e.g. Mackie & Dewar v. Director-General of Fair Trading*, 1995 S.L.T. 1028.

[7] Cases are reported in the ordinary series of reports and also in *Law Reports*, Restrictive Practices series (1958–). See, *e.g. Re Wholesale and Retail Bakers of Scotland Association's Agreement*, 1960 S.L.T. 130; (1959) L.R. 1 R.P. 347.

[8] *e.g.* social security appeal tribunals.

tribunals are accordingly frequently called administrative tribunals, dealing with matters between state departments and citizens; but in other cases tribunals have been established to deal with issues between one person and another which could well have been dealt with by the ordinary courts,[9] because of parliamentary suspicions and dislike of lawyers and courts and in the belief that cases would be disposed of more quickly and fairly than in ordinary courts. These tribunals have developed in a very disorderly way and they vary considerably as to composition, powers and appeals; some deal with cases at first instance only; others with appeals; there is no consistent pattern, no uniformity as to membership or procedure and no settled rules as to right of appeal from their decisions.[10] The membership of statutory tribunals is very varied. There may be requirements that members be chosen from panels of suitable persons, or possess certain professional qualifications. Usually members are appointed for a specified period by the Minister concerned with the subject-matter; if a legally-qualified chairman is required, as is frequently prescribed, it is usual to prescribe that he be appointed by the Lord President of the Court of Session or, in England, the Lord Chancellor or, in Northern Ireland, the Lord Chief Justice of Northern Ireland.

There is frequently now provision for appeal from a tribunal exercising original jurisdiction to a superior level of tribunal, and frequently provision for appeal, usually by stated case on a point of law only, from a tribunal to the superior civil court.

The Tribunals and Inquiries Act 1992, superseding the similar Acts of 1958, 1966 and 1971, which had given effect to some of the recommendations of the (Franks) Committee on Administrative Tribunals and Inquiries,[11] provides that the chairmen of certain tribunals specified in the Act have to be selected by the appropriate Minister from panels appointed by, in Scotland, the Lord President, and no person's membership of any of the tribunals listed in the Schedule to the Act might be terminated without the approval of, in Scotland, the Lord President.

Unless exempted, scheduled tribunals are required, when requested, to give reasons for their decisions, though these may be withheld on grounds of national security. The Act also enlarged the range of tribunals from which appeal lay on a point of law to the Court of Session, which court might be empowered by Rules of Court to substitute its own decision for that of the tribunal from which appeal had been brought.

---

[9] *e.g.* industrial tribunals.

[10] The development of administrative tribunals was greatly stimulated by the development from 1911 of what we now call the Welfare State. Thus the National Health Insurance Act 1911 introduced unemployment tribunals.

[11] Cmnd. 218 (1957).

The Council on Tribunals

Following a recommendation of the Franks Committee there was established the Council on Tribunals.[12] It consists of from 10 to 15 members appointed by the Lord Chancellor and the Lord Advocate, one of whom is chairman.[13] It has a Scottish Committee of two or three members, together with three or four non-members appointed by the Lord Advocate. The Parliamentary Commissioner for Administration is *ex officio* a member of the Council and of its Scottish Committee. All members serve part-time and they include not only lawyers but also persons with experience of business, public administration, trade unions and consumer interests.

The Council is not an appellate body. Its functions are to keep under review the constitution and working of the tribunals listed in the Schedule to the 1992 Act (to which many additions have been made by other Acts), to consider and report on particular matters referred to it by the Lord Chancellor and the Lord Advocate with regard to any tribunal other than the ordinary courts of law, whether or not specified in the Schedule, and to consider and report on such matters as may be referred or as the Council may consider to be of special importance with respect to administrative procedures which may involve the holding of a statutory inquiry by or on behalf of a Minister. It makes an Annual Report to the Lord Chancellor and Lord Advocate. Members visit various tribunals to see them in operation and make written reports thereon.

Schedule 1, Part I to the 1992 Act lists the types of tribunals which are subject to the surveillance of the Council, and in practice the Council delegates to its Scottish Committee its powers in relation to the operation of these tribunals in Scotland, and Schedule 1, Part II specifies tribunals operating in Scotland subject to the particular supervision of the Scottish Committee.[14]

The Council does not have functions in relation to the appointment of tribunal chairmen or the appointment of members, but may make general recommendations as to membership of the tribunals in the Schedule, or the panels from which members are to be selected, and the appointing Minister must have regard to such recommendations. Nor does it have power to formulate procedural rules for tribunals, but it must be consulted by a rule-making authority before procedural rules are made for any scheduled tribunal. It must also be consulted before any scheduled

---

[12] Tribunals and Inquiries Act 1992, ss. 1, 4, replacing Tribunals and Inquiries Acts 1958, 1966 and 1971.

[13] He is frequently a member of the House of Lords who can speak for the Council there.

[14] Information on alterations to the Scheduled List are contained in the Annual Reports of the Council on Tribunals and in the *Parliament House Book*, Div. N.

tribunal can be exempted from the requirement of giving reasons for its decisions on request.[15]

Particular Tribunals

It is very difficult to classify tribunals in any rational way. Some of those discussed hereafter are United Kingdom tribunals, divisions of which sit also in England; some are peculiar to Scotland.[16] The practical importance of tribunals varies very much, from tribunals which sit in divisions in various places and handle, in total, many thousands of cases a year to tribunals which are rarely, if ever, called on to sit. The following list is deliberately incomplete but seeks to include most of the tribunals of substantial importance. In every case, reference must be made to the constituting statute and any subordinate legislation for the composition, powers, procedure and other attributes of the particular tribunal.

While appeal from a tribunal to the ordinary courts may or may not be allowed in particular cases, it is thought that an aggrieved individual may always, by the procedure for judicial review, bring a decision of a tribunal before the Court of Session for the exercise of its supervisory jurisdiction, but only on such grounds as refusal to exercise jurisdiction or acting in excess of jurisdiction, substantial disconformity to prescribed procedure, or breach of natural justice.

REVENUE GROUP

Bookmakers' Levy

Bookmakers at race meetings are assessed for a levy under a scheme made by the Horserace Betting Levy Board in accordance with declarations made by the bookmaker. Appeals against levy are referred to an appeal tribunal for Scotland consisting of a legally qualified chairman appointed by the Lord President, and two members appointed by the Secretary of State. The Lord President may prescribe procedure. It may confirm, increase or reduce the assessment or give the appellant a certificate of exemption. Its decision is final.[17]

Commissioners of Income Tax

Income tax, corporation tax and capital gains tax are assessed on individuals by inspectors who are officers of the Commissioners of Inland Revenue. There are appointed Commissioners for the General Purposes

---

[15] See also the Special Report by the Council on *The Function of the Council on Tribunals* (Cmnd. 7805 (1980)). In 1991 the Council suggested a comprehensive collection of model procedural rules for the use of Departments and tribunals: *Model Rules Report* (Cm. 1434 (1991)).

[16] The attempt has been made here to group tribunals according to the area of law involved. But, however it is done, there remains a substantial "Miscellaneous" category.

[17] Betting, Gaming and Lotteries Act 1963, ss. 27–29.

of the Income Tax (General Commissioners) acting for divisions of the country and appointed by the appropriate local authority; they are unpaid. Sheriffs principal and sheriffs are *ex officiis* General Commissioners.[18] The Treasury also appoints persons as Commissioners for the Special Purposes of the Income Tax Acts (Special Commissioners). They are full-time, salaried officers with considerable professional experience of tax law. One is Presiding Special Commissioner.[19] Appeal may be brought by written notice against an assessment to tax, to the Special Commissioners in specified kinds of cases and to the General Commissioners in other cases; in some cases the taxpayer may elect.[20] The General Commissioners hear the majority of appeals against assessments; at least two sit. Appeals to the Special Commissioners are usually heard by two Commissioners. Parties may be represented by counsel or solicitors and evidence may be led. After an appeal is determined, either party may require the Commissioners to state a case on a question of law for the opinion of the Court of Session as court of Exchequer, which may reverse, affirm or amend the determination. Further appeal lies to the House of Lords.[21] Questions of law are usually questions of statutory interpretation, *e.g.* is a particular activity "charitable"? Is a receipt or payment of the nature of income or of capital?

Value Added Tax Tribunals

Value Added Tax is administered by the Commissioners of Customs and Excise, and persons trading must make returns to them. There are Value Added Tax Tribunals directed by a legally qualified President. Each tribunal is chaired by the President or one of a panel of chairmen appointed by the Lord President, alone or with one or two members selected from the appropriate panel of persons appointed by the Treasury. The Commissioners prescribe procedure. Appeals are competent with respect to registration or cancellation of registration, the tax chargeable on the supply of any goods or services, and various other matters affecting liability.[22]

Social Security Group

The Appeals Service

This Service (formerly the Independent Tribunal Service) is responsible for the functioning of tribunals hearing appeals concerning child support

---

[18] Taxes Management Act 1970, s. 2.

[19] *Ibid.*, s. 3. On the origins of the Commissioners, who first appeared in 1799, see H. H. Monroe, *Intolerable Inquisition? Reflections on the Law of Tax* (Hamlyn Lectures, 1981). On the functions of General Commissioners see *Inland Revenue v. Barrs*, 1961 S.C.(H.L.) 22.

[20] *Ibid.* s. 42 and Sched. 2.

[21] *Ibid.* s. 56. Many cases are reported both in the Court of Exchequer and the House of Lords, *e.g. Inland Revenue v. Glasgow Police Athletic Association*, 1953 S.C.(H.L.) 13.

[22] Value Added Tax Act 1983, s. 40 and Sched. 8.

assessments, social security benefits and vaccine damage payments. Judicial authority rests with the President, but administrative responsibility is exercised by the Appeals Services Agency, which is an executive agency of the Department of Social Security.

War Pensions

Appeals against rejection of war pensions claims by members of the forces go to a Pension Appeal Tribunal, consisting of a legally qualified chairman, a doctor and a person with experience of the same service as the claimant, with further appeal on a matter of law to a single judge nominated by the Lord President.[23]

Adjudication Officers, Social Security Appeal Tribunals and the Commissioners

Under the Social Security Acts certain questions may be determined by the Secretary of State and a question of law may be referred to the Court of Session. Normally claims are determined by an adjudication officer, subject to appeal to a local tribunal consisting of a person appointed by the Secretary of State to be chairman, and two persons, one chosen from a panel representing employers and one from a panel representing employees. Further appeal lies to persons appointed full-time from experienced lawyers as Chief Social Security Commissioner and Social Security Commissioners.[24] A Commissioner may require the assistance of an assessor or assessors drawn from a panel, or may refer a question to a doctor for examination and report. Any decision of an adjudication officer or tribunal or Commissioner may be reviewed by an adjudication officer, tribunal or Commissioner in the event of fresh evidence or of a change of circumstances.[25] Disablement questions are determined by a medical board or a medical appeal tribunal with an appeal on a question of law to a Commissioner.[26] A question of law of special difficulty may be heard by a tribunal of three Commissioners.[27] Appeal lies, with the leave of the Commissioner to the Court of Session, on a question of law only.[28]

Child Support Officers, Appeal Tribunals and Support Commissioners

Each parent of a child is responsible for maintaining him, and a parent not living in the same household as the child must make periodical

---

[23] Pensions Appeal Tribunal Act 1943.

[24] Social Security Acts 1975, ss. 93–96; 1980, ss. 12–13; Health and Social Security Adjudications Act 1984; Social Security Administration Act 1992.

[25] *Ibid.*, ss. 97–104. See Micklethwait, *The National Insurance Commissioner* (Hamlyn Lectures, 1976).

[26] *Ibid.*, s. 108.

[27] *Ibid.*, s. 116.

[28] *e.g. Burns v. Secretary of State for Social Services*, 1985 S.L.T. 351; *Ruddick v. Secretary of State for Social Services*, 1988 S.L.T. 707; *Ferguson v. Secretary of State for Social Services*, 1989 S.L.T. 117; *Chief Adjudication Officer v. Combe*, 1997 S.C. 297.

payments as determined under the Child Support Act 1991. Maintenance assessments may be made by Child Support Officers and must be reviewed by them. Appeal may be taken to a child support appeal tribunal of three persons with further appeal to the Chief Child Support Commissioner and other Child Support Commissioners (who are legally qualified) on a question of law.[29] A further appeal lies with the leave of the Commissioner on a question of law to the Court of Session. Disputes about parentage go to a court in the first instance. Maintenance payments are enforceable by deductions from earnings order or by diligence.

Independent Review Service for the Social Fund

The Social Fund Commissioner is appointed by the Secretary of State for Social Services and appoints Social Fund Inspectors, who provide an independent review of decisions made by Social Fund Officers in the Benefits Agency of the Department of Social Security.

Health Group

The National Health Service is in Scotland managed by the Scottish Executive through a network of Health Boards, committees and other bodies.

Inefficient Practitioners

There is a National Health Service Tribunal (Scotland) to inquire into cases where representations are made by a Health Board that the continued inclusion of a medical or dental practitioner, opthalmic optician, dispensing optician or pharmacist in the lists is prejudicial to the efficiency of the service. It consists of a practising lawyer appointed by the Lord President, a person appointed by the First Minister after consultation with the body representative of Health Boards, and a practitioner member chosen from an appropriate panel. It inquires into the case and may remove the practitioner's name from the list. Appeal lies to the First Minister from any direction of the Tribunal.[30]

Complaints

Health Boards set up committees to consider complaints against practitioners of various classes with appeal to the Tribunal.

Misuse of Drugs

Directions may be given prohibiting the prescribing or supply of controlled drugs by medical practitioners or pharmacists in certain circumstances. Where grounds for giving such a direction are thought to exist,

---

[29] See Child Support Commissioners (Procedure) Regs. 1992 and 1995: S.I. 1992 No. 2640; S.I. 1995 No. 2907.
[30] National Health Service (Scotland) Act 1978, s. 29 and Sched. 8.

the Secretary of State may refer the case to a tribunal to consider and report. The Tribunal consists of five, a legally qualified person appointed by the Secretary of State and the Lord President, who is chairman, and four persons nominated from members of the respondent's profession by the appropriate medical colleges. The quorum is the chairman and two members.[31]

Vaccine Damage

A person who claims that he was severely disabled as a result of vaccination against any of certain diseases may claim from the Secretary of State. Independent medical tribunals may be established by regulations to determine the extent of disablement, whether it resulted from the vaccination, and whether the disability amounts to severe disablement. The Secretary of State may reconsider a determination on certain grounds.[32]

Mental Welfare Commission

The Mental Welfare Commission is a body of at least 10 persons, including at least three women, and three must be medically qualified and one legally qualified. It has to exercise protective functions in relation to persons mentally affected, to make inquiries, visit patients and bring to the attention of hospitals cases of ill-treatment, improper detention, or loss of property. Many actions affecting mentally disordered persons and patients must be reported to the Commission, and it may order discharge of a patient from hospital or from guardianship.[33]

Mental Health

The managers of a mental hospital have various discretionary powers, including that of transferring a patient to another hospital. An appeal by a patient lies to the sheriff.[34]

Employment Group

Employment (formerly Industrial) Tribunals

Industrial tribunals were first established under the Industrial Training Act 1964. Since then they have been given jurisdiction in an expanding range of issues connected with employment and are now established under the Employment Tribunals Act 1996. Each comprises a legally qualified chairman and two lay members, one drawn from a panel representative of employers and one from a panel representative of employees. Some

---

[31] Misuse of Drugs Act 1971, s. 16 and Sched. 3.
[32] Vaccine Damage Payments Act 1979.
[33] Mental Health (Scotland) Act 1984, Pt. II.
[34] *F. v. Ravenscraig Hospital Managers*, 1989 S.L.T. 49.

chairmen are permanent and serve full-time but others sit part-time. Their procedure is determined by regulations.[35] Matters referred to employment tribunals include claims arising from the entitlement of women to equal pay,[36] complaints that a person has committed an act of sex discrimination,[37] complaints that a person has committed an act of racial discrimination,[38] complaint that an employee has not been given written particulars of employment, or notice of a change therein, or an itemised pay statement, or an employer has failed to pay full remuneration or taken action against a person on account of trade union membership or activities, or failed to pay maternity pay, or unfairly dismissed an employee, or as to redundancy payment,[39] complaints by a union about not being allowed a secret ballot[40] or by a person about unreasonable exclusion from a trade union,[41] and a great variety of cases formerly heard by certain other tribunals.[42] There is statutory power to confer on employment tribunals claims of damages for breach of contract.[43]

Employment Appeal Tribunal

The Employment Appeal Tribunal consists of judges of the High Court in England nominated by the Lord Chancellor, at least one judge of the Court of Session nominated by the Lord President, and lay members having special knowledge of industrial relations appointed as representatives of employers or representatives of workers. One of the judicial members is appointed President. It is a superior court of record with its main office in London but may sit anywhere in Great Britain as a single tribunal or in two or more divisions concurrently.[44] A sitting comprises a judicial member and two or four lay members. Appeal lies on a question of law from a decision of an employment tribunal under many provisions of employment legislation and from decisions of the Certification Officer under the Trade Union Acts. Further appeal lies on questions of law with the leave of the Tribunal or of the Court of Session, to the Court of Session[45] and to the House of Lords.[46]

---

[35] 1978 Act, Sched. 9 and Employment Act 1989, s. 20; Employment Tribunals (Constitution and Rules of Procedure) Regulations 1993, as amended.

[36] Equal Pay Act 1970, s. 2.

[37] Sex Discrimination Act 1975, ss. 63–65.

[38] Race Relations Act 1976, ss. 54–56.

[39] Employment Protection Consolidation Act 1978, ss. 11, 22, 24, 36, 43, 67, 108, 112, 124.

[40] Employment Act 1980, s. 2.

[41] *Ibid.* s. 4.

[42] 1978 Act, Sched. 10.

[43] *Ibid.* s. 131.

[44] Employment Protection Act 1975, now Employment Tribunals Act 1996.

[45] *e.g. Ladbroke Racing v. Arnott*, 1981 S.C. 159; *Spook Erection v. Thackray*, 1983 S.L.T. 630; *Greater Glasgow Health Board v. Mackay*, 1989 S.L.T. 729; *Nairne v. Highlands Fire Brigade*, 1989 S.L.T. 754; *Walmsley v. Ferguson*, 1989 S.L.T. 258; *Rennie v. N.C.B.*, 1989 S.L.T. 799.

[46] *e.g. Melon v. Hector Powe*, 1981 S.C.(H.L.) 1; *Litster v. Forth Dry Dock Co.*, 1989 S.L.T. 540.

Advisory, Conciliation and Arbitration Service

The Advisory, Conciliation and Arbitration Service (A.C.A.S.) is directed by a Council of seven, a full-time chairman and nine other members, three appointed after consultation with employers' organisations and three after consultation with workers' organisations; there may be up to three deputy chairmen appointed from the members or in addition, and possibly two other members. It maintains offices in major towns. Its function is to promote the improvement of industrial relations and the extension of collective bargaining. In case of trade disputes it may seek to assist by conciliation through its conciliation officers, or, on request, refer the dispute to arbitration by an independent person or by the Central Arbitration Committee. It also offers advice on a wide range of employment matters, holds inquiries into industrial relations, issues Codes of Practice giving guidance on industrial relations and otherwise seeks to promote good industrial relations.[47]

The Central Arbitration Committee

The Central Arbitration Committee consists of a chairman, deputy chairman and members appointed by the Secretary of State from persons nominated by A.C.A.S. as experienced in industrial relations. It may deal with an application by a trade union that an employer is not complying with recommendations of A.C.A.S. or his failure to disclose information to a trade union, and it acts as a voluntary arbitration panel.[48]

Certification Officer

The Certification Officer is appointed to discharge functions as registrar under the Trade Union Acts, to maintain a list of trade unions, to certify that a union is an independent trade union (refusal being appealable to the Employment Appeal Tribunal), and to have custody of annual returns and accounts of trade unions. He is also in charge of the administrative arrangements relating to the provision of the funds for trade union ballots.[49]

Land Group

Agricultural Holdings

Under various provisions relative to agricultural holdings, obtaining the consent of the Land Court is requisite, but these are not appeals. In the case of rent review arbitrations, there may be appeal to the Land Court both on fact and law, and a case may be stated in the course of arbitration

---

[47] Employment Protection Act 1975, s. 1 and Sched. 1.
[48] *Ibid.*, s. 10 and Sched. 1, Pt. II. It replaced the Industrial Court and the later Industrial Arbitration Board.
[49] *Ibid.* s. 7 and Sched. 1, Pt. III.

proceedings to the Land Court on any question of law, its decision being final.[50] In the case of rent variation arbitrations, there is appeal by stated case on a point of law to the sheriff court and then to the Court of Session.[51]

Crofters Commission

The Crofters Commission is charged with reorganising, developing and regulating crofting and promoting the interests of crofters. Appeal lies to the Scottish Land Court against a refusal to issue a decrofting direction, and to the Secretary of State against a refusal to grant a reletting proposal.[52]

Forestry Commission

The Forestry Commissioners have to develop afforestation and the production and supply of timber in Great Britain. They may grant felling licences, and their refusal may be referred to a committee; so, too, with felling directions.[53]

Lands Tribunal for Scotland

The Lands Tribunal for Scotland consists of a President and other members appointed by the Lord President, the President being an experienced lawyer[54] and the others being lawyers or persons experienced in the valuation of land. It has jurisdiction to determine questions of disputed compensation for land acquired compulsorily, to hear appeals by public sector housing tenants as to delay in or refusal of their offers to buy their houses[55] and may act as an arbiter under a reference by consent. It also deals with applications under the Conveyancing and Feudal Reform (Scotland) Act 1970, for variation or discharge of conditions in feu-charters under which land is held. Jurisdiction may be exercised by one or more members. Its decisions are final on fact[56] but an aggrieved person may require it to state a case on a point of law for the decision of the Court of Session; there is no further appeal, save by leave of that court.[57]

Rent Assessment Committees

Rent assessment committees are drawn from a panel of persons appointed by the Secretary of State; each consists of a chairman and one

---

[50] Agricultural Holdings (Scotland) Act 1949, s. 75(1A) added by Agricultural Holdings (Amendment) (Scotland) Act 1983, s. 5.

[51] *Ibid.* s. 75.

[52] Crofters (Scotland) Act 1955, ss. 16, 16A.

[53] Forestry Act 1967, s. 27

[54] The office of President is at present held by the person who is also Chairman of the Scottish Land Court.

[55] Housing (Scotland) Act 1987, s. 71.

[56] Decisions are reported in S.L.T. (Lands Tr.). See, *e.g. N.E. Fife District Council v. Lees*, 1989 S.L.T. (Lands Tr.) 30.

[57] Lands Tribunal Act 1949; *McLaren's Tr. v. Secretary of State for Scotland*, 1989 S.L.T. 83; *Campbell v. Western Isles Islands Council*, 1989 S.L.T. 603. For an appeal to the House of Lords see *Woolfson v. Strathclyde R.C.*, 1978 S.C.(H.L.) 90.

or two members. Applications for registration of rent under regulated tenancies may be made by either or both parties to the lease and may be determined by the rent assessment committee.[58]

Valuation

Local authorities appoint assessors to prepare and maintain valuation rolls for all heritable property on which, formerly, rates and from 1993, council charge is levied. Each valuation area must have a valuation appeal committee constituted in accordance with a model scheme made by the First Minister and made up from members of local valuation panels constituted in accordance with the model scheme and appointed by the sheriff principal.[59] In a year of revaluation, appeal may be lodged by a proprietor, tenant or occupier; in intervaluation years, appeal is more limited. Since 1984 difficult or legally complicated cases may be referred to the Lands Tribunal for determination.[60] Parties dissatisfied with the decision of the valuation appeal committee or the Lands Tribunal for Scotland may appeal to the Lands Valuation Appeal Court by stated case, which is final as to the facts found and stated. The latter court's decision is final on the law.[61]

Building Control

Local authorities grant warrants for the construction or demolition of buildings or for change of use of a building to ensure that they comply with health and safety requirements. Appeal against refusal lies to the sheriff court.[62] Local authorities may also require certain repairs to be done or the demolition of unsafe buildings.[63]

Planning Control

Town and country planning is effected by the First Minister and local authorities and practically every "development" of land requires planning consent. Appeal lies to the First Minister against many planning decisions of local authorities.[64] Appeal also lies to the court against a decision of a First Minister's reporter on an appeal relative to enforcement.[65]

---

[58] Rent (Scotland) Act 1984, ss. 43, 54, 65, 72, 77, and Sched. 4. See, *e.g. Learmonth Property Investment Co. v. Aitken*, 1970 S.C. 223.

[59] Local Government (Scotland) Act 1975, s. 4; Valuation (Local Panels and Appeal Committees Model Scheme) (Scotland) Order 1975 (S.I. 1975 No. 1220). They may not proceed entirely on their local knowledge: *Central Region Assessor v. Binnie*, 1984 S.L.T. 393.

[60] Rating and Valuation (Amendment) (Scotland) Act 1984, s. 12. See *I.C.I. plc. v. Central Region Valuation Appeal Committee*, 1988 S.L.T. 106; *Civil Aviation Authority v. Argyll and Bute Valuation Appeal Committee*, 1988 S.L.T. 119.

[61] Valuation of Lands (Scotland) Amendment Act 1879, as amended.

[62] Building (Scotland) Act 1959, s. 16.

[63] *e.g. G.U.S. Property Management v. City of Glasgow D.C.*, 1989 S.L.T. 390.

[64] Town and Country Planning (Scotland) Act 1972, s. 33, as amended; *Lakin v. Secretary of State for Scotland*, 1988 S.L.T. 780. See also Young (ed.), *Scottish Planning Appeals, 1978–90* and monthly *Scottish Planning Appeal Decisions.*

[65] *Glasgow D.C. v. Secretary of State for Scotland*, 1989 S.L.T. 256; *Strathclyde R.C. v. Secretary of State for Scotland*, 1990 S.L.T. 149. See also *Adam v. Secretary of State for Scotland*, 1988 S.L.T. 300.

Transport Group

The Traffic Commissioner

There is a Traffic Commissioner for Scotland who may grant Public Service Vehicle operators' licences, which are needed to operate vehicles as stage, express or contract carriages, carrying passengers for reward.[66] He also grants PSV drivers' licences[67] and may grant the necessary licences for the operation of heavy goods vehicles.

Transport Tribunal

The Transport Tribunal is the successor of the Railway and Canal Commission and the later Railway Rates Tribunal. It is a court of record and consists of a number of members, the President and two or more chairmen being experienced lawyers, and two or more others having experience in transport.[68] It has jurisdiction to hear appeals from the decisions of the Traffic Commissioners and may sit anywhere in Great Britain. It may, before or during a hearing, refer a question arising to a member or officer of the Tribunal for report after holding a local inquiry. Decision is by a majority and the Tribunal must give reasons.[69] Appeal lies from the Transport Tribunal to the Court of Session on a point of law[70] and this is final.

Civil Aviation

The Civil Aviation Authority may grant, suspend, vary or revoke an air transport licence which is necessary for the operation of carriage by air, only after a public hearing. Appeal lies to the Secretary of State. An air travel organiser's licence may be granted, with appeal to the sheriff against an unfavourable decision.[71]

Commercial Group

Banking Tribunal

An institution aggrieved by the Bank of England's decision to refuse its application for authorisation as a bank, or revoke or restrict its authorisation, or in certain other circumstances may appeal to a tribunal. Certain persons may also appeal against decisions that they are not fit and proper persons to manage a bank. The Treasury makes regulations governing appeals. The Tribunal consists of a legally experienced chairman

---

[66] Public Passenger Vehicles Act 1981; Civic Government (Scotland) Act 1982.

[67] See *Johnstone v. Traffic Commissioner*, 1990 S.L.T. 409.

[68] Transport Act 1985, Sched. 4.

[69] *Merchandise Transport Co. v. B.T.C.* [1962] 2 Q.B. 173.

[70] See *Clarke v. Edinburgh and District Tramways Co.*, 1919 S.C.(H.L.) 35; *Strathclyde Passenger Executive v. McGill*, 1984 S.L.T. 377.

[71] Civil Aviation Act 1982, ss. 64 *et seq.*

appointed by the Lord Chancellor in consultation with the Lord Advocate and two other members with experience of accountancy and banking, respectively. It determines its own procedure; the hearing is in private, unless the chairman directs otherwise. The Tribunal may confirm or reverse the decision, but has only limited power to vary it. A further appeal lies to the Court of Session on a question of law arising from the Tribunal's decision and further with the leave of that court or the House of Lords, to the House of Lords.[72]

Financial Services Tribunal

This tribunal was established to handle appeals against decisions of the Secretary of State or the Securities and Investment Board. It consists of at least 10 persons appointed by the Secretary of State, some having legal qualifications and others suitably qualified. When a case is referred the Secretary of State will nominate three from the panel, one (who must be legally qualified) as chairman. Appeal to the Tribunal is open to persons refused authorisation to carry on investment business or having their authorisation withdrawn or suspended, or in certain other cases. It reports to the Securities and Investment Board which must then decide in accordance with the Tribunal's report.[73]

Building Societies Tribunal

A building society aggrieved by the decision of the Building Societies Commission to refuse or revoke authorisation or impose conditions or as to conditions imposed, may appeal to a tribunal consisting of a legally qualified chairman and two members having experience of accountancy and of building societies or financial institutions. A further appeal lies to the Court of Session on a point of law.[74]

Insolvency Practitioners Tribunal

A person must be a qualified insolvency practitioner to act as permanent trustee in the sequestration of an individual[75] or the winding up of a company;[76] this requires him to be a solicitor or an accountant or to hold an authorisation from the Secretary of State. If the authority proposes to refuse or withdraw authorisation, the aggrieved person may make representations to the authority and require the case to be referred to the Insolvency Practitioners Tribunal. It consists of panels of experienced lawyers nominated by the Lord President and of persons experienced in

---

[72] Banking Act 1987, ss. 27–28, 31.
[73] Financial Services Act 1986, ss. 96–100.
[74] Building Societies Act 1986, ss. 46–48.
[75] Bankruptcy (Scotland) Act 1985, s. 24.
[76] Insolvency Act 1986, s. 230.

insolvency matters; a sitting consists of a legal chairman and two drawn from the panel, who must investigate the case in private and report thereon.[77]

Intellectual Property Group

Patents

The Comptroller-General of Patents, Designs and Trade Marks has extensive powers to grant letters patent conferring rights in new inventions capable of industrial applications. Appeal lies from most decisions of the Comptroller-General to the Patents Court which consists of one or more judges of the High Court in England nominated by the Lord Chancellor or an Outer House judge of the Court of Session. Further appeal lies in a limited range of cases or where the ground is that the decision of the single judge is wrong in law.[78]

Industrial Designs

In respect of registration of industrial designs the Comptroller-General, as registrar, exercises powers of registration, subject to appeal to the Appeal Tribunal which is a judge of the Court of Session.[79]

Trade Marks

In respect of trade marks the Comptroller-General, as registrar, has powers of registration subject to review by the Court of Session.[80]

Plant Varieties

The Controller of the Plant Variety Rights Office may grant plant breeder's rights. There is a Plant Variety Rights Tribunal consisting of an experienced legal chairman appointed by the Lord President, and two members drawn from panels of persons with specialised knowledge, to hear appeals against decisions of the Controller.[81]

Copyright

The Copyright Tribunal, which has replaced the Performing Right Tribunal, consists of a chairman and two deputy chairmen, all experienced lawyers appointed by the Lord Chancellor after consultation with the Lord Advocate, and from two to eight members appointed by the First Minister. Each sitting consists of the chairman or a deputy and at least two members, with a quorum of three. It has jurisdiction in relation to

---

[77] *Ibid.* ss. 390–396.
[78] Patents Act 1977, ss. 96–98.
[79] Registered Designs Act 1949, ss. 28, 45.
[80] Trade Marks Act 1938, ss. 51, 66.
[81] Plant Varieties and Seeds Act 1964, s. 10 and Sched. 4.

licensing schemes, applications relating to royalties or the term of copyright licences, and other matters relating to copyright. An appeal lies on a point of law to the Court of Session.[82]

Miscellaneous Group

Children's Hearings

Children under 16 who are beyond parental control, falling into bad associations or exposed to moral danger through lack of parental care, or suffering lack of care, have been victims of offences or where members of the same household have been victims of offences, have failed to attend school regularly, have committed offences, or in certain other cases, are deemed in need of compulsory measures of care, including protection, control, guidance and treatment. Children under 16 are not now prosecuted except on the instructions of the Lord Advocate or at his instance.[83] In each local authority area there are constituted children's panels of such size as is appropriate, appointed by the First Minister; he also appoints a chairman and deputy chairmen. Suitable persons are proposed by the local Children's Panel Advisory Committee. The First Minister has to make arrangements for training panel members.

Children's hearings, consisting of sittings of three members of the panel, both sexes being represented, are held in private to consider cases of children who may require compulsory care. Cases are brought before the hearing by an officer of the local authority unit of the Scottish Children's Reporter Administration called the Reporter[84] and his deputies, who make initial investigation and, if he thinks necessary, arranges a children's hearing. If the chairman considers it necessary to protect the interest of the child, he may appoint a person as "safeguarder" to do so.[85] If the child or his parents do not accept the ground stated by the reporter for the referral, the Reporter makes application to the sheriff for a finding as to whether the grounds for referral are established. The sheriff, sitting in chambers, may discharge a referral or find on the evidence that the grounds for referral have been established and remit the case back to hearing.[86] The hearing is then to proceed to consider what course they should adopt in the best interests of the child, discharging the referral, continuing the case for further investigation, requiring the child to submit to supervision or to reside in a residential establishment. Supervision

---

[82] Copyright, Designs and Patents Act 1988, ss. 145–152. *e.g. Performing Rights Society v. British Entertainment and Dancing Assoc.* [1993] E.M.L.R. 325.

[83] Social Work (Scotland) Act 1968, ss. 30–58 and Sched. 3. See further, Kearney, *Children's Hearings and the Sheriff Court.*

[84] On Reporters' qualifications see *Miller v. Council of the Law Society of Scotland,* 2000 S.L.T. 513.

[85] *Ibid.* s. 34A(1) as amended. See *Catto v. Pearson,* 1990 S.L.T. (Sh.Ct.) 77.

[86] *e.g. Ferguson v. P.,* 1989 S.L.T. 681; *Sloan v. B.,* 1991 S.L.T. 530.

requirements must be reviewed when the local authority recommends, at intervals if required by the child or his parents, and in any event yearly.

The child or his parents may appeal to the sheriff in chambers against a decision, in which case the sheriff may confirm the decision, remit the case for reconsideration or discharge the child.[87] Appeal lies from a decision of the sheriff to the Court of Session by way of stated case on a point of law[88] or in respect of any irregularity in the conduct of the case.[89] Where the sheriff has remitted a case for reconsideration, the child or his parents may appeal against the reconsidered decision. Where a child is found guilty of an offence in a criminal trial the court may remit the cases for disposal by a children's hearing, or request a children's hearing to obtain advice on disposal.

Immigration

A person who is refused leave to enter the United Kingdom by an immigration officer may generally appeal to an adjudicator appointed by the Secretary of State against the decision that he requires leave, against the refusal of leave, or against the refusal of a certificate of patriality or an entry certificate. A person dissatisfied with an adjudicator's determination may appeal to the Immigration Appeal Tribunal, generally only with the leave of the adjudicator or the Tribunal. It is constituted by persons appointed by the Lord Chancellor; the President must be legally qualified and the quorum is three. Procedure is provided by regulations.[90] The Special Immigration Appeals Commission was created to hear appeals in certain matters otherwise excluded from appeal. After it has made a final determination, a party may take a further appeal to the Court of Session on a question of law.[91]

Data Protection

The Data Protection Commissioner has to register and supervise data users and computer bureaux to ensure that personal data held on computer tape are used only in conformity with the data protection principles. The Data Protection Tribunal consisting of a legally qualified chairman and equal numbers of lay persons representing the interests of the data-users and data subjects hears appeals against certain decisions of the Data Protection Commissioner and against certain notices issued by him.[92]

---

[87] *e.g. M. v. Children's Hearing for Strathclyde*, 1988 S.C.L.R. 592.
[88] *e.g. McGregor v. H.*, 1983 S.L.T. 626; *B. v. Harris*, 1990 S.L.T. 208; *Mitchell v. S,* 2000 S.C. 334.
[89] *Sloan v. B.*, 1991 S.L.T. 530.
[90] Immigration Act 1971, s. 12 and Sched. 5. Cases are reported in Immigration Appeal Reports. See also *Nawaz v. Lord Advocate*, 1983 S.L.T. 653.
[91] Special Immigration Appeals Commission Act 1997.
[92] Data Protection Act 1984, s. 3 and Sched. 2 as amended.

Interception of Communications

Under the Interception of Communications Act 1985 it is an offence to intercept a communication by post or a public telecommunications system, but the secretary of state may by warrant allow it in particular circumstances. There was established a Tribunal to carry out investigations to determine whether there was a warrant or certificate authorising an interception, and a Commissioner was appointed to keep under review the carrying out by the secretary of state of his functions under the Act and the Tribunal in its functions and to report contraventions to the Prime Minister.

Liquor Licensing

Local councils, and sometimes divisions thereof, have licensing boards consisting of a quarter of the members of the council. Boards elect their own chairman[93] and meet at least four times a year. There are numerous different types of licence and the chief constable[94] and other persons may object to a grant. Boards also deal with applications for regular or occasional extension of permitted hours. They must give written reasons for decisions on certain matters. There is a general right of appeal to the sheriff against certain decisions[95] but the grounds of appeal are limited to error in law, decisions based on an incorrect material fact,[96] conduct contrary to natural justice[97] and unreasonable exercise of discretion.[98] Thereafter there is a right of appeal in limited cases to the Court of Session on a point of law. It is uncertain if further appeal to the House of Lords is competent.[99] Relief may also be sought by judicial review where there has been unfair procedure.[1]

Certificates of registration of clubs allowing them to sell liquor are granted by a sheriff.[2]

Licensing of Betting, Gaming and Lotteries

Licensing boards created for liquor licensing are also licensing authorities for granting bookmakers' permits, betting agency permits and betting office licences,[3] licensing gaming premises[4] and issuing permits for gaming machines or amusements in public houses and licensed hotels.[5]

---

[93] Licensing (Scotland) Act 1976, s. 1.

[94] *e.g. Stephen v. Aberdeen District Licensing Board*, 1989 S.L.T. (Sh.Ct.) 94.

[95] Licensing (Scotland) Act 1976, s. 39; *e.g. Barnett v. Bute and Cowal Divisional Licensing Board*, 1989 S.L.T. 572. It is to the sheriff or sheriff principal, not to both: *Troc Sales v. Kirkcaldy District Licensing Board*, 1982 S.L.T. (Sh.Ct.) 77.

[96] *Fitzpatrick v. Glasgow Licensing Board*, 1978 S.L.T. (Sh.Ct.) 63.

[97] *Moughal v. Motherwell Licensing Board*, 1983 S.L.T. (Sh.Ct.) 84.

[98] *Collins v. Hamilton Licensing Board*, 1984 S.L.T. 230.

[99] *Sutherland v. Edinburgh Licensing Board*, 1984 S.L.T. 241.

[1] *Tait v. Glasgow District Licensing Board*, 1987 S.C. 4; *Bury v. Kilmarnock Licensing Board*, 1989 S.L.T. 110; *CRS Leisure v. Dumbarton Licensing Board*, 1990 S.L.T. 200.

[2] Licensing (Scotland) Act 1976, Pt. VII.

[3] Betting, Gaming and Lotteries Act 1963, ss. 2, 9.

[4] Gaming Act 1968, s. 11; *Noble Organisation v. Glasgow D.C.*, 1990 S.L.T. 557.

[5] *Ibid.* s. 34.

Other Licensing

Local authorities have extensive powers to control many activities by requiring licensing and registration.[6] These include the use of premises for film or theatrical performances,[7] pet shops, selling game, the operation of taxis,[8] window cleaners and many other trades. Similarly local authorities may allow or prohibit public processions.[9]

Appeal against refusal may generally be made to the sheriff by summary application, but only on the grounds that the authority erred in law, founded on an incorrect material fact, acted contrary to natural justice[10] or exercised its discretion in an unreasonable manner,[11] and thereafter to the Court of Session.[12]

Licensing of Consumer Credit Businesses

Persons carrying on businesses of or involving lending money, pawn-broking, granting credit, letting goods on hire or hire-purchase, and related businesses require licences from the Director-General of Fair Trading, who may also vary, renew or continue licences. There are various categories of licences. There is a right of appeal to the Secretary of State[13] against the Director-General's decision on the issue of a licence with a further appeal to the Court of Session on a point of law.[14]

Registration of Establishments

Under the Social Work (Scotland) Act 1968, Sched. 5, the First Minister has to appoint a panel from which to create an appeal tribunal as may be required to hear appeals by a person wishing to carry on an establishment providing non-residential accommodation for the purposes of that Act and refused registration by the local authority. Each tribunal is to consist of the sheriff principal and two other persons appointed from the panel by the First Minister.

Schools

It is the duty of education authorities to comply with parents' requests as to their children's schooling. The authority's refusal may be appealed to an appeal committee of three, five, or seven members of the education committee and parents, the latter to be in a majority, with a further appeal to the sheriff. There is similarly an appeal against a decision to exclude a pupil from school.[15]

---

[6] Civic Government (Scotland) Act 1982, ss. 9–44.
[7] *Gerry Cottle's Circus v. Edinburgh D.C.*, 1990 S.L.T. 235.
[8] *City Cabs (Edinburgh) v. Edinburgh D.C.*, 1988 S.L.T. 184.
[9] *Aberdeen Orange Lodge v. Grampian R.C.*, 1988 S.L.T. (Sh.Ct.) 58.
[10] *Thomson v. Motherwell D.C.*, 1989 S.C.L.R. 175.
[11] *Holt v. Watson*, 1983 S.L.T. 588.
[12] *Piper v. Kyle and Carrick D.C.*, 1988 S.L.T. 217.
[13] Consumer Credit Act 1974, s. 41.
[14] *Ibid.* s. 42.
[15] Education (Scotland) Act 1980, ss. 28D–28H and Sched. A1, inserted by Education (Scotland) Act 1981.

Professional conduct committees

Many professions have bodies which can censure or discipline members for professional misconduct and even have them expelled from the profession.[16]

Scottish Solicitors' Discipline Tribunal

This is an independent statutory body consisting of a panel of 18, ten of whom are solicitors, appointed by the Lord President, with the function of considering complaints of misconduct by solicitors in Scotland and with powers to fine or strike off the Roll of Solicitors.[17]

Domestic tribunals

Professional and trading organisations frequently create tribunals to enforce standards and discipline among their members. Such bodies must act fairly and observe the main principles of natural justice.[18]

THE SHERIFF AS APPELLATE TRIBUNAL

Quite apart from his function as a civil and criminal judge the sheriff is constituted by numerous statutes the authority to authorise or order many kinds of acts, and in other cases made an appellate tribunal from the decisions of many kinds of bodies and persons. The approach to him is frequently to be made by summary application. There is, however, no uniformity or standard pattern in the statutory provisions.[19] Thus, the Civic Government (Scotland) Act 1982 requires local authorities to license many kinds of activities and gives an individual aggrieved by a refusal an appeal to the sheriff. The appellate powers under statutes seem to fall into three classes, where the sheriff may reconsider the decision complained of not only as to jurisdiction, powers or error of law, but also on the merits and expediency of the decision,[20] or where the sheriff may uphold the decision only if he finds certain matters of fact existing,[21] or where the sheriff can consider only specified grounds of appeal, such as jurisdiction, powers, error of law or of procedure.[22]

It similarly depends in every case on the particular legislation whether the sheriff may reach a fresh decision, or if not satisfied can only remit the case back for reconsideration[23] and whether any further appeal lies to the

---

[16] *e.g. Carr v. U.K. Central Council for Nursing,* 1989 S.L.T. 589; *Tehrani v. Argyll and Clyde Health Board,* 1989 S.C. 342

[17] *Paterson v. Scottish Solicitors' Discipline Tribunal,* 1984 S.L.T. 3.

[18] *Rennie v. Scottish Milk Records Association,* 1985 S.L.T. 272; *Tait v. Central Radio Taxis (Tollcross) Ltd,* 1989 S.C. 4.

[19] See Macphail, *Sheriff Court Practice,* Chaps. 26–27.

[20] *e.g. Glasgow Corp. v. Glasgow Churches Council,* 1944 S.C. 97.

[21] *e.g. Glasgow Corp., supra.*

[22] *e.g. Cigaro (Glasgow) Ltd. v. Glasgow District Licensing Board,* 1982 S.C. 104.

[23] *e.g. Botterills of Blantyre v. Hamilton District Licensing Board,* 1986 S.L.T. 14.

Court of Session, either by way of appeal or by stated case on a point of law.[24] Where a right of appeal to the sheriff is given and the statute says nothing about review of his decision, the presumption is that "the sheriff's decision" is final.[25]

But unless jurisdiction to review the decision of a body such as a housing authority is conferred on a sheriff, he cannot exercise review jurisdiction.[26]

CRIMINAL COURTS

Criminal jurisdiction is divided into solemn and summary jurisdiction, the former being exercised by trial on indictment before a judge or sheriff sitting with a jury of 15[27] and the latter by trial on complaint by sheriff or magistrate or by one or more justices of the peace sitting alone, without a jury. The determination whether a case is to be prosecuted under solemn or under summary procedure depends on any statutory prescription which is applicable to the offence in question and on the gravity of the offence. If statute is silent the prosecutor has a discretion, but that discretion is limited by the fact that procedure in the sheriff's summary court and in magistrates' courts is regulated by the Criminal Procedure (Scotland) Act 1995, which excludes from the jurisdiction of these courts a number of the more serious crimes, and limits the powers of these courts to punish offenders. Furthermore, it is a general principle that justices of the peace cannot deal with statutory offences unless jurisdiction is conferred on them expressly or by implication in the statute in question.[28] There are accordingly four modes of trial: (i) magistrate or one or more justices alone (summary offences); (ii) sheriff alone (summary offences); (iii) sheriff[29] and jury; (iv) judge of the High Court and jury.

The prosecution of crimes and offences is almost exclusively in the hands of the Lord Advocate in the High Court, and of procurators-fiscal, acting on instructions from the Lord Advocate, in the sheriff and district courts. Private prosecution, though possible, is practically unknown,[30] and

---

[24] *e.g. Arcari v. Dunbartonshire C.C.*, 1948 S.C. 62; *Kaye v. Hunter*, 1958 S.C. 208.

[25] *T. v. Secretary of State for Scotland*, 1987 S.C.L.R. 65.

[26] *Brown v. Hamilton D.C.*, 1983 S.L.T. 397.

[27] Notice that the Scottish criminal jury numbers 15, the Scottish civil (like the English) jury 12.

[28] *McPherson v. Boyd*, 1907 S.C.(J.) 42. The sheriff's summary court is accordingly the commonest forum for prosecutions in Scotland.

[29] Sheriff principal or sheriff (permanent or part-time).

[30] *J. & P. Coats v. Brown*, 1909 S.C.(J.) 29; *McBain v. Crichton*, 1961 J.C. 25; *X v. Sweeney*, 1982 J.C. 70. The concurrence of the Lord Advocate must be sought though the High Court may permit the prosecution without his concurrence. It is wholly incompetent for a private prosecutor to prosecute on indictment in the sheriff court: *Dunbar v. Johnston* (1904) 7 F. 40. A county council has no title to institute a private prosecution: *McKinstry v. Lanark C.C.*, 1962 J.C. 16. Certain public bodies such as British Railways had statutory powers to bring what are technically private prosecutions; see, *e.g. British Railways Board v. Dick*, 1965 S.L.T.(Sh.Ct.) 25.

while certain officials, such as officers of Customs and Excise, may prosecute summary offences they do so in the public interest, and even in such cases the procurator-fiscal is usually asked to act. The police do not in any circumstances prosecute in Scotland. Crimes are reported to the local procurator-fiscal in the first place and he decides, in serious cases in consultation with the Crown Office in Edinburgh, whether to prosecute and in what form. In High Court cases, the indictment is settled by the Lord Advocate, the Solicitor-General or one of the advocates-depute appointed by the Lord Advocate, and one of these conducts the case for the Crown in the High Court and in important cases in the sheriff court. In other sheriff court cases and in summary offences, the procurator-fiscal conducts the prosecution case.[31]

The District Court

A court consisting of a stipendiary magistrate (in Glasgow) or one or more justices of the peace, has a criminal jurisdiction extending over the area having a distinct commission of the peace for which the justices are appointed[32] and extending to all breaches of the peace and certain minor charges under statute. A local authority has power[33] to secure the appointment of a stipendiary magistrate, who must have been legally qualified for five years and who has the same jurisdiction as the sheriff in his summary court in respect of offences committed within the district. Only in Glasgow has this power been used, where four stipendiaries sit in the district courts.[34] The sheriff has jurisdiction within his sheriffdom concurrent with the justices in regard to all offences triable by them. Prosecutions are conducted by one of the procurators-fiscal and procedure is summary, there being no jury.

These courts have strictly limited powers of punishment,[35] so although numerous cases are brought before them, they are not serious cases.

Appeal lies to the High Court of Justiciary by way of a stated case, which sets out the facts admitted or proved and raises a question of law only, or by bill of advocation (at the instance of the prosecutor) or by bill of suspension (at the instance of the accused). As a criminal court, the district court is very much less important in Scotland than are magistrates' courts in England; it deals only with the most ordinary cases and not even with the bulk of them.

---

[31] See further, Milne, *The Scottish Office*, 206–208; Gordon, in *Source Book of Administrative Law*, Chap. 5. For statistics, see the annual *Criminal Statistics, Scotland*.

[32] The District Court was created in 1975 and replaced the former Burgh Police Courts (in burghs) and Justice of the Peace Courts (in counties): District Courts (Scotland) Act 1975. For history of the justices' jurisdiction see *Wright v. Bell* (1905) 8 F. 291. For jurisdiction see Criminal Justice (Scotland) Act 1980, s. 7.

[33] District Courts (Scotland) Act 1975, s. 5.

[34] On stipendiary magistrates' status see *Maclean v. Glasgow City Council*, 1999 S.L.T. 11.

[35] Criminal Procedure (Scotland) Act 1995. A stipendiary magistrate has the same powers of punishment as a sheriff and usually tries the more serious cases.

The Sheriff Court

As in civil matters, the sheriff court is the most generally important lower criminal court and it can try any crime or offence committed within the sheriffdom, not reserved to the High Court, including cases which might be heard in the district court.[36] In criminal cases no distinction need be taken between the sheriff principal and the sheriffs since their powers are co-extensive and no appeal lies from the one to the other. The sheriff principal or sheriff may, sitting alone, deal with cases prosecuted on complaint under the Criminal Procedure (Scotland) Act 1995 and, when sitting with a jury of 15, deal with cases prosecuted on indictment.[37] In the latter case the procedure followed is identical with that followed in the High Court of Justiciary. The selection of the mode of trial appropriate is determined by the prosecutor, and the accused has no right to elect jury trial. In either case, the prosecution is prepared and conducted by the procurator-fiscal or one of his deputes, though in difficult cases an advocate-depute may appear for the Crown. Counsel may always, and frequently do, appear for the accused. In other cases, the accused is normally represented by a solicitor, but he may defend himself. As compared with the High Court, however, the sheriff's power of punishment is limited, in cases on indictment, to three years' imprisonment or an unlimited fine, unless the offence is under a statute which imposes a limit on the fine, and in summary cases, to three months' imprisonment unless there are previous convictions or a particular statute confers wider powers, or a fine of £5000, unless a particular statute confers wider or narrower powers.[38] In cases on indictment the sheriff may remit a convicted person to the High Court for sentence if he regards his powers as inadequate in the circumstances.[39] The sheriff court has concurrent jurisdiction with other lower courts within the sheriffdom in regard to all offences which can be tried in such courts, and its jurisdiction is practically universal in that it need not be expressly conferred by the statute creating the offence, but it is limited in that the most serious crimes of all, such as murder and rape, may be tried only in the High Court, and by the fact that its powers of punishment are limited. Nevertheless the sheriff court, either summarily or on indictment, deals with an immense number of offenders and

---

[36] If a statute speaks of an offence being prosecuted in "a court of summary jurisdiction," jurisdiction is conferred on district and sheriff courts, but if it speaks of the offence being punishable "on summary conviction," or does not name the court, jurisdiction is conferred only on the sheriff court: *McPherson v. Boyd*, 1907 S.C.(J.) 42.

[37] About 90 per cent of prosecutions on indictment and more than 50 per cent of prosecutions on complaint are dealt with in the sheriff courts.

[38] Criminal Procedure (Scotland) Act 1995, s. 5.

[39] Criminal Procedure (Scotland) Act 1995, s. 195. In such a case the High Court is not bound to impose a heavier sentence than the sheriff could have imposed. The sheriff cannot remit if the maximum penalty for the offence charged is within the sheriff's competence: *H.M. Advocate v. Stern*, 1974 S.L.T. 2. An accused may also notify his intention to plead guilty and ask for his case to be expedited, in which case the sheriff may sentence him or remit him to the High Court for sentence: Criminal Procedure (Scotland) Act 1995, s. 76.

with practically every kind of crime and offence, and it is by far the most important of the inferior criminal courts.

An appeal from the sheriff sitting summarily lies to the High Court of Justiciary by the way of stated case or bill of advocation (at the instance of the prosecutor) or bill of suspension (at the instance of the accused) and, from the sheriff sitting with a jury, under solemn procedure, to the High Court of Justiciary in its capacity as Court of Criminal Appeal under the Criminal Appeal (Scotland) Act 1926 (now the Criminal Procedure (Scotland) Act 1995).

The High Court of Justiciary

The High Court was established in 1672, replacing the Court of the Justiciars, and consisted until 1887 of seven judges—the Lord Justice-General, Lord Justice-Clerk and five Lords Commissioners of Justiciary.[40] The office of Lord Justice-General was long hereditary, becoming vested in the sixteenth century in the Dukes of Argyll. In 1628 the Duke resigned this office to the King, retaining the office of Justice-General for Argyll and the Isles. The office of Lord Justice-General was held from 1628 to 1836 by various noblemen, but since 1836 has been held by the Lord President of the Court of Session.

The Lord Justice-Clerk was originally the clerk of the criminal court but became the normal president since the Act 1672 provided that he should preside when the Lord Justice-General did not sit, which regularly happened down to 1836, while the latter office remained honorary.[41]

Since the Criminal Procedure (Scotland) Act 1887, the court consists of the Lord Justice-General, Lord Justice-Clerk, and all the other (30) Lords of Session as Lords Commissioners of Justiciary.[42] Persons appointed as temporary judges of the Court of Session are also temporary Lords Commissioners of Justiciary.[43]

It has jurisdiction over all Scotland and in respect of all crimes, unless its jurisdiction is expressly or impliedly excluded by the terms of a statute. It has exclusive jurisdiction to try the most serious crimes, such as treason

---

[40] When sitting as Lords Commissioners of Justiciary the judges wear scarlet robes faced with white, decorated with scarlet crosses. The Lord Justice-General's robe is faced with ermine and the Lord Justice-Clerk's robe has rows of square holes in the white satin facings to give the appearance of ermine. The judges always wear their justiciary robes for state functions, and public occasions.

[41] See further, *Introduction to Scottish Legal History*, Chap. 31; Malcolm, "The Lord Justice-Clerk of Scotland" (1915) 27 J.R. 342, 375; Hannay, "The Office of the Justice-Clerk" (1935) 47 J.R. 311.

[42] This gave rise in *H.M. Advocate v. Sugden*, 1934 J.C. 103, to the interesting question whether a decision of a Full Bench of 1773 of seven judges could be overruled by that of a Full Bench of 1934 consisting of 12 judges (the total strength being then 13, and one being absent). It was held that it could. So, too, in *Muir v. Hart* (1912) 6 Adam 601 the question was raised whether a Full Bench of seven judges could overrule a decision of a Full Bench of five judges of 1855, when five judges was the usual bench to consider cases of difficulty.

[43] Law Reform (Miscellaneous Provisions) (Scotland) Act. 1990, Sched. 4, para. 8.

and murder, and in practice deals with all the more serious cases of crime even though some of these might also have been tried by sheriff and jury.

The High Court as Court of Trial

The High Court is both a court of first instance and a court of appeal. As a court of first instance, sittings of the High Court are held in Edinburgh and also on circuit as required. Scotland is divided into four circuits, Home, West, North and South,[44] and courts are held for these districts at (i) Edinburgh; (ii) Glasgow, Stirling and Oban (formerly Inveraray); (iii) Inverness, Aberdeen, Dundee and Perth; and (iv) Dumfries, Jedburgh and Ayr. Sittings are not, however, restricted to these towns and a sitting may be held in any town which is convenient to or near the locality of a crime. Sittings on circuit are appointed to be held quarterly but no circuit need be held if there is no business.[45] On the other hand, the volume of business at Glasgow requires monthly sittings there. As a rule only one judge needs to go on circuit, but in Glasgow two courts sits concurrently and two judges go on the West circuit. They may be replaced at a convenient stage in the sittings by colleagues. The Lord Justice-General does not go on circuit and the Lord Justice-Clerk only for exceptionally important cases. As a rule, only one judge sits at a trial but in cases of difficulty or importance two or more, usually three, may sit.[46] Procedure is always solemn (on indictment) and with a jury.

The jurisdiction of the court extends to all cases of crime except where its jurisdiction has been excluded by statute, and it is exclusive in the case of the most serious crimes, namely, treason, murder and rape, incest, certain offences under the Official Secrets Act, deforcement of messengers-at-arms and breach of duty by magistrates. In practice, all the most serious cases are tried in the High Court, particularly since its powers of punishment are greater than those of any inferior courts.

The prosecution is invariably conducted by one of the Law Officers or one of the Advocates-Depute, and the accused is invariably defended by counsel (unless, as sometimes happens, he refuses or dismisses counsel).

The High Court as Appellate Court—Summary Trials

Appeals from courts of summary criminal jurisdiction lie to the High Court of Justiciary in Edinburgh and are heard by three or more Lords

---

[44] The circuit areas are defined in Act of Adjournal (High Court Sittings and Juries) 1975 (S.I. 1975 No. 717).

[45] Lord Cockburn's *Circuit Journeys* gives a delightful picture of the circuit system in the early 19th century.

[46] *e.g.* trial of Madeleine Smith where L.J.C. Hope, Lords Handyside and Ivory all sat. Three or more judges also sit to dispose of any difficult or important point raised before trial, for deciding points raised at trials on circuit and certified to the High Court (see, *e.g.* H.M. Advocate v. Bickerstaff, 1926 J.C. 65), and for disposing of petitions to the *nobile officium* of the court. In *H.M. Advocate v. Hay,* 1968 S.L.T. 334, three judges sat to dispose of a point of admissibility of evidence arising during a trial in Edinburgh.

Commissioners of Justiciary. A person convicted may appeal against conviction or sentence or both on the ground of miscarriage of justice. The prosecutor may appeal on a point of law against acquittal or sentence. The normal modes of appeal are by way of stated case or bill of advocation or bill of suspension.

In a stated case, the sheriff or other judge of the inferior court is requested by either party to prepare a statement of the facts found by him to be admitted or proved[47] and to formulate a question or questions of law raising the issue the accused wishes to have argued. Questions of evidence and matters of fact and the inferences therefrom are for the inferior court and cannot be raised in a stated case.[48] The appeal is thus only on points of law and in this way authoritative rulings are given on many points, particularly on the interpretation of statutes and instruments creating offences. Thus the phrase, "in charge of" a vehicle, has been elucidated several times, when the High Court has held in stated cases that a sheriff was or was not entitled in particular circumstances to hold that an accused was "in charge of" a vehicle, so as to render him liable to certain penalties. The question in such a case is not whether the inferior court was *correct* in its decision, which is a matter for it on the evidence, but whether the lower court was *entitled in law* to do what it did on the basis of the facts found to have existed.

The High Court may remit the case to the inferior court with its opinion, affirm the verdict, quash the conviction or substitute an amended verdict, or set aside the verdict and authorise a new prosecution. It may pass another, not more severe, sentence. On appeal against acquittal it may convict and sentence, or remit with instructions to convict and sentence, or remit the case with its opinion.

Appeal by bill of advocation is appropriate where the prosecutor seeks to bring a decision under review of the High Court or to appeal against an acquittal on the ground of miscarriage of justice. The High Court may pass the bill or remit the case to the lower court to proceed as directed, or may set aside a verdict and authorise a new prosecution.

Appeal by bill of suspension is appropriate to raise an issue of jurisdiction, incompetency of proceedings or another matter extrinsic to the complaint or the facts adduced, or where the appeal is an attack on the judicial character of the proceedings (such as an allegation of oppression), or fundamental irregularity or radical defect in the proceedings.[49] A Bill is prepared by the accused's advisers, narrating the conviction and the objection to it, and is served on the procurator-fiscal as respondent; he usually lodges written answers and appears by counsel at

---

[47] *Gordon v. Allan,* 1987 S.L.T. 400.
[48] *Strain v. Herron,* (1973) S.C.C.R. Supp. 42.
[49] *Fairley v. Muir,* 1951 J.C. 56, 60; *MacGregor v. MacNeill,* 1975 J.C. 57, 60; *Handley v. Pirie,* 1976 J.C. 65.

the hearing to uphold the conviction. The High Court may pass the Bill and suspend the sentence, or refuse the Bill, or amend the conviction and sentence. At such sittings of the High Court the presiding judge has no vote unless the other judges are equally divided in opinion,[50] and if the court consists of four judges who are equally divided the judgment will be contrary to that of the presiding judge.[51]

The High Court as Appellate Court—Trials on Indictment

Up until 1926 no appeal lay to the High Court from trials on indictment (*i.e.* under solemn procedure, with a jury, whether before a judge or a sheriff), but in that year, in consequence of the miscarriage of justice in the case of Oscar Slater[52] the Scottish court of criminal appeal was established. It consists of three or more[53] judges of the High Court of Justiciary and is consequently another aspect of the appellate work of the High Court.[54] Appeal may be brought by written note of appeal stating all the grounds of appeal against conviction, or against the sentence, unless it is one fixed by law,[55] or against both conviction and sentence. By appeal a person may also bring under review any alleged miscarriage of justice.[56] The appellant, or counsel on his behalf, may present argument, and a Law Officer or advocate-depute will appear for the Crown.

The court may hear additional evidence, remit to a person to inquire and report on any matter, or appoint a person with expert knowledge to act as assessor. It decides by a majority, including the vote of the presiding judge. The court may allow the appeal, set aside the verdict and quash the conviction, or it may refuse the appeal, or amend the verdict or modify the sentence. The court has power to authorise a new prosecution[57] and it may also do so when sitting as Courts-Martial Appeal Court.[58]

Secretary of State's Reference

There is also provision for the First Minister to refer a case to the High Court or to refer a point to the court for its opinion.[59]

---

[50] *Campbell v. Maclennan* (1888) 1 White 604; *Muir v. Hart* (1912) 6 Adam 601.

[51] *Ross v. Johnston* (1886) 1 White 171.

[52] See *Trial of Oscar Slater*, ed. Roughead (Famous Trials Series) and *Slater v. H.M. Advocate*, 1928 J.C. 94.

[53] *e.g.* in *H.M. Advocate v. Kirkwood*, 1939 J.C. 36, 13 judges sat.

[54] In practice what usually happens is that every three or four weeks either the First or the Second Division of the Court of Session does not sit as such but three of its members (the Lord President or Lord Justice-Clerk and two others) don their justiciary gowns and sit as the High Court, and then, having disposed of the Criminal Appeal Roll, sit on for disposal of the Justiciary Roll, *i.e*, appeals from summary cases. The fourth judge of the Division may be absent or unwell or on circuit, but, if available, is usually set to assist the Outer House judges in civil business.

[55] *e.g.* the penalty of death for treason.

[56] 1995 Act, ss. 106 and 112.

[57] 1995 Act, s. 118. See, *e.g. Mackenzie v. H.M. Advocate*, 1983 S.L.T. 220.

[58] Courts-Martial (Appeals) Act 1968, s. 19.

[59] For an example, see *Gallacher v. H.M. Advocate*, 1951 J.C. 38, footnote to p. 49. See also *McDonald v. Secretary of State for Scotland*, 1996 S.L.T. 16.

Lord Advocate's Reference

Where a person tried on indictment has been acquitted, the Lord Advocate may refer a point of law which arose in relation to that charge to the High Court for its opinion.[60] The person acquitted may elect to appear personally or be represented at the hearing; if he does not, the High Court appoints counsel to act as *amicus curiae.*[61] The Reference procedure is intended to enable the court to give an opinion which will elucidate the law for future similar cases. The opinion it delivers on the point referred does not affect the acquittal.[62]

No further appeal lies from the High Court to the House of Lords,[63] so that this court has final responsibility for disposing of cases and for settling the law, and has given many judgments of great importance and value for the development of Scottish criminal law.

Scottish Criminal Cases Review Commission

The Commission is an independent body which took over, from the Secretary of State, powers to consider alleged miscarriages of justice and refer cases satisfying stated criteria to the High Court for review.[64] Members are appointed by the First Minister.

Criminal Injuries Compensation Authority (formerly Board)

The Criminal Injuries Compensation Board was set up under the prerogative in 1964 on an experimental and non-statutory basis and established by statute in 1988.[65] From 1996 it became the Criminal Injuries Compensation Authority. It is composed of a chairman and a number of members, all legally qualified, some being members of the Scottish Bar, appointed by the Home Secretary and the Secretary of State for Scotland.[66] It may sit in England, Scotland or elsewhere as necessary. It submits an annual report and accounts to Parliament.

---

[60] If the accused had been convicted the point could have been raised in an appeal.

[61] *i.e.* friend of the court. The object is to secure that argument from the accused's side is presented to the court.

[62] See, *e.g. Lord Advocate's Reference No. 1 of 1983,* 1984 J.C. 52; *Lord Advocate's Reference No. 1 of 1985,* 1987 S.L.T. 187.

[63] *Bywater v. Lord Advocate* (1781) 2 Pat. 563; *Mackintosh v. L.A.* (1876) 3 R.(H.L.) 34; Criminal Procedure (Scotland) Act 1887, s. 72; but appeal lies from the High Court sitting in the capacity of Courts-Martial Appeal Court: Courts-Martial (Appeals) Act 1968, Pt. III. The House did consider an appeal in *Elgin Magistrates v. Elgin Ministers* (1713) Robert. 69. In 1773 two sheep-stealers appealed to the House of Lords but a Committee of the Lords ruled that the House of Lords could not receive appeals from the High Court of Justiciary: *H.M. Advocate v. Murdison and Miller,* (1773) MacLaurin 557; *Boswell for the Defence,* 1769–1774 (ed. Wimsatt and Pottle), p. 156. See also MacLean, "The House of Lords and Appeals from the High Court of Justiciary, 1707–1887," 1985 J.R. 192.

[64] The Review Commission's remit has been extended to summary proceedings: Scottish Criminal Cases Review Commission (Application to Summary Proceedings) Order 1999 (S.I. 1999 No. 1181).

[65] Criminal Justice Act 1988, ss. 108–117, replaced by Criminal Injuries Compensation Act 1995.

[66] *Ibid.*

The Board exists to deal with claims for compensation for injuries or death suffered in circumstances amounting to criminal injury[67] caused by conduct constituting one of the listed offences, sustained in Great Britain, where in many cases the assailant is not identified or is not worth suing for damages. Compensation may be claimed by a person who has sustained a qualifying injury or a dependant of one who died after sustaining such an injury. Awards may be made for the injury and for any loss or damage to property which occurred in the course of sustaining it. The claimant must satisfy the board that he had taken all reasonable steps to inform the police and had co-operated with the police in bringing to justice any person responsible, and that there is no possibility that a person responsible for causing the injury will benefit from an award.[68] The board may make interim awards, or a further interim award if the victim's condition deteriorates. It may refuse or limit an award for provocation or other conduct of the claimant. Awards were assessed generally on the same bases as civil claims for damages for personal injuries or wrongful death at common law, but awards below a statutory minimum are excluded. From 1996, awards are assessed under a tariff-based scheme. There is a separate avenue of appeal to the Criminal Injuries Compensation Appeals Panel.

Appeal on any ground involving a question of law alone, lies to the Court of Session and, with leave, to the House of Lords.[69] In England several questions of interpretation of the scheme have been tested by the procedure of judicial review.[70]

Where a person has been convicted of an offence and the board has made an award of compensation in respect of injury which is a criminal injury by virtue of the offence—*e.g.* rape, assault—the sheriff may, on application by the board, require the offender to reimburse the board in whole or in part.

SPECIAL CRIMINAL COURTS

Courts-Martial and the Courts-Martial Appeal Court

Offences against naval, military or air force law are dealt with either summarily, by the accused's commanding officer, or in more serious cases by courts-martial constituted under the respective codes of discipline for the several forces.[71] The offences in question are mostly "service" ones, such as mutiny, desertion or other breach of discipline, but include also

---

[67] *R. v. Criminal Injuries Compensation Board, ex p. Johnson,* 21 B.M.L.R. 48.

[68] This will exclude many claims arising from "wife battering."

[69] s. 113. *Rae v. C.I.C.B.,* 1997 S.L.T. 291; *Young v. C.I.C.B.,* 1997 S.L.T. 297.

[70] *R. v. Criminal Injuries Compensation Board, ex p. P.* [1995] 1 All E.R. 870.

[71] Naval Discipline Act 1957; Naval Disciplinary Courts (Procedure) Orders 1958; Army Act 1955; Rules of Procedure (Army) 1996; Air Force Act 1955; Rules of Procedure (Air Force) 1996. Acts continued by Armed Forces Act 1996. See further, Halsbury's *Laws of England,* tit. "Royal Forces."

offences punishable by the ordinary law,[72] though the most serious crimes, unless committed on active service, must not be tried by a court-martial if they can with reasonable convenience be tried by an ordinary court.[73]

While it is no doubt desirable to have a common code of service law for all personnel, it is unfortunate that the code adopted is based entirely on English criminal law, which may cause difficulties for Scottish counsel or solicitors defending and may give rise to problems of great difficulty on appeal, since Scottish judges do not profess to know English criminal law.

If preliminary investigation within the unit discloses a prima facie case, a court-martial will be convened by an authorised convening officer.

In the Navy, commanding officers of ships have very extensive powers of summary punishment and there is only one type of court-martial—Naval Court-Martial—which deals with all offences under the Naval Discipline Act which cannot be dealt with summarily. An officer prosecutes and an officer or lawyer acts as "accused's friend." An officiating judge-advocate is appointed at each court-martial to advise on law and procedure and to secure that the proceedings are fair. The minutes of every defended court-martial and any legal questions of importance are always referred to the Judge-Advocate of the Fleet, who advises the Board of Admiralty as to the validity of procedure, evidence, finding and sentence, whereupon the Board decide whether to uphold or quash the conviction and to uphold or reduce the sentence.

In the Army and Air Force there are General Courts-Martial, consisting of not fewer than five officers, which try officers and also other ranks in the most serious cases, and District Courts-Martial, consisting of not fewer than three officers, which try other ranks. The president is usually of the rank of colonel or brigadier and the members are drawn, so far as possible, from different corps and units. Women officers must be represented on the court if a female member of the forces is being tried. No member of the court need have any legal experience but must have certain minimum periods of commissioned service. On service the Field General Court-Martial, consisting of three officers, is the usual tribunal.

A judge-advocate[74] must, in the case of general courts-martial, and in other cases may, be appointed by the Judge-Advocate General of the Army and Air Force to attend to advise the court on law, procedure and powers of punishment. He sums up the evidence and advises the court before it deliberates on its findings. The prosecution is conducted by an officer, but counsel[75] may be instructed on his behalf, and the accused may

---

[72] *i.e.* the criminal law of *England.*

[73] Thus murder or assault in Britain, especially if perpetrated on a civilian, would be tried by the ordinary criminal courts. But murder committed on a foreign station would be tried by court-martial at that station; *e.g. R. v. Page* [1953] 3 W.L.R. 895.

[74] Judge-advocates are advocates or barristers employed whole-time in the legal branches of the services.

[75] In this context "counsel" includes Scottish advocates and solicitors, and they may appear wherever the trial be held; *e.g.* a Scottish advocate may appear at Aldershot.

be represented by an officer or by counsel or solicitor. Courts-martial normally sit in public and the procedure, which is based on English criminal procedure, is largely regulated by the printed form used to record proceedings, which sets out the stages of the trial. Findings of guilt and sentence are subject to confirmation by the convening authority.[76]

A person convicted by court-martial may petition the confirming or reviewing authority to quash or vary his conviction or sentence before or even after confirmation, and in some cases the proceedings may be submitted to Her Majesty or to the Defence Council. Apart from these prerogative petitions, a convicted person must petition to have his conviction quashed before he may apply for leave to appeal; he is entitled to apply for leave to appeal within 10 days of the dismissal of his petition or the end of the period for disposing of his petition.

The Courts-Martial (Appeals) Act of 1951 (now the Courts-Martial (Appeals) Act 1968) constituted a Courts-Martial Appeal Court consisting, in Scotland,[77] of such Lords Commissioners of Justiciary as the Lord Justice-General may nominate, being uneven in number and not less than three. The Lord Chancellor may appoint other persons of legal experience to be judges of the Court. A person convicted by court-martial in any of the services may, with the leave of the Appeal Court, and subject to certain conditions, appeal against his conviction.

The practice of the High Court of Justiciary sitting as Court of Criminal Appeal is followed[78] and the powers of the court are similar.[79] The court will allow an appeal if it thinks that the finding of the court-martial, under all the circumstances of the case, is unsafe or unsatisfactory, or involves a wrong decision on a point of law, or that there was a material irregularity in the course of the trial, but the court may dismiss an appeal on a technical point if it considers that, in the circumstances, no miscarriage of justice has occurred. In certain cases the court may authorise a retrial. The court's decision is final but appeal lies to the House of Lords by leave of the court or of the House of Lords, which shall be granted only if the Appeal Court certifies that a point of law of general public importance is involved and that it appears to the court or the House of Lords that the point ought to be considered by the House of Lords.[80]

---

[76] As to powers of confirming authorities, see Criminal Appeal Act 1966, Sched. 1, Pt. II.

[77] When this court sits in England the judges are the *ex officio* and ordinary members of the Court of Appeal and certain judges of the Queen's Bench Division nominated by the Lord Chief Justice, and when it sits in Northern Ireland the judges are such of the judges of the Supreme Court of Judicature in Northern Ireland as the Lord Chief Justice of Northern Ireland may nominate. The Act also makes provision for "such other persons, being persons of legal experience, as the Lord Chancellor may appoint" being appointed judges of the court for such term as may be determined by the Lord Chancellor.

[78] See *R. v. Houghton* [1952] C.L.Y. 159; *R. v. Condon* (1952) 36 Cr.App.R. 130; *Hendry*, 1955 S.L.T. (Notes) 66.

[79] Powers are regulated by the statutes regulating the powers of the [English] Court of Appeal, Criminal Division, *viz.* Criminal Appeal Act 1968; Courts-Martial (Appeals) Act 1968.

[80] Administration of Justice Act 1960, ss. 1, 10 and Sched. 1; now Courts-Martial (Appeals) Act 1968, s. 39.

Standing Civilian Courts

Standing civilian courts are established for the trial outside the United Kingdom of civilians subject to the Army or Air Force Acts for offences triable by court-martial or which constitute offences by English law. Procedure is prescribed by Order. Finding or sentence may be reviewed by a reviewing authority and appealed to a court-martial.

ECCLESIASTICAL COURTS[81]

The courts of the Church of Scotland are legally established courts of the realm within their own field whereas courts of other Churches have jurisdiction only so far as conferred by their own constitutions and the adherence of their members.[82] Church courts have jurisdiction only over their own members and in matters affecting church discipline, ritual and membership.

The constitution and powers of the courts of the Church of Scotland are founded on the General Assembly Act 1592, confirmed by the Confession of Faith Ratification Act 1690, which in turn was ratified by the Protestant Religion and Presbyterian Church Act 1706, which is incorporated into the Treaty of Union with England. These courts are supreme, and independent of the civil and criminal courts in matters ecclesiastical and spiritual,[83] so that no claim of damages lies in the Court of Session against a Church court for a judgment in a proper case of discipline duly brought before it.[84] The civil courts are bound to assist the Church courts in making their decrees effectual, but cannot review their decisions in matters falling within their jurisdiction.[85]

The courts of the Church are the Kirk-Session, composed of the minister and elders of the parish, which has a general power of discipline over members; the Presbytery, which consists of all the ministers of parishes within its bounds and an elder from each Kirk-Session and has a general supervisory responsibility, power to censure, suspend or depose ministers after due trial,[86] and the duty of hearing appeals and references from inferior courts; and the General Assembly.[87]

---

[81] See further, Donaldson, "The Church Courts," in *Introduction to Scottish Legal History*, Chap. 27; Cox, *Practice and Procedure in the Church of Scotland*, 6th ed.; the *Church of Scotland Year Book*; Taylor, "Church and State in Scotland," 1957 J.R. 121; King Murray, "Constitutional Position of the Church of Scotland" [1958] Pub.L. 155.

[82] *McMillan v. General Assembly of the Free Church of Scotland* (1859) 22 D. 290; (1861) 23 D. 1314; *Brentnall v. Free Presbyterian Church of Scotland*, 1986 S.L.T. 471.

[83] *Lockhart v. Presbytery of Deer* (1851) 13 D. 1296; *Wright v. Presbytery of Dunkeld* (1870) 8 M. 921.

[84] *Sturrock v. Greig* (1849) 11 D. 1220.

[85] *Logan v. Dumbarton Presbytery*, 1995 S.L.T. 1228.

[86] *Logan, supra.*

[87] Until 1992 there were also Provincial Synods, intermediate between Presbyteries and the General Assembly.

The General Assembly is both the legislature[88] and the Supreme Court of the Church. It consists of ministers and elders elected by presbyteries, universities and royal burghs and meets in Edinburgh for a week in May each year. It is presided over by the Moderator, who is elected annually, and the Queen is represented by a Lord High (now Queen's) Commissioner who has no voice in the deliberations of the Assembly but is the official medium of communication between the Sovereign and the Assembly.[89]

The judicial functions consist of hearing and deciding appeals and complaints from inferior courts and adjudicating on petitions from members and congregations. Legal representation is permitted. Forms of libels in the Church courts are similar to those of indictments in the High Court. The procedure is regulated by Acts of Assembly.[90]

PROFESSIONAL DISCIPLINARY TRIBUNALS

The professional bodies exercising most completely "internal" domestic jurisdiction are the Faculty of Advocates and the Inns of Court, each of which has jurisdiction over their members in matters of discipline and professional conduct to the extent, if need be, of disbarring counsel. At least in England there is, by custom, an appeal to the judges.[91] So, too, the committee of the Stock Exchange has disciplinary powers over the members. But in all these cases it is likely that the courts would interfere to ensure that the requirements of natural justice[92] are complied with, though not further.

Statutes have in many cases established various tribunals with powers to control and discipline members of particular professions. Thus, the Professional Conduct Committee of the General Medical Council can remove a practitioner's name from the Medical Register, subject to appeal to the Privy Council.[93] Similar provisions apply to dentists,[94] opticians,[95]

---

[88] The legislation is printed in the Acts of Assembly. *The Booke of the Universall Kirk of Scotland* (Bannatyne Club, 1839–45) contains many Acts 1560–1618. Other volumes contain Acts of Assemblies of 1638–49, 1690, 1692, 1638–1842 while the printed Acts of each year are maintained in many libraries.

[89] In 1969 the Queen attended personally and there was no Lord High Commissioner.

[90] Acts of Assembly 1707, XI and 1889, XIX.

[91] *Re Marrinan* [1957] C.L.Y. 2747; *R. v. Visitors to the Inns of Court, ex p. Calder* [1993] 3 W.L.R. 287; see *R. v. Gray's Inn* (1780) 1 Doug.K.B. 353. In 1874 E. V. H. Kenealy, Q.C., was disbenched and disbarred by Gray's Inn. In 1961 Mr. Victor Durand, Q.C. was suspended from practice for three years by the Benchers of the Inner Temple. On appeal five judges reduced this to one year. See further, Halsbury's *Laws of England*, tit. "Barrister."

[92] The requirements of natural justice are vague and undefined, but certainly cover the requirements that the person charged should be acquainted with the charge against him, be allowed to hear the evidence against him, and be heard in his own defence, and that the members of the tribunal be not biased or personally interested in the outcome of the dispute.

[93] Medical Act 1983, ss. 36, 40 (first established by the Medical Act 1858). See *Daly v. G.M.C.* [1952] 2 All E.R. 666; *Fox v. G.M.C.* [1960] 3 All E.R. 225; *Libman v. G.M.C.* [1972] A.C. 217; *Muqit v. General Medical Council,* 1999 S.C.L.R. 924.

[94] Dentists Act 1984, ss. 27, 29.

[95] Opticians Act 1989, ss. 17, 23.

veterinary surgeons,[96] and professions supplementary to medicine.[97] In some other cases appeal lies to the Court of Session.[98]

The Solicitors (Scotland) Act 1980 empowered the Council of the Law Society to make rules for regulating professional practice, conduct and discipline of solicitors[99] and to act where inadequate professional services have been rendered.[1] The Act created the Scottish Solicitors Discipline Tribunal of ten to fourteen solicitors and eight non-lawyers, with a quorum of four, including at least one lay member. It has power on complaint to it to hear evidence and order that a solicitor be struck off the roll or suspended from practice, or fined or censured, or both censured and fined.[2] The Tribunal also has powers where complaint has been made that professional services provided by a solicitor were inadequate, and may reduce his fee, require him to rectify an error, omission or deficiency at his own expense, and to refund or waive any fee.[2] It also has powers to hear certain appeals against determinations or directions by the Council of the Society in relation to inadequate professional services.[3] Appeal from the Tribunal lies to the Court of Session, which has similar powers and which is final.[4]

The same Act[5] empowered the Secretary of State to appoint a non-lawyer, called the Lay Observer, to examine any written complaints by members of the public about the Society's treatment of a complaint about a solicitor. This office is now superseded by that of the Scottish Legal Services Ombudsman.[6] A person complaining that a solicitor has been guilty of professional misconduct or has provided inadequate professional services, complains first to the Law Society which investigates and reports to the complainer and the practitioner and must comply with a request from the Scottish Legal Services Ombudsman for information or a report. If the ombudsman reports to the Law Society; it has to consider whether any further action needs to be taken on the complaint and reports to the complainer and the ombudsman.

The Scottish Conveyancing and Executry Services Board has powers, whether or not following complaint, if satisfied that a practitioner licensed

---

[96] Veterinary Surgeons Act 1966, ss. 16, 17.

[97] Professions Supplementary to Medicine Act 1960, s. 9.

[98] Architects Registration Act 1931, ss. 7–9; Pharmacy Act 1954, ss. 8, 10; Teaching Council (Scotland) Act 1965, s. 11; Insurance Brokers (Registration) Act, 1977, ss. 13–20; Nurses, Midwives and Health Visitors Act 1979, ss. 12, 13. See, *e.g. Johnstone v. General Teaching Council for Scotland*, 1981 S.C. 51; *Carr v. U.K. Central Council for Nursing, Midwifery and Health Visiting*, 1989 S.L.T. 580.

[99] 1980 Act, ss. 50–55 and Sched. 4.

[1] s. 42A added by Solicitors (Scotland) Act 1988, s. 1. See, *e.g. Ramage v. Matthew,* 1998 S.C. 167; *Matthew v. Law Society of Scotland,* 1998 S.C. 306.

[2] s. 53A added by 1988 Act, s. 3.

[3] s. 53B added by 1988 Act, s. 3.

[4] 1980 Act, s. 55. See, *e.g. Council of the Law Society of Scotland v. Docherty*, 1968 S.L.T. 133; *A and B, Petrs.*, 1978 S.L.T. (Notes) 71; *Sharp v. Law Society*, 1984 S.L.T. 313; *MacColl v. Law Society*, 1987 S.L.T. 524.

[5] s. 49 and Sched. 5.

[6] On him see 338, *infra.*

by it was guilty of professional misconduct, has provided inadequate professional services, failed to comply with regulations made by the Board or has been convicted of a criminal offence rendering him no longer fit to provide conveyancing or executry services, to take action against him, including cutting his fee, directing him to secure rectification of any error or omission at his own expense, suspend or revoke his registration, order compensation or fine or censure him.[7] The Board may be called on by the Scottish Legal Services Ombudsman to report on what action it has taken. The Police (Scotland) Act 1967 provides for appeals to a police appeals tribunal against disciplinary action.[8]

DOMESTIC TRIBUNALS

In many cases groups of individuals engaged in some common activity or the promotion of some common interest have formed associations—such as clubs, societies, guilds, trade unions[9]—with rules and established domestic tribunals to enforce the rules, regulate the members' activities and discipline them. These tribunals are based not on statute or common law but on the contract of association between the members of the body, whereby those joining agree, in return for what they see as certain benefits of membership, to submit to the rulings and discipline of the tribunal or committee established by them all.[10] There may be provision in the disciplinary rules for appeal; if not, no appeal lies, unless the supervisory jurisdiction of the Court of Session can be invoked in a case of serious breach of the terms of the contract of association or of the rules of natural justice.[11]

PARLIAMENTARY COMMISSIONERS AND OMBUDSMEN

The title Ombudsman was given in Scandinavia to an official appointed, outside the court system, to deal with complaints and grievances brought up by members of the public. The idea was adopted in Britain and, while initially other titles were given, the title Ombudsman is now increasingly being given by statutes.

The Parliamentary Commissioner

The Parliamentary Commissioner for Administration is not a judge nor does he hold a court, but he should be considered in the context of courts

---

[7] Law Reform (Miscellaneous Provisions) (Scotland) Act 1990, s. 20.

[8] See also Police (Conduct) (Scotland) Regulations 1996 (S.I. 1996 No. 1642); Police Appeal Tribunal (Scotland) Rules 1996 (S.I. 1996 No. 1644).

[9] *e.g. Walker v. A.U.E.W.*, 1969 S.L.T. 150.

[10] See, *e.g. Lee v. Showmen's Guild* [1952] 2 Q.B. 329; *Abbott v. Sullivan* [1952] 1 K.B. 189; *Byrne v. Kinematograph Renters Society* [1958] 2 All E.R. 579; *Rennie v. Scottish Milk Records Assoc.*, 1985 S.L.T. 272.

[11] *St. Johnstone F.C. v. S.F.A. Ltd.*, 1965 S.L.T. 171; *Tait v. Central Radio Taxis (Tollcross)*, 1989 S.L.T. 217.

and tribunals because his function is equally to provide redress for grievances. The office was created by the Parliamentary Commissioner Act 1967 on the general model of that of the Ombudsman of the Scandinavian countries, and now subsists under the Parliamentary and Health Service Commissioners Act 1987[12], extended by the Parliamentary Commissioner Act 1994. Under the Acts, the Queen may appoint a person to be Parliamentary Commissioner for Administration. He may not be a member of the House of Commons, nor of either house of the Parliament of Northern Ireland, but is *ex officio* a member of the Council on Tribunals and of the Scottish Committee thereof.

He may investigate any action[13] taken by or on behalf of any of the government departments or other authorities listed in Schedule 2 to the 1987 Act,[14] including the Ministers, members or officers of that department or authority, being action taken in the exercise of administrative functions of that department or authority, in any case where (a) a written complaint is made to a member of the House of Commons by a member of the public who claims to have sustained injustice in consequence of maladministration[15] in connection with the action so taken, and (b) the complaint is referred, with the complainer's consent, to the Commissioner by a member of the House with a request to conduct an investigation thereon. The Commissioner is not, however, to conduct an investigation in respect of any action in respect of which the aggrieved person has or had a right of appeal, reference or review to or before a tribunal, or a remedy by way of proceedings in any court of law, unless he is satisfied that in the particular circumstances it was not reasonable to expect the complainer to have resorted to it, and he may not investigate any of the actions or matters described in Schedule 3 to the Act.[16] He may use his own discretion whether or not to initiate, continue or discontinue any investigation.

Complaints may be made by any individual or body of persons, but not by local authorities or bodies constituted for the public service, or by a personal representative or member of the aggrieved person's family, and must be made to a member of the House of Commons within 12 months of the date when the person first had notice of the matters alleged in his complaint. Investigations are to be conducted in private in such manner as

---

[12] On these, see Rowat, *The Ombudsman.*

[13] "Action" includes failure to act: 1967 Act, s. 12 (1).

[14] The list may be amended. As framed the list does not include all the central government departments, and does not include public corporations or local authorities or departments thereof.

[15] Not defined by the Act.

[16] These include matters involving the royal prerogative, the commencement or conduct of civil or criminal proceedings before any court in the United Kingdom, matters relating to contractual or other commercial transactions of a department or authority, and matters relating to the armed forces.

the Commissioner thinks fit, and he has wide powers of calling for information and witnesses. Where the Commissioner investigates or decides not to investigate he must report the results to a member of the House of Commons, and where he has investigated he must report to the head of the department or authority concerned. If after investigation it appears to the Commissioner that injustice has been done to the person aggrieved in consequence of maladministration and that the injustice has not been, or will not be, remedied, he may lay before each House of Parliament a special report on the case. He must report annually to Parliament on the performance of his functions generally.[17]

Nothing in the Act authorises or requires the Commissioner to question the merits of a decision taken without maladministration by a government department or other authority in the exercise of a discretion vested in it.

The Commissioner maintains a Scottish office and may also investigate alleged maladministration by the Scottish Executive, the Parliamentary Corporation and a range of public bodies involved in affairs devolved to Scotland.

Health Service Commissioner for Scotland

Under the National Health Service (Scotland) Act 1972, Pt. VII (now 1978, Pt. VI),[18] there is a Health Service Commissioner for Scotland, a salaried officer who may not be an M.P. but may be the same person as the Parliamentary Commissioner. He may investigate any alleged failure in service or action taken by or on behalf of health authorities where a complaint is made that a person claims to have sustained injustice or hardship in consequence of the failure or of maladministration in connection with the action so taken. Excluded are matters in respect of which there is a right of appeal or review before a tribunal, or a remedy by way of court proceedings, and certain specified kinds of matters.[19] Procedure for complaints is laid down and the results of an investigation must be reported to the complainer, the body investigated, the person complained against and the First Minister. The Commissioner must also make a general report annually.

Commissioner for Local Administration in Scotland

Under the Local Government (Scotland) Act 1975, Part II, amended by the Scottish Legal Services Ombudsman and Commissioner for Local Administration in Scotland Act 1997, there is a Commissioner for Local

---

[17] From 1980 HMSO has also published *Selected Cases* investigated by the Parliamentary Commissioner. Some cases, if involving EEC law, are also reported in *Common Market Law Reports, e.g. Re Slaughter of Hill Cattle in Scotland* [1979] C.M.L.R. 505.
[18] Amended by Parliamentary and Health Service Commissioners Act 1987 and Health Service Commissioners (Amdt.) Act 1996.
[19] 1978 Act, s. 93 and Sched. 14.

Administration in Scotland appointed by the Crown, now on the advice of the First Minister, who may investigate complaints in relation to local authorities, committees and joint committees and other specified bodies by a member of the public who claims to have suffered injustice in consequence of maladministration in connection with action taken in the exercise of the authority's administrative functions. Certain matters are excepted. He investigates privately and reports to the complainer and to the authority. The report is normally made public, and he makes an annual report. There is no right of appeal but it has been held in England that a local authority is entitled to judicial review of the exercise of the Commissioner's jurisdiction.[20]

Scottish Legal Services Ombudsman

The Secretary of State may appoint a non-lawyer to examine any written complaint by or on behalf of a member of the public concerning the treatment by the Faculty of Advocates, the Council of the Law Society of Scotland or the Scottish Conveyancing and Executry Services Board, of a complaint made by a member of the public that a practitioner has been guilty of professional misconduct or has provided inadequate professional services. This post replaces that of the Lay Observer under earlier legislation. He must make such investigation as seems appropriate and reports *ad interim*, or finally, to the complainer and the organisation. He does not have power to penalise a practitioner; that is for the relevant organisation. On receipt of a report to it from the Ombudsman, the organisation must consider whether any further action requires to be taken in relation to the complaint and report the result to the complainer and the ombudsman.[21]

Adjudicator's Office

The Adjudicator's Office investigates complaints about the way the Inland Revenue and Customs and Excise have handled an individual's affairs and responds to complaints about the way in which these departments have treated taxpayers and may recommend settlements.[22]

Pensions Ombudsman

The Pensions Ombudsman handles complaints of maladministration by trustees or managers of personal pension schemes.[23]

European Union Ombudsman

The European Parliament has established an Ombudsman of the European Union.[24]

---

[20] *R. v. Local Commissioner for Administration for the South, ex p. Eastleigh* [1988] Q.B. 855.

[21] Law Reform (Miscellaneous Provisions) (Scotland) Act 1990, ss. 33–34. Scottish Legal Services Ombudsman and Commissioner for Local Administration in Scotland Act 1997. There is a corresponding officer for England under the Courts and Legal Services Act 1990.

[22] [1993] C.L.Y. 3446.

[23] Pension Schemes Act 1993.

[24] European Parliament Decision 95/376: 12 July 1995: O.J. L 225/17. See further p. 355.

Other Ombudsmen

In addition to direct statutory creations, certain associations and bodies providing services have created officers, sometimes called ombudsmen, to deal with complaints more simply than by action in court.[25]

Financial service

The Financial Services Authority under the Financial Services Act 2000, established a new regulatory regime representing a merger of nine former regulatory bodies, the Building Societies Commission, the Friendly Societies Commission, the Insurance Directorate of the Department of Trade and Industry, the Registry of Friendly Societies, the Securities and Futures Authority, the Securities and Investments Board, the Supervision and Surveillance Division of the Bank of England, the Personal Investment Authority, and the Investment Management Regulatory Organisation, all of which had been established under earlier Acts. The new Authority has draconian powers. This does not, however, include all the bodies regulatory of various financial transactions.

Banking

The Banking Ombudsman deals with complaints about bank charges and interest, forged cheques, cash dispensing machines and the like. The Deposit Protection Board under the Banking Act 1987, s. 50, has power to make payments of compensation from the Deposit Protection Fund to a depositor in the event of a bank becoming insolvent.

Insurance

There is an Insurance Ombudsman, incorporating also the Unit Trust Ombudsman Scheme, who deals with disputes about terms in all kinds of insurance policies and about the administration of insurance and unit trust schemes.

Corporate Estate Agents

The Corporate Estate Agents Ombudsman deals with complaints of inconvenience, unfair treatment or maladministration.

Commercial Businesses

A number of associations of persons engaged in particular kinds of business—*e.g.* motor dealers—have adopted schemes providing for various kinds of conciliation or consumer arbitration schemes for the resolution of complaints or disputes about the services of their members as alternatives to litigation. These schemes apply only to members and cannot exclude a complainer's liberty to go to law instead, but frequently provide a simpler and cheaper mode of securing redress.

---

[25] There is a Housing Association Ombudsman for Scotland.

II.—ENGLAND AND WALES

While the courts and legal system of England have no direct or immediate jurisdiction over transactions or legal problems arising entirely in and affecting Scotland only, the Scot may frequently have to consider whether legal action should or must be taken in England, while the references to English courts and procedure in legal books, documents and statutes are so common that he must be cognisant of the main features of the English system of courts and their respective competence in broad outline.[26]

CIVIL COURTS

Magistrates' Courts

A court of summary jurisdiction consisting of two or three justices of the peace has limited civil as well as substantial criminal jurisdiction.[27] They authorise recovery of certain civil debts such as income tax and electricity charges and may make adoption orders, affiliation orders in bastardy cases, grant judicial separation between husband and wife, grant a wife a maintenance order, as well as exercising many ministerial functions particularly with regard to licensing. Domestic proceedings are heard separately from other business and the public is excluded.[28] Appeals in these cases generally lie to a Divisional Court of the Family Division, to the Court of Appeal and the House of Lords, but certain appeals are heard by the Crown Court.

County Court

The main local courts for small causes are the county courts instituted in 1846.[29] England and Wales are divided into some 400 districts, grouped into circuits, each with one or more circuit judges, formerly called county court judges.[30] These are full-time salaried judges who have had considerable experience in practice. Every judge of the Court of Appeal or High Court and every Recorder is, *ex officio*, capable of sitting as a judge for any county court district. Circuit judges hold courts regularly in the principal towns of the district, about 400 places in all.[31] Divorce jurisdiction has been conferred on certain designated county courts, to hear any undefended matrimonial cause.[32] Personal injury claims for less than £50,000 must start in the county courts. Other claims for less than £25,000 must, and for claims up to £50,000 may, be tried in the county court. They have no criminal jurisdiction.

---

[26] On these, see generally Halsbury's *Laws of England*, tit. "Courts."
[27] The principal statute is the Magistrates' Courts Act 1980.
[28] Matrimonial Proceedings (Magistrates' Courts) Act 1960.
[29] For the modern jurisdiction, see County Courts Act 1984 as amended.
[30] The full title is His Honour Judge X, and they are addressed as "Your Honour".
[31] For the districts, judges and court towns, see the annual *Bar List of the United Kingdom*.
[32] Matrimonial Causes Act 1967, s. 1.

In the City of London the county court is called the Mayor's and City of London Court, replacing an old special court of that name. The judge is known as the judge of the Mayor's and City of London Court.

The district judge has limited jurisdiction to try cases, subject to appeal to the circuit judge, and there is provision for small claims.

Appeal lies to the Court of Appeal on a matter of law, or, in cases involving the larger sums of money, on matters of fact or law except in bankruptcy matters, where appeal lies to a Divisional Court of the Chancery Division. The amount of work dealt with in the county courts is very great because procedure is relatively simple and inexpensive. Both solicitors and counsel have the right of audience in county courts.

High Court

The superior civil courts are the High Court of Justice and the Court of Appeal, both of which are branches of the single Supreme Court of England and Wales.[33] In 1875 the High Court replaced, and assumed the jurisdiction possessed by, the former separate Courts of Kings Bench, Common Pleas, Exchequer, Chancery, Admiralty, and Probate, Divorce and Matrimonial Causes,[34] together with that of certain others, such as the Assize Courts and the Courts of Common Pleas at Lancaster and Durham, but excepting the Chancery Courts of the Counties Palatine of Lancaster and Durham. The High Court was for convenience divided in 1875 into five Divisions, Queen's Bench, Common Pleas, Exchequer, Chancery, and Probate, Divorce and Admiralty Division; in 1881 the first three were amalgamated into the Queen's Bench Division, and in 1971 the Probate, Divorce and Admiralty Division was renamed the Family Division. Also in 1971, the Chancery Courts of the Counties Palatine of Lancaster and Durham were merged in the High Court.

All Divisions are empowered to grant all remedies and to try all kinds of actions, but certain matters were originally assigned to each Division, corresponding roughly to the jurisdiction of the courts they had replaced, and in practice work is distributed among the Divisions according to subject-matter, the Queen's Bench dealing with actions of contract and tort, the recovery of land and commercial litigation, and Admiralty and prize jurisdiction, the Chancery Division with trusts, mortgages, wills and estates, partnership, companies and bankruptcy, contentious probate business, revenue matters, town and country planning and landlord and tenant cases, and the Family Division dealing with matrimonial causes, legitimacy, adoption, guardianship, maintenance orders and related topics. The Admiralty Court is now part of the Queen's Bench Division. The

---

[33] The main Acts are the Judicature Acts 1873–75, later amended in detail, notably by the Courts Act 1971 and now the Supreme Court Act 1981. The Supreme Court also includes the Crown Court, which is the superior criminal court, on which see p. 346, *infra*.

[34] This is why pre-1875 English reports are of cases decided in one or other of these courts.

Commercial Court, formerly only a list of cases dealt with by a particular judge, is now a part of the Queen's Bench Division, dealing with matters entered in the commercial list. A judge of the Commercial Court may, in a dispute of a commercial character, accept appointment as a sole arbitrator, or as umpire, under an arbitration agreement. The Patents Court is part of the Chancery Division. In certain cases the jurisdictions of the Divisions overlap. There are minimum but no maximum pecuniary limits to High Court jurisdiction and cases are allocated to county courts or the High Court according to substance, importance and complexity. The Divisions are staffed by judges[35] under the presidency respectively of the Lord Chief Justice of England (Q.B. Division), the Lord Chancellor[36] (who very seldom sits in the High Court at all, the working president of the Division being the Vice-Chancellor) (Chancery Division), and the President (Family Division). The main sittings are at the Royal Courts of Justice in the Strand, but the High Court may sit anywhere in England and Wales.

Divisional Courts

Divisional Courts are constituted of such number of the judges of the Division as the president of the Division with the concurrence of at least two other judges thinks expedient. The number is normally two.

A Divisional Court of the Queen's Bench Division is a tribunal of two or more judges of that Division, which has a jurisdiction partly original and partly appellate. Its original jurisdiction includes the issue of the writ of habeas corpus and orders of certiorari, mandamus and prohibition, which are important in the judicial control of inferior courts and certain administrative bodies,[37] and the appellate jurisdiction covers the decision of questions of law raised by cases stated by magistrates' courts, the decision of appeals from the justices of the peace in landlord and tenant cases, and certain other appeals from a judge sitting in chambers. The work of the Queen's Bench Divisional Court is, however, mainly criminal or administrative rather than civil.[38] A Divisional Court of the Chancery Division deals with appeals from county courts in bankruptcy matters, and a

---

[35] The proper title is, *e.g.* Mr. Justice Smith, notwithstanding that on appointment they receive knighthoods, and the printed contraction is Smith J. The plural is, *e.g.* Smith and Jones JJ. A female High Court judge is known as Mrs. Justice X. Judges other than the heads of the three Divisions are known as "puisne" (pronounced "puny") judges. The maximum number is now (2000) 106, but the number may be increased by Order. A judge of the Court of Appeal, a Circuit judge or Recorder may be requested to sit as a judge of the High Court. The Lord Chancellor may appoint any person qualified for the appointment to be a Deputy Judge of the High Court. For the current number and names of the judges, see the *Bar List of the United Kingdom*.

[36] This is a relic of the historical fact that the system of equity, which is the basis of the jurisdiction of the Chancery Division, was developed by succesive Lord Chancellors in their courts of Chancery.

[37] See de Smith, *Judicial Review of Administrative Action*.

[38] On this see p. 345, *infra*.

similar court of the Family Division hears appeals from magistrates' courts, in separation and maintenance orders and in certain other civil cases.

In all these civil cases there is an appeal from the Divisional Court to the Court of Appeal, and, with leave, to the House of Lords. There is a right of appeal from the Divisional Court by way of judicial review on an application for a prerogative order in a criminal case direct to the House of Lords.[39]

The Court of Appeal (Civil Division)

The Court of Appeal consists (apart from certain *ex officio* judges who rarely sit) of the Master of the Rolls and up to 35 Lords Justices of Appeal[40] normally sitting in a number of courts each of three, or, for certain purposes, two, judges;[41] the courts all have the same powers and are not related to particular subject-matter. A judge of the High Court may sit to make up a quorum and conversely a Lord Justice may sit as an extra judge in the High Court. The civil jurisdiction extends to hearing appeals from all Divisions of the High Court, county courts, the Restrictive Practices Court, the Lands Tribunal and certain local courts and various tribunals.[42] Further appeal lies to the House of Lords, but only with the leave of the Court of Appeal or of the House of Lords. For the great majority of cases, the Court of Appeal is the final stage and its judgments command great respect as authoritative statements of the law of England.

House of Lords

The House of Lords as the supreme court of appeal from English courts in civil business is the same court and constituted in the same way as the House sitting as the supreme court of appeal from Scottish courts in civil business, and it acts subject to the same rules and conventions. Scottish Lords of Appeal may sit even for the hearing of English appeals.[43] There is now, in certain circumstances, with the consent of all parties, a right of appeal direct from the High Court to the House of Lords, the so-called "leap-frog" appeal.[44]

---

[39] *R. v. Manchester Crown Court, ex p. D.P.P.* [1993] 1 W.L.R. 1524.

[40] The titles are, *e.g.* Lord Blank, Master of the Rolls, abbreviated as Blank M.R., and, *e.g.* Lord Justice Smith, printed as Smith L.J. The plural is, *e.g.* Smith and Jones L.JJ. They are appointed by the Queen on the recommendation of the Prime Minister and are sworn of the Privy Council. For the names of the present judges, see the *Bar List of the United Kingdom*.

[41] A "full court" of five or more members may hear appeals on novel or difficult points: see, *e.g. Young v. Bristol Aeroplane Co.* [1944] K.B. 718.

[42] On the work of the courts, see Lord Evershed M.R., *The Court of Appeal in England*; Asquith L.J., "Some Aspects of the Work of the Court of Appeal" (1950) 1 J.S.P.T.L.(N.S) 350; Cohen L.J., "Jurisdiction, Practice and Procedure of the Court of Appeal" (1951) 11 Camb.L.J. 3.

[43] This gives rise to the complaint among English lawyers that Scottish Lords have sometimes mishandled the law of England. But it has to be remembered that the Scottish Law Lords are hardly ever in a majority in the House, particularly when dealing with English appeals, so that the chance of their ever affecting English law detrimentally is small.

[44] Administration of Justice Act 1969, ss. 12–16. For an example of its use see *Ealing London Borough v. Race Relations Board* [1972] 1 All E.R. 105. On the practice see Drewry, "Leap-frogging—and a Lords Justices' Eye View of the Final Appeal" (1973) 89 L.Q.R. 260.

COURTS OF SPECIAL JURISDICTION;
STATUTORY COURTS AND TRIBUNALS;
ECCLESIASTICAL COURTS

Some of the special courts and many of the statutory tribunals found in
Scotland are found also in England. In some cases there is no parallel and
in other matters England has special courts of her own. These include a
number of anomalous survivals of old local courts, and Coroners' Courts,
which deal principally with ascertaining the causes of sudden deaths. Most
of the Scottish administrative tribunals, domestic and *ad hoc* tribunals,
have their English counterparts with corresponding jurisdiction.[45] There
are also ecclesiastical courts which have jurisdiction in relation to the
Church of England, its clergy and property.

CRIMINAL COURTS

The essential distinction is into courts which may deal only with petty
offences punishable on summary conviction (tried on information without
a jury), and those which deal with indictable offences, tried on indictment
before a jury. Some offences may be tried either way. Magistrates' courts
deal with summary proceedings only. Judged by the number of cases dealt
with, the magistrates' courts are by far the most important in the country,
though the more serious crimes can be tried only by higher courts. All
proceedings on indictment are brought before the Crown Court which,
along with the Court of Appeal and the High Court, forms the Supreme
Court of England and Wales. Reorganisation of the courts in 1971
abolished the former courts of quarter sessions and assizes. In theory
there is no restriction on private prosecution, but in practice most
prosecutions are now initiated and conducted by the Crown Prosecution
Service, a force of lawyers employed full-time on prosecution work.[46] The
Director of Public Prosecutions is head of the Service and Crown
prosecutors work under his direction. He is concerned with prosecutions
in the most serious cases of indictable offences only.

Magistrates' Courts
    Justices of the peace are appointed in every county in England and
Wales and the counties are divided into petty sessional divisions.[47] Certain
persons are also *ex officio* justices. One such magistrate sitting alone has

---

[45] See generally Halsbury's *Laws of England*, tit. "Courts."
[46] Prosecution of Offences Act 1985. The Act does not affect the right of private prosecution
in England and Wales.
[47] The office of justice dates from 1361 in England, and is now regulated by the Justices of
the Peace Act 1949. Jurisdiction and procedure are regulated by the Magistrates' Courts Act
1980 and rules made thereunder.

very limited powers, but he may not act as a court of trial. The function of the examining justice or justices is to conduct a preliminary inquiry to decide whether or not there is sufficient evidence against the accused to justify committing him for trial, and the justices must commit for trial if there is evidence on which a reasonable jury could convict. Only if there is no such evidence can the justices discharge him.

A magistrates' court as a court of trial of offences tried summarily, is constituted by two to seven justices of the peace, one of whom acts as chairman. The court is assisted and advised by their legally qualified clerk. It tries criminal cases of minor importance, such as road traffic offences. The power of punishment is in general limited. The court has power to commit the defendant to the Crown Court for sentence if it thinks the case warrants such disposal, and in certain other cases.

Young persons charged with crimes other than homicide, who need care or protection, who are truants, or who are beyond control are dealt with summarily in "care proceedings."[48]

Stipendiary and Metropolitan Magistrates

Cities may obtain the appointment of a legally qualified stipendiary magistrate who, sitting alone, has all the powers of a magistrates' court. He may also sit with, and act as a chairman of, a bench of justices. In London there are a number of metropolitan stipendiary magistrates who sit in the various courts, whilst additional acting magistrates may be appointed when there is pressure of business.

Appeals from Magistrates' Courts

At the instance of the accused, appeal lies to the Crown Court against conviction or sentence, or if he pleaded guilty, against sentence only. There is no right of appeal against a conviction or order unless it is specifically conferred by statute. For hearing an appeal, the Crown Court is composed of a judge of the High Court, or a Circuit judge or Recorder, sitting with at least two, and not more than four, justices of the peace. Where justices sit, the decision of the court is by a majority, the regular judge having a casting vote in case of equal division.

Queen's Bench Divisional Court

A Divisional Court of the Queen's Bench Division, consisting of two or three judges of the Division, exercises appellate jurisdiction in respect of the proceedings of magistrates' courts by hearing and deciding cases stated on points of law for its opinion. Either prosecutor or defendant may ask for a case to be stated. The Divisional Court will hear counsel and may reverse, affirm or amend the determination of the lower court in respect

---

[48] Children and Young Persons Act 1969.

of which the case was stated, or remit the matter to the justices with the court's opinion thereon, or make such other order as may seem just. Either party to any order, judgment or other decision of the Crown Court, other than one relating solely to trial on indictment, may also apply for a case to be stated to the Divisional Court on the ground that the decision is wrong in law or in excess of jurisdiction. The Divisional Court may deal with such an appeal in the same way as an appeal from a magistrates' court. In criminal matters the decision of the Divisional Court may be appealed by either party to the House of Lords, with the leave of that court or of the House of Lords, if a point of law of general public importance is involved in the decision and it appears that the point ought to be considered by the House.

The Crown Court

The Crown Court established in 1971 is part of the Supreme Court and the superior criminal court; it may sit at any place in England and Wales.[49] The judges are (a) all the judges of the High Court; (b) persons holding the office of Circuit judge or Recorder, and (c) a judge of the High Court, a Circuit judge or Recorder, sitting with justices of the peace. A judge of the Court of Appeal, deputy High Court judge or deputy circuit judge, may sit as a judge of the Crown Court at the request of the Lord Chancellor. Circuit judges must be barristers of 10 years' standing or have held the office of Recorder for three years. They are capable, *ex officio*, of sitting as judge for any county court district.[50] Recorders are legally qualified persons (barristers or solicitors) appointed to act for limited periods as part-time judges of the Crown Court.[51] Justices of the peace must sit in the Crown Court for the hearing of any appeal or of proceedings on committal by a magistrates' court to the Crown Court for sentence, but any jurisdiction or power of the Crown Court may be exercised by a regular judge sitting with not more than four justices.

For the purposes of trial in the Crown Court offences are classified[52] into (1) offences such as treason or murder, which must be tried by a High Court judge and jury; (2) offences such as manslaughter or rape, which must be tried by a High Court judge and jury unless a particular case is released by the High Court judge with special responsibility for the circuit;

---

[49] It sits at about 90 centres, classified as first tier centres, where High Court and Circuit judges sit and where the High Court also takes civil business; second tier centres where High Court and Circuit court judges sit; and third tier centres where circuit judges and Recorders sit.

[50] Holders of various existing judicial offices abolished by the Court Act 1971, automatically became Circuit judges thereby.

[51] Circuit judges and recorders (unless sitting as a judge of the High Court, or at the Central Criminal Court) are addressed in court as "Your Honour." Judges of the Court of Appeal, High Court, Central Criminal Court, and the honorary recorders of Liverpool and Manchester are addressed as "My Lord" or "My Lady": Practice Note [1977] 1 W.L.R. 1435.

[52] Practice Notes [1987] 1 W.L.R. 1671; [1995] 1 W.L.R. 1083.

(3) indictable only offences, which may be tried by a High Court judge or Circuit judge or Recorder, in each case with a jury, and (4) offences which may be tried either on indictment or summarily and which, if tried on indictment, will normally be tried by a circuit judge or Recorder, in each case with a jury.

At the trial, a jury is empanelled and evidence led, counsel address the jury and the presiding judge sums up. The jury give their verdict and, if the accused is found guilty on any part of the indictment, sentence is passed. The defendant may ask the court to take into consideration other offences still untried or even unknown.

Central Criminal Court

The Central Criminal Court, popularly known as the "Old Bailey," is a sitting of the Crown Court. Sessions are held at the Old Bailey in London four times a year, which in practice means continuous session, for the disposal of criminal cases from Greater London or committed on the high seas. The Lord Mayor and Aldermen of London may sit as judges with any judge of the High Court or Circuit judge or Recorder in this court, but in practice cases are tried by one of the judges of the High Court, the Recorder of London,[53] the Common Serjeant[53] or one of the circuit judges, always with a jury. A panel of counsel known as Treasury Counsel prosecute in cases directed by the Director of Public Prosecutions.

Court of Appeal (Criminal Division)

Prior to 1907 criminal appeals were heard by the Court for Crown Cases Reserved or by appeal by writ of error to the Queen's Bench Division. From 1907 to 1966 the Court of Criminal Appeal, consisting of the Lord Chief Justice and all the judges of the Queen's Bench Division, heard appeals.[54] Since 1966 appeal against conviction on indictment lies to the Criminal Division of the Court of Appeal.[55] This is composed of the Lord Chief Justice and the Lords Justices of Appeal. The Lord Chief Justice may call on any judge of the Queen's Bench Division to sit as a member of the Criminal Division of the Court of Appeal. Two or more courts of the Criminal Division may sit simultaneously; each consists of three or a greater, uneven, number of judges usually including at least one judge of the Queen's Bench Division.[56] A "full court" of five or more judges may sit to hear especially difficult points, but has no wider powers than a normal court. Appeal may be brought by a person convicted on indictment against conviction, on any question of law, or under certain conditions on

---

[53] These are ancient offices of the City of London and now rank as Circuit judges.
[54] See Goddard, "The Working of the Court of Criminal Appeal" (1952) 2 J.S.P.T.L.(N.S.) 1; Knight, "The Court of Criminal Appeal and Binding Precedent" (1963) 113 L.J. 589.
[55] Criminal Appeal Act 1968.
[56] A single judge may hear applications for leave to appeal.

a question of fact, or a mixed question of fact and law, or against sentence. The court must allow an appeal if they think the verdict of the jury should be set aside on the ground that it is unsafe. The court may substitute a verdict of guilty of an alternative offence. It may reduce or vary the sentence passed. It may receive fresh evidence unavailable at the trial, quash the conviction and order a new trial. The Crown cannot appeal against an acquittal but can, without affecting the acquittal, refer a point of law to the Court of Appeal for opinion.[57] In such a case, that court may refer the point to the House of Lords. Normally only one judgment is delivered by the court except in the case of a question of law where, in the presiding judge's opinion, it is convenient that separate judgments should be pronounced. Many of the judgments of this court are of great importance. The court acts also as Courts-Martial Appeal Court for England and Wales.

House of Lords

Any case brought on appeal to the Court of Appeal (Criminal Division) or a Divisional Court of the Queen's Bench Division in a criminal matter may be appealed by either prosecutor[58] or defendant to the House of Lords with the leave of the court below or of the House of Lords, if it is certified by the court below that a point of general public importance is involved and that court or the House gives leave on the ground that the point is one which ought to be considered by the House.[59] Appeal lies also from the Courts-Martial Appeal Court for England and Wales under the same conditions. The House is constituted as for the hearing of civil appeals.

Attorney-General's Reference: Criminal Cases Review Commission

The Attorney-General may refer a point of law arising in a case to the Court of Appeal, Criminal Division, for its opinion even though the defendant was acquitted and without prejudice to that acquittal. The Court of Appeal may refer the point to the House of Lords. This procedure is designed to secure examination and clarification of the point of law and to avoid a mistake being repeated.[60] The Criminal Cases

---

[57] Criminal Justice Act 1972, s. 36; see *e.g. Re Att.-Gen. Reference (No. 1 of 1974)* [1974] Q.B. 744.

[58] Thus in *D.P.P. v. Beard* [1920] A.C. 479, the Court of Criminal Appeal reduced a conviction of murder to one of manslaughter and the House of Lords restored it to one of murder. (The death penalty was not carried out.)

[59] Administration of Justice Act 1960, ss. 1–10. Cases heard under this provision include *Joyce v. D.P.P.* [1946] A.C. 347 (the trial of Lord Haw-Haw). See also *R. v. Hancock* [1986] 1 All E.R. 641. Until 1960 appeal required the certificate of the Attorney-General that the decision involved a point of law of exceptional public importance. This was not always granted as a matter of course. The jurisdiction of the House of Lords in criminal cases is discussed in Blom-Cooper and Drewry, *Final Appeal*, Chap. 13.

[60] Criminal Justice Act 1972. See *Att-.Gen. Reference No. 1 of 1985* [1986] 2 All E.R. 219.

Review Commission may in certain cases refer a conviction or sentence to the Court of Appeal.

III.—NORTHERN IRELAND

CIVIL COURTS

The courts are in general organised on the English model. The Supreme Court of Judicature of Northern Ireland consists of the Court of Appeal, the High Court, and the Crown Court.[61] Resident magistrates hold courts for minor civil cases, but the main inferior court is the county court (in Belfast and Londonderry called the Recorder's Court) which has a limited jurisdiction in common law, equity and probate matters. There are no juries. Appeals may be taken to the High Court.

The High Court is divided into a Queen's Bench Division, Chancery Division, and Family Division, as in England. Appeal lies to the Court of Appeal and a further appeal from the Court of Appeal to the House of Lords, and there is also an appeal on the constitutionality of a Northern Ireland statute to the Judicial Committee of the Privy Council, whose decision on such a point is binding on the House of Lords.

CRIMINAL COURTS

The resident magistrates, like stipendiary magistrates, try summary offences at petty sessions and also act as examining magistrates in more serious crimes. Lay magistrates have no criminal jurisdiction. Appeal lies from a magistrates' court to the county court. There is a Director of Public Prosecutions who initiates criminal proceedings in certain circumstances and a separate set of penal establishments.

The judges of the Crown Court go on circuit to hold the Crown Court for the trial of serious crimes; trial is before a jury, save that some offences are tried before a judge alone. Appeal from the Crown Court lies to the Court of Appeal, which consists of all the judges of the Supreme Court, with a further appeal to the House of Lords.

IV.—JUDICIAL COMMITTEE OF THE PRIVY COUNCIL

This body[62] consists of the Lord Chancellor, the Lord President of the Council, ex-Lords President, the Lords of Appeal in Ordinary and all Privy

---

[61] Judicature (N.I.) Act 1978. The High Court consists of the Lord Chief Justice of Northern Ireland and not less than two nor more than six puisne judges, and the Court of Appeal of the Lord Chief Justice and three Lords Justices of Appeal. The puisne judges may be called on to serve as extra judges of the Court of Appeal, and the three Lords Justices of Appeal frequently sit in the High Court. The Crown Court consists of the Lord Chief Justice, and all the judges of the Court of Appeal or the High Court and the county court judges. See further, MacDermott, "The Supreme Court of Northern Ireland—Two Unusual Jurisdictions" (1954) 2 J.S.P.T.L.(N.S) 201, and "Law and Practice in Northern Ireland," 10 N.I.L.Q. 47.

[62] It is regulated by the Judicial Committee Acts 1833 and 1844, the Appellate Jurisdiction Acts 1876–1947 and other statutes. For development see Howell, *The Judicial Committee of the Privy Council*. See also, Normand, "Judicial Committee of the Privy Council" (1950) 3 C.L.P. 1.

Councillors who hold or have held high judicial office in the United
Kingdom, together with certain distinguished Commonwealth judges.
There is an age limit of 75. In practice the Lords of Appeal in Ordinary
usually sit so that the judicial composition of this body is very much the
same as that of the House of Lords. Appeals are heard at the bar of the
Privy Council by at least three, and usually five, members of the Judicial
Committee, who sit unrobed. The Committee is still in theory a branch of
the Privy Council so that its decisions are tendered, not as judgments, but
in the form of humble advice to Her Majesty to allow or dismiss an
appeal. By convention this advice is accepted and implemented by an
Order in Council. Until recently dissents were not voiced and only one
opinion was delivered, but dissenting opinions may now be delivered in
open court.[63]

As an appellate court it hears appeals from the Dominions and colonies,
a jurisdiction now considerably reduced since many parts of the Commonwealth, on attaining independence, have abolished appeals to the Privy
Council from their own Supreme Courts.[64]   It is not a court of appeal in
ordinary cases from United Kingdom courts but only in certain matters
from the English ecclesiastical courts, from the Admiralty Court of the
Queen's Bench Division of the High Court in prize cases, from the courts of
the Channel Islands and the Isle of Man, in certain constitutional matters
from Northern Ireland, and under statute from certain professional disciplinary tribunals, notably the General Medical Council. Under the Scotland
Act 1998 certain persons may refer to the Judicial Committee the question
of whether a Bill of the Scottish Parliament would be within the legislative
competence of that Parliament (s. 33), and devolution issues arising in
proceedings before certain courts may, and sometimes must, be referred to
the Judicial Committee (Sched. 6).[65] In hearing proceedings under the 1998
Act, only Lords of Appeal in Ordinary, past or present, or holders of high
judicial office in the United Kingdom, may sit (s. 103).

Any other disputed matter, not necessarily arising from a judicial
decision, may be referred to it by the Crown for hearing and opinion.[66]

In view of the personal eminence of its judges, decisions of the Judicial
Committee are entitled to careful consideration in so far as they seem
relevant to any matter of United Kingdom law. Their authority is,
however, never more than highly persuasive.

V.—THE EUROPEAN COURT

The Court of Justice of the European Communities (CJEC) sitting at
Luxembourg consists of 15 judges who must have the qualifications for the

---

[63] Judicial Committee (Dissenting Opinions) Order in Council 1966. See, *e.g. Madzimbamuto*
v. *Lardner-Burke* [1968] 3 All E.R. 561.

[64] *cf. Attorney General for Ontario v. Attorney General for Canada* [1947] A.C. 127.

[65] *Brown v. Stott,* 2001 S.L.T. 59.

[66] *e.g. Re Piracy Jure Gentium* [1934] A.C. 586; *Re Macmanaway* [1951] A.C. 61.

highest judicial offices in their own countries, or be jurisconsults of recognised competence, appointed by agreement among the member states for renewable six-year terms.[67] In practice each state nominates one so that all the states' legal systems are represented. The judges themselves elect the President of the Court from among themselves for renewable three-year terms. Presidents of Chambers are elected by the judges for one year. The Court is assisted by eight Advocates-General who must possess the same qualifications as the judges[68] and whose function is, acting impartially and independently, to make reasoned submissions in open court on cases brought before the Court, to assist the Court in the performance of its functions.[69]

Every judge and Advocate-General has a *cabinet* or small team of assistants and legal secretaries, who assist with research and preparation of cases. The Advocates-General serve in turn for a year as First Advocate-General. The Court may sit in plenary session and must do so when hearing actions by a member state or a Community institution, but has also formed Chambers of three to five judges to undertake preparatory inquiries or to adjudicate on particular classes of case. The quorum for the Court is seven and for a Chamber three. There is no appeal from a Chamber to the full Court.

The procedure is divided into two stages, written pleadings containing both averments of fact and legal arguments and submissions, and oral procedure, including oral testimony, the reading of the report for the hearing prepared by the Judge Rapporteur assigned to the case, oral argument and submissions on behalf of the parties[70] and the reading of the opinion of the Advocate-General. The language of the case is any one of the, at present, eleven official languages of the EC selected by the applicant, plus Irish, but a case against a state must be in that state's language. The decision of the Court is in that language though the judges use French among themselves when discussing a proposed judgment and judgments are usually drafted in French. Everything is translated into all the languages for their editions of the Reports. Judgments are delivered following secret deliberations. The Court is not bound to follow the view

---

[67] The judges appointed from the U.K. have been Lord Mackenzie Stuart (from the Scottish Bench) (1973–88), President of the Court, 1984–88, Sir Gordon (later Lord) Slynn (from the English Bench) (1988–92) and Professor D.A.O. Edward, Q.C. (from the Scottish Bar) (1992–).

[68] The four big states each nominate one; the eleven smaller states nominate the other Advocates-General in rotation. The Advocates-General appointed from the U.K. have been Mr J.P. Warner (1973–81) later a judge of the High Court, Sir Gordon Slynn (1981–88) later a judge of the European Court (1988–1992) and then a Lord of Appeal in Ordinary, and Professor F.G. Jacobs Q.C. (1988–) from London University.

[69] On the functions of the Advocates-General see Warner, "The Role of the Advocate-General" (1975) 20 J.L.S. 47. He is not an advocate for any party but somewhat like a judge of first instance, giving an opinion which is frequently adopted by the court.

[70] This is brief and must not exceed 30 minutes in the full Court or 15 minutes in a Chamber.

of the Advocate-General. Judgment is given in open court as a unanimous and anonymous statement and neither concurring nor dissenting opinions are announced. The judgment summarises the facts, sets out the reasons and the decision of the Court. The Court is not bound by any of its prior decisions, still less by any opinion of an advocate-general. The Court has no machinery for enforcing its judgments.

The Court's function is to ensure that, in the interpretation and application of the Community Treaties, the law is observed.[71] Its powers may vary according to whether the case comes under the ECSC, EEC or Euratom Treaty. It also has jurisdiction conferred by certain other agreements. The Court has jurisdiction in several kinds of case. The first is a direct action by the Commission against a member state[72] or by a member state against another[73] for failure to fulfil an obligation under EC law, or by the Commission, Council or a member state, or even by the Parliament or sometimes by a person affected, to annul an act of a Community institution,[74] or by an institution or member state to compel one of the institutions to do what it is bound to do[75] or to require the Community to pay damages for loss or damage unlawfully caused.[76] The second is to give preliminary rulings on the interpretation of a point of EC law which has arisen before a national court.[77] Such a ruling is preliminary to the disposal of the case by the national court. Where a question of the interpretation of a Treaty, the validity and interpretation of acts of the Community institutions, or the interpretation of the statutes of bodies established by an act of the Council, where these statutes so provide, is raised before any court or tribunal[78] of a member state, that court or tribunal may, if it considers that a decision on the question is necessary to enable it to give judgment, request the Court to give a ruling thereon; if the question is raised before a court against whose decisions there is no judicial remedy under national law, that court must refer the matter to the Court.[79]

This is different from an appeal to a higher court, *e.g.* Outer House to Inner House. It is a reference out of the Scottish judicial system for a ruling; when the ruling is received the case comes back to the Scottish court which referred it, which must accept the ruling and dispose of the case accordingly. But there may still be an appeal within the Scottish

---

[71] See further Mackenzie Stuart, *The European Communities and the Rule of Law* (1977).
[72] EEC Treaty, Art. 169
[73] EEC Treaty, Art. 170
[74] EEC Treaty, Art. 173
[75] EEC Treaty, Art. 175
[76] EEC Treaty, Art. 178; H. G. Schermers, *Non-contractual Liability of the European Communities* (1988).
[77] ECSC Treaty, Art. 41; EEC Treaty, Art. 177; Euratom Treaty, Art. 150.
[78] Difficult questions may arise as to whether a body is a "court or tribunal."
[79] On the advantage of getting a ruling from the Court see *Customs and Excise v. Samex* [1983] 1 All E.R. 1042.

system. Or there could be an appeal first and the higher court seek a ruling from the European Court. References may be made from any kind of national court or tribunal[80] but if there is no appeal from that court or tribunal[81] it must refer. English decisions[82] formulated guidelines to assist the decision whether to refer, but these have been criticised.

It is for the national judge to decide whether to refer or not,[83] and how to frame the question which he refers. He must think a ruling is "necessary." If the national judge thinks the point is clear and does not require interpretation he need not refer.[84] An appeal may be taken on the question whether a sheriff was wrong in seeking a preliminary ruling.[85] A preliminary ruling is binding on the court which referred in the case referred, but not in later identical cases, though national courts usually accept previous rulings as applying to later similar cases,[86] but they are free to refer the same point again in a later case.

The Court may, thirdly, deal with a challenge by a person affected by the legality of an act of a Community institution, where it is in issue in an action before the Court and, lastly, it may give an opinion on the compatibility with the Treaty of a proposed agreement between the Community and a third state or group of states, and it may have jurisdiction conferred on it by the Convention on Jurisdiction and the Enforcement of Judgments of 1968 incorporated in Scots law by the Civil Jurisdiction and Judgments Act 1982.

Decisions of the Court cannot be overruled by an act of the Council of the EC, though the Court can overrule acts of the Council.

An institution whose act has been declared void or whose failure to act has been declared by the Court to be contrary to the Treaties, must take the necessary measures to comply with the Court's judgment. Judgments of the Court are enforceable by the courts of the countries concerned and enforcement may be suspended only by a decision of the Court.

In United Kingdom courts, judicial notice must be taken of any decision of, or expression of opinion by, the Court on any question as to the

---

[80] *e.g.* Chancery Division: Case 41/74 *Van Duyn* [1978] 3 All E.R. 190; Court of Appeal, Criminal Division: *R. v. Thompson* [1980] 2 All E.R. 102; Crown Court: Case 175/78 *Saunders*; Magistrates' Court: Case 30/77 *Bouchereau*; National Insurance Commissioner: Case 17/76 *Brack*; Special Commissioners of Income Tax: Case 208/80 *Lord Bruce*; Sheriff court (criminal) Case 24/83 *Gewise v. Mackenzie*, 1984 S.L.T. 449; Case 370/88 *P.F. v. Marshall* [1988] 1 C.M.L.R. 657; Court of Session: *Brown v. Secretary of State for Scotland*, 1989 S.L.T. 402.

[81] *e.g.* the House of Lords in civil and English criminal matters, *e.g. R. v. Henn & Darby* [1980] 1 C.M.L.R.; [1980] 2 All E.R. 166; the High Court of Justiciary in Scottish criminal matters. Some lower courts may be final if, in the kind of case in issue, no appeal lies, *e.g.* because of its small monetary value. See, *e.g. S.A. Magnavision N.V. v. General Optical Council* [1987] 2 C.M.L.R. 262.

[82] *Bulmer v. Bollinger* [1974] Ch. 401; *Irish Dairy Board v. Milk Marketing Board* [1984] 2 C.M.L.R. 584.

[83] *Prince v. Secretary of State for Scotland*, 1985 S.L.T. 74; [1984] 1 C.M.L.R. 723.

[84] *C.I.L.F.I.T. v. Ministro della Sanita* [1983] 1 C.M.L.R. 472; *S.A. Magnavision, supra.* This is called the "doctrine of *acte clair*."

[85] *Wither v. Cowie*, 1990 S.C.C.R. 741.

[86] See *Re Sandhu* [1985] C.L.Y. 1408 (H.L.).

meaning or effect of any of the Treaties or the validity, meaning or effect of any Community instrument. This includes decisions or opinions arising from cases which originated in other member states. For the purpose of proceedings in any United Kingdom court, any such question must be treated as a matter of law and, if not referred to the European Court, be treated as a question of law in accordance with the principles laid down by any relevant decision of the Court.[87] "That court is moulding the law of Europe into a single whole which every country of the nine must obey."[88] In case of conflict, European law has priority over national law.[89]

The important distinction in practice is between interpreting a provision of the Treaties, the supreme tribunal for which is the European Court, and applying the treaties to a case arising, which remains the function of Scottish and English courts, which have to find the facts, state the issues in dispute, give judgment and see that the judgment is enforced.[90]

The Court of First Instance

The Court of First Instance of the European Communities was created in 1988 by the Council of Ministers under the Single European Act of 1986 and began to function in 1989. It has 15 judges[91] but no Advocates-General, though any judge may be called on to perform the task of Advocate-General in a particular case. It sits in chambers of three or five, but in cases of importance or legal difficulty or justified by special circumstances, in plenary session. In this case it must be assisted by an Advocate-General designated by the President from the members of the court. It deals at present only with (a) staff cases, (b) certain competition cases, and (c) certain cases under the ECSC Treaty relating to levies, steel production quotas and pricing practices. It has framed its own Rules of Procedure.[92] If the Court of First Instance holds that it does not have jurisdiction it must refer the case to the CJEC, which may refer it back, in which case the Court of First Instance must deal with the case; if the CJEC finds that a case before it falls within the jurisdiction of the Court of First Instance it must refer it to that court. Decisions of the Court of First Instance are subject to appeal to the CJEC on a point of law.[93]

The European Union Ombudsman

It was agreed in 1992 to create a new remedy for persons entitled to petition the European Parliament. The Parliament was to appoint an

---

[87] *Bulmer, supra*, 1237.
[88] *Application des Gaz v. Falks Veritas* [1974] 3 All E.R. 51, 57, *per* Lord Denning M.R.
[89] *Sirena SRL v. Eda SRL* [1975] 1 C.M.L.R. 409.
[90] *Bulmer, supra*, 1232.
[91] The first UK judge was Mr D.A.O. Edward Q.C. of the Scottish Bar, who had been Salvesen Professor of European Institutions in the University of Edinburgh (1989–1992) and the second, Christopher Bellamy Q.C. of the English Bar.
[92] O.J. C 136, 5.6.90, p.1.
[93] *e.g. E.C. Commission v. BASF* [1994] E.C.R. 1–2555.

Ombudsman after each election of the Parliament, for its lifetime. He has the same rank as a judge of the European Court and is based in Strasbourg. He may make inquiries into complaints of alleged malad-ministration in Community institutions or bodies and has to report on action taken, and also, annually, to the European Parliament, but has no powers of enforcement of his decisions.[94]

VI.—THE EUROPEAN COURT OF HUMAN RIGHTS

A European Convention for the Protection of Human Rights and Fundamental Freedoms was concluded under the auspices of the Council of Europe in 1950 and came into force in 1953. There are five later protocols. It provided for the establishment of a Commission of Human Rights (1954) to hear complaints between parties to the Convention[95] and by individuals against parties.[96] In 1959 there was also established a European Court of Human Rights composed of judges elected by the Parliamentary Assembly of the Council of Europe from persons nomi-nated by Member States. Its jurisdiction extends to all matters concerning the interpretation and application of the Covention and protocols.

The Court sits in committees of three judges, in Chambers of 7 judges and a Grand Chamber of 17 judges. Chambers decide on the admissibility and merits of applications. It may give advisory opinions.[97] The Court is not an appellate body from the ordinary British courts, but resort must be had to the ordinary courts and domestic remedies exhausted before resorting to the Court[97a]. Decisions of the Commission and the Court are not enforceable in British law but have considerable moral force[98] and influence on governments. The final sanction, if a Member State does not enforce a decision of the Court of Human Rights, is suspension, or even expulsion, from the Council of Europe.

VI.—ARBITRATION

Arbitration is the submission by parties of any controversy or matter in dispute between them to the decision of a third party rather than resorting

---

[94] See O.J. 1994, L. 54; Marias (ed.) *the European Ombudsman* (1994).

[95] *e.g. Ireland v. U.K.,* E.C.H.R., Series A, No. 25, 1976; (1978) 2 E.H.R.R. 25.

[96] *e.g. Handyside v. U.K.,* E.C.H.R., Series B, No. 22, 1979. The Commission rejected most applications as inadmissible under the Convention and these did not come before the Court. It was abolished in 1999.

[97] Selected decisions of the Commission were published in the Collection of Decisions of the European Commission of Human Rights and the Yearbook of the Convention and decisions of the Court are published in the European Court of Human Rights, Series A (Judgments and Decisions) and Series B (Pleadings, Arguments and Documents).

[97a] *Malone v. Metropolitan Police Commissioner (No. 2)* [1979] 2 All E.R. 620; *Kaur v. Lord Advocate,* 1980 S.C. 359; *Moore v. Secretary of State for Scotland,* 1985 S.L.T. 38.

[98] *Ahmad v. Inner London Education Authority* [1978] Q.B. 36.

to the courts. The arbiter may be anyone who is independent and not biased.[99] Reference to arbitration is commonly contractual, where the parties bind themselves by a clause in their contract to refer disputes of any particular kind arising between them out of the contract to the decision of a particular third person. The reference may also be made by a statutory provision that disputes arising in certain specified circumstances are to be determined not by resort to the courts but by arbitration. Under the Agricultural Holdings (Scotland) Act 1991, questions and differences between landlord and tenant of an agricultural holding arising out of the tenancy fall to be determined by arbitration. Again the reference may be made, when a dispute has arisen, by deed expressing the agreement of parties to having their dispute decided by a person as arbiter rather than by the ordinary courts.

The advantages of arbitration are that in many cases the reference may be to an expert in the subject-matter of dispute, the procedure can be less formal and better suited to the controversy, is not bound by rules of court procedure, and the issue may be determined more quickly than in the courts, and in private. The expense, however, may be greater because the arbiter and his clerk have to be remunerated, while counsel and solicitors are required as for a court and witnesses may have to be called as to a court. Nevertheless, commercial men frequently prefer quick arbitration by an expert to the lengthy process of a court action and various chambers of commerce, and professional and trade associations have established arbitration panels to deal with disputes arising in their trade or business. The Law Society of Scotland operates an arbitration service and has issued Arbitration Rules and forms of submission and agreement.

Who may Arbitrate

Parties may submit their disputes to the arbitration of whomever they care to name. It is competent[1] in the contract to provide for arbitration by a specified and named person, or by the holder for the time being of a particular office, or by a person nominated by the holder for the time being of a particular office, or by a person designated in any similar way. A judge may, with the consent of the Lord President, act as arbiter in a commercial dispute.[2] Sometimes the reference is to a sole arbiter, or to two arbiters, one chosen by each party, in which case the two arbiters have power, unless there is provision to the contrary, to appoint an oversman. If the parties cannot agree as to the choice of a single arbiter, or if one party

---

[99] Questions of crime, personal status and issues involving the public interest cannot be the subject-matter of arbitration. Apart from that practically any issue can be referred to arbitration, though contractual and commercial issues are the commonest topics.

[1] Prior to the Arbitration (Scotland) Act 1894, the rule was that reference to an unnamed arbiter was not binding.

[2] Law Reform (Miscellaneous Provisions) (Scotland) Act 1980, s. 17.

does not nominate an arbiter where the reference is to two, the court may make an appointment on the application of any party interested.[3] So, too, the court may appoint an oversman if the two arbiters cannot agree in nominating one.[4] The person designated must be fair and unbiased, and have no interest in the subject-matter in dispute or in the outcome of the arbitration. He may stipulate for a fee, and a man acting in a matter involving his professional knowledge and experience is in practice recognised as entitled to a fee. A lay arbiter may be assisted by a legal assessor and appoints a clerk to the arbitration.

Effect of Submission

The effect of the contractual or statutory submission of any matter to arbitration is that the jurisdiction of the ordinary courts is excluded as to that matter, and if one party does appeal to the courts, the other may object; the court will decline to consider the merits of the dispute and will sist the action to await the result of the arbitration.[5] In case of doubt as to the interpretation of the reference, it is for the court to decide,[6] as a problem of the interpretation of the deed or statute in question, whether the dispute is one covered by the reference to arbitration or not,[7] in which case the court may proceed to deal with the merits of the dispute. The scope of the submission depends on the terms used; it may be of specified or incidental matters only or of all questions arising between those parties out of their contract. If one party repudiates the contract completely, that does not exclude the jurisdiction of the arbiter if there was a reference to arbitration of all questions that may arise under the contract, and it will be for the arbiter to say whether the repudiation was justified or not. But the arbiter's jurisdiction will be excluded if the contract referred only specified matters to arbitration.[8]

Powers of Arbiter

In statutory arbitrations the powers of the arbiter, including any matter of appeal to the courts from his decision, are regulated by the relevant statute. In non-statutory arbitrations the decision of the arbiter, or of the oversman if two arbiters differ, is final both on questions of fact and of law save that he may, and must if directed by the court, state a case for the opinion of the Court of Session on any question of law arising in the arbitration.[9] In

---

[3] Arbitration (Scotland) Act 1894, ss. 1–3.

[4] *Ibid*. s. 4.

[5] *Hamlyn v. Talisker Distillery* (1894) 21 R.(H.L.) 21.

[6] See, *e.g. Brodie v. Ker*, 1952 S.C. 216.

[7] *Crudens v. Tayside Health Board*, 1979 S.C. 142.

[8] *Sanderson v. Armour*, 1922 S.C.(H.L.) 117; *Heyman v. Darwins* [1942] A.C. 356; *Mauritzen v. Baltic Shipping Co.*, 1948 S.C. 646.

[9] Administration of Justice (Scotland) Act 1972, s. 3; *Clydebank District Council v. Clink*, 1977 S.L.T. 190; *Fairlie Yacht Slip v. Lumsden*, 1977 S.L.T. (Notes) 41. Such an opinion cannot be appealed to the House of Lords: *McGregor v. Grampian Regional Council*, 1991 S.L.T. 365.

statutory arbitrations the Act may provide for the arbiter stating a case to the sheriff or the Court of Session on a matter of law.[10] Stating a case is not an appeal but a request for guidance on a matter of law. An arbiter has no power to find either party liable in damages unless there is express provision for that,[11] and he has no power to enforce his decision by civil diligence, though it is usual to insert in deeds providing for arbitration a clause consenting to the registration of the award for preservation and execution, and in such a case diligence may proceed on an extract of the award from the register. If there is no such clause, an action in court for decree conform is necessary. An arbiter does have an implied power to award interest from the date of final award (but not from an earlier date without express power),[12] and to award expenses. Under the Arbitration Act 1975, awards made in a state other than the United Kingdom which is a party to the New York Convention on Recognition and Enforcement of Foreign Arbitral Awards of 1958 are enforceable in the United Kingdom by action or, if the award has been registered in the Books of Council and Session for execution, by summary diligence.

Consumer Arbitration Agreements

In the case of a "consumer contract" to which sections 16 to 18 of the Unfair Contract Terms Act 1977 apply an agreement to refer future differences arising out of the contract to arbitration cannot, if it is a domestic arbitration agreement,[13] be enforced against the consumer save with his written consent after the difference between the parties has arisen, or where he has submitted to arbitration in pursuance of the agreement or by virtue of an order under the 1988 Act.[14] The Court of Session or the sheriff may order that the 1988 Act is not to apply, but only if satisfied that it would not be detrimental to the interests of the consumer if the difference were to be referred to arbitration in pursuance of the arbitration agreement. The court has to have regard to certain factors in so deciding. No order is to be made where the alternative to arbitration would be a small claim.[15]

Appeal

An arbiter's award is generally final on both the facts and the law and cannot be appealed to a court. It may, however, be challenged either at common law on the ground of breach of an express or implied term of the submission, as where it does not exhaust the submission or is ambiguous

---

[10] *e.g. Miller v. Edinburgh Corp.,* 1978 S.C. 1; *Johnson v. Gill,* 1978 S.C. 74.

[11] *Mackay & Son v. Leven Police Commissioners* (1893) 20 R. 1093.

[12] *McGregor v. Grampian R.C.,* 1991 S.L.T. 136

[13] Defined by Arbitration Act 1975, s. 1.

[14] Consumer Arbitration Agreements Act 1988.

[15] On this see p. 537, *infra*.

or unclear or the arbiter exceeded his jurisdiction,[16] or under the Articles of Regulation 1695, Art. 25, on the ground that the arbiter was guilty of corruption, bribery or falsehood.[17]

An arbiter may on the application of a party to the arbitration, and if the Court of Session so directs, must state a case for the opinion of the Court of Session on any question of law arising in the arbitration.[18] The arbiter is then bound to apply the law as stated to him by the Court; if he disregards it he is guilty of misconduct.[19] The award of an arbiter appointed by the First Minister or the Land Court in a statutory rental arbitration under the Agricultural Holdings (Scotland) Act 1991, as amended, may be appealed on fact and law, including the amount of the award, to the Land Court.[20]

International Commercial Arbitration

By statute[21] the UNCITRAL Model Law on International Commercial Arbitration adopted by the UN Commission on International Trade Law in 1985[22] has the force of law in Scotland and the documents of the Commission and its working group relating to the preparation of the Model Law may be considered in ascertaining the meaning or effect of any of the provisions thereof.[23] The parties to an arbitration agreement may, notwithstanding that it would not be an international commercial arbitration within the meaning of the Model Law, agree that it shall apply.

VII.—ALTERNATIVE DISPUTE RESOLUTION

Alternative Dispute Resolution (ADR)[24] is a quick and cheap method of resolving disputes. Parties agree to seek a solution assisted by a mediator. The Law Society of Scotland has accredited a number of experienced solicitors with skills as mediators and also provides an ADR service called ACCORD, under which guidance is given on the suitability of a dispute for mediation, and assistance is given to prepare a timetable and find suitable premises.[25] There are also panels of Family Law Mediators and Comprehensive Accredited Lawyer Mediators.

---

[16] *e.g. Farrans v. Roxburgh C.C.,* 1969 S.L.T. 35; *Crudens v. Tayside R.C.,* 1979 S.C. 142.

[17] *Johnson v. Lamb,* 1981 S.L.T. 300.

[18] Administration of Justice (Scotland) Act 1972, s. 3; *Haley v. Dumfries and Galloway Regional Council,* 1985 S.L.T. 109; *McGregor v. Grampian Regional Council,* 1989 S.L.T. 299.

[19] *Mitchell Gill v. Buchan,* 1921 S.C. 390.

[20] *e.g. Aberdeen Endowments Trust v. Will,* 1985 S.L.T. (Land Ct.) 23; *Earl of Seafield v. Stewart,* 1985 S.L.T. (Land Ct.) 35.

[21] Law Reform (Miscellaneous Provisions) (Scotland) Act, 1990, s. 66.

[22] Set out in Sched. 7, adapted for application in Scotland. "International" and "commercial" are defined by Arts. 1 and 2 of the Model Law. On registration and enforcement see A.S. (Rules of Court, International Commercial Arbitration) 1991.

[23] These *travaux préparatoires* are voluminous. The Model Law was prepared in six official languages (English, French, Spanish, Russian, Chinese and Arabic) and the wording had to be capable of expression in all of these.

[24] Discussed in Mackay, *The Administration of Justice* (1994) Lect. 4.

[25] For further information, consult the Law Society of Scotland Professional Practice Department.

FURTHER READING

Scottish Courts
Dobie: *Sheriff Court Practice.*
Gibb: *Law from Over the Border.*
Hannay: *The College of Justice.*
Mackay: *Practice of the Court of Session.*
Maclaren: *Court of Session Practice.*
Maxwell: *Court of Session Practice.*
Renton and Brown: *Criminal Procedure.*

English Courts
Archer: *The Queen's Courts.*
Blom-Cooper and Drewry: *Final Appeal.*
Cornish: *The Jury.*
Devlin: *The Criminal Prosecution in England.*
    Trial by Jury.
Halsbury's *Laws of England*, tit. "Courts."
Holdsworth: *History of English Law*, Vol. 1.
Jackson: *The Machinery of Justice in England.*
Plucknett: *Concise History of the Common Law.*
Stevens: *Law and Politics.*
Walker and Walker: *The English Legal System.*

Special Courts and Administrative Tribunals
Allen: *Law and Orders.*
    Administrative Jurisdiction.
Bell: *Tribunals in the Social Services.*
Denning: "Courts and Tribunals" (1954) 1 B.J.Adm.L. 107.
Hene: "Domestic Tribunals of Great Britain" (1956) 2 B.J.Adm.L. 24.
Mitchell: "Domestic Tribunals and the Courts" (1956) 2 B.J.Adm.L. 80.
Robson: *Justice and Administrative Law.*
de Smith: *Judicial Review of Administrative Action.*
Street: *Justice in the Welfare State.*
Wraith and Hutchesson: *Administrative Tribunals.*

European Court
Arnull: *The European Union and its Court of Justice.*
Brown and Jacobs: *The Court of Justice of the European Communities.*
Collins: *European Community Law in the United Kingdom.*
Hartley: *The Foundations of European Community Law.*

Human rights
Clayton and Tomlinson: *The Law of Human Rights.*
Janis, Kay and Bradley: *European Human Rights Law.*
Livingstone: *The European Convention on Human Rights.*

CHAPTER 9

THE PERSONNEL OF THE LAW

THE personnel of the law comprise many classes and grades of persons all concerned with some function of administering justice through law.

The Judiciary

The office of judge is one of great honour and dignity as well as of immense constitutional and legal importance, and calls for the noblest moral and mental qualities and the highest standards of intelligence, scholarship and diligence.

The Judicial Function

The judicial function is to apply principles and rules of law to issues brought before the court or tribunal to the effect of deciding the issue and ordering the legal consequences, remedy, penalty or other. In case of doubt or dispute this frequently involves deciding what happened and was said or done (the facts), and determining what principle or rule applies and what in the circumstances it means and directs or forbids or authorises (the law). In many cases the judicial function involves exercising discretion, in determining what it seems right to do in the circumstances.[1]

The College of Justice

The College of Justice in Scotland, established in 1532, comprises the judges of the Court of Session (who are designated Senators of the College), and advocates, Writers to the Signet, clerks of session, keepers of the rolls, macers and certain other persons, who are members of the College.[2] The judges are invariably, and sheriffs principal and sheriffs are frequently, chosen from among the senior advocates, but on appointment to the Bench, apart from temporary appointments as sheriff, members of the judiciary become public officers and cease to be practising members of

---

[1] There was set up in 1997 a Judicial Studies Committee under Lord Ross, retired Lord Justice-Clerk, to promote training for the judiciary, both of the Supreme Courts and sheriff courts.

[2] See further, Mackay's *Practice*, Chap. 3. Though designated Senators of the College of Justice the judges are officially addressed, *e.g.* in petitions, as Lords of Council and Session, a title reflecting the origins of the court. The Law Society of Scotland and its members are not members of the College of Justice: see *Law Society of Scotland*, 1955 S.L.T.(Lyon Ct.) 2.

the legal profession, though they do not relinquish their membership of their professional organisation.

Appointment as a judge of the Court of Session and a Lord Commissioner of Justiciary is made[3] by selection hitherto from the practising bar, frequently of a Law Officer or ex-Law Officer, or senior Advocate-Depute, or the Dean or Vice-Dean of the Faculty of Advocates.[4] Eligibility for appointment extends to sheriffs principal and sheriffs who have held office as such for five years, advocates, and solicitors who have had for at least five years right of audience in both the Court of Session and High Court of Justiciary.[5] The person appointed has frequently had previous judicial experience as a part-time chairman of a tribunal or as a sheriff;[6] there seem, at least in modern times, to be no instances of the promotion of an academic jurist.[7] The judges are accorded the courtesy title of Lord —— or Lady ——, the title being either taken from their estates or a part of the country with which they have connections, or, more frequently today, merely their family names. They are not peers[8] nor are they even knighted

---

[3] The appointment was made by the Queen on the nomination of the Secretary of State for Scotland who consulted the Lord Advocate. The Lord Advocate might, and frequently did, propose himself for promotion to the Bench. Under the Scotland Act 1998, s. 95, the Prime Minister on the nomination of the First Minister, recommends a person for appointment as Lord President or Lord Justice-Clerk. The First Minister, after consulting the Lord President, recommends appointments of judge of the Court of Session, sheriffs principal and sheriffs. On the induction ceremony see J.T. Aitken, "Making a Judge" (1989) 34 J.L.S. 176.

[4] For holders of the office see Brunton and Haig's *Senators of the College of Justice* continued by lists in 1972 S.L.T.(News) 233 and 1979 S.L.T.(News) 323. Of the present (2000) 29 three had held the offices of Lord Advocate or Solicitor-General; two of Dean of Faculty; and the others were promoted from the senior Bar, and of these several had previously been Advocates-Depute. Extra appointments were made in 2000 because Lord Justice-Clerk Cullen was to hold an inquiry into a rail disaster and four judges were to be away trying persons accused of having caused the Lockerbie air disaster.

[5] Law Reform (Miscellaeous Provisions) (Scotland) Act 1990, Sched. 4, para. 1.

[6] T.D. King Murray was a sheriff-substitute but later returned to practice and took silk. In 1938 he became Chairman of the Scottish Land Court as Lord Murray. He resigned in 1941, became Solicitor-General and became a judge of the Court of Session in 1945 as Lord Birnam. H.S. Wilson was a sheriff-substitute but resigned in 1965 to become Solicitor-General and later (1967) Lord Advocate. He was made a Life Peer in 1969. In 1970 on a change of government he resumed duty as a sheriff-substitute and in 1972 became Director of the Scottish Courts Administration. In 1975 he became sheriff principal of Glasgow and Strathkelvin. Philip Caplan was a solicitor, then an advocate, then a sheriff (1979) and then a sheriff principal before appointment to the Bench in 1988. Alexander Philip was made Chairman of the Scottish Land Court in 1994 and transferred to the Court of Session in 1996. J.F. Wheatley was a sheriff, then a sheriff principal, before being appointed to the Court of Session in 2000.

[7] There were one or two cases of this in the eighteenth century but in those days professorships were not full-time posts. The most notable is David Hume who became a Baron of the Scottish Court of Exchequer in 1822. Appointment of an academic jurist has occasionally been made in America, Canada and elsewhere and several judges of the European Court were professors before becoming judges. See also J.B. Stewart, "Judicial Appointments" (1989) 34 J.L.S.S. 254.

[8] A judge may be made a peer, before or after promotion to the Bench, but he does not become one by becoming a judge. Judges promoted to be Lords of Appeal in Ordinary, *i.e.* to the House of Lords, receive a life peerage, and occasionally a Lord of Session receives a peerage; instances are Lord President Balfour (1899–1905), created Lord Kinross in 1902, Lord

on appointment.[9] A judge may, however, have been knighted or ennobled previously for public services or for political reasons. All judges have the same rank and title and promotion to the Inner House from the Outer House is by selection on a vacancy occurring and no judge is appointed direct, though he may be promoted, to the Inner House over his brethen,[10] except in the cases of the chairs of the two Divisions. There is now a retirement age of 75.[11]

The Lord President and Lord Justice Clerk are appointed by the Queen on the nomination of the First Minister and the recommendation of the Prime Minister; the First Minister must consult the current Lord President or Lord Justice-Clerk.[12]

The Lord President presides over the First Division. Since 1837 the formerly separate offices of Lord President and of Lord Justice-General of Scotland have been held by the same person. The latter office under the name of Justiciar goes back to the thirteenth century. The Lord Justice-Clerk ranks next to the Lord President in judicial status and presides in the Second Division. His title is derived from the office of Clerk and assessor to the criminal court prior to 1663, when the Justice-Clerk was added to the judges. In 1672 when the Court of Justiciary was instituted, the Justice-Clerk was made the deputy of the Justice-General. Appointment as Lord President[13] or Lord Justice-Clerk[14] has frequently been made direct from the Bar, usually by the promotion of a Law officer.[13, 14] Only

---

President Cooper (1947–55), created Lord Cooper of Culross in 1954, Lord Wheatley (1954–85) and Lord President Emslie (1970–89), created life peers in 1970 and 1980. Interlocutors and correspondence are signed by the judges in their professional names unless they have been made peers. An index of territorial titles of judges is in Grant: *The Faculty of Advocates in Scotland*, 1532–1943 (Scottish Record Society.) and in Brunton and Haig, *Senators of the College of Justice*, Appendix. The courtesy title of Lady was conferred on judges' wives and widows only by Royal Warrant of 1905, which also allowed retired judges to continue to use the style of, *e.g.* The Honourable Lord Blank.

[9] All English judges are knighted on appointment to the High Court bench.

[10] Law Reform (Miscellaneous Provisions) (Scotland) Act 1990, Sched. 4, para. 4. In these respects the court differs markedly from the High Court and Court of Appeal in England where a barrister may be appointed direct to the Court of Appeal.

[11] Judicial Pensions Act 1959; Judicial Pensions and Retirement Act 1993.

[12] Scotland Act 1998, s.95(1), (2) and (3).

[13] Thus in the present century Alexander Ure, Lord Strathclyde (1913–20), was Lord Advocate 1909–13; James Avon Clyde (1920–35) was Lord Advocate 1916–20 and also Dean of the Faculty of Advocates; Wilfrid Guild Normand (1935–47) was Lord Advocate 1933–35; Thomas Mackay Cooper (1947–54) was Lord Advocate 1935–41 and Lord Justice-Clerk 1941–47; James Latham Clyde (1955–72) was Lord Advocate 1951–55; J.A.D. Hope was Dean of Faculty, 1986–89. A list of Lords President is in *Introduction to Scottish Legal History*, App. 2, and 1972 S.L.T.(News) 233.

[14] *e.g.* L.J.C. Aitchison (1933–41) was Lord Advocate 1929–33; L.J.C. Cooper (1941–47) was Lord Advocate 1935–41; L.J.C. Moncrieff (1947) was promoted from the Bench; L.J.C. Thomson (1947–62) was Lord Advocate 1945–47; L.J.C. Grant (1962–72) was Lord Advocate 1960–62; L.J.C. Wheatley (1972–85) had been a Lord of Session since 1954; L.J.C. Ross (1985–96) and L.J.C. Cullen (1977–) were promoted from the Bench. A list of Lords Justice-Clerk is in *Introduction to Scottish Legal History*, App. 3. and 1972 S.L.T.(News) 233. See also, Malcolm, "The Lord Justice-Clerk of Scotland" (1915) 27 J.R. 342, 375.

occasionally has the Lord Justice-Clerk been promoted Lord President[15] and until recently it has been rare for a judge already on the Bench to be promoted Lord President or Lord Justice-Clerk.[16]

The two places among the Lords of Appeal in Ordinary usually filled by Scottish lawyers are filled by the Queen on the advice of the Prime Minister. They are normally filled by promotion from the Court of Session bench, from the office of Lord President[17] or from the Inner House[18] or Outer House,[19] but may be filled by promotion direct from the Bar.[20] They must now retire at 75.[21]

Since 1850 only three out of 46 holders of the office of Lord Advocate have failed to ascend the bench of the Court of Session or go to the House of Lords, and only a few of those holders of the office of Solicitor-General for Scotland who did not later become Lord Advocate have failed to do so. These officers are political appointments given, save exceptionally, to supporters or at least adherents of the party in power, though it is fair to say that promotions of Law Officers or ex-Law Officers have not always been made by their own party. Since 1850 only a few holders of the office of Dean of Faculty have not attained the Bench, though only a few of the holders of the office of Vice-Dean have done so. As these offices are filled by election by the Faculty of Advocates, this road to the Bench is a means whereby professional standing and esteem among peers are recognised in judicial appointments. Service as an advocate-depute is frequently an element in the career of a person appointed judge.

It is apparent that promotion to the Bench is frequently the reward for political service or support, and there was too little chance of promotion to the Bench for the advocate who was politically inactive, unless he should attain the office of Dean or Vice-Dean of Faculty, though it is undeniable that the system has brought to the offices of Lord President

---

[15] The only instances are: Thomas Miller of Barskimming and Glenlee (L.J.C. 1766–87, L.P. 1787–89); Charles Hope (L.J.C. 1804–11, L.P. 1811–41); David Boyle (L.J.C. 1811–41, L.P. 1841–52); John Inglis (L.J.C. 1858–67, L.P. 1867–91); T.M. Cooper (L.J.C. 1941–47, L.P. 1947–55).

[16] Duncan McNeill (later Lord Colonsay) was appointed in 1851, promoted Lord President in 1852 and elevated to the House of Lords as Lord Colonsay in 1867; Alexander Moncrieff, appointed in 1926, was promoted Lord Justice-Clerk in 1947. He retired later in the same year. George Emslie was appointed in 1970 and promoted Lord President in 1972. John Wheatley was appointed in 1954 and promoted Lord Justice-Clerk in 1972. Donald Ross was appointed in 1977 and promoted Lord Justice-Clerk in 1985. A.F. Rodger was appointed in 1995 and promoted Lord President in 1996. Douglas Cullen was appointed in 1986 and promoted Lord Justice-Clerk in 1997.

[17] *e.g.* Lord Robertson (1899); Lord Dunedin (1913); Lord Normand (1947); Lord Hope (1996).

[18] *e.g.* Lord Keith of Avonholm (1953); Lord Fraser (1975); Lord Clyde (1996).

[19] *e.g.* Lord Guest (1961); Lord Kilbrandon (1971); Lord Keith of Kinkel (1977); Lord Mackay of Clashfern (1985); Lord Jauncey of Tulliechettle (1987).

[20] *e.g.* Lord Gordon (1876); Lord Watson (1880); Lord Shaw (1909); Lord Thankerton (1929); Lord Macmillan (1930); Lord Reid of Drem (1948); he was then Dean of Faculty and an M.P., and had previously been Lord Advocate, 1941–45.

[21] Judicial Pensions and Retirement Act 1993.

and Lord Justice-Clerk and to the Bench some outstanding lawyers whose contributions to the development of Scots law have been of permanent value. Some others have been merely adequate and legal ability does not always reach the Bench.[22] It would be beneficial if more with experience of the Sheriff Court were appointed.

Retired judges who have not reached the retirement age (75) may be recalled as temporary judges, and any person qualified for permanent appointment may be appointed a temporary judge for such time as the Secretary of State may determine without prejudice to any other appointment he may hold.[23]

A judge of the Court of Session and the Chairman of the Scottish Land Court may be removed from office by the Queen, on the recommendation of the First Minister, which may be made only if a Parliament, on a motion by the First Minister resolves that it should be made. Provision is made for a tribunal to investigate and report on whether a judge of the Court of Session or the Chairman of the Scottish Land Court is unfit for office by reason of inability, neglect of duty or misbehaviour and for the report to be laid before the Scottish Parliament.[24] A judge may at any time resign his office.

Sheriff Court

Appointment as a sheriff principal is made from Q.C.s or advocates or solicitors or sheriffs of at least 10 years' standing, and as sheriff from Q.C.s, advocates or solicitors of at least 10 years' standing. The First Minister after consulting with the Lord President, recommends a person to the Queen for appointment as a sheriff principal or sheriff.[25] Persons having these qualifications may be appointed temporary sheriffs principal or temporary sheriffs. Sheriffs principal are sometimes transferred from one sheriffdom to another and sheriffs are sometimes moved from one town to another. Retirement of full-time sheriffs principal and sheriffs on pension is now compulsory at 72.[26] A sheriff may resign office and resume practice. A sheriff, if reported by the Lord President and Lord Justice-Clerk to be unfit for office, may be removed by the Secretary of State for Scotland.[27]

---

[22] See also, Wilton, "The Scottish Judiciary" (1923) 35 J.R. 73; Willock "Scottish Judges Scrutinised," 1969 J.R. 193; "The Judiciary," 1972 S.L.T.(News) 217; Campbell, "Judicial Selection and Judicial Impartiality," 1973 J.R. 255; Styles, "The Scottish Judiciary, 1919–1986", 1988 J.R. 41; Paterson, "The Scottish Lords of Appeal, 1876–1988" 1988 J.R. 231; Griffith, *The Politics of the Judiciary*. For personal memories see Lord Walker, "The Scottish Judiciary in the first half of the Twentieth Century," 1968 S.L.T.(News) 9.

[23] Law Reform (Miscellaneous Provisions) (Scotland) Act 1990, Sched. 4, paras. 5–11.

[24] Scotland Act 1998, s.95(6) to (11).

[25] Scotland Act 1998, s.95(4) and (5).

[26] Sheriffs' Pensions (Scotland) Act 1961; Judicial Pensions and Retirement Act 1993.

[27] In 1977 Sheriff Peter Thomson of Hamilton was removed from the Bench for open involvement in political activity, promoting plebiscites on home rule. In 1992 Sheriff Ewen Stewart of Wick was removed for inability: [1992] C.L.Y. 6410. This was challenged unsuccessfully: *Stewart v. Secretary of State for Scotland*, 1995 S.L.T. 895; 1996 S.L.T. 1203; 1998 S.C. (H.L.) 81.

Stipendiary Magistrates and Justices of the Peace

Stipendiary magistrates are appointed by a local authority from among qualified legal practitioners. Justices of the peace are partly appointed by local councils, which may nominate one-quarter of their members as justices; the rest are appointed by the Secretary of State for Scotland on the recommendation of local committees which try to secure that justices are broadly representative of the local community; they need have no qualifications.[28]

Women are eligible for all judicial appointments equally with men. In Scotland Miss M. H. Kidd Q.C. became the first lady part-time Sheriff Principal in 1960, and Miss I. L. Sinclair Q.C. the first lady full-time sheriff in 1965. Ms Hazel Aronson was appointed a sheriff in 1979, took silk in 1991, and was appointed a judge of the Court of Session in 1996 under her married name of Lady Cosgrove. Mrs Ann Paton, who had served as an advocate-depute, was made a judge in 2000 as Lady Paton.

Legal Practitioners[29]

In Scotland the legal profession is divided into advocates and solicitors,[30] each body having exclusive functions, rights and privileges in certain aspects, and concurrent functions and rights in others. While an individual may move from either branch to the other, no one may belong to or practise simultaneously in both.[31] The two branches of the profession have developed separately[32] and each has its own governing body, qualifications for entry, *esprit de corps* and etiquette. As compared with countries where the legal profession is undivided, the terms "counsel" (both denoting the singular and as a collective noun) and "the Bar" are properly used in United Kingdom countries of advocates and their counterparts only, and not of the whole legal profession.

The distinction between the two branches is broadly that between the specialist or consultant, particularly in relation to possible or actual litigation, or other disputed issue, and the general adviser.[33] The advocate

---

[28] District Courts (Scotland) Act 1975, ss. 5 and 9. There is a Central Advisory Committee on Justices of the Peace which monitors the provision of local training courses. There are about 4,500 J.P.s in Scotland of whom about 1,500 are aged over 70 and are on the Supplementary List. Of the rest about half are available only for signing forms and about half take their turns of sitting in the district courts.

[29] *cf.* Rodger and others, "The Future of the Legal Profession in Scotland," 1991 J.R. 1.

[30] This division of the profession is not found in the USA nor in some Commonwealth countries. It is arguable whether division or fusion is theoretically better: see Sweet, "Fusion in the Legal Profession" (1890) 2 J.R. 147; Walker, "Fusion of the Profession" (1956) 72 S.L.R. 25; Jackson, *Machinery of Justice in England*, Chap. 4; Report of the Royal Commission on Legal Services in Scotland, 229 (which recommended continuance of the divided profession). Where the profession is fused, some lawyers in fact practise only as court lawyers.

[31] It is, of course, also incompetent to be a Scottish solicitor and an English barrister simultaneously, and vice versa, though one may be enrolled simultaneously in the *same* branch of the profession in two or more countries of the United Kingdom.

[32] See further, Henderson Begg, *Treatise on Law Agents*, Chap. 1.

[33] There are about 650 advocates, including judges, sheriffs and others, and about 400 in active practice. There are about 9000 solicitors, including sheriffs, procurators-fiscal, those employed and those in active practice.

specialises in advice on complicated issues of law, the framing of pleadings and the conduct of proceedings, oral and written, before courts and tribunals on behalf of the client. In England to a substantial extent, but in Scotland to a rather lesser extent, particular counsel specialise in particular branches of law and acquire reputations for expertise in those areas of law. The solicitor alone comes into personal contact with the client and concerns himself generally with advice, business negotiations, commercial work such as the formation of companies, taxation questions, conduct of the legal formalities relating to the sale and transfer of property, the drawing up of wills, and pleading in the inferior courts as well as much preliminary work in cases coming before superior courts. To an increasing extent solicitors are specialising in particular fields of law. The solicitor is to a large extent the general legal practitioner, the primary adviser, the negotiator and the man of business, whereas the advocate is called in in cases of difficulty, for advice in tricky or important business, and in all cases where there is litigation of any consequence in prospect or in train.[34] The two branches of the profession call for slightly different training, and appeal to different types of people. The advocate has to be the legal expert, the quick thinker, the fluent and persuasive debater, usually involved in matters of controversy, whereas the solicitor has much more routine work to do and spends much time in consulting clients, negotiating and carrying through business, frequently non-contentious, and attending to everyday business affairs. Many solicitors are employed by other solicitors, by local authorities, and by large commercial and industrial concerns, to attend to business having legal connections and implications.

Most papers and pleadings in the Court of Session must be signed by counsel; the most important exception is a summons, which is signed by a solicitor, but it is customary to have all papers and pleadings for the superior courts prepared or revised by counsel.

Advocates

The Faculty of Advocates[35] is the Scottish Bar, and members of Faculty have a status and function corresponding to that of barrister in England or Northern Ireland.[36]

---

[34] The distinction is not unlike that between medical specialist or consultant (particularly connected with a hospital), and general medical practitioner, and that between consultants and general practitioners in other professions.

[35] See Wilson, "The Faculty of Advocates Today," 1965 *Acta Juridica*, 227. The Society of Advocates in Aberdeen is a local body of solicitors and quite distinct from the Faculty.

[36] In England persons are called to the Bar, *i.e.* become barristers, after passing examinations and "keeping terms" at one or other of the four Inns of Court (Lincoln's Inn, The Middle Temple, The Inner Temple and Gray's Inn). In Northern Ireland there is an Inn of Court of Northern Ireland. On the Inns, see further, Jackson, *Machinery of Justice in England*, Chap. 4, and generally, Halsbury's *Laws of England*, tit. "Barrister." Some advocates do in fact possess the additional qualification of barrister and could therefore appear in both Scottish and English courts. Apart from that, a barrister cannot appear in the Court of Session or an advocate in the High Court in England.

The Faculty is by prescriptive right an autonomous corporation and as such dates from at least the early sixteenth century, having its origin in the group of pleaders who regularly appeared before the courts which preceded the foundation of the Court of Session.[37] Admission is by election after the intrant has petitioned the court, paid certain fees, and satisfied the Faculty Examiners as to his qualifications in both general scholarship and in law.[38] The principal officer of the Faculty is the Dean, who takes precedence over all members of the Bar except the Lord Advocate for the time being.[39] He is assisted by a Vice-Dean[40] and other officers, all being elected annually at the anniversary meeting of the Faculty held in January, and in practice usually re-elected so long as they are willing to serve. The affairs of the Faculty are managed by an elected Bar Council. The Dean, acting through Discipline Panels and an Investigating Committee, exercises strict control over the professional discipline and etiquette of all members of Faculty and may censure, fine or even disbar a member guilty of professional or other serious misconduct.[41]

Senior and Junior Counsel

An advocate or junior counsel remains a junior from the date of his call to the Bar until he becomes a Queen's Counsel, otherwise known as senior counsel.[42] Senior counsel thus consist of such members of the Bar as have, after a number of years of practice and the acquisition of considerable experience and legal skill, been appointed by the Queen, on the recommendation of the Lord Justice-General, to the rank and dignity of Her Majesty's Counsel learned in the law.[43] Queen's Counsel take precedence

---

[37] The right of advocates to plead was secured by law in the time of Alexander III: A.P.S. I, 425; and there is frequent mention in records from the 13th century onwards of forespeakers (*prolocutores* or *praelocutores*) and advocates. See, *e.g.* Acts 1318, c. 17 and c. 18; 1320, c. 28; 1425, c. 24; 1429, c. 16; Bankton IV, 3, 1 *et seq.*; Mackay's *Practice of the Court of Session* I, 102 *et seq.*; Henderson Begg, *Treatise on Law Agents*, 5 *et seq.*

[38] See further, Sturrock "Training Advocates" 1996, 41 J.L.S.S. 30. In 2000 there were about 650 advocates of whom about 100 held judicial and other public offices and about 400 were in practice in the courts. Much information about "devilling," as pupillage is often miscalled in Scotland, about the formalities of call to the Scottish Bar, and life and work thereat, is in Lord Macmillan's *A Man of Law's Tale*, 26 *et seq.* See also, Guthrie, "R.L. Stevenson" (1920) 32 J.R. 7.

[39] A list of Deans of Faculty from 1698 is in 1972 S.L.T.(News) 233 and 1979 S.L.T.(News) 323.

[40] A list of Vice-Deans of Faculty from 1754 is in 1972 S.L.T.(News) 233 and 1979 S.L.T.(News) 323.

[41] For an example, see 1968 S.L.T.(News) 47; sequel to *Lee v. H.M.A.*, 1968 S.L.T. 155.

[42] In England also sometimes called "leading counsel," or "leaders."

[43] A roll of Queen's Counsel in Scotland was created only in 1897; until then the dignity was conferred only on Law Officers and the Dean of Faculty. For the full story, see "The Faculty of Advocates and Queen's Counsel" (1896) 4 S.L.T. 47, 51, 55, 60, 143, 169, 254. Only advocates in active practice are normally appointed Q.C. but the honour is usually conferred on advocates of the requisite standing who are M.P.s, sheriffs promoted sheriff principal, if they do not already hold that rank, but only occasionally on sheriffs or academic lawyers of distinction. When the sovereign is a King, they are designated King's Counsel (K.C.); Demise of the Crown Act 1901.

inter se according to the dates of their respective patents, except that the Lord Advocate for the time being has precedence over all others and is entitled to a seat "within the Bar," *i.e.* in the well of the court, at the clerk's table on the judges' right side. The Dean of Faculty ranks next in precedence and has his seat at the centre of the Bar. The Solicitor-General for Scotland for the time being ranks third and has his seat within the Bar, at the left side of the clerk's table. Thereafter rank ex-law officers of the Crown and other Q.C.s according to the dates of their patents. As in England, a Q.C. wears a silk gown,[44] and he is entitled in court to lead any other counsel not of that rank, whatever may be his date of call to the Bar. In courts where Scottish and English or other Q.C.s appear, they have precedence according to the dates if their respective patents of creation.[45] It was formerly the rule that a Q.C. might not draw or revise pleadings, nor appear in any "court," nor before a Provisional Order Inquiry, Board of Trade Inquiry, a Royal or Parliamentary Commission or a Departmental Inquiry unless accompanied by a junior counsel. Accordingly a party who wished to instruct a Q.C. had in these cases to instruct a junior as well, and this was customary in the House of Lords, the Inner House and in all cases of importance. In cases not covered by the general rule senior counsel might appear alone, provided that junior counsel had neither drawn nor revised pleadings or that junior counsel had not previously advised as to the preparation of the case. The rule requiring that a junior be instructed along with a Q.C. did not apply to criminal cases or arbitrations, nor to written opinions. A senior might, for not more than one year after taking silk, continue to write in any case in which he was previously instructed as a junior, and be instructed to appear in court unaccompanied by a junior.[46] Since 1977[47] there has been no requirement also to engage a junior when senior counsel is instructed, though the senior may, if he considers the case warrants it, insist that a junior be instructed. In some cases two juniors are instructed, one of whom acts as senior counsel, or a senior counsel may be assisted by two juniors. In exceptional cases several counsel may be instructed for one party, but there must always be at least one junior among them.

It was originally the rule, at least in England, that senior counsel must not be employed against the Crown without special licence, which was

---

[44] Hence the phrase "taking silk," signifying promotion to the rank of Q.C.

[45] In *Burmah Oil Co (Burma Trading) Ltd v. Lord Advocate*, 1964 S.C.(H.L.) 117, a Scottish appeal, an English Q.C. led a Scottish Q.C. whose patent was later. In *Whitworth Street Estates (Manchester) Ltd v. Miller*, [1970] A.C. 583, an English appeal, a Scottish Q.C. led an English Q.C. whose patent was later. See also, *Attorney General v. Lord Advocate*, (1834) 2 Cl. & F., 481; *Stewart v. Kennedy*, (1890) 17 R.(H.L.) 1.

[46] Rulings by the Dean of Faculty: [1970] C.L.Y. 3405.

[47] In consequence of a report by the Monopolies and Mergers Commission: *Advocates' Services* (HMSO, 1976).

refused only if the Crown desired to be represented by the Q.C. concerned.[48]

Function of Counsel

The major function of counsel is to represent a party in proceedings before any court or tribunal, unless representation is barred by statute. Representation includes advising on whether to bring a claim, in what court and for what remedy, or whether to defend, drafting and revising all necessary pleadings and papers for the court or tribunal, advising on what evidence is necessary and should be sought, advising on procedure, appearing at all necessary stages, arguing points of law orally, examining and cross-examining witnesses and generally presenting the client's case to the court, advising on appeal, negotiating a settlement of a claim[49] and generally seeking to safeguard the client's interests. The rule is that no advocate, without very good cause[50] may refuse to act for any person tendering a reasonable fee, under pain of deprivation of his office of advocate.

Counsel is also frequently consulted in matters not, or not yet, the subject of litigation, as when he is asked to give his opinion on certain documents or issues. This opinion may be accepted as a basis for action or as settling a controversy without litigation. In such cases a Memorial is normally prepared by a solicitor, setting out the facts which raise the legal problem, and sent with all the relevant documents and information to one or more counsel with certain questions formulated, to which answers are desired. The answers are returned in the form of a written Opinion, which deals *seriatim* with the questions, usually giving reasons for the answers with references to cases and statutes.

Relations between Counsel

Usually, every counsel, both junior and senior, works entirely independently, and is dependent for his income on his own exertions and ability. The collaboration which exists between a senior and the junior instructed by a party in one case subsists in respect of that case only, and the two counsel may simultaneously be instructed to appear on opposite sides in another case. Hence every counsel is alone personally and solely responsible for the whole work of his practice and for every opinion, note or pleading which he writes. It says much for the sense of honour and

---

[48] With the great increase in litigation against the Crown and Crown Departments in modern times, this rule was abrogated in 1920, and Q.C.s were granted a general dispensation to appear against the Crown without a licence. For the development of the status of Q.C. in England, where it originated in the 16th century, see Plucknett, *Concise History of the Common Law* (5th ed.), 230; Holdsworth, "Rise of the Order of King's Counsel" (1920) 36 L.Q.R. 212.

[49] See *Brodt v. King*, 1991 S.L.T. 272.

[50] *e.g.* acting for a party with contrary interest, or in another case in another court at the same time.

camaraderie of the Bar that such a system works smoothly and is not productive of personal enmities. The settled tradition is that disagreement and opposition are confined to the court room and are never carried over into personal relationships.

Partnership with another advocate or any other person for the purpose of jointly offering professional services has been permissible since 1990.[51]

In the conduct of a litigation the junior counsel is responsible for all drawing and adjusting of pleadings,[52] incidental motions and procedure, and advice on evidence, and generally all steps leading up to the trial of the action, though on all matters he may consult with his senior, and the senior will frequently in complicated cases revise the pleadings before they are finally closed. At a hearing in court the senior counsel normally conducts the examination and cross-examination of most of the witnesses and certainly of all the important and difficult witnesses, while the junior counsel is noting the substance of the evidence, taking care that his senior is supplied with any maps, books or documents to which he may be referring, and trying to ensure that no point of substance is overlooked in the examination. There are, however, no rigid rules about the apportionment of work at a hearing and the two counsel may divide it as they choose.

Instruction of Counsel

A client may normally instruct counsel only through an enrolled solicitor, and if he has a consultation with counsel the solicitor will be present.[53] The choice of counsel lies with the client, but he normally leaves the choice to the solicitor, who is usually better acquainted with the personality and experience of the different counsel in practice and with their special experience in particular fields. Some counsel have special expertise in particular fields, such as tax, planning or valuation cases. Instructions should always be in writing and counsel is not bound to appear unless properly instructed. Exceptionally an advocate may accept instructions from persons not practising solicitors, namely from chartered accountants or chartered surveyors on advisory work, including giving opinions, drafting or revising documents, and doing administrative or investigative work, from patent agents, in matters relating to patents or trade marks and designs, parliamentary agents, clerks to local authorities, in non-contentious matters or for the purposes of appearance at local inquiries, or lawyers furth of Scotland in matters in which no litigation in Scotland is contemplated or in progress.[54]

---

[51] Law Reform (Miscellaneous Provisions) (Scotland) Act 1990, s. 31.

[52] Hence, in Scotland, prior to the introduction of a roll of Queen's Counsel, an advocate was said to "give up writing" (*i.e.* pleadings) when he began to undertake only senior practice.

[53] A country agent may put before counsel a Memorial for opinion without the intervention of an Edinburgh agent: *Journal of Jurisprudence*, XIV, 148, 206, In general, consultations are held at the advocate's chambers, which in most cases is Parliament House, but may be held in a solicitor's office or other convenient place.

[54] Ruling by Dean of Faculty [1970] C.L.Y. 3405.

An advocate is presumed to have a mandate to appear for a person from the bare fact of his appearance[55] and this can be rebutted only by a disclaimer.[56] He is not responsible for the consequences if he acts on the instructions of a practising solicitor.[57] Once he has accepted instructions to act in a case he must remain free to act according to his judgment and discretion[58] so that he may take a particular course of action or even abandon or compromise a claim on his own responsibility,[59] unless he has been expressly instructed not to, though it is advisable to consult the client before taking any drastic step. "The nature of an advocate's office makes it clear that in the performance of his duty he must be entirely independent and act according to his own discretion and judgment in the conduct of the cause for his client. His legal right is to conduct the case without any regard to the wishes of his client, so long as his mandate is unrecalled, and what he does bona fide according to his own judgment will bind his client and will not expose him to any action for what he has done, even if the client's interests are thereby prejudiced."[60]

Special rules apply to "retainers," *i.e.* to instructions with reference to any particular cause (special retainer), or retainer by virtue of instructions to draw or revise pleadings or to appear for a party in court (implied retainer), or retainer whereby the services of a particular counsel are secured in all cases in Scottish courts, but not in arbitrations or in the House of Lords, in which the person retaining him is concerned as a party (general retainer). A special retainer lapses after one year unless renewed, or if the client instructs other counsel. A general retainer endures for the lifetime of the client and the counsel, but falls if the client instructs another counsel. General retainers rank according to their dates so that if a counsel holds retainer from two parties who come together on opposite sides in a case he must act for the one whose retainer is earlier in date, provided that party sends a special retainer for that case. Detailed rules have been formulated from time to time by the Dean of Faculty.[61]

Since mutual confidence is of the essence of the professional relationship, the client remains free at any time to instruct another counsel and the counsel to return his papers at any stage in the course of employment. The advocate is not bound to disclose information which he has obtained in the course of the employment, unless the client waives the privilege.

---

[55] Ersk., III, 3, 333; Maclaren's *Practice*, 16; *Ballantine v. Edgar* (1676) Mor. 348; *Marchmont and Morison v. Home* (1715) Mor. 358.

[56] *Ogston v. Turnbull* (1875) 13 S.L.R. 69; see also *Ferguson, Davidson & Co. v. Peterson & Dobbie* (1898) 1 F. 227.

[57] *Wallace v. Miller* (1821) 1 S. 40.

[58] *Batchelor v. Pattison and Mackersy* (1876) 3 R. 914.

[59] *Mackintosh v. Fraser* (1860) 22 D. 421; *Duncan v. Salmond* (1874) 1 R. 329; *Ballach v. Kelly* (1900) 8 S.L.T. 52. *cf. Strauss v. Francis* (1866) L.R. 1 Q.B. 379.

[60] *Batchelor v. Pattison and Mackersy* (1876) 3 R. 914, 918.

[61] Printed in *Parliament House Book*, Div. A.

Each advocate belongs to one of 12 groups ("stables") each of which is serviced by a clerk, who receives instructions, distributes work and deals with solicitors on behalf of advocates, while a service company, Faculty Services Ltd., exists to provide secretarial and supporting services. Most advocates now have their chambers address at the Advocates Library in Parliament House, and all have a "box" in the Parliament House to which papers may be delivered by solicitors.

On grounds of public policy and by long-settled custom an advocate was not liable in damages for wrong advice in law, negligence, mistake, indiscretion, error of judgment, or the mismanagement of a cause,[62] unless in case of an express agreement, or if he has acted fraudulently or treacherously;[63] nor is a solicitor liable who acts upon the advice of counsel in matters connected with the conduct of a suit.[64]

Complaints against advocates are considered by the Dean of Faculty, who may consult his Council. He may censure an advocate if he finds misconduct proved.

The Law Officers

The Crown has long had two official advisers or Law Officers for Scotland, the Lord Advocate and the Solicitor-General for Scotland.[65] Nowadays they are appointed by the First Minister and go out of office with the government.[66] Either or both may be M.S.P.s and, if in the Parliament, advise on legal issues and assist the Scottish Executive in handling government business.[67] If either is not an M.S.P. he may

---

[62] *Fell v. Brown* (1791) 1 Peake 131; *Purves v. Landell* (1845) 12 Cl. & F. 91, 103: *Burness v. Morris* (1849) 11 D. 1258 *Swinfen v. Lord Chelmsford* (1860) 5 H. & N. 890; *Batchelor v. Pattison and Mackersy* (1876) 3 R. 914; but see *Rondel v. Worsley* [1969] 1 A.C. 191; *Saif Ali v. Mitchell* [1980] A.C. 198; *Hall v. Simons*, [2000] 3 W.L.R. 543.

[63] *Swinfen, supra*, at p. 920.

[64] *Megget v. Thomson* (1827) 5 S. 275; *Dixon v. Rutherford* (1863) 2 M. 61.

[65] Their English counterparts are the Attorney-General and the Solicitor-General. Despite his title the Solicitor-General is a Q.C. not a solicitor. Lists of the holders of the offices of Lord Advocate and Solicitor-General are in Milne, *The Scottish Office*, 218–221; 1972 S.L.T.(News) 233 and 1979 S.L.T.(News) 323. See also, Mackay, *Practice*, I, 119; Omond, *The Lord Advocates of Scotland*, 3 vols. Green's *Encyclopaedia, s.v.* Criminal Administration; "Law Officers of Scotland." 1924 S.L.T.(News) 43; Malcolm, "The Solicitor-General for Scotland" (1942) 54 J.R. 67, 125; Dickinson, "The Office of Lord Advocate," 1980 S.L.T.(News) 69; *King's Advocate v. Lord Dunglas* (1836) 15 S. 314, 318 (discussing history of the office); *Dumfries C.C.* v. *Phyn* (1895) 22 R. 538; *McBain v. Crichton*, 1961 J.C. 25; *Hester v. Macdonald*, 1961 S.C. 370.

[66] Scotland Act 1998, ss. 44 and 48. A person may be appointed Lord Advocate, or Solicitor-General, on a non-political basis, in which case he advises the Government but is not committed to supporting it in any political context. The office of Lord Advocate was held on this basis by H.P. Macmillan in 1924–25 (appointed a Law Lord in 1930) and I. H. Shearer in 1962–64 (appointed a judge as Lord Avonside in 1964) and that of Solicitor-General by D. P. Blades in 1945–47 (appointed a judge as Lord Blades in 1947).

[67] In 1969 the Lord Advocate (H. S. Wilson, Q.C.), not being an M.P., was made a Life Peer, so as to assist the then Government in Parliament. In 1979 J.P.H. Mackay was made Lord Advocate and given a life peerage (as Lord Mackay of Clashfern) to represent the Government in the House of Lords, the Solicitor-General being in the Commons. In 1987 the Lord Advocate, having lost his seat in the Commons at an election, was made a life peer, to be able to answer in the Lords.

participate in the proceedings of the Scottish Parliament but may not vote.[68] They advise the Crown and represent it in civil cases and the Lord Advocate is the head of the system of public prosecution in the criminal courts, and he or the Solicitor-General appears for the Crown in important cases. He has full power over and complete discretion in the prosecution of crimes in any court in Scotland.[69]

To assist him in the ordinary business of prosecuting in the High Court the Lord Advocate appoints a number of Advocates-Depute (at present 13). One of these, the "Home Depute," is a Q.C. and deals with Edinburgh cases. The others may be senior or junior counsel, and exchange circuits every six months so as to share the work evenly. These appointments formerly fell when the Lord Advocate went out of office, but in 1970 the rule was established that the appointment of advocates-depute should not fall automatically with a change of Lord Advocate, but that they would be continued by the new incumbent. The Scotland Act 1998, s. 87 created the office of Advocate General for Scotland with the function of advising the government of the United Kingdom and the United Kingdom Parliament on Scottish legal matters.[70]

Standing Junior Counsel

Various advocates are also appointed to be standing junior counsel to various government departments and boards, such as the Inland Revenue and the Foreign Office, and act as advisers to and counsel for these offices. These appointments are non-political, but a standing junior counsel relinquishes office when he takes silk.

The Lord Advocate's Office

The Lord Advocate's Office[71] is a small group of advocates and solicitors employed in the Civil Service to assist the Lord Advocate and Solicitor-General and to advise the staff of any Government department which has no Scottish legal adviser of its own. The Scottish Executive Justices Department includes the Office of the Scottish Parliamentary Counsel, who act as Parliamentary Draftsmen, drafting Bills and parts of Bills applicable to Scotland for consideration and enactment by Parliament and consulting with the Parliamentary Counsel to the Treasury on Scottish aspects of legislation to be applicable throughout the United Kingdom. Their work includes work, under the direction of the Scottish Law Commission, on Law Reform Bills and Bills for the consolidation or

---

[68] Scotland Act 1998, s. 27.
[69] It was observed in *McDonald v. H.M.A.*, 1988 S.L.T. 713, that the Lord Advocate could be criminally responsible for his own actings in directing prosecutions, but was not responsible for Crown counsel, the Crown Office or procurators-fiscal.
[70] See also ss. 32, 33, 102 and Sched. 6.
[71] The main office of the Department is now in Edinburgh.

revision of statute law affecting Scotland. The Justice Department also includes the Private Legislation Office, concerned with legislation under the Private Legislation Procedure (Scotland) Act 1936.

Solicitors

The other, and much larger, branch of the legal profession in Scotland consists of solicitors, formerly known as writers or law agents.[72] While many solicitors practise individually or in partnership, many also are employed by large businesses or public or local authorities, as full-time employees, to conduct their legal transactions, or in managerial or secretarial capacities.[73] Admission to the Roll of Solicitors kept by the Registrar of Solicitors is by petition following the taking of a law degree at a Scottish university or the passing of professional examinations in lieu thereof, the obtaining of a Diploma in Legal Practice at a Scottish university, and a period of practical training with a practising solicitor.[74] A solicitor in practice must take out a practising certificate annually.[75]

The professional organisation is the Law Society of Scotland, established in 1949, which comprises all practising solicitors in Scotland, conducts the professional examinations, acts as Registrar of Solicitors, and makes rules as to professional practice, conduct and discipline.[76] In addition there are various smaller professional societies of considerable antiquity and high professional status, of which the principal are the Society of Writers to the Signet (1594),[77] the Society of Solicitors in the Supreme Courts (1797),[78] the Royal Faculty of Procurators in Glasgow (1796),[79] and the Society of Advocates in Aberdeen (1774)[80] (which last is a body of solicitors and is not to be confused with the Faculty of Advocates).[81]

---

[72] Some individuals and firms adhere to the older designations, but since the Solicitors (Scotland) Act 1933, "solicitor" has been the correct term. On the history of the profession, see Henderson Begg, *Treatise on Law Agents*, Chap. 1. See also Cooper, "The Future of the Legal Profession," in *Selected Papers*, 153.

[73] See further, Lynex, "The Role of the Employed Lawyer in Industry" (1954) 2 J.S.P.T.L.(N.S.) 214.

[74] See Admission as Solicitor (Scotland) Regulations 1976 and 1986 printed in *Parliament House Book,* Div. F.

[75] See Solicitors (Scotland) Act 1980 and Solicitors (Scotland) Practising Certificate Rules 1951, printed in *Parliament House Book,* Div. F.

[76] It is now regulated by the Solicitors (Scotland) Act 1980 as amended.

[77] See *History of the Society of Writers to H.M. Signet* (revised ed., 1936); Haldane, "The Society of Writers to H.M. Signet" (1970) 15 J.L.S.S. 35.

[78] Anon., "The Society of Solicitors in the Supreme Courts" (1971) 16 J.L.S.S. 66; J.B. Barclay, *The S.S.C. Society, 1784–1984.*

[79] Anon., "The Faculty of Procurators in Glasgow" (1969) 14 J.L.S.S. 295; Muirhead, *The Old Minute Book of the Faculty of Procurators in Glasgow* (1948).

[80] Anon., "The Advocates of Aberdeen" (1969) 14 J.L.S.S. 325.

[81] On these bodies, see further, Mackay, *Practice,* I, 128 *et seq.* and list in Report of Royal Commission on Legal Services in Scotland, p. 237 and *The Scottish Law Dictionary.* On their precedence, see *Law Society of Scotland,* 1955 S.L.T.(Lyon Ct.) 2.

The employment of a solicitor is regulated by the general principles of the law of agency and a formal mandate is seldom necessary.[82] The extent of the solicitor's authority depends on the kind of work he has been instructed to perform.[83] He is entitled to a measure of discretion in the conduct of litigation, subject to the directions of counsel where one has been retained,[84] though he may not abandon a claim without authority from the client,[85] and various extraordinary steps, such as entering into a judicial reference, require express authority. His actings are binding on the client as long as they do not go beyond what is necessary for the accomplishment of the work he was employed to perform, or what is usual in the exercise of the authority conferred.[86] The nature of solicitor's work is very varied. It includes general business advice, sale and purchase of land and houses, income tax affairs, winding up of the estates of deceased persons, administration of trusts, advice to companies on reconstructions, take-overs, buy-outs and other transfers, advice to banks and other traders, representation of clients in sheriff courts and tribunals, preparation of cases for the Court of Session, and practically any kind of work which has legal implications. Solicitors must comply with the Solicitors (Scotland) Accounts Rules and produce annually an accountant's certificate that their accounts have been kept in accordance with the Rules.[87]

By accepting employment, solicitors undertake to perform the business entrusted to them with due diligence and skill[88] and will be liable in damages for loss sustained by the client in consequence of breach of this duty.[89] There are many decisions on what constitutes professional negligence in various circumstances.[90] Solicitors must be covered by insurance against claims.[91] The profession maintains a Scottish Solicitors' Guarantee Fund from which grants are made to persons suffering loss in consequence of a solicitor's dishonesty.[92] A solicitor will not, however, be held liable in damages for giving incorrect advice on a doubtful point of law where there has been no clear rule or practice, since that is properly the function of

---

[82] For the cases where one is necessary, see Begg on *Law Agents*, pp. 75–78.

[83] See further, Begg, *op. cit.*, Chaps. 8 and 9. On authority see *Swan v. Blaikie*, 1992 S.C.L.R. 405.

[84] *Buchanan v. Davidson & Stevenson* (1877) 14 S.L.R. 233.

[85] *Thoms v. Bain* (1888) 15 R. 613.

[86] *Sanderson v. Campbell* (1833) 11 S. 623.

[87] 1980 Act, ss. 35–42. For rules see *Parliament House Book*, Div. F. *cf. Law Society v. Docherty*, 1968 S.C. 104; *Sharp v. Law Society*, 1984 S.L.T. 313.

[88] *Frame v. Campbell* (1839) McL. & Rob. 595; *Bell v. Ogilvie* (1863) 2 M. 336; See Bell's *Prin.* §§ 153–154.

[89] *Evans v. Stool* (1885) 12 R. 1295; *Stewart v. McLean, Baird & Neilson*, 1915 S.C. 13. See also *Rondel v. Worsley* [1969] 1 A.C. 191.

[90] See Begg on *Law Agents*, Chap. 18; cases in *Faculty Digest, s.v.* "Agent and Client," and in *Scots Digest, s.v.* "Agency." See also, Eddy, *Professional Negligence*.

[91] See Solicitors (Scotland) Professional Indemnity Insurance Rules, 1988, in *Parliament House Book*, Div. F.

[92] 1980 Act, s. 43 and Sched. 3; Guarantee Fund Rules in *Parliament House Book*, Div. F.

counsel.[93] Nor will he be held liable if he follows the usual course of practice even if it should be held in the end to be incorrect.[94] Nor is it professional misconduct to bring an action if that is advised by counsel.[95] Advice on doubtful or difficult matters of law is properly the province of counsel, and the proper course in such a case is to submit such points to counsel in a Memorial containing a full and accurate statement of facts and to act upon the opinion obtained. Neglecting to obtain counsel's opinion may in some cases be enough to render a solicitor liable in damages for breach of duty and he is protected against such a claim by bona fide reliance on counsel's opinion, at least in matters which do not fall within the exclusive province of the solicitor.[96]

Special Services

An Accredited Specialists' Scheme has been developed by the Law Society of Scotland to enable general practitioners to refer clients to specialists in difficult or complex cases without losing the client to the specialist. So far, 13 areas of specialisation have been recognised, such as agricultural law, employment law, and intellectual property law. There are also panels of Authorised Insolvency Practitioners, Solicitor Mediators, Family Law Mediators, Comprehensive Accredited Lawyer Mediators and a Personal Injury Panel, who in a "no win, no fee" case can offer an insurance scheme which meets a pursuer's expenses in personal injuries cases.

Partnerships

It is very common for solicitors to practise in partnership. This has the advantages of moderating office and other overhead expenses and permitting a measure of specialisation, some partners dealing with corporate work, others with conveyancing, others with litigation and so on. Provision was made in 1985[97] for bodies corporate, *i.e.* companies, carrying on businesses consisting of the provision of professional services, the members of which were restricted to solicitors, executors of solicitors, and other incorporated practices, to be recognised by the Council of the Law Society of Scotland and regulated by it. There is no statutory prohibition on such an incorporated body being incorporated with limited liability. An incorporated practice is subject to the same disciplinary controls as ordinary practices and the same rules for the protection of clients.[98]

---

[93] *Cooke v. Falconer's Reps.* (1850) 13 D. 157; *Blair v. Assets Co.* (1896) 23 R.(H.L.) 36.

[94] *Hamilton v. Emslie* (1868) 7 M. 173.

[95] *X Insurance Co. v. A. and B.*, 1936 S.C. 225, 240. Contrast *W.S. Society v. Mackersy*, 1924 S.C. 776.

[96] Mackay's *Practice of the Court of Session*, I, 138. The practical aspects of conveyancing are possibly the only subject which is peculiarly the solicitor's province.

[97] Solicitors (Scotland) Act 1980, s. 34(1A) added by Law Reform (Miscellaneous Provisions) (Scotland) Act 1985, Sched. 1, para. 12.

[98] See also Solicitors (Incorporated Practices) Practice Rules 1987, in *Parliament House Book*, Div. F. Very few firms have so far incorporated.

Multi-disciplinary Partnerships

Until 1990 it was forbidden for a solicitor to form a partnership with a non-solicitor[99] but this is now permitted, and indeed there may be multi-disciplinary partnerships including, *e.g.* solicitors, accountants, stock-brokers, chartered surveyors or others.[1] But no partnership is ever likely to be so wide as to enable a client to get all the professional assistance he may require in the one office.

Multi-national Practices

Solicitors and incorporated practices may also enter into multi-national practices with registered foreign lawyers.[2] Any foreign lawyer may apply to the Law Society of Scotland to be registered as such and the Council, if satisfied, may register him as such. This will enable a Scottish practice to open offices in, say, New York or Paris or Moscow with New York or French or Russian lawyers, locally qualified and resident there, as partners of the Scottish firm, just as readily as a practice can have offices in Edinburgh and Stornoway with partners at each place of business.

Cross-border Practices within the United Kingdom

Persons qualified in Scotland who have also qualified and been called to the Bar or admitted as solicitor in England and Wales or Northern Ireland, or secured equivalent qualifications elsewhere, may practise in the other jurisdiction, subject to compliance with the practice rules of the other jurisdiction, and conversely.[3] The First Minister, after consulting the Lord President, may prescribe circumstances in which, and conditions subject to which, practitioners qualified to practise in England and Wales or Northern Ireland may, in such capacity as may be prescribed, exercise in Scotland prescribed rights of audience or prescribed rights to conduct litigation without being otherwise entitled to do so, *i.e.* without being called or admitted in Scotland.[4]

Practice in other EU Countries

An EC Council Directive of 1977[5] required Member States to permit lawyers from another Member State to offer legal services within their jurisdictions, subject to certain conditions, and this was implemented in

---

[99] 1980 Act, s. 27.

[1] Law Reform (Miscellaneous Provisions) (Scotland) Act 1990, s. 31(3).

[2] *Ibid*., s. 32. "Foreign lawyer" is defined by Sched. 8, para. 29(15)(*a*).

[3] This covers, *e.g.* barristers who have also been called to the Bar in Scotland.

[4] Law Reform (Miscellaneous Provisions) (Scotland) Act 1990, s. 30. This covers, *e.g.* barristers who have not been called to the Scottish Bar. It includes also persons falling within such category as may be prescribed by regulations made by the First Minister after consultation with the Lord President, which might extend to English licensed conveyancers. See also Cross-Border Code of Practice Rules, 1989, in *Parliament House Book*, Div. F.

[5] 77/249/EEC.

the United Kingdom by statutory instrument.[6] This covers provision of temporary services in another Member State. A Council Directive of 1988[7] required Member States to recognise as equivalent comparable professional qualifications obtained in another Member State. The practical difficulties about legal practice in another EU country are the language, and in particular the technical terms, changes in the law, and lack of familiarity with the professional customs and conventions, usages, forms, practices and procedures of the other state. A lawyer from one state seeking to establish himself and provide legal services in another Member State may be required by the government of the host country to undergo an aptitude test or a period of supervised practice, but not both. The United Kingdom government has chosen the aptitude test for foreign-trained lawyers, and the Faculty of Advocates and the Law Society of Scotland have specified the requirements for such a test.[8]

Notaries Public

The office of notary public is very ancient and has survived as a distinct office in some legal systems.[9] In Scotland his functions were and are the authentication of various categories of formal deeds, particularly in relation to the title to heritable property, notes of which were formerly made in his protocol book.[10] In mercantile matters the noting and protesting of bills of exchange, the execution of maritime protests, and the swearing of affidavits in bankruptcy, are all notarial business, while deeds executed in Scotland for use abroad have frequently to be executed before and authenticated by a notary public. In modern times, in consequence of legal changes, his services have increasingly been dispensed with and the powers conferred also on enrolled solicitors, while since 1896 admission to the roll of notaries public has been restricted to enrolled solicitors. Admission is by petition to the First Division of the Court of Session[11] or by petition for admission as solicitor and as a notary public.[12]

---

[6] European Communities (Services of Lawyers) Order 1978 (S.I. 1978, No. 1910), amended by S.I. 1980, No. 1964). European Communities (Lawyer's Practice) (Scotland) Regulations 2000 (S.S.I. 2000 No. 121). One state cannot prevent a lawyer from another state providing services in its country: Case 427/385: *Commission v. Federal Republic of Germany*; see also Case 292/86: *Gullung v. Conseil de l'Ordre des Avocats de Colmar*.

[7] 89/48/EEC. It is supplemented by Directive 92/51.

[8] See generally *Council of European Bars and Law Societies Cross Border Practice Compendium* (1992).

[9] See, *Ars Notariatus; or the Art and Office of a Notary Public as practised in Scotland* (1740–1821); Murray, *Law of Scotland relating to Notaries Public* (1890); Brown, "Origin and Early History of the Office of Notary" (1935) 47 J.R. 201, 335; "The N.P.," 1923 S.L.T.(News) 103; "Mottoes of Notaries Public," 1926 S.L.T.(News) 54; "The Notary Public," 1970 S.L.T.(News) 77; see also *Sources and Literature of Scots Law* (Stair Society), 289–300.

[10] These accordingly frequently contain valuable information about lands, families and legal practice and some have been edited and published by the historical clubs.

[11] See Solicitors (Scotland) Act 1980, Pt. V. On taking the oath see *Chiene, Petr.*, 1984 S.L.T. 323.

[12] 1980 Act, s. 87, amended Law Reform (Miscellaneous Provisions) (Scotland) Act 1990, s. 37.

Qualified Conveyancers and Executry Practitioners

In 1990 the government sought to strike at monopolistic practices in the legal profession[13] by establishing two inferior categories of persons providing certain kinds of legal services only. There was established in 1991 the Scottish Conveyancing and Executry Services Board, comprising a chairman and between six and nine other members appointed by the First Minister, appointed for five-year terms, to regulate the provision of conveyancing services, or of executry services, by persons other than solicitors or by unqualified persons who may draw and prepare documents relating to heritable estate and confirmations and, in the case of executry services, by recognised financial institutions.[14] The Board has to maintain a register of qualified conveyancers, being natural persons who have satisfied the Board that they are fit and proper persons to provide conveyancing services and comply with the Board's rules as to educational qualifications and practical training. Where a qualified conveyancer informs the Board that he intends to provide conveyancing services[15] to the public for reward, and satisfies the Board as to his arrangements for satisfaction of claims against him arising out of his provision of services or participates in the Board's insurance scheme for that purpose, the Board will recognise him as an independent qualified conveyancer.[16] It is an offence for anyone other than an independent qualified conveyancer, a solicitor, an incorporated legal practice[17] or a multi-disciplinary practice[18] to employ a qualified conveyancer to provide conveyancing services to other parties. The Secretary of State may make regulations designed to maintain appropriate standards of conduct and practice among independent qualified conveyancers, with particular reference to the manner in which they conduct the provision of conveyancing services, conflicts of interest, contractual obligations, the holding of clients' money and the disclosure of and accounting for commissions. The Board has to maintain suitable procedures for dealing with complaints to it in connection with the provision of conveyancing services by such conveyancers. Falsely pretending to be a qualified conveyancer or an independent qualified conveyancer are offences.[19]

The Board must similarly maintain a register of executry practitioners, who have complied with its conditions, including those as to education and

---

[13] The wickedness of the monopoly consisted in insisting that legal services for reward were offered only by persons who had undergone education, training and examination and were deemed competent.

[14] Law Reform (Miscellaneous Provisions) (Scotland) Act 1990, s. 16. The constitution, duties, powers and status of the Board are set out in Sched. 1, Pt. I to the Act. The Board is to be financed by the income from persons licensed by it.

[15] Defined, s. 23.

[16] Qualified conveyancers, that is, may be employed by solicitors or firms or practise independently.

[17] Under the Solicitors (Scotland) Act 1980, s. 34.

[18] Under 1990 Act, s. 31.

[19] 1990 Act, s. 17.

practical training and insurance against clients arising from their provision of executry services.[20] Falsely pretending to be an executry practitioner is an offence.[21]

Recognised financial institutions, such as banks, building societies and insurance companies and subsidiaries thereof are entitled to perform executry work if they have notified the Board, complied with the Secretary of State's requirements with respect to the educational qualifications and practical training of their employees who will be engaged in the work, and participate in a scheme for dealing with complaints.[22]

The Board has disciplinary powers where a qualified conveyancer or executry practitioner (but not a financial institution offering executry services) has been guilty of professional misconduct, has provided inadequate professional services,[23] failed to comply with regulations seeking to maintain appropriate standards of conduct or practice, or been convicted of a criminal offence rendering him no longer a fit and proper person to provide these services. This includes powers to suspend or revoke his registration, to impose a fine and to order compensation to the client. These are without prejudice to a civil claim for professional negligence.[24] The Board may intervene if, after inquiry, it appears desirable to protect the interests of a client and take the client's affairs and assets out of the hands of the conveyancer or executry practitioner and transfer them to a trustee. The practitioner may appeal to the Court of Session.[25]

RIGHTS OF AUDIENCE IN COURT

The rules determining what classes of persons have right of audience before particular courts have evolved gradually. Any court in relation to any proceedings has power to hear a person who would not otherwise have a right of audience, or to refuse to hear a person for reasons which apply to him as an individual, who would otherwise have a right of audience before the court in relation to these proceedings, but if a court so refuses it must give its reasons for that decision.[26]

Any living person of full age and sound mind who is a party to a case brought before a court or tribunal may appear and present his own case personally. But an individual may not appear or speak for his spouse[27] or parent[28] or his employer[29] or a firm of which he is a partner[30] or a company

---

[20] s. 18.
[21] s. 18(13).
[22] s. 19.
[23] Defined, s. 23.
[24] s. 20.
[25] s. 21.
[26] Solicitors (Scotland) Act 1980, s. 25A(13) added by Law Reform (Miscellaneous Provisions) (Scotland) Act 1990, s. 24.
[27] *Gordon v. Nakeski-Cumming*, 1924 S.C. 939.
[28] *Rush v. Fife R.C.*, 1984 S.L.T. 391.
[29] *Scottish Gas Board v. Alexander*, 1963 S.L.T.(Sh.Ct.) 27; *Dana v. Stevenson*, 1989 S.L.T.(Sh.Ct.) 43.
[30] *Macbeth and Maclagan v. Macmillan*, 1914 S.C.(J.) 165.

of which he is a director[31] or a club of which he is treasurer[32] unless he is legally qualified, and in all such cases the party must be legally represented. The reasons for the development of such restrictions on representation are the need to ensure that representatives are familiar with the law, the procedures and practices of the court, the duties of assisting the court, the appropriate modes of presenting arguments, and that they are subject to the codes of honour and of discipline of professional organisations.

Advocates

Advocates have rights of audience before the European Court, the House of Lords, Judicial Committee of the Privy Council, parliamentary committees, the Court of Session,[33] High Court of Justiciary,[34] sheriff and district courts and all inferior courts and tribunals, inquiries and other hearings, unless they are excluded by express rule of law.

Solicitors

Prior to 1991 solicitors had rights of audience in the European Court, the sheriff and district courts and all tribunals, inquiries and other hearings, unless they were excluded by an express rule of law. By the Law Reform (Miscellaneous Provisions) (Scotland) Act 1990, section 24,[35] a solicitor may obtain right of audience in the Court of Session, House of Lords and Judicial Committee, or in the High Court of Justiciary by completing to the satisfaction of the Council of the Law Society a course of training in evidence and pleading in relation to procedure in those courts, showing that he has such knowledge of the practice and procedure of, and professional conduct in regard to, those courts as appears to the Council to be appropriate, and has satisfied the Council that he is otherwise a fit and proper person to have right of audience in those courts. Accordingly, a solicitor may now acquire right of audience in the superior civil courts or superior criminal courts or both.[36] If a solicitor has right of audience in any of these courts and is instructed to appear in that court, these instructions take precedence over any of his other professional obligations.[37]

---

[31] *Equity and Law Life Assurance Socy. v. Tritonia Ltd.*, 1943 S.C.(H.L.) 88.

[32] *Strathclyde Regional Council v. Sheriff Clerk, Glasgow*, 1992 S.L.T.(Sh.Ct.) 79.

[33] A solicitor has right of audience before a vacation judge: Court of Session Act 1988, s. 48(2), and in such other circumstances as may be prescribed: Law Reform (Miscellaneous Provisions) (Scotland) Act 1990, Sched. 8, para. 38.

[34] A solicitor has right of audience before a single judge for special purposes: Criminal Procedure (Scotland) Act 1995, s. 103(8).

[35] Adding s. 25A to Solicitors (Scotland) Act 1980.

[36] A solicitor who does so is called a Solicitor-Advocate. The President for the time being of the Law Society of Scotland is given right of audience in the Court of Session solely for the purpose of introducing to the Court solicitors who have acquired right of audience and inviting the Lord Ordinary to administer the appropriate declaration: [1993] C.L.Y. 5612.

[37] *Ibid.*, s. 25A(6).

Members of other Bodies

Any professional or other body[38] may, for the purpose of enabling any of their members who is a natural person to acquire rights to conduct litigation on behalf of members of the public and rights of audience, may make application to the Lord President and the First Minister with a draft scheme specifying the courts, categories of proceedings, nature of business, and rights of litigation and representation sought, and giving certain other information.[39] If a scheme is approved, any member of the body who has complied with the terms of the scheme and who appears to that body to be a fit and proper person, shall have the right to conduct litigation or have the rights of audience to which that compliance entitles him, but the court still has a discretion whom to hear or not to hear.[40] Pretending to have right of audience is an offence.

Laymen, Friends, etc.

In some cases in lower courts and tribunals, a party has for long been allowed to be represented by a person who is not a lawyer. In the sheriff court a party to proceedings arising solely under the Debtors (Scotland) Act 1987 is entitled, except in appeals to the sheriff principal, to be represented by a non-lawyer, provided the sheriff is satisfied that the person is suitable and duly authorised.[41] The power of the Court of Session to make rules for sheriff court summary causes and small claims includes making rules permitting a party to such a cause, in such circumstances as may be specified in the rules, to be represented by a person who is neither an advocate nor a solicitor.[42] At the first calling of a summary cause a party may be represented by a non-lawyer if the court is satisfied that the person is suitable and is duly authorised. If the action is not defended on the merits, such representation is allowed at later diets unless the court has directed otherwise at the first calling. Under this rule, trainees may appear. In cases under the Debtors (Scotland) Act 1987 a person may be so represented at any stage.[43] In cases under the Small Claims Rules a person may be represented by a non-lawyer at the preliminary hearing if the representative is suitable and authorised.[44]

In an appeal to the Special or General Commissioners of Income Tax, the Commissioners have to permit any barrister or solicitor to plead before them on behalf of any party and hear any accountant, and on an

---

[38] Not defined. This might include, *e.g.* the Institute of Chartered Accountants, an association of social workers or trade union officers or consumer protection officers.

[39] Law Reform (Miscellaneous Provisions) (Scotland) Act 1990, ss. 25–29.

[40] *Ibid.*, s. 27.

[41] Sheriff Court Ordinary Cause Rules, r. 2.

[42] Sheriff Courts (Scotland) Act 1971, s. 36.

[43] Summary Cause Rules, r. 17(2); Act of Sederunt (Amendment of Summary Cause Rules) 1991 (S.I. 1991 No. 821).

[44] Small Claims Rules, r. 30.

appeal under Schedule B, the Commissioners have to permit an agent appointed by the appellant to plead before them. Any officer of the Board of Inland Revenue may attend every appeal and seek to support the decision appealed against.[45]

Any person may appear before an industrial tribunal in person or be represented by counsel, by a solicitor or by a representative of a trade union or an employer's association, or by any other person whom he desires to represent him.[46]

A reporter to the Children's Panel, or his deputy with at least one year's experience, appearing before a children's hearing or a sheriff on reference from a hearing, need not be legally qualified.[47]

Professional Discipline: Complaints

Professional discipline and the investigation of complaints of professional misconduct or inadequate professional services are made in the first instance to the Faculty of Advocates,[48] or the Law Society of Scotland and the Scottish Solicitors Discipline Tribunal,[49] or the Scottish Conveyancing and Executry Services Board,[50] or any body which has secured acceptance of a scheme under which its members have rights of litigation and audience,[51] according to which body the alleged delinquent belongs. The Scottish Legal Services Ombudsman[52] may seek to secure that complaints are followed up.

OTHER LEGAL OFFICERS

The Crown Agent

The Crown Agent is the permanent head of the Crown Office, Edinburgh, solicitor to the Lord Advocate's department and chief permanent official of the system of criminal administration. To his office come reports from procurators-fiscal in each sheriffdom, and in reply go instructions, requests and general guidance on prosecutions. He also acts in certain civil actions where the Lord Advocate is a party in the public interest, but not where he appears on behalf of a Government department.

---

[45] Taxes Management Act 1970, s. 50.

[46] Employment Protection Consolidation Act 1978, Sched. 9, para. 6.

[47] Reporters (Conduct of Proceedings before the Sheriff) (Scotland) Regulations 1975 (S.I. 1975 No. 2251); overruling *Kennedy v. O.*, 1975 S.L.T. 235. See also *C. v. McGregor*, 1976 S.L.T.(Notes) 13.

[48] Law Reform (Miscellaneous Provision) (Scotland) Act 1990, s. 33.

[49] Solicitors (Scotland) Act 1980, ss. 42A, 49–56; 1988, ss. 1, 3; 1990 Act, s. 33. See, *e.g. MacColl v. Law Society of Scotland*, 1987 S.L.T. 524; *Law Society of Scotland v. J.*, 1991 S.L.T. 662; *MacDonald v. Law Society of Scotland*, 1992 S.L.T. 353; *Doran v. Law Society of Scotland*, 1992 S.L.T. 456; *Gray v. Law Society of Scotland*, 1993 S.C. 126; *Gordon Coutts Thomson (A Firm) v. Law Society of Scotland*, 1999 S.C.L.R. 823.

[50] 1990 Act, ss. 20–21, 33.

[51] *Ibid.*, ss. 25, 33.

[52] p. 338, *supra.*

Solicitor to the Advocate General

This small office provides solicitor services to the Advocate General, who advises the United Kingdom Government, and to United Kingdom departments in Scotland.

The Scottish Courts Administration

This is a small office established in 1971 responsible to the Scottish Ministers for the general oversight of the Supreme and sheriff courts, their administration, staffing and efficient operation, and for policy in relation to civil court procedure, diligence, arbitration and dispute resolution, law reform, and other related matters.

Scottish Court Service

This is an executive agency within the Scottish Courts Administration, established in 1995 and responsible to the Scottish Ministers for the provision of staff, court buildings and associated services for the Supreme and sheriff courts.

The Procurator-fiscal Service

The procurator-fiscal service[53] is a body of lawyers, a few advocates, mostly solicitors, employed full-time as civil servants and located at the various sheriff courts throughout Scotland and responsible for investigating and instituting proceedings for criminal offences within their districts, and for presenting the cases in court. They also prosecute in the district courts. The more serious crimes are reported to the Crown Office for the consideration and instructions of Crown Counsel. They are also responsible for inquiry into sudden and suspicious deaths, and conduct Fatal Accident Inquiries and have other miscellaneous functions. In country districts procurators-fiscal are sometimes local solicitors, employed only part-time on procurator-fiscal duties. Young lawyers are also frequently employed as temporary procurators-fiscal in busy courts. The procurator-fiscal is an independent person prosecuting in the public interest, not one acting on behalf of the sheriff.[54]

In each sheriffdom there is a regional procurator-fiscal with supervisory control over all the procurators-fiscal in the sheriffdom.

The procurator-fiscal also has the duty of investigating all sudden, suspicious and unexplained deaths in his district. If the death resulted from accident in the course of employment or the deceased was in legal custody, the Lord Advocate will direct the holding of a public Fatal Accident Inquiry.

---

[53] *Dumfries C.C. v. Phyn* (1895) 22 R. 538; Reid, "Origins of the Office of Procurator-fiscal in Scotland," 1965 J.R. 154.

[54] *Green v. Smith*, 1988 S.L.T. 175. On the relationship between procurators-fiscal and the police, see *Smith (James) v. H.M. Advocate*, 1952 J.C. 66, 71.

Messengers-at-Arms and Sheriff Officers

Messengers-at-arms are part of the corps of Her Majesty's officers-of-arms, headed by the Lord Lyon and consisting of heralds, pursuivants, macers and messengers-at-arms. A messenger holds a public office under the Crown. Messengers-at-arms are appointed by Lyon, after petition to the Court of Session and recommendation by it, and examination by Lyon, macer or a senior messenger.[55] All messengers must have been sheriff officers for at least a year, and they must lodge a bond of caution for their acts. They practise independently or in partnership and are remunerated by fees from those who instruct them. A person ceasing to be a sheriff officer ceases to be entitled to be a messenger-at-arms.

The insignia of office are a wand (now an ebony rod about six inches long), and a blazon, a silver disc bearing the royal arms and attached to the wand by a ring. If a messenger-at-arms is deforced, by being threatened or prevented from performing his functions, he "breaks" the wand by moving the ring and blazon to the other end of the rod. Messengers-at-arms must carry and exhibit an official identity card. The function of messengers-at-arms is to execute warrants granted by the Court of Session, High Court of Justiciary or Lyon Court, on the instructions of the party in right of the warrant. Writs under the signet, with some exceptions, notably summonses, may be executed only by messengers. A messenger is accountable to Lyon for things done under his commission and under the Rules of Court. He is obliged to execute with care and diligence the instructions of those instructing him, but the person instructing is liable to the debtor for acts done by a messenger-at-arms on his instructions. Messengers are not entitled to assistance from procurators-fiscal or the police.[56]

Sheriff officers are officers of the sheriff court, appointed by commission from the sheriff principal, after examination[57] to practise in the sheriffdom, or a sheriff court district or an administrative district in the sheriffdom. They have to find caution and carry an identity card and are paid by fees for work done. They may practise independently or in partnership. Their function is to serve the lieges by executing warrants granted by the sheriff court, such as to do diligence by executing poindings, selling poinded goods ("warrant sales") proceeding on decrees, and decrees arbitral, awards of tribunals and deeds registered for execution in the Sheriff Court Books. A sheriff officer has all the powers of a messenger-at-arms in specified matters in places where there is no resident practising messenger-at-arms.[58]

---

[55] Debtors (Scotland) Act 1987, s. 77. On criteria for the grant or refusal see *MacPherson, Petr.*, 1989 S.L.T.(Sh.Ct.) 53.

[56] *Caldwell v. Caldwell*, 1983 S.C. 137.

[57] Debtors (Scotland) Act 1987, s. 86.

[58] Execution of Diligence (Scotland) Act 1926, as amended.

There is now an Advisory Council of Messengers-at-Arms and Sheriff Officers which advises the Court of Session on all matters relating to officers of court.[59]

Solicitor to the Scottish Executive

The Solicitor's Office which has a large staff of solicitors, who are civil servants, is a branch of the Scottish Executive Secretariat based in Edinburgh and acts in legal matters for all the departments of the Scottish Executive and for numerous other Government departments and offices, including United Kingdom departments such as the Treasury which have functions in Scotland. The functions are general legal advice, drafting and submission to Parliament of Scottish delegated legislation, instructions for Bills to be drafted by the Lord Advocate's Department, conveyancing and reparation work and management of land and other property belonging to departments for which the Solicitor acts. Members of the staff appear before the Scottish Land Court, tribunals, arbitrations and in some sheriff courts.

The Accountant of Court

The Accountant of Court is an officer of the Court of Session appointed by the Secretary of State on the nomination of the Lord Advocate. He supervises the conduct of persons judicially appointed by the Court of Session or Sheriff Court to be judicial factor or *curator bonis* to administer the estates of persons incapable of doing so themselves, and annually audits and reports on their accounts and fixes their remuneration. He also supervises persons appointed trustees on sequestrated estates.

The Accountant in Bankruptcy

The Accountant in Bankruptcy has the functions of supervising interim trustees, permanent trustees in bankruptcy and commissioners and maintaining registers of bankruptcies, trust deeds and other matters. Trustees have to report to him and seek his authority for various steps.[60]

The Queen's and Lord Treasurer's Remembrancer

This officer[61] is the Treasury representative in Scotland and the Accounting Officer for the Vote for Law Charges and Court of Law, Scotland. He makes payments from the Consolidated Fund of legal salaries and from the various Votes of Parliament administered by the Scottish Departments, and carries out functions relating to banking and receipts and payments such as the Paymaster-General does in England.

---

[59] Debtors (Scotland) Act 1987, s. 77; Act of Sederunt (Messengers-at-Arms and Sheriff Officers Rules) 1988 (S.I. 1988 No. 2097).

[60] Bankruptcy (Scotland) Act 1985.

[61] The office is an amalgamation of the two old offices in the former Court of Exchequer.

He audits the criminal accounts of procurators-fiscal and sheriff clerks and the expenses of returning officers at elections, and has certain functions of examining Court of Session and Sheriff Court books. He is *ex officio* administrator of treasure trove and of estates which fall to the Crown by reason of failure of heirs or as *bona vacantia*. By warrant of the Department of Trade he is Registrar of Companies, Registrar of Limited Partnerships and Registrar of Business Names. He is also Keeper of the *Edinburgh Gazette* and responsible on behalf of the Great Officers of State for the custody of the Regalia of Scotland in Edinburgh Castle. In 1981 the Crown Agent was appointed also to be Queen's and Lord Treasurer's Remembrancer.

The Keeper of the Registers of Scotland

The Keeper is appointed by the Secretary of State with the consent of the Lord President and is head of the Registers of Scotland which is an executive agency of the Scottish Executive Justice Department and is concerned with the maintenance of 16 separate registers and with the registration therein of a large variety of deeds and documents relating to various legal processes. The registers are the General Register of Sasines, the Register of Inhibitions and Adjudications, of Hornings, of Deeds, of Entails, of Protests, of Service of Heirs, of the Great Seal, of the Quarter Seal, of the Prince's Seal, of the Cachet Seal, of Crown Grants, of Sheriffs' Commissions, of English and Irish Judgments, of European Court Judgments and the Land Register of Scotland. The most important of these is the General Register of Sasines in which are registered all writs relating to rights in land. The Land Register of Scotland, which will record all interests in land, will in time completely replace the General Register of Sasines.[62] The Keeper's refusal to amend the Land Register may be challenged by seeking an order for rectification of the Register.[63] Legal registers, together with the records of the Court of Session, are periodically transmitted to the Scottish Record Office for preservation along with other public records and many private collections of material of historical interest.[64]

The Registrar General

The Registrar General of Births, Deaths and Marriages for Scotland, acting through a network of district registrars, registers births, deaths, marriages, adoptions and related events and collects statistical information.[65] Some district registrars are authorised to perform marriages.[66]

---

[62] Public Registers and Records (Scotland) Act 1948; Land Registration (Scotland) Act 1979. For information about the individual Registers, see *Guide to the National Archives of Scotland* (1994).

[63] *Short's Tr. v. Keeper of the Registers of Scotland*, 1996 S.L.T. 166 (H.L.).

[64] Public Records (Scotland) Act 1937; Public Registers and Records (Scotland) Act 1948.

[65] Registration of Births, Deaths and Marriages (Scotland) Act 1965.

[66] Marriage (Scotland) Act 1977.

The Police

The police are not a branch of the Civil Service nor a national force, but eight separate forces administered by police boards for council areas as police authorities.[67] The Scottish Executive Justice Department is responsible for police legislation and generally guides and co-ordinates the work of the police forces; it administers the police grant, maintains a central establishment for the training of police officers and maintains contact through Her Majesty's Inspectors of Constabulary who report to the First Minister on the efficiency of police forces. The function of the police is to preserve law and order, to enforce a great volume of legislation, to search out and apprehend criminals and to report crimes detected to the appropriate procurator-fiscal. In Scotland the police do not themselves decide whether to prosecute, nor do they initiate or conduct prosecutions. Each force has its own special constabulary made up of part-time volunteers. There are also the British Transport Police, the Ministry of Defence Police and the United Kingdom Atomic Energy Authority Constabulary.

The Prison Service

The Scottish Executive Justice Department, acting through the Scottish Prison Service, administers prisons, Young Offenders Institutions and other penal establishments in Scotland, through four directorates concerned with custody, strategy and corporate affairs, human resources and finance and information systems.[68] There is a Chief Inspector of Prisons, and local authorities appoint visiting committees to visit prisoners and to hear complaints, and sheriffs and Justices of the Peace may visit prisons. There is a Scottish Prisons Complaints Commission to hear prisoners' grievances. The Parole Board for Scotland advises the First Minister on the release of prisoners under licence. The probation service has since 1968 been part of a local authority's social work service.

The Fire Service

The Scottish Executive Justice Department has overall responsibility for fire services. There are two fire boards and six joint fire boards for council areas, which act as fire authorities for areas. There is a H.M. Inspectorate of Fire Services.

JURIES

In various kinds of legal investigations a part is played by a jury.[69] The main cases are criminal trials under solemn procedure (jury of 15) and

---

[67] Police (Scotland) Act 1967, as amended.
[68] See also Prisons (Scotland) Act 1989.
[69] For a modern evaluation of jury trial, particularly in England, see Cornish, *The Jury*. It is a very uncertain and questionably just mode of trying cases.

some civil trials of certain actions, mainly for damages for personal injuries or death, or defamation in the Court of Session (jury of 12). The jurors are persons chosen by lot from a larger number of qualified persons summoned for the purpose by the Clerk of Justiciary, Principal Clerk of Session or Sheriff-Clerk from those named in the General Jury Book of the District. The qualifications are to be between 18 and 65, ordinarily resident in the United Kingdom for at least five years and registered as an elector. Both men and women are eligible to serve but many categories of persons, *e.g.* doctors in practice, are exempted.[70]

In criminal cases the prosecutor or the accused may challenge three jurors peremptorily and any number on cause shown. But there should be no general questioning by judge or on behalf of either party to ascertain whether any person cited could or should be excused from a particular trial. It is not a sufficient cause for a juror to be excused that he is of a particular race, religion, political belief or occupation, or that he might be prejudiced either way. The essence of the jury system is of a number of individuals chosen at random.[71]

It is very improper for a juror, while a case is in progress, to discuss the case, or anything relating to it, with any outsider.[72]

In all cases the function of the jury is to have regard to the evidence and, subject to the directions in matters of law of the presiding judge or sheriff, to return a verdict on one or more questions of fact, or of mixed fact and law, *e.g.* in a criminal case, the question: Are you satisfied beyond reasonable doubt that the accused committed the crime charged? Or in a civil case: Are you satisfied on the balance of probabilities that the accident to the pursuer was caused by the fault of the defender? If so, at what sum do you assess the damages?[73] In all cases a majority verdict is competent. The jury verdict is announced orally by the chancellor, chosen from among themselves by the jurors, in response to a question from the clerk of court. Jurors are entitled to compensation for loss of earnings and to travelling and subsistence allowances.

PROFESSIONAL ETHICS AND ETIQUETTE

Both branches of the legal profession have a profound *esprit de corps* and regard for the ethics of the profession, and also a distinct code of professional etiquette. Most of these rules are rules dictated by prudence and the desire that justice should, so far as humanly possible, both be

---

[70] Law Reform (Miscellaneous Provisions) (Scotland) Act 1980, Sched. 1.
[71] *M. v. H.M. Advocate*, 1974 S.L.T.(Notes) 25.
[72] *Pike v. H.M. Advocate,* 1987 S.L.T. 488.
[73] A jury may, exceptionally, be directed to bring a special verdict, *i.e.* answers to specific questions, the legal effect of which is later decided by the court after argument.

done and be manifestly seen to be done. Some matters of professional etiquette, relating to the relations between the two branches of the profession, have already been touched on. No comprehensive code of professional ethics exists and much of it is simply absorbed by experience[74]; nevertheless the administration of justice depends in large part on the integrity and honour of the profession.

It is difficult to generalise but the overriding consideration, applicable equally to both branches of the profession, is that an advocate or solicitor, if consulted or instructed, must invariably apply his whole mind and devote his fullest energies to the business entrusted to him, and seek to use his ability, ingenuity and knowledge towards achieving by honest means a fair and just conclusion of the issue without regard to his personal advantage or belief. He must retain his own professional integrity and opinions and not subordinate them to the client's opinions or interests, and if a client should insist on doing what the legal adviser believes is imprudent or wrong or unjust or illegal, he must be free to withdraw from the employment; he is not bound to aid in some foolish or wrongful escapade, still less to advise or abet some unjust or illegal enterprise. "An advocate in undertaking the conduct of a cause in this court enters into no contract with his client, but takes on himself an office in the performance of which he owes a duty, not to his client only, but also to the court, to the members of his own profession, and to the public. . . . The position of an agent is somewhat different. There is a contract of employment between him and his client, by virtue of which the client, for certain settled rates of remuneration, is entitled to require from the agent the exercise of care and diligence, and professional skill and experience. . . . The agent, of course, cannot be asked to follow the client's instructions beyond what is lawful and proper. For the agent, as well as the counsel, owes a duty to the court. . . . He is also bound by that unwritten law of his profession which embodies the honourable understanding of the individual members as to their bearing and conduct towards each other."[75]

Duties to the Court

A lawyer owes to any court of law or tribunal a duty to treat it with proper respect and to make any criticisms in a moderate and respectful

---

[74] The American Bar Association has adopted a code of Canons of Professional Ethics for the guidance of its members and in some states an oath must be taken on admission to the Bar to observe the highest moral principles in the practice of the profession. The "Canons of Professional Ethics" are printed in Moreland, *Equal Justice Under Law*. The Annual Statements of the [English] Bar Council, summarised in *Current Law Year Books*, contain rulings on points of ethics and etiquette. See also, Lord Macmillan, "The Ethics of Advocacy," in *Law and Other Things*, p. 36; Stone, *Law and its Administration*, 162–165; Rogers, "Ethics of Advocacy" (1899) 15 L.Q.R. 259; Webster, *Professional Ethics and Practice for Scottish Solicitors* (1976); Boulton, *Conduct and Etiquette at the [English] Bar*, 1975; Solicitors' (Scotland) Code of Conduct, 1989, in *Parliament House Book*, Div. F. The Conseil des Barreaux de la Communauté Européenne adopted in 1988 a Code of Conduct for lawyers in the European Communities.

[75] *Batchelor v. Pattison and Mackersy* (1876) 3 R. 914, 918, *per* Lord President Inglis.

manner. Disrespectful or insulting conduct in the face of a court is punishable as contempt of court. Any attempt to exert personal influence on the court, or even to discuss privately with a judge any pending matter is very improper.

The lawyer, moreover, is present in court not merely to present his client's case but to assist the court, by argument and criticism of opposing contentions, to arrive at a just and legally correct decision. "He is there to help the judge, and, when there is a jury, to help the jury, to arrive at a proper result in the dispute between the parties."[76] Hence his conduct must be characterised by candour and fairness. It is professionally disgraceful to resort to or be a party to any fraud, deception or trickery,[77] such as fabricating documents or deliberately withholding evidence, or knowingly to misquote the substance of a document, a witness's testimony, an opposing argument, or a decision or textbook. An advocate is bound to bring to the notice of the court authorities known to bear on the subject of a debate, whether or not they are in his client's favour.[78] He must not cite as authoritative a decision known to have been overruled or a statute repealed or amended, nor assert as fact what has not been proved. Nor should pleading or argument include any scandalous or irrelevant matter[79] or matter merely prejudicial, or statements designed to sway a jury emotionally or on grounds other than legal.

Counsel must accept a brief offered "and do all he honourably can on behalf of his client. I say 'all he honourably can' because his duty is not only to his client. He has a duty to the court which is paramount. It is a mistake to suppose that he is the mouthpiece of his client to say what he wants; or his tool to do what he directs. He is none of these things. He owes allegiance to a higher cause. It is the cause of truth and justice. He must not consciously mis-state the facts. He must not knowingly conceal the truth. He must not unjustly make a charge of fraud, that is, without evidence to support it. He must produce all the relevant authorities, even those that are against him. He must see that his client discloses, if ordered, the relevant documents, even those that are fatal to his case. He must disregard the most specific instructions of his client, if they conflict with his duty to the court. The code which requires a barrister to do all this is not a code of law. It is a code of honour. If he breaks it, he is offending against the rules of the profession and is subject to its discipline; but he cannot be sued in a court of law."[80]

Both the court and other parties must be able to rely on the honesty and to trust the word of legal advisers. Moreover, in some cases issues are

---

[76] *Beevis v. Dawson* [1956] 3 All E.R. 837, 839.
[77] *cf.* Annual Statement of the [English] Bar Council, 1953, p. 16, quoted in [1954] C.L.Y. 2514.
[78] *Glebe Sugar Refining Co. v. Greenock Harbour Trustees*, 1921 S.C.(H.L.) 72.
[79] See *Wardrope v. Hamilton* (1876) 3 R. 876; *A. v. B.* (1895) 22 R. 402; *H. v. P.* (1905) 8 F. 232; *M. v. S.*, 1909 1 S.L.T. 192; *A. v. C.*, 1922 S.L.T. 34.
[80] *Rondel v. W.* [1966] 3 All E.R. 657, 665, *per* Lord Denning M.R.

decided on the *ex parte* statements of one party,[81] so that it is important that only such statements be made as are true to the best of the adviser's belief and knowledge. It is quite improper to assert in argument a personal belief in the innocence of the client or the justice of his cause.

It is part of the duty to the court to treat opposing parties and witnesses with fairness and consideration, and not to indulge in abuse, to suggest improprieties, or to make any personal attack, even at the instance of the client, except in so far as any such conduct may be necessitated by the circumstances of the case. Thus, sometimes one has to put to the other side's witnesses the suggestion that they are lying.

When initiating proceedings in court, counsel and solicitors owe a duty to the court and also to the other party involved to consider seriously whether there is any prospect of success. It is professional misconduct, at least on a solicitor's part, to raise and maintain an action without belief that it has any reasonable prospect of success,[82] but counsel and agents need not go so far as to be fully convinced of the rightness or substantial justice of the client's case.[83] So, too, in presenting appeals to the High Court from conviction by a jury it has been observed that where counsel considers there are no statable grounds of appeal, he acts properly in performance of his duty to the court as well as to his client in refusing to act further in the case.[84]

In arguing a case, counsel or solicitor is entitled to take any point which is fairly or reasonably arguable, because it is for the court, not for him, to say whether the point is good or bad. But it is misconduct knowingly to take a bad point, or to take it merely to cause confusion or waste time.[85]

Counsel or procurator-fiscal engaged in conducting a criminal prosecution has the primary duty not of securing a conviction but of assisting the court and trying to secure that justice is done. Hence, he must not press the prosecution case unduly and may properly afford the defence reasonable facilities to prepare their defence.[86] "The Crown counsel is a representative of the State, 'a minister of justice'; his function is to assist the jury in arriving at the truth. He must not urge any argument that does not carry weight in his own mind, or try to shut out any legal evidence that would be important to the interests of the person accused. 'It is not his duty to obtain a conviction by all means; but simply to lay before the jury the whole of the facts which compose his case, and to make these perfectly intelligible, and to see that the jury are instructed with regard to the law

---

[81] *e.g.* the granting of *interim* interdict.

[82] *X Insurance Co. v. A. and B.*, 1936 S.C. 225.

[83] So, too, a litigant is not liable in damages to his opponent for judicial proceedings which are unsuccessful or unfounded so long as there is no malice or fraud: *Ormiston v. Redpath* (1866) 4 M. 488; *Davies v. Brown* (1867) 5 M. 842; *Kinnes v. Adam* (1882) 9 R. 698.

[84] *Scott, J.N. v. H.M. Advocate*, 1946 J.C. 68. *Cf. Monteath v. H.M. Advocate*, 1965 J.C. 14.

[85] *cf. Abraham v. Jutsun* [1963] 2 All E.R. 402.

[86] *cf. Smith v. H.M. Advocate*, 1952 J.C. 66.

and are able to apply the law to the facts.'[87] 'It cannot be too often made plain that the business of counsel for the Crown is fairly and impartially to exhibit all the facts to the jury. The Crown has no interest in procuring a conviction. Its only interest is that the right person should be convicted, that the truth should be known, and that justice should be done.'[88] "[89]

When defending on a criminal charge a lawyer is entitled to act independently of his personal opinion as to the guilt of the accused and he is entitled, and even bound, to present every legal defence which he can reasonably rely on, so that no person shall be convicted save after due process of law and after guilt has been satisfactorily proved by competent evidence, to a competent tribunal. As regards confessions of guilt, if the confession is made before proceedings have commenced, no harm can be done by requesting the accused to retain another advocate. But if the confession is made during proceedings, the advocate should continue and must continue the defence by all legitimate means, though he may not set up an affirmative case inconsistent with the confession, for example by suggesting that another person committed the crime.[90]

Duties to the Profession

A lawyer owes it to his profession, to the abstract idea of Law and all that it stands for, and to the ideal of Justice, that he does nothing in his professional practice of which a moral, skilful, diligent and upright person need be ashamed. Advertisement is permissible, within limits,[91] though restriction does not extend to the insertion of names and addresses in the recognised Law Lists, nor giving name and qualifications as the author of legal books and articles, or articles in the press or broadcasts in which the person is named or given his professional designation. Touting for business is unethical.[92] A lawyer must not engage "on the side" in any other business or activity which is inconsistent with his professional standing.[93] The sharing of fees with an unqualified person is also forbidden.[94]

It is a duty to the profession to take a share in assisting individuals in need of legal assistance even though they may be unable to pay, or may require legal aid,[95] and to accept instructions in a cause from the first person who tenders instructions to him with the customary fee, even

---

[87] Sir J. Holker, Att.-Gen. (*The Times*, Feb. 25. 1880).
[88] Lord Hewart C.J. (1941) 25 Cr.App.R. at p. 115.
[89] Kenny, *Outlines of Criminal Law* (16th ed.), 504–505.
[90] Annual Statement of the [English] Bar Council, 1915, p. 14, approved by the then Attorney-General.
[91] See Solicitors (Scotland) (Advertising) Practice Rules, 1987, in *Parliament House Book*, Div. F.
[92] *Scottish Law Agents Society v. Lawrence*, 1940 S.C. 196.
[93] *Gillespie & Sons v. Gardner*, 1909 S.C. 1053; *Aitken v. Campbell's Trs.*, 1909 S.C. 1217.
[94] This is subject to the rule permitting multi-disciplinary partnerships.
[95] On legal aid, see p. 402, *infra*.

though he might prefer to act on the other side or not to be involved in that case at all. The duty to defend on a criminal charge takes priority over a competing engagement in a civil case.[96]

Other members of the profession must be treated as persons of honour and not abused, ridiculed or condemned, and undertakings, promises and assurances given one to another must be fulfilled. Thus, if counsel's fees are paid by the client to the solicitor, it is a debt of honour to remit them to counsel. Again any ill feeling between parties should not be allowed to affect or influence their advisers in their conduct towards one another or the parties.

Duties to the Client

The lawyer's first duty to his client is to perform with requisite skill and due diligence the business entrusted to him.[97] The relationship of advocate and client is that of mandatary and mandant and the fee paid is theoretically an honorarium, and is not recoverable by law. The relationship of solicitor and client is that of agent and principal, the fee is impliedly due under the contract and it is recoverable by law.[98] Beyond the general duty to perform business with due skill, care and diligence it is difficult to state duties in detail.

It is not, however, a lawyer's duty to do whatever may enable him to win his client's case, but only to utilise any remedy, claim or defence which is permitted by law and which may be used honourably and honestly, and he is entitled, and indeed bound, to prevent his client from taking any action which he himself ought not to take, such as fabricating or suppressing evidence or suborning witnesses. If a client does anything disgraceful or improper the lawyer should terminate his employment.[99]

The fiduciary character of the relationship between solicitor and client necessarily imposes restrictions on their transacting one with another in view of the possible conflict of interests. Contracts between them are liable to reduction, as contrary to public policy, and in any such transaction the client should be advised by another and independent solicitor.[1] Even gifts[2] or bequests[3] to the solicitor are scrutinised closely and suspiciously, while he may not make any secret profit at the client's expense in dealing with third parties.[4] So, too, if a solicitor acts as a trustee he may not, unless expressly authorised by the trust deed or all the beneficiaries,[5] take any remuneration for his services. Nor may a lawyer

---

[96] *cf.* Denning, *The Road to Justice*, 53.
[97] *Bell v. Ogilvie* (1863) 2 M. 336. For details, see Begg on *Law Agents*, Chaps. 18 and 24.
[98] *cf. Rondel v. Worsley* [1969] 1 A.C. 191.
[99] Bankt., IV, 3, 13.
[1] *McPherson's Trustees v. Watt* (1877) 5 R.(H.L.) 9.
[2] *Long v. Taylor* (1824) 2 Sh.App. 233.
[3] *Grieve v. Cunningham* (1869) 8 M. 317.
[4] *Tyrrell v. Bank of London* (1862) 10 H.L.C. 26.
[5] *Lewis's Trustees v. Pirie*, 1912 S.C. 574. This even extends to the solicitor-trustee's partner: *Mitchell v. Burness* (1878) 5 R. 1124.

divulge secrets or confidences obtained during employment or when acting subsequently for others, utilise knowledge gained in a previous professional connection.

Again it is quite improper to accept instructions from a client if there is any conflict of interest between that client and another client. Accordingly, one advocate or solicitor should not act for two persons whose interests do, or even may, conflict.[6] Thus it is forbidden for one solicitor to act for both buyer and seller of property; he can properly protect the interests of one or other only. He cannot act for both in settling the price.[7] If he acts for both lender and borrower (which is allowable only exceptionally) he is responsible to both parties for any failure in duty[8] and may be liable for recommending a security which turns out to be inadequate, quite apart from any failure in the legal validity of the security.[9]

Privilege

Neither advocate nor solicitor can be obliged to disclose information obtained by him in his professional capacity unless the client consents,[10] and it is a breach of professional confidence to do so voluntarily. Memorials to, and the opinions of, counsel are protected.[11] But anything which is part of the events in a crime or fraud is not protected.[12] The privilege certainly covers communications having reference to a contemplated action or an action in progress and probably also all communications made in a professional capacity, whether or not any dispute has yet arisen.[13]

Advocates and solicitors are absolutely privileged in their written and oral pleading in court, in commenting on the evidence and the conduct of parties, and in all other matters relevant to the cause,[14] while litigants have qualified privilege only and will accordingly be liable to an action for defamation if personal malice can be proved.[15] But counsel and solicitors

---

[6] *Oastler v. Dill, Smillie & Wilson* (1886) 14 R. 12; *MacClure, Naismith, Brodie & MacFarlane* v. *Stewart* (1887) 15 R.(H.L.) 1; *Ellis's Trustees v. Ellis* (1898) 1 F. 4 (two parties to a special case); *Stewart v. McLean, Baird & Neilson*, 1915 S.C. 13; *Dunlop's Trustees v. Farquharson*, 1955 S.L.T.(Notes) 80. See further, Solicitors (Scotland) Practice Rules 1986 in *Parliament House Book*.

[7] *McPherson's Trustees v. Watt* (1877) 5 R.(H.L.) 9.

[8] *McLeod v. McDonald* (1835) 13 S. 287; *Haldane v. Donaldson* (1840) 1 Rob.App. 226; *Oastler, supra.*

[9] *Cleland v. Brownlie, Watson & Beckett* (1892) 20 R. 152; *Wernham v. McLean, Baird & Neilson*, 1925 S.C. 407.

[10] *Forteith v. Earl of Fyfe* (1821) 2 Mur. 467; *Noble v. Scott* (1843) 5 D. 723; *Hay v. Edinburgh & Glasgow Bank* (1858) 20 D. 701.

[11] Bell, *Prin.* § 2254; *Thomson's Trustees v. Clark* (1823) 2 S. 262; *Clark v. Spence* (1824) 3 Mur. 454.

[12] *McCowan v. Wright* (1852) 15 D. 229, 494.

[13] *Ibid.*; *Munro v. Fraser* (1858) 21 D. 103.

[14] *Drew v. Mackenzie* (1862) 24 D. 649, 662; *Williamson v. Umphray and Robertson* (1890) 17 R. 905.

[15] *Williamson, supra.*

are liable to censure for improper or insulting conduct in court and the Court of Session may punish by censure, suspension or even deprivation of the office of advocate.[16] Counsel and agent are also privileged in respect of matters alleged or put in pleadings with the authority and on the instructions of the client, so long as pertinent to the matter in issue.[17]

Professional Negligence

Professional negligence is the failure to take the care, show the knowledge and skill, or use the diligence to be expected of a reasonably competent practitioner. It was formerly thought that a solicitor could be,[18] but an advocate could not be, liable for professional negligence, because in the advocate's case he was a mandatary and could not sue for his fees.[19] It has now been held in England[20] that a barrister or solicitor as advocate is no longer immune from liability for negligence in the conduct and management of court business, but that he may be liable for negligent opinion, advice, drawing of pleadings or other pre-trial or non-litigious work. These decisions would probably be followed in Scotland. In either case the ground of action may be breach of an implied term of the contract to provide services, or harm caused by negligence. It is accordingly for advocates and solicitors to be covered by indemnity insurance against claims for professional negligence.

PROFESSIONAL FEES

An advocate's fees are, as in the Roman law, regarded as honoraria, not as fees, and used to be presumed to have been paid at the time he was instructed.[21] There is no scale of counsel's fees, except for work done on legal aid, and fees are subject to negotiation with counsel's clerk. The practice used to be for the solicitor to send the appropriate fee with each letter instructing a particular step to be taken,[22] but fees were sometimes noted and paid in a lump sum afterwards.[22] There are no fixed scales of fees for counsel though in practice the fees for various standard types of business are conventionally fixed within limits, depending largely on the

---

[16] A.S. Dec. 21, 1649; July 26, 1699; June 23, 1756.

[17] *Ramsey v. Nairne* (1833) 11 S. 1033. *cf. Bayne v. Macgregor* (1862) 24 D. 1126; (1863) 1 M. 615.

[18] *Frame v. Hart* (1839) McL. & R. 595; *Haldane v. Donaldson* (1840) 1 Robin. 226; *Robertson v. Fleming* (1861) 4 Macq. 167; *Simpson v. Kidstons, Watson, Turnbull & Co.*, 1913, 1 S.L.T. 74; *Robertson v. Bannigan*, 1965 S.C. 20; *Midland Bank Trust Co. v. Hett. Stubbs & Kemp* [1978] 3 All E.R. 571; *Bristol and West Building Society v. Aitken Nairn, W.S.* 2000 S.L.T. 763.

[19] *Landell v. Purves* (1845) 4 Bell 46; *Swinfen v. Lord Chelmsford* (1860) 5 H. & N. 890; *Batchelor v. Pattison and Mackersy* (1876) 3 R. 914.

[20] *Hall v. Simons* [2000] 3 W.L.R. 543, disapproving *Rondel v. Worsley* [1969] 1 A.C. 191; *Saif Ali v. Mitchell* [1980] A.C. 198.

[21] *Batchelor v. Pattison and Mackersy* (1876) 3 R. 914.

[22] Mackay's *Practice*, I, 115.

value and importance of the cause, on its complexity, and on the time involved.[23] There is no rule in Scotland that the fee of junior counsel should be two-thirds of the fee of any senior counsel with whom he is instructed to appear.[24] It is always open to a client to pay counsel more than the conventional fee, though a successful litigant, if awarded expenses against his opponent, will be allowed by the Auditor of Court to recover from his opponent not what he may have paid but what was reasonably necessary in the circumstances to secure the services of competent counsel.[25]

Fees cannot be recovered by action since they are honoraria,[26] unless in the exceptional case where a solicitor has received payment of his professional account from the client and has failed to transmit counsel's fee to him,[27] or in the case of a salary as standing counsel, which may be sued for.[28] An advocate is probably entitled to retain a fee sent to him even though he has not had to render any services.[29] It is illegal to take a proportion of the subject of a litigation in lieu of a fee, or to buy up any debatable rights which are still in dependence,[30] but quite legitimate to act on the basis that there will be no remuneration unless in the event of success.[31]

In 1971 a new system was adopted. A company, Faculty Services Ltd., was formed to obtain payment of counsel's fees.[32] When work has been done, it sends to the instructing solicitor a note of the work done and the fee counsel proposes to charge. If solicitor and counsel's clerk are unable to agree on a fee, the Auditor of the Court of Session adjudicates on what is a reasonable fee. In case of failure to pay counsel's fee the Dean of Faculty may request the Law Society to take disciplinary action against the solicitor.

In the case of the solicitor on the other hand, fees are in the same category as the fees of other professional men in that the fact of employment implies an undertaking by the client to pay professional fees

---

[23] For examples, see cases in *Faculty Digest, s.v.* "Expenses." It should be observed that, overall, counsel are not highly paid for their work and much of it, particularly of the kind given to young junior counsel, is very poorly renumerated, and there are many instances where counsel gets no fee at all, or only a token fee. See also, Lord Macmillan, *A Man of Law's Tale,* pp. 130–140 (an exceptionally successful advocate).

[24] Ruling by Dean of Faculty [1970] C.L.Y. 3405.

[25] See *Elas v. Scottish Motor Traction Co.*, 1950 S.C. 570; *Macnaughton v. Macnaughton*, 1949 S.C. 42.

[26] *Batchelor v. Pattison and Mackersy* (1876) 3 R. 914.

[27] *Cullen v. Buchanan* (1862) 24 D. 1132; *Keay v. A.B.* (1837) 15 S. 748n.

[28] *McKenzie v. Town of Burntisland* (1728) Mor. 11421.

[29] Mackay, *Manual of Court of Session Practice*, 28.

[30] Land Purchase Act 1594, c. 220.

[31] *X Insurance Co. v. A. and B.*, 1936 S.C. 225, 238–239, 250–251.

[32] See 1971 S.L.T.(News) 197; Scheme for Accounting for and Recovery of Counsel' Fees (1987).

at the ordinary rate[33] and they may be recovered by action.[34] Fees in most cases are based in the case of conveyancing and property transactions, generally, on a percentage of the value of the property concerned, and in the case of litigious business, on the complexity and time occupied. The client is always entitled to have the account remitted for taxation to the Auditor of the Court of Session or of the local sheriff court before paying it.[35] Solicitors are also, of course, entitled to recover all outlays and expenses properly incurred on account of the client.[36] A solicitor may charge less than is permitted by the Table of Fees and he may act gratuitously for a poor client, taking his chance of recovering his fees and outlays from any award of damages and expenses made against the opposite party.

It is doubtful whether the Roman law rule of *pactum de quota litis* (the prohibition on a legal adviser taking as a fee a share of the property in dispute) is applicable in Scotland,[37] but the principle seems to be followed, as the practice is highly undesirable.[38] But a non-professional man may advance money to carry on a litigation on the basis of receiving a share of any sum recovered. An advocate and the person instructing him may agree to undertake a litigation on a speculative basis, *i.e.* no win, no fee, and in that case may agree that, if the litigation is successful, the fee shall be increased by an agreed percentage, not exceeding such limit as the court may prescribe.[39]

Transacting with Clients

A solicitor is not debarred from transacting with a client so long as he is not acting as legal adviser in that same transaction, but he must show that he made full disclosure and gave full value,[40] and it is desirable to have the client separately advised by a completely independent solicitor. A bequest in a will to the solicitor who drew up the will may be valid,[41] but the onus is on the solicitor to show that the testator was in full possession of his faculties and made the bequest freely and in knowledge of its effect.[42] If a solicitor has been instructed by a client to find a purchaser for property, he

---

[33] Bell, *Prin.*, § 226; *Manson v. Baillie* (1855) 2 Macq. 80; *Goodsir v. Carruthers* (1858) 20 D. 1141; *Bell v. Ogilvie* (1863) 2 M. 336; *Winton v. Airth* (1868) 6 M. 1095.

[34] *Bell v. Ogilvie* (1863) 2 M. 336.

[35] Rules of the Court of Session 1994, Chap. 42, as amended; Act of Sederunt (Fees of Solicitors in the Sheriff Court) 1993 (S.I. 1993 No. 3080, as amended).

[36] *Carrick v. Manford* (1854) 16 D. 410; *Dingwall's Trs. v. Earl of Kintore* (1862) 24 D. 427.

[37] Contrast Stair, I, 10, 8; Bell, *Prin.*, § 36; with *Johnston v. Rome* (1831) 9 S. 364.

[38] *Farrell v. Arnott* (1857) 19 D. 1000; Land Purchase Act 1594, c. 220.

[39] Law Reform (Miscellaneous Provisions) (Scotland) Act 1990, s. 36; similarly with solicitors; Solicitors (Scotland) Act 1980, s. 61A, added by 1990 Act, s. 36.

[40] *McPherson's Trustees v. Watt* (1877) 5 R.(H.L.) 9; *Cleland v. Morrison* (1878) 6 R. 156; *Gillespie & Sons v. Gardner*, 1909 S.C. 1053; *Aitken v. Campbell's Trustees*, 1909 S.C. 1217.

[41] *Rooney v. Cormack* (1895) 22 R. 761.

[42] *Weir v. Grace* (1899) 2 F.(H.L.) 30; *Rigg's Exrx. v. Urquhart* (1902) 10 S.L.T. 503; *Stewart v. Maclaren*, 1920 S.C.(H.L.) 148; *Matthew v. Law Society of Scotland*, 1998 S.C. 306.

may not purchase himself without the client's express authority and without divesting himself of the character of agent for sale.[43] The same applies in a case of agency to purchase. Again, the notarial execution of a will by a solicitor on behalf of a client is invalid if the solicitor or a partner of his takes any benefit thereunder or is nominated as executor or trustee.[44]

All these limitations arise from the policy of the law that there must be no conflict of interest between legal adviser and client and there must be no suspicion of the one gaining improper benefit for himself at the other's expense.[45]

Accounts

Solicitors are under strict obligations with regard to the care of clients' money which comes into their hands in the course of their actings on behalf of the clients. Under the Solicitors' (Scotland) Accounts Rules 1992,[46] made by the Law Society of Scotland, money in excess of £50 received from or held on behalf of a client must be paid into a client account, and books and accounts must be kept showing all dealings with the money of each separate client. The Law Society is empowered to institute the investigation of any solicitor's books by an accountant to discover whether the rules are being complied with.

Regular and accurate books must be kept and business accounts, which should be rendered periodically or, in the case of employment for one transaction, at the conclusion of that transaction, must be fair transcripts of the entries therein,[47] and give all the information necessary to enable the client and the auditor to examine it.[48]

The Law Society has power[49] to withdraw the practising certificate of a solicitor who is failing to comply with the Accounts Rules. Every solicitor must balance his books at least once every practice year and within six months thereof deliver an accountant's certificate that the books appear to be in order.[50]

Provision is made[51] for a guarantee fund from which to compensate persons who suffer pecuniary loss by reason of dishonesty on the part of a solicitor. It is improper to do anything which can reasonably be regarded as touting, advertising or calculated to attract business unfairly, or to share profits with an unqualified person, with certain exceptions.[52]

---

[43] *Cunningham v. Lee* (1874) 2 R. 83.
[44] *Ferrie v. Ferrie's Trustees* (1863) 1 M. 291; *Finlay v. Finlay's Trustees*, 1948 S.C. 16.
[45] See further, cases discussed in Begg on *Law Agents*, Chap. 21.
[46] Printed in *Parliament House Book*, Div. D.
[47] *Stewart v. Scott* (1844) 6 D. 889.
[48] *Grant v. Alcock* (1870) Guthrie's Sel.Shf.Ct.Cas. 11.
[49] Solicitors (Scotland) Act 1980, s. 40. See also *Hill v. Law Society of Scotland*, 1996 S.C. 491.
[50] *Ibid*. s. 37; Solicitors' (Scotland) Accountants' Certificate Rules 1964, amended 1966.
[51] *Ibid*. s. 43, and Scottish Solicitors' Guarantee Fund Rules 1951, printed in *Parliament House Book*, Div. D.
[52] Solicitors' (Scotland) Practice Rules 1964.

Expenses in Litigation

Every civil court has an inherent common-law discretionary right to award expenses in any cause which comes before it, unless that right has been qualified or abrogated by statute.[53] In practice a pursuer usually includes an express conclusion for expenses in his summons, the justification for this being that he has been put to the expense and trouble of litigation by the defender's failure spontaneously to satisfy the pursuer's requests. The award of expenses is in the discretion of the court and accordingly, while an appeal may be taken on the question of expenses, an appellate court will not interfere unless it be shown that the judge making the award had erred in principle.

While the award of expenses is always in the discretion of the court, the court usually exercises its discretion in accordance with principles worked out in previous cases, and a large volume of case-law has developed on the subject.[54] Expenses can be awarded even if not claimed. Counsel moves for an award of expenses when judgment has been given after any hearing. In the sheriff court the sheriff may certify the case as justifying the employment of counsel.[55]

Accordingly, as a rule, expenses will be awarded to the successful party against the unsuccessful party, but sometimes expenses are modified or refused, sometimes no expenses are found due to or by either party and, commonly in cases arising out of a will or the disposal of an estate, all parties' expenses are made payable out of the estate. There are many special rules affecting particular categories of litigants and particular kinds of cases.

To say, however, that the court may award the successful party expenses does not mean that he will be reimbursed by the unsuccessful party to the full extent of his expenditure in the litigation. Where expenses are awarded the solicitor for the party awarded expenses must make up his itemised account and submit it to the Auditor of the Court of Session[56] for taxation. The purpose of taxation is to strike out and disallow all items of expenditure considered to have been unnecessary or excessive for the pursuit of the claim. Hence, if a party chooses to employ an unnecessary number of counsel, or pay higher fees than are warranted by ordinary practice, the extra expense will not be allowed against the other party. The auditor will allow only such expenses as are necessary for conducting litigation in a proper manner but with due regard to economy. Parties' solicitors may attend before the auditor and contend that certain items of expenditure were justifiable, and appeal may be taken to the court against the auditor's decision.

---

[53] *Rooney v. Cormack* (1895) 23 R. 11; *Thomson v. Kerr* (1901) 3 F. 355.

[54] See Maclaren on *Expenses*, and cases in the Digests, *s.v.* "Expenses."

[55] Compare *Smith v. B.R. Engineering*, 1985 S.L.T. 463 with *McPherson v. B.R. Board*, 1985 S.L.T. 467.

[56] Or, in the sheriff court, the Auditor of the Sheriff Court.

In taxing an account, the auditor may proceed on any one of three bases, expenses as between party and party,[57] which allows only such expenses as are absolutely necessary for conducting the litigation in a proper manner with due regard to economy; expenses between solicitor and client chargeable against the opposite side, which is rather more generous; and expenses between solicitor and own client, which is still more generous and allows all expenses reasonably incurred by the solicitor for the protection of his client's interest, even though such expenses could not be recovered from the opposite party, and any extraordinary expenses specially authorised by the client.[58]

LEGAL AID AND ADVICE

A system of free legal aid for the poor has existed in Scotland since 1424.[59] Latterly the practice was for the Faculty of Advocates annually to appoint a number of advocates as counsel for the poor, while the W.S. and S.S.C. Societies appointed agents for the poor. A committee of reporters on *probabilis causa litigandi* considered applications, which had to be supported by certificates of poverty, and could admit to the benefit of the poor's roll, which conferred the privileges of obtaining the services of counsel and solicitors for the poor gratuitously and the right to litigate without payment of any court dues.[60] This scheme was superseded in the civil courts by the establishment of the Legal Aid Scheme in 1950,[61] intended to make legal aid more readily available for persons of small or moderate means. The general administration of the scheme was in the hands of the Law Society of Scotland.

Legal aid is now managed by the Scottish Legal Aid Board.[62] It consists of 11 to 15 members appointed by the First Minister, one to be chairman, and including at least two advocates, at least two solicitors and at least one person having experience of the procedure and practice of the courts.[63] It administers the Scottish Legal Aid Fund from which are paid sums to

---

[57] When expenses are awarded without qualifications by the court, the taxation is between party and party.

[58] Apart from the question of paying another party's expenses, every client is entitled to have his solicitor's account of judicial expenses taxed by the auditor and need not pay any more then the taxed amount.

[59] Stoddard, *Law and Practice of Legal Aid in Scotland*; "Short History of Legal Aid in Scotland," 1979 J.R. 170.

[60] See further, Maclaren, *Court of Session Practice*, 274 *et seq.*; Dobie, *Sheriff Court Practice*, 491.

[61] Legal Aid and Solicitors (Scotland) Act 1949, later amended.

[62] Legal Aid (Scotland) Act 1986, amended by the Legal Aid Act 1988, Sched. 4. Numerous sets of regulations are made under the Act. For those see *Parliament House Book*, Div. G. Legal aid costs about £100 million a year, largely in criminal cases. The major defect of the system is that the upper limits of eligibility in civil cases are so low that only people of very moderate means can benefit. For most people litigation is a dangerously risky luxury.

[63] 1986 Act, s. 1 and Sched. 1.

counsel and solicitors for fees and outlays, expenses awarded to litigants and other payments.

Advice and assistance are available to a person whose disposable income does not exceed a stated sum, or if he is in receipt of certain social security benefits, and his disposable capital does not exceed a small sum. Regulations may prescribe for assistance by way of representation in certain cases at various stages. In certain cases clients must make contributions.[64]

Civil legal aid means representation by a solicitor and, if necessary, counsel in most ordinary and special jurisdiction civil courts in proceedings other than those concerned with defamation or verbal injury, election petitions and simplified divorce applications, if on application made to the Board it is satisfied that the applicant has *probabilis causa litigandi* and it appears that it is reasonable that he should receive legal aid.[65] It is available to persons with less than stated sums of disposable income and disposable capital.[66] Sums recovered as expenses by a legally assisted person are paid to the Fund, and legally assisted persons may be required by the Board to contribute to the Fund, as determined by the Board. The liability of an assisted person under an award of expenses in favour of an unassisted person is not to exceed the amount which in the opinion of the court is reasonable for him to pay, and certain assets are to be ignored. The court may make an award out of the Fund to an unassisted person of any of the expenses incurred by him, but it must consider an award of expenses against the legally assisted person.[67]

Criminal legal aid applies in all courts and is available in summary proceedings after the first diet at which the accused has tendered a plea of not guilty. It consists of representation by solicitor and, if need be, by counsel, and by a solicitor at an identification parade. It is available automatically for identification parades, in cases under solemn procedure until an application for legal aid has been determined or he is admitted to bail or committed until liberated in due course of law, and in cases under summary procedure, if he is in custody or has been liberated by the police on an undertaking to appear, until the first diet, or if he has pled guilty, until his case is disposed of, or if he is in custody under summary procedure and has pled not guilty, until his application for legal aid has been determined, and in certain other cases.[68]

---

[64] *Ibid.*, ss. 6–12. See *Drummond & Co., W.S. v. Scottish Legal Aid Board* 1991 S.L.T. 758.

[65] On relevant factors, see *McTear v. Scottish Legal Aid Board,* 1997 S.L.T. 108.

[66] Attempting to obtain legal aid by fraud is criminal at common law and under the Act: *McGhee v. H.M. Advocate*, 1987 S.C.C.R. 702.

[67] *Ibid.*, ss. 13–20. See *MacDonald v. Galson Estates*, 1990 S.C.L.R. 128. As to taxation of account see *Milne, Mackinnon and Peterkins v. Scottish Legal Aid Board*, 1989 S.C.L.R. 464.

[68] *Ibid.*, ss. 21–22.

It is available on application to the court in prosecutions under solemn procedure or where the court is considering a first sentence of imprisonment.[69]

The Scottish Legal Aid Board has to prepare annually a duty plan for every district court and every sheriff court of first instance, providing that at all times there will be available duty solicitors for attending identification parades, and advising persons in custody and acting for them in the first instance.

The court cannot review the decision of a sheriff or magistrate to refuse legal aid merely because it thought that the judge was wrong.[70]

In summary proceedings it is available on application to the Board if it is satisfied that refusal would cause undue hardship.[71]

It is available also in criminal appeals on application to the Board.[72] The Board may employ solicitors to give advice and assistance, act for persons receiving legal aid or provide any of various services.[73] The Public Defence Solicitors' Office is an office of solicitors employed by the Scottish Legal Aid Board to provide summary criminal legal assistance in Edinburgh Sheriff and District Courts. Certain accused persons must use this service unless a waiver of direction has first been obtained.

Legal aid is also available in certain proceedings relating to children.[74] A person to whom legal aid is granted may himself select the solicitor to advise or act for him and the counsel, but the Faculty of Advocates or the Law Society may exclude any advocate or solicitor from acting in a legal aid case. When legal aid is granted the solicitor or counsel may not take any payment from the client but is paid out of the Fund fees and outlays at prescribed rates.[75]

CONTEMPT OF COURT

Contempt of court includes a wide variety of acts insulting to the court, flouting its authority, or prejudicial to the fair administration of justice.[76] It includes disorderly or unseemly behaviour in court by members of the public, witnesses, parties or their agents or counsel,[77] including refusal to answer competent questions[78] or prevarication by a witness,[79] though not

---

[69] *Ibid.*, s. 23.

[70] *McLachlan, Petr.*, 1987 S.C.C.R. 195.

[71] *Ibid.*, s. 24. It is competent by petition for judicial review to challenge the Board's refusal of legal aid in a case under s. 24: *K. v. Scottish Legal Aid Board*, 1989 S.L.T. 617.

[72] *Ibid.*, s. 25.

[73] *Ibid.*, s. 26.

[74] *Ibid.*, ss. 29–30.

[75] *Ibid.*, ss. 31–32.

[76] See also Contempt of Court Act 1981.

[77] *cf. Morris v. The Crown Office* [1970] 1 ALL E.R. 1079.

[78] *Kerr* (1822) Shaw Just. 68; *Smith*, 1987 S.C.C.R. 726.

[79] *Macleod v. Speirs* (1884) 11 R.(J.) 26; *Wylie v. H.M. Advocate,* 1966 S.L.T. 149.

necessarily an inadvertent failure to attend court.[80] It includes also attempts to exert improper influence on the course of justice, including verbal attacks on judges, intimidation of witnesses[81] and particularly the publication of reports, articles or letters in the press or elsewhere which may tend to prejudice the fair trial of any pending cause[82] (though it is not contempt to report,[83] or comment subsequently, even in unfavourable terms, on, the merits or conduct of proceedings then completed)[84] or the publication of pleadings or documents in cases before the court.[85] Contempt also covers disobedience to orders of the court, such as failure to obey a citation as a witness,[86] breach of a solemnly given undertaking to the court,[87] a letter implying refusal to obey a court order,[88] and refusal to give up or state the whereabouts of children.[89] A breach of interdict is not properly a contempt of court but is a distinct offence of impeding the course of justice.[90]

The court itself must determine whether conduct amounts to a contempt of its authority[91] and contempt committed in face of the court is usually dealt with summarily by the judge himself. The power to punish contempt is inherent in every court, civil or criminal, superior or inferior,[92] and may be exercised by admonition, fine or imprisonment, or in the case of legal practitioners, suspension from office.[93] It should be exercised with care and discretion.[94] Sentences for contempt may be appealed to the Court of Session,[95] High Court of Justiciary,[96] or House of Lords.[97]

FURTHER READING

Boulton: *Conduct and Etiquette at the Bar*, 6th ed.

---

[80] *Pirie v. Hawthorn*, 1962 J.C. 69; *Morrison v. Jessop*, 1989 S.L.T. 86.

[81] *Forbes v. Weir* (1897) 5 S.L.T. 194.

[82] *Watson v. Murray* (1820) Shaw Just. 9; *Henderson v. Laing* (1824) 3 S. 384; *McLauchlan v. Carson* (1826) 5 S. 147; *Miller v. Mitchell* (1835) 13 S. 644; *Smith v. Mitchell* (1835) 14 S. 172; *Smith v. Ritchie* (1892) 20 R.(J.) 52; *Cowie v. Outram*, 1912 J.C. 14; *MacAlister v. Associated Newspapers*, 1954 S.L.T. 14; *Atkins v. London Weekend Television Ltd.*, 1978 J.C. 48. See also *Att.-Gen. v. Times Newspapers* [1973] 3 All E.R. 54; *Att.-Gen. v. London Weekend Television* [1972] 3 All E.R. 1146; *Adams*, 1987 S.C.C.R. 650; *H.M. Advocate v. News Group Newspapers*, 1989 S.C.C.R. 156.

[83] But see Judicial Proceedings (Regulation of Reports) Act 1926.

[84] *Glasgow Corp. v. Hedderwick*, 1918 S.C. 639.

[85] *Richardson v. Wilson* (1879) 7 R. 237; *Young v. Armour*, 1921, 1 S.L.T. 211.

[86] *H.M. Advocate v. Bell*, 1936 J.C. 89.

[87] *Graham v. Younger*, 1955 J.C. 28.

[88] *Simpson, Boath & Co.*, 1981 S.C. 153.

[89] *Leys v. Leys* (1886) 13 R. 1223; *Guthrie v. Guthrie* (1906) 8 F. 545.

[90] *Johnson v. Grant*, 1923 S.C. 789; see also *Stark's Trs. v. Duncan* (1906) 8 F. 429.

[91] *McLeod v. Lewis J.P.s* (1892) 20 R. 218.

[92] Stair, IV, 36, 7; Ersk., I, 2, 8.

[93] *Hamilton v. Anderson* (1856) 18 D. 1003.

[94] *Milburn*, 1946 S.C. 301, 315; *Royle v. Gray*, 1973 S.L.T. 31.

[95] *Hamilton, supra*; *Munro v. Matheson* (1877) 5 R. 308; *Milburn*, 1946 S.C. 301.

[96] *Macleod v. Speirs* (1884) 11 R.(J.) 26; *Graham v. Younger*, 1955 J.C. 28; *Cordiner*, 1973 S.L.T. 125.

[97] *Hamilton v. Caledonian Ry.* (1850) 7 Bell 272.

Cardozo: *Nature of the Judicial Process.*
      Growth of the Law.
      The Paradoxes of Legal Science.
Drinker: *Legal Ethics.*
Forsyth: *Hortensius: Historical Essay on the Duties of an Advocate.*
Halsbury's *Laws of England*, tit. "Barrister."
Hannay: *The College of Justice.*
Henderson Begg: *Treatise on Law Agents,* 2nd ed.
Hilbery: *Duty and Art in Advocacy.*
Laws of Scotland, tit. "Legal Profession".
Mackay: *Practice of the Court of Session*, Vol. I.
MacPhail: *Sheriff Court Practice.*
Muirhead: "From Attorneys to Solicitors," 68 S.L.R. 25.
Phillips: *Professional Ethics for Scottish Solicitors.*
Singleton: *Conduct at the Bar and Some Problems of Advocacy.*
Slesser: *The Art of Judgment.*
      The Judicial Office and Other Matters.
Stoddart: *Law and Practice of Legal Aid in Scotland.*
Wasserstrom: *The Judicial Decision.*
W.S. Society: *History of the Society of Writers to H.M. Signet*, 1936.

CHAPTER 10

THE SOURCES OF SCOTS LAW

THE phrase "sources of the law" has several meanings which have to be carefully distinguished.[1] There are, firstly, historical sources, which are the events and incidents in legal history which have given rise to the principle or rule in question. Thus historical sources of various rules may be that the rule was laid down by Justinian and adopted into Scots law,[2] or enacted by Parliament in response to certain needs of that time, or developed by the courts over a particular period.[3] Common historical sources include ancient customs, the Roman law, the Bible and the Christian church, the canon law, feudal law, the medieval law merchant and maritime law, foreign (including English) rules and many of the major events in constitutional and legal history. Every principle and rule of law has an historical source somewhere, even though it may not be known, but the principle or rule does not draw any validity or binding force from that source. The historical source merely explains when and how that rule came to be established. It frequently helps also to explain why the rule took a particular form.

Secondly, every principle and rule has a social, political, economic, moral or religious source in that some fact or set or state of facts, moral, political, economic or other, have provoked or given rise to that rule.[4] Thus some rules of law were enacted or developed for social reasons, such as the legislation on race relations, others for political reasons, such as the law regulating trade unions, others for economic reasons, such as the law of companies, others for moral reasons, such as those relating to punishment of cruelty and neglect of children, and so on. Some rules have been made law because they have been thought to be "human rights" of individuals.[5] Again, every principle and rule has such a philosophical source, though it may be forgotten or difficult to discover, but again the philosophical source does not give the rule any legal validity but merely gives a justification for the rule. That justification, moreover, may later

---

[1] See further, Salmond, *Jurisprudence,* Chap. 6; Allen, *Law in the Making,* Introduction; Pound, *Jurisprudence,* Chap. 16; Smith, "Sources of Scots Law" (1904) 16 J.R. 375; Dove Wilson, "Sources of Scots Law" (1892) 4 J.R. 1.

[2] See, *e.g. Central Motors v. Cessnock Garage Co.*, 1925 S.C. 796.

[3] Many examples of historical sources of the latter two kinds may be found in Chap. 4.

[4] See, *e.g.* the Incest Act 1567, adopting the substance of Leviticus, c. 18, into Scots law.

[5] Human Rights Act 1998, ss. 1 and 11. See further, Perry, *The Idea of Human Rights.*

disappear or seem unsound or inadequate to a later generation, but the rule is not thereby abrogated.[6]

Thirdly, the statements in enactments, decisions, books and documents and the usages of persons from which a court may derive a principle for the decision of a case are sometimes spoken of as material sources, and again every principle or rule has such a source, but these are better described as the materials for formulating a decision and which determine the content of a principle or rule derived from them. Thus if a judge adopts a principle from Roman law or a textbook, that is the material source of his decision; it supplies the material for his decision.

It would be better if the term "source" were not used in all these senses and instead one talked of historical origins of rules, philosophical bases of rules and material grounds of rules.

Legal or Formal Sources from which are drawn Authoritative Precepts of Law

The only true "sources" of legal principles and rules are the legal or formal sources.[7] The legal or formal sources of the law are the answer to the question: where do I find authoritative statements of the principles and rules which the courts must apply to determine my rights and duties, my remedies and liabilities, in various circumstances? Legal validity, and authority compelling obedience, attach to a principle or rule of law only by virtue of its being drawn from a legal source, one recognised by the legal system itself as a reservoir of valid authoritative and binding principles and rules of law, and it is with these legally authoritative sources that this chapter is concerned. It is to these legal sources only that one may resort to find a rule or principle of law for the application to and solution of a legal controversy or problem raised by certain facts. To put it another way: how does one distinguish a precept of law from a precept of non-law? The answer is that the first issues from a legal source, the second from what is not recognised as a legal source. Thus if a precept of conduct such as: You must give up your seat on a bus to a lady, can be shown to be drawn from a legal source, it is a precept of law; if it is drawn from a non-legal source such as generally accepted good manners, it is a precept of non-law. The importance of identifying the legal sources of principles and rules of law is that this furnishes the criterion of recognition and identification of valid statements of law.

The ultimate legal source of all Scots law, that which confers the authority on all principles and rules to make them determinative of rights and decisive of controversies, is the power of the state, that is, of the

---

[6] See further, Dicey, *Lectures on the Relation between Law and Public Opinion in the Nineteenth Century, passim.*

[7] They are called formal because they give form to statements of law.

legally organised community of the United Kingdom. The state issues authoritative statements of principles and rules through its legislature and courts, and the immediate practical sources of principles and rules recognised in Scots law as legally authoritative are the Treaties establishing the European Communities and rules made thereunder,[8] the statutes of the former Parliaments of Scotland and of Great Britain, of the Parliament of the United Kingdom and of the Scottish Parliament, subordinate legislation authorised by such statutes, judicial decisions of the superior courts of the United Kingdom, certain books recognised by the courts as of authority, accepted customs, and principles of equity and certain other extraneous sources. No other sources give rise to principles and rules having legal validity and authority recognised by the courts of this country. The recognised forms of law in Scotland are accordingly legislation, case law, statements in certain recognised books, accepted customs, and principles drawn from equity and other extraneous sources.

The facts that rules embodied in statute law and case law themselves have historical origins, philosophical bases, and material grounds are matters of interest and concern to historical and philosophical legal study, but do not by themselves confer any validity or authority on the rules. Thus the condemnation of the slave trade gave rise to valid and authoritative rules of law only when and because Parliament proscribed it by statute, not because of the historical steps towards, or the moral justifications for, the abolition of slavery. The principle that an employer must take reasonable care for the safety of his employees is a valid principle only because the superior courts have said so in many cases, not because such a principle is socially, economically or morally justifiable. Moreover, the sources rank in the order stated, in that a provision of any one of these kinds of authority supersedes and overrules an inconsistent provision drawn from one of the other kinds ranking lower in the list.[9] EU law overrules United Kingdom law, even statutes; statutory provision overrules a judicial decision; a judicial decision overrules a statement in a book and so on. The legal sources, moreover, are the only sources from which new principles or rules can be added to the body of law.

Sources of Knowledge of the Law—Legal Literature

These legal sources must be sharply distinguished from legal literature, books on the law. Books on law are, in general, *not* authoritative sources of the law on any matter but only means of our knowledge of the law, to which we turn to discover not what the principles of law are, but what the

---

[8] These were incorporated into U.K. law by the European Communities Act 1972 and amending Acts.

[9] The ranking has changed in the course of time. Stair ranked custom higher than legislation. Legislation has risen in the ranking since the early 19th century. EU law only entered the ranking from 1973.

author of the book believes the principles and rules to be, having regard to the statutes and cases which appear to him applicable to his subject-matter. Certain books, as has been indicated and as will appear later, are in a privileged position, have substantial authority and may be described as literary sources of law, as distinct from the general body of legal literature (legal encyclopedias, textbooks, periodicals, legal histories, etc.), but in general any court may quite freely ignore as unauthoritative what is written in a textbook.[10] The function of the textbook is to collect and present in logical form a statement of the rules of law on a given topic, drawn from the authoritative sources, the relevant statutes and scattered cases, and to suggest their cumulative effect and how they appear to the author to apply in different circumstances. Textbooks are of great value for their synthesis and reasoned statement of the rules drawn from different legal materials, and for their criticism of rules and their conjectures of suitable developments to solve problems which have not yet arisen. They may supply, or help to supply, materials for a decision. If a court accepts the view of a text-writer, that view becomes authoritative, not because the text-writer wrote it but because the court has adopted and approved it, and it thereby acquires the authority of case-law; in future the rule is authoritative because of the case and the judicial adoption, and not because of being stated in the book. Parliament and the courts are always entirely free to ignore formulations of legal principle or doctrine in a textbook, however highly esteemed it or its learned author may be. Textbooks are, in general, therefore, only secondary authorities and useful in so far as they completely and accurately present rules laid down in the primary authorities, *i.e.* the statutes and cases, on any topic.

"The Authorities"

The sources which yield authoritative statements of principle and rules for application in a particular case are generally referred to as "the authorities." Thus: "Counsel referred us to a number of authorities including . . . Counsel said that these authorities showed that . . . The authorities, both the writers of the textbooks and the decided cases, now accept it."[11] In this sense an "authority" is a statement in a source having legal authority and compelling, or at least influencing, a judge or lawyer to the view that the rule of law on the point in question is to a particular effect.

---

[10] Lord Wrenbury, who, when still young Mr. Buckley at the Bar, had written a book on Companies, once remarked from the Bench when Buckley's *Companies Acts* was cited to him: "You must not substitute for the judgments of the court the irresponsible conjectures of a textbook writer." This emphasises that textbooks are not infrequently written by comparatively young and inexperienced men, and many contain statements which are tentative, conjectural or even simply wrong.

[11] *Dundee Corp. v. Marr*, 1971 S.C. 96, 102–103.

The Problems in Relation to Legal Sources

Having determined what are the legally recognised sources of authoritative rules of law it will be evident that two problems exist in relation to each class of legal source, namely, how and where to recognise and find the expressions of rules of law which come from these various sources, and, secondly, how to interpret the statements therein so as to draw from them a rule suitable for the resolution of the particular problem or controversy which is in issue, or for advice on that issue.

PRIMARY OR AUTHORITATIVE SOURCES

I.—LEGISLATION

A—LEGISLATION COMMON TO COUNTRIES OF THE EUROPEAN UNION

In certain spheres, mainly economic, there is a body of law common to all the countries which are members of the European Union. The sources of this body of law are (1)(*a*) the Treaties which established the European Communities and certain subsidiary Conventions and treaties, and (*b*) the bodies of administrative Regulations, Directives and Decisions[12] made by the Council and the Commission of the Communities in pursuance of their powers under the Treaties and for the furtherance of policies agreed upon to give effect to the purposes of the Communities; and (2) rulings and decisions of the Court of Justice of the Communities interpreting the Treaties and administrative legislation and filling the gaps left by them in the law. All legislation may be reviewed by the Court of Justice and may be held invalid. The general principles of the law common to the member states and general principles of international law may be referred to as subsidiary sources.

DISCOVERY OF RELEVANT LEGISLATION

EU legislation is most conveniently found in the *Encyclopaedia of European Community Law*. EU Regulations and ECSC general decisions come into force on the date specified in them or, if no date is specified, on the 20th day following publication.[13] Directives and decisions, and ECSC general decisions and recommendations, take effect on being notified to their addressees.[13] Where, as in the case of directives, EU legislation requires to be implemented by national law, it cannot come into force until implementing legislation by statute or statutory instrument is passed

---

[12] To these correspond under the ECSC Treaty General Decisions, Recommendations and Individual Decisions respectively.

[13] EEC Treaty, Art. 191; Euratom Treaty, Art. 163; ECSC Treaty, Art. 15 and ECSC High Authority Decision 22/60.

and does so from the date when that legislation is effective.[14] EU legislation may be retrospective.

CONSTRUCTION OR INTERPRETATION OF EU LEGISLATION

It is a fundamental principle that directly applicable or directly effective EU legislation prevails over inconsistent rules of national law.[15]

In interpreting EU legislation, the Court of Justice and national courts must seek to give full effect to the provisions and also the unwritten principles on which the EU are founded. In particular, since EU legislation is drafted in several languages all equally authentic[16] interpretation requires comparison of the different language versions. Also, some legal concepts and terms do not have the same meanings in EU law as in national systems. Provisions of EU law must be looked at in context and interpreted in the light of EU law as a whole. Hence the Court of Justice and national courts interpret EU law in the light of its purpose, general scheme and the objectives of the Treaties and the particular legislation before the court. While the wording of the legislation is the starting point, the literal meaning is not necessarily the true meaning. It is more important to discover the purpose and seek to give effect to it. Principles and concepts common to the laws of member states may be considered in interpretation, but not if inconsistent with the apparent meaning of the principle in the EU legislation.

Though the Court of Justice is not bound in any case to follow an interpretation it gave to a provision in a previous case, it is likely to follow it. When it gives an interpretation on a request for a preliminary ruling from a national court, that interpretation is binding on that national court,[17] and other national courts may follow that interpretation, though they are free to seek a separate preliminary ruling.[18] It has been held in Germany that a court had acted unconstitutionally in failing to follow a ruling of the Court of Justice and that it must make a fresh reference to the Court of Justice stating why it doubted the Court of Justice's previous preliminary ruling.[19]

B—LEGISLATION APPLICABLE TO SCOTLAND

As has been explained[20] legislation comprises statutes or Acts of Parliament, prerogative legislation, and subordinate or delegated legislation

---

[14] European Communities Act 1972, s. 2(2).
[15] *Costa v. ENEL* [1964] E.C.R. 585; *Amministrazione delle Finanze v. Simmenthal* [1978] E.C.R. 629; *R v. Secretary of State for Transport, Ex p. Factortame* [1991] 1 A.C. 603.
[16] Save that the sole authentic text of the ECSC Treaty is the French one.
[17] *Milch Eierkontor GmbH v. Hauptzollamt Saarbrucken* [1969] E.C.R. 165.
[18] *CILFIT Srl v. Ministry of Health* [1982] E.C.R. 3415.
[19] *Re VAT Exemption* [1989] 1 C.M.L.R. 113.
[20] Chap. 6, *supra*.

made by Ministers of the Crown, local authorities, courts and other bodies.

A statute is an authoritative declaration of the will of the Queen in Parliament as to some matter of law, usually prescribing some general rule for the future regulation of conduct. It may, however, be specific and relate to only one or a few limited cases only. The body of statute law which is of relevance in Scotland comprises the body of statutes or Acts of the Parliaments of Scotland down to 1707, of the Parliament of Great Britain from 1707 to 1800, of the Parliament of the United Kingdom since 1801, and of the Scottish Parliament since 1999, in all cases so far as these statutes are still in force and have been amended but not repealed or cancelled by subsequent legislation.

To use legislation as a source from which possibly to find a rule resolving a doubt or deciding a dispute, it is necessary first to discover what statutory provisions, if any, are relevant to the matter under consideration and then to resort to the process of construction or interpretation to determine what the words thought to be relevant mean in the circumstances.

Discovery of Relevant Legislation

The discovery of what, if any, provisions of statute law are relevant to a particular matter includes the discovery of whether each piece of legislative material which is relevant has or has not been brought into force, is or is not applicable to Scotland, has or has not been amended or repealed or has expired.[21] In the case of subordinate legislation it includes also the question whether the legislation is invalid for any reason.[22]

Construction or Interpretation of Legislation

The process of construction[23] or interpretation is that whereby a legal adviser or a court seeks to discover, in a particular factual context, whether a given statutory provision is applicable to the set of facts, and, if so, what meaning and effect has to be given to it. It is in essence the problem of finding the meaning of certain statutory expressions in the context of certain circumstances. This is a problem which arises very frequently, raises many and difficult issues, and is one of the most thorny

---

[21] Chap. 6, *supra*.

[22] *e.g. Edinburgh D.C. v. Secretary of State for Scotland*, 1985 S.L.T. 551. The invalid part of a statutory instrument may be severable: *Dunkley v. Evans* [1981] 3 All E.R. 285. The validity of an Act of Parliament cannot be challenged: *Sillars v. Smith*, 1982 S.L.T. 539.

[23] From the verb "construe," not from "construct." A distinction has sometimes been drawn between "construction" or the process of resolving uncertainties or ambiguities in a statute, and "interpretation" or the process of assigning a meaning to the words in a statute. See, *e.g. Franklin v. Att.-Gen.* [1974] Q.B. 185, 199.

with which any adviser or court can be faced. It is always a question of law, not of fact, to be decided by the court, not the jury, to be decided after legal argument, not on evidence.[24] It arises frequently, not only in contentious proceedings in court, but in the course of advising or deciding on the legality or competency of some projected course of action, past or proposed. Construction or interpretation are necessary because the words used in statutes may be ambiguous, *i.e.* susceptible of two meanings,[25] or be indefinite or uncertain in scope and application.[26] Thus it has been said[27]: "The word 'office' is of indefinite content. Its various meanings cover four columns of the New English Dictionary, but I take as the most relevant for purposes of this case the following . . . " A considerable volume of principles of construction, presumptions and guides has grown up in practice and much depends on which is followed, since the application of different guides may produce diametrically opposite consequences.[28] As has been observed: "The English language is not an instrument of mathematical precision. Our literature would be much poorer if it were. This is where the draftsmen of Acts of Parliament have often been unfairly criticised. A judge, believing himself to be fettered by the supposed rule that he must look to the language and nothing else, laments that the draftsmen have not provided for this or that, or have been guilty of some other ambiguity. It would certainly save the judges trouble if Acts of Parliament were drafted with divine prescience and perfect clarity. In the absence of it, when a defect appears a judge cannot simply fold his hands and blame the draftsman. He must set to work on the constructive task of finding the intention of Parliament, and he must do this not only from the language of the statute, but also from a consideration of the social conditions which gave rise to it and of the mischief which it was passed to remedy and then he must supplement the written word so as to give force and life to the intention of the legislature."[29] It has to be remembered that Parliament in enacting any provision, or a department or local authority in enacting subordinate legislation, cannot foresee every contingency or set of circumstances which

---

[24] *Mason v. Bibby* (1864) 2 H. & C. 881; *Re Energy Conversion Devices* [1982] Com. L.R. 219.

[25] For examples of ambiguity see *Renfrewshire Assessor v. Hendry*, 1969 S.C. 211, 213; *Gordon v. Kirkcaldy D.C.*, 1990 S.L.T. 644.

[26] *e.g.* Is a residential caravan a "dwelling-house" for the purpose of removal of rubbish? See *Gordon, supra.*

[27] *McMillan v. Guest* [1942] A.C. 561, 566 quoted in *I.R.C. v. Brander & Cruickshank*, 1970 S.C. 116, 121.

[28] The principal guides are Craies' treatise on *Statute Law* (7th ed., 1971); Maxwell on *The Interpretation of Statutes* (11th ed., 1961) and Odgers, *The Construction of Deeds and Statutes* (4th ed., 1956). See also Willis, "Statute Interpretation in a Nutshell" (1938) 16 Can. Bar Rev. 1; Davies, "Interpretation of Statutes in the Light of Their Policy by the English Courts" (1935) 35 Col.L.R. 519; Friedmann, "Statute Law and its Interpretation in the Modern State" (1948) 26 Can. Bar Rev. 1277.

[29] *Seaford Court Estates Ltd v. Asher* [1949] 2 K.B. 481, 499, *per* Denning L.J. criticised on appeal ([1950] A.C. 508, 530) as stated much too widely.

may arise, and may never have considered at all the kind of case which has arisen, so that it is not surprising that the language used seldom fits every possible case. Indeed the perversity of circumstances is such that, as soon as a carefully phrased piece of legislation comes into force, a case seems to arise which the words do not seem particularly apt to cover. Thus it is an offence to be in charge of a vehicle while under the influence of drink.[30] Do the words "in charge of" cover a drunken person put in the back seat of his car in a car-park, the car having been immobilised,[31] a drunken person in the front passenger seat while another person, who held only an expired provisional licence, had started the engine,[32] a drunken person in the driving seat of a stationary car but who had arranged for another person to drive it to that person's garage,[33] or a drunken person sitting beside a "learner" who was driving?[34]

The overriding purpose is to discover the intention of Parliament as expressed in the statute. The work of interpreting a statute is not a mechanical function: "the duty of the courts is to ascertain and give effect to the will of Parliament as expressed in its enactments. In the performance of this duty the judges do not act as computers into which are fed the statute and the rules for the construction of statutes and from which issue forth the mathematically correct answer. The interpretation of statutes is a craft as much as a science and the judges, as craftsmen, select and apply the appropriate rules as the tools of their trade. They are not legislators, but finishers, refiners and polishers of legislation which comes to them in a state requiring varying degrees of further processing."[35]

If possible a statute should be construed in a way which makes it operative and not unworkable or nonsensical, and it should be assumed that words are not used unnecessarily or incorrectly.

The Two Approaches to Interpretation

There are two general approaches or attitudes discernible in statutory interpretation, the one favouring a literal, strict or narrow construction, and the other a more liberal or broader construction.[36] The choice between them is a matter for the individual judge and much depends on

---

[30] Road Traffic Act 1972, s. 5(2) (formerly Road Traffic Acts 1930, s. 15 and 1960, s. 6).

[31] *Dean v. Wishart*, 1952 J.C. 9.

[32] *Winter v. Morrison*, 1954 J.C. 7.

[33] *Macdonald v. Kubirdas*, 1955 S.L.T.(Sh.Ct.) 50.

[34] *Clark v. Clark*, 1950 S.L.T.(Sh.Ct.) 68. It has been observed (*Fraser v. Caledonian Ry.*, 1911 S.C. 145, 159) that some older statutes were badly drafted, with contempt, or ignorance, or both, of Scots law.

[35] *Corocraft Ltd v. Pan-American Airways* [1969] 1 Q.B. 616, *per* Donaldson J.

[36] There are sometimes said, particularly in English cases, to be three rules of interpretation, the literal rule, to adhere to the words, the golden rule, to adhere to the literal approach unless it produces absurdity, in which case another meaning must be adopted, and the mischief rule, to discover the defect in the law which the statute was meant to remedy and to give effect to the remedy.

his general attitude to the law and legal development, and more particularly on his subjective view of the case and the Act and on whether he thinks that the statute should cover the circumstances of the case before him or not. This renders prediction of the court's attitude to a particular provision difficult, may give rise to inconsistencies between similar cases or similar statutory provisions, and has given rise to accusations of judicial bias against certain kinds of legislation, as of giving an unduly narrow construction to some social welfare legislation. These criticisms seem quite unjustified, but the analysis of this belongs to jurisprudence, and need not be pursued further here.

The Literal Approach

The literal approach stresses the need for close and careful scrutiny of the actual words enacted by the legislature and has little regard for anything but the relevant words or phrases, the context and any other relevant provision of the Act itself. It is appropriate where the statute is unambiguous and the words adequately indicate what Parliament intended.[37] Words are to be construed in their ordinary sense, as the words were used when the Act was passed. The general effect of adopting this approach is that an Act will not be held to affect, or to be intended to have affected, anything not dealt with expressly or by clear implication even if the result of this attitude may be obviously absurd or inconsistent with the commonsense idea of what Parliament meant to do.[38] This approach is frequently buttressed with such arguments as that if Parliament had meant to cover this case it could and should have said so, or that it is not for the courts to legislate or to usurp the function of Parliament or to speculate what Parliament might have intended and to write this into the Act. For example, at common law a wife was entitled to exact a share of her husband's moveable estate, called *jus relictae*, when he died or she divorced him. The Married Women's Property (Scotland) Act 1881 gave a husband a corresponding right of *jus relicti*, but it was held exigible only on death, not on divorce, because the Act says "the husband of any woman who may *die*,"[39] and the court declined to apply the fiction that divorce had the same effect as death in view of the literal terms of the Act, though this was commonly quoted as the basis for the wife's claim. The result was a legal anomaly; it is likely that Parliament had merely overlooked the case of divorce and had not intended to exclude it.

Objections have been stated to the literal approach, particularly that words do not have plain, ordinary meanings apart from their context, that, as dictionaries show, most words have several meanings, that the plain-

---

[37] *Westminster Bank v. Zang* [1966] A.C. 182.
[38] *Glasgow Court House Commrs v. Lanarkshire C.C.* (1900) 3 F. 103.
[39] *Eddington v. Robertson* (1895) 22 R. 430.

meaning approach is inappropriate for general words, which can obviously mean several things, and that judges sometimes differ as to what the plain meaning is.[40] To put undue emphasis on the literal meaning of words is to assume unattainable perfection in draftsmanship.

The Liberal Approach

The liberal approach lays stress on the need for the courts to try to appreciate the overriding intention of the legislation, the general policy behind the Act, and the need to further remedies and not to take refuge in pettifogging verbal objections.[41] Thus in *Taff Vale Ry.* v. *A.S.R.S.*,[42] the House of Lords examined the policy of successive Trade Union Acts as a means of deciding that Parliament must have meant that trade unions could be sued for tort in their registered names. The discovery of the general purpose and intention of legislation is, however, difficult and subject to two serious handicaps. The court can most easily and readily discover Parliament's intention from what Parliament has enacted, that is, from an examination of the literal form and wording of the enactment, and, secondly, the court is not at liberty to read into a statute phrases or provisions which are quite clearly not there, however much the general policy might seem to render them desirable.

The desire to give effect to the general policy expressed in literal terms in the Act underlines what is sometimes called "the golden rule" of statutory interpretation. "The only rule for the construction of Acts of Parliament is that they should be construed according to the intent of the Parliament which passed them. If the words of the statute are in themselves precise and unambiguous, then no more can be necessary than to expound these words in their natural and ordinary sense. The words themselves alone do in such case best declare the intention of the lawgiver."[43] "It is a very useful rule in the construction of a statute to adhere to the ordinary meaning of the words used, and to the grammatical construction, unless that is at variance with the intention of the legislature to be collected from the statute itself or leads to any manifest absurdity or repugnance, in which case the language may be varied or modified so as to avoid such inconvenience, but no further."[44] A court may not disregard the plain meaning merely because it produces an anomaly, but only if it produces an absurdity.[45] It remains of course difficult in many cases to say what the intention of Parliament seems to have been, and it may well be a

---

[40] *e.g. Ellerman Lines v. Murray* [1931] A.C. 126.
[41] *Ferguson v. Secretary of State for Social Services*, 1989 S.L.T. 117.
[42] [1901] A.C. 426.
[43] *Sussex Peerage Case* (1844) 11 Cl. & F. 85, 143, *per* Tindal C.J.
[44] *Becke v. Smith* (1836) 2 M. & W. 191, 195, *per* Parke B. *cf. Caledonian Ry. v. N.B. Ry.* (1881) 8 R.(H.L.) 23; *Campbell's Trs. v. O'Neill*, 1911 S.C. 188; *I.R.C. v. Luke*, 1963 S.C.(H.L.) 65, 80.
[45] *Stock v. Jones* [1978] 1 All E.R. 948.

matter of opinion whether the ordinary meaning does or does not lead to absurdity or repugnance, so that this rule does not take the discussion much further. Or the intention may be plain, but the words clearly do not give effect to the intention.

Another version of the liberal approach is what is sometimes called the "mischief rule," that where a statute was passed to remedy some mischief and defect in the law, the interpretation should be adopted which corrects the mischief. Thus liberal interpretation is appropriate where an Act is clearly intended to protect a class of persons, such as consumers.[46]

Interpretation Act

Some guidance is given by the Interpretation Act 1978,[47] which assigns meanings to a number of words commonly found in statutes and provides, for example, that words importing the masculine shall include the feminine, that words in the singular shall include the plural and vice versa,[48] that "person" includes any body of persons corporate or unincorporate, and so on. These definitions, however, may always have to give way to contrary indications in the context of a particular Act,[49] and this Act is accordingly far from providing a comprehensive code of interpretation. Its only real value is in fact to abbreviate statutes by permitting the omission of such phrases as "he or she," "person or persons or body of persons."

A few definitions of general application are contained in Acts other than the Interpretation Act 1978.

Interpretation Sections

In many modern Acts there is, usually near the end, an interpretation section which gives definitions of certain words used in the Act[50] and provides that they shall have in the Act the particular meaning thereby assigned to them, which may be wider or narrower than the ordinary dictionary meaning of the word.[51] The section may provide that certain words shall "mean" something, which explains, defines and limits the words used, or it may provide that certain words shall "include" or "exclude" particular cases, in which case the definition is extensive or restrictive of the usual meaning. The meanings thus statutorily assigned to particular words hold for that Act only, though subsequent legislation may refer back to that definition by providing in another context that a word

---

[46] *McCrone v. Boots Farm Sales*, 1981 S.C. 68, 74.

[47] Replacing earlier Acts of 1850 and 1889.

[48] See, *e.g. Griffiths v. Ferrier*, 1952 J.C. 56, and generally *20 Cannon St. v. Singer* [1974] 2 All E.R. 577.

[49] *e.g. Payne v. Barratt Developments Ltd* [1985] 1 All E.R. 257.

[50] *e.g.* Sale of Goods Act 1979, s. 61(1).

[51] For these, see Stroud's *Judicial Dictionary* and Saunders' *Words and Phrases Legally Defined*.

shall bear the meaning assigned to it in a specified prior Act. An interpretation section which extends the meaning of a word does not thereby abolish the ordinary, popular and natural sense of the word where that is properly applicable but merely enables the word, when there is nothing in the context or subject-matter to the contrary, to be applied to some things to which it would not ordinarily be applicable.[52] Moreover, the interpretation section is not to be taken as defining the terms mentioned in all circumstances but only as defining what may be comprehended by the term where the circumstances require that it should be so comprehended.[53] Sometimes there are separate interpretation sections for separate Parts of an Act. Some modern statutes have instead a Glossary of Expressions.[54]

Subsidiary Principles

It is apparent that courts get little assistance in the task of interpretation from the Interpretation Act and any interpretation section in the Act under consideration and that they have to draw a meaning out of the statutory passage in the circumstances which have given rise to the controversy primarily by reference to the words enacted, and also to what the court or judge thinks, on a consideration of the whole legislation in issue, Parliament intended. Sometimes one factor rather than the other weighs more with the court. But numerous subsidiary principles have been developed to assist the court in its scrutiny of the language employed.

In the first place the usual dictionary meaning of a word is taken, as at the time when the statute was passed, and if the word has a legal or technical connotation the usual technical meaning is taken. Parliament is presumed to be familiar with, and to use, the ordinary and, if applicable, usual legal or technical meanings of words.[55] Any unusual or restricted or extended sense of a word calls prima facie for a mention in the interpretation section. Words which are permissive or empowering may be shown in particular circumstances to be really imperative, and it has been said that prima facie where powers are conferred by statute for the public benefit, they must be exercised.[56]

Secondly, the usual meaning is taken subject to the context in which the word is used, so as to attribute to the word or phrase a meaning consistent with the rest of the section and even of the whole Act or series of Acts on the subject.

Reference to Whole Act

Interpretation must have regard, moreover, not merely to the immediate verbal context, but to the whole of the Act in which the phrase under

---

[52] *Robinson v. Barton Eccles Local Board* (1883) 8 App.Cas. 798.
[53] *Meux v. Jacobs* (1875) L.R. 7 H.L. 481; *Strathern v. Padden*, 1926 J.C. 9.
[54] Social Security Act 1975, Sched. 20.
[55] *Clerical Assurance Co. v. Carter* (1889) 22 Q.B.D. 444.
[56] *Walkinshaw v. Orr* (1860) 22 D. 627; *Julius v. Bishop of Oxford* (1880) 5 App.Cas. 214; *Black v. Glasgow Corp.*, 1958 S.C. 260.

construction appears, because regard to the whole Act may reveal an underlying scheme or legislative purpose which helps to give a meaning to a particular phrase. Where a literal interpretation produces an absurd result the court must seek an interpretation more consistent with the scheme of the Act.[57] Sections of Acts frequently refer back and forward to other sections and, even without express reference, one interpretation of a word may be more consistent with another section of the Act than is the alternative interpretation. Thus if one section provides for notice being "given" and another for the notice being "served on or left with" a person, it is apparent that written notice was contemplated and that this meaning will fit both sections while oral notice would fit only the earlier section; one does not "serve" or "leave" an oral notice with a person. Reference to the whole Act, or at least the whole of that part of the Act, will therefore tend to give an interpretation consistent with the rest of the Act. Moreover, where there is a series of Acts dealing with the same subject-matter they should be looked at as a continuous code.[58]

Reference to Context

The fact that a particular word or phrase has to be construed does not justify ignoring the verbal context in which the word is used, and three principles have been recognised in this connection:

(a) *Noscitur a sociis*, that is, a vague word takes a shade of meaning from the accompanying words; thus in the context of "houses for public refreshment, resort and entertainment," the last word was held to be limited to physical and not mental gratification,[59] because that meaning, it was felt, agreed better with the earlier part of the phrase than the other or wider meaning which might have covered a theatrical or musical performance.

(b) *Expressio unius est exclusio alterius.* Under this the express mention of one thing or category and not of another similar or related thing or category tends to indicate the implied exclusion of the latter. It is inapplicable to a situation other than one where there is only a choice between two persons or objects.[60] But the exclusion of the other may be the result of inadvertence or accident, so that the principle cannot be rigidly applied,[61] and is indeed of very limited value.

(c) *Ejusdem generis.* Where several things or specific items are enumerated, all of the same kind or having some distinct characteristic in common, and this enumeration is followed by general words

---

[57] *I.R.C. v. Luke*, 1963 S.C.(H.L.) 65; *Hirsch v. Crowthers Cloth* [1990] S.T.C. 174.

[58] *Hamilton v. N.C.B.*, 1960 S.C.(H.L.) 1.

[59] *Muir v. Keay* (1875) L.R. 10 Q.B. 594.

[60] *R. v. Palfrey* [1970] 2 All E.R. 12.

[61] *Stevenson v. Hunter* (1903) 5 F. 761. *cf. Dean v. Wiesengrund* [1955] 2 Q.B. 120.

such as "or otherwise," "or other things," "or other person," it has to be presumed that the general words are limited to other things or items or persons having the same common characteristic or of the same kind or class or category as the items specifically mentioned.[62] It is clear, accordingly, that the rule has no application where the specific words have no common category or characteristics,[63] or if the concluding general words are so very general as to include every other case or, at least, the case under discussion, *e.g.* "any other place *whatsoever.*" Thus in a provision that traffic signs should include "all signals, warning signposts, direction posts, signs or devices," it was held that "devices" must be *ejusdem generis* with the previous words and could not cover a painted white line.[64] A prohibition on "all houses and every other building whatever" did not extend to a low parapet wall and iron railing.[65] Before the rule can be applied, accordingly, one must be able to discover a *genus* common to all the specific words and also to assign a meaning to the concluding general words consistent with their limitation to that same *genus.*

Further indications of the appropriate shade of meaning to give to a word may sometimes be gathered from one or more of two sets of indications, which are distinguished as internal and external aids to construction.

Internal Aids to Construction

Internal aids are those indications which may be drawn from the statute under construction itself to assist in arriving at a true interpretation of its provisions. The principal are:

(*a*) *Title.* It is now accepted that the long title is part of an Act and may legitimately be used to assist in interpreting the Act as a whole and in ascertaining its scope.[66] The short title cannot be used as an aid to construction.[67]

---

[62] *Mortimer v. Samuel B. Allison Ltd,* 1959 S.C.(H.L.) 1. *Gray v. Crofters Commission,* 1980 S.L.T.(Land Ct.) 2.

[63] *e.g. Crichton Stuart v. Ogilvie,* 1914 S.C. 888.

[64] *Evans v. Cross* [1938] 1 K.B. 694.

[65] *Partick Police Commrs. v. G.W. Steam Laundry Co.* (1886) 13 R. 500; see also *Moss' Empires v. Glasgow Assessor,* 1917 S.C.(H.L.) 1; *Cormack v. Crown Estates Commrs,* 1985 S.L.T. 426.

[66] *Fielden v. Morley Corp.* [1899] 1 Ch. 1, 3; *Fenton v. Thorley* [1903] A.C. 443, 447; *Millar & Lang v. Macniven & Cameron* (1908) 16 S.L.T. 56; *Vacher v. London Society of Compositors* [1913] A.C. 107, 128; *Magistrates of Buckie v. Dowager Countess of Seafield's Trs.,* 1928 S.C. 525; *Kelly v. Nuttall,* 1965 S.C. 427, 438, 449; *Black-Clawson Int. Ltd v. Papierwerke AG* [1975] A.C. 591.

[67] *Re Boaler* [1915] 1 K.B. 21.

(b) *Preamble.* This again is part of the Act and may be resorted to, to explain the meaning of an Act.[68] But a preamble cannot cut down or control or qualify a clear and unambiguous provision in the body of the Act.[69]

(c) *Headings.* Headings prefixed to groups of sections or parts of an Act may, like preambles, be taken as a guide but only for the purpose of explaining doubtful expressions or ambiguities in the body of the sections or part of the Act.[70]

(d) *Marginal notes.* These have been said both to be not part of a statute and the courts cannot look at them,[71] and to be part of a statute but a most unsure guide to construction.[72]

(e) *Punctuation.* Modern statutes are punctuated, but punctuation is regarded not as forming part of the statute but rather as a kind of *contemporanea expositio*.[73] Sometimes it has been referred to,[74] but punctuation is not authoritative.

(f) *Interpretation sections.* These can certainly, and must, be considered, though the meaning of a word is determined more by its use in the context in which it appears. Interpretation sections may extend or restrict the ordinary meanings of words for the purposes of the particular Act, or part of an Act.

(g) *Examples.* A few Acts give examples of the application of the Act. Examples may be looked at, but cannot override words in a section of the Act.[75]

(h) *Schedules.* These are part of the Act and may be looked at to resolve ambiguities,[76] though mere forms contained in a Schedule cannot limit or qualify words of enactment in the Act. If there is conflict between a section of the Act and a Schedule, the section must prevail.[77]

---

[68] *L.C.C. v. Bermondsey Bioscope Co.* [1911] 1 K.B. 445, 451; *Vacher, supra*; *Renfrewshire C.C. v. Orphan Homes of Scotland* (1898) 1 F. 186; *Incorporated Council of Law Reporting v. Att.-Gen.* [1971] Ch. 626.

[69] *Powell v. Kempton Park Racecourse Co.* [1899] A.C. 143, 157, 184; *Att.-Gen. v. Prince Ernest of Hanover* [1955] Ch. 440; [1957] A.C. 436; *Kemp v. Robertson*, 1967 S.C. 229; *Oliver v. Douglas*, 1981 S.C. 192, 199.

[70] *Martins v. Fowler* [1926] A.C. 746, 750; *Buckie Magistrates v. Seafield's Trustees*, 1928 S.C. 525; *R. v. Surrey (N.E. Area) Assessment Committee* [1948] 1 K.B. 28, 32; *D.P.P. v. Schildkamp* [1969] 3 All E.R. 1640; *Hill v. Orkney Islands Council*, 1983 S.L.T.(Lands Tr.) 5.

[71] *Nixon v. Att.-Gen.* [1930] 1 Ch. 566, 593.

[72] *D.P.P. v. Schildkamp, supra.*

[73] *Duke of Devonshire v. O'Connor* (1890) 24 Q.B.D. 468, 478; *I.R.C. v. Hinchy* [1960] A.C. 748.

[74] *Alexander v. Mackenzie*, 1947 J.C. 155; *D.P.P. v. Schildkamp, supra.*

[75] Consumer Credit Act 1974, s. 188 and Sched. 2.

[76] *Ellerman Lines v. Murray* [1931] A.C. 126; see also *Jacobs v. Hart* (1900) 2 F.(J.) 33.

[77] *Kerr v. H.M. Advocate*, 1986 S.C.C.R. 81.

External Aids to Construction

External aids are those sources of information outside the Act under construction which may be sought to be invoked to assist interpretation. The principal external aids are:

(a) *Prior state of the law*. Parliament must be presumed to know the state of the law existing when the Act in question was passed, and the intention of the later legislation may sometimes be discovered by examination of the previous state of the law. This includes the previous common law, any prior Acts, and the known defects of the previous state of the law.[78] This is sometimes comprehensively called the parliamentary history of the Act. Only prior statutes *in pari materia* relating to the same subject-matter can be regarded, so closely related that they can fairly be said to form one system of legislation, and not other statutes or other statutes vaguely relating to kindred topics.[79] Reference to prior statutes is particularly appropriate in the case of a group of Acts relating to one topic, such as housing or merchant shipping, where the legislation is practically a code in itself.[80] Even subsequent legislation *in pari materia* may be looked at in the same way.

(b) *Earlier statutes repealed and consolidated by statute under construction.* Prior statutes repealed but reproduced in substance in consolidated form may be looked at[81] and judicial decisions on a repealed statute are treated as applicable to substantially identical provisions in the repealing Act.[82] This is justifiable on the basis that consolidation and re-enactment are both designed to restate rather than to change the law. Earlier legislation is of much less value as an aid to construction if the later legislation is professedly amending or clearly makes extensive changes, since there is then no presumption that Parliament intended the earlier interpretation to be continued.

(c) *Subsequent Acts*. Subsequent legislation may be looked at in order to find the proper construction to be put on an earlier and ambiguous Act,[83] since Parliament may in a later Act on the same

---

[78] *Bank of England v. Vagliano* [1891] A.C. 107, 144; *Re Mayfair Property Co.* [1898] 2 Ch. 28, 35; *Eastman Photographic Co. v. Comptroller-General of Patents* [1898] A.C. 571, 575; *Macmillan v. Dent* [1907] 1 Ch. 107, 120; *Keates v. Lewis Merthyr Consolidated Collieries* [1911] A.C. 641, 642; *Avery v. N.E. Ry.* [1938] A.C. 606, 612, 617; *Armah v. Govt. of Ghana* [1968] A.C. 192; *Black-Clawson Int. v. Papierwerke AG* [1975] A.C. 591.

[79] *Sharp v. Morrison*, 1922 S.L.T. 272.

[80] *Lord Advocate v. Sprot's Trustees* (1901) 3 F. 440.

[81] Thus in interpreting the Companies Act 1985, reference may be made in many cases to decisions on similar sections of the 1948, 1929, 1908, and earlier Companies Acts.

[82] *Smith v. Baker* [1891] A.C. 325; *Boyle v. Wilson* [1907] A.C. 45, *sub nom. Walsh* v. *Pollokshaws Magistrates*, 1907 S.C.(H.L.) 1; *Farrell v. Alexander* [1977] A.C. 59.

[83] *Att.-Gen. v. Clarkson* [1900] 1 Q.B. 156, 163; *Re Macmanaway* [1951] A.C. 161; *Att.-Gen.* v. *Prince Ernest Augustus of Hanover* [1957] A.C. 436.

subject-matter expressly give a meaning to what was doubtful in an earlier Act, or may, more commonly, do so by implication, as by making further provision which is consistent with or inconsistent with the construction of the earlier Act proposed by the court.

(d) *Cases.* Decided cases which construe the words of an Act of Parliament[84] establish principles and rules of law whereby its scope and effect may be interpreted.[85] A precedent on interpretation of a statutory provision is as much authoritative or persuasive on that point in a later case as is a precedent on a point of common law.[86] This makes for uniformity of interpretation in different courts. This principle is not without its defects because some statutory provisions have been interpreted in many cases, and the task in a subsequent case may be more obscured than helped by the quest for a meaning consistent with the earlier cases. But it is only if the actual words under construction have been previously construed in the same or a closely analogous statute that there is any scope for case-law doing any more than laying down general principles. The law is contained in the Act, not in what previous judges have said the Act meant.[87] Reference to cases where a similar question has arisen on Acts differently framed is of little value, since they merely illustrate a general principle.[88] Moreover, when Parliament uses in an Act a term which has already received judicial interpretation in a case, it is presumed that the term is used in the sense in which it has been judicially interpreted, unless a contrary intention appears.[89] But while a court will be slow to differ from a decision when Parliament has re-enacted a statutory provision in the same terms, it may do so, and is not *bound* to apply the same meaning as before.[90] This presumption has been heavily criticised by some judges and is not very strong.[91]

In connection with cases interpreting particular statutory words and phrases it should be noted that the courts take the view that

---

[84] Thus the phrase "merchantable quality" in the Sale of Goods Act 1893 (now 1979) has been discussed in many cases; see, *e.g. B. S. Brown v. Craiks*, 1970 S.C.(H.L.) 51. Many of the interpretations put in past cases on particular words in particular statutory and factual contexts are collected in Gibb and Dalrymple's *Scottish Judicial Dictionary*; Stroud's *Judicial Dictionary*; Saunders' *Words and Phrases Legally Defined* and in *Current Law, s.v.* "Words and Phrases."

[85] *Re Aeronautics in Canada* [1932] A.C. 54, 70.

[86] *Nicol's Trs.* v. *Sutherland*, 1951 S.C.(H.L.) 21.

[87] *Hochstrasser v. Mayes* [1960] A.C. 376, 391; *Ogden Industries Ltd v. Lucas* [1970] A.C. 113; *Chalmers v. Peterhead Harbour Trs.*, 1991 S.L.T. 98.

[88] *Reid v. Reid* (1886) 31 Ch.D. 402, 405.

[89] *Webb v. Outrim* [1907] A.C. 81; *Barras v. Aberdeen Steam Trawling Co.*, 1933 S.C.(H.L.) 21; Winder, "Interpretation of Statutes subject to Case Law" (1946) 58 J.R. 93; *Zimmerman* v. *Grossman* [1971] 1 All E.R. 363. This was said in *Haigh v. Ireland*, 1974 S.C.(H.L.) 1, not to apply to a consolidation statute.

[90] *Royal Crown Derby Porcelain Co. v. Russell* [1949] 2 K.B. 417; *R. v. Bow Road Domestic Proceedings Court* [1968] 2 All E.R. 89.

[91] *Paisner v. Goodrich* [1955] 2 Q.B. 353, 358; [1957] A.C. 65; *F. v. Kennedy*, 1988 S.L.T. 404.

statutes so far as common to Scotland and England should be interpreted to the same effect in both countries, so that cases from the other jurisdiction are relevant guides to interpretation. So, too, a phrase in a Scottish Act may sometimes be elucidated by a case construing the corresponding provision in the equivalent English Act,[92] though here there may be more room for diversity, but English cases construing the same word or phrase in a statute not also applicable to Scotland and not the counterpart of the Scottish provision, may be of very little value indeed. The value of interpretative cases from the other jurisdiction is greatest in such matters as taxation, where parity of application throughout the United Kingdom is clearly desirable.[93] In cases concerning international conventions incorporated in British law, it is permissible in aid of interpretation to refer to cases from superior courts in other countries which are parties to the convention.[94]

(e) *Usage and contemporanea expositio.* Where it appears that a statutory provision has long been understood and acted upon in a certain sense the court will adopt that sense unless it appears manifestly wrong.[95] If the meaning of the statute is clear, no usage to the contrary will prevail[96] and any such understanding or practice or usage must have been generally accepted, not merely prevalent.[97] These aids are particularly relevant to the construction of ancient statutes but have much less weight in more modern statutes.[98] The principle is accordingly relevant in the construction of old Scots Acts.[99] Similarly, in interpreting the older Scots statutes, equitable considerations have been admitted[1] and some have been interpreted very broadly.[2]

(f) *Textbooks.* A statement in an established textbook as to the meaning of a statutory provision has no binding force on any court, but if there is doubt and the view of the text-writer has been

---

[92] *cf. Oliver v. Douglas*, 1981 S.C. 192, 198, where a Scottish Act was intended to enact for Scotland provisions similar to these enacted by earlier Acts for England.

[93] *Income Tax Commrs v. Pemsel* [1891] A.C. 531; *Lord Advocate v. Earl of Moray's Trs.* (1905) 7 F.(H.L.) 116; *I.R.C. v. Glasgow Police Athletic Assocn*, 1953 S.C.(H.L.) 13; *Secretary of State for Employment v. Clarke Chapman & Co.* [1971] 2 All E.R. 798.

[94] *Fothergill v. Monarch Airlines* [1980] 2 All E.R. 696.

[95] *Gorham v. Bishop of Exeter* (1850) 15 Q.B. 52, 73; *Migneault v. Malo* (1872) L.R. 4 P.C. 123; *Welham v. D.P.P.* [1961] A.C. 103.

[96] *Magistrates of Dunbar v. Duchess of Roxburghe* (1835) 3 Cl. & F.335, 354; *Northam Bridge Co. v. R.* (1886) 55 L.T. 759; *Walker Trs. v. Lord Advocate*, 1912 S.C.(H.L.) 12.

[97] *Bank of Ireland v. Evans' Charity* (1855) 5 H.L.C. 389, 405.

[98] *Clyde Navigation Trustees v. Laird* (1883) 10 R.(H.L.) 77.

[99] *Montrose Peerage Case* (1853) 1 Macq. 401; *Graham v. Irving* (1899) 2 F. 29; *cf. Middleton v. Tough*, 1908 S.C.(J.) 32. Comments in Mackenzie's *Observations on the Acts of Parliament* are valuable.

[1] *Mill's Trs v. Mill's Exrs.*, 1965 S.C. 384, 388, 393.

[2] *Thomas v. Thomson* (1865) 3 M.1160, 1165.

accepted as law for a substantial period of time, the court will probably accept it as correct. This is particularly true of very old statutes commented on by text-writers of high repute.[3] In the case of international conventions, reference may be made to foreign textbooks by jurists of high reputation.[4]

(g) *Dictionaries.* In case of doubt as to the ordinary scope or sense of particular words, standard dictionaries may be consulted. Their definitions are not authoritative but are valuable evidence of the ordinary and accepted connotation of particular words and accordingly may be of assistance, but the court is quite free to hold that Parliament has used a word with another meaning than that which is usual.[5] Where an international convention has to be interpreted it is permissible to examine foreign language dictionaries.[6]

(h) *International law.* If legislation is clear it must be given effect to even if that conflicts with general international law or with treaty obligations.[7] But if the legislation is not clear it is presumed that Parliament did not intend to legislate in breach of international law or of specific treaty obligations, and the meaning consonant with the treaty obligations is to be preferred.[8]

(j) *International conventions.* When a statute is passed to give effect in the United Kingdom to an international convention to which the United Kingdom has become a party, the convention may be referred to if scheduled to the Act[9] and, even if not expressly referred to in the Act, may be looked at for the purpose of resolving ambiguities and obscurities, certainly where the terms of the convention and of the Act are so similar that there is an irresistible inference that the statute was intended to embody the convention.[10]

(k) *EU law.* In case of doubt, a United Kingdom statute should be construed in a way consistent with relevant provisions of EU law.[11]

---

[3] *Mayor of Newcastle v. Att.-Gen.* (1845) 12 Cl. & F. 402; *Bastin v. Davies* [1950] 1 All E.R. 1095.

[4] *Fothergill v. Monarch Airlines* [1980] 2 All E.R. 696.

[5] *Camden v. I.R.C.* [1914] 1 K.B. 641. *Cf. Heriot's Trust v. Matson,* 1920 J.C. 34, 45; *McVittie v. Bolton Corpn.* [1945] 1 K.B. 281; *Rutherford v. Miln,* 1941 S.C. 125, 143; *Inland Revenue v. Russell,* 1955 S.C. 237, 240; *Mills v. Cooper* [1967] 2 Q.B. 459; *Thornton v. Fisher & Ludlow Ltd* [1968] 2 All E.R. 241; *I.R.C. v. Brander & Cruickshank,* 1970 S.C. 116, 121. In *Lord Advocate v. Mirrielees' Trs.,* 1945 S.C.(H.L.) 1, when considering the words "common soldier" the House was led by the O.E.D. to discuss Shakespeare's use of the phrase.

[6] *Fothergill, supra.* In this case the French text of the convention in question was declared by the British statute to prevail, if inconsistent with the English text.

[7] *Mortensen v. Peters* (1906) 8 F.(J.) 93; *Ellerman Lines v. Murray* [1931] A.C. 126.

[8] *Salomon v. Commissioners of Customs and Excise* [1966] 3 All E.R. 871.

[9] *e.g.* Carriage by Air Act 1961; see *Fothergill v. Monarch Airlines, supra.*

[10] *Salomon, supra; P.O. v. Estuary Radio Ltd* [1969] 2 Q.B. 740; *The Banco* [1971] 1 All E.R. 524. As to the use of *travaux préparatoires* in interpreting international conventions see *Fothergill, supra; Gatoil International v. Arkwright-Boston Ins. Co.,* 1985 S.L.T. 68 (H.L.). See also *State of Norway's Application* [1989] 1 All E.R. 737, 751.

[11] *Garland v. B.R. Engineering* [1982] 2 All E.R. 402.

Where an Act or regulations have been enacted to comply with a Directive or other provision of EU law British courts should follow the practice of the Court of Justice and give it a purposive construction.[12]

(*l*) *Royal Commission and other Reports.* Reference may not be made to Royal Commission, Committee, Law Commission or other Reports, on the subject-matter of the legislation, since these are merely proposals put before Parliament and there is no certainty that Parliament accepted the recommendations in whole or in part or intended to accept or enact any part of the suggestions. Parliament has sometimes accepted a minority report and rarely accepts and enacts everything exactly as recommended by a Commission or Committee.[13] But it is permissible to look at such a report which led up to the legislation under consideration to discover the defects in the law which the legislation had then set out to remedy.[14]

(*m*) *Hansard, White Papers, etc.* Similarly no reference is generally permitted to *Hansard* (the Parliamentary Debates),[15] or to White Papers[16] or memoranda circulated in Parliament,[17] or to memoranda issued by a Department of State,[18] since these have no authoritative verbal form, nor do they necessarily represent the finally agreed will of Parliament, while, particularly in the case of *Hansard*, the volume of words is considerable, there is no certainty which speech could be taken as authoritative since the speeches are argument rather than expression of will, and each argument can usually be matched by a counter-argument. But in *Pepper v. Hart*[19] the House of Lords held that where legislation was obscure or ambiguous, reference to statements made by a minister, reported in *Hansard*, could be referred to, where such statements were sufficiently clear. This is a very dangerous exception to the

---

[12] *Marshall v. Southampton Health Authy.* [1986] 2 All E.R. 584, 592; *Litster v. Forth Dry Dock Co.*, 1989 S.L.T. 540.

[13] *Assam Ry. Co. v. I.R.C.* [1935] A.C. 445; *Inglis v. British Airports Authority*, 1978 S.L.T.(Lands Tr.) 30; *Elantosh v. Edinburgh Licensing Board*, 1984 S.L.T. 92.

[14] *Heatons Transport v. T. & G.W.U.* [1973] A.C. 15; *Black-Clawson Int. Ltd v. Papierwerke Waldhof-Aschaffenburg AG* [1975] A.C. 591; *Fothergill, supra; Keith v. Texaco*, 1977 S.L.T. (Lands Tr.) 16.

[15] *Black-Clawson Int. Ltd, supra; Davis v. Johnson* [1979] A.C. 317. Some judges have on occasion clearly looked at *Hansard*: *Re Aeronautics in Canada* [1932] A.C. 54; *R. v. I.R.C., ex p. Rossminster* [1979] All E.R. 385, 399. See also *Davis, supra*, at 276.

[16] *Viscountess Rhondda's Claim* [1922] 2 A.C. 339; *McCormick v. Lord Advocate*, 1953 S.C. 396; *Katikiro of Buganda v. Att.-Gen.* [1961] 1 W.L.R. 119.

[17] *Escoigne Properties Ltd v. I.R.C.* [1958] A.C. 549.

[18] *Inglis v. British Airports Authority*, 1978 S.L.T.(Lands Tr.) 30.

[19] [1993] A.C. 593. This principle was invoked in *Short's Tr. v. Keeper of the Registers of Scotland*, 1994 S.L.T. 65. It was extended to interpreting the intention behind a particular statute in *Three Rivers D.C. v. Bank of England* [1996] 2 All E.R. 363.

principle because it may lead to substitution for the question of the meaning of what Parliament has enacted by the question of the meaning which the minister intended, or thought Parliament was enacting. A minister's words have no authority.

(*n*) Schemes made under authority of a statute and to give effect to it are not part of the statute and may not be consulted, except to confirm an interpretation of the words of the statute itself.[20]

Presumptions

There is also a considerable body of presumptions which can be invoked in various cases and which have greater or lesser weight depending on the statute in question and the composition of the court. These are only, be it noted, presumptions which may be applied in the absence of contrary indications and must give way to any clear indication that they should not apply. The principal are:

(*a*) The Crown, Crown officials, and Crown departments are not bound by statute to their prejudice unless that is provided expressly or by necessary implication.[21] Hence some modern statutes provide that the Act shall bind the Crown.[22]

(*b*) It is presumed that fundamental principles of constitutional law or of the common law of the land will not be altered by implication but only expressly.[23] It is difficult to say what are "fundamental principles" in this sense and it might be more helpful to phrase the presumption in the form that extensive and far-reaching changes in the law require to be made expressly, or that there is a presumption against interference with existing common law rights.[24]

(*c*) It is to be presumed that a British statute does not intend to infringe international law.[25] It may do so, but for reasons of international peace and comity the presumption is to the contrary.

(*d*) It is presumed that the jurisdiction of the ordinary courts applies and that an individual aggrieved may resort thereto and bring

---

[20] *Howgate v. Att.-Gen.* [1951] 1 K.B. 265. *cf. Jackson v. Hall* [1980] 1 All E.R. 177.

[21] *Cooper v. Hawkins* [1904] 2 K.B. 164; *Tamlin v. Hannaford* [1950] 1 K.B. 18; *Somerville v. Lord Advocate* (1893) 20 R. 1050; *Schulze v. Steele* (1890) 17 R.(J.) 47; *Edinburgh Magistrates v. Lord Advocate*, 1912 S.C. 1085; *Lord Advocate v. Strathclyde R.C.* [1990] 1 All E.R. 1.

[22] *e.g.* Crown Proceedings Act 1947; Road Traffic Act 1960, s. 250. *cf. Salt v. MacKnight*, 1947 J.C. 99.

[23] *e.g. Nairn v. University Courts of St. Andrews and Edinburgh*, 1909 S.C.(H.L.) 10 (decided when women did not have the vote and had just been admitted to university degrees, but university graduates had a vote: argued that women could be graduates, and graduates could vote, *ergo* women graduates could vote. *Held* that if Parliament meant to confer the franchise on any woman it must do so expressly); *Nokes v. Doncaster Amalgamated Collieries* [1940] A.C. 1014; *National Assistance Board v. Wilkinson* [1952] 2 Q.B. 648.

[24] *Rendall v. Blair* (1890) 45 Ch.D. 139; *Central Control Board (Liquor Traffic) v. Cannon Brewery Co. Ltd* [1919] A.C. 744.

[25] *Mortensen v. Peters* (1906) 8 F.(J.) 93.

actions and appeals in the usual way.[26] Hence, if appeal to the ordinary courts is to be limited or excluded, that should be stated expressly.

(e) An interpretation is to be preferred which makes a statutory provision meaningful, purposeful and operable, rather than one which renders it nugatory and inoperable. Nothing short of impossibility should allow the court to declare a statute unworkable.[27]

(f) Statutes are presumed to have prospective effect only and not retrospective, *i.e.* to deal with future cases and not past ones.[28] A provision may, of course, be expressed to be retrospective, and indeed a statute may be passed deliberately to abrogate rights declared by a court decision,[29] or it may be held that such must have been the intention of Parliament, and this presumption is much weaker in the case of statutes extending remedies or rights than in the case of statutes limiting liberty or imposing penalties.[30]

(g) A strict construction will be given to penal statutes, which impose a prohibition or a penalty, and they will not be held to extend to cases not clearly covered by the words used.[31] So, too, there is a presumption against any interference with individual liberty.

(h) In penal statutes or those creating criminal offences, it is presumed that *mens rea* (intention, guilty knowledge) is required for the commission of the offence and not merely the ignorant or inadvertent doing of the prohibited conduct.[32] But the words used frequently rebut this presumption and many modern statutes have infringed it.[33]

(j) A strict construction is to be given to statutes restrictive of personal liberty or encroaching on the property rights of individuals.[34] This presumption is weaker in times of national emergency[35] and weaker than it used to be in view of the impact of social welfare legislation. So, too, the intention to take away property

---

[26] *Dunbar v. Scottish County Investment Co.*, 1920 S.C. 210; *Chester v. Bateson* [1920] 1 K.B. 829; see also *Portobello Magistrates v. Edinburgh Magistrates* (1882) 10 R. 130.

[27] *Murray v. Inland Revenue*, 1918 S.C.(H.L.) 111; *Nokes v. Doncaster Amalgamated Collieries* [1940] A.C. 1014; *Kelly v. Nuttall*, 1965 S.C. 427, 438.

[28] *Gardner v. Beresford's Trs* (1878) 5 R.(H.L.) 105; *Wilson v. Wilson* 1939 S.C. 102; *Scott v. Aberdeen Corp.*, 1976 S.C. 81; *R. v. Kirk* [1985] 1 All E.R. 453.

[29] *e.g.* War Damage Act 1965, overruling retrospectively *Burmah Oil Co. Ltd v. Lord Advocate*, 1964 S.C.(H.L.) 117.

[30] *Wilson v. Wilson*, 1939 S.C. 102; *Bell v. Hay*, 1979 S.C. 237.

[31] *I.R.C. v. Hinchy* [1960] A.C. 748; *H.M. Advocate v. R.M.*, 1969 J.C. 52, 59; *Zimmerman v. Grossman* [1971] 1 All E.R. 363; *I.R.C. v. Ruffle*, 1979 S.C. 371.

[32] *Younghusband v. Luftig* [1949] 2 K.B. 354; *Sweet v. Parsley* [1970] A.C. 132.

[33] *e.g. Mitchell v. Morrison*, 1938 J.C. 64.

[34] *Scott v. Aberdeen Corp.*, 1976 S.C. 81.

[35] *Liversidge v. Anderson* [1942] A.C. 206.

from an individual without compensation is not to be imputed to Parliament unless that intention is clearly expressed.[36]

(k) A strict construction is to be given to statutory provisions imposing taxes on the public; such imposts must be clearly imposed, if at all,[37] though the courts are not keen to stretch this to the length of letting evasive transactions escape if they are within the spirit, if not the exact words, of the section.[38]

(l) Unless they do so clearly, statutes should not be construed so as to take away the jurisdiction of the superior courts[39] or to enlarge it by giving a right of appeal from inferior courts[40] or to confer jurisdiction on inferior courts, government departments or *ad hoc* authorities.[41]

(m) When a branch of law is codified by statute, the statute is to be interpreted by seeking the natural meaning of the words, uninfluenced by considerations based on the previous state of the law, and not presuming that it was intended to leave the former law unaltered.[42] Similarly, when Parliament re-enacts statutory provisions it does not thereby necessarily approve decisions on the former repealed provisions; there is a weak presumption that it does, but no more.[43] It is also presumed that comprehensive legislative codes are complete in themselves.[44]

(n) In accordance with the maxim *quilibet potest renunciare juri pro se introducto*, unless the contrary is stated, a person may renounce or contract out of a provision for his benefit,[45] but the reverse is the rule where the public has an interest to have the provision implemented.[46]

(o) It should be presumed that Parliament intended to legislate in conformity with the European Convention on Human Rights.[47]

Other presumptions of greater or lesser weight are sometimes enumerated, but the foregoing are the principal ones. Some of them are imprecise and of doubtful status, and they may conflict.

---

[36] *Central Control Board (Liquor Traffic) v. Cannon Brewery Co. Ltd* [1919] A.C. 744; *Malloch v. Aberdeen Corp.*, 1971 S.C.(H.L.) 53; 1974 S.L.T. 245; *R. v. I.R.C., ex p. Woolwich Building Society* [1990] 1 W.L.R. 1400.

[37] *I.R.C. v. Wolfson* [1949] 1 All E.R. 865.

[38] *Howard de Walden v. I.R.C.* [1942] 1 K.B. 389, 397; contrast *I.R.C. v. Levene* [1928] A.C. 217, 227. See also *Ross and Coulter v. Inland Revenue*, 1948 S.C.(H.L.) 1; *Edinburgh Life Assurance Co. v. Solicitor of Inland Revenue* (1875) 2 R. 394.

[39] *Pyx Granite Co. v. Ministry of Housing* [1960] A.C. 260.

[40] *Edwards v. Roberts* [1891] 1 Q.B. 302.

[41] *R. v. Board of Education* [1910] 2 K.B. 165.

[42] *Bank of England v. Vagliano Bros.* [1891] A.C. 107; *Haigh v. Ireland*, 1974 S.C.(H.L) 1.

[43] *Royal Crown Derby Porcelain Co. v. Russell* [1945] 2 K.B. 417; *R. v. Bow Road Justices* [1968] 2 Q.B. 572.

[44] *Pioneer Aggregates v. Secretary of State for the Environment* [1984] 2 All E.R. 358, 363.

[45] *Kennedy v. Johnstone*, 1956 S.C. 39, 49; *Elder v. Elder*, 1985 S.L.T. 471.

[46] *Ayr Harbour Trs. v. Oswald* (1883) 10 R. (H.L.) 85; *Johnson v. Moreton* [1980] A.C. 37, 60.

[47] *T., Petr.* 1996 S.C.L.R. 897.

Acts of the Scottish Parliament

Any provision of an Act of the Scottish Parliament or of subordinate legislation made by the Scottish Executive which could be read in such a way as to be outside legislative competence is to be read as narrowly as is required for it to be within competence, if such a reading is possible, and to have effect accordingly.[48]

Interpretation of human rights legislation

A court or tribunal determining a question which has arisen in connection with a Convention right must take into account any (a) judgment, decision, declaration or advisory opinion of the European Court of Human Rights; (b) opinion of the Commission given in a report adopted under Article 31 of the Convention; (c) a decision of the Commission in connection with Article 26 or 27(2) of the Convention; or (d) decision of the Committee of Ministers taken under Article 46 of the Convention, whenever made or given, so far as, in the opinion of the court or tribunal, it is relevant to the proceedings in which the question has arisen.[49]

So far as it is possible to do so, primary legislation and subordinate legislation must be read and give effect in a way which is compatible with Convention rights. This applies to primary legislation and subordinate legislation whenever enacted, does not affect the validity, continuing operation or enforcement of any incompatible primary or subordinate legislation if in the latter case (disregarding any possibility of revocation) primary legislation prevents removal of incompatibility.[50]

Special Considerations in Interpretation of International Conventions

When the court has to interpret the treaties establishing the European Communities, or legislation made thereunder,[51] or an international convention incorporated into British law, it would be absurd to interpret it differently from the courts of other countries which also are parties to the treaty or convention, and the courts should adopt the European method of looking at the design and purpose of the legislation and interpreting the legislation to have the desired effect,[52] or in a manner less constrained by technical rules of English or Scottish law or by legal precedent but on broad principles of general acceptance. If the convention is expressed in more than one language it is legitimate to look for assistance to the foreign language text, certainly if the English text is ambiguous.[53] It may

---

[48] Scotland Act 1998, s. 101.
[49] Human Rights Act 1998, s. 2.
[50] *Ibid.*, s. 3.
[51] *Bulmer v. Bollinger* [1974] Ch. 401.
[52] *Buchanan v. Babco Forwarding & Shipping Co.* [1977] Q.B. 208; *Fothergill v. Monarch Airlines* [1980] 2 All E.R. 696.
[53] *Buchanan, supra,* on appeal [1978] A.C. 141; *Fothergill, supra.* Note the approval in *Fothergill* of examination of foreign language dictionaries, textbooks and articles.

be permissible to look at the *travaux préparatoires* leading up to the convention.[54]

Conclusions on Statute Law

It will be apparent that statutory interpretation is neither a mechanical task nor an exact science. It is more of an art and many factors enter into the final decision: the inherent vagueness and inexactness of the ordinary words of the English language; grammatical difficulties; the draftsman's human failure to foresee all possible cases; the immense variety and complexity and unusual character of the circumstances which may arise; the temperament of the judge or court before whom the matter comes; and the judges' philosophy and their social, moral and other beliefs, their sympathy or lack of it for the parties, their judicial caution in adhering to a safe interpretation or valour in boldly extending a provision to cover a new case.

Too much attention should not be devoted to so-called rules of construction since "it must be remembered that the courts have laid down, indeed, not rigid rules, but principles which have been found to afford some guidance when it is sought to ascertain the intention of Parliament,"[55] and so conflicting are these in many cases that one is driven to the view that "a court invokes whichever of the rules produces a result that satisfies its sense of justice in the case before it."[56] In particular the courts cannot discover Parliament's intention, nor give effect to it, save by regard to the words enacted, and can never reach a conclusion which cannot be reconciled with the words used.

The Scottish and English Law Commissions made a joint study of the interpretation of statutes[57] and proposed that reference be permitted to a wider range of materials to ascertain Parliament's intention, and that specially prepared material be provided to ascertain the context in which statutory provisions were to be read, explanatory statements issued with the Act. The proposals seem as likely to complicate the process of interpretation as to facilitate it, and have not been acted on.

---

[54] *Gatoil International v. Arkwright-Boston Ins. Co.*, 1985 S.L.T. 68 (H.L.). The Civil Jurisdiction and Judgments Act 1982, giving effect in the U.K. to a Convention on Jurisdiction and the Enforcement of Judgments in Civil and Commercial Matters of 1968 provides by s.3 that a question of the meaning or effect of any provision of the Convention is to be determined in accordance with the principles laid down by and any relevant decisions of the European Court and two reports by Mr. P. Jenard on the 1968 Convention and a Protocol on its interpretation by the European Court of 1971, and by Professor P. Schlosser on the Accession Convention of 1978, by which the U.K. acceded to the 1968 Convention (both printed in the Official Journal of the European Communities) may be considered in interpreting the Convention.

[55] *Cutler v. Wandsworth Stadium* [1949] A.C. 398, 410, *per* Lord du Parcq.

[56] Willis, "Statute Interpretation in a Nutshell" (1938) 16 Can. Bar Rev. 1, 16.

[57] Law Com. No. 21; Scot. Law Com. No. 11, 1969.

II.—JUDICIAL PRECEDENTS OR CASE LAW

The reasons or principles justifying the decisions of judges of the superior courts in past cases are also important sources of principles and rules of law.[58] A judicial precedent is a previous judicial decision embodying a principle capable of subsequent application. Judicial precedents have an authority as sources of principles and rules of law for application in later cases, second only to relevant statutory provisions, and of highest authority in the absence of relevant statutory provisions. Every judicial decision is in the first place the determination of a litigated controversy between two parties; secondly, it is an example of the application of some principle of law to certain facts, and as such, apart from its value to students and jurists, will naturally be looked at as a guide when a court again has to deal with a similar problem, since judges naturally wish to utilise the wisdom and experience of their predecessors and to give decisions consistent with those previously given in like cases. Thirdly, under the modern system of *stare decisis*, discussed later, it may in certain circumstances provide an authoritative ruling on the law which *must* be applied in a subsequent case raising a similar problem of law. What is important in Anglo-American countries, as contrasted with civil law countries, is not that precedents are referred to or followed, but that in certain cases they *must be* followed.[59] The acceptance of even single decisions as settling the law and binding later courts to adopt the same principle is, in Scotland, a modern development, largely under English influence, superseding the native rule that a train of decisions was very persuasive but that one decision was merely an example.[60] To Stair[61] and Mackenzie[62] a train of decisions was good evidence of custom.[63] Erskine denied that decisions obliged the judges to follow them but held that a uniform series of decisions could make a usage which became part of our unwritten law. But in 1828 a Division of the Court of Session accepted that a prior decision of the whole Court was binding on it.[64]

"Our common law system consists in the applying to new combinations of circumstances those rules of law which we derive from legal principles and judicial precedents; and for the sake of obtaining uniformity, consistency and certainty, we must apply those rules where they are not plainly

---

[58] See generally, Gardner, *Judicial Precedent in Scots Law*; and "Judicial Decisions as a Source of Scots Law" (1941) 53 J.R. 33; Smith, *Judicial Precedent in Scots Law*; Cross, *Precedent in English Law*.

[59] See, *e.g. Re Automatic Telephone Co.'s Agreement* [1965] 1 All E.R. 206, following *Re Schweppes Ltd's Agreement* [1968] 1 All E.R. 195, decided earlier on the same day.

[60] Smith, *Judicial Precedent in Scots Law*, 1–14.

[61] *Inst.,* I, 1, 16.

[62] *Inst.,* I, 1, 10.

[63] *Inst.,* I, 1, 47.

[64] *Rose v. Drummond* (1828) 6 S. 945.

unreasonable and inconvenient, to all cases which arise; and we are not at liberty to reject them, and to abandon all analogy to them, in those to which they have not been judicially applied, because we think that the rules are not as convenient and reasonable as we ourselves could have devised."[65] Reference to previous decisions makes for consistency of treatment of similar cases and permits extension and development of principles by analogy. It also makes the law on particular points fairly predictable or certain. But it may sometimes cause a bad rule to be perpetuated.

Precedents are prior decisions embodying statements of principles of *law*, or rulings on disputed points of *law*. Previous decisions on questions of fact, *e.g.* that X was negligent in driving at 30 m.p.h. in fog, are not precedents to be followed in later similar cases,[66] because the facts of every case are unique and must be examined individually,[67] but decisions on some matters of fact, such as the sum of damages which may reasonably be awarded, are sometimes assisted by the citation of other decisions where similar injuries have been sustained.[68] So, too, previous decisions as to criminal penalties may give guidance, but are never binding authorities which have to be followed. A jury verdict on certain facts is never a precedent, even where very similar facts recur. Earlier cases on similar facts can only show how a basic rule has been applied to situations of a particular class.[69]

The use of judicial precedents as a source of law depends on several factors, the general practice in the superior courts (at least in cases of any difficulty or complexity or legal interest) of the judge or judges not merely issuing a decision but delivering an opinion explaining how and why they reached their decision and what rules or principles of law they have applied[70]; the long-established practice of reporting judicial decisions and the judges' reasons, and in later times the existence of a system of publishing reliable reports of the decisions of the superior courts; and the existence of a settled hierarchy of courts, in which the decisions of the higher courts carry greater weight than those of the lower.

---

[65] *Mirehouse v. Rennell* (1833) 1 Cl. & F. 527, 546.

[66] *L. & Y. Ry. v. Highley* [1917] A.C. 352; *G.W. Ry. v. S.S. Mostyn* [1928] A.C. 57; *cf. Beith's Trs. v. Beith*, 1950 S.C. 66.

[67] *Qualcast (Wolverhampton) Ltd v. Haynes* [1959] A.C. 743, 757–759; *Cavanagh v. Ulster Weaving Co.* [1960] A.C. 145; *Brown v. Rolls-Royce Ltd*, 1960 S.C.(H.L.) 22.

[68] *Waldon v. War Office* [1956] 1 W.L.R. 51; *Allan v. Scott*, 1972 S.C. 59.

[69] *Hazell v. B.T.C.* [1958] 1 W.L.R. 169.

[70] Note that in the sheriff court in civil cases, the sheriff is bound by the Sheriff Courts Act 1907, Sched. 1, r. 82, to make findings in fact and in law separately, and to add a note giving his reasons. For examples, see the Sheriff Court Reports. In higher courts the practice is only customary. Note also that in the Privy Council the opinion, or majority opinion, is couched in the form of advice from the Privy Council to Her Majesty to dismiss or allow the appeal. See Privy Council cases in the volumes of *Appeal Cases. cf. Jacobs v. L.C.C.* [1950] A.C. 361, 369: "While it is the primary duty of a court of justice to dispense justice to litigants, it is its traditional role to do so by means of an exposition of the relevant law."

Judicial Opinions

In the superior courts it is customary in all but the simplest cases for the judge or judges to deliver or issue an opinion stating the relevant facts and explaining why he or they have found for the one party rather than the other, with references to the statutes and cases relied on and justifying the decision. The practice is very valuable as affording the parties the legal justification for the actual decision, and affording lawyers generally an explanation and discussion of the principles and rules of law thought applicable to the case and others raising the same issue of law. "It is not the function of noble and learned Lords or indeed of any judges to frame definitions or to lay down hard and fast rules. It is their function to enunciate principles and much that they say is intended to be illustrative or explanatory and not to be definitive. When there are two or more speeches they must be read together and then it is generally much easier to see what are the principles involved and what are merely illustrations of it."[71]

Reports

There is no official series of law reports, though *Session Cases* in Scotland and the *Law Reports* in England enjoy a rather more favoured status than do other series, in that the printed opinions are revised by the judges, which is not always the case with other reports. There is nothing, however, to prevent other reports being published or cited in court[72] and sometimes reports in other series are preferable or include cases or points omitted from the main series.[73] Not all cases are reported; probably on average only about 5 per cent to 10 per cent of cases decided in the Inner House,[74] so that an unreported decision can sometimes be found

---

[71] *Cassell v. Broome* [1972] 1 All E.R. 801, 836, *per* Lord Reid.

[72] *Renshaw v. Dixon* [1911] W.N. 40; Megarry, "Reporting the Unreported" (1954) 70 L.Q.R. 246; Allen, *Law in the Making* (6th ed.), 257, 355. In the House of Lords the *Law Reports* should normally be cited if the case is in that series; there is no practice in revenue cases to cite *Tax Cases* instead: *National Bank of Greece v. Westminster Bank Executor Co.* [1970] W.L.R. 1400.

[73] Thus *Robertson's Tutor v. Glasgow Corp.* is reported in 1950 S.C. 502, but not in S.L.T.; *Donnelly v. Glasgow Corp.* is in 1949 S.L.T. 362 and not in S.C.; in *Lawrence v. Scott*, 1965 S.C. 403, 406, a passage is referred to which is omitted from the S.C. report of the precedent cited. *cf.* also *Coats's Trs. v. Lord Advocate*, 1965 S.C.(H.L.) 45, 66, *per* Lord Guest; *Duke of Buccleuch v. I.R.C.* [1967] 1 All E.R. 129, 133; *Lamb v. Lord Advocate* 1975 S.L.T. (Notes) 78. There are today many series of reports, many dealing only with cases on particular topics, such as employment cases.

[74] Walker, "The Mass of Reports" (1953) 69 S.L.R. 222. Decisions unreported at the time may subsequently be exhumed and reported either fully, *e.g. Walker v. Walker* (1949) in 1953 S.C. 297; or as a note appended to the report of a later case: see, *e.g. McNamara v. Laird Line* (1924), reported in a note to *McKay v. Scottish Airways*, 1948 S.C. 254, 265; *Cremin v. Thomson* (1941) reported in [1953] 2 All E.R. 1185 and 1956 S.L.T. 357; *Brown v. Redpath Brown & Co.* (1952) reported in 1963 S.L.T. 219; *Robertson v. Lord Advocate* (1950), reported in a note to *Ayr Town Council v. Secretary of State for Scotland*, 1965 S.C. 394, 400; *Hunter v. Bradford Property Trust* (1960) reported in 1970 S.L.T. 173; *Glasgow Heritable Trust v. Donald* (1971) reported in *Albyn Properties v. Knox*, 1977 S.C. 108, 113.

useful.[75] A report, moreover, may deal with only one aspect or one stage of a case, and other points, the ultimate result and the disposal of a case may remain unknown.[76] There are instances of cases being cited from newspapers,[77] textbooks,[78] a shorthand report of the judgment,[79] and the personal recollection of the judge and a report may be supplemented when it is considered in a later case by reference to the Session Papers, pleadings and other documents in the case.[80] At least in England there is a salutary rule that only reports prepared and initialled by a member of the Bar may be cited.[81] The House of Lords has criticised the citation of cases which merely illustrated accepted principles of law.[82] Mere notes of cases are of little use.[83]

The Form of Reports

The standard modern form of report consists of several parts.[84] There are first certain head-words or catch-words printed in italics and separated by dashes, chosen to indicate very briefly by reference to recognised legal headings and sub-heads what legal topics are dealt with in the case, mentioning first the principal ones and then the subordinate or more detailed matters,[85] and what statutes have been discussed or interpreted in the case. This is followed by the rubric or headnote, which is a concise

---

[75] The proportion of cases decided by a single judge in the Outer House or in the sheriff court and not reported is much higher: so also in England. In *Leighton v. Harland & Wolff*, 1953 S.L.T.(Notes) 36, it was observed that it was counsel's duty to refer the court to unreported as well as reported cases on the point in issue. But the discovery of unreported decisions on a point may be fortuitous.

[76] Thus *McGhie v. B.T.C.* is reported at one stage and on one point in 1964 S.L.T. 25. The Lord Ordinary's unreported decision on another point is referred to and printed in part, in *Russell's Exrx. v. British Railways Board*, 1965 S.C. 422, 424.

[77] *R. v. Labouchere* (1884) 12 Q.B.D. 320, 328; *Barras v. Aberdeen Steam Trawling Co.* 1933 S.C.(H.L.) 21; *Overstone Ltd v. Shipway* [1962] 1 All E.R. 52; *Wills' Trs. v. Cairngorm School Ltd*, 1976 S.C.(H.L.) 30, 162, but on the dangers of this, see *Mahon v. Osborne* [1939] 2 K.B. 14.

[78] *Bush v. Whitehaven Trustees*, reported only in Hudson on *Building Contracts*, cited in *Davis Contractors Ltd v. Fareham U.D.C.* [1956] A.C. 696; *Cowe v. Millar*, reported only in Connell on *The Agricultural Holdings Act*, cited in *Smith v. Grayston Estates Ltd*, 1960 S.C. 349, 354.

[79] *Renshaw v. Dixon* [1911] W.N. 40; *Perez v. C.A.V. Ltd* [1959] 2 All E.R. 414.

[80] *Grant v. Duke of Gordon* (1781) Mor. 12820, examined in *Wills' Trs., supra*; *Société du Gaz de Paris v. Les armateurs francais*, 1926 S.C.(H.C.) 13, examined in *Credit Chimique v. Scott* 1979 S.C. 406, 414.

[81] *Rivoli Hats v. Gooch* [1953] 1 W.L.R. 1190; *Birtwistle v. Tweedale* [1954] 1 W.L.R. 190.

[82] *Lambert v. Lewis* [1982] A.C. 225, 274; *Roberts Petroleum Ltd v. Kenny* [1983] 2 A.C. 192, 200.

[83] *Birtwistle v. Tweedale* [1954] 1 W.L.R. 190 (*Estates Gazette* rejected); *Rivoli Hats Ltd v. Gooch* [1953] 1 W.L.R. 1190 (*Current Law* rejected); see also, *Mahon v. Osborne* [1939] 2 K.B. 14; *Chapman v. Chapman* [1954] A.C. 429. In *Re Alsopp* [1967] 2 All E.R. 1056, it was said to have been the practice to ignore reports in *Weekly Notes* on matters of construction of wills and in *Johnson v. Agnew* [1979] 1 All E.R. 883, 891, Lord Wilberforce thought it contrary to sound practice to cite *Weekly Notes* at all. In *Maitland*, 1961 S.C. 291, and *McLaughlin*, 1965 S.C. 243, a prior case reported without opinions only in S.L.T. (Notes) was said to be valueless as a precedent in future.

[84] *cf.* Newark, "Anatomy of a Law Report" (1965) 16 N.I.L.Q. 371.

[85] These catch-words are of great importance for determining where the case will be placed in the Digests.

statement of the facts, of the point of law in issue, and of the court's decision, which last element is usually preceded by the word "Held." There is also an indication of any dissenting or divergent opinions by particular judges and of any specially noteworthy remarks or observations, and sometimes a mention of the attitude adopted to certain previous cases.[86] It has to be noticed that the head-words and rubric are compiled by the reporter under the supervision of the editor of the series of reports, and they have no authority at all. They may contain mistakes or misleading statements[87] and judges sometimes have occasion to criticise the rubric of previous reports.[88] The rubric is only the reporter's summary, his view of what the case decided. There may be two or more sets of head-words and rubrics where the case has raised two or more distinct matters for argument and decision, as where there have been debatable points on procedure, on law and on evidence.

Then follows a narrative of the facts of the case and of the material steps in the litigation, sometimes with quotations from the written pleadings of the parties or from the evidence heard at an earlier stage. Sometimes this is done by incorporating that part of a judge's opinion which states the facts, or by reference to his opinion which, in the reporter's view, adequately states the facts. This information should make clear what the controversy is about, and everything that has gone before in its progress through the courts. It should, but may not, contain all factual information about the case which enables the reader to understand it and to evaluate or criticise the decision and judicial opinions. But some facts are sometimes tantalisingly omitted.

This is followed by a brief account of the arguments put forward by counsel on each side with a note of the cases, statutes and books referred to by them. Sometimes important or valuable statements are made in argument, or made by the Bench in reply to an argument. Moreover, it may be very important in a later case to know whether the court was referred in argument to a particular case or statute, as there have been instances of decisions arrived at in ignorance of a case or statute in point, and a decision is of lesser authority for the future if relevant prior cases were not cited in argument.[89]

Lastly there are printed the opinions of the judges, usually in full, but sometimes with omissions. It should be noted that another series of

---

[86] *e.g.* that some precedent case has been "applied" or "followed" or "not followed" or "distinguished" or "overruled." For the significance of these terms, see p. 472, *infra*.

[87] Thus in *Victoria Laundry v. Newman* [1949] 2 K.B. 528 it was pointed out that the rubric in *Hadley v. Baxendale* (1854) 9 Ex. 341 was incorrect in a material respect.

[88] Thus in *Hamilton v. Hamilton*, 1954 S.L.T. 16, the report of *Robb v. Robb*, 1953 S.L.T. 44, was severely criticised.

[89] *Penrikyber Navigation Colliery Co. v. Edwards* [1933] A.C. 28; in *Aldridge v. Simpson-Bell*, 1971 S.C. 87, an earlier decision was not followed on the ground that the point in question had not been argued.

reports may include passages omitted in one report,[90] or may give a slightly different version of a passage.[91]

Some reported decisions are merely instances of the application of an existing rule of law, reported for the interest of the circumstances or the value of the judicial expression of an old and settled principle of law, while others are really creative of new law, as where a new rule is laid down or an existing rule reformulated, modified, extended or limited, or applied to a fresh set of circumstances. The former kind of cases are merely applications of law, the latter in some measure create new law or define or delimit the applicability of some principle or rule of law in a sphere previously vague. Cases of the former sort may be, but are rather unlikely to be, authoritative or binding in a future case, but cases of the latter sort are much more likely to be authoritative in future.

Reports Held on Database

In addition to printed reports, the legal database, *Lexis*, includes modern decisions of the Scottish superior courts[92] and more recent unreported decisions, and a wider range of decisions of English courts. This raises the danger of too many reports being available and the English courts have warned of the dangers of too many reports being liable to be cited.[93]

The Principle of Stare Decisis

While, as has been pointed out, it is a natural and commonsense practice to have regard, when deciding a case, to reported decisions in prior cases raising the same issue of law, the modern British system goes further by its insistence on *stare decisis*, that is, on the principle of abiding by authorities or decided cases, so that in certain circumstances the doctrine derived from a precedent case or series of cases *must* be followed and applied, even though the judge in the subsequent case might not have been disposed of his own accord to apply that doctrine. The habit of referring to precedents in point and applying them has grown into the rule that a precedent in point *must* be applied.[94] This is not a rule of law, but a settled practice and usage adopted and accepted by the courts.

---

[90] Thus the report of *Leadbetter v. N.C.B.*, 1952 S.L.T. 179 deals with a matter omitted from 1952 S.C. 19. *cf. Barras, supra*, at p. 50, *per* Lord Macmillan and *Lawrence v. Scott*, 1965 S.C. 403, 406, *per* L.P. Clyde, in each case quoting a passage from one report of a case, absent from another report.

[91] Thus there are four different reports of *Holmes v. Mather* in 1875 (L.R. 10 Ex. 261; 44 L.J.Ex. 176; 33 L.T. 361; 23 W.R. 869) which show important verbal differences: two are set out in parallel columns for comparison in Pollock on *Torts* (15th ed.), 132.

[92] *Session Cases* and S.L.T. from 1950, S.C.C.R. from 1981.

[93] *Lambert v. Lewis* [1982] A.C. 225, 274; *Roberts Petroleum Ltd v. Kenny* [1983] 2 A.C. 192, 200.

[94] See also Salmond, "Theory of Judicial Precedents" (1900) 16 L.Q.R. 376.

This principle of *stare decisis* may be justified on the ground that it makes for certainty and consistency of the law, that it makes for the disposal in the same way of similar cases (and equality of treatment is a commonly accepted element in justice), that it tends to limit or exclude judicial mistakes, prejudices and faulty formulations of an appropriate rule of law to apply to the facts, and that it tends to make the law predictable, so as to enable a legal adviser to forecast what rule a court would probably apply to a given set of facts.

On the other hand, as will appear later, there are countervailing disadvantages: adherence to *stare decisis* may make the law rigid, inflexible and impervious to social change; the discovery of the doctrine enunciated by a precedent is difficult and may be impossible; it tends to make the quest for a ground of decision the quest for a prior similar case, rather than for the appropriate principle; it leads judges to make tediously long quotations from previous cases in their opinions; judicial distaste for, or disinclination to be regulated by, a particular precedent produces much verbal juggling, sophistry, false reasoning and the drawing of fine, or even invisible, distinctions; and a decision may come to depend too much on the finding or not finding of an apt precedent in the reports.

Nevertheless, this is the modern British rule[95]: a precedent which is both *in point and binding must* be applied; a precedent which is *in point and persuasive* should be considered and *may be adopted* and applied; a precedent which is *not in point may be ignored*. Much accordingly depends on the criteria for deciding whether a particular precedent is in point or not and, in the circumstances before a particular court, whether it is binding or merely persuasive.

When is a Precedent "In Point"?

A prior decision is a precedent in point when there was raised, argued and decided in it as applicable to a certain set of facts some issue of law which is the same issue of law as arises in the instant case in relation to a different set of facts of the same general kind.[96] Similarity of facts between the precedent and the instant case is not enough and may, indeed, matter very little. One case about sale of a car may have no relation in law to another case about sale of a car. But a decision about the sale of a car or a book may contain a statement of principle on an issue of law relevant to a later case about the sale of a car or a horse raising the same issue of law. Decisions on questions of fact do not make precedents though they may give some guidance in a later case of what courts currently do.[97] What is

---

[95] The rule is English in origin and has been accepted in Scotland only since 1800, largely under the influence of the House of Lords: see Smith, *Judicial Precedent*, 10–17.

[96] In *Dick v. Falkirk*, 1976 S.C.(H.L.) 1, 4, 5, 7 judges wrongly stressed similarity of facts.

[97] *Waldon v. War Office* [1966] 1 All E.R. 108.

important is the raising in a subsequent case of the same issue of law as was decided in the precedent case, as, for example, whether artificial insemination by a donor amounts to legal adultery or not,[98] or what amounts in law to fraudulent misrepresentation inducing a contract.[99] Thus the precedent about fraudulent misrepresentation is in point in a later case of a contract of sale or of hiring, even though the precedent related to the contract to take shares in a company, but is not necessarily in point in relation to fraudulent misrepresentation inducing a marriage, since marriage is a relationship distinct from a commercial contract.[1]

As will be seen later, much ingenuity is sometimes devoted to arguing that a precedent is not "in point" or not "on all fours with" the instant case, on the ground that the precedent dealt with a different legal issue or that the facts are sufficiently different from those of the precedent to make the issue of law materially different. When it is remembered that facts never exactly reproduce themselves and that possible combinations of facts raising legal issues are limitless, it will be apparent that it is frequently difficult to say whether a given prior case is really in point or not, and that in most cases it is really a matter of degree, the decision being that the prior case is or is not sufficiently similar in the legal issue raised to the instant case to be treated as having raised the same point of law and, accordingly, to be a precedent for the decision of the instant case.

Binding and Persuasive Precedents

Even of prior decisions which are in point, not every one is binding on a subsequent court, or authoritative. Some are merely persuasive.

A precedent in point is authoritative or binding when judges in a subsequent case raising the same issue of law *must* follow and apply it to the facts before them, irrespective of their views as to its soundness.[2]

A precedent in point is persuasive when judges in a subsequent case will take it into consideration, when they will attach such weight to it as they think the precedent deserves, having regard to its value, the personal eminence of the judges who decided it, the place in the judicial hierarchy from which it comes, and the extent to which it is in point in the later case, but which they are *not bound* to follow and apply. It may persuade them to apply it, but if it does so, it does so on its merits, and not because it is authoritative.

The question whether any given precedent which is "in point" is authoritative or merely persuasive in a subsequent case depends primarily on where it emanated from in the hierarchy of courts and, secondly, on

---

[98] *MacLennan v. MacLennan*, 1958 S.C. 105.

[99] *Derry v. Peek* (1889) 14 App.Cas. 337.

[1] *Lang v. Lang*, 1921 S.C. 44. In *MacQueen v. Hodge* 1990 S.L.T. 266 the Lord Ordinary held a House of Lords decision of 1861 was "directly in point" and not distinguishable.

[2] *Ferguson v. Littlewoods Pools Ltd*, 1997 S.L.T. 309; *Lindsay v. H.M. Advocate* 1997 J.C. 19.

certain factors affecting its evaluation. These two elements must now be considered.

The Hierarchy of Courts

The regular courts of the United Kingdom form a systematic hierarchy in which appeals generally lie from inferior courts to courts superior to them in their own line of ascent. In considering whether any given court is bound or subject to persuasion by a precedent emanating from another court in the hierarchy, it is essential to have in mind the place of each court in the hierarchy. The authority of a prior decision does not depend on whether an appeal lies from the court considering the precedent to the court which issued judgment in the precedent case. It depends on the place in the hierarchy held by the court from which the precedent came, relative to the place in the hierarchy held by the later court considering the precedent.

The hierarchy of United Kingdom regular courts consists of six parallel lines, comprising respectively the civil and criminal courts of Scotland, England and Wales, and of Northern Ireland. These are set out in the following table, in which courts shown on the same horizontal line are of generally corresponding standing and authority. The lowest courts can be omitted from consideration since their decisions are very seldom reported and are of negligible value as precedents.

The general principle is that any court is bound by prior decisions in point pronounced by courts superior to it in its own vertical line of authority, normally treats as binding precedents in point pronounced by a prior court of its own rank in its own vertical line, and that prior decisions in point of courts of equal or higher rank in other vertical lines of authority are persuasive in varying degree.[3] Decisions of courts of lower rank in any vertical line of authority may be ignored but may sometimes be of some persuasive value. But this general statement must now be examined in more detail in relation to the main courts because practice is not uniform in all courts. Moreover the practice in Scotland is less strict and rigid throughout than in England.

The Principle of Stare Decisis in Operation

The way in which the principle of *stare decisis* operates varies slightly in different courts and must be examined in relation to the different Scottish and English courts separately.

---

[3] "In the hierarchical system of courts which exists in this country, it is necessary for each lower tier . . . to accept loyally the decisions of the higher tiers": *Cassell v. Broome* [1972] 1 All E.R. 801, 809, *per* Lord Hailsham. An inferior court cannot disregard a decision of a superior court, however sure that it was wrongly decided: *Farrell v. Alexander* [1977] A.C. 59.

SCOTLAND		ENGLAND & WALES		N. IRELAND	
Civil	*Criminal*	*Civil*	*Criminal*	*Civil*	*Criminal*
H.L. Ct. of Session (Inner Ho.)	— High Court (appeals)	H.L. Ct. of Appeal[4] (Civil Division)	H.L. Ct. of Appeal[5] (Criminal Division)	H.L. Ct. of Appeal (Civil Division)	H.L. Ct. of Appeal (Criminal Division)
Ct. of Session (Outer Ho.)	High Court (trials)	Divisional Court High Court[6]	Divisional Court Crown Court[7]	Divisional Court High Court[8]	Divisional Court Crown Court[9]
Sheriff Principal	Sheriff and jury		Crown Court		Crown Court
Sheriff	Sheriff (summarily)	County Court			

EUROPEAN COMMUNITIES LAW

Court of Justice of the European Communities

On matters of the interpretation of the Treaties, the validity and interpretations of acts of the Community institutions, and of the interpretation of the statutes of bodies established by an act of the Council, the Court of Justice is the supreme tribunal and its decisions are binding on all United Kingdom courts.[10] The Court of Justice does not however regard itself as bound by its own previous decisions though it does not readily depart from principles previously laid down.[11]

Where a United Kingdom court has referred a point to the Court of Justice for a preliminary ruling its ruling must be accepted by the court which requested it but not by that court in other cases nor by other courts which, if they doubt the ruling, may request a further ruling.

Decisions on points of European law by other courts in the United Kingdom or courts in other member states are not binding on a Scottish court but are persuasive.

---

[4] Including the Court of Exchequer Chamber which was the predecessor of the Court of Appeal.

[5] Including the former Court for Crown Cases Reserved (1846–1906) and Court of Criminal Appeal (1906–66).

[6] Including the pre-1875 separate Courts of Queen's Bench, Common Pleas, Exchequer, Admiralty and Matrimonial Causes.

[7] Including the Central Criminal Court.

[8] Including the former courts replaced by the High Court of Northern Ireland.

[9] Including the former courts replaced by the Crown Court.

[10] European Communities Act 1972, s. 3.

[11] Case 28–30/62: *Da Costa v. Nederlandse Belastingadministratiè* [1963] C.M.L.R. 224, cited in *Bulmer v. Bollinger* [1974] Ch. 401; Case 4/69 *Lütticke GmbH v. EC Commission* [1971] E.C.R. 325. Difficulties arise where the Court does not make plain whether it is differing from a previous decision.

SCOTLAND

House of Lords

The House of Lords, when sitting as the final court of civil appeal from Scotland, sits as a Scottish court[12] and normally considers itself bound by precedents of its own pronounced in Scottish appeals,[13] or by decisions in appeals relating to questions of general jurisprudence[14] and not turning on specialities of English law,[15] but not by its own precedents pronounced in English or Irish appeals,[16] nor by dicta on questions of Scots law raised incidentally in such appeals.[16] Such precedents will, however, be persuasive.[17] Decisions of the House in English appeals on statutory provisions common to England and Scotland are probably binding,[18] but not if the statute is peculiar to England.

In July 1966[19] the Lord Chancellor announced on behalf of himself and the Lords of Appeal in Ordinary that their Lordships regarded the use of precedent as an indispensable foundation upon which to decide what is the law and its application to individual cases, and providing at least some degree of certainty upon which individuals can rely in the conduct of their affairs, as well as a basis for orderly development of legal rules. Their Lordships nevertheless recognised that too rigid adherence to precedent might lead to injustice in a particular case and also unduly restrict the proper development of the law, and they therefore proposed to modify their previous practice and, while treating former decisions of the House as normally binding, to depart from a previous decision when it appeared right to do so. In this connection they would bear in mind the danger of disturbing retrospectively the basis on which contracts, settlements of property and fiscal arrangements had been entered into and also the special need for certainty as to the criminal law.[20] The announcement was stated as not intended to affect the use of precedent elsewhere than in the House.

---

[12] *Concha v. Murietta* (1889) 40 Ch.D. 543, 550; *cf. Cooper v. Cooper* (1888) 15 R.(H.L.) 21; *Elliot v. Joicey*, 1935 S.C.(H.L.) 57. But see *Virtue v. Alloa Police Commissioners* (1873) 1 R. 285, 296.

[13] *Gordon v. Marjoribanks* (1818) 6 Dow 87, 112; *Houldsworth v. City of Glasgow Bank* (1880) 7 R.(H.L.) 53, 62; *Oliver v. Saddler*, 1929 S.C.(H.L.) 94, 97; as to England, see *London Tramways Co. v. L.C.C.* [1898] A.C. 375; Landau, "Precedents in the House of Lords" (1951) 63 J.R. 222.

[14] What these are may be matter of dispute.

[15] *Orr Ewing's Trustees v. Orr Ewing* (1885) 13 R.(H.L.) 1.

[16] *Glasgow Corp. v. Central Land Board*, 1956 S.C.(H.L.) 1; and see discussion in 19 M.L.R. 427; *McIntyre v. Armitage Shanks Ltd*, 1980 S.C.(H.L.) 46, 62.

[17] *Virtue v. Alloa Police Commissioners* (1873) 1 R. 285; *Blacks v. Girdwood* (1885) 13 R. 243; Henderson, "English Cases as Scots Authorities" (1900) 12 J.R. 304.

[18] *I.R.C. v. Glasgow Police Athletic Association*, 1953 S.C.(H.L.) 13; *Dalgleish v. Glasgow Corp.* 1976 S.C. 32, 52.

[19] Note [1966] 3 All E.R. 77. On this see Lord Kilbrandon, "The House of Lords and the Scottish Law Commission" (1967) 83 L.Q.R. 176; Paterson, *The Law Lords*, 146–151.

[20] The House does not deal with criminal appeals from Scotland, save from the Courts-Martial Appeal Court.

The House has, so far, been very cautious in overruling any of its own previous decisions.[21] It has indicated that the power should be used sparingly and not as a method of law reform.[22]

Decisions of the House in Scottish appeals are binding on all civil courts in Scotland, as are decisions in non-Scottish appeals on United Kingdom statutes having equal or similar applicability in both countries; but decisions of the House in other appeals, on statutes not common to the United Kingdom, and on grounds of general jurisprudence raised in non-Scottish appeals are persuasive only, though in a high degree.[23] It is always difficult to determine what are questions of "general jurisprudence", particularly in view of the tendency of English Lords of Appeal to assume that much English law is general, and that the same principles apply in Scotland. The Court of Session has, on occasion, declined to follow an old House of Lords decision, decided in the context of conditions which no longer apply.[24]

Court of Session, Inner House

Either Division of the Inner House of the Court of Session, or an Extra Division, is normally bound by decisions of the House of Lords in Scottish appeals,[24] by a decision of seven or more judges of the Court of Session, and by a previous decision of either Division or an Extra Division.[25] There is no fixed rule that even the whole court is bound by its own previous decisions, but it is certainly not the rule that decisions of a Division have the same weight as decisions of the full court.[26] In exceptional cases a precedent in point of either Division may not be followed, but doubtful precedents or conflicts of precedent are normally resolved by convening a fuller court of seven or more judges.[27] A court of seven judges may quite

---

[21] It declined to do so in *Jones v. Secretary of State for Social Services* [1972] A.C. 944 but did so in *British Railways Board v. Herrington* [1972] A.C. 877; *Miliangos v. George Frank (Textiles) Ltd* [1976] A.C. 443; *The Johanna Oldendorff* [1974] A.C. 479; and *Dick v. Burgh of Falkirk*, 1976 S.C.(H.L.) 1.

[22] *McKendrick v. Sinclair*, 1972 S.C.(H.L.) 25, 55.

[23] *Virtue v. Alloa Police Commrs* (1873) 1 R. 285; *Orr Ewing's Trs. v. Orr Ewing* (1885) 13 R.(H.L.) 1; *Glasgow Corp. v. Central Land Board*, 1956 S.C.(H.L.) 1, 16; *Dalgleish v. Glasgow Corp.*, 1976 S.C. 32, 51.

[24] In *Commerzbank AG v. Large*, 1977 S.C. 375 a Full Bench declined to follow *Hyslops v. Gordon* (1824) 2 Shaw's App. 451, as decided in conditions which no longer applied and because a more recent House of Lords case, *Miliangos v. George Frank (Textiles) Ltd* [1976] A.C. 443, had taken an opposite view. But see *Weir v. J.M. Hodge & Son*, 1990 S.L.T. 266.

[25] *e.g. Garden's Exor. v. More*, 1913 S.C. 285; *Heavyside v. Smith*, 1929 S.C. 68; *Cameron v. Glasgow Corp.*, 1935 S.C. 533; *Galloway v. Galloway*, 1947 S.C. 330; *Marshall v. Scottish Milk Marketing Board*, 1956 S.C.(H.L.) 37, 39 (revd. by H.L., *ibid.*, 40–48). In *Hargrave's Trs. v. Schofield* (1900) 3 F. 14 there were expressions of dissent from this principle.

[26] As is the case in England under *Young v. Bristol Aeroplane Co.* [1944] K.B. 718. In *Yuill's Trs. v. Thomson* (1902) 4 F. 815, 819, it was said to be contrary to practice for the whole court to reconsider a question considered by seven judges, seven judges having the same authority as the whole court, but not all the judges accepted that proposition.

[27] In *Drummond v. Inland Revenue*, 1951 S.C. 482, it was doubted whether it was competent for the court, when sitting as Court of Exchequer, to convene a larger court to reconsider a precedent, and the view was expressed that this should be done by the House of Lords.

freely overrule a precedent of either Division.[28] There are, however, expressions of the view that a Division is not necessarily bound by a single decision of either Division.[29] A decision has been held not binding where it had been decided in ignorance of a prior and higher decision.[30] Moreover even when a precedent is directly in point it may be disregarded if the social and economic background has so changed that the precedent is quite outmoded.[31]

Decisions of the House of Lords in English or Irish appeals are not binding but may be very strongly persuasive,[32] and of the English or Irish Courts of Appeal strongly persuasive, the degree of persuasiveness depending largely on the similarity of Scots to English or Irish law on the point in issue.[33] Decisions of lower English or Irish courts are weakly persuasive, though rather more so when construing a statute common to Scotland and to England or Ireland.

High Court of Justiciary as Court of Criminal Appeal

The High Court is not bound by decisions of the House of Lords in a criminal matter, even when dealing with a United Kingdom criminal statute,[34] and still less by the (English) Court of Appeal, Criminal Division, or the predecessors of that court,[35] though such decisions are persuasive if the matter is one common to United Kingdom law.[36] Normally any precedent doubted is reviewed by a larger, or even a full, bench.[37] A full bench can probably overrule a precedent decided by a prior full bench.[38] A larger full bench can overrule a prior decision of a smaller full bench,[39] and any full bench can overrule a mere quorum of three.[40]

---

[28] *e.g. Cochrane's Exrx. v. Cochrane*, 1947 S.C. 134; *McElroy v. McAllister*, 1949 S.C. 110; *Smith v. Stewart & Co.*, 1960 S.C. 329; *Scottish Discount Co. v. Blin*, 1986 S.L.T. 123.

[29] *Lord Advocate v. Young* (1898) 25 R. 778; *Earl of Wemyss v. Earl of Zetland* (1890) 18 R. 126, 130.

[30] *Mitchell v. Mackersy* (1905) 8 F. 198, where *Gray's Trs. v. Royal Bank* (1896) 23 R. 199 was overruled as decided in ignorance of the House of Lords' decision of *Globe Insurance Co. v. Mackenzie* (1850) 7 Bell 296, which had been accepted as authoritative in *Stewart's Tr. v. Stewart's Exrx.* (1896) 23 R. 739.

[31] *Beith's Trustees v. Beith*, 1950 S.C. 66. *cf.* Lord Carmont's reasons in *Macdonald v. Glasgow Western Hospitals*, 1954 S.C. 453, 484 for refusing to hold the First Division bound by the First Division's decision in *Reidford v. Aberdeen Magistrates*, 1933 S.C. 276 and *Commerzbank AG*, *supra*. In *Donnelly v. Donnelly*, 1959 S.C. 97, Lord Justice-Clerk Thomson (p. 102) refused to regard a case of 1561, however much in point, as binding, but Lord Patrick (p. 103) accepted the case as an authority.

[32] *Glasgow Corp. v. Central Land Board*, 1956 S.C.(H.L.) 1, 16; *Dalgleish v. Glasgow Corp.*, 1976 S.C. 32, 52.

[33] *e.g. I.R.C. v. Ferguson*, 1968 S.C. 135, 151 (revd. 1969 S.C.(H.L.) 103).

[34] *Ritchie v. Pirie*, 1972 J.C. 7, 14; *Brennan v. H.M. Advocate*, 1977 J.C. 38.

[35] *Kelly v. MacKinnan*, 1982 J.C. 94; *Thomson v. H.M. Advocate*, 1983 S.L.T. 682.

[36] *Dalgleish, supra.*

[37] *e.g. Kirkwood v. H.M. Advocate*, 1939 J.C. 36 (11 judges).

[38] *Sugden v. H.M. Advocate*, 1934, J.C. 103. A "full bench" may be any court larger than the essential quorum of three, and may consist of five (*e.g. McFadyan v. Stewart*, 1951 J.C. 164), seven (*e.g. Mitchell v. Morrison*, 1938 J.C. 64), 11 (*e.g. Kirkwood, supra*), 12 (*e.g. Sugden, supra*), or other, normally uneven, number.

[39] *Smith v. Macnab*, 1975 J.C. 48; *Brennan, supra.*

[40] *Macmillan v. McConnell* 1917 J.C. 43; *Marshall v. Clark*, 1957 J.C. 68.

Decisions of a quorum are binding on later courts.[41] Decisions of the High Court on appeal are normally binding on High Court judges presiding at trials, and on sheriffs.

Court of Session, Outer House

A Lord Ordinary sitting alone in the Outer House is bound by decisions of the House of Lords in Scottish appeals,[42] by decisions of seven or more judges,[43] or of either Division or an Extra Division of the Inner House.[44] He is not bound by decisions of another Outer House judge, though he treats such decisions with respect.[45] But he may decline to follow them, leaving it to a higher court at a later date to decide which view is right.[46] Decisions of the House of Lords in English or Irish appeals are very persuasive,[47] of the English or Irish Courts of Appeal strongly persuasive, and of the English or Irish High Courts mildly persuasive,[48] the degree depending on the similarity of the legal systems on the point in issue. If a Lord Ordinary intends to base his judgment on a case not cited in argument, he should give counsel an opportunity to comment on it before finalising his judgment.[49]

High Court of Justiciary (as court of trial)

A single Lord of Justiciary usually accepts the law laid down previously on appeal by a bench of the High Court, but single-judge rulings, though very persuasive, are not binding on other single judges.[50] Decisions of the English superior criminal courts are highly persuasive, and of English trial judges mildly persuasive, but only if the legal systems are similar on the point in issue.

Sheriff Principal and Sheriff (civil)

Sheriffs principal and sheriffs are bound by decisions of the House of Lords[51] and Inner House of the Court of Session, and regard English and

---

[41] *McAvoy v. Cameron*, 1917 J.C. 1; *Ritchie v. Pirie*, 1972 J.C. 7.

[42] Even if the House of Lords decision was at variance with subsequent developments of the common law: *Weir v. J.M. Hodge & Son*, 1990 S.L.T. 266.

[43] *Munro's Trs. v. Munro*, 1971 S.C. 280, 284; *American Express Europe Ltd v. Royal Bank of Scotland*, 1989 S.L.T. 266.

[44] e.g. *Hunter v. Glasgow Corp.*, 1971 S.C. 220, 231; *American Express Europe Ltd v. Royal Bank of Scotland*, 1989 S.L.T. 266. This is so even when it proceeded on a concession in law by counsel: *Elder v. Elder*, 1985 S.L.T. 471.

[45] e.g. *Galbraith v. Galbraith* 1971 S.C. 65; *Bain v. Bain*, 1971 S.C. 146, 151; *Collins v. S.S.E.B.*, 1977 S.C. 13; *Eastern Marine v. Dickson*, 1981 S.C. 355, 361.

[46] *Blackwood v. André*, 1947 S.C. 333, not following *McDaid v. Clyde Navigation Trustees*, 1946 S.C. 462; *Blackwood* was later approved by the House of Lords in *B.T.C. v. Gourley* [1956] A.C. 185. cf. *McKenzie v. McKenzie*, 1960 S.C. 322 and *Breen v. Breen*, 1961 S.C. 158, 175, 188.

[47] See *Spencer v. Macmillan's Trs.*, 1958 S.C. 300, 303.

[48] e.g. *Hunter, supra.*

[49] *Lees v. N.E. Fife D.C.*, 1987 S.L.T. 769; *Osborne v. British Coal Property*, 1996 S.L.T. 736.

[50] *H.M. Advocate v. Higgins* (1914) 7 Adam 229.

[51] *Boomsma v. Clark and Rose Ltd*, 1983 S.L.T.(Sh.Ct.) 67.

Irish decisions as persuasive in varying degrees,[52] depending on the rank of the court and the subject-matter. They are not bound by decisions of the Outer House, though they treat them with respect,[53] nor are they bound by one another; one sheriff principal is not bound by another,[54] though a sheriff will usually follow the decisions of his sheriff principal.[55] One sheriff's decision does not bind another.

Sheriff and Jury; Sheriff's Summary Court (criminal)

A sheriff presiding at a trial by jury or trying a case summarily must accept law laid down by the High Court sitting as Court of Criminal Appeal[56] but is not necessarily bound by previous rulings of a single trial judge, whether Lord of Justiciary or sheriff, though he will normally follow such rulings.[57] English and Irish criminal decisions are persuasive, depending on the status of the court which pronounced them and on the similarity or difference between Scots and English or Irish law on the matter.[58]

District Courts

A magistrate sitting in a district court is probably bound by rulings of any superior criminal court or of a single judge or sheriff.

Lord Advocate's References

The purpose of a reference is to secure guidance for future courts and the opinions on a reference must be taken to be binding in all Scottish criminal courts.[59]

Precedent in Courts of Special Jurisdiction

The Court of the Lord Lyon treats decisions of the House of Lords in Scottish cases and of the Court of Session as binding though it may distinguish them,[60] but it is not bound by its own previous decisions though it treats them as persuasive.[61] The Lands Valuation Appeal Court is not bound by the House of Lords[62] but it may accept its decisions when they are relevant[63] and it will generally follow the Court of Session on general

---

[52] *More v. Boyle*, 1967 S.L.T.(Sh.Ct.) 38.

[53] *Foster v. Craigmillar Laundry Ltd*, 1980 S.L.T. (Sh.Ct.) 100; *Lossie Hydraulic Co. v. Ecosse Transport Ltd*, 1980 S.L.T. (Sh.Ct.) 94, 96; *Farrell v. Farrell*, 1990 S.C.L.R. 717.

[54] *Spencer v. Spencer*, 1983 S.L.T. (Sh.Ct.) 87.

[55] *Edwards v. Lothian R.C.*, 1980 S.L.T. (Sh.Ct.) 107. *Lothian R.C. v. T.*, 1984 S.L.T.(Sh.Ct.) 74.

[56] *Farrell v. Stirling*, 1975 S.L.T. (Sh.Ct.) 71; *Herron v. Nelson*, 1976 S.L.T. (Sh.Ct.) 42.

[57] *Tudhope v. Grubb*, 1983 S.C.C.R. 350; *Jessop v. Stevenson*, 1988 S.L.T. 223.

[58] *Lockhart v. Smith*, 1979 S.L.T.(Sh.Ct.) 52.

[59] *Lord Advocate's Reference (No. 1 of 1983)* 1984 S.L.T. 337; *Lord Advocate's Reference (No. 1 of 1985)* 1986 S.C.C.R. 329

[60] *Smollett of Bonhill*, 1959 S.L.T. (Lyon Ct.) 3.

[61] *MacDonald of Keppoch*, 1989 S.L.T. (Lyon Ct.) 2.

[62] *Glasgow Parish Council v. Glasgow Assessor*, 1912 S.C. 818, 835.

[63] *Aberdeen Assessor v. Collie*, 1932 S.C. 304.

matters of private law, *e.g.* whether subjects are heritable. It is not bound by its own previous decisions.[64] The Court of Exchequer is bound by decisions of the House of Lords in Scottish appeals[65] and by its own decisions,[66] and generally follows the Court of Session on matters of private law.[67] In view of the desirability of the incidence of taxation being the same in Scotland as in England it treats relevant English decisions as highly persuasive. Indeed, in relation to charities and what is "charitable" the court has to have regard to a great range of English decisions on that subject and probably treat them as binding even though they are inconsistent with Scots law.[68] It has been doubted whether it is competent for the Court of Session sitting as Court of Exchequer to convene a larger court to reconsider a precedent challenged.[69] The Registration of Voters Appeal Court follows the House of Lords and the Court of Session on matters of general law and generally follows its own decisions. Its decisions are binding on sheriffs hearing appeals from electoral registration officers.[70] The Scottish Land Court treats as binding decisions of the House of Lords[71] and the Court of Session[72] while English decisions are persuasive,[73] and it usually follows its own decisions but is not bound to do so.[74] A divisional court of the Land Court follows the views of the Full Court.[75] The Restrictive Practices Court is a United Kingdom court though appeal lies in Scotland to the Court of Session, and, accordingly, when sitting in Scotland it treats decisions from any part of the United Kingdom as equally binding[76] and follows the general trend of its own decisions,[77] but it is empowered to discharge its own previous declarations and orders.[78]

Precedent in Tribunals

In tribunals the rules of precedent do not apply with the same rigour, and to some extent tribunals have been established to avoid this feature of British judicial technique. Where reports of tribunal decisions are published there is a natural tendency to have regard to prior cases. Where

---

[64] *Aberdeen Assessor, supra; Inverness-shire Assessor v. Cameron,* 1938 S.C. 360; *National Commercial Bank v. Fife Assessor,* 1963 S.C. 197.
[65] *Clark's Trs. v. Lord Advocate,* 1972 S.C. 177; *Cleveleys Investment Trust v. I.R.C.,* 1975 S.C. 283; *Thomson's Trs. v. I.R.C.,* 1978 S.C. 206.
[66] *Drummond v. I.R.C.,* 1951 S.C. 482.
[67] *Allan's Trs. v. Lord Advocate,* 1970 S.C. 10.
[68] *I.R.C. v. Glasgow Police Athletic Association,* 1958 S.C.(H.L.) 13.
[69] *Drummond, supra.*
[70] *Dumble v. Borders Electoral Registration Officer,* 1980 S.L.T.(Sh.Ct.) 60.
[71] *Haddo House Trs. v. Davidson,* 1982 S.L.T. (Land Ct.) 14.
[72] *Cameron v. Argyll's Trs.,* 1981 S.L.T. (Land Ct.) 2.
[73] *Cameron, supra.*
[74] *Niven v. Cameron* (1938) 27 S.L.C.R. 23.
[75] *Fulton v. Noble,* 1938 S.L.T. (Land Ct.) 40.
[76] *Re Scottish Master Monumental Sculptors' Association's Agreement* (1965) L.R. 5 R.P. 437.
[77] *Re Scottish Daily Newspapers' Society's Agreement* (1971) L.R. 7 R.P. 379.
[78] Restrictive Trade Practices Act 1976, s. 4.

appeal lies from a tribunal to the ordinary courts it seems probable that tribunals hold themselves bound by decisions on points of principle on appeal. The Commissioners of Income Tax hold themselves bound by decisions of the courts in tax cases. The Pensions Appeal Tribunal follows reported decisions and in one case[79] the English tribunal held that it should follow a later Court of Session decision on appeal, in preference to an earlier English High Court decision on a similar point. Social Security tribunals are not bound by court decisions[80] but adjudication officers and Social Security Appeal Tribunals must follow decisions of a Social Security Commissioner or a tribunal of Commissioners, giving more weight to a decision of the latter kind, normally relying only on reported decisions.[81] A single Commissioner must follow a decision of a tribunal of Commissioners and should normally follow decisions of other single Commissioners. Adjudication officers, SSATs and Commissioners are bound to follow decisions on matters of general law reached by the superior courts, Scottish and English. A SSAT is certainly bound by a decision of a court exercising supervisory jurisdiction.[82] Employment tribunals are bound in Scottish matters by the House of Lords and the Court of Session and by decisions of the Employment Appeal Tribunal in Scottish or English appeals, but not by decisions of other employment tribunals; the purpose of such tribunals is to reach decisions on facts and to apply Acts in a commonsense manner. The Employment Appeal Tribunal is a British court and bound by the House of Lords and the Court of Session on Scots law, and by the House of Lords and the Court of Appeal on English law, and tends to follow its own decisions, whether sitting in Scotland or in England, but it is not bound by decisions of single judges or of its predecessor (the National Industrial Relations Court) or its own earlier decisions, though all of these are persuasive.[83] The Lands Tribunal for Scotland considers itself bound by the House of Lords and the Court of Session on general questions of Scottish private law and its practice is to follow its own precedents.[84] A decision by a small tribunal might be reviewed by a later, larger one.[84] The Transport Tribunal should not regard itself as bound by its own decisions.[85]

---

[79] *Minister of Pensions v. Higham* [1948] 2 K.B. 153.

[80] *Chief Supplementary Benefit Officer v. Leary* [1985] 1 All E.R. 1061.

[81] Micklethwait, *The National Insurance Commissioners*, 73–75; Ogus and Barendt, *Law of Social Security*, 595–596.

[82] *Chief Supplementary Benefit Officer, supra.* On the desirability of consistency of decisions see *R. v. National Insurance Commr, ex p. Michael* [1977] 2 All E.R. 420, 425.

[83] *Portec (U.K.) Ltd v. Mogensen* [1976] 3 All E.R. 565.

[84] *Robertson v. Church of Scotland Gen. Trs.*, 1976 S.L.T. (Lands Tr.) 11.

[85] *B.T.C. v. Bristow Ltd* (1955) 30 Traff. Cas. 217, 232; *Merchandise Transport Ltd v. B.T.C.* [1962] 2 Q.B. 173.

House of Lords

Decisions of the House of Lords when pronounced in an English appeal are normally binding on the House itself for the future[86] and that even though the House were equally divided so that the decision appealed against stands unreversed[87] "This House has debarred itself from ever reconsidering any of its own decisions. It matters not how difficult it is to find the *ratio decidendi* of a previous case, that *ratio* must be found. And it matters not how difficult it is to reconcile that *ratio* when found with statutory provisions or general principles; that *ratio* must be applied to any later case which is not reasonably distinguishable."[88] A binding precedent cannot be disregarded merely because it was inadequately argued or considered, nor because their Lordships disagree with it,[89] nor even can it be disregarded on the ground that it was based on industrial and social conditions which have changed.[90] The decision is probably not binding if decided *per incuriam*, in ignorance of the terms of a statute or statutory instrument.[91] The House was formerly forced in many cases to resort to "distinguishing" its own previous decisions if it wished not to be bound to follow them.[92] It seems probable also that if a conflict be found between two previous decisions of the House, the House could follow either and would not be bound to follow one because it was earlier or later.[93] But a dictum patently wrong and unnecessary to the decision of the precedent may be disapproved,[94] and it has been suggested that when a particular

---

[86] *Beamish v. Beamish* (1861) 9 H.L.C. 274, 338; *London Tramways Co. v. L.C.C.* [1898] A.C. 375; *Radcliffe v. Ribble Motor Services* [1939] A.C. 215; *Nash v. Tamplin* [1952] A.C. 231. On history of this, see Salmond on *Jurisprudence*, 11th ed., 175–184. In *Niddrie and Benhar Coal Co. v. Dee*, 1927 S.C.(H.L.) 47, Lord Dunedin dissented. In *Ocean Coal Co. v. Davies* [1927] A.C. 271, which raised the same point and was decided later on the same day, he accepted that the law was settled by the view of the majority in the earlier case. See also Dworkin, "*Stare Decisis* in the House of Lords" (1962) 25 M.L.R. 163; Cross, "*Stare Decisis* in Contemporary England" (1966) 82 L.Q.R. 203. The Lord Chancellor's announcement (p. 443) that the House will exceptionally consider itself free to disregard its own precedents applies to English and Irish Appeals also. See also Brazier, "Overruling House of Lords Criminal Cases" [1973] Crim. L.R. 98.

[87] *Att.-Gen. v. Dean of Windsor* (1860) 8 H.L.C. 369; *R. v. Millis* (1844) 10 Cl. & F. 534; *Beamish v. Beamish* (1861) 9 H.L.C. at 338; *I.R.C. v. Walker* [1915] A.C. 509, 519. As to other courts equally divided, see *The Vera Cruz* (1884) 9 P.D. at 98.

[88] *Nash v. Tamplin & Sons Brewery* [1952] A.C. 231. This dictum is now qualified by the Lord Chancellor's announcement in 1966 (*supra*).

[89] *London Transport Executive v. Betts* [1959] A.C. 213; *Jones v. Secretary of State for Social Services* [1972] 1 A.C. 944. *Cf. Fitzleet Estates v. Cherry* [1977] 3 All E.R. 996.

[90] *Radcliffe v. Ribble Motor Services* [1939] A.C. at 245–246. But on this, see Lord Evershed M.R., *The Court of Appeal in England*, p. 18.

[91] *London Tramways, supra*, at p. 379. "*Per incuriam*" has been said (*Morelle v. Wakeling* [1955] 2 Q.B. 379) to cover only decisions given in ignorance or forgetfulness of some inconsistent statutory provision or of some authority binding on the court concerned.

[92] On "distinguishing," see p. 472, *infra*.

[93] This is the rule in the Court of Appeal.

[94] *Public Trustee v. I.R.C.* [1960] A.C. 398.

precedent, even of the House, conflicts with a fundamental principle, also of the House, the latter must prevail.[95] It has also been said *obiter*[96] that there are at least three circumstances in which the the House can question or limit the *ratio decidendi* of a previous House of Lords decision: namely where the decision (a) is obscure; (b) is out of line with other authorities or established principles; and (c) is much wider than was necessary for the decision so that it becomes a question of how far it is proper to distinguish the earlier decision. Nor is the House bound to follow a previous decision of its own, merely because it is indistinguishable on the facts; the decision is binding only because it lays down some principle of law, or for its reasoning on particular facts.[97]

The House has stated that the power to depart from its own previous decisions should only be sparingly exercised, and rarely on a matter of statutory interpretation.[98] The power should not be used where the effect would be to abolish an offence, certainty being important in the criminal law and abolition the function of Parliament.[99] It has in fact only rarely overruled previous decisions of its own.[1]

In respect of decisions pronounced in Scottish or Irish appeals, the House is clearly technically not bound in a subsequent English case, but it has been accepted that it will normally be so bound where the Scottish case was decided in the House on the same principles as apply in English law.[2] Thus it has always been accepted in England that *Donoghue v. Stevenson*[3] is binding on the House and on lower English courts, but strictly it is not, being a Scottish appeal. And the House can, in an English appeal, choose between previous decisions of its own in a Scottish and in an English appeal, and elect to follow the Scottish one, where the law is or is assumed to be the same in both countries.[4] The decisions of the House of Lords are binding on all inferior English courts,[5] and must be loyally observed by the Court of Appeal and all lower English courts.[6] An inferior

---

[95] *London Transport Executive, supra*, 247, *per* Lord Denning.

[96] *Scruttons v. Midland Silicones Ltd*. [1962] 1 All E.R. 1, *per* Lords Reid and Keith.

[97] *Chancery Lane Safe Deposit Co. v. I.R.C.* [1966] A.C. 85.

[98] *Jones v. Secretary of State for Social Services* [1972] 1 All E.R. 145.

[99] *Knuller v. D.P.P.* [1972] 2 All E.R. 898.

[1] *Herrington v. B.R. Board* [1972] A.C. 877, not following *Dumbreck v. Addie's Collieries*, 1929 S.C. (H.L.) 51; *The Johanna Oldendorff* [1974] A.C. 479, overruling *The Aello* [1961] A.C. 135; *Miliangos v. George Frank (Textiles) Ltd* [1976] A.C. 443, not following *Re United Railways of Havana Ltd*. [1960] 2 All E.R. 332; *Dick v. Burgh of Falkirk*, 1976 S.C.(H.L.) 1, overruling *Darling v. Gray* (1892) 19 R.(H.L.) 31.

[2] *R. v. Minister of Health, ex p. Yaffé* [1931] A.C. at 502; *Heyman v. Darwins Ltd* [1942] A.C. at 401. In the leading case (*London Tramways, supra*) the House held itself bound by its previous decision in a Scottish appeal, *Edinburgh Street Tramways v. Edinburgh Magistrates* (1894) 21 R.(H.L.) 78.

[3] 1932 S.C.(H.L.) 31. In that case the Lords said that the principles applicable were common to Scots and to English law. But this is a dangerous doctrine.

[4] *Heymans v. Darwins Ltd* [1942] A.C. 356.

[5] *Att.-Gen.* v. *Dean and Canons of Windsor* (1860) 8 H.L.Cas. 369; *G.W. Ry. v. S.S. Mostyn* [1928] A.C. 57.

[6] *Cassell v. Broome* [1972] 1 All E.R. 801, 809, 835.

court can justifiably refuse to follow what has been said in the House if what was said was *obiter* or where there are two clearly inconsistent decisions of the House, and the lower court has then to choose which to follow.[7]

Court of Appeal (Civil Division)

The Court of Appeal is bound by decisions of the House of Lords in English civil appeals,[8] even if they were decided *per incuriam*,[9] but not if the House of Lords decision discloses no discernible *ratio decidendi*.[10] The Court of Appeal has also held that it is bound by its own previous decisions[11] unless (a) the prior decision was arrived at *per incuriam, i.e.* in ignorance or forgetfulness of some inconsistent statutory provision or of some authority binding on the court,[12] or without full citation of authorities,[13] or there was some manifest slip or error, especially if the case would not go to House of Lords,[14] or (b) is inconsistent with and expressly or impliedly overruled by a later decision of the House of Lords,[15] or (c) when there are several conflicting previous decisions of its own, in which case it may select and follow one of them, and this selection probably binds later Court of Appeal cases.[16] Full binding force attaches even to unreported decisions of the court,[17] and a full court of five judges has no greater powers than the usual court of three.[18] The court must follow its own previous decisions even though a point was less fully argued in the previous case,[19] though it be argued that in the previous decision it had

---

[7] *Cassell, supra,* 854.

[8] *Conway v. Rimmer* [1967] 2 All E.R. 1260; *Miliangos v. George Frank (Textiles) Ltd* [1976] A.C. 443; *Davis v. Johnson* [1979] A.C. 264, 317.

[9] *Cassell, supra.*

[10] *Harper v. N.C.B.* [1974] 2 All E.R. 441.

[11] *Perrin v. Morgan* [1943] A.C. 399; *Young v. Bristol Aeroplane Co,* [1944] K.B. 718; affd. [1946] A.C. 163, 169; *Gallie v. Lee* [1969] 1 All E.R. 1082, 1072, 1062; affd. [1970] 3 All E.R. 961; *Davis v. Johnson* [1978] 1 All E.R. 1132, and see Goodhart, "Precedents in the Court of Appeal" (1947) 9 C.L.J. 349; Gooderson, "Precedents in the Court of Appeal" (1950) 10 C.L.J. 432; Mason, "*Stare Decisis* in the Court of Appeal" (1956) 19 M.L.R. 136.

[12] *Morelle Ltd. v. Wakeling* [1955] 2 Q.B. 379. *Per incuriam* is relevant only to the right of an appellate court to decline to follow one of its own previous decisions, not to its rights to disregard a decision of a higher court: *Cassell v. Broome* [1972] 1 All E.R. 801, 874; *Miliangos, supra,* 495.

[13] *A. & J. Mucklow Ltd v. I.R.C.* [1954] Ch. 615, *cf. Bryers v. Canadian Pacific Steamships Ltd* [1957] 1 Q.B. 134.

[14] *Williams v. Fawcett* [1985] 1 All E.R. 787.

[15] *Noble v. Southern Ry.* [1940] A.C. 583, 598; *Fitzsimmons v. Ford Motor Co.* [1946] 1 All E.R. 429; *Williams v. Glasbrook Bros.* [1947] 2 All E.R. 884. See also *Worcester Works Finance v. Cooden Eng. Co.* [1971] 3 All E.R. 708.

[16] *Craddock v. Hampshire C.C.* [1958] 1 W.L.R. 202; *Ross-Smith v. Ross-Smith* [1961] P. 39; *Tiverton Estates Ltd v. Wearwell* [1975] Ch. 146. There are possibly some other exceptions to the rule of *Young v. Bristol Aeroplane Co.*: see Lord Denning, M.R. in *Davis, supra,* and the case of *Doughty v. Turner Manufacturing Co.* [1964] 1 Q.B. 518 in which the Court of Appeal followed a Privy Council decision in preference to a previous Court of Appeal decision.

[17] *Gibson v. South American Stores* [1950] Ch. 177; *cf. King v. King* [1943] P. 91.

[18] *Morelle Ltd v. Wakeling* [1955] 2 Q.B. 379; *Tiverton Estates Ltd, supra.*

[19] *Critchell v. Lambeth B.C.* [1957] 2 Q.B. 535; *Amanuel v. Alexanders* [1986] 1 All E.R. 278.

misunderstood a House of Lords precedent,[20] and even though another case on the same point is under appeal to the House of Lords,[21] but it can overrule one of the grounds of a prior Court of Appeal decision, leaving that decision to stand on its other ground.[22]

A decision arrived at by the court being equally divided is not binding[23] and a ruling by a court of two Lords Justices is not binding on the court.[24] Decisions of the Court of Appeal are binding on judges of the High Court in civil cases, on the Divisional Court in cases where an appeal lies from it to the Court of Appeal, and on county court judges.[25] Similar weight attaches to decisions of the former Court of Exchequer Chamber and Court of Appeal in Chancery, which were superseded by the Court of Appeal in 1875.

Court of Appeal (Criminal Division)

This court is bound by decisions of the House of Lords in English criminal appeals. Decisions of the old Court for Crown Cases Reserved, which was the predecessor (until 1906) of the Court of Criminal Appeal, are entitled to similar weight.[26] This court also will normally follow decisions of its predecessor, the Court of Criminal Appeal (1906–66) and its own decisions[27] but, since the liberty of the subject is at stake in its decisions, it does not apply the doctrine of *stare decisis* with the same rigidity as in its civil jurisdiction[27] and may, if sitting as a full court, reconsider a previous decision if it finds that the law was misunderstood or misapplied in the earlier case.[28] Accordingly, it is not always or absolutely bound by a prior decision.[29] It may also reconsider a decision which was not argued on both sides.[30] Its decisions are binding on the Queen's Bench Divisional Court in criminal matters, even though no appeal lies,[31] and certainly bind judges of the Crown Courts and Central Criminal Court.

Divisional Courts

A Divisional Court of the High Court is certainly bound by decisions of the House of Lords and by decisions of the Court of Appeal in civil

---

[20] *Williams v. Glasbrook Bros.* [1947] 2 All E.R. 884.
[21] *Re Yates' Settlement Trusts* [1954] 1 W.L.R. 564.
[22] *Betty's Cafés Ltd v. Phillips Furnishing Stores Ltd.* [1959] A.C. 20, 53.
[23] *The Vera Cruz* (1884) 9 P.D. 96.
[24] *Boys v. Chaplin* [1968] 2 Q.B. 1, 11.
[25] *Consett Industrial Socy. v. Consett Iron Co.* [1922] 2 Ch. 135.
[26] *R. v. Cade* [1914] 2 K.B. 209, 211; *R. v. Porter* [1949] 2 K.B. 128, 132.
[27] *R. v. Gould* [1968] 1 All E.R. 849.
[28] *R. v. Taylor* [1950] 2 K.B. 368, overruling *R. v. Treanor* (1939) 27 C.A.R. 35. In this case seven judges sat instead of the usual three. It is not certain whether it needs the larger court to exercise this power or whether the number was summoned simply to obtain the benefit of extra opinions. A court of five judges may, certainly in relation to the discretion as to sentencing, depart from a recent earlier view of a court of three: *R. v. Newsome* [1970] 3 All E.R. 455, 458.
[29] See Winder, "The Rule of Precedent in Criminal Courts" (1941) 5 J.C.L. 242; Zellick, "Precedent in the Court of Appeal, Criminal Division" [1974] Crim. L.R. 222.
[30] *R. v. Ettridge* [1909] 2 K.B. at 27; *R. v. Norman* [1924] 2 K.B. at 322.
[31] *Ruse v. Read* [1949] 1 K.B. 377, 384; *Russell v. Smith* [1958] 1 Q.B. 27.

matters,[32] though it has held itself free[33] to disregard a precedent in the Court of Appeal[34] in which two prior decisions, of the House of Lords and the Privy Council respectively, had not been cited. The Divisional Court is bound in criminal matters by House of Lords decisions in criminal cases and by the Court of Criminal Appeal, and now by the Court of Appeal, Criminal Division.[35] It seems now to hold itself bound by its own decisions,[36] whether exercising civil or criminal jurisdiction, unless, probably, the prior decision was inconsistent with the decision of a higher court or obviously reached by mistake.[37] It may, however, exceptionally, depart from a previous decision.[38]

In civil matters the Divisional Court probably ranks no higher than a single judge of the High Court and its decisions cannot bind him, though only exceptionally would a single judge differ from the Divisonal Court's view of the law.[39] In criminal matters its rulings probably bind inferior criminal courts.

High Court

Judges of the High Court are certainly bound by decisions of the House of Lords and the Court of Appeal,[40] but probably not by Divisonal Court decisions. If a single judge is faced with a series of decisions of higher courts which are difficult to reconcile, he must follow any one which is indistinguishable, failing which he must try to apply the principles which can be extracted from the reported decisions as a whole.[41]

A decision of one High Court judge does not bind another[42] and a High Court judge may even decline to follow a previous decision of his own.[43] It

---

[32] *Read v. Joannon* (1890) 25 Q.B.D. 300, 302.

[33] In *R. v. Northumberland Compensation Tribunal* [1951] 1 K.B. 711; *cf. Nicholas v. Penny* [1950] 2 K.B. 466. This is implicity disapproved by the House of Lords in *Cassell v. Broome* [1972] A.C. 1004.

[34] *Racehorse Betting Control Board v. Secretary of State for Air* [1944] Ch. 114.

[35] *Carr v. Mercantile Products Ltd.* [1949] 2 K.B. 601. In *Hawke v. Mackenzie* [1902] 2 K.B. 225, 232, 233 the D.C. took the view that it was bound by decisions of the former Court for Crown Cases Reserved, the predecessor of the C.C.A., and in *Russell v. Smith* [1958] 1 Q.B. 27 a D.C. held itself bound by the C.C.A.

[36] *Huddersfield Police Authority v. Watson* [1947] K.B. 84 (civil); *Younghusband v. Luftig* [1949] 2 K.B. 354; *Russell v. Smith* [1958] 1 Q.B. 27 (criminal); see further, Winder, "Divisional Court Precedents" (1949) 9 M.L.R. 257; Stone, "*Stare Decisis* in the Divisional Court"(1951) 14 M.L.R. 219.

[37] *Melias Ltd.* v. *Preston* [1957] 2 Q.B. 380; *Cogley v. Sherwood* [1959] 2 Q.B. 311.

[38] *R. v. Fulham Rent Tribunal* [1951] 1 T.L.R. 423; *R. v. Greater Manchester Coroner* [1984] 3 All E.R. 240.

[39] *Chandris v. Isbrandtsen-Moller Inc.* [1951] 1 K.B. 240, 243; but see *Huddersfield Police Authority v. Watson* [1947] K.B. 842, 848, *per* Lord Goddard C.J.

[40] *Cackett v. Cackett* [1950] P. 253, 258.

[41] *Re House Property and Investment Co. Ltd* [1954] Ch. 576. See also *Miliangos v. George Frank (Textiles) Ltd* [1975] 1 Q.B. 487; [1976] A.C. 443, 477; *Moodie* v. *I.R.C.* [1991] C.L.Y. 2115.

[42] *Forster v. Baker* [1910] 2 K.B. 636, 638; *Green v. Berliner* [1936] 2 K.B. 477, 493; *Alma Shipping Co. v. Salgaoncar* [1954] 2 Q.B. 94, 104; *Receiver for Metropolitan Police v. Croydon Corp.* [1957] 2 Q.B. 154; *Colchester Estates v. Carlton Estates* [1984] 2 All E.R. 601.

[43] *Andrews v. Styrap* (1872) 26 L.T. 704, 706.

is, however, unusual, for reasons of judicial comity, to refuse to follow a decision of another High Court judge unless there seems good reason for doing so,[44] particularly in such a matter as the interpretation of a statute or a common commercial document,[45] and that even though the previous single-judge decision has been doubted in a dissenting judgment in the Court of Appeal.[46] Even where the matter is one for the exercise of judicial discretion, there is a strong tendency to conform to practice and give decisions consistent with those of other judges. In the event of one judge declining to follow another, two contradictory precedents stand in the books until a superior court in a later case resolves the conflict by approving one and overruling the other. The later one rules unless the third judge believes that it was wrong.[47] The principles applicable to a single judge also apply to the supervisory jurisdiction of the High Court exercised by one judge or a Divisional Court.[48] Decisions of High Court judges are probably binding on county court judges in civil cases, though appeal lies not to the High Court but direct to the Court of Appeal.

Crown Court

Judges of the Crown Court are bound by rulings of the House of Lords, the Court of Appeal (Criminal Division), and probably by the Divisional Court in its criminal jurisdiction. The decisions of judges of the Crown Court in criminal matters probably bind magistrates' courts, though no appeal lies. In cases of any consequence appeal is usually taken by case stated from magistrates' courts to the Queen's Bench Divisonal Court for a ruling on the law.

Scottish and Irish Decisions in English Courts

Decisions of Scottish and Irish courts are not binding on English courts but are treated with respect, particularly in matters where the law is the same or very similar to English law.[49]

NORTHERN IRELAND

The doctrine of binding precedent is accepted in Northern Ireland so that decisions of the House of Lords in Northern Ireland cases, of the Court of Appeal, Court of Criminal Appeal and of the High Court of Northern Ireland are binding on lower courts. The Court of Appeal is bound by its

---

[44] *Receiver for Metropolitan Police District v. Croydon Corpn.* [1956] 1 W.L.R. 1113; contrast *Monmouthshire C.C. v. Smith* [1956] 1 W.L.R. 1132; *The Makedonia* [1958] 1 Q.B. 365.

[45] *Alma Shipping Co. v. V.M. Salgaoncar E. Irmaos Ltda.* [1954] 2 Q.B. 94.

[46] *Re Cohen* [1960] Ch. 179.

[47] *Colchester Estates, supra.*

[48] *R. v. Greater Manchester Coroner, supra.*

[49] *Kahn v. Newberry* [1959] 2 Q.B. 1; *Andrew v. Philby* [1960] Ch. 27; *Westward Television v. Hart* [1969] 1 Ch. 212.

own previous decisions[50] under the principles laid down in *Young v. Bristol Aeroplane Co.*[51] Decisions of the English and Scottish superior courts have persuasive value and decisions of the Irish courts prior to 1921[52] have high persuasive value. Decisions of the Irish courts are entitled to the highest respect but are never binding on Scottish or English courts.[53]

PRIVY COUNCIL

Judgments of the Privy Council, except in those few cases where it sits as a court of appeal from a United Kingdom court,[54] are not binding on any United Kingdom court,[55] though highly persuasive and entitled to great weight because of the personal eminence of the lawyers who form the Judicial Committee.[56] The Privy Council is, moreover, not bound by its own previous judgments and may reconsider points decided in previous appeals to the Board.[57] What attitudes the Judicial Committee will adopt to references from the Scottish Parliament[58] remains to be seen.

Decisions of the Judicial Committee in proceedings under the Scotland Act are made binding in all legal proceedings (other than proceedings before the Committee).[59] A decision of the House of Lords is not likely to be disregarded by the Judicial Committee unless for special reasons.[60]

The European Court

The Court of Justice is not bound by its own previous decisions, still less by an opinion of an advocate-general, but it usually follows its own previous decisions. It is not settled whether the Court of First Instance or a chamber of the Court is bound by a decision of the full court.

OTHER JURISDICTIONS

There has been a growing tendency, particularly in England, to cite decisions from Commonwealth countries and the United States of

---

[50] *Parkinson v. Watson* [1956] N.I. 1.

[51] [1944] K.B. 718.

[52] Prior to 1921 there was one set of superior courts for all of Ireland.

[53] *Re Parsons* (1890) 45 Ch.D. 51.

[54] *Combe v. Edwards* (1877) 2 P.D. 354.

[55] *Dulieu v. White* [1902] 2 K.B. 669; *Venn v. Tedesco* [1926] 2 K.B. 227; *Lynn v. Bamber* [1930] 2 K.B. 72; *Brown v. John Watson Ltd*, 1914 S.C.(H.L.) 44; *Duncan v. Cammell Laird & Co.* [1942] A.C. 624.

[56] *Leask v. Scott* (1877) 2 Q.B.D. 376, 380. Thus the decision of the Privy Council in *Overseas Tankship (U.K.) Ltd v. Morts Dock & Engineering Co.* [1961] A.C. 388, has been repeatedly treated by English courts as authoritative as to English law. In *Doughty v. Turner Manufacturing Co.* [1964] 1 Q.B. 518 the Court of Appeal followed it in preference to an earlier decision of its own.

[57] *Re Transferred Civil Servants (Ireland) Compensation* [1929] A.C. 242; *Mercantile Bank of India v. Central Bank of India* [1938] A.C. 287; see also Raney, "The Finality of Privy Council Decisions" (1926) 4 Can.B.R. 307.

[58] Scotland Act 1998, s. 33 and Sched. 6, paras 10–13.

[59] Scotland Act 1998, s. 103.

[60] *De Lasak v. De Lasak* [1979] 2 All E.R. 1147; *Tai Hing Cotton Mill v. Lim Chong Hing Bank* [1985] 2 All E.R. 947.

America.[61] Some such decisions, if on points where it is desirable that the law should be the same throughout the English-speaking world, may be valuable, but can never have priority over statute or Scottish precedent, and are never binding on any Scottish or British court.

EVALUATION OF PRECEDENTS

Binding Precedent

The foregoing paragraphs indicate that, of prior decisions in point in a later case, the category of binding precedents is determined for any given court primarily by the place in the hierarchy of the court which decided the precedent case in relation to the place held by the court which subsequently has to consider the applicability of the prior decision to a case before it. The only precedents absolutely binding are those decided by a higher court in the same vertical line of the hierarchy.

Persuasive Precedent

The category of persuasive precedents includes all precedents other than those which may be held binding under the foregoing principles. Thus any case decided by a court in another vertical line of the judicial hierarchy will be persuasive in greater or lesser degree, depending on the status of the court which decided it. So will a case from a court of equivalent or even lower status, in the same or another line, though little weight attaches in the latter case.

Other persuasive precedents include judgments of the Privy Council when sitting as the final court of appeal from the colonies, and formerly from the dominions[62]; judgments of superior courts in Ireland[63] and countries of the Commonwealth[64]; judgments of superior courts in America[65] and judgments of foreign courts[66]; while rather similar persuasive force attaches to judicial dicta,[67] to statements in reputable books[68] and articles in standard legal periodicals,[69] and to the civil[70] and canon

---

[61] Megarry, *Lawyer and Litigant in England* (1962), 163.

[62] *Leask v. Scott* (1877) 2 Q.B.D. 376, 380.

[63] *Re Parsons* (1890) 45 Ch.D. 51.

[64] *Chester v. Waverley*, 62 C.L.R. 1 (Australia) cited in *Bourhill v. Young*, 1942 S.C.(H.L.) 78; *cf. Hughes and Vale Pty. Ltd v. State of N.S.W.* [1955] A.C. 241, 307; *Midland Silicones Ltd v. Scruttons Ltd* [1961] 1 Q.B. 106, 128; *Conway v. Rimmer* [1967] 2 All E.R. 1260, 1262–1263; *Morgan Guaranty Trust Co. v. Lothian R.C.*, 1995 S.C. 145.

[65] *Castro v. R.* (1881) 6 App.Cas. at 249; *Scaramanga v. Stamp* (1880) 5 C.P.D. at 303; *Cory v. Burr* (1882) 9 Q.B.D. at 469; *Donoghue v. Stevenson*, 1932 S.C.(H.L.) 31; *Haynes v. Harwood* [1935] 1 K.B. at 156–157, 163, 167; *Walsh v. Lord Advocate*, 1956 S.C.(H.L.) 126; *Midland Silicones Ltd v. Scruttons Ltd, supra.* But see cautions voiced in *Re Missouri* (1889) 42 Ch.D. at 330; *Fender v. Mildmay* [1938] A.C. at 25; *A/B Karlshamns Oljefabriker v. Monarch S.S. Co.*, 1949 S.C.(H.L.) 1.

[66] *Sugden v. H.M. Advocate*, 1934 J.C. 103.

[67] As to judicial dicta, see p. 469, *infra*.

[68] *e.g.* Dicey, *Conflict of Laws*.

[69] *e.g. Gold v. Essex C.C.* [1942] 2 K.B. 293.

[70] *e.g. Taylor v. Caldwell* (1863) 3 B. & S. 826; *Cantiere San Rocco v. Clyde Shipbuilding Co.*, 1923 S.C.(H.L.) 105.

laws[71] and the opinions of the standard commentators thereon.[72] Judgments of the Scottish courts are persuasive in England and elsewhere, particularly when interpreting a United Kingdom statute or discussing a point of general jurisprudence.[73] In matters of commercial law it is particularly desirable that there should be uniformity of decision in common law jurisdictions.[74]

On points of European law a decision of the Court of Justice on a reference from a United Kingdom court is binding on the referring court, and other decision are highly persuasive in all United Kingdom courts.

On the interpretation of the Human Rights Act 1998, a court or tribunal determining a question as to a Convention right must "take into account" any judgment, decision, declaration or advisory opinion of the European Court of Human Rights, and certain other opinions, if relevant.[75]

Factors Affecting the Evaluation of Precedents

Quite apart from the formal questions whether a precedent is authoritative and binding or merely persuasive, its value as a guide in a future case is affected by various other factors which are all of relevance when one has to evaluate a precedent. The importance of the factors affecting evaluation arises particularly when a court is trying to find a reason for not holding itself bound or is dealing with persuasive authority.

A precedent in general gains authority from its antiquity and the lapse of time since it was decided. This is particularly so if it has been approved, followed and applied in other cases, but even if it has stood unquestioned and unreversed for a substantial time, a precedent may have acquired such authority that a later court will hesitate to overrule it, even though it could, in view of the upset to the law and to expectations and transactions founded on the precedent.[76] If it has been considered as establishing the

---

[71] *e.g. Annan v. Annan*, 1948 S.C. 532.

[72] *e.g.* Pothier: *McLean v. Clydesdale Bank* (1883) 11 R.(H.L.) 1.

[73] *Minister of Pensions v. Higham* [1948] 2 K.B. 153, 155; *Murdoch Lownie v. Newman* [1949] 2 All E.R. 783; *Newman v. Lipman* [1951] 1 K.B. 333, 337; *Regional Properties v. Frankenschwerth* [1951] 1 K.B. 631; *Trickers (Confectioners) v. Barnes* [1955] 1 W.L.R. 372; *Cording v. Halse* [1955] 1 Q.B. 63; *R. v. Minister of Agriculture* [1955] 2 Q.B. 140; *Watson v. Nikolaisen* [1955] 2 Q.B. 286; *Wiseburgh v. Domville* [1956] 1 W.L.R. 312; *Kahn v. Newberry* [1959] 2 Q.B. 1; *Abbott v. Philbin* [1960] Ch. 27 (revd. [1961] A.C. 352); *Secretary of State for Employment v. Clark Chapman & Co.* [1971] 1 W.L.R. 1094, but see *Lord Advocate v. Babcock & Wilcox*, 1972 S.C.(H.L.) 1, 17. See also *McLean v. Clydesdale Bank, supra.*

[74] *Midland Silicones Ltd v. Scruttons Ltd* [1961] 1 Q.B. 106, 128.

[75] Human Rights Act 1998, s. 2.

[76] *Wilson's Trs. v. Pagan* (1856) 18 D. 1096, 1103; *West Ham Union v. Edmonton Union* [1908] A.C. 1; *Baird v. Baird's Trs.*, 1956 S.C.(H.L.) 93, 107–108; *Brownsea Haven Properties Ltd v. Poole Corp.* [1958] Ch. 574; *cf. Fortington v. Lord Kinnaird*, 1942 S.C. 239, 266: "[The precedent] has been cited and quoted too often down to very recent times to be open to challenge." So, too, in *Baird v. Baird's Trs.*, 1956 S.C.(H.L.) 93, 107, it was said that it was too late to reconsider *Alves v. Alves* (1861) 23 D. 712, but it was distinguished; *Jacksons (Edinburgh) v. Constructors John Brown*, 1965 S.L.T. 37, following *Duncan v. Arbroath* (1668) Mor. 10075; *Shand's Trs. v. Shand's Trs.*, 1966 S.C. 178, 184; *American Express Europe v. Royal Bank (No. 2)*, 1989 S.L.T. 650 following *Gordon v. Murray* (1765) Mor. 16818.

law and been acted upon, a later court will not interfere with it.[77] An old case may be re-established as sound despite later criticism.[78] Approval by institutional writers strengthens an old decision.[78]

Conversely, however, an older precedent may be of small value if inadequately reported,[79] repeatedly criticised,[80] not followed, or distinguished, or if in the course of time it becomes inconsistent with modern views and doctrines or is inconsistent with or superseded by later legislation. It may thus become practically obsolete and inoperative.[81]

Something depends, too, on whether the court in the precedent case was unanimous or divided and, in the latter case, whether the dissents were substantial and on weighty grounds.[82] Approval by a subsequent court (especially if a higher one), affirmation on appeal, approval by academic jurists, consultation with other judges[83] or the presence of a larger bench[84] and the passage of a subsequent statute which does not interfere with the decision,[85] all tend to strengthen a precedent.

The personal eminence of the judges has also to be borne in mind. Some decisions can be characterised as of a "strong bench," not so much in number of judges as of high judicial quality. Other cases are of the

---

[77] *Pugh v. Golden Valley Ry.* (1880) 15 Ch.D. at 334; *Smith v. Keal* (1882) 9 Q.B.D. at 352; *Bourne v. Keane* [1919] A.C. 815, 857; *Admiralty Commissioners v. S.S. Valverda* [1938] A.C. 173, 194; see also *Ridsdale v. Clifton* (1877) 2 P.D. 306; *Foakes v. Beer* (1884) 9 App.Cas. 630; *Queen v. Edwards* (1884) 13 Q.B.D. 590; *Re Wallis* (1890) 25 Q.B.D. 180; *Admiralty Commissioners v. S.S. Amerika* [1917] A.C. 38, 55; *Weld Blundell v. Stephens* [1920] A.C. 956, 987; *French Marine v. Campagnie Napolitaine* [1921] 2 A.C. 494, 511; *Gibaud v. G.E. Ry.* [1921] 2 K.B. 426, 432; *Triefus & Co. v. Post Office* [1957] 2 Q.B. 352.
[78] *Morgan Guaranty Trust Co. v. Lothian R.C.*, 1995 S.C. 145.
[79] *Wilson v. Wright* (1816) Hume 537 criticised as mistakenly reported in *Wilson's Tr. v. Pagan* (1856) 18 D. 1096, 1103; *Leslie v. Mollison*, 15 Nov. 1808, F.C. criticised as incorrect in *Johnson v. Tillie, Whyte & Co.*, 1917 S.C. 211, 219–20; *Stirling v. Lauderdale* (1733) disregarded in *Glasgow Corp. v. Lord Advocate*, 1959 S.C. 203, 231; *Logan v. Wood* (1561) regarded as not binding in *Donnelly v. Donnelly*, 1956 S.C. 97; *Bell's Exor.*, 1960 S.L.T. (Notes) 3 said not to be binding in *McLaughlin*, 1965 S.C. 246. In *Pickin v. B.R. Board* [1974] A.C. 765, the H.L. dismissed a report of a Scottish H.L. case in 1752 as a mere note, not a reason for the decision. In *Wills' Trs. v. Cairngorm School*, 1976 S.C(H.L.) 30 the H.L. examined original records to find the basis for the decision in *Grant v. Duke of Gordon* (1782) 2 Paton 582. So, too, in *Morgan Guaranty Trust Co. v. Lothian R.C.*, 1995 S.C. 145. One report may contain matter omitted from another: thus *Wood v. Gray* [1892] A.C. 576 includes a speech omitted from the report of the case, *sub nom. Darling v. Gray* in (1892) 19 R.(H.L.) 31.
[80] *cf. Barras v. Aberdeen Steam Trawling Co.*, 1933 S.C.(H.L.) 21, 38.
[81] *Laing and Irvine v. Anderson* (1871) 10 M. 74; *Rawlence v. Spicer* [1935] 1 K.B. at 435; *Matthews v. Kuwait Bechtel Corpn.* [1959] 2 Q.B. 57, *cf.* also the observations in *R. v. Jackson* [1891] 1 Q.B. 671, that a husband's right to chastise his wife is now obsolete, and *Winchester v. Fleming* [1958] 1 Q.B. 259. *cf.* also *Beith's Trustees v. Beith*, 1950 S.C. 66; *Sutherland Estates v. Sutherland*, 1988 S.L.T.(Land Ct.) 37.
[82] *cf.* Lord Blanesburgh in *Barras, supra,* at p. 42, evaluating *Ex p. Union Bank of Manchester* (1871) L.R. 12 Eq. 354.
[83] *e.g.* where the judges of one Division of the Court of Session consult with the other Division before giving their judgment, as in *Connell v. Connell*, 1950 S.C. 505.
[84] As in cases argued before seven judges.
[85] *cf., Thorne v. Motor Trade Association* [1937] A.C. 797, 806.

converse.[86] In modern times judgments of Lord President Inglis,[87] Lord Dunedin (both as Lord President and later as Lord of Appeal)[88] and Lord President Cooper[89] are always entitled to especial respect. In the House of Lords judgments of Lords Cairns, Halsbury, Watson, Macmillan, Atkin, Wright and Reid have similarly had special value and are not lightly to be disregarded.

Precedents are of less value if it appears that the case was not fully argued,[90] as where only one party appeared, or if some points passed unnoticed or were not argued,[91] or were conceded[92] or if it appears from the printed arguments of counsel in the report that certain relevant cases or statutes were not cited or considered in the precedent,[93] particularly if they were to a contrary effect, or if no reasoned judgments were delivered,[94] or if there were powerful dissenting judgments, or if the case were compromised or settled,[95] or if the report is defective,[96] or if the judges differ as to their reasons or if these seem defective, or the decision has been criticised in textbooks[97] or if the decision has apparently been reached on some specialty, such as to avoid hardship or injustice, or on the particular terms of a deed or contract or statute. In some cases, judges have examined Session Papers, pleadings, earlier judge's notebooks and other materials to discover what a precedent really decided,[98] or have obtained personal information from a judge who heard a case or was counsel in it.[99]

---

[86] *cf.* Kennedy, "The Second Division's Progress" (1896) 8 J.R. 268, where he criticises the Second Division of his day.

[87] See Crabb Watt, *John Inglis*, Chap. 13.

[88] "Dunedin, the greatest master of the principles of Scots Law in our time": *per* Lord Macmillan, *Stewart v. L.M.S. Ry.*, 1943 S.C.(H.L.) 19, 38.

[89] See Smith, "The Contribution of Lord Cooper of Culross to Scottish Law" in (1956) 67 J.R. 249 and in Lord Cooper's *Selected Papers*, xxix.

[90] *R. v. Ettridge* [1909] 2 K.B. at 27 (C.C.A.): *Edwards v. Jones* [1947] 1 All E.R. 830 (D.C.); *Nicholas v. Penny* [1950] 2 K.B. 466. *cf. Sugar v. Ridehalgh* [1931] 1 Ch. 310. In *Bell v. Bell*, 1941 S.C.(H.L.) 5, an undefended divorce case, in view of the importance of the principle of law in issue, the Solicitor-General appeared in the House of Lords, at the House's request, and was heard, so that the House had the benefit of argument on both sides.

[91] *Rahimtoola v. Nizam of Hyderabad* [1958] A.C. 379; *Aldridge v. Simpson-Bell*, 1971 S.C. 87.

[92] *O'Shea v. O'Shea and Parnell* (1890) 15 P.D. 59, 64; *Young v. Sealey* [1949] 1 All E.R. 92, 108.

[93] *e.g. Racecourse Betting Control Board v. Secretary of State for Air* [1944] Ch. 114, not followed in *R. v. Northumberland Compensation Appeal Tribunal, ex p. Shaw* [1952] 1 K.B. 338.

[94] As in some old cases.

[95] *Sagar v. Ridehalgh* [1931] 1 Ch. 310.

[96] Some reports prior to 1800 are so brief and defective that it is not really possible to say what the basis for the decision was: such a precedent is of little value.

[97] *Cochrane's Exrx. v. Cochrane*, 1947 S.C. 134, 140, 147.

[98] *Wilson's Trs. v. Pagan* (1856) 18 D. 1096, 1103; *Hutchison v. Hutchison* (1872) 11 M. 229; *Tweeddale's Trs. v. Tweeddale* (1905) 8 F. 264, 274; *Sinclair's Trs. v. Sinclair*, 1942 S.C. 362; *Korner v. Shennan*, 1950 S.L.T. 215, 219; *Will's Trs. v. Cairngorm School*, 1976 S.C.(H.L.) 30.

[99] *Lindsay v. Giles* (1844) 6 D. 771; *Clark v. Beattie*, 1909 S.C. 299.

What is it that is Binding or Persuasive?

Decisions are cited in textbooks for various reasons, sometimes as examples, sometimes for the form of action chosen, sometimes for points which are implicit in the case, sometimes for the interest of the decision reached, and sometimes for other reasons. But all these reasons are of little or no value when the matter in issue is whether a later court is, in the circumstances, bound to follow or is subject to persuasion to follow the principle of law enunciated or developed in the precedent, because the importance of precedents as a source of law is that earlier cases lay down and develop principles, rules and doctrines of law capable of future application.[1] The problem is: what is it in a precedent that a later court must, or should consider carefully whether to, follow and apply?

A reported case is of value as a precedent for guidance in future cases, whether authoritative or persuasive, only in respect of the principle of law, if any, which can be derived from it, as that on which it was decided,[2] and which must, or may, be used again to decide a later case. Not every reported case contains a statement of a principle; it may be reported for the interest of the factual situation, or simply as an example of how the court applied a particular principle in certain circumstances, or because of a ruling on evidence or pleading or procedure, or because of the application of an accepted principle to a new or unusual set of facts. Again it may not be apparent on what principle the judges proceeded, but in many cases a statement of a principle of law can be discerned as expressed or implied in the decision reached in the circumstances, and it is this statement of principle alone which is valuable in subsequent cases. "When any tribunal is bound by the judgment of another court, either superior or co-ordinate, it is, of course, bound by the judgment itself. And if from the opinions delivered it is clear—as is the case in most instances—what the *ratio decidendi* was which led to the judgment, then that *ratio decidendi* is also binding."[3] "The inevitable first question, then, with which the court must deal is:—Is a certain general *ratio* laid down and at the root of [the precedent]; and is it to be approved and applied?"[4]

The Ratio Decidendi

This underlying principle of a judicial decision is termed the *ratio decidendi* and it is only this element of the decision which is binding or

---

[1] "The only use of authorities or decided cases is the establishment of some principle which the judge can follow out in deciding the case before him": *Re Hallett* (1879) 13 Ch.D. 696, 712, *per* Jessel M.R.; *cf. Smith v. Harris* [1939] 3 All E.R. 960, 965.

[2] "The only thing in a judge's decision binding as an authority upon a subsequent judge is the principle on which the case was decided": *Osborne to Rowlett* (1880) 13 Ch.D. 774, 785, *per* Jessel M.R. *cf. Craig v. Glasgow Corp.*, 1919 S.C.(H.L.) 1, 10.

[3] *G.W. Ry. v. Owners of S.S. Mostyn* [1928] A.C. 57, 73, *per* Lord Dunedin, quoted in *Beith's Trs. v. Beith*, 1950 S.C. 66, 70 and *Douglas Hamilton v. Duke and Duchess of Hamilton's Trs.*, 1961 S.C. 205, 229.

[4] *Fortington v. Lord Kinnaird*, 1942 S.C. 239, 269, *per* Lord Mackay; *cf.* Lord Wark at 281.

persuasive upon a subsequent judge. It has been defined as "the reason or ground on which a judgment is rested,"[5] "the underlying principle which forms the authoritative element [of a judicial decision],"[6] or "the conclusion reached by the judges on the basis of the material facts and on the exclusion of the immaterial ones,"[7] or "the proposition of law which was necessary for the decision, or can be extracted from the decision,"[8] or "the enunciation of the reason or principle on which a question before a court has been decided is alone binding as a precedent,"[9] or "that part of [any judgment of any court] . . . which is considered to have been necessary to the decision of the actual issue between the litigants,"[10] or "any rule of law expressly or impliedly treated by the judge as a necessary step in reaching his conclusion, having regard to the line of reasoning adopted by him, or a necessary part of his direction to the jury . . . [It] is generally the proposition of law for which that case may be cited as authority, but it is the practice of the judges to interpret a decision in the light of the facts of the case and the decision in other cases."[11] Finding the *ratio* of a case is a process of abstracting principle from a mass of allegations, facts, arguments, opinions and judgment. *Ratio* should *not* be translated as "the reason *for* the decision," because a decision yielding a sound *ratio* may be reached, overtly or tacitly, for a bad reason, *e.g.* because the judge disapproved of the pursuer's morals, or felt sorry for him.[12] "The reason which the judge gives for his decision is never the binding part of the precedent."[13]

The *ratio* of a precedent is distinct from the facts of and the actual decision of the precedent case, and from the judgments or judicial opinions delivered by the judges when justifying their decision, because these are all concerned with the actual circumstances of the particular case, whereas the *ratio* is the underlying principle which was used in and is exemplified by the decision and opinions. The *ratio*, though so distinct, must be a general proposition of law which supports the actual decision of the particular case. Thus in *Bourhill v. Young*[14] Mrs. B claimed damages from Y's executor, alleging that while removing her basket from the

---

[5] *Wauchope v. Hope,* Dec. 15, 1767 F.C., 122; Bell's *Law Dictionary,* 884; *cf.* Fraser Tytler's *Memoirs of Lord Kames,* I, 114; " . . . the *ratio decidendi,* or rule of law on which the judgment rests."

[6] Salmond, *Jurisprudence* (11th ed.), 223.

[7] Paton, *Jurisprudence* (2nd ed.), 160, following Goodhart, *Essays,* 22.

[8] Dias & Hughes, *Jurisprudence,* 72.

[9] Halsbury's *Laws of England,* tit. "Judgments," para. 1682.

[10] Allen, *Law in the Making* (6th ed.), 247; *cf. Re Hetherington* [1989] 2 All E.R. 129, 133.

[11] Cross, *Precedent in English Law,* 75–76.

[12] In *Priestley v. Fowler,* (1837) 3 M. & W. 1, the judge's first stated reason was that any other decision than the one he had reached would be absurd, which was nonsense, but the *ratio* of the decision lasted until 1948.

[13] Goodhart, "Determining the *Ratio Decidendi* of a Case," in *Essays in Jurisprudence and the Common Law,* 1, and (1930) 40 Yale L.J. 161.

[14] 1942 S.C.(H.L.) 78.

platform of a tramcar, Y had passed the tramcar on the other side on his motorcycle, had collided with a car and killed himself, and had caused Mrs. B. shock by the noise and the sight of blood on the road. It was decided that her claim failed. According to the opinions this was because, in the place where she had been, Y could not have realised or foreseen that, if he was involved in a collision, a person where Mrs. B. was might in consequence be injured or shocked. The *ratio* or general proposition derivable from the decision is probably: one person is not entitled to damages from another for injuries or shock unless the other should, as a reasonable person, have realised or foreseen that his conduct was liable to harm a person in the claimant's place[15]; or it may be expressed as: the range of liability of an alleged causer of harm is limited to those whom he should reasonably have foreseen were liable to be harmed by his wrongful conduct.[16]

The determination of the *ratio decidendi* of a precedent is the task of the judge in a subsequent case, or of the legal adviser when trying to discover the law applicable to a problem before him. He has to try to determine what general proposition of law the precedent expressly or impliedly stated or proceeded on, apart from the court's application of that proposition in the circumstances of the prior case to produce the court's actual disposal of the case.[17] It is a task of extreme importance and considerable difficulty for which unfortunately no settled formula or rule of thumb can be suggested; it cannot be done mechanically; it is an art rather than a science.[18]

Finding the Ratio Decidendi

It should be noted first that the *ratio* of a decision is not necessarily contained in the rubric of the report, since that is compiled by the reporter and is not authoritative; nor is it necessarily to be found in any phrase or

---

[15] In this case the wrongful conduct was riding recklessly and crashing into the car. It should be noted that while Mrs. B.'s claim failed it was observed that a claim by the persons in the car would have succeeded, because injury or shock to them should reasonably have been foreseen.

[16] In strict logic a general proposition can only be inferred from at least two particular propositions or decisions; many general propositions may justify one particular proposition or decision.

[17] There is a considerable periodical literature on this topic. The most important are: Goodhart, "Determining the *Ratio Decidendi* of a Case," in *Essays in Jurisprudence and the Common Law*, 1; Paton and Sawer, "*Ratio Decidendi* and *Obiter Dictum* in Appellate Courts" (1947) 63 L.Q.R. 461; Gooderson, "*Ratio Decidendi* and the Rules of Law" (1952) 30 Can.B.R. 892; Montrose, "*Ratio Decidendi* and the House of Lords" (1957) 20 M.L.R. 124; Montrose, "*Ratio Decidendi* of a Case" (1957) 20 M.L.R. 587; Simpson, "*Ratio Decidendi* of a Case" (1957) 20 M.L.R. 413; (1958) 21 M.L.R. 155; Goodhart, "*Ratio Decidendi* of a Case" (1959) 22 M.L.R. 117; Simpson, "*Ratio Decidendi* of a Case" (1959) 22 M.L.R. 453; Stone, "The *Ratio* of the *Ratio Decidendi*" (1959) 22 M.L.R. 597; Simpson "The *Ratio Decidendi* of a Case and the Doctrine of Binding Precedent", *Oxford Essays on Jurisprudence* (1961), 148.

[18] In *Will's Trs. v. Cairngorm School*, 1976 S.C.(H.L.) 30, where an important, but old, case was briefly reported the courts examined the materials which had been before the court in that case in order to discover the legal basis of the decision. See pp. 118, 130, 138, 161.

passage of any of the opinions delivered in the case. It is not necessarily expressed anywhere in the report.[18] It is the proposition of law which is the ground or basis of the decision, or was necessary for the decision of the precedent, necessarily underlying and inherent in the decision reached on the facts alleged or found proved,[19] a generalised statement of law which justifies the decision on the facts of the precedent case, neither more nor less.[20] A judgment must always be read as applicable to the facts of the case in which it was delivered and the generality of expressions used are qualified by the facts of the case and are not necessarily more widely applicable.[21] Every judgment, that is, is to be read *secundum subjectam materiam*.[22]

According to Wambaugh[23] the *ratio* is a general rule without which the case must have been decided otherwise, but he gives little guidance on how to extract the *ratio* from the actual decision and the opinions. But it is true that the *ratio* must be a proposition which justifies what the court actually decided.

According to Goodhart[24] one must first determine what facts were averred for the purposes of the argument (in a debate on pleadings) or were found to have been proved (in a decision after proof) and segregate these facts into facts necessary for or material to the decision and facts immaterial to the decision. It is impossible to lay down in the abstract what averments or facts can be treated as immaterial. Any averment or fact may be material, but normally such averments or facts as the name, age, sex, status or condition of the parties, time, date, place, or weather conditions of the happenings, and all merely coincident and concomitant circumstances will be immaterial, though in particular cases any one or more of these factors may be material. If the judge treats any factor as material, either expressly or impliedly, in his opinion, then it must be accepted as material. The material averments or facts must then be set down in relation to the actual decision of the court and the *ratio* formulated in terms of a general proposition of law which takes account of all, but no more than, the material averments or facts and of the ultimate

---

[19] In Scottish practice, when the precedent is of a decision on relevancy (as to which see p. 523, *infra*) the facts averred and accepted for the purposes of argument are material, but when the precedent is of a decision arrived at after proof or trial, the material facts are those which have been held proved.

[20] In logic, of course, an indefinitely large number of general propositions can be thought of, all of which would justify the particular decision on the actual facts of the precedent. No general proposition can be deduced from one particular proposition. But, in fact, the possible general propositions are limited by the court's opinion and by the accepted context of that branch of the law and other cases on related points. On this point, see further, Stone, *The Province and Function of Law*, 186 *et seq.*; Patterson, *Jurisprudence*, 306 *et seq.*

[21] *Quinn v. Leathem* [1901] A.C. 495, 506, *per* Lord Halsbury.

[22] *Neilson* (1890) 17 R. 608, 613; *Fortington v. Kinnaird*, 1942 S.C. 239, 271; *Price v. Watson*, 1951 S.C. 359; *Inverurie Mags. v. Sorrie*, 1956 S.C. 175, 181.

[23] *The Study of Cases.*

[24] "Determining the *Ratio Decidendi* of a Case," *supra.*

decision. Thus the *ratio* of *Donoghue v. Stevenson*[25] might be expressed as follows: A person who claims to have suffered injury in consequence of drinking a bottled drink containing an impurity is entitled to claim damages direct from the manufacturer thereof where there was no reasonable possibility of intermediate inspection of the product between manufacture and consumption.

The more averments or facts that are held to be material and therefore necessarily incorporated in the *ratio*, or the more narrowly they are stated, the narrower will be the resulting *ratio* and the more limited its scope of application in future cases.[26] Conversely, the fewer the essential material averments or facts, or the more broadly they are stated, the wider will be the principle and the more readily available for later cases. It follows also from this insistence on material facts that a case may yield a *ratio* even if there is only a judgment on certain facts, with no opinion delivered and no reasons given.

This technique of seeking to determine material facts and elicit a *ratio* therefrom may also tend to produce a statement of a *ratio* which is very closely related to the facts of a case and dependent on its specialities. Also, relating the *ratio* so closely to the material facts of a case means that the *ratio* is not strictly applicable to any future case unless it has the same material facts or averments, and this theory of *ratio* may produce a state in which every case has its own *ratio*, which is not necessarily applicable to any other case.

Alternatively, one can approach the problem by searching the opinions of the judges for a statement of principle which that judge held to subsume and to justify his decision on the facts or averments of the case before him. This depends on a close analysis of the opinions and no more detailed guidance than that can be given.[27] On this basis, examination of the opinions in *Donoghue v. Stevenson* shows that Lord Macmillan considered the case to fall within this principle: "A person who for gain

---

[25] 1932 S.C.(H.L.) 31. It has to be remembered that *Donoghue's* case was decided, even in the House of Lords, on the basis of facts averred to have happened, and not proved to have taken place. The main averments were that Mrs. D. was bought a ginger-beer (manufactured and put out in an opaque bottle by S.) by a friend in a café. She drank some of it and when emptying the rest of the bottle into her glass, the remains of a decomposed snail floated out of the bottle. She was shocked and made sick, and sued S. for damages. In law, could she recover? This was the question for debate, it being necessarily assumed for the purpose of that debate that Mrs. D. could, if called on, prove by evidence that there had in fact been a decomposed snail in the bottle. As the case was finally settled by agreement, Mrs. D. was never called on to try to prove the existence of the snail, and that it had caused her sickness. The case is familiarly known as the "Snail in the bottle" case.

[26] Thus a *ratio* which starts "A married person . . . " is narrower than one starting "A person . . . " and one including the fact of sex, *e.g.* "A married female person . . . " is narrower still. A formulation of the *ratio* of *Donoghue* which says "a bottled drink" is narrower than one which says "food or drink," and narrower still than one which says "manufactured product" (which could include clothing, vehicles, etc.).

[27] See the attempt in *Muirhead v. Industrial Tank Specialities* [1985] 3 All E.R. 705, 711, 714, 715, to discover the *ratio* of *Junior Books v. Veitchi Co.*, 1982 S.C. (H.L.) 244.

engages in the business of manufacturing articles of food and drink intended for consumption by members of the public in the form in which he issues them is under a duty to take care in the manufacturing of these articles," and Lord Atkin under this: "A manufacturer of products which he sells in such a form as to show that he intends them to reach the ultimate consumer in the form in which they left him with no reasonable possibility of intermediate examination, and with the knowledge that the absence of reasonable care in the preparation or putting up of the products will result in an injury to the consumer's life or property, owes a duty to the consumer to take that reasonable care."

This kind of approach to the problem of finding the *ratio* implies that there is no *ratio* where a case is decided without opinions being expressed,[28] and it tends to produce *rationes* which are broader than required for, or sometimes justified by, the circumstances of the case argued and decided, and which may in literal terms cover sets of circumstances never contemplated by the judges, since judges commonly express their opinions more generally than the facts of the case demand. In fact, even if no opinions are delivered, a *ratio* may exist and can be inferred from the facts taken along with the actual judgment or disposal of the case. It is essential to remember that no proposition can ever be said to be the *ratio* if the court's actual decision and disposal of the case is not consistent with or does not follow from that proposition.

Any formulation of the *ratio* of a precedent must, moreover, be construed in the light of cases subsequent to the precedent and what may appear to be, or even be clearly indicated as, part of the *ratio*, may have been explained in later cases as inaccurate or unnecessary.[29]

Multiple Rationes

It is, of course, apparent that one precedent may contain decisions and rulings on several separate points of dispute, and any one of these separately may be a valuable precedent in a later case, even though the other points decided in the precedent may have no relevance. Thus if a precedent contains rulings on (a) the jurisdiction of the court, (b) a matter of pleading, (c) the merits of the claim, (d) the kind of remedy, and (e) the expenses of the cause, the *ratio* on point (c) may be extracted and used in a subsequent case for which the precedent is in point, even though the other points argued and decided in the precedent did not arise in the subsequent case. One case may, that is, be authority for several points of

---

[28] Lord Dunedin in *G.W. Ry. v. S.S. Mostyn* [1928] A.C. 57, 73 suggested that in such a case the judgment on the facts might be binding, apart from any *ratio* or principle discoverable. So, too, if there are opinions delivered which do not seem to yield any clear statement of the principle on which the case was decided.

[29] See, *e.g.* the explanation of the *ratio* of *Barwick v. English Joint Stock Bank* (1866) L.R. 2 Ex. 259 in *Lloyd v. Grace, Smith & Co.* [1912] A.C. 716.

law on widely different topics, and may consequently be referred to in a textbook in several different contexts. It follows also that a decision may be superseded or overruled on one point but remain good law on another.[30]

But even on a single point a judge sometimes gives two or more reasons for his decision or formulates his ruling on the law in two or more ways. Each formulation is regarded as a separate *ratio decidendi* and both are binding; a later court cannot pick one and ignore the other[31]; but one may be *obiter* or merely tentative, and merely tentative indications of opinion do not amount to *ratio*.[32] One ground of decision may subsequently be overruled, leaving the decision to rest on the other ground.[33] If a court gives two reasons for its decision and a later court finds that one of the reasons was right and the other wrong, they are entitled to accept the right reasons and reject the wrong, and the case is authority for the right reason.[34] It is also difficult where a judge discusses several possible grounds of decision and finally, looking at the case as a whole, arrives at a decision without making clear which ground is really the basis of decision. Probably in such a case a subsequent court must accept each of the grounds of decision as being the *ratio* of the case. "It is well established that if a judge gives two reasons for his decision, both are binding. It is not permissible to pick out one as being supposedly the better reason and ignore the other one; nor does it matter for this purpose which comes first and which comes second. But the practice of making judicial observations *obiter* is also well established. A judge may often give additional reasons for his decision without wishing to make them part of the *ratio decidendi*; he may not be sufficiently convinced of their cogency as to want them to have the full authority of precedent, and yet may wish to state them so that those who later may have the duty of investigating the same point will start with some guidance. This is a matter which the judge himself is alone capable of deciding and any judge who comes after him must ascertain which course has been adopted from the language used and not by consulting his own preference."[35]

A rather similar problem arises in the event of discrepancy or conflict between the opinions delivered and the interlocutor pronounced as the operative part of the court's decision. On principle the *ratio* has to be

---

[30] Thus in *Oliver v. Douglas* 1981 S.C. 191, it was held that (a) the Act founded on applied to fraudulent representations only, and accordingly the action was dismissed against the directors; (b) an accountant did owe a duty of care, and accordingly proof before answer was allowed against the accountant.

[31] *Behrens v. Bertram Mills Circus Ltd.* [1957] 2 Q.B. 1, 24.

[32] *Jacobs v. L.C.C.* [1950] A.C. 361, 369. "There is no justification for regarding as *obiter dictum* a reason given by a judge for his decision because he has given another reason also." *cf. Landon Jewellers v. Attenborough* [1934] 2 K.B. 206, 222.

[33] *Betty's Cafés Ltd v. Phillips Furnishing Stores Ltd.* [1959] A.C. 20, 53.

[34] *Re Holmden's Settlement Trusts* [1966] 2 All E.R. 661, 666.

[35] *Behrens v. Bertram Mills Circus* [1957] 2 Q.B. 1, 25, *per* Devlin J.

consistent with the operative decision, whatever the opinions may appear to say.[36]

Ratio in Appellate Courts

It is likewise obviously a problem of great difficulty to determine the *ratio* of the decision of an appellate court, where several opinions may be delivered (apart from any dissents), and different judges may formulate principles differently or proceed on the basis of different facts being material.[37] If a majority apply one *ratio* and a minority another, the *ratio* is that of the majority of the court. It is possible for several judges of an appellate court each to arrive at the same decision and to concur in the disposal of the case, but for different reasons, and each judge's opinion may yield a quite distinct *ratio*, possibly inconsistent with the others.[38] In such a case there cannot be said to be any *ratio*, and the case is not authority for any more than its actual decision.

If the *ratio* common to all, or at least to the majority, of the judges is obscure, a subsequent court is probably entitled to consider itself influenced by the decision itself and to choose for itself the *ratio* of the precedent.[39]

Cases where there is no Useful Ratio

There are some few cases which are decided on their own pleadings or facts and which are not authority for anything more than the particular decision of that case. Among such cases are decisions on matters of fact, on the sentence or measure of damages appropriate in the circumstances, on the way judicial discretion is being exercised in the particular case, or those decided on the terms of a particular trust deed or will, or on the precise terms of particular pleadings, or in the precise factual circumstances of a particular case.[40] They are decisions on their own facts and do not purport to lay down any general rules or principles, and are unlikely to be of any value at all as precedents unless in the very unlikely event of precisely similar circumstances arising again. The decisions are merely choices between two or more possible interpretations of words or facts and proceed on no legal basis capable of wider application. Every such

---

[36] See, however, *Pollock School v. Glasgow Town Clerk*, 1946 S.C. 373 and 1947 S.C. 605.

[37] Paton and Sawer, "*Ratio Decidendi* and *Obiter Dictum* in Appellate Courts" (1947) 63 L.Q.R. 461; Cross, "The *Ratio Decidendi* and a Plurality of Speeches in the House of Lords" (1977) 93 L.Q.R. 378.

[38] *e.g. Republica de Guatemala v. Nunez* [1972] 1 K.B. 669; *Boys v. Chaplin* [1971] A.C. 356; *Junior Books v. Veitchi Co.*, 1982 S.C. (H.L.) 244.

[39] *G.W. Ry. v. S.S. Mostyn* [1928] A.C. 57, 73, where the House of Lords abandoned the attempt to discover the *ratio* of *River Wear Commrs v. Adamson* (1877) 2 App.Cas. 743. See further, Paton and Sawer, "*Ratio Decidendi* and *Obiter Dictum* in Appellate Courts" (1947) 63 L.Q.R. 461. See also the observations of L.P. Cooper in *McDonald v. Glasgow Western Hospitals*, 1954 S.C. 453, 474 on *Reidford v. Aberdeen Magistrates*, 1933 S.C. 276.

[40] *e.g.* later criticisms of *Junior Books v. Veitchi Co.*, 1982 S.C. (H.L.) 244.

case has, of course, its own individual *ratio*, but it is so special to the terms and circumstances of that case that it is of little or no use as a precedent for the future. Thus in *Mair's Trustee* v. *Aberdeen Royal Infirmary*[41] a testatrix made certain bequests and directed finally that "what money is left over" was to go to a charity. It was held that, while the word "money" might sometimes cover heritable property, it did not do so *in the will under construction,* and accordingly that a bequest of heritage which had lapsed did not fall under this residuary bequest of "money." Accordingly, one way of avoiding being bound by or distinguishing a precedent is to hold that it was decided on its particular facts only.[42]

There is again no useful *ratio* where the judgments delivered are so unclear that a subsequent court cannot find the *ratio*,[43] and where a case has been so frequently distinguished or doubted that it cannot be taken as more than a decision on its own special facts.[44] If no *ratio* is discernible the decision for or against the pursuer may be binding.[45]

Ratio and Obiter Dictum

All statements by the judges which are outwith the *ratio* or are not necessary for the *ratio* fall to be classed as *obiter dicta* (things said by the way). Such dicta thus include all statements of law which go beyond the occasion, as where a rule is laid down for "animals" in a case dealing with a horse; or which lay down a rule irrelevant to the problem before the court, as where in the case of a limited company a judge says, "It would be competent for a local authority . . . "; or which are stated as analogies, as where a judge remarks, "Similarly in cases of . . . the same would apply"; or which deal with the opposite case, as where a judge remarks, "Conversely, the rule would not apply to . . . "; or which deal with hypothetical cases, as where a judge states the law: "if the pursuer had proved . . . then I should have been prepared to hold that . . . "; or which are mere observations made in the course of argument.[46] Other kinds of *obiter dicta* are statements of law by a judge who dissents, and statements leading to one conclusion which the court then does not adopt for a

---

[41] 1946 S.L.T. 88.

[42] *e.g. Dundee Magistrates* v. *Morris* (1858) 3 Macq. 135, 155; *Turner's Trs.* v. *Turner,* 1961 S.L.T. 319, 321.

[43] The famous example is *River Wear Commrs.* v. *Adamson* (1877) 2 App.Cas. 743; in *G.W. Ry.* v. *S.S. Mostyn* [1928] A.C. 57 the House of Lords abandoned the attempts to find its *ratio*. In *Harper* v. *N.C.B.* [1974] 2 All E.R. 441, the Court of Appeal held that there was no discernible *ratio* in the House of Lords decision in *Central Asbestos Co.* v. *Dodd* [1973] A.C. 518.

[44] Thus *McLachlan* v. *McLachlan,* 1945 S.C. 382 has been distinguished in *Swan* v. *Swan* [1953] P. 258; *Jamieson* v. *Jamieson,* 1951 S.C. 286; *Scott* v. *Scott,* 1960 S.C. 36 and *Breen* v. *Breen,* 1961 S.C. 158 and can now be regarded as limited to its own special circumstances, if not indeed wrongly decided.

[45] *Harper* v. *N.C.B.* [1974] 2 All E.R. 441.

[46] Practice Note [1942] W.N. 89.

particular reason.[47] There can be no complete catalogue of what will be dicta rather than part of the *ratio* and these are only examples. Subsequent judges sometimes condemn as mere dicta statements which others have thought were part of the *ratio* of a prior decision.[48]

Dicta are of varying weights and varying value, from mere casual observations, possibly unconsidered, possibly even erroneous, to carefully considered statements which are not, however, part of the *ratio* as going outside or beyond the circumstances of the case before the court.[49] They may be highly important as persuasive precedent in future,[50] but they are never binding.[51] A distinction has also been drawn[52] between *obiter dicta*, judicial *dicta*, and other *dicta*.

Drawing the distinction between *ratio* and *obiter dictum* is clearly also an art rather than a science; different men may differ as to what is *ratio* and what is dictum in a precedent, and while to stigmatise something as merely dictum is one of the easiest ways to avoid being bound by an incovenient precedent, that is not always practicable. All that can be said is that the *ratio* is the central and essential part of the decision while the dicta are collateral and inessential, but in certain cases have to be weighed and regarded carefully. Cross[53] sums it up as follows: "The *ratio decidendi* of a case is any rule of law expressly or impliedly treated by the judge as a necessary step in reaching his conclusion, having regard to the line of reasoning adopted by him, or a necessary part of his direction to the jury. In arriving at it regard must be had to the facts of the case, the issues raised by the pleadings and arguments, and the previous state of the law. Further guidance may sometimes be obtained from the observations in prior and subsequent cases by judges who were members of the court in the case the *ratio decidendi* of which is to be determined. It is open to question whether the decision of any issue in a case in favour of the party against whom the court order is made can constitute part of the *ratio decidendi* of that case. The *ratio decidendi* of a case is generally the proposition of law for which that case may be cited as authority, but it is

---

[47] Thus in *Hedley Byrne & Co. v. Heller* [1964] A.C. 465 the House of Lords laid down that the maker of a statement in certain cases owed a duty of care to persons relying on it, but then held the defendants not liable, because they were protected by their disclaimer of liability. See discussion of this in *Rondel v. Worsley* [1967] 1 Q.B. 443.

[48] *Morgan Guaranty Trust Co. v. Lothian R.C.,* 1995 S.C. 145. A great judicial luminary once told a Lord Justice: "The rule is quite simple: if you agree with the other bloke you say it's part of the *ratio*, if you don't you say it's *obiter dictum* with the implication that he is a congenital idiot": (1950) 1 J.S.P.T.L. (N.S.) 359.

[49] *Slack v. Leeds Industrial Co-operative Society* [1923] 1 Ch. 431, 451.

[50] *cf. Re House Property and Investment Co.* [1953] 3 W.L.R. 1037. In *Hedley Byrne v. Heller* [1964] A.C. 465 the H.L. adopted and approved *obiter dicta* in the dissenting judgment of Denning L.J. in *Candler v. Crane, Christmas & Co.* [1951] 1 All E.R. 426.

[51] "A dictum of a judge of first instance is not binding even upon himself": *Kwei Tek Chao* v. *British Traders and Shippers* [1954] 3 W.L.R. 496, *per* Devlin J.

[52] *West v. Dick* [1969] 1 All E.R. 289, 292, *per* Megarry J.

[53] *Precedent in English Law,* pp. 75–76.

the practice of the judges to interpret a decision in the light of the facts of the case and the decisions in other cases. Accordingly, in order to ascertain the proposition of law for which a case is authority at a later date, regard must be had to subsequent cases in which it has been considered."

Ratio and Principles of Law

The *ratio* of a case is accordingly the proposition of law necessary to the decision of the case. It is not the same as a general principle of law but is an example and application of such a principle to certain pleadings and facts, and general principles of law have in fact been, particularly in England, largely built up by the generalisation from a number of specific *rationes* or principles of particular cases, whereas in Scotland *rationes* have also frequently been deductions from overriding general principles of law. The *ratio* or principle of a case is thus related to, but distinct from, those broader and more general principles. Thus to say that a man is entitled to recover damages from one who has caused him loss, injury or damage without legal justification is a general principle from which may be deduced, in the circumstances of an actual case, the *ratio* that if a defender has caused another person loss and damage by knocking him down with his car, an action lacking legal justification, the other person may recover damages from the defender. The *ratio* of *Donoghue v. Stevenson*[54] is distinct from, and a specific instance of, the more general principle that a person is liable in damages to another if it was foreseeable that his act or omission might cause injury to that other, and if his act or omission has actually so caused injury.

The possibility exists of conflict between a binding precedent and a fundamental principle, in which case it has been said that the fundamental principle must prevail,[55] but this involves the difficult task of formulating verbally the fundamental principle as well as the *ratio* of the precedent.

The Application of Precedents in Later Cases

When a precedent is cited in a later case the later court has several things to do before it can accept and apply it or reject it. It has to decide first of all what the *ratio* of the precedent is and then, comparing the material issues of the precedent with those of the instant case, to decide whether the precedent is in point or not. If it is not in point, if the material issues do not coincide in all respects, the precedent is not exactly in point and is not decisive, though it may remain highly persuasive. Now it has to be accepted that precedents are hardly ever absolutely in point, exactly on all fours, agreeing in all material issues. They will always differ,

---

[54] 1932 S.C.(H.L.) 31.
[55] *London Transport Executive v. Betts* [1959] A.C. 213, *per* Lord Denning.

if only in point of time, and usually in some other respects too, from the instant case, and this question comes to be whether a particular precedent is, if not exactly, at least sufficiently closely in point to be treated as influential. Secondly, the court must consider from what place in the judicial hierarchy the precedent has come and whether it is binding under the rules of *stare decisis* or merely persuasive, and in the latter case, how highly persuasive it is, having regard to the status of the court and the other factors affecting evaluation. Thirdly, the court must decide how far the precedent is to be influential in its decision. Is the later court going to accept it and apply it to the case before the court or follow it or to try to avoid that course?

The court may *apply* the precedent by accepting the *ratio*, if it is binding on that court, and applying it to the material facts of the instant case, in effect saying that the rule of Case X (the precedent) governs the present facts also.[56] Or the court may *follow* the precedent, if it is merely persuasive, applying it by analogy or by extension to the instant case, or adopting its reasoning as leading to the decision of the instant case.

A court may also *not follow* a precedent. This can be done only in the case of a precedent which is not binding or proceeds from a court of co-ordinate or lower jurisdiction.[57] It is plain indication that the second court has serious doubts about the correctness of the precedent. In such a case the precedent and the later case both stand in the reports as representing divergent views as to the law and this divergence can be solved only by a later superior court accepting one decision and overruling the other,[58] or possibly by reconciling both by means of an explanation or formula which allows each to stand as correct in its own circumstances. Even plainer is the action of a superior court when it *reserves its opinion on the soundness of* a decision not binding on it.[59]

Alternatively, the court may *distinguish* the precedent by pointing to differences between the precedent and the instant case in certain material issues. It may decline on that ground to consider the precedent to be in point and to be either binding or even persuasive.[60] To distinguish a

---

[56] See, *e.g. Lockhart v. Barr*, 1943 S.C.(H.L.) 1.

[57] Thus in *Blackwood v. André*, 1947 S.C. 333 a judge of the Outer House did not follow another judge of the Outer House in *McDaid v. Clyde Navigation Trustees*, 1946 S.C. 462.

[58] In *British Transport Commission v. Gourley* [1956] A.C. 185, *McDaid* was approved and *Blackwood* disapproved.

[59] Thus the House of Lords in *O'Hanlon v. Stein*, 1965 S.C.(H.L.) 23 reserved its opinion on *Sinclair v. N.C.B.*, 1963 S.C. 586 which was not so closely in point as to require to be followed or overruled.

[60] "It must, however, in my opinion, always be open to a party to contend that the differences between the facts in the case then under discussion and those in the case on which the decision in the House of Lords proceeded are so material as to prevent his case from falling within the *ratio decidendi* of the House, even though the opinions of the noble and learned lords who decided the case in the House are so worded as to seem to apply equally to the facts in the case then under discussion": *Houldsworth v. City of Glasgow Bank* (1880) 7R.(H.L.) 53, 62 *per* Lord Blackburn.

decision does not mean that it was wrongly decided but merely that it is not in point in the instant case or in the circumstances not binding. The technique of distinguishing is much resorted to where a judge or court does not in fact wish to be bound by or to follow or apply a particular precedent.[61] It tends to produce hair-splitting distinctions when courts point to slight or even imaginary differences in facts to avoid being required to follow the precedent.[62] It may be a matter of argument whether a precedent is really distinguishable or not.

If a court *approves* a precedent, the precedent must have been one accepted on its merits as a valuable guide though not binding, either because it comes from an inferior court or one in a different line of descent.[63] If the court *disapproves* a precedent, the precedent must be one not binding in the circumstances and not so closely in point as to require the court either not to follow or to overrule it.[64] Weaker than disapproval is the action of a court when it *doubts* a precedent, which can be done only in the case of a merely persuasive precedent, or one not sufficiently in point to be binding but which is on an analogous point. The effect of this is to suggest that the doubted case may not be good law. A case which has been doubted may be overruled in a later case[65] or may be reconsidered and the doubts rejected as unjustified.[66]

Other modes of dealing with precedents, as where they are *considered, explained, discussed, questioned, observed upon* or *commented on*, are self-explanatory; all are appropriate to precedents which are not in the circumstances both in point and binding.

Lastly, a superior court may *overrule* a precedent of a lower court in the same line of descent by declaring expressly or impliedly that the precedent is bad law and no longer of any authority on the point in question.[67] A

---

[61] For example, what did *Manners v. Whitehead* (1898) 1 F. 171 really decide and was it binding in *Eastern Marine v. Dickson*, 1981 S.C. 355, 359, and *Twomax v. Dickson*, 1982 S.C. 113?

[62] See, *e.g. Donoghue v. Stevenson*, 1932 S.C.(H.L.) 31, Lord Atkin at pp. 49–56, Lord Macmillan at pp. 65–69.

[63] Thus the Inner House might approve an Outer House precedent or an English precedent but it is not for the Inner House to "approve" a House of Lords decision, whether it is binding or not, since it comes from a superior court. It could only apply it or follow it or distinguish it.

[64] Thus the Court of Session may disapprove an English Court of Appeal decision, and conversely. See, *e.g. Dempster's Trs. v. Dempster*, 1949 S.C. 92. In *National Commercial Bank v. Fife Assessor*, 1963 S.C. 197 the Lands Valuation Appeal Court disapproved *Simpson v. Selkirk Assessor*, 1948 S.C. 270. In *Johnstone v. Irvine*, 1984 S.L.T. 209, the O.H. disapproved a sheriff court decision.

[65] *e.g. Greig v. Macleod*, 1908 S.C.(J.) 14, doubted in *Thornley v. Hunter*, 1965 J.C. 22, and overruled in *Noble v. Heatly*, 1967 S.L.T. 26.

[66] *e.g.*, opinions were reserved on *Traill v. Dalbeattie* (1904) 6 F. 798 in *Smith v. Stewart*, 1960 S.C. 329, but it was approved as good law in *Cole-Hamilton v. Boyd*, 1963 S.C.(H.L.) 1.

[67] Thus, *Horn v. N.B. Ry.* (1878) 5 R. 1055 was overruled in *McElroy v. McAllister*, 1949 S.C. 110. In *H.M. Advocate v. Cunningham*, 1963 J.C. 80, the High Court of Justiciary overruled *H.M. Advocate v. Ritchie*, 1926 J.C. 45. In *I.R.C. v. Ferguson*, 1969 S.C.(H.L.) 103, the House of Lords overruled *Blount v. Blount* [1916] 1 K.B. 230. In *Scottish Discount Co. v. Blin*, 1986 S.L.T.

precedent overruled becomes of no value for the future so far as concerns the *ratio* on which it has been overruled, but other points decided in the same case may still continue to be accepted as good law, and the actual decision, as affecting the parties, is unaffected.[68]

Moreover, a precedent disapproved or even overruled may be reinstated as good law if the overruling case is itself later overruled: thus a case of 1888[69] was disapproved by a case in 1893[70] which was itself disapproved in 1963[71] and the case of 1888 thereby restored as a sound decision.

A court is sometimes faced with the difficult task of *reconciling* precedents, and trying to derive from two or more binding precedents a doctrine which subsumes them both or all. "What is the duty of a judge when he is confronted with a series of decisions which are difficult to reconcile? In my judgment it depends: if there is a decision which cannot be distinguished from the case before him, even if it is a decision of a judge of first instance, *a fortiori*, of course, if it is a decision of the Court of Appeal or House of Lords, he ought to apply it—expressing maybe his doubts whether it is still good law, but leaving a superior tribunal to overrule it."[72] Sometimes it is possible to reconcile, sometimes one decision or group of decisions can be distinguished and the other followed, sometimes one can be set aside as inconsistent with a later decision of a superior court, but sometimes a court or judge may be faced with two equally binding precedents of equal status which cannot be reconciled, in which case the only course open is to follow what appears the better or preferable.[73]

Obiter dicta may be applied, followed or approved, doubted or disapproved but do not need to be distinguished or overruled.[74]

---

123 the court overruled *Cliffplant v. Kinnaird*, 1981 S.C. 9. In *Dick v. Falkirk*, 1976 S.C.(H.L.) 1 the H.L. overruled *Darling v. Gray* (1892) 19 R.(H.L.) 31. In *Morgan Guaranty Trust Co. v. Lothian Regional Council*, 1995 S.L.T. 299 the Inner House approved a case of 1733 and overruled two modern cases. In *McCue v. Scottish Daily Record*, 1998 S.L.T. 983, five judges overruled several precedents. Notice that overruling a precedent is quite distinct from reversing a prior decision of the instant case (not a precedent) by a lower court. Also, overruling a precedent does not affect the decision of the earlier case as between the parties to it, since it was decided on what was then believed to be the law, but is now found to have been an incorrect statement of the rule. Old cases cannot be reopened on this ground. In *Davie v. New Merton Board Mills* [1959] A.C. 604, the House of Lords, in an English appeal, purported to overrule *Donnelly v. Glasgow Corp.*, 1953 S.C. 107. This is, strictly, a misstatement; all that the House could do in an English appeal was to disapprove a Scottish case.

[68] The *Digests* and the *Current Law Case Citator* volumes disclose whether cases have been applied, followed, distinguished, overruled or otherwise handled in later cases.

[69] *Cann v. Willson* (1888) 39 Ch.D. 39.

[70] *Le Lievre v. Gould* [1893] 1Q.B. 491.

[71] *Hedley Byrne v. Heller* [1964] A.C. 465.

[72] *Re House Property Investment Co.* [1953] 3 W.L.R. 1037.

[73] See, *e.g. Angus's Exrx. v. Batchan's Trs.*, 1949 S.C. 335, where one prior decision was followed and the other overruled.

[74] See, *e.g.* treatment of dicta in *Eastern Marine v. Dickson*, 1981 S.C. 355.

Conclusions on Case-law

Possibly even more than with statutory law, it will be apparent that the handling of case-law is an art rather than a mechanical process. Lord Wright, indeed, observed that it was partly intuition.[75] Such rules as there are are not by any means settled or unchanging. In the last resort a great deal depends on judicial temperament, on whether the judge agrees with and wishes to follow a precedent or whether he disagrees with it, wants to avoid it, and can find a way of avoiding being bound, on whether he values more highly consistency of decisions or what he conceives to be the requirements of justice in the circumstances. It is undoubtedly true that the rigidity of some of the modern rules leads to much false reasoning, narrow verbal distinctions, excessive refinements of rules and doctrines and hypocrisy in "distinguishing" cases, when the truth is that the later court does not wish to apply the rule of the precedent. Nevertheless, despite the rules there is still considerable scope for judicial discretion and the creative function of the judge, developing the law according to current trends, beliefs and policies.

But while these difficulties arise in marginal cases, it has to be remembered that principles worked out and laid down in cases of the higher courts suffice for the decisions of hundreds of cases in lower courts, in which those precedents are accepted as undoubtedly in point and equally undoubtedly authoritative, and, on the whole, the advantages of consistency, certainty and predictability of the law justify in large measure the existence of the rule of *stare decisis*. What is, however, very doubtful is whether not only the House of Lords but possibly also the Inner House and corresponding courts, should have the power to overrule their own previous decisions, and whether any binding force should ever attach to a single decision of a single judge. But the discussion of this belongs to jurisprudence.

III.—LITERARY SOURCES—BOOKS OF AUTHORITY

Statements as to the law made by legal writers have varying degrees of authority, but always less than that of statute or case-law in that, in case of conflict, the rule laid down by statute or worked out by the courts has undoubtedly to be given effect to, notwithstanding anything in the books. The highest degree of authority attaches to the writings of a small number of writers, all of bygone ages, who all treated in their works of the whole law of Scotland, or at least of very large tracts of it. These are known as the institutional writings,[76] and a statement in one of them, in default of

---

[75] "Precedents," 8 C.L.J. 138.

[76] Because most of them were modelled on the *Institutes* of Justinian and were entitled *Institutions, Institute* or *Institutes*. On the development of the category of "institutional" see Blackie, "Evaluation of the Institutions," *Stair Tercentenary Studies* (Stair Society, 1981). On the institutional writers see David, *Introduction a l'Etude du Droit Ecossais*, 295–380; Cairns, "Institutional Writings in Scotland Reconsidered" (1983) 4 J.L.H. 76.

higher authority, will almost certainly be taken as settling the law.[77] Among the institutional writers on civil matters are *always included*[78] Sir Thomas Craig (*Jus Feudale,* 1655); Viscount Stair (*The Institutions of the Law of Scotland,* 1681),[79] Andrew McDouall, Lord Bankton (*An Institute of the Laws of Scotland,* 3 volumes, 1751–53); Professor John Erskine (*An Institute of the Law of Scotland,* 2 volumes, 1773); and Professor George Joseph Bell (*Commentaries on the Law of Scotland and the Principles of Mercantile Jurisprudence,* 1804,[79] and *Principles of the Law of Scotland,* 1829).

To these are sometimes added Sir George Mackenzie (*The Institutions of the Law of Scotland,* 1684)[80] and Henry Home, Lord Kames (*Principles of Equity,* 1760), but not all authorities concede the privileged status of institutional writings to these works.

In criminal law, Sir George Mackenzie (*The Laws and Customs of Scotland in Matters Criminal,* 1678), Baron David Hume (*Commentaries on the Law of Scotland respecting Crimes,* 2 volumes, 1797) and Archibald Alison (*Principles of the Criminal Law of Scotland,* 1832, and *Practice of the Criminal Law of Scotland,* 1833) are also regarded as institutional writers. Various other texts have on occasion been referred to as "institutional," but the status is not generally conceded to them. Most of these institutional writings are the Scottish instances of a widespread trend in Western Europe in the sixteenth to eighteenth centuries for writers to seek to expound the developing legal systems of rising nation-states, based on native rather than Roman law sources, but frequently based on the general pattern of Justinian's *Institutes.*[81]

The authority of statements in institutional writings depends on recognition by the courts of the weight and value of their views. The authority of a statement in an institutional writing[82] is probably about equal to that of a decision of either Division of the Inner House. It has been said,[83] "Stair, Erskine and Bell are cited daily in the courts, and the court will pay as

---

[77] "When on any point of law I find Stair's opinion uncontradicted I look upon that opinion as ascertaining the Law of Scotland": *Drew v. Drew* (1870) 9 M. 163, 167, *per* Lord Benholme. See also, *Kennedy v. Stewart* (1889) 16 R. 421, 430 on Kames. On Stair see further *Stair Tercentenary Studies* (Stair Society, 1981).

[78] The dates given are of the first publication of the books in question.

[79] First published in 1800–04 as *Treatise on the Law of Bankruptcy in Scotland.*

[80] *Lord Advocate v. Aberdeen University,* 1963 S.C. 533, 559. H.L. MacQueen, "Mackenzie's *Institutions* in Scottish Legal History" (1984) 29 J.L.S. 498.

[81] K. Luig, "The Institutes of National Law in the Seventeenth and Eighteenth Centuries," 1972 J.R. 193; K. Luig, "Stair from a Foreign Standpoint" in *Stair Tercentenary Studies* (Stair Society, 1981).

[82] A distinction may have to be taken between what the writer himself wrote and what a later editor may have added. Hence reference to the last edition *by the author* is sometimes made. But editors' notes may themselves sometimes have considerable weight and value. See *Fortington v. Kinnaird,* 1942 S.C. 239.

[83] Lord Normand, *The Scottish Judicature and Legal Procedure* (Holdsworth Club, Birmingham, address, 1941). See also *Routledge v. Carruthers,* May 19, 1812, F.C.; *Ross v. Heriot's Hospital,* June 6, 1815, F.C.

much respect to them as to a judgment of the House of Lords, though it is bound to follow a judgment of the House of Lords whatever the institutional writers may have said."[84] Institutional writings may also be referred to as authority reinforcing older judicial decisions.[85] Courts have sometimes approved or disapproved particular statements in institutional writings.[86] The authority of institutional writings does not, however, extend automatically to all the writer's works, so that Erskine's *Principles*, written as a textbook for students, is not institutional,[87] and Hume's *Lectures on Scots Law*,[88] not finally revised or published by him, are not entitled to the same weight as his *Commentaries on Crimes*.[89] These other works are merely legal literature though very valuable specimens of it in view of the personal eminence of the writer. The institutional writings have been immensely influential in the past and have guided many past decisions of the courts, so that their importance is not confined to the somewhat spasmodic reference to them today.

SECONDARY SOURCES

IV.—STANDARD TEXTBOOKS AND OTHER LEGAL LITERATURE

Writers on law other than the institutional writers, whose writings are legal literature rather than literary sources of the law, are technically not authorities at all and, according to an English view, could not be quoted in court during their lifetimes,[90] unless possibly they were elevated to the Bench, and even then their writings were of less weight than their judgments.[91] Such writings could only be "adopted" in argument as

---

[84] For recent instances of substantial reliance on institutional writings see *Widenmeyer v. Burn, Stewart & Co.*, 1967 S.C. 85; *Wills' Trs. v. Cairngorm School Ltd*, 1976 S.C.(H.L.) 30; *Crown Estates Commrs v. Fairlie Yacht Ltd.*, 1976 S.C. 161; *Sloan's Dairies Ltd v. Glasgow Corp.*, 1977 S.C. 223; *Wolifson v. Harrison*, 1977 S.C. 384; *Precision Relays v. Beaton*, 1980 S.C. 220, 223.

[85] *Morgan Guaranty Trust Co. v. Lothian Regional Council*, 1995 S.L.T. 299.

[86] *L. v. Wilson*, 1995 S.L.T. 673, approving Hume and disapproving Alison; *Burns v. H.M. Advocate*, 1995 S.L.T. 1090, criticising Hume and Macdonald's *Criminal Law*.

[87] In *Wills' Trs., supra*, at 117 Lord Wilberforce includes Erskine's *Principles*; this is inaccurate.

[88] Ed. Paton, Stair Society, 6 vols.

[89] *Fortington v. Kinnaird*, 1942 S.C. 239, 253; but Hume's *Lectures* have nevertheless frequently been cited since then; see also *Pettigrew v. Harton*, 1956 S.C. 67; *MacLennan v. MacLennan*, 1958 S.C. 105; *Thomson v. Cuthbert's Co-operative Association Ltd*, 1958 S.C. 380, 394, 398; *N.C.B. v. Thomson*, 1959 S.C. 353, 383; *Cole-Hamilton v. Boyd*, 1962 S.C. 247, 257; *Mill's Trs. v. Mill's Trs.*, 1965 S.C. 384, 394; *Balshaw v. Balshaw*, 1967 S.C. 63, 83; *Wills' Trs., supra*; *Sloan's Dairies, supra*, 240; *Wolifson, supra*, 391. On More's *Notes on Stair*, see *Forrest v. Forrest* (1863) 1 M. 806.

[90] Hence Lord Wright, speaking of (the then still-living) Sir Frederick Pollock's *Law of Torts*, called it "fortunately not a work of authority": *Nicholls v. Ely Beet Sugar Factory* [1936] 1 Ch. 343, 349. The restriction is not observed in the Scottish courts: Bell and Hume were cited repeatedly in court in their lifetimes.

[91] A distinction may also be taken between a work written by a judge when he was young and an inexperienced advocate at the Bar and a work written in the days of his maturity.

representing part of the speaker's contention as to the law. "The law books give no assistance because the work of living authors, however deservedly eminent, cannot be used as authority, although the opinions they express may demand attention."[92] Their writings are secondary and not primary sources of the law. But in fact in modern practice many writers are nowadays cited in argument and judgment notwithstanding that in many cases they are neither dead nor have been on the Bench.[93] Thus in one case[94] a judge said: "In support of their argument, pursuer's counsel relied mainly on (1) certain cases such as . . . ; (2) certain English authority; (3) certain Scottish textbooks, including . . . ; and (4) the case of . . . " and continued: "I turn, therefore, to the law . . . as expounded by text-book writers and judicially in Scotland. . . . " In another[95]: "There remain for consideration the commentaries and text-book writers." In another the judge stated that in the absence of judicial authority, academic authority demonstrated certain principles.[96] While many such books are referred to in argument and even sometimes quoted in judgments, they are only statements of what the jurist in question *believes* the law to be, what he submits is the result of the statutes and decided cases, and any court is quite free to differ from him and to lay down the true rule otherwise.[97] Such books do not state the law as authoritatively as the institutional writings do, but are only persuasive and state what the writer thinks is the law on a particular subject.[98] If a court follows a text-writer his statement becomes authoritative by virtue of the approval. There is further a gradation of books, from books regarded in the profession as standard treatises on various branches of law with established reputations, down to books such as mere students' textbooks with no reputation and no influence on the court. Some books are in fact highly regarded, almost as highly as are institutional writings, and their views usually accepted and

---

[92] *Donoghue v. Stevenson*, 1932 S.C.(H.L.) 31, 35, *per* Lord Buckmaster.

[93] *cf.* Lord Reid, "The Judge as Lawmaker" (1972) 12 J.S.P.T.L.(N.S.) 22.

[94] *Stein v. Beaverbrook Newspapers*, 1968 S.C. 272, 278.

[95] *Wills' Trs. v. Cairngorm School*, 1976 S.C.(H.L.) 30, 80.

[96] *Baring Bros. & Co. v. Cunninghame District Council* [1996] 11 C.L. 592.

[97] Thus, in cases on vesting, the courts repeatedly have referred to Candlish Henderson's *Principles of Vesting* with approval. On questions of international private law modern textbooks are regularly cited. Standard textbooks are more frequently cited in Scotland than in England. But textbooks may equally be criticised. See *e.g. Bell v. Blackwood Morton & Sons Ltd*, 1960 S.C. 11, 23, disapproving a passage in Glegg on *Reparation*; *Carter v. Allison*, 1966 S.C. 257; *Highland Engineering Ltd v. Thomson*, 1972 S.C. 87, 91; *Mitchell v. McCulloch*, 1976 S.C. 1, 9; *Gibson v. Carson*, 1980 S.C. 360; *Allan v. Paterson*, 1980 J.C. 57, 60, approving some and disapproving other textbooks. *cf. Bastin v. Davies* [1950] 2 K.B. 579, where Lord Goddard C.J. said: "If a statement has appeared in a well-known textbook for a great number of years and has never been dissented from by a judicial decision, it would be most unfortunate to throw doubt on it after it had been acted on . . . for so long." For criticisms of statements in textbooks, see also *Re H.L. Bolton Engineering Co. Ltd* [1956] Ch. 577; *Beevis v. Dawson* [1957] 1 Q.B. 195, 207; *Bentley v. Macfarlane*, 1964 S.C. 76. See also *Leon v. Leon* [1967] P. 275, where the court disapproved a statement in one textbook but applied principles stated in two others.

[98] *cf. Mitchell, supra*, at 9: "While the comments of current academic writers are of persuasive effect only, it is interesting to note the conclusions they have drawn from these cases."

followed,[99] while approval of a decision by the text-writers may be taken as supporting its soundness,[1] or disapproval as shaking its authority[2]; but it is important to remember that these books do not impose law on the Bench, but merely may be voluntarily accepted for their clarity and accuracy of statement. The precise degree of regard paid to a particular book depends on the writer's reputation,[3] the esteem in which the book is held in the profession, and its age, for on the one hand it takes some time for any book to acquire reputation and on the other all books tend to become out of date, and if not revised may become practically valueless by the passing of time and the progress of the law, as new statutes and cases arise. But, if in point, a statement in a standard treatise carries weight comparable to, but rather lesser than, a single-judge decision. English textbooks have lesser weight unless the principles in question are the same in both legal systems.

Legal literature, of course, serves an invaluable purpose in presenting, for student or practitioner or judge, a connected, coherent and systematic account of the law on its topic, and in collecting in its text and footnotes references to the main statutes, cases and other primary sources of the rules of law on the subject. It is only in legal literature that one can find a coherent systematised account of any branch of law; without the textbooks the law is a jumble of disconnected statutory provisions and decisions. Many textbooks have done much to clarify and systematise the law and by generalisations from cases, examination of terms and doctrines, constructive suggestions, criticism of unsatisfactory decisions and interpretations of statutes, and indications of desirable developments have influenced courts and judges in subsequent cases.[4] "The judges discover the law either from the words of relevant statutes or, so far as the common law offences are concerned from earlier decisions of other courts which are binding on them or have persuasive authority. They may often be assisted by eminent writers of commentaries or by academic writers, in so far as they have distilled the essence of judicial decisions. Judges should, however, be careful to disregard those parts of their writings which suggest what the law ought to be but is not."[5]

---

[99] Such books include Gloag on *Contract*, Rankine on *Land Ownership*, Rankine on *Leases*, Graham Stewart on *Diligence*, Goudy on *Bankruptcy* and a number of others. See the authorities cited in *Wills' Trs. v. Cairngorm School*, 1976 S.C.(H.L.) 30 at all stages.

[1] *cf. Dempster's Trs. v. Dempster*, 1949 S.C. 92, *per* Lord Jamieson: "The decision . . . has been accepted by the text writers as settling the law,"; *Dick v. Falkirk*, 1976 S.C.(H.L.) 1, 22–23.

[2] Thus *Machado v. Fontes* [1897] 2 Q.B. 231 has been almost universally condemned by the text-writers: see *McElroy v. McAllister*, 1949 S.C. 110, 135, where L. P. Cooper noted this consensus of disapproval. See also *Dick v. Falkirk*, 1976 S.C.(H.L.) 1, 23, 28.

[3] See, *e.g. Coats's Trs. v. Lord Advocate*, 1965 S.C.(H.L.) 45, 69 on an article in Green's *Encyclopaedia*. See also the reliance on, and discussion of, Gloag on *Contract* in *Errol v. Walker*, 1966 S.C. 93 (which was wrongly decided).

[4] Thus the completely unofficial *Restatement of the Law*, published by the American Law Institute, has considerable influence: it was cited in *e.g. McPhail v. Lanark C.C.*, 1951 S.C. 301.

[5] *R. v. Howe* [1986] 1 All E.R. 833, 836–37, *per* Lord Lane C.J.

In the present century the influence of legal literature has extended also to the chief legal periodicals; courts and judges have shown themselves sensitive to criticism by academic jurists in these journals, and have with increasing frequency considered and paid respect and attention to opinions expressed therein. Everything depends on the personal standing and reputation of the writer, without which matter in a legal journal carries no weight.[6]

V.—CUSTOM

Among other sources, mention must be made of custom,[7] which was historically a very important source but now plays a much smaller part as a source than it formerly did, in that many older customs have now been embodied in legislation or cases or books of authority. Many general customs have accordingly been incorporated long ago in the common law of Scotland. Thus the "legal rights" of spouses on death and the common-law rules governing the relationship of landlord and tenant are based on very old customs. But apart from these customs, now absorbed into the law, custom may still be alleged in a particular case and, if proved, will be a valid source of a new rule of law. Such a custom must be (*a*) in some sense an exception to or qualification of the ordinary rule of law, yet not run completely counter to, or be contradictory of, an already established rule of statute or case-law. It must, that is, be an exception to, yet still consistent with, the existing general body of law.[8] It may, for example, be confined to a locality; (*b*) definite and certain. It cannot be a custom if it is not known what it is, or is vague or if it is not habitually observed; (*c*) fair and reasonable; hence a claim for an exaction by a landlord for which nothing was given in return has been held unreasonable[9]; (*d*) generally accepted for so long as to justify the inference that it has long been accepted as law, as the binding rule. No particular period of time must be proved.[10]

The basis on which the court in an appropriate case will enforce the custom as law is that it has been shown to have been so certain, settled and established that it was in fact accepted as law and treated as binding even though it had not previously been before the courts or obtained express judicial recognition. If it is proved that a particular custom is accepted as law it will rule notwithstanding that either party is ignorant of it; *ignorantia juris neminem excusat*.[11] The importance of this kind of custom as a source of new rules of law is clearly limited.

---

[6] For example of the influence of periodicals, see *Haynes v. Harwood* [1935] 1 K.B. 146.

[7] See Cameron, "Custom as a Source of Law in Scotland" (1964) 27 M.L.R. 306.

[8] *Walker Trustees v. Lord Advocate*, 1912 S.C.(H.L.) 12; *McCann v. Anderson*, 1981 S.L.T.(Lands Tr.) 13.

[9] *Bruce v. Smith* (1890) 17 R. 1000.

[10] Ersk., I, 1, 44; *secus* in England.

[11] *Learmonth v. Sinclair's Trs.* (1878) 5 R. 548.

Possibly distinct from this kind of custom is the kind of custom or usage, sometimes sought to be proved, particularly in mercantile matters, to assist in interpreting a contract or implying a term into one. In this case, evidence may be allowed to explain or supplement a mercantile contract, not on the basis that the custom is a rule of law, but on the ground that parties must have known of, and must be taken to have intended to act in accordance with, some particular trade usage. Since the basis for this kind of custom is implied agreement of parties to be bound by the custom, notice to or knowledge of the usage on the part of the person against whom it is pleaded must be proved.[12] Such a usage must be reasonably fair[13] and at least generally recognised in the trade in question.[14] Thus, under this rule it has been proved that by the custom of the rabbit trade "one thousand" meant 1,200,[15] or that a provision in a contract for oil for the reference of disputes to "arbitration in Glasgow" meant, by the custom of the oil trade, a reference to an arbiter appointed by each party with an oversman chosen by them.[16] Moreover, unless a contract is made expressly subject to some usage, proof of usage is not permitted to contradict the plain meaning of express words in the contract. Thus a contract to supply "the whole of the steel for [a bridge], the estimated quantity to be 30,000 tons," was held to be a contract for the whole amount of steel, despite an alleged usage of the steel trade that the words meant 30,000 tons only.[17]

Parties may also contract in general terms by reference to, *e.g.* the custom of a particular port, and in that case they will be bound by the custom even though they did not know of its precise terms.[18]

The importance of this kind of custom as a source of law is considerable and in many cases mercantile contracts still have to be interpreted in accordance with customs and usages of particular ports, or particular trades. Similarly in industrial relations custom or usage of trade may supplement the express terms of employment or assist its interpretation.[19]

VI.—EQUITY

Equity has several distinguishable meanings, as natural law, as fairness or justice, as flexibility and discretion opposed to rules of strict law, and as a

---

[12] *Holman v. Peruvian Nitrate Co.* (1878) 5 R. 657.

[13] *Devonald v. Rosser* [1906] 2 K.B. 728.

[14] *Hogarth v. Leith Cottonseed Oil Co.*, 1909 S.C. 955; *Dick v. Cochrane & Fleming*, 1935 S.L.T. 432.

[15] *Smith v. Wilson* (1832) 3 B. & Ad. 728.

[16] *United Creameries Co. v. Boyd & Co.*, 1922 S.C. 617.

[17] *Tancred, Arrol & Co. v. Steel Co. of Scotland* (1887) 15 R. 215; (1890) 17 R.(H.L.) 31; *MacLellan v. Peattie's Trustees* (1903) 5 F. 1031; *Affréteurs Réunis v. Walford* [1919] A.C. 801.

[18] *Strathlorne S.S. Co. v. Baird*, 1915 S.C. 956; revd. 1916 S.C.(H.L.) 134; *Cazelet v. Morris*, 1916 S.C. 952. *cf. Forget v. Baxter* [1900] A.C. 467; *Clydesdale Bank (Moore Nominees) Ltd v. Snodgrass*, 1939 S.C. 805.

[19] See, *e.g. Sagar v. Ridehalgh* [1931] 1 Ch. 310; *Marshall v. English Electric Co.* [1945] 1 All E.R. 653; *Heaton's Transport v. T. & G.W.U.* [1973] A.C. 15; *Hardwick v. Leeds Health Authority* [1975] I.R.L.R. 319.

body of principles distinct from those of law administered by separate courts.[20] Scottish courts have always administered an undivided system of law and equity and many of the principles commonly applied by the courts are as much equitable as legal in origin and justification.[21] Many doctrines of Scots law have been modified by equity, in the sense of the force of reason and natural justice, to rectify or avoid an excessive strictness or rigidity. In many fields of law this influence has so exercised itself in the past that the legal and equitable elements in the modern doctrine have been completely blended and the boundary is not perceptible. But equity remains a valid and unexhausted source of Scots law in that it is still open to a court to delimit a rule or interpret a principle in the light of what seems consistent with reason and natural justice.[22]

Apart from instances where the rule of law has been modified by equitable ideas in the course of its development, the Court of Session and, to some extent, the High Court of Justiciary[23] retain an ultimate residuary equitable power to provide a remedy where justice requires it and to intervene to prevent unduly rigorous law working injustice. This power, the *nobile officium*, has of late come to be much restricted and is, as a rule, exercised now only in circumstances for which there is precedent or analogy.[24]

Moreover, in many fields of law a judge is expressly or impliedly enjoined to keep equitable considerations, the concepts of what is reasonable and conform to natural justice, in mind. He is endowed with discretion, which has to be exercised consistently with these principles and not arbitrarily, though in practice the exercise soon tends to become limited by the ways in which the exercise has been done in past cases, and repeatedly he finds that he has to do what is "just and reasonable" or "fair," or otherwise finds a standard fixed which has to be applied to the facts of the case having in mind the equitable considerations of providing a remedy for any obvious wrong, of avoiding the injustice of excessively rigid application of law, and of rewarding care, diligence and honesty.

---

[20] Until 1875 England had courts of common law which administered law and courts of equity which gave equitable remedies. The distinction still persists in some Commonwealth countries. Since 1875 all courts in England may give both legal and equitable remedies but it is doubtful how far law and equity have been merged; the merger is still incomplete. On English Equity, see further, Levy-Ullmann, *The English Legal Tradition*, Pt. 3; Plucknett, *Concise History of the Common Law*, 675 *et seq.*; Potter, *Historical Introduction to English Law* (4th ed.), 569 *et seq.*; Allen, *Law in the Making*, Chap. 5.

[21] See further, Brown, "Equity" (1914) 26 J.R. 338; Walker, "Equity in Scots Law" (1954) 66 J.R. 103; art. "Equity" in Green's *Encyclopaedia*; Lord Wark, "The Law of Nature," in (Stair Society) *Sources and Literature of Scots Law,* 249; *The Laws of Scotland*, Vol. 22, paras 394 *et seq.*

[22] As a factor in interpreting the old Scots prescription statutes, see, *e.g. Earl of Fife v. Duff* (1888) 15 R. 253; *Mill's Trs.*, 1965 S.C. 384, 388.

[23] See, *e.g. Wylie v. H.M.A.*, 1966 S.L.T. 149.

[24] See Green's *Encyclopaedia*, art. "Nobile Officium"; *The Laws of Scotland*, Vol. 22, para. 426.

VII.—EXTRANEOUS SOURCES

Extraneous sources include all those other sources to which a judge may resort, in default of guidance from the sources already discussed, and from which he may draw or adapt a principle or rule to apply to a new problem before him.

Other Systems of Law

If the sources from which rules and principles of Scots law are normally drawn, those already discussed, yield nothing or nothing very satisfactory, it is permissible and proper to look at other systems of law in which the problem may have arisen and which may, accordingly, be able to suggest a suitable rule. Among other systems, regard should first be had to Roman law, particularly in questions of obligations and moveable property. Roman law has long been, and may still be, a good quarry for the material of legal decisions and it would be consistent with the traditions of Scots law if resort were made more to the Roman law instead of always running to the English books.[25] Modern systems of law which have drawn heavily on the Roman law, such as the Roman-Dutch law of South Africa, and later commentators on the Roman law, such as Voet, may also usefully be referred to.

In consistorial matters the old Roman canon law and the great mass of learned commentaries thereon is likewise a traditional, and still valuable and highly reputable source.

Especially in matters of commercial and industrial law, the laws of England, the Commonwealth countries, and the United States may usefully be looked at. But one has always to keep in mind the very different history, development and working-out of English rules and doctrines. In particular the different approaches of common law and of equity to the same problems prior to 1875, and the continuing results of that dichotomy since then, make English law a very unsafe guide unless in the hands of a scholar who understands both systems. Immense harm has been done to Scots law by the uncritical culling from English law of decisions which appear applicable equally to Scotland but which have really been misunderstood. Moreover, the more remote the legal system from which guidance is being sought, the greater the danger of failing to

---

[25] Ersk. I, 1, 41, speaks of the Roman law as "of great weight in all cases not fixed by statute or custom, and in which the genius of our law will suffer us to apply it." See also *Wills' Trs.* v. *Cairngorm School Ltd,* 1976 S.C.(H.L.) 30, 140; *Sloan's Dairies Ltd v. Glasgow Corp.,* 1977 S.C. 223.

appreciate the background of the decision or the rule and of importing an unsound principle. Continental law is also occasionally referred to.[26]

Dissenting judgments, *obiter dicta*, and arguments by analogy from principles accepted in other contexts may also give assistance.

Ideals of Justice

In default of all other sources, the judge is thrown back on his own moral conscience, his beliefs as to what is fair and right and reasonable in the circumstances; in short, on his idea of what justice requires.[27] In the House of Lords it has been said[28]: "In the end and in the absence of authority binding this House, the question is simply: 'What does justice demand in such a case as this?'" Failing other authority the broad principles of justice, as the judge sees it, are not a bad basis for decision, and such principles can also sometimes be appealed to in support of a conclusion based also on another ground. Thus conduct has been stigmatised as "morally and socially wrong,"[29] or it has been held that something was "contrary to natural justice,"[30] or "opposed to the fundamental principles of justice."[31] Where a judge is entitled to exercise discretion, his exercise must be determined largely by his view of what is just in the circumstances.[32]

Akin to ideals of justice, and indeed only facets of justice under other names, are those considerations of morality and public policy sometimes invoked to justify a decision, reflecting the fact that an important characteristic of any acceptable system of law is that it will promote what is generally beneficial and good and discourage the contrary.[33] Again a decision may be reached on grounds of policy or what is believed to be in the general public interest.[34]

---

[26] For examples of reference to foreign law, see, *e.g. Donoghue v. Stevenson*, 1932 S.C.(H.L.) 31 (English and U.S. cases); *A/B Karlshamns Oljefabriker v. Monarch S.S. Co.*, 1949 S.C.(H.L.) 1 (U.S. case); *Drummond's J.F. v. H.M. Advocate*, 1944 S.C. 298 (English and French law); *Cantiere San Rocco v. Clyde Shipbuilding Co.*, 1923 S.C.(H.L.) 105; *Glasgow Corp. v. Lord Advocate*, 1959 S.C. 203 (Roman law); *Sugden v. H.M.A.*, 1934 J.C. 103 (Dutch jurists, French and Roman law); *Collins v. Collins* (1884) 11 R.(H.L.) 19; *Purves' Trustees v. Purves* (1895) 22 R. 513; *Annan v. Annan*, 1948 S.C. 532; *Imre v. Mitchell*, 1958 S.C. 439, 464 (all canon law); *Walsh v. Lord Advocate*, 1956 S.C.(H.L.) 126 (U.S. case); *Breen v. Breen*, 1961 S.C. 158 (Roman and canon law); *Burmah Oil Co. v. Lord Advocate*, 1965 S.C.(H.L.) 117 (international jurists, legal history and U.S. law); *Wills' Trs. v. Cairngorm School Ltd*, 1976 S.C.(H.L.) 30 (Roman, French and Canadian Law); *Junior Books v. Veitchi*, 1982 S.C.(H.L.) 244.

[27] See further, Cardozo, *Nature of the Judicial Process*; *Ingle v. Ingle's Tr.*, 1999 S.L.T. 650.

[28] *National Bank of Greece and Athens S.A. v. Metliss* [1958] A.C. 509, 525, *per* Viscount Simonds.

[29] *Wilson v. Glossop* (1888) 20 Q.B.D. 354.

[30] *Valentini v. Canali* (1889) 24 Q.B.D. 166.

[31] *Robinson v. Continental Insurance Co.* [1915] 1 K.B. 155.

[32] Robertson, *Judicial Discretion in the House of Lords*.

[33] For cases where considerations of morality and public policy have been in issue, see, *e.g. R. v. Bourne* [1939] 1 K.B. 687; *Steel v. Glasgow Iron & Steel Co.*, 1944 S.C. 237; *Fender v. Mildmay* [1938] A.C. 1; *Beresford v. Royal Insurance Co.* [1938] A.C. 586.

[34] *Smart v. H.M. Advocate*, 1975 S.C. 30, 34; *Brennan v. H.M. Advocate*, 1977 J.C. 38, 44; *Hill v. Chief Constable of West Yorkshire* [1988] 2 All E.R. 238, 243.

Conclusions

These, then, are the sources, and it will be seen that the legal adviser must sometimes have to search long and deeply for the basis for his advice, and the judge at least as far and widely for the ground of his decision and its justification in the eyes of critical jurists and subsequent judges. Frequently, no ready-made proposition of law can be found directly applicable to the facts in issue, and the search must be for the materials with which the court may fashion a proposition for application to those facts. Increasingly, moreover, the courts in their decisions put the stamp of authority on propositions which in part they work out and formulate themselves, but in large part they select and develop from doctrinal writings. New problems keep on turning up and every now and then a case arises which raises some quite fundamental point and requires for its solution long and careful research in these sources and sometimes outward from them into history or social science or some other branch of learning which might at first sight appear remote from the law. The inevitable conclusion is that nothing can be ignored by the lawyer as irrelevant to his main study and that the wider his background knowledge the better. Moreover, even when matter bearing on the problem can be found in the statutes or cases or books, the matter must be interpreted to see what light it casts on the problem, and to decide whether it supplies the answer or merely a guide to the answer.

FURTHER READING

Sources Generally
Allen: *Law in the Making.*
Gray: *Nature and Sources of the Law.*
Holdsworth: *Sources and Literature of English Law.*
Holland: *Jurisprudence*, Chap. 5.
The Laws of Scotland, tit. Sources of Law (Formal).
        Sources of Law (General and Historical).
Paton: *Jurisprudence,* Chaps. 6–10.
Patterson: *Jurisprudence*, Chaps. 9–11.
Pound: *Jurisprudence*, Chap. 16.
Salmond: *Jurisprudence*, Chaps. 5–9.
Stair Society: *Sources and Literature of Scots Law.*
Sweet and Maxwell: *Guide to Law Reports and Statutes.*

Sources of European Communities Law
Hartley: *Foundations of European Community Law.*

Legislation
Allen: *Law and Orders.*
Carr: *Delegated Legislation.*
Craies: *Treatise on Statute Law.*
Cross: *Statutory Interpretation.*

Griffith and Street: *Principles of Administrative Law.*
Halsbury's Laws of England, tit. Statutes.
Ilbert: *Legislative Methods and Forms*, 1901.
    Methods of Legislation, 1911.
Maxwell: *The Interpretation of Statutes.*
Thring: *Practical Legislation.*

Case Law
Cross and Harris: *Precedent in English Law.*
Daniel: *History and Origin of the Law Reports.*
Ellis Lewis: "History of Judicial Precedent" (1930) 46 L.Q.R. 207, 341; (1931) 47
    L.Q.R. 411; (1932) 48 L.Q.R. 230.
Frank: *Courts on Trial.*
    Law and the Modern Mind.
Gardner: *Judicial Precedent in Scots Law.*
    "Judicial Precedent in American and Scots Law" (1940) 52 J.R. 144.
Gibb: *Law from over the Border.*
Goldstein: *Precedent in Law.*
Goodhart: "Precedent in English and Continental Law" (1934) 50 L.Q.R. 40.
Jensen: *The Nature of Legal Argument.*
Levi: *Introduction to Legal Reasoning.*
Moran: *The Heralds of the Law.*
Ram: *The Science of Legal Judgment*, 1871.
Smith: *Judicial Precedent in Scots Law.*
Stone: *The Province and Functions of Law*, Chaps. 6 and 7.
    Legal System and Lawyer's Reasoning, Chap. 7.
Wallace: *The Reporters*, 4th ed., 1982.
Wambaugh: *Study of Cases*, 2nd ed., 1984.

Institutional Writings
Black: "The Institutional Writers" in (Stair Society) *Sources and Literature of Scots
    Law.*
Cooper: "Some Classics of Scottish Legal Literature" in *Selected Papers.*
Fifoot: *Judge and Jurist in the Reign of Queen Victoria.*
Walker: *The Scottish Jurists.*

Custom
Institutional writers.

Equity
Allen: *Law in the Making.*
Kames: *Principles of Equity.*
Walker: "Equity in Scots Law" (1954) 66 J.R. 103.

Extraneous Sources
Cardozo: *Nature of the Judicial Process.*
Frank: *Courts on Trial.*
Mackintosh: *Roman Law in Modern Practice.*
Oliver: "Roman Law in Modern Cases," in *Cambridge Legal Essays*, 243.
Stein and Shand: *Legal Values in Western Society.*

CHAPTER 11

THE REPOSITORIES OF SCOTS LAW

A DISTINCTION has been drawn between the legally authoritative sources of the law and legal literature, or books about the law, which are sources of our knowledge of the law, setting out only the author's view of what the law is on the subject discussed in his work. Legal literature has no binding authority at all and is only a secondary source of the law, though some books may in fact enjoy a high reputation and exercise an influence on a court not much, if at all, inferior to that of a judicial decision. The whole corpus of books which contain the written law, both the authoritative sources, and the unauthoritative books about the law or literary or secondary sources, forms the repositories of the law, to which the inquirer must resort to search out the law applicable to some precise point. A knowledge of these repositories is essential; the lawyer must know where and how to look for the law.[1]

PRIMARY OR AUTHORITATIVE SOURCES

I.—LEGISLATION

A—LEGISLATION COMMON TO COUNTRIES OF THE EUROPEAN UNION

The primary sources of EU law, the treaties, are published by the Office for Official Publications of the EU and by the Stationery Office as *European Communities* and in the Sweet & Maxwell/W. Green *Encyclopaedia of European Community Law*, Series B.[2] United Kingdom sources relevant to the incorporation of EU law into United Kingdom law are in the same *Encyclopaedia*, Series A. Community secondary legislation is published in the *Official Journal* of the Communities, which is published regularly in all the official languages of the EU, since 1968 in two series, "L" (legislation) and "C" (information and notices),[3] and also in the

---

[1] Every lawyer and student should become familiar with the Legal Bibliographies and Reference Books listed on p. 508. See also Colquhoun, *Finding the Law.*

[2] This is a loose-leaf, regularly updated collection of texts with commentary.

[3] The English edition, abbreviated O.J., runs from January 1973. Prior to 1973, before English was an official language, material appeared in the *Journal Officiel* (J.O.). All earlier EC secondary legislation still in force in 1973 was later reissued in an English language Special Edition of the O.J., cited "S.Edn." and by the Stationery Office as *European Communities: Secondary Legislation, 1952–72.* The proceedings of the European Parliament are also published in the O.J., Series C.

Encyclopaedia, Series C. The Supplement to the *Official Journal* appears irregularly and contains items such as Public Works Contracts.

B—Legislation Applicable to Scotland

Scots Acts prior to 1707 are to be found in *The Acts of the Parliaments of Scotland, 1124–1707*,[4] and also in Murray of Glendook's *Laws and Acts of Parliament, 1424–1681*,[5] while Scots Acts still in force in 1908 were reprinted in *Scots Statutes Revised, 1424–1707*,[6] and those still in force in 1964 were reprinted in the *Acts of the Parliaments of Scotland, 1424–1707*.[7]

Statutes of the Parliament of England prior to 1707 are contained in the *Statutes of the Realm, 1225–1713*,[8] and in various editions of the *Statutes at Large*.[9] Legislation during the Interregnum is collected in the *Acts and Ordinances of the Interregnum, 1642–60*.[10]

Acts of the Parliaments of Great Britain, 1707–1800, and of the Parliaments of the United Kingdom since 1801 are also in the *Statutes at Large*. There is also an edition of statutes 1806–69 in 63 volumes, and since 1831 the Queen's Printer has published annually the *Public General Statutes*.[11]

The *Statutes Revised*, third edition (1235–1948)[12] prints, in chronological, not classified, order, the statutes (excepting Acts of the pre–1707 Scottish Parliaments) so far as still in force and as amended to the end of 1948. Each volume has a chronological table which lists all Acts within the period it covers and gives the reason for omissions, and an index to subjects dealt with in the volume. This is continued to the present by

---

[4] Ed. Thomas Thomson and Cosmo Innes, 11 vols. in 12, and Index Vol., 1814–75, cited, *e.g.* A.P.S. II, 345. This is known as the Record edition, having been published by the Commissioners on the Public Records.

[5] Folio, 1681; duodecimo, two volumes, 1682; cited, *e.g.* Act 1449, c. 18. A third volume continues to the Union. The texts of the Acts, and the numbering, is not the same in the A.P.S. and Glendook's editions; the former is the better.

[6] 1908.

[7] Second revised edition, HMSO, 1966. This edition gives also the short titles conferred on the surviving Scots Acts by the Statute Law Revision (Scotland) Act 1964, Sched. 2, and references to the chapter numbers of both the Record edition and Glendook's edition.

[8] Published by the Record Commissioners, 9 vols. in 10, large folio, 1810–22, with alphabetical index, 1824, and chronological index, 1828, reprinted 1963. It includes private Acts to 1539 and the titles of private Acts thereafter, and there are valuable introductions and editorial notes.

[9] The best are Ruffhead's (1215–1764) in 9 vols. with 9 supplementary vols. covering 1763–1800; Runnington's new edition of Ruffhead (1215–1785) in 10 vols. with 4 supplementary vols. covering 1785–1800; Tomlins and Raithby's (1215–1800) in 10 vols. quarto, or 20 vols. octavo, continued by a Queen's Printer's edition 1801–69 in 29 vols.; and Pickering's (1215–1761) in 24 vols., continued to 1806 by 22 supplements.

[10] Ed. Firth and Rait, 3 vols. 1911.

[11] The Statutory Publications Office also issues annually *Annotations to Acts*, in the form of adhesive slips containing substituted provisions which can be attached to older Acts affected by the year's new legislation.

[12] (1235–1948) in 32 vols. There is also a uniform volume of [English] *Church Assembly Measures Revised*.

annual volumes of *Public General Statutes*. The *Scots Statutes Revised*[13] includes only Acts applicable to Scotland, as amended to the date of each volume. This is continued by *Scots Statutes*[14] and *Scottish Current Law Statutes*.[15] There are other editions, such as the Blackwood edition,[16] while reprints of statutes were issued with the *Scots Law Times* from 1901 to 1948 and with the [English] *Law Reports* from 1865 to 1950.

When they receive Royal Assent new Acts of Parliament are first published by the Stationery Office as single Acts, known as Queen's Printer's copies. The Acts passed during a calendar year are collected in chronological order of passing in several volumes, with alphabetical and chronological lists and an index to all the Acts of the year, as *Public General Acts and Measures, 19—* . The last volume of each year's Acts also contains tables of the derivations of Acts consolidated, *i.e.* tables showing from what sections of older Acts each section of the consolidating Act has been derived, of the destinations of the Acts consolidated, *i.e.* tables showing where sections of the older Acts consolidated are to be found in the new consolidating Act, the effect of the legislation of the year, by amendment, repeal or otherwise of older Acts, and the textual amendments of Acts made by Statutory Instruments during the year.

Publication was made in 1972–1981 of *Statutes in Force*, a new official revised edition of the statutes in which each Act (including Acts of the Parliaments of Scotland) in force is printed as a separate booklet. Booklets containing Acts dealing with related subjects, *e.g.* Shipping, are grouped chronologically in loose-leaf binders. When an Act is heavily amended the booklet is replaced by a new one containing an amended print of the Act. A cumulative amendments booklet issued annually, lists all the amendments not yet incorporated in the edition. In respect of some groups of Acts there are separate Scottish and English groups and in such cases Acts extending to both Scotland and England may be included in both groups. There are indexes to groups or large sub-groups of the recommended arrangement, and there will ultimately be an index to the whole work. Cumulative lists of the Acts in the edition, both alphabetical and chronological, are published from time to time. The booklets are held in loose-leaf binders and may be included therein in any order the user or library may choose, though there is a recommended arrangement prepared by the Editorial Board on the advice of a working party. Repealed Acts are simply removed from the binders. In this way this edition will be

---

[13] (1707–1900) in 10 vols.
[14] (1901–1948) in 12 vols.
[15] (1949–), annual volumes. Acts of Sederunt and Acts of Adjournal are also printed therein.
[16] (1707–1847) in 3 vols., and annual vols. 1848–1947.

constantly self-renewing and will be constantly substantially up-to-date.[17] It supersedes *Statutes Revised*.

Halsbury's *Statutes of England*[18] contains the public general Acts applicable to the United Kingdom and to England, classified under alphabetical subject-headings, and annotated. There are also various books containing statutes relevant to particular topics published by commercial publishers,[19] and annotated editions of particular Acts included in textbooks.

None of the foregoing includes local or private Acts. There is a separate annual volume of *Local and Personal Acts* (with tables and index). *Current Law Statutes* now includes local and private Acts, and some cities have published volumes containing their own local Acts. The Stationery Office is now releases on the Internet summaries of some Acts of Parliament from 1984 and plans to publish the text of all new Acts on the Internet. A Statute Law Database is in preparation.

Acts of the Scottish Parliament since 1999 are included in Greens *Current Law Statutes*, in print and on CD ROM.

Indexes to Legislation

Statutes can be traced through the *Index to the Statutes in Force, 1235–*,[20] and the *Chronological Table of the Statutes, 1235–*.[21] The *Index* groups under selected headings, arranged alphabetically, entries relating to the whole of the general statute-law in force. It is analytical within each heading, and provides a subject-matter index to every provision in any Act of Parliament in operation at the date of the *Index*; it has to be noticed that some headings are duplicated, such as Education (England) and Education (Scotland), where there are two distinct bodies of statute-law referring to the two countries. Headings are not duplicated where the statute-law is entirely or largely common to the two countries. The *Chronological Table* gives a list of public general Acts (since 1966 including Scots Acts) from 1235 to the date of the edition, in chronological order showing, for repealed Acts, by what Act they were repealed, and,

---

[17] Individual holdings of *Statutes in Force* may be complete, or contain Acts applicable to Scotland, or to England and Wales, or to Northern Ireland, or be limited to the particular groups or sub-groups of Acts which are of interest to the library or holder of the set in question. Individual Acts may be purchased in the *Statutes in Force* edition. These are preferable to the original Queen's Printer's edition as they show amendments to the original legislation.

[18] 3rd ed., 41 vols. (in progress).

[19] *e.g.* the annual *Butterworths Yellow Tax Handbook* and *Butterworths Company Law Handbook*.

[20] 2 volumes, annually.

[21] 2 volumes, annually. These volumes act as the general Table and Index of the *Statutes Revised*, as continued by the annual *Public General Statutes*, and the *Statutes in Force*. There is also published annually *Annotations to Acts*, a volume of notes by means of which the effect of each year's legislation can be noted up briefly on any set of statutes to keep them up to date, and this includes gummed printed sheets, called "annexes," for lengthier entries, which can be stuck in at the appropriate places.

for Acts still in operation, the effect on each section of all subsequent amendments and modifications, both by Act of Parliament and by Statutory Instrument.[22] It now includes also a table of Local and Personal Acts amended or repealed since 1973.

There is a *Chronological Table of Local Legislation, 1797–1994.*[23]

There is a separate *Index to Local and Personal Acts, 1801–1947*, a *Supplementary Index to the Local and Personal Acts, 1948–1966* continued by an annual table and index and an *Index to the Local and Personal Acts 1850–1995.*[24]

Whether Legislation Repealed or Amended

The *Current Law Legislation Citator* volumes and the monthly parts of *Current Law* show whether particular sections of particular Acts have been repealed in whole or in part, and by what later Act, or have been amended, and by what Act. They also disclose cases in which particular sections have been judicially considered, which may be helpful on their interpretation.

Whether Legislation is in Force or not

Much legislation does not come into force on the passing of the Act but is to be brought into force by the responsible Minister by statutory instrument. The annual *Is It In Force?*[25] lists under each year from 1965 the Acts of that year, showing, unless the Act has been repealed, the date of royal assent, provisions in the Act dealing with commencement, any date or dates appointed for particular provisions of that Act to come into force and an indication where any provision is not yet in force. It distinguishes between commencement in Scotland and in England on the same or different dates. This shows that, *e.g.* section 82 of the Consumer Credit Act 1974 was brought into force on April 1, 1977, by S.I. 1977 No. 325. To check possible Commencement Orders after the date of the volume of *Is It In Force?* it is necessary to check the Table of Dates of Commencement in *Current Law*.

Subordinate Legislation

Orders in Council and Statutory Rules and Orders have been issued since 1890 in annual volumes, collected under the same headings of legal

---

[22] The *Acts of Parliaments of Scotland* (second revised ed., HMSO, 1966) has a similar chronological table of the Scots statutes, 1424–1707.

[23] Four volumes, the Stationery Office, 1996. Local legislation prior to 1797 is included in the *Chronological Table of the Statutes.* The effect of legislation from 1974 on earlier local, personal and private Acts is in section 4 of the *Chronological Table of Statutes* and in a volume supplementary to the *Chronological Table of Local Legislation.*

[24] Four volumes, the Stationery Office, 1996.

[25] Published by Butterworths and correct to the end of the previous calendar year. The Preface should be studied to discover how to use the book effectively.

subjects as in the *Indexes to the Statutes in Force*. Since 1948 the annual volumes have been entitled *Statutory Instruments*.

The *Statutory Rules and Orders and Statutory Instruments Revised*[26] reprints all S.R. and O.s and S.I.s of a permanent nature and still in force, as amended, arranged, not numerically or chronologically, but under subject-headings. The last volume contains a list of subject-headings, a numerical table, and a table of effects.

Halsbury's *Statutory Instruments*[27] also collect the orders and instruments under subject-headings and include annotations, but neglect purely Scottish matters, so that they must be used only cautiously. Green's *Scottish Statutory Instruments Service* gives annotated texts of Scottish subordinate legislation.

Acts of Sederunt passed by the Court of Session to regulate procedure are collected in various older collections[28] but the *Codifying Act of Sederunt* of 1913[29] collected those relative to procedure then in force, and was itself superseded by the *Rules of Court 1936*, revised edition 1994.[30] Modern Acts of Sederunt, and Acts of Adjournal passed by the High Court of Justiciary to regulate criminal procedure[31] are also published in *Scottish Current Law Statutes*, the *Scots Law Times* and *Parliament House Book*.

Indexes to Subordinate Legislation

Subordinate legislation can be traced by recourse to the *Index* (formerly *Guide*) *to Government Orders*,[32] the *Table of Government Orders*,[33] and the *S.I. Effects*.[34] The *Index* contains a Table of Statutes which shows all statutory powers to make subordinate legislation, under classified subject-headings under which those powers are indexed. The Index, under the subject-headings, *e.g.* Factories, lists powers to make subordinate legislation and gives particulars of all instruments under it current at the stated date of the volume, showing the date, title and number of the instrument

---

[26] (1904–1948) 25 vols.

[27] 24 vols. and Supplements.

[28] See Sweet and Maxwell's *Legal Bibliography*, Vol. 5, for details. They are cited by date, *e.g.* A.S. March 9, 1951.

[29] Cited by book, chapter and section, *e.g.* C.A.S., A, ii, 2.

[30] Cited by book and number, or number, *e.g.* R.C. II, 134 or R.C. 134. They are reprinted as amended in the *Parliament House Book*.

[31] Cited, *e.g.* A.A. February 2, 1921.

[32] The Stationery Office. Published in alternate years with a supplement in the intervening years. This acts as Index to the *S.R. & O.s and S.I.s Revised*, as continued by the annual *Statutory Instruments*.

[33] The Stationery Office, annually, with half-yearly Supplement.

[34] The Stationery Office, annually. This volume comprises a table showing the effect of the statutory instruments of the year on previous statutory rules and orders and statutory instruments, showing which have been revoked or amended, and which have become spent or have ceased to operate. It does not cover instruments made under emergency legislation. The Stationery Office also publishes daily, monthly and annual lists of S.I.s.

and a reference where it can be found in the *S.R. & O.s and S.I.s Revised 1948*, by volume and page or (in the case of a post-1948 exercise) to the annual volume and page of S.I. The *Table of Government Orders* shows in chronological order, with the exception of certain categories, the titles, numbers and volume references of all S.R. & O.s and S.I.s still in operation, and which have been amended or revoked and by what authority.

The Stationery Office also publishes a *Daily List of Government Publications* (which includes S.I.s, and monthly and annual lists of S.I.s and Statutory Rules.

II.—CASE-LAW

A—Case-Law of the European Court

The official reports of the decisions of the Court of Justice of the European Communities are the *European Court Reports*, (cited E.C.R.) which are published simultaneously in all the Community languages. There is also a *Recueil de la Jurisprudence de la Cour*. In the United Kingdom, *Common Market Law Reports* (from 1962, cited C.M.L.R.) contain major decisions of the Court of Justice and a selection of decisions of national courts which deal with issues of EU law. Its translations are, however, unofficial. Selected cases are also reported in *European Commercial Cases* (from 1978) and *All England Law Reports European Cases*. Judgments of the Court of Justice in cases referred by United Kingdom courts are also printed in the Scottish and English reports.

Cases on particular points can be found in the *Guide to EC Court Decisions*, published by the TMC Asser Institute. The Court of Justice has published an incomplete *Digest of Case Law* relating to the European Communities. The *Gazetteer of European Law* (ed. N. M. Hunnings, published by the European Law Centre) contains references to all judgments of the Court of Justice and to selected judgments of national courts, with alphabetical, chronological, citation and subject-matter indexes.

B—Case-Law of United Kingdom Courts

Scottish Reports

Down to the eighteenth century the only reports were notes of cases contained in volumes of *Practicks*, or notes made by private individuals, frequently judges, for their own use and sometimes later published.[35]

---

[35] There are various volumes of *Practicks* still unedited and unpublished.

The published volumes of *Practicks* are:

Name	Vols.	Period	Citation
Balfour's *Practicks* (1754)[36]	1	1469–1579	Balf.Prac.
Spotiswoode's *Practicks* (1716)	1	1541–1637	Spot.Prac.
Hope's *Minor Practicks* (1726, 1734)	1	1608–33	Hope, Min.Prac.
Hope's *Major Practicks* (1937–38)[37]	2	1608–33	Hope, Maj.Prac.

In the seventeenth century individuals, frequently judges, made collections of notes of decisions and later published them. These private reports are cited by volume and page with an abbreviation of the reporter's name. The following is a list of the old private reports:

Reporter	Vols.	Period	Citation
Sir Alexander Gibson, Lord Pres. Durie	1	1621–42	Durie
Decisions of the English Judges during the Usurpation	1	1655–61	Eng.Judg.
Sir John Gilmour, Lord Pres. Craigmillar	1	1661–66	Gil. & Fal.
Sir David Falconer, Lord Pres. Newton		1681–86	
Sir James Dalrymple, Lord Pres. Stair	2	1661–81	Stair
Sir John Nisbet, Lord Dirleton	1	1665–77	Dirl.[38]
Sir John Lauder, Lord Fountainhall	2	1678–1712	Fount.
Sir Roger Hog, Lord Harcarse	1	1681–91	Harc.
Sir Hew Dalrymple of North Berwick, Lord Pres.	1	1698–1718	Dalr.
William Forbes, Faculty Reporter	1	1705–13	Forbes[39]

---

[36] Reprinted in facsimile by the Stair Society in 1962–63.

[37] Ed. Lord Clyde, Stair Society and cited by Part, Title and paragraph number.

[38] These reports are normally bound up along with Dirleton's *Doubts*, but separately paginated.

[39] This volume is entitled *A Journal of the Session*. Some further reports by Forbes, 1713–14, were included in Lord Kames' *Folio Dictionary*.

Reporter	Vols.	Period	Citation
Alexander Bruce,			
Faculty Reporter	1	1714–15	Bruce[40]
Henry Home, Lord Kames	2	1716–28	Kames Rem.Dec.[41]
		1730–52	
John Edgar, Faculty Reporter	1	1724–25	Edgar
Patrick Grant, Lord Elchies	2	1733–54	Elchies[42]
Alexander Home,			
Clerk of Session	1	1735–44	Cl. Home
Sir James Fergusson,			
Lord Kilkerran	1	1738–52	Kilk.[43]
David Falconer,			
Faculty Reporter	2	1744–51	D.Falc.
Henry Home, Lord Kames	1	1752–68	Kames Sel.Dec.[44]
Sir David Dalrymple,			
Lord Hailes	2	1766–91	Hailes
David Hume, Professor, later			
Baron of Exchequer	1	1781–1822	Hume
Robert Bell,			
Clerk to the Signet	1	1790–92	Bell Oct.Cas.[45]
do.	1	1794–95	Bell Fol.Cas.[45]

In 1705 the Faculty of Advocates first appointed a reporter of decisions.[46] From 1752 there appeared three series of their reports, known as the *Faculty Collection* or *Faculty Decisions*, namely, the Old Series in 14 volumes (1752–1808), the New Series in seven volumes (1808–25) and the Octavo Series in 16 volumes (1825–41). The first two series are cited by the date of the decision with the letters F.C. added, *e.g.* 10th Jan., 1793, F.C., and the Octavo Series by volume and page, *e.g.* 9 Fac.Dec. 123.[47]

Most of the older cases are summarised in Kames' and Woodhouselee's *Dictionary* (five volumes covering cases 1540–1796 and cited Fol.Dic. or K.

---

[40] Bruce's *Decisions* are frequently found bound with Vol. 1 of Kames' *Remarkable Decisions* and cited as Bruce and Home's *Decisions*. Further decisions reported by Bruce, 1716–17, are printed in Vol. 3 of the *Faculty Collection* (1760–64).

[41] The volume is entitled *Remarkable Decisions in the Court of Session*.

[42] Vol. 1 consists of reports of cases and was printed by Morison as Appendix II to his *Dictionary of Decisions*. Vol. 2 consists of notes of cases from which the reports were compiled.

[43] Additional cases noted by Kilkerran, 1735–59, are printed in Brown's *Supplement*, Vol. 5. On Kilkerran, see Fergusson, "Background to a Lord of Session," 1974 S.L.T.(News) 1.

[44] The volume is entitled *Select Decisions of the Court of Session*.

[45] These are known, from the sizes of the volumes, as Bell's Octavo and Folio cases, respectively.

[46] The Faculty reporters were in succession Forbes (later Professor of Law at Glasgow) (1705–13), Bruce (1714–15), Edgar (1724–25) and Falconer (1744–51), and from 1714 to 1744 the work was very inadequately done, but the collections of Lords Elchies, Kames and Kilkerran and of Clerk Home supply most of the defects.

[47] There are several editions of some of the volumes, and variations in binding. Halkerston's *Compendium* (1819, and Supplement 1820) contains indexes of the decisions in *Faculty Collection* (1752–1817).

& W.Dic.) and reprinted in Morison's *Dictionary of Decisions* (22 volumes)[48] cited M. or Mor. or sometimes Dict., with Morison's *Synopsis* 1808–16 (two volumes) and *Indexes* (one volume) and Tait's *Index* (one volume).[49] Brown's *Supplement to the Dictionary of Decisions* in five volumes (1622–1794) includes most of the cases omitted by Morison, and also some not previously printed, and is cited, *e.g.* 3 B.S. or Brown's Supp. Brown also published in four volumes Brown's *Synopsis of Cases*, 1540–1827, contained in Morison's *Dictionary*, Brown's *Supplement* and in some other reports down to 1827.

Session Cases

From 1821 to 1906 five series of *Session Cases* were issued, distinguished by the initial letter of the editor's or chief reporter's name. These are:

First Series—	Shaw[50]	16 vols. 1821–38	*e.g.* 5 S. 390[51]
Second Series—	Dunlop[52]	24 vols. 1838–62	*e.g.* 7 D. 436.
Third Series—	Macpherson	11 vols. 1862–73	*e.g.* 10 M. 120.[53]
Fourth Series—	Rettie	25 vols. 1873–98	*e.g.* 17 R. 931.
Fifth Series—	Fraser	8 vols. 1898–1906	*e.g.* 4 F. 297.

From 1907 the *Session Cases* were issued by the Faculty of Advocates.[54] In 1957 the Scottish Council of Law Reporting was formed to take over the responsibility for publishing *Session Cases*. From 1907 these reports are cited by the year and page of the annual volume, *e.g.* 1975 S.C. 471.[55]

House of Lords Cases

The older House of Lords decisions in Scottish appeals are in private reports. These are set out in the following list:

---

[48] Vols. 20 and 21 consist of a Synopsis or Digest of the cases in the previous 19. This is distinct from Morison's *Synopsis* 1808–16. Vol. 22 is a Supplemental volume. Appendix I to the Dictionary is usually bound into it, each title after the title in the Dictionary, but sometimes bound as two separate volumes. The Dictionary is paginated consecutively throughout the work and cited, *e.g.* (1540) Mor. 5932 or (1714) M. 12345. At some places the pagination is inaccurate.

[49] The notes at the end of Tait's *Index* supply much valuable bibliographical information about the older Scottish reports and reporters.

[50] Occasionally known as Shaw and Dunlop's reports and cited S. & D.

[51] There are two editions of the first five volumes of Shaw which do not coincide in pagination.

[52] The earlier volumes are sometimes known as Dunlop, Bell and Murray's reports, and cited as D.B. & M.

[53] Distinguish this reference from Morison's *Dictionary*. These volumes are sometimes cited, *e.g.* 3 Macph. 617.

[54] Short notes of cases were also issued, 1925–48, as *Session Notes*. They were frequently, but not always, superseded by fuller reports in *Session Cases*.

[55] Where the date is an essential part of the reference to the volume (*i.e.* since 1906), it is *not* in brackets. Where the date is not essential (*i.e.* before 1907), it is put, if at all, in round brackets. Square brackets are *never* used in references to Scottish but only in references to English reports, for which see *infra*.

Reporter	Vols.	Period	Citation
David Robertson	1	1707–27	Rob. or Robert.
Thomas S. Paton	6	1726–1821	Pat.[56]
Patrick Shaw	2	1821–26	Sh.App.
James Wilson and Patrick Shaw	7	1825–35	W. & Sh.
Patrick Shaw and Charles H. Maclean	3	1835–38	Sh. & Macl.
Charles H. Maclean and Geo. Robinson	1	1839	Macl. & R.
Geo. Robinson	2	1840–41	Rob. or Robin
Sydney S. Bell	7	1842–50	Bell
John F. Macqueen	4	1851–65	Macq.[57]
James Paterson	2	1851–73	Paters.[58]

From 1850 House of Lords decisions are reported and bound in with the annual volumes of *Session Cases* but separately paginated,[59] as follows:

Dunlop	12 vols. 1850–62	*e.g.* (1850) 13 D.(H.L.) 5.[60]
Macpherson	11 vols. 1862–73	*e.g.* (1862) 1 M. (or Macph.) (H.L.) 6.
Rettie	25 vols. 1873–98	*e.g.* (1874) 1 R.(H.L.) 21.
Fraser	8 vols. 1898–1906	*e.g.* (1898) 1 F. (H.L.) 7.
Session Cases (annual)	1907–	*e.g.* 1950 S.C.(H.L.) 17.

Some Scottish appeals are also reported in the English volumes covering the same period, in *Law Reports* (*Appeal Cases*) and *All England Reports*.[61]

Justiciary (Criminal) Cases

Some early criminal reports have been published independently.[62] Separate series of criminal reports by private reporters appeared from 1819 to 1916. They are set out in the following list:

---

[56] Craigie and Stewart collaborated with Paton in the first volume and it is sometimes cited as Craigie, Stewart and Paton.

[57] These reports are contemporaneous with reports in 13 D.(H.L.) to 3 M.(H.L.).

[58] This series is a revised reprint of the House of Lords reports in the *Scottish Jurist*. It is also contemporaneous with reports in 13 D.(H.L.) to 11 M.(H.L.).

[59] It follows that since 1874, volumes of Scottish reports contain three sets of reports, each separately paginated (House of Lords, Justiciary and Court of Session). Hence 1958 S.C.(H.L.) 1; 1958 J.C. 1 and 1958 S.C. 1 are all different reports, in different series, but contained in the one volume.

[60] House of Lords decisions are included in Dunlop's reports only from Vol. 13.

[61] Information on which of the older series of English House of Lords cases contain Scottish appeals may be found in Stair Society, *Sources and Literature of Scots Law*, pp. 57–58.

[62] Collections of earlier criminal cases, more used in legal history than in modern law, are Pitcairn's *Criminal Trials*, 3 volumes bound in 7, 1488–1624; Arnot's *Celebrated Criminal Trials in Scotland*, 1536–1784; McLaurin's (Lord Dreghorn's) *Arguments and Decisions in Remarkable Cases before the High Court of Justiciary*, 1670–1733; Scott-Moncrieff's *Justiciary Court Records*, 1661–78 (S.H.S., 2 vols.); *Justiciary Cases*, 1624–50 (ed. Gillon and Irvine Smith, 3 vols., Stair Society) and *Argyll Justiciary Records*, 1664–1742 (ed. Cameron and Imrie, 2 vols., Stair Society).

Reporter	Vols.	Period	Citation
Patrick Shaw	1	1819–31	Shaw Just. or P. Shaw
David Syme	1	1826–29	Syme
Archibald Swinton	2	1835–41	Swin.
Archibald Broun	2	1842–45	Broun
Patrick Arkley	1	1846–48	Arkley
John Shaw	1	1848–51	J. Shaw
Alex. Forbes Irvine	5	1851–68	Irv.
Charles T. Couper	5	1868–85	Coup.[63]
James C. White	3	1885–93	White[63]
Edwin Adam	7	893–1916	Adam[63]

From 1874 Justiciary cases have also been published in the annual volumes of *Session Cases* but paginated separately,[59] as follows:

Rettie	25 vols. 1874–98	*e.g.* (1874) 1 R.(J.) 19.
Fraser	8 vols. 1898–1906	*e.g.* (1898) 1 F.(J.) 24.
Session Cases	11 vols. 1907–16	*e.g.* 1907 S.C.(J.) 17.[64]
Justiciary Cases (annual)	1917—	*e.g.* 1917 J.C. 8.[64]

Since 1917 these Justiciary cases, as well as being bound in with *Session Cases*, are sometimes found bound separately, five years to a volume. The citation remains the same.

Collateral Reports and Reprints

The *Scots Revised Reports* includes in 45 volumes a reprint of the principal decisions down to 1873, as follows: Morison's *Dictionary*, two volumes; *Faculty Collection*, 1807–25, two volumes; House of Lords Appeals, 10 volumes; Shaw, six volumes; Dunlop, 13 volumes; Macpherson, 11 volumes; cases reported only in the *Scottish Jurist*, volumes 1–37 (1829–65), one volume.

At various times other series of reports have been issued and are frequently of value in reporting other cases and supplying information on matters omitted from the reports already mentioned. These include Murray's *Jury Court Reports* (five volumes, 1815–30) and McFarlane's *Jury Court Reports* (one volume, 1838–39), Shaw's *Teind Court Decisions* (one volume, 1821–31), Deas and Anderson's reports (five volumes, 1829–33), Fergusson's *Consistorial Cases* (one volume, 1811–17) and Stuart, Milne and Peddie's *Reports* (two volumes, 1851–53). More important are the *Scottish Jurist* (45 volumes and five parts, 1829–73, cited S.J. or Sc.Jur.), the *Scottish Law Reporter* (61 volumes, 1866–1924, cited S.L.R.),[65] and the

---

[63] From 1874 reports of some of the same cases are also to be found in Rettie (Justiciary), Fraser (Justiciary) and Session Cases (Justiciary) reports.

[64] The change in the abbreviated citation after 1916 should be noted.

[65] Distinguish references to the *S.L. Reporter* from those to the *S.L. Review*, which contains the Sheriff Court reports (1885 to 1963).

Scots Law Times, since 1893. This last is cited from 1893 to 1908 by volume, *e.g.* (1900) 7 S.L.T., and thereafter by the year only.[66] The last three include House of Lords, Justiciary and Court of Session cases, while the S.L.T. now has also separately paginated sections of reports of Sheriff Court cases, Lyon Court cases, Land Court cases and Lands Tribunal for Scotland cases.[67] Some Scottish appeals to the House of Lords are also reported in current English series of reports.

Greens Weekly Digest contains brief reports of recent cases, many of which are later fully reported in the *Scots Law Times*.

Scottish Criminal Case Reports (1981–) contains reports of criminal cases with critical notes. A *Supplement* (1950–80) contains a selection of cases not previously reported but of interest and importance.

Scottish Civil Law Reports (1987–) contains similar reports of civil cases from all level of civil courts.

Selected sheriff court cases are found in Guthrie's *Select Cases in the Sheriff Courts*,[68] sheriff court reports printed in the *Scottish Law Review*,[69] and sheriff court cases in the *Scots Law Times*.[70]

Selected decisions of Lyon Court have been printed in the *Scots Law Times* since 1959.[71]

Decisions of the Scottish Land Court were published as a Supplement to the *Scottish Law Review*,[72] and now appear in the Land Court portion of the *Scots Law Times*.

Decisions also appear in special-subject series such as Green's *Reparation Law Reports*.

Decisions of Scottish courts of special jurisdiction and tribunals are only sometimes reported: some may be found in the ordinary series, some in specialised series. The government publishes *Tax Cases, Value Added Tax and Duties Reports, Value Added Tax Tribunal Reports, Immigration Appeal Reports*, and selected decisions of Social Security Commissioners.

The Royal Institution of Chartered Surveyors publishes *Scottish Lands Valuation Appeal Reports*.

The *Session Papers* are sets of the papers in cases which came before the Court of Session, preserved by various judges for their own use and frequently later bound up.[73] Many were annotated by the judges in the

---

[66] From 1909 to 1916 there are two volumes in each year, cited, *e.g.* 1912 1 S.L.T.—and 1912 2 S.L.T.—.

[67] It formerly also included Notes of Recent Decisions, frequently but not always later superseded by a full report.

[68] Two vols., 1861–78 and 1879–85.

[69] 1885 to 1963; cited, *e.g.* (1954) 70 Sh.Ct.Rep.—.

[70] Latterly these are separately paginated and cited, *e.g.* 1955 S.L.T.(Sh.Ct.)—.

[71] Cited, *e.g.* 1965 S.L.T.(Lyon Ct.)—.

[72] 1913 to 1963: cited, *e.g.* (1951) 40 L.C.— or 40 S.L.C.R.—; continued since 1964 by S.L.T.(Land Ct.) Reports.

[73] The collections are mostly unindexed so that finding the papers in a case is largely a matter of luck.

course of debates. Many of the cases were never reported but the *Papers* contain notes of the arguments and decisions. The Advocates Library has a valuable collection of *Session Papers*, bound in about 3000 volumes, comprising 45 discrete but overlapping collections covering the period 1660 to 1868. The Signet Library has another collection.

English Reports

The practice of noting cases began early in England[74] and from the later twelfth century to 1536 there is a series of Year Books, notes made in law-French of points of procedure and pleading, probably for the writer's own information, but later copied and printed. Reports proper begin in the sixteenth century. Down to 1865 reporting was in the hands of private reporters and the reports vary greatly in value;[75] they were usually printed some time afterwards, sometimes from inaccurate or even stolen notes. Round about 1800 the practice developed of judges revising copies of their judgments and even supplying copies to the reporters, and one reporter in each court tended to be favoured as the "authorised" reporter, though this was never official, and the practice of revising judgments was extended to other series also. The various series of private reports are usually cited by initials or abbreviations of the reporters' names, though in some instances other abbreviations, sometimes confusing, are used.[76] Three reprints of the older reports have to be noticed: *The Revised Reports* (1785–1865) in 149 volumes (plus Table of Cases (one volume) and *Index-Digest* (two volumes)), which omits some obsolete cases, cited, *e.g.* 110 R.R. 345, the *English Reports* (1220–1865) in 178 volumes, which is a

---

[74] On the older English reports and reporters, see Holdsworth, *Sources and Literature of English Law*, 74–104, and "Law Reporting in the Nineteenth and Twentieth Centuries," in *Essays in Law and History*, 284; Wallace, *The Reporters*; Winfield, *Chief Sources of English Legal History*, 145–199; Bolland, *The Year-Books*; Pollock, *First Book of Jurisprudence*, Chap. 5; Veeder, "The English Reports," in (1901) 15 H.L.R. 1, 109, reprinted in part in *Select Essays in Anglo-American Legal History*, II, 123; Daniel, *History and Origin of the Law Reports*. On reporting, see also Moran's *Heralds of the Law*; Lindley, "History of the Law Reports" (1885) 1 L.Q.R. 137; Mews, "The Present System of Law Reporting" (1893) 9 L.Q.R. 179; Pollock, "English Law Reporting" (1903) 19 L.Q.R. 451; Goodhart, "Reporting the Law" (1939) 55 L.Q.R. 29; O'Sullivan, "Law Reporting" (1940) 4 M.L.R. 104; Burrow, "Law Reporting" (1942) 58 L.Q.R. 96.

[75] This has given rise to many stories about reports and reporters, some of which can be read in Williams' *Learning the Law* and in Allen's *Law in the Making*.

[76] Lists of these abbreviations can be found in Sweet and Maxwell's *Where to Look for your Law*, Sweet and Maxwell's *Guide to Law Reports and Statutes*, Raistrick's *Index to Legal Citations and Abbreviations*, and prefaced to Halsbury's *Laws of England*, Vol. I, volume I of the *Digest*, or to any volume of *The Laws of Scotland*. The date is not an essential of the reference to a pre-1865 report, but if inserted it is put in round brackets, *e.g.* (1842) 10 M. & W. 546.

literal reprint with a few annotations,[77] cited, *e.g.* 137 E.R. 234, and the *All England Reports Reprint* (1558–1935), which reprints only selected cases, and is cited, *e.g.* [1775–1802] All E.R. Rep. 266. All are generally reliable and very useful.

In 1866 the Incorporated Council of Law Reporting began to publish the *Law Reports*, and these quickly superseded all the old private reporters though not the series of reports issued by various legal journals. The *Law Reports* have no exclusive privilege of citation but are usually preferred for purposes of citation and references.[78] They have been issued in three series, 1866–75, 1876–90, 1891 to date.[79]

Other Series

Other series of reports, now discontinued, are the *Law Times Reports* (New Series, 177 volumes, 1859–1947, cited, *e.g.* (1934) 150 L.T.—), the *Law Journal Reports* (127 volumes, 1822–1949, cited, *e.g.* (1930) 99 L.J.—),[80] both now incorporated in the *All England Law Reports*, and *The*

---

[77] A chart supplied with the set in a slim volume to itself shows in which volume is to be found any particular volume of the old reports. The spine of each volume of the E.R. lists which of the older volumes are reprinted within. This chart is not perfect and some of the old reports are known under variant names; this can be found in *Where to Look for your Law*. Volumes 177–178 contain a complete index of cases under the names of the parties. Lists in *Where to Look for your Law* and the *Guide to Law Reports and Statutes* indicate in which volumes of *Revised Reports* and/or *English Reports* private reports are reprinted. Another table in the *Guide* shows what volumes of what series relate to particular calendar years from 1810 onwards.

[78] See *Fairman v. Perpetual Investment Building Socy.* [1923] A.C. 74; *Practice Note* [1931] W.N. 121.

[79] The series comprise the following; First Series: Admiralty and Ecclesiastical (4 vols.); Crown Cases Reserved (2 vols.); Common Pleas (10 vols.); Chancery Appeals (10 vols.); English and Irish Appeal [House of Lords] (7 vols.); Equity (20 vols.); Exchequer (10 vols.); Privy Council Appeals (6 vols.); Probate and Divorce (3 vols.); Queen's Bench (10 vols.); Scotch and Divorce Appeals (2 vols.). These are cited, *e.g.* (1875) L.R. 7 H.L.—; (1875) L.R. 10 Q.B.—.
Second Series: Appeal Cases (15 vols.); Chancery Division (45 vols.); Common Pleas Division (5 vols.); Exchequer Division (5 vols.); Probate Division (15 vols.); Queen's Bench Division (25 vols.). These are cited, *e.g.* (1890) 15 App.Cas.—; (1890) 25 Q.B.D.—.
Third Series: Appeal Cases; Chancery Division; Queen's (Kings, 1901–1952) Bench; Probate Division (1891–1971) and Family Division (1972–). These are cited, *e.g.* [1959] A.C.—. Sometimes there is more than one volume for each court in one year, *e.g.* [1958] 2 Q.B.—.
The Law Reports also issued a series of reports of the Restrictive Practices Court 1957–72, 7 vols. (cited (1959) L.R. 1 R.P.—) and a series for the National Industrial Relations Court 1971–74 called *Industrial Court Reports*, continued by *Industrial Cases Reports*, 1975–.
For correct abbreviations, see *Where to Look for your Law* and *Guide to Law Reports and Statutes*.
Note that L.R. precedes the volume number in the First Series only, and that D. after Q.B., Ch., C.P., Ex. and P. is found only in the Second Series.
Prior to 1891 the date is not an essential of the reference to the Law Reports and goes in round brackets. After 1890 the year is essential and is put in square brackets.

[80] From 1947 the volumes were cited, *e.g.* [1949] L.J.R.—. The Old Series covered 1822–31 in 9 volumes, the New Series 1831–1949 in 118 volumes. Many volumes of *Law Journal* are separately paginated within the volume for the different courts, *e.g.* for L.J.C.P. and L.J.Ch.

Times Law Reports (71 volumes, 1884–1952, cited, *e.g.* (1910) 26 T.L.R.—).[81]

Other series now current are the *All England Law Reports* (since 1936,[82] cited, *e.g.* [1980] 2 All E.R.—) and the *Weekly Law Reports* (since 1953, cited, *e.g.* [1953] 1 W.L.R.—), which replaced the earlier *Weekly Notes* (1865—1952, cited, *e.g.* [1945] W.N.—)[83] while brief reports and notes are to be found in many of the legal journals and periodicals.

Series of reports concentrating on particular topics include *Commercial Cases* (1895–1941), *Lloyd's List Reports* (1919–50), *Lloyd's Reports* (1951–67), and *Lloyd's Law Reports* (1968–), *Reports of Patent, Design, Trade Mark and Other Cases* (1884–), *Railway and Canal Traffic Cases* (1855–1934) continued by *Traffic Cases* (1935–), *Cox's Criminal Cases* (1843–1948), *Criminal Appeal Reports* (1908–), *Criminal Appeal Reports (Sentencing)* (1979–), *Tax Cases* (1875–), *Annotated Tax Cases* (1922–), *Simon's Tax Cases* (1973–), *Butterworths Company Law Cases* (1983–), *Financial Times Law Reports* (1982–), *Fleet Street Patent Law Reports* (1963–), *Industrial Court Reports* (1972–75)[84] continued by *Industrial Cases Reports* (1975–),[84] *Industrial Relations Law Reports* (1972–), *Industrial Tribunals Reports* (1966–) and *Knight's Industrial Reports* (1967–74) continued as *Managerial Law* (1975–). But there are now innumerable series of reports and journals dealing with specific areas of law.[85]

Special series of reports and Irish and Commonwealth Series may be traced through the *Guide to Law Reports and Statutes* and *Current Law*.

Cases in the European Court of Human Rights are reported in the publications of the Court, *viz.* E.C.H.R. Series A (Judgments and Decisions) and Series B (Pleadings and Documents) with, in either case, the number of the case, and in the *European Human Rights Reports* (1979–) while some decisions are in the annual *Yearbook of the European Convention on Human Rights* (1959–).

Digests of Case-Law

The finding of case-law is greatly facilitated by the Digests of case-law which arrange the reported cases under main and subordinate subject-headings on an analytical basis, the main headings being arranged in

---

[81] The 1950 volume was cited 66 T.L.R. Part 1 and Part 2, and the 1951 and 1952 volumes, *e.g.* [1951] 1 T.L.R. and [1951] 2 T.L.R.

[82] Reports of selected cases 1558–1935 have now been published by All E.R. in a series called *All E.R. Reprints*, cited, *e.g.* [1904–7] All E.R.Rep. 438. The selection is based on the frequency of citation of the cases in later judgments and the cases are reprinted from the private reports down to 1843 and from the *Law Times* thereafter.

[83] On the authority of *Weekly Notes*, see *Re Loveridge* [1902] 2 Ch. 859; *Re Smith's Settlement* [1903] 1 Ch. 373; *Re Allsop* [1967] 2 All E.R. 1056, 1060.

[84] Incorporating Restrictive Practices Court cases.

[85] See Table of Abbreviations in any monthly part of *Current Law*.

alphabetical order. Each entry gives a brief account of the case and the legal propositions which can be inferred from it, but the entries are so brief that they are not a substitute for the full reports. It is usually necessary to follow up a point by searching the relevant headings in the main part of the Digest and then in each supplementary volume down to the latest published. There is considerable variation in the headings and sub-headings used[86] so that a search must frequently be made under several different headings, but experience greatly increases familiarity with the system used.

The older Scottish cases are mostly to be found, grouped under alphabetical subject-headings, in Kames's *Folio Dictionary*, 1540–1728 (two volumes) Woodhouselee's continuation thereof to 1796 (two volumes) and McGrugar's Supplement thereto (one volume), Morison's *Dictionary of Decisions*, 1540–1808 (22 volumes), Morison's *Synopsis* of the cases in the *Dictionary* (two volumes), Brown's *Supplement* to Morison's Dictionary, 1628–1794 (five volumes), Brown's *Synopsis* of the cases in Morison's *Dictionary*, Brown's *Supplement* thereto, the reports of Elchies, Hailes, Bell and the *Faculty Decisions* down to 1827 (four volumes), Halkerston's *Compendium*, digesting the cases in the *Faculty Decisions* 1752–1817 (one volume), and Bell's *Dictionary of Decisions*, 1808–33 (two volumes). Shaw's *Digest of Cases* (three volumes)[87] contains House of Lords decisions from 1726 to 1868 and decisions of the Scottish superior courts from 1800 to 1868. This is carried on by the *Faculty Digest* from 1868.[88] The *Scots Digest* contains House of Lords cases from 1707–1947 and cases from the Scottish superior courts from 1800–1947.[89] The *Sheriff Court Digest* covers 1885–1944 in five volumes dealing with consecutive periods, and there is a *Digest of Sheriff Court Cases* reported in S.L.T., 1893–1943.

English cases are digested in the *Digest*, formerly called the *English and Empire Digest*, which contains English cases from early times with Scottish and Commonwealth decisions in footnotes on each page,[90] in Mews' *Digest of English Case-Law*[91] (which includes some Scottish cases) and in the *Law*

---

[86] Thus the *Faculty Digest* includes all criminal cases under the heading Justiciary; *Shaw's Digest* puts such cases under the heading Crime. There are, of course, many cross-references to assist the searcher, but much ingenuity and some luck is sometimes requisite for the search. Of course, there may not be any cases closely in point: the *Digest* only contains what has been reported in the main series of reports.

[87] This consolidates earlier Digests covering parts of the period.

[88] 1868–1922, 6 vols., supplementary volumes 1922–30, 1930–40, 1940–50, 1951–60, 1960–70, 1970–80 and 1980–90.

[89] 1800–73, 4 vols.; 1873–1904, 2 vols.; supplementary volumes 1904–14, 1914–23, 1923–30, 1930–37, 1937–44, and supplementary parts to 1947. Superseded by *Scottish Current Law* thereafter.

[90] 48 volumes, with supplements, replaced by the "Blue-Band" edition in 56 volumes, which incorporates material in earlier supplements. This is being replaced by the "Green-Band" edition. There are also Continuation Volumes and Annual Cumulative Supplements.

[91] Second ed., 24 volumes (to end of 1924) and annual supplementary volumes to 1970.

Reports Digest of Cases, 1865–1949,[92] continued by the *Law Reports Index* in decennial volumes.

Modern Digests also contain such additional reference tools as an index of statutes, showing in what cases statutory provisions have been interpreted, an index of cases commented on in later cases, an index of words and phrases discussed in particular cases, and an index of parties' names whereby a case known by name can be traced to its classified subject. Very recent cases are found in *Current Law*.

Current Law

This publication appears in booklet form each month and each monthly part contains in separate sets of pages concerned with United Kingdom, English and EU, Northern Irish, and Scots law respectively, digested under subject-headings, notes of all statutes, statutory instruments and other subordinate legislation, cases and articles published during the previous month. There are also Tables of Quantum of Damages, Words and Phrases Judicially Considered, Progress of Bills in Parliaments, Dates of Royal Assent, Dates of Commencement of Statutory Provisions, Statutes passed, amended, repealed or judicially discussed, Statutory Instruments issued and European legislation implemented by Statutory Instrument. The indexes are cumulative, including references to matter included in any of the monthly parts for the current year. Much information from miscellaneous sources such as Royal Commission reports is also summarised. It has to be noted that all matters applicable to the United Kingdom generally are included in the English section of *Current Law*, so that the Scottish lawyer cannot ignore that section of the publication entirely.

Each summer the matter contained in the 12 Monthly Digests of the previous calendar year's *Current Law* is brought together, revised, reprinted and issued in consolidated form as the *Current Law Year Book*.[93] There are indexes of cases, statutes and subjects. The volumes for 1956, 1961, 1966 and 1971 (Master Volumes 1948–56, 1957–61, 1962–66 and 1967–71) contain cumulative references to matters covered in detail in the annual volumes 1948–56, 1957–61, 1962–66 and 1967–71.

The *Scottish Current Law Statute Citator*, 1948–1971 lists all statutes passed, amended, applied, repealed or otherwise affected by legislation in

---

[92] 12 volumes, covering 1866–1950 continued by *Index to Law Reports*, 1951–60, 1961–70 and 1971–80.

[93] There were down to 1990 two editions of both monthly parts and Year Book, the Scottish and the English. The Scottish was a complete reprint of the English edition with the addition of pages, printed on green paper in the monthly parts, of exclusively Scottish material. The English pages contain (a) exclusively English matter, and also (b) United Kingdom and EU matter also applicable in whole or in part to Scotland. Both sets of pages must accordingly be looked at. From 1991 there is only one edition which contains in separate sets of pages United Kingdom, English and EU matter, Northern Irish matter, and Scottish matter. From 1992 there is also a *European Current Law* digesting legal materials from every country in Europe, consolidated into *European Current Law Yearbooks*.

the period 1948–71, together with statutory instruments made under rule-making powers contained in statutes, and cases decided on the statutes. The *Scottish Current Law Case Citator*, 1948–1976, lists separately for England and for Scotland all the reports of each case decided in the period and indicates by reference to paragraph numbers in what other cases the case under consideration was applied or distinguished or otherwise treated, or discussed in the periodicals. The references in the *Citator Volumes* are to the *Current Law Consolidation* volume 1947–51,[94] which contains United Kingdom and English matter only, and for matters subsequent to 1951 to the annual volumes of the *Scottish Current Law Year Book*.

These volumes are continued by the *Scottish Current Law Legislation Citator*, 1972–1988 and 1989–1996, and the *Scottish Current Law Case Citator*, 1977–1988 and 1989–1996, each of which is continued by annual Supplements. From 1991 the Supplements are common to all parts of the United Kingdom.

Reading the monthly parts frequently brings to the reader's attention developments such as new statutes or cases, which he had not otherwise noticed. Searching *Current Law* down to the latest available monthly part is an essential means of seeking to discover the latest developments in any field of law being investigated.

Use of Computers to Store and Find Law

Westlaw UK and *Lexis/Nexis* are computer databases maintained in London and accessible by telephone line from dedicated terminals in law libraries and major offices. The materials held on the databases are constantly updated and include statutes, cases, including a wide range of unreported cases, and Scottish cases, as well as a considerable range of material from the United States and Commonwealth jurisdictions. However, in the case of *Lexis/Nexis* as the database does not include older material it does not supersede older repositories and older methods of searching in cases where older materials may be relevant. Access to the Internet provides a link to an ever-increasing amount of material. Increasingly materials are being made available on CD-Rom. These include House of Lords Hansard (1992–   ) and House of Commons Hansard (1988–   ), *Scots Law Times*, 1893–2001, and various "books on screen".

---

[94] *Current Law* began in England in 1947 and in Scotland in 1948. The *Current Law Consolidation* deals with matter in the English *Current Law*, 1947–51, and has no Scottish equivalent, but United Kingdom and English matters for 1948–51 are found in the U.K. and English sections of the *Scottish Current Law Year Books*, 1948–49–50–51, and a paragraph reference to the C.L.C. (unless it relates to 1947) can be traced through the indexes to these years of the *Scottish Current Law Year Book*. The preface to each volume gives guidance on the use of these volumes.

III.—INSTITUTIONAL WRITINGS

The standard editions in modern use are:

Craig's *Jus Feudale and the Books of the Feus*, translated by J.A. (Lord President) Clyde, two volumes, 1934; Stair's *Institutions*,[95] sixth edition by Professor D.M. Walker, 1981; Mackenzie's *Institutions*, eighth edition, 1758 and in his *Collected Works* (two volumes, 1716–22)[96]; Bankton's *Institute*, only edition, three volumes, 1751–53,[97] Erskine's *Institute*, new (eighth) edition, with notes by J. Badenach Nicolson,[98] two volumes, 1871,[96] Kames's *Principles of Equity*, fifth edition 1825; Bell's *Commentaries*, seventh edition, by John (later Lord) McLaren, two volumes, 1870[99]; and Bell's *Principles*, tenth edition by Sheriff William Guthrie, 1899.[1]

On criminal law the standard editions are: Mackenzie's *Laws and Customs*, second edition, 1699, and in his collected *Works* (two volumes, 1716–22); Hume's *Commentaries*,[2] fourth edition with supplement by B.R. Bell, two volumes, 1844[99]; and Alison's *Principles* and *Practice*, only editions 1832 and 1833.[99, 3]

SECONDARY SOURCES

IV.—LEGAL LITERATURE

These sources comprise all commentaries, books and other writings, about the law or any topic thereof, other than institutional writings, which are not themselves authoritative but which may give a court, or an inquirer, valuable guidance on where to find the authoritative primary sources of a principle of law relevant to the problem before him, on the interrelation of several relevant primary sources, such as several statutes and cases, and on the interpretations which have hitherto been placed by the courts on the primary authorities. Legal literature is also valuable as giving a

---

[95] In *Fortington v. Kinnaird*, 1942 S.C. 239, 265. Lord Justice-Clerk Cooper attached importance to the views expressed in More's Notes to his (fifth) edition of Stair (2 vols. 1832) and Lord Mackay (at p. 276) said that the Notes "carries almost the authority of a separate Institution."

[96] These books are cited by Book, title and section, *e.g.* Stair, I, 1, 16.

[97] Reprinted by the Stair Society in 1993–1995. Bankton is also cited by Volume, page and section.

[98] In *Fortington, supra*, Lord Cooper attached importance also to Lord Ivory's Notes to Erskine, which are printed in Lord Ivory's (sixth) edition of Erskine, and reprinted in Badenach Nicolson's edition.

[99] These books are cited by volume and page.

[1] This book is cited by the section number.

[2] In *H.M. Advocate v. Grant* (1848) J. Shaw, 17, 92, Lord Justice-Clerk Hope spoke of Hume as of great authority. See also Paton's Biography of Baron Hume (*Lectures* (Stair Society) VI) at 350.

[3] Reprints of the last editions of Erskine, Bell, Hume and Alison have been published by Butterworths.

coherent account of all the law on a topic, with the legislation, case-law, views of the institutional writers, and later comment and criticism brought together into a related whole and presented, so far as possible, as a reasoned and systematic body of related principles and rules.

The writing of legal literature, of commentaries and treatises on the law and various branches of it, has from the time of Gaius been an important function of the academic jurists. The literary sources are the essential means of legal study, the starting point of research for the answer to some problem, and the means of obtaining a general conspectus of the law on any topic.

Some books are written expressly for students, or for particular groups of students, others for legal practitioners as reference books and guides through the tangle of statutes and cases. A knowledge of what books there are on each subject and what they cover, their relative sizes and values, their standing, is a necessary part of a lawyer's knowledge, and with these books his investigation of any problem starts.

On every topic the distinction between Scottish and English books must be kept in mind, since the latter do not usually cite statutes applicable to Scotland or Scottish cases, ignore specialities of Scottish procedure, and are all, to a greater or less degree, depending on whether the topic is one on which Scots and English law diverge much or little, unreliable guides in Scottish practice. But many English books have to be considered, if only *faute de mieux*, in default of any, or any modern, Scottish book.[4]

A—EUROPEAN LAW

General

Encyclopaedia of European Community Law.

Kapteyn and Verloren van Themaat: *Introduction to the Law of the European Communities.*

Lasok and Bridge: *Introduction to the Law and Institutions of the European Communities.*

Hartley: *Foundations of European Community Law.*

Lipstein: *Law of the E.E.C.*

Parry and Hardy: *E.E.C. Law.*

Collins: *European Community Law in the United Kingdom.*

Vaughan: *Law of the European Communities*, 2 vols.

Wall: *Court of Justice of the European Communities.*

B—SCOTS LAW

GENERAL BOOKS

Legal Bibliographies and Reference Books

---

[4] In the following lists the prefix E denotes a book written from the English standpoint.

Institute of Advanced Legal Studies: *Bibliographical Guide to U.K. Law.*
Manual of Legal Citations, Part I.
Stair Society: *Sources and Literature of Scots Law.*
Sweet & Maxwell Ltd.: *Guide to Law Reports and Statutes* (4th ed., 1962).
Where to Look for Your Law (14th ed., 1962).
Legal Bibliography of the British Commonwealth—
Vol. 1—*English Law to* 1800.
Vol. 2—*English Law 1800–1954.*
Vol. 5—*Scots Law and Roman Law, to* 1955.
Price and Bitner: *Effective Legal Research* (U.S.A.)
Raistrick: *Index to Legal Citations and Abbreviations.*
Lawyer's Law Books.

Dictionaries
Bell: *Dictionary and Digest of the Law of Scotland.*
Beaton: *Scots Law Terms and Expressions.*
Gibb: *Students' Glossary of Scottish Legal Terms.*
E   Wharton: *Law Lexicon.*
E   Jowitt: *Dictionary of English Law.*
Walker: *Oxford Companion to Law.*

Maxims
Trayner: *Latin Maxims and Phrases.*
E   Broom: *Legal Maxims.*

Words and Phrases
Gibb and Dalrymple: *Scottish Judicial Dictionary.*
E   Stroud: *Judicial Dictionary of Words and Phrases* (5th ed.), 4 vols. and Supp.
E   Saunders: *Words and Phrases Legally Defined*, 5 vols. and Supp.

Interpretation
E   Bennion: *Statutory Interpretation.*
E   Craies: *Statute Law.*
E   Maxwell: *Interpretation of Statutes.*

Encyclopaedias and General Textbooks
The Laws of Scotland: Stair Memorial Encyclopaedia, 25 vols. and looseleaf updating service.
E   *Halsbury's Laws of England* (4th ed.) 56 vols. and annual cumulative supplements.
Erskine: *Principles of the Law of Scotland* (21st ed., 1911).
Gloag and Henderson: *Introduction to the Law of Scotland* (10th ed., 1992).
Walker: *Principles of Scottish Private Law* (4th ed., 4 vols. 1988–89).

Older Books, not Institutional but still Valuable.[5]
Balfour: *Practicks' or System of the More Ancient Law of Scotland*, 1754 and (Stair Society) 1962–63.

---

[5] The dates given are those of first publication and, where applicable, of a modern edition. In some cases there were several early editions, for which see the bibliographies.

Brown, M.P.: *Law of Sale*, 1821.

Brown, R.: *Sale of Goods Act, 1893*, 1895, 1911.

Burnett, J.: *Criminal Law of Scotland*, 1811.

Clark, F.W.: *Law of Partnership and Joint Stock Companies*, 2 vols., 1866.

Craigie, J.: *Digest of the Scottish Law of Conveyancing: Heritable Rights*, 1887, 1899.
       Digest of the Scottish Law of Conveyancing: Moveable Rights 1888, 1894.

Dallas, George, of St. Martin's: *Stiles of Writs*, 1697, 1774.

Dickson, W.G.: *Law of Evidence in Scotland*, 2 vols., 1855, 1887.

Dirleton, Sir J. Nisbet, Lord: *Doubts and Questions in the Law*, 1698, 1762.

Fergusson, James: *Consistorial Law of Scotland*, 1829.

Forbes, Prof. Wm.: *Institutes of the Law of Scotland*, 2 vols. 1722–30.

Fraser, Patrick, Lord: *Husband and Wife*, 2 vols. 1876–78.
       Master and Servant, 1872, 1882.
       Parent and Child, 1866, 1906.

Gloag, W.M. and Irvine, J.M.: *Rights in Security and Cautionary Obligations*, 1897.

Hermand, George Fergusson, Lord: *Consistorial Decisions* (ed. Walton, Stair
       Society), 1940.[6]

Hope, Sir Thomas: *Major Practicks* (ed. Lord Clyde, Stair Society), 2 vols., 1937–38.
       Minor Practicks, 1726, 1734.

Hume, Prof. (later Baron) David: *Lectures on the Law of Scotland* (ed. Paton, 6 vols.,
       Stair Society), 1939–58.[7]

Hunter, R.: *Law of Landlord and Tenant*, 2 vols., 1833, 1876.

Kames, Henry Home, Lord: *Elucidations Respecting the Common and Statute Law of
       Scotland*, 1777, 1800.
       Historical Law Tracts, 1758, 1817.
       Principles of Equity, 1760, 1825.
       Statute Law of Scotland Abridged, 1757.[8]

Macdonald, Sir J.H.A.: *Criminal Law of Scotland*, 1867, 1948.

Mackenzie, Sir Geo.: *Observations on the Acts of Parliament*, 1686 and in *Works*,
       1716–22.
       Science of Heraldry, 1680, and in *Works*.

McLaren, John, Lord: *Law of Wills and Succession*, 1862, 1894.

McLaurin, John, Lord Dreghorn: *Arguments and Decisions in Remarkable Cases
       before the High Court of Justiciary*, 1774.

Menzies, A.: *Lectures on Conveyancing according to the Law of Scotland*, 1856, 1900.

Menzies, A.J.P.: *Law of Scotland affecting Trustees*, 1893, 1913.

Montgomery Bell, A.: *Lectures on Conveyancing*, 2 vols., 1867, 1882.

More, Prof. J.S.: *Lectures on the Law of Scotland* (ed. McLaren), 2 vols., 1864.

Rankine, Sir John: *Law of Land Ownership in Scotland*, 1879, 1909.
       Law of Leases in Scotland, 1887, 1916.
       Law of Personal Bar, 1921.

Regiam Majestatem (ed. Skene), 1597, 1609, 1774; (ed. Cooper, Stair Society), 1947.

Skene, Sir John: *De Verborum Significatione*, 1597.[9]

Ross, George: *Leading Cases in the Law of Scotland—Land Rights*, 3 vols., 1849–51.
       Leading Cases in the Commercial Law of England and Scotland, 3
       vols., 1853–57.

---

[6] On the authority of this, see *Fortington v. Kinnaird*, 1942 S.C. 239, 277.

[7] On the authority of Hume's *Lectures*, see *Fortington v. Kinnaird*, above, at 253, 265.

[8] Kames also published various volumes of essays and decisions.

[9] Reprinted in Skene's *Lawes and Acts of Parliament*, 1597, and in R. Bell's *Dictionary of the Law of Scotland*.

Steuart, Sir J.: *Answers to Dirleton's Doubts in the Laws of Scotland*, 1715, 1762.
Stewart, J. Graham: *Law of Diligence*, 1898.
Wallace, G.: *System of the Principles of the Law of Scotland*, vol. 1, 1760.[10]
Wood, J.P.: *Lectures on Conveyancing*, 1903.

Modern Textbooks

The range of modern textbooks on particular subjects of law is too great usefully to list. They must be traced from references in the more general books, bibliographies and library catalogues.

Other Reference Books

The *Parliament House Book*, first published in 1821, is an invaluable compendium of statutes and subordinate legislation in the major areas of private law, and of the sets of rules of procedure of the different courts. It is now published in five loose-leaf binders and updated at least twice a year.

Other Government Publications

Many other government publications are of relevance to the study and practice of law.

Parliamentary Papers

Parliamentary papers are all the papers which are put before members of either House of Parliament in the course of their work. House of Commons Papers bear to be "ordered by the House of Commons to be printed" and are numbered from H.C. 1 onwards within each parliamentary session and cited, *e.g.* H.C. 1990–91 (127). They include reports and returns which have to be presented to the House, financial statistics, reports of Select Committees and Minutes of Standing Committees. They are listed as presented in the Votes and Proceedings and the Journal of the House and are available to members on demand at the Vote Office. Bills are a separate series. House of Lords papers include bills and are numbered in one sequence, *e.g.* H.L. 1990–91 (234).

Command Papers

Command Papers are papers presented to Parliament by command of the Queen, printed on the authority of the department presenting them.[11]

---

[10] No more ever published. On the authority of this book, see *Kerr v. Martin* (1840) 2 D. 752, 776, 792.

[11] Command Papers are numbered and cited as follows: 1836–69: first series, no prefix, but year and number [1]–[4222]; 1870–99: second series, prefix C. with year and number [1]–[9550]; 1900–18: prefix Cd. with number [1]–[9239]; 1919–56: prefix Cmd. with number [1]–9889; 1956–86, prefix Cmnd. with number 1–9756; 1986 to date: Cm. with number 1–. The use of square brackets round the number was discontinued in 1922. Some reports, published as Command Papers, are familiarly known by the name of the chairman, *e.g.* The Beveridge Report on Social Insurance (Cmd. 6404). On these see Richard: *British Government Publications: An Index to Chairmen and Authors*, 1900–1940; Morgan, *British Government Publications: An Index to Chairmen and Authors 1941–1966*; HMSO *Index to Chairmen of Committees* (quarterly).

They include Reports of Royal Commissions, Departmental Committees, commissions of inquiry, annual reports by various officers and bodies to ministers under various statutes, Law Commission and Scottish Law Commission recommendations, reports dealing with foreign and Commonwealth affairs and many other kinds of documents. The more bulky ones are commonly called Blue Books, from the colour of their paper covers. White papers are not bulky enough to get blue covers and commonly contain statements of proposed government action. Green papers contain proposals for public discussion. In the Foreign and Commonwealth Office there are various series, the EC series, Treaty series, "Country" series (dealing with relationships with particular countries), and Miscellaneous series. These are numbered in the Command Paper series and also within the particular series to which they belong.[12]

The Gazettes

The *London Gazette* is the world's oldest continuously published registered newspaper. It is published every weekday. Many kinds of notices have by statutory requirements to be published in it, *e.g.* notices of bankruptcies, and many kinds of public notices are published in it. Occasional supplements are published for the announcement of the New Year and Queen's Birthday Honours Lists. The *Edinburgh Gazette* is published twice weekly and contains similar notices.

Parliamentary Debates

There have been five series of *Parliamentary Debates* since 1803, commonly known as Hansard, from an early printer of these reports. They are published daily, collected in weekly pamphlets and issued later in bound volumes reporting the debates of the Parliamentary session with a sessional index. They are cited by volume, House, series, date and column number. Written answers to parliamentary questions are in a separate sequence at the end of volumes.

Legal Periodicals

Periodicals have various functions, to keep the jurist, practitioner and student acquainted with recent changes and developments in the law, and

---

[12] They are catalogued in the annual *Government Publications* and the *General Index to Parliamentary Papers*, 1900–49. There is also *Hansard's Catalogue and Breviate of Parliamentary Papers*, 1696–1834, a *General Index to the reports of Select Committees printed by Order of the House of Commons*, 1801–52, a *General Index to the Accounts and Papers printed by Order of the House of Commons and to the papers presented by command*, 1801–52, and a *General Index to the Bills, Reports, Estimates, Accounts and Papers printed by order of the House of Commons and to the papers printed by command*, 1852–69. See also P. and G. Ford's *Select List of British Parliamentary Papers*, 1833–99, *Breviate of Parliamentary Papers*, 1900–54 (3 vols.) and *Select List of British Parliamentary Papers*, 1955–64. A classified reprint of the *British Parliamentary Papers* commenced in 1968.

to enable him to bring his search for any matter of law right up to date, to keep members of the profession in touch with changes affecting them and matters of common interest, and to serve as an outlet for academic thinking and a forum for the discussion of doctrines and critical analysis of developments.

The first function of the periodical, that of the professional journal, is performed by several journals many of which include also notes, or full reports, of cases and reviews of legislation.[13]

Articles and notes in periodicals of the second kind, *fora* for scholarly discussion, may be persuasive authority and may have considerable influence on judicial thinking; articles vary from highly theoretical to very practical but the general theme is of scholarly analysis, discussion and criticism. There are many journals of this kind, both general[14] and specialised,[15] and a few of the major United States' and other foreign periodicals also sometimes contain matter of interest in this country.

Articles in legal periodicals can be traced through the special indexes thereto.[16]

---

[13] The main ones are the *Scots Law Times* (1893–); the *Scottish Law Review* (1885–1963); the *Scottish Law Gazette* (1933–); the *Journal of the Law Society of Scotland* (1956–) and the *Conveyancing Review* (1957–1963) now incorporated in the *Journal of the Law Society of Scotland* and the *Scottish Law and Practice Quarterly* (1982–). In England there are the *Law Journal* (1822–1965); the *Law Times* (1843–1965) merged in the *New Law Journal* from October 1965; the *Solicitors' Journal* (1857–) and the *Law Society's Gazette* (1904–).

[14] The principal are the *Juridical Review* (1888–1955); the *Juridical Review; The Law Journal of the Scottish Universities* (1956–), the *Edinburgh Law Review* (1998–), and in England, the *Law Quarterly Review* (1885–); the *Cambridge Law Journal* (1921–); the *Modern Law Review* (1937–); the *Journal of the Society of Public Teachers of Law* (1924–38 and, New Series, 1947–80); *Legal Studies* (1981–); the *British Journal of Law and Society* (1974–); *The Journal of Legal History* (1980–); *The Oxford Journal of Legal Science* (1981–). Articles of legal relevance also appear in non-legal journals.

[15] The principal are *Public Administration* (1923–); the *British Journal of Administrative Law* (1954–57) merged with *Public Law* (1956–); *Justice: The Journal of the International Commission of Jurists* (1958–); the *Journal of Criminal Law* (1937–); the *Journal of Criminal Science* (1948–); the *Criminal Law Review* (1954–); *The British Journal of Delinquency* (1950–60) incorporated in the *British Journal of Criminology* (1960–); the *Howard Journal* (1921–); the *Medico-Legal Journal* (1901–); *Medicine, Science and the Law* (1960–); the *Journal of Family and Social Welfare Law* (1978–); the *Business Law Review* (1954–); the *Journal of Business Law* (1957–); the *Industrial Law Review* (1946–60); the *Industrial Law Journal* (1972–); the *European Law Review* (1976–); the *Statute Law Review* (1980–); the *Conveyancer and Property Lawyer* (1936–); the *Journal of Planning and Environment Law* (1948–); the *British Tax Review* (1956–); the *Construction Law Journal* (1985–); the *Civil Justice Quarterly* (1982–); the *European Law Review* (1976–); the *Journal of Comparative Legislation and International Law* (1896–1951), combined with the *International Law Quarterly* (1947–51) into the *International and Comparative Law Quarterly* (1951–); also the annual *British Yearbook of International Law* (1921–); and *Current Legal Problems* (1948–). There are many more periodicals, mostly concerned with particular branches of the law.

[16] See Jones-Chipman, *Index to Legal Periodical Literature*, 1803–1937, 6 vols.; *Index to Legal Periodicals* (1908–); *Index to Foreign Legal Periodicals* (1960–); *International Index to Periodicals*, 1907–55; *International Index*, (1955–65); *Social Sciences and Humanities Index* (1965–74); *Social Sciences Index* (1974–) and *Humanities Index* (1974–); *Subject Index to Periodicals* (1951–61) and *British Humanities Index* (1962–); *Legal Journals Index*.

Apart from periodicals there are various annuals which frequently contain valuable information and articles[17] and many volumes of collected essays and studies, sometimes by one author, sometimes by several, and sometimes contributed by many hands to make a volume in honour of a distinguished jurist.[18]

FURTHER READING

General Reference Books
Bell: *Dictionary and Digest of the Law of Scotland* (ed. Watson).
Broom: *Legal Maxims*.
Gibb and Dalrymple: *Scottish Judicial Dictionary*.
Jowitt: *Dictionary of English Law*.
Saunders: *Words and Phrases Legally Defined*.
Stair Society: *Sources and Literature of Scots Law*, 1936.
Stroud: *Judicial Dictionary*.
Trayner: *Legal Maxims and Phrases*.
Walker: *Oxford Companion to Law*.
Wharton: *Law Lexicon*.

Statute-law
Craies: *Statute Law.*
Stair Society: *Sources and Literature of Scots Law*, Chap. 1.
Sweet & Maxwell: *Guide to Law Reports and Statutes*.

Case-law
Institute of Advanced Legal Studies: *Manual of Legal Citations, Part I.*
Price and Bitner: *Effective Legal Research.*
Raistrick: *Index to Legal Citations and Abbreviations.*
Stair Society: *Sources and Literature of Scots Law*, Chaps. 3 and 4.
Sturgess and Hewitt: *Dictionary of Legal Terms, Statutory Definitions and Citations.*
Sweet & Maxwell: *Guide to Law Reports and Statutes.*
Tait: *Index to Morison's Dictionary of Decisions.*
Wallace: *The Reporters.*

Institutional Writings and Text-books
Institute of Advanced Legal Studies: *Bibliographical Guide to United Kingdom Law.*
Sweet & Maxwell: *Legal Bibliography of the British Commonwealth of Nations,*
    Vols. 1 and 2—English Law
    Vol. 5—Scots Law.
Raistrick and Rees: *Lawyers' Law Books.*
Walker: *The Scottish Jurists.*

---

[17] The chief are the *U.N. Yearbook*; the *European Yearbook*; and the *Yearbook of World Affairs*.

[18] These are more common in Germany, where they are known as *Festschriften* or *Festgaben*, in Italy, where they are usually entitled *Studi in onore di—*, and in France, where they are called, *Mélanges* or *Études*.

Government Publications
Government Publications (daily, monthly, annual, five-yearly).
Pemberton, J. E.: *British Official Publications.*

CHAPTER 12

THE RESOLUTION OF CIVIL DISPUTES

A CIVIL dispute arises whenever two or more parties are at issue on any matter of fact or of law or of both, which affects their legal rights and duties. Such controversies may sometimes be resolved by compromise or agreement or by accepting the opinion of counsel or other third party. But in the last resort controversies as to legal rights or duties can be resolved only by application to the appropriate court or tribunal for a ruling, or, in certain cases, to arbitration. Such applications are regulated by the several bodies of law of procedure, civil and administrative, and the principles of pleading and the principles and rules of the law of evidence are accessory thereto. These subjects are too complicated to discuss here in detail. The following pages merely indicate in very broad outline the course of procedure followed in the commoner kinds of cases to obtain an author-itative ruling on matters in controversy and the main ways in which effect may be given to such rulings.[1] An understanding of procedure is also important in that to understand the law stated in reported decisions it is necessary to understand how the issue had been raised before the court and what stage it had reached at the point at which it is reported.

In civil or administrative proceedings, where the individual has a grievance or claim, he must initiate and press the claim himself, because the failure to satisfy his grievance or claim is a harm to him alone, whereas in the case of conduct stigmatised as criminal, it is prejudicial to the general welfare of the community and the claim to have the wrongdoer punished will be taken up and pressed by a public officer on behalf of the community. In a few cases a question of choice may arise, but normally the questions of who is to initiate the claim, and by what procedure, civil, administrative or criminal, will depend on the nature of the claim involved and its legal classification.

In all cases it is important to observe how disputed issues of law and disputed issues of fact are elucidated and at what stages one or the other may be investigated.

---

[1] This examination of civil procedure is not designed to teach the reader procedure but to explain it sufficiently to enable him to read reports of cases with understanding. It should be noted that reports are frequently concerned with one stage only of the case and do not disclose who ultimately won or how the case ended. They deal, that is, with one battle, and that not necessarily the last, in the war. Hence, also, cases may be reported several times at different stages, after different battles.

I.—CIVIL PROCEEDINGS

In certain cases an individual may legally act at his own hand and need not invoke the help of the court. Thus a man may eject a trespasser, or rescind a contract if the other party is in breach thereof, in each case without the court's intervention. In some cases, too, a contract between the parties provides for remedies in the event of breach of the contract. But in most cases he must seek a remedy from a court.

Civil proceedings are undertaken to obtain a civil remedy. Civil remedies may be classified according to their purposes into:

(i) declaratory judgments, whereby the court declares that particular rights do or do not exist, without necessarily making any order as to consequential action, as where it declares that a pretended marriage was null;

(ii) reduction, whereby the court reduces or sets aside as invalid a contract, will, decree or other writing which is prejudicial to the pursuer's rights;

(iii) prevention, whereby the court stops a threatened legal wrong, or the continuance of the perpetration of a legal wrong or some illegality, before any, or any further, harm is done to the pursuer, as where it issues an order of interdict against commission of a nuisance;

(iv) protection or the securing of possession of property;

(v) enforced performance, whereby the court gives redress by ordering the doing of what should have been done voluntarily by the defender in performance of his legal duty, as by ordering payment, delivery or other action;

(vi) damages, or substitutional redress in the shape of pecuniary compensation, for loss caused or injury or harm done by the failure to implement some legal duty owed to the pursuer by the defender, as where the court awards damages in compensation for loss caused by the defender's breach of contract or for personal injuries resulting from the defender's fault;

(vii) consistorial remedies, as where it judicially separates two spouses or decrees dissolution of a marriage on the ground of the breakdown of the marriage;

(viii) admiralty remedies, being those peculiar to maritime cases;

(ix) remedies competent under particular statutes in particular cases;

(x) administrative remedies, as where the court appoints a judicial factor, or new trustees, or sequestrates an estate or appoints a receiver; and

(xi) miscellaneous remedies, such as applications to the *nobile officium*.

Before proceedings are initiated many preliminary problems have to be decided. Such problems include that of jurisdiction, *i.e.* which country's courts, and, within that country, which court or tribunal is appropriate and can issue a valid decree against the defender or otherwise deal with the case; that of choice of law, *i.e.* whether Scots or some other system of law falls to determine the rights and duties of parties; that of competency, whether that court can take account of the claim, or by way of the kind of proceedings contemplated; that of choice of remedy; that of relevancy, namely, what will have to be alleged and proved to justify the court in granting the remedy sought; and that of evidence, of what evidence must and can be adduced to establish any facts alleged but disputed or in doubt but which must be established if the claim is to succeed. Such preliminary consideration may convince the aggrieved person or his legal adviser that he has no remedy, or is unlikely to be able to establish it. Nobody should rush into court without careful preliminary consideration.

In all proceedings the distinction between questions of fact and questions of law must be kept in mind.[2] Disputed questions of fact must be alleged in the written pleadings and are decided by the judge, or jury if there is one, after hearing and considering evidence.[3] Disputed questions of law must be raised by appropriate pleas-in-law and are decided by the judge after hearing legal argument.[4] Disputed questions of mixed fact and law are determined by the judge after hearing evidence of fact and legal argument as to the effect of the evidence being interpreted in one way or another, though sometimes a jury verdict is the decision of a mixed question of fact and law.

COURT OF SESSION PROCEEDINGS

The Court of Session has jurisdiction to decide all civil claims brought in Scotland save where statute has directed that such a claim may only be dealt with in the sheriff court or a court of special jurisdiction or a statutory tribunal. It also has appellate jurisdiction, supervisory jurisdiction and certain special common law and statutory powers.

It has power, by Act of Sederunt, to regulate its own procedure.[5]

Proceedings in the Court of Session are usually initiated in the Outer House by *summons*, occasionally by *petition* and more rarely by other forms of application to the court. A summons[6] is a writ running in the

---

[2] See p. 103, *supra*.

[3] Thus if the pursuer alleges that the defender drove fast round the corner and knocked him down, and the defender alleges that he drove slowly and carefully round the corner and could not avoid hitting the pursuer who ran out in front of his car without looking, there is a disputed issue of fact, which must be determined after hearing evidence.

[4] Thus whether facts alleged *can* amount in law to cruelty justifying divorce, or to fraud justifying reduction of a contract, or to negligence justifying damages, are questions of law. If it is held that they *can*, whether they *do* is a question of fact.

[5] A.S. (Rules of Court, Consolidation and Amendment) 1965 (S.I. 1968 No. 321), frequently later amended.

[6] For form, see *Rules of Court*, 1994, Appx. form 1, and Appx. A to this book.

name of the Queen and passing the Royal Signet, prepared by the pursuer's legal advisers, setting out the demand of one party, the *pursuer*, against another, the *defender*, and summoning the defender to appear in court to answer the pursuer's demand, with the warning that the pursuer may proceed to take decree in absence against the defender if he does not appear to defend. The first page of a summons is a printed form with certain blanks completed in typewriting. The remainder consists of typewritten sheets setting out the substance of the claim.

After the formal printed introduction identifying the parties (the *instance*) and summoning the defender to appear, the summons contains *conclusions*, or brief statements of the precise remedies claimed,[7] a *condescendence*, or statement in numbered paragraphs of the facts which the pursuer alleges to exist and on which he relies as justifying his claim (but not of the evidence thereof nor of arguments on the relevant law), and *pleas-in-law*, which are brief propositions of law, stating the legal grounds on which the pursuer rests his case.[8]

The summons is signed by a solicitor entitled to practise before the Court of Session, signeted at the court offices,[9] and *citation* of the defender is effected by serving a copy of the summons on him by post or personally. After the *induciae* or warning interval has expired the summons is *called* by being published in the Rolls of Court and at the same time various papers known collectively as *the process* are lodged for the use of the court.

Pleadings

If the defender ignores the summons, the pursuer may take *decree in absence* against him.[10] If he wishes to defend, he must *enter appearance* and lodge *defences*, which are a typed statement of facts, and which must answer, statement by statement, every material allegation in the pursuer's condescendence, and which are completed by *pleas-in-law for the defender* and are signed by defender's counsel. The defences may be defences on the facts, in the form of statements contradictory or explanatory of the pursuer's averments in his condescendence, or defences in point of law, in the form of pleas-in-law challenging the legal basis of the pursuer's claim, or the defences may be both as to fact and law. A defender may also lodge a *counterclaim* with his defences.

An *open record*[11] is now made up, a duplicated pamphlet reproducing the summons, conclusions, the paragraphs of the pursuer's condescendence followed each by the corresponding paragraph of the defender's

---

[7] See *Rules of Court* Appx. form 2, for specimens.

[8] For specimens of summons, see *Encyclopaedia of Scottish Legal Styles, s.v.* "Action."

[9] On signeting and registration of the cause in the offices of the Court of Session see *Practice Notes* [1976] C.L.Y. 3329.

[10] In consistorial actions, exceptionally, even if the defender does not seek to defend, the pursuer may not obtain decree in absence but must prove the facts averred, formerly in an undefended proof in open court but now by lodging affidavits by pursuer and witnesses. A judge considers these and grants decree if satisfied.

[11] In this sense pronounced "recórd."

defences, the pleas-in-law for the pursuer and the pleas-in-law for the defender. Counsel now *adjust the record*[11] by each making alterations in their written pleadings to meet points made by the other, so as to narrow down the matters in dispute and focus clearly the matters of disagreement. The solicitors for the parties communicate to each other the adjustments made. New statements may be added to condescendence and defences, or existing statements altered, and pleas-in-law added or deleted. The pursuer may, for example, add a plea challenging the legal basis of the defences. The careful framing of written pleadings is an essential preliminary to proof or jury trial. Pleadings must (1) give the other side fair warning of the grounds of claim or defences thereto[12]; (2) focus the issue in dispute; moreover (3) evidence at proof or jury trial will be limited to issues raised in the pleadings and of which each party has thereby given the other fair notice, so as to enable him to prepare his answer, and to plan his examination and cross-examination of witnesses.[13]

When counsel have completed their adjustments, or earlier if delay is taking place, the Lord Ordinary will pronounce an *interlocutor*[14] *closing the record*[11]; and appointing further procedure. This completes the written pleadings.[15] A *closed record*[11] is then made up, which is a reprint of the open record but embodying all the adjustments made on the open record, and copies are duplicated.[16]

Summary Decree

The Court may grant summary decree in favour of a pursuer if satisfied that there is no defence to the action or a part of it. Thus it may grant decree as to an injured pursuer's claim for breach of statutory duty, but allow proof to proceed on the pursuer's common law claim.[17] The test is whether the pleadings disclose a defence.[18]

---

[12] Pleadings which are too general and lacking in specification will not be admitted to probation, *e.g. Crown Estates v. Fairlie*, 1979 S.C. 156, 178–179; *Eadie Cairns v. Programmed Maintenance Painting*, 1987 S.L.T. 777.

[13] *e.g. Hill v. N.C.B.*, 1976 S.C. 138.

[14] An interlocutor is an order made by a judge giving effect to his ruling on any matter, and disposing of the whole or any part of a case. In most cases there are many interlocutors before the case is finished.

[15] Alterations to either party's written pleadings can thereafter only be made by *Minute of Amendment*, with the leave of the court. Amendment may be penalised by an award of expenses caused thereby to the other side, particularly if it has caused delay or wasted effort. Amendment may be attempted at a late stage, or even after proof or jury trial, and indeed at any stage until final judgment, but it is in the court's discretion whether to allow it or not; see, *e.g. Thomson v. Glasgow Corp.*, 1962 S.C.(H.L.) 36. The decision to allow or refuse an amendment may be appealed to the Inner House and to the House of Lords; *e.g. Thomson, supra*; *Duke of Argyll v. Duchess of Argyll*, 1962 S.C.(H.L.) 88.

[16] Portions of pleadings from the closed record are frequently reprinted in reported cases. For a specimen Closed Record see Appx. A. (This is included as a *specimen*, as illustration, not presented as a model of good pleading.)

[17] *Frew v. Field Packaging Scotland*, 1994 S.L.T. 1193.

[18] *Cooper v. Northern Scaffolding Group*, 1997 S.L.T. 157; *Keppie v. Marshall Food Group*, 1997 S.L.T. 305.

CHART OF PROCEDURE IN

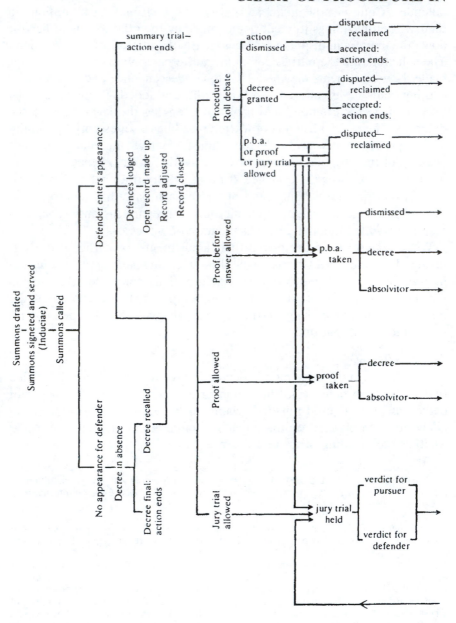

OUTER HOUSE STAGES

COURT OF SESSION ACTION

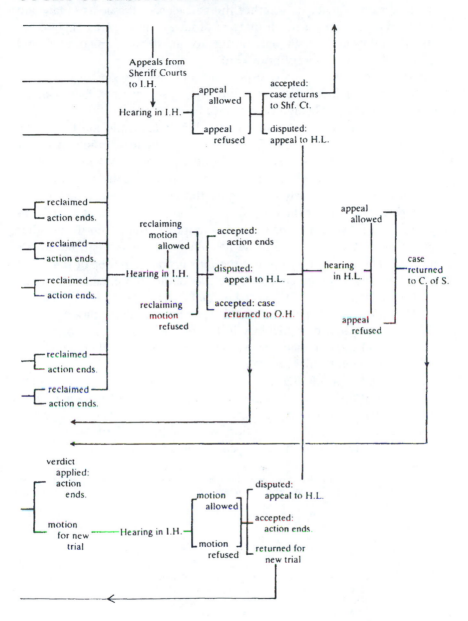

Appeals from
Sheriff Courts
to I.H.

Hearing in I.H. —
- appeal allowed
  - accepted: case returns to Shf. Ct.
- appeal refused
  - disputed: appeal to H.L.

reclaimed — action ends.

reclaimed — action ends.

reclaiming motion allowed
- accepted: action ends
- disputed: appeal to H.L.

Hearing in I.H. —
reclaiming motion refused
- accepted: case returned to O.H.

reclaimed — action ends.

reclaimed — action ends.

reclaimed — action ends.

appeal allowed

hearing in H.L.

case returned to C. of S.

appeal refused

verdict applied: action ends.

motion for new trial — Hearing in I.H. —
motion allowed
- disputed: appeal to H.L.
- accepted: action ends.

motion refused
- returned for new trial

INNER HOUSE STAGES   **H.L. STAGE**

Debate

The next step depends on whether the parties are at issue as to law and have tabled *preliminary pleas* on matters of law, or have pleas only *on the merits*, when they are at issue only on fact, or are at issue on both law and fact, when they have pleas of both kinds.

If parties are at issue on a question of fact only, the court will order a *proof* (*i.e.* trial by judge alone) or *jury trial*,[19] so that the facts can be determined by the production of evidence.

If parties are at issue on law, or on both fact and law, the court will send the case to the Procedure Roll[20] for discussion of the legal points raised by the pleas-in-law which have been tabled in the pleadings. When the case is called on Procedure Roll the legal debate proceeds by way of legal argument only and the party challenging the legal sufficiency or basis of the other's case must, for the purposes of his argument, accept as true his opponent's narrative of the facts. His contention is that, even if the other party can prove the facts to be as he has alleged, he is not entitled in law to succeed. The debate may discuss the *jurisdiction* or power of the court to grant the remedy in the circumstances,[21] whether the pursuer has a *title to sue* for the remedy sought, the legal *competency* of the remedy sought, the *specification* or adequacy of the averments or allegations of either party, or the *relevancy* or sufficiency in law of the averments of one party or the other to justify his claim or establish his defence, on the assumption that the facts stated by him are true.[22]

If the defender pleads that *the action is incompetent* he is contending that this kind of claim cannot be made at all,[23] or cannot be made by that kind of pursuer, *e.g.* because the right had been cut off by lapse of time,[24] or because only criminal prosecution was competent,[25] or because the matter of dispute was by the contract referred to arbitration,[26] or the

---

[19] Jury trial is competent only on defined and limited grounds, on which see *Robertson v. Bannigan*, 1965 S.C. 20, 28. The institution is much criticised and civil jury trial is now much less popular than it was.

[20] Formerly there were separate Procedure and Debate Rolls to which were assigned cases raising different kinds of legal issues.

[21] *e.g. Scotmotors v. Dundee Petrosea*, 1980 S.C. 351.

[22] See *Jamieson v. Jamieson*, 1952 S.C.(H.L.) 44, 50, 63; Walker, "The Theory of Relevancy" (1951) 63 J.R. 1; and on the theory of pleading, Michael and Adler, "The Trial of an Issue of Fact" (1934) 34 Col.L.R. 1224. A famous example of a debate on relevancy is *Donoghue v. Stevenson*, 1932 S.C.(H.L.) 31, where the legal question was whether, even if the pursuer's story could be proved true, she was entitled in law to the remedy sought; it was held that, if the pursuer's averments were proved true, she was entitled to the remedy claimed. In fact the case was compromised, so that the pursuer never required to prove by evidence that her narrative was in fact true, and it remains unknown whether the narrative could have been proved or not and consequently whether Mrs. Donoghue was or was not entitled to her remedy. But the House of Lords' ruling on the law, that such a claim was good in law, is a valid and valuable precedent for later similar cases, quite apart from the fate of that particular claim.

[23] *e.g. McLaren v. Lothian Procurator Fiscal*, 1991 S.C.L.R. 872.

[24] *e.g. B.R. v. Strathclyde R.C.*, 1981 S.C. 90.

[25] *e.g. Reid v. Minicabs*, 1966 S.C. 137.

[26] *Crudens v. Tayside R.C.*, 1979 S.C. 142.

pursuer was not entitled to the remedy claimed but only another remedy,[27] or the pursuer could not claim in that legal capacity.[28] In effect the plea is: You can't do that. If the defender pleads that *the action is irrelevant* he is contending that the summons is not good in law and even if the pursuer can prove all that he has averred, he is still not, in law, entitled to the remedy he has claimed.[29] If the pursuer's case is held irrelevant it falls to be dismissed at once[30]; if the court repels the plea to the relevancy it will allow a proof or a proof before answer.[31] A particular instance of the plea to the relevancy is the plea that the pleadings are *lacking in specification*, *i.e.* that they do not disclose adequately in what respects the defender is alleged to have been in fault.[32] The modes of disposing of this plea are the same. In effect the defender is saying to the pursuer: Well, even if you proved your story, so what? Similarly, the pursuer may table a plea to the relevancy of the defences, contending that *the defences are irrelevant*, which is the contention that, even if the defender can prove all that he has averred, his defence is not sufficient in law,[33] *e.g.* if a man pleads that he has not paid a sum due because he had lost his money gambling. If the defences are held irrelevant the pursuer is entitled to decree *de plano*.[34] If the court repels the plea it will allow a proof or a proof before answer.[35] Each party may have a plea to the relevancy of the other's pleadings.[36]

Such debates proceed by counsel bringing to the judge's attention statutory provisions thought to be relevant, principles laid down, and dicta uttered, in cases, passages in institutional writings and authoritative textbooks, and basing arguments thereon, trying to lead the judge to one view or the other on the issue or issues of law being debated. Such arguments frequently raise problems of the interpretation of statutory provisions, or of the discovery of the true *ratio* of one or more cases and sometimes of the effect on the *ratio* of one case of the *ratio* or of *dicta* in another, or the meaning or weight to be attached to a statement by an institutional or authoritative text-writer. The discovery of the materials for

---

[27] *Hoey v. Butler*, 1975 S.C. 87; *Marchmont v. Clayton*, 1989 S.L.T. 725, *B.M.A. v. Greater Glasgow Health Bd.*, 1989 S.L.T. 493.

[28] *Dick v. Falkirk*, 1976 S.C.(H.L.) 1.

[29] *Jamieson v. Jamieson*, 1952 S.C.(H.L.) 44, 50, 63. In the specimen Closed Record in Appx. A the defender's plea to the relevancy would raise the questions (1) Can a seller complain if by his own error he sells too cheaply? (2) Is there any legal duty on a buyer to know, and pay, the true value of a thing if the seller is willing to sell at the price offered?

[30] *e.g. Glasgow D.C. v. Secretary of State for Scotland*, 1981 S.C. 188; *Oliver v. Douglas*, 1981 S.C. 192, 196.

[31] *e.g. Daejan v. Armia*, 1981 S.C. 48; *Hostess Catering v. Scott*, 1981 S.C. 185.

[32] *e.g. Eadie Cairns v. Programmed Maintenance Painting*, 1987 S.L.T. 777; *Rowallan Creamery v. Dawes*, 1988 S.L.T. 95.

[33] *Mackay v. Campbell*, 1966 S.C. 237.

[34] *e.g. McPhail v. Lothian R.C.*, 1981 S.C. 119, 124–125.

[35] *Bermans & Nathans v. Weibye*, 1981 S.C. 42; *Lord Advocate v. Reo Stakis Organisation*, 1981 S.C. 104.

[36] *e.g. Baker v. Glasgow D.C.*, 1981 S.C. 258; *Glenlight Shipping v. Excess Ins. Co.*, 1981 S.C. 267.

argument raises again the importance of knowing the sources and the repositories of the law and of diligently digging out materials relevant to each point in debate. How to arrange and present an argument is a skill born of experience.

During or after a debate on competency or relevancy, the party under attack may seek leave to amend his pleadings to try to cure the defects disclosed by his opponent.[37] Thereafter there may be a further hearing.

After the debate the judge may give judgment at once but will normally make *avizandum*[38] and subsequently give judgment, when he will issue an *interlocutor* disposing of the points raised[39] and an opinion on the law involved. The judge may grant decree in favour of the pursuer if the parties were at issue on the law alone and the judge holds that the defences, even if proved, would not be adequate in law. He may dismiss the action where the court has no jurisdiction to hear the action; where the pursuer has no title to sue for the remedy claimed; where the pursuer's claim is incompetent, *e.g.* where the pursuer claims a remedy which the court is unable to grant; or where the pursuer's case is irrelevant (*i.e.* insufficient in law), even if the facts were proved to be true as stated.[40] If the parties were at issue on both fact and law, the judge will rule as to the law and, if convinced by the defender's argument on the law, may dismiss the action. If he is convinced by the pursuer's argument on the law, he may order either a *proof or a jury trial* to allow the pursuer to try to prove the facts he has averred. Alternatively, if the judge feels unable to rule on the law without hearing the facts more fully, he can order a *proof before answer* and reserve judgment on the issues of law until the facts have been elucidated.[41]

The advantage of such debates on preliminary pleas is that it is sometimes possible to dispose of the case quickly and without the necessity to hear all the evidence.

Down to this point, one party may request the court to remit the case to the sheriff court as more appropriate, but it is not bound to do so.[42]

---

[37] *e.g. Wilson v. Mersey Insulation Co.*, 1987 S.L.T. 238.

[38] That is, reserve the case for consideration; the word is derived from medieval Latin *avizare*, to consider.

[39] This normally takes the form of his upholding certain pleas-in-law for one party or repelling certain pleas-in-law for the other party. He may also grant decree, dismiss the action, or appoint further procedure.

[40] Appeal may be, and frequently is, taken at this stage, and this may finally dispose of the case, or it may be further appealed to the House of Lords and it may come back to the Outer House, the judge's ruling having been upheld or reversed. Thus in *Junior Books v. Veitchi Co.*, 1982 S.C.(H.L.) 244, 245, 253, 258, a decision on relevancy was reclaimed to the Inner House and then appealed to the House of Lords, and then returned to the Outer House for proof before answer.

[41] See *Forbes v. Forbes's Trs.*, 1957 S.C. 325.

[42] *Westcott v. Dickie*, 1991 S.L.T. 200.

Proof

When the case is called in court on the date fixed for the diet of proof, counsel for both parties appear. There is no opening speech outlining the case and counsel for the pursuer[43] proceeds at once to call his witnesses. There is no need to prove any matter of fact admitted in the pleadings. Failure in the pleadings to deny an averment of fact within a party's knowledge is to be construed as an admission of that fact but denial is not an implied admission merely because the party denying has been less than frank or candid.[44] Each witness is in turn sworn by the judge, *examined-in-chief* by counsel, *cross-examined* by the defender's counsel, and, if thought necessary, *re-examined* by pursuer's counsel to clear up any matter left in doubt. After all the witnesses for the pursuer have been heard the defender's witnesses are in turn sworn, *examined-in-chief* by the defender's counsel, *cross-examined*, and, if need be, *re-examined*. The rules of evidence determine what must be proved, and by what means, and incidental argument may arise as to the admissibility or pertinency of some of the evidence.[45]

There must be a basis in the pleadings of the parties for evidence led by them and parties will not be allowed to lead evidence on matters not made the subject of averment on record.[46] Nor may a judge rely on evidence as to a matter not averred on record.[47] Evidence is of various kinds: *observation evidence*, given by the parties and independent witnesses of what they severally saw, heard and did at the material times; *opinion or expert evidence* by skilled persons such as physicians, engineers, architects, accountants, chemists and other persons of skill of what they observed, found, measured or tested and of what inferences they drew and what conclusions they reached on the basis of their measurements and tests as interpreted in the light of their professional knowledge and experience, *e.g.* as to cause, nature and extent of injuries, cause of explosion, effect of wind-pressure, and so on; *real evidence*, such as production of a broken support or a burst tyre; *circumstantial evidence*, of facts and circumstances bearing on a matter in dispute, as of the state of goods; *written evidence*, such as correspondence, invoices, contract notes, title-deeds, plans and other kinds of documents which tend to establish facts. Evidence of the first four kinds is given orally, sometimes supported by production of things, or photographs of them; written evidence, if probative or *in re mercatoria*, proves itself and need only be lodged in court, but the other kinds of written evidence must be proved by oral evidence to have been executed by the person who bears to have executed the writing.

---

[43] Exceptionally, the defender may be ordained to lead in the proof.
[44] *Gray v. Boyd*, 1996 S.L.T. 60.
[45] *e.g. Young v. N.C.B.*, 1960 S.C. 6.
[46] *Parker v. Lanarkshire Health Board*, 1996 S.C.L.R. 57.
[47] *Robertson v. Cowe*, 1970 S.C. 29.

The purpose of examination-in-chief is to ascertain from the witness what he knows favourable to the case of the party calling him as a witness. The purpose of cross-examination is to test the veracity, accuracy of observation and correctness of the witness's evidence, to find whether he will qualify or retract it and to ascertain what he knows favourable to the other side's case. If the other side has a different explanation of any matter in dispute, this explanation must be put to the witness in cross-examination to see whether he agrees with it or not. Any point on which a witness is not cross-examined is taken as accepted. Leading questions, *i.e.* questions so framed as to indicate the answer desired, are allowed only in cross-examination. The evidence is recorded by a shorthand writer and the judge makes notes for his own use. Evidence is supplemented by *judicial knowledge*, *i.e.* those facts which judges are assumed to know without need for evidence, and may be affected by *presumptions*, *i.e.* rules to the effect that in certain circumstances some state of fact must, or may, be treated as if proved.

Unless parties agree to dispense with it and the court agrees, the evidence is recorded by a shorthand writer and his notes are later extended in typed form.[48]

At the conclusion of the evidence, or at an adjourned *hearing on evidence*, counsel address the court and make their submissions to the judge on the effect of the evidence and on what inferences should be drawn from it. The assessment or weighing of evidence is a difficult job. It involves deciding which witnesses are honest, which lying, which exaggerating, which confused, or inaccurate, or forgetful, which truthful, accurate and reliable, and trying to build up from the whole body of evidence a coherent picture of what happened. This involves accepting some evidence, discarding some and trying to piece it all together. There may be gaps in the evidence, things not observed, periods as to which there is silence and so on, and questions may arise of how far a judge can draw an inference from incomplete evidence. The judge may give judgment at once or may make *avizandum*,[49] in which case the cause is called again a few days later for judgment, when junior counsel attend, the judge reads his judgment and, on the motion of counsel, awards or reserves expenses. While the judge's opinion contains his reasons, the operative part of his judgment is the *interlocutor*, which sustains and gives effect to one or more of the pleas in law for one party and repels contrary pleas, or the *decree* which he pronounces, determining the cause, granting the pursuer the remedy sought, or assoilzieing[50] the defender.

---

[48] A proof may be lengthy. In *McColl v. Strathclyde*, 1983 S.L.T. 616, the proof lasted 201 days, the evidence extended to 5.3 million words and the Lord Ordinary's judgment occupied 392 pages. In *Elf Enterprise Caledonia v. London Bridge Engineering* (1993–96), the proof lasted 391 days and the evidence extended to 13 million words.

[49] *i.e.* take the case for private consideration.

[50] The "z" is not pronounced. The word means "absolving" and the decree is called "absolvitor."

Procedure where proof before answer has been allowed is the same, save that legal issues are kept open for argument when counsel is heard on the evidence, and they will then make submissions both on the law and on the evidence. Each party will argue to the judge that, on the evidence, he, should hold it proved that certain facts were, or were not, established, that the facts established did, or did not, amount to legal cruelty or breach of contract or negligence or whatever be the case, and that in consequence the judge should find the defender liable, or not liable. In such cases evidence and legal argument are closely interwoven. Thus in *B.S. Brown v. Craiks*[51] B sued C for damages for breach of a contract of sale of cloth by delivery of defective cloth. At a proof, evidence was led of the contract, the delivery, the quality of the cloth and its defects, and the pursuers argued that the cloth supplied with the defects proved was not of "merchantable quality" within the meaning of the Sale of Goods Act 1893, s. 14(1), and that the sellers were therefore in breach of contract and should be held liable in damages. The Lord Ordinary found the facts[52] and reached the conclusion[53] that the pursuers had failed to prove the facts necessary to establish their claim under section 14(1) and also, after examination of the cases to determine what "merchantable quality" in section 14 meant, held[54] that the pursuers had failed to prove that the cloth was not of "merchantable quality." He therefore assoilzied the defenders. The case was appealed on the legal issue only to the First Division[55] and to the House of Lords[56] and both courts agreed with the Lord Ordinary.

Optional Procedure

Claims for reparation for injuries may be brought under an optional procedure[57] which provides for speedy reference to proof before answer. A case brought under optional procedure may be transferred to the ordinary roll, but not thereafter transferred back.[58]

Summary Trial

Parties may petition the Outer House to have a case, other than one affecting status, decided by a particular Lord Ordinary in a summary way. The procedure is such as the parties, with the consent of the Lord Ordinary, may agree, or such as he may order. The Lord Ordinary may hear and determine any such case in chambers. His decree is final and not appealable.[59]

---

[51] 1970 S.C.(H.L.) 51.
[52] p. 53.
[53] p. 55.
[54] p. 61.
[55] pp. 61–70.
[56] pp. 71–80.
[57] R.C. 43.21; *e.g. Dalson v. Tayside Health Board*, 1998 S.L.T. 1304.
[58] *Anderson v. British Coal Corpn.*, 1992 S.L.T. 398.
[59] Administration of Justice (Scotland) Act 1933, s. 10; *McGeachy v. Standard Life Assurance Co.*, 1972 S.C. 145; *Britain Steamship Co. v. Lithgows Ltd*, 1975 S.C. 110.

Jury Trial

Jury trial is competent only in specified types of actions and the Court may be persuaded that even in an action of one of the specified types, special cause exists for hearing the case by proof rather than by jury trial.[60] It is normally done with Issues. An *Issue* is a question of fact precisely formulated in writing by the pursuer for the jury to answer; there may also be a *Counter-Issue* for the defender.[61] Issue and counter-issue, if any, are designed to obtain an answer from the jury to the major matters of fact on which the parties are in dispute, such as whether the pursuer's injuries were caused by the defender's fault.

The jury numbers 12 and both sexes are usually represented. The members are drawn by lot from a larger number cited for the purpose. The jury is sworn and junior counsel for the pursuer makes an opening speech to the jury outlining the case.[62] Evidence for the pursuer is then led as in a proof. As at a proof, the evidence is recorded in shorthand and the judge makes his own notes. At the conclusion of the pursuer's case, counsel for the defence may submit that there is no case to answer and that the case should be withdrawn from the jury.[63] Unless this is acceded to, the defence case is opened by junior counsel and evidence for the defence led in the same way. If the motion to withdraw the case from the jury is acceded to, the pursuer may move the Inner House to allow a new trial.[64]

After the conclusion of the evidence, senior counsel for the pursuer and for the defender successively address the jury, each trying to commend his client's case to the jury. Each counsel must, after addressing the jury, make any special requests or submissions in law to the judge, such as requests for a particular direction to the jury in point of law.

The judge then charges the jury; he instructs them that they are sole masters of the facts and judges of the credibility of witnesses, of the cogency, value and weight to be attached to their evidence, and of the inferences which may be drawn from conduct, circumstantial evidence or the absence of evidence or explanations. He will explain to them as simply as possible the points of law which are involved[65]; he will indicate the main points in the evidence, to assist the jury to have the evidence clearly before their minds; he must point out the value of corroborative testimony. Lastly he will indicate what elements have to be taken into account

---

[60] *McKechnie's C.B. v. Gribben*, 1996 S.L.T. 136; *Meechan v. McFarlane*, 1996 S.L.T. 208; *Johnston v. Clark*, 1997 S.L.T. 923; *Gibson v. McAndrew Wormald*, 1998 S.L.T. 562.

[61] For specimens, see *Hayden v. Glasgow Corp.*, 1948 S.C. 143; *McLean v. The Admiralty*, 1960 S.C. 199; *McKeown v. Arrol*, 1974 S.C. 98; *Kirkland v. B.R. Board*, 1978 S.C. 71; *McAllister v. Abram*, 1981 S.L.T. 85.

[62] On this speech, see *Robertson v. Federation of Iceland Co-operative Societies*, 1948 S.C. 565; *Lawrie v. Glasgow Corp.*, 1952 S.C. 361.

[63] *McDonald v. Duncan*, 1933 S.C. 737; *Grant v. W. Alexander & Sons*, 1937 S.L.T. 572.

[64] *Mulligan v. Caird (Dundee)*, 1973 S.L.T. 72.

[65] The jury must accept his view of the law: *Gelot v. Stewart* (1871) 9 M. 957.

if the jury come to consider damages, and what principles should be followed in their assessment, and he will refer to the Issue, and Counter-Issue, if there is one, indicating the possible answers according to the possible views of the evidence.

If counsel for either party objects to any part of the charge or wishes any further or other direction to be given to the jury, he must say so at the end of the charge. The jury is directed to withdraw and counsel addresses the judge, indicating the direction desired, and if the judge refuses to give it, counsel must there and then tender a *Note of Exceptions*, formulating the exception taken by him and stating the substance of the direction desired and this note, recording the judge's determination thereon is certified by him.[66] The judge may accept counsel's proposition and give further or other directions to the jury in the sense requested.

At the conclusion of the charge the jury may at once give its verdict but usually retires to the jury room to deliberate before doing so. They may return to court to request further directions from the judge on any point, or to request that some portion of evidence be read over to them from the notes.

The verdict may be given unanimously or by a majority at any time, but if after three hours the jury has been unable to agree upon some verdict, the judge may order them to be discharged and order the case to be tried afresh with another jury. The verdict is normally a *General Verdict, i.e.* such answers to the Issue, and Counter-Issue, if any, as amount to a general finding for or against the pursuer, but do not answer specific points as to grounds of liability or otherwise. A *Special Verdict, i.e.* a series of answers to specific questions on points of fact formulated by the trial judge, is competent but rare. The verdict is recorded and the jury discharged. Subsequently counsel for the party favoured by the verdict moves the court to apply the verdict, *i.e.* convert it into a decree, and to deal with expenses. Difficulties occasionally arise when juries return self-contradictory or incomprehensible verdicts.

Commercial Actions

Actions of a commercial character, concerned with export or import, carriage, insurance, banking and similar disputes, are under the direction and control of a judge designated as commercial judge. Pleadings are abbreviated and such actions are sought to be processed rapidly.[67]

Settlement of Actions

At any stage the parties may settle the action, as where the defender offers a sum in settlement of the pursuer's claim and the pursuer accepts

---

[66] For an example, see *Power v. Central S.M.T. Co.*, 1949 S.C. 376; see also *Bain v. Fife Coal Co.*, 1935 S.C. 681; *Robertson v. Federation of Iceland Co-operative Societies*, 1948 S.C. 565; *Glacken v. N.C.B.*, 1951 S.C. 617; *Douglas v. Cunningham*, 1964 S.C.(H.L.) 112; *McArthur v. Weir Housing Corp.*, 1970 S.C. 135.

[67] *Rules of Court*, Chap. 47; [1994] C.L.Y. 6104. On reclaiming, see *Highland and Universal Properties v. Safeway*, 1996 S.C. 424.

it. Settlement may be extra-judicial, *i.e.* not appearing in the pleadings[67a] or judicial, where the defender makes an offer in his defences or in a separate minute[67b] to make payment to settle the action. When this happens the action is abandoned or the court grants decrees in terms of a joint minute agreed by the parties.

Abandonment of Action

A pursuer who sees no prospect of success may abandon his action.[68]

Petitions

Petition is the proper mode of approaching the court and seeking its authority for some action, or some administrative remedy, or some appointment which only the court can make. Petitions must be prepared on the prescribed official printed form. They contain an address to their Lordships, a statement of facts, and a prayer craving the remedy sought. Thus a petition is appropriate for the appointment of a judicial factor, for the appointment of new trustees, to obtain power for trustees to sell heritage, to wind up a company or effect an arrangement between a company and its creditors, and in various other cases. Petitions are frequently non-contentious and uncontested.

Most petitions are presented to the Outer House, some to the Inner House. The authority of the court is necessary before the petition is served on the persons who may wish to object, or advertised or otherwise intimated. If no answers are lodged by the respondents called, the petition appears on the rolls, counsel appears before the court and may have his petition granted at once. In some cases, the court remits to a member of the Bar or to a solicitor of experience[69] to inquire into the facts alleged and to report before it disposes of the petition. In other cases, a proof is ordered, which proceeds in the same way as the proof in an action.

If the petition should be opposed, *Answers* are lodged and the court may hear parties, have a proof, or remit to a reporter and hear parties on his report before disposing of the application. A party affected by the petition but not desiring to oppose it may lodge a minute and crave to be heard on some point.

An important class of petition in modern practice is the petition for judicial review, whereby an aggrieved person asks the court to strike down some act by a public authority or to declare its conduct unlawful or to stop its conduct. It takes a special form which requires a statement not only of

---

[67a] *e.g. Lawrence v. Knight*, 1972 S.C. 26.
[67b] *e.g. Smeaten v. Dundee Corporation*, 1941 S.C. 600; *Avery v. Cantilever Shoe Co.*, 1942 S.C. 469.
[68] *Frost v. Unity Trust Bank*, 1997 S.L.T. 1358.
[69] See, *e.g. Scotstown Moor Children's Camp*, 1948 S.C. 630; *City Property Investment Trust Corp. Ltd*, 1951 S.C. 570.

facts but of the arguments, statutes and precedents founded on by the petitioner and contains pleas-in-law. Judicial review is a procedure developed to allow an aggrieved individual to challenge the act of an administrative person or authority as legally unjustified. The issue must be one of public rather than private law,[70] such as a decision to deport a person,[71] or to detain in a metal hospital,[72] or to refuse a student a degree,[73] or to challenge the findings of a Fatal Accident Inquiry.[74] It is not an additional mode of appeal against a civil or criminal decision but is a challenge of the legality of what was done. It is not normally competent if a statutory remedy or form of appeal exists and has not been exhausted.[75]

Motions

Incidental applications to the court are made by *motion*, which may be opposed, argued, and appealed.[76] Motions include motions that a case be remitted to the sheriff court.[77]

Special Forms of Action

Certain kinds of action have special procedural features.

Report to the Inner House

An Outer House judge, faced with a point of general importance or particular difficulty, may report the case to the Inner House with an opinion. The point is then argued before one of the Divisions which delivers an opinion, giving guidance to the Lord Ordinary, and returns the case to him.[78]

Appeal to the Inner House—Reclaiming Motion

The decision of a judge pronounced in the Outer House after debate or proof may be appealed to the Inner House by way of *reclaiming motion*, which brings under the review of the Inner House the whole or any part of the cause as decided down to that point. Only exceptionally need the leave of the Outer House judge be obtained. Copies of the pleadings and

---

[70] *Criper v. Edinburgh University*, 1991 S.L.T. 129; *West v. Secretary of State for Scotland*, 1992 S.L.T. 636; *Kyle & Carrick D.C. v. Kerr*, 1992 S.L.T. 629; *Blair v. Lochaber*, 1995 S.L.T. 407; *Maclean v. Glasgow C.C.*, 1999 S.L.T. 11.

[71] *Sokha v. Secretary of State for the Home Department*, 1992 S.L.T. 1049.

[72] *R v. Lothian Health Board*, 1991 S.L.T. 282.

[73] *Saleh v. Dundee University* [1993] C.L.Y. 5252.

[74] *Smith v. Lord Advocate*, 1995 S.L.T. 379.

[75] *Tarmac v. Lothian Assessor*, 1991 S.L.T. 77; *Simpson v. I.R.C.*, 1992 S.L.T. 1069; *Shanks & McEwan (Constructors) v. Mifflin*, 1993 S.L.T. 1124; *Strathclyde Buses v. Strathclyde R.C.*, 1994 S.L.T. 724; *Ingle v. Ingle's Tr.*, 1999 S.L.T. 650.

[76] *e.g. Harley v. Kinnear Moodie & Co.*, 1964 S.C. 99.

[77] *e.g. Hamilton v. British Coal Corp.*, 1990 S.L.T. 287.

[78] *e.g. Kerr v. John Brown & Co.*, 1965 S.C. 144.

documents used in the Outer House and of the Lord Ordinary's opinion are lodged for the court, and, where appropriate, duplicated transcripts of evidence extended from the shorthand-writer's notes. It is now normal for the court to order the reclaimer to intimate his grounds of appeal, stating the points to be raised. Most cases challenge the Lord Ordinary's view of the relevant law, but a reclaimer may challenge his view of the facts,[79] or the way he exercised discretion.[80] In due course the case appears in the rolls assigned to either the First or the Second Division and is argued. If the reclaiming motion is from the decision of an Outer House judge on a point debated in Procedure Roll, there is purely legal argument on the pleadings, there being no evidence. In this case the pleadings and the Lord Ordinary's opinion are read and criticised by the reclaimer and supported by the respondent. If the reclaiming motion is against a Lord Ordinary's decision after proof, the evidence which has been heard in the Outer House is not reheard but the judges and counsel have duplicated copies of the shorthand-writer's transcript of the evidence and this, or the relevant parts of it, is read to the court. Junior counsel for the reclaimer opens the case and is replied to by junior counsel for the respondent. Thereafter, senior counsel for the reclaimer and for the respondent respectively address the court.

At the end of the hearing judgment may be given at once. One of the judges may deliver extempore a leading opinion and the others concur or add short opinions. In more difficult cases, the court will *make avizandum*, *i.e.* reserve the case for consideration, in which event the case will be called on a later date for "Advising," when judgment will be given, each judge reading the opinion he has prepared. Any judge may dissent in whole or in part from his brethren. The decision of the court will subsequently be translated into an *interlocutor*, which will be signed by the presiding judge. At advising, expenses fall to be dealt with on counsel's motion. The decision normally takes the form of adhering to the Lord Ordinary's interlocutor, *i.e.* refusing the appeal, or of recalling his interlocutor and pronouncing a fresh one in different terms, *i.e.* allowing the appeal in whole or in part. There is no power to order a fresh proof.

The Division before which the case is heard has power, if equally divided or in doubt as to a matter of complexity and difficulty, to consult the judges of the other Division,[81] or to order a rehearing before five[82] or seven judges,[83] or even before the whole court.[84]

---

[79] *e.g. Thomas v. Thomas*, 1947 S.C.(H.L.) 45; *Islip Pedigree Breeding Centre v. Abercromby*, 1959 S.L.T. 161.

[80] *e.g. Thomson v. Glasgow Corp.*, 1962 S.C.(H.L.) 36.

[81] *e.g. Connell v. Connell*, 1950 S.C. 505.

[82] *e.g. Houston v. Buchanan*, 1937 S.C. 460.

[83] *e.g. Yuill's Trustees v. Thomson* (1902) 4 F. 815; *Brodie v. Ker*, 1952 S.C. 216.

[84] *e.g. Lang v. Bruce* (1832) 10 S. 777; see also *Baird v. Stevenson*, 1907 S.C. 1259.

The case may now be at an end, or it may be remitted to the Outer House for further procedure.[85] or there may be a further appeal to the House of Lords.

Motion for New Trial

After a jury trial has taken place, a party dissatisfied with the verdict may enrol a motion in the Inner House for the granting of a new trial on specified and limited grounds. The court will not grant the motion for a new trial merely if it disagrees with the jury's verdict but only if the verdict is in its view so flagrantly wrong that no reasonable jury discharging their duty honestly under proper direction would have given it.[86] The jury is accordingly allowed a considerable latitude and its verdict will not be interfered with if there was some evidence before it on which a reasonable jury could have reached the verdict complained of, or unless its award of damages is grossly excessive or inadequate.[87] Nor will a new trial be allowed on the ground of misdirection unless the charge taken as a whole was misleading.[88]

The case is heard before either of the Divisions of the Inner House, and the judge who presided at the jury trial in the Outer House formerly also sat with the Division for the hearing of the motion. As in the case of reclaiming motions, any evidence necessary is read from duplicated transcripts of the shorthand-writer's notes. While two counsel are usually instructed, only one speech is heard from each side.

The court delivers judgment in the usual way, allowing or refusing a new trial and remitting the case to the Outer House for the verdict to be entered up, or to have a fresh jury summoned and the case retried.[89] Sometimes, by consent of parties, the court itself decides the issue instead of allowing a new trial, and in certain circumstances it may set aside the verdict and enter judgment for the party unsuccessful at the trial.[90] The

---

[85] Thus in *Bourhill v. Young*, 1941 S.C. 395, the pursuer's claim was dismissed as irrelevant in the Outer House (p. 398), reclaimed to the Inner House, which allowed a proof before answer (p. 403), dismissed after proof in the Outer House (p. 405), and this decision was affirmed in the Inner House (p. 407), and, on appeal, in the House of Lords (1942 S.C.(H.L.) 78). In *Boyd and Forrest v. G.S.W. Ry.* the action was thrice before the Inner House (1911 S.C. 37 and 42, 1914 S.C. 472) and twice before the House of Lords (1912 S.C.(H.L.) 93 and 1915 S.C.(H.L.) 20).

[86] *Campbell v. Scottish Education News Co.* (1906) 8 F. 691; *McGinley v. Pacitti*, 1950 S.C. 364; *Kirkland v. B.R. Board*, 1978 S.C. 71; *MacArthur v. Strathclyde Chief Constable*, 1989 S.L.T. 517.

[87] *Elliot v. Glasgow Corp.*, 1922 S.C. 146; *McKinlay v. Glasgow Corp.*, 1951 S.C. 495; *Girvan v. Inverness Farmers Dairy*, 1998 S.C.(H.L.) 1.

[88] *McArthur v. Weir Housing Corp.*, 1970 S.C. 135.

[89] Sometimes a third trial is necessary, and there is theoretically no limit, but the court rarely grants a third trial and there seems to be no record of a fourth ever being granted: see *Watson v. N.B. Ry.* (1904) 7 F. 220; *McKnight v. General Motor Carrying Co.*, 1936 S.C. 17; *McCallum v. Paterson*, 1969 S.C. 85.

[90] Court of Session Act 1988, s. 30; *Mills v. Kelvin & White*, 1913 S.C. 521; *Collum v. Carmichael*, 1957 S.C. 349; *Potec v. Edinburgh Corp.*, 1964 S.C.(H.L.) 1. For an unusual example of practice, see *Moyes v. Burntisland Shipbuilding Co.*, 1952 S.C. 429.

exercise of the court's discretion in allowing or refusing a new trial, or setting aside the verdict and entering judgment for the other party, may be challenged by way of appeal to the House of Lords,[91] which may itself exercise similar powers.[92]

Appeals from the Sheriff Court

Appeals from the sheriff court are heard by the Inner House and disposed of in very much the same way as reclaiming motions. The case appears in the rolls of either Division of the Inner House and the judges have before them prints of the sheriff court record, the interlocutors of the sheriff, and of any evidence heard and documents produced in the sheriff court. Argument is heard from one or two counsel on each side and the sheriff's interlocutor appealed from may be adhered to, or recalled and a different interlocutor substituted, or the court may make different or additional findings in fact or in law. The appeal may thus be allowed or dismissed, and the action may, if necessary, be remitted to the sheriff court. The court may order additional proof to be heard.

In sheriff court summary causes, appeal is by way of stated case and a point not argued in the sheriff court and not in the stated case cannot be argued on appeal.[93]

Other Inner House Appeals

Other Inner House appeals brought under particular statutes commonly proceed in the same general manner as appeals from the sheriff court. In some cases, particularly appeals to the Court of Session as Court of Exchequer, the appeal is by way of *stated case*, in which procedure the parties frame a case setting forth the facts found or agreed and formulating certain questions of law for the opinion of the court thereon.[94] Legal argument is heard in the usual way and the court delivers opinions containing answers to the questions of law raised by the case.

Petitions

Certain kinds of petitions are presented directly to the Inner House.

Special mention must be made of petitions to the Inner House to exercise the *nobile officium* of the Court. This is an extraordinary equitable remedy, competent only where there has been revealed a *casus improvisus* in statutory procedure, or a situation has arisen which requires exceptional relief to avoid a deadlock. It is not generally available if any ordinary remedy is competent, nor as a mode of appeal failing, or after,

---

[91] *e.g. Potec, supra*; *Douglas v. Cunningham*, 1964 S.C.(H.L.) 112.
[92] Administration of Justice (Scotland) Act 1972, s. 2.
[93] *Verrico v. Hughes*, 1980 S.C. 179; *Hart v. Kitchen*, 1990 S.L.T. 54.
[94] For an example, see *Inland Revenue v. Glasgow Police Athletic Association*, 1952 S.C. 102 (reversed by H.L., 1953 S.C.(H.L.) 13).

any ordinary appeal, nor can it be invoked to extend or override a statute.[95] The Court tends to limit its use to circumstances for which there is precedent or at least analogy. Examples of competent applications[96] have included retrospective authorisation of trustees' acts,[97] authorising the correction of a public register,[98] allowing acts prohibited by interdict,[99] authorising a Clerk of Session to sign a deed for persons who have gone abroad,[1] setting aside a court decree[2] and allowing children's evidence in a referral from a children's hearing to be taken at a court other than that of the district.[3]

Special Cases

Apart from those petitions which are presented direct to the Inner House, the most important business originating in the Inner House is the *special case*. The essential feature of the special case is that the parties are in agreement as to the facts and are submitting differences as to law only, for the opinion, or opinion and judgment, of a Division of the Court. The case is settled by counsel for the parties and sets out all the relevant facts, printing any relevant documents in an Appendix, and formulating several *questions in law* for the court, which raise the legal difficulties which they wish to have determined. The special case is commonly used where parties are agreed as to the facts but in doubt or dispute as to the interpretation of a document, such as a will, or trust deed, *e.g.* has the legacy to B been revoked, is Y's share to be divided into two or three shares in the circumstances, and so on? Many important questions in the law of wills and succession are accordingly decided in special cases.[4]

Appeal to the House of Lords

Appeal to the House of Lords is competent, unless expressly excluded by statute, against most Inner House judgments and, as a rule, without leave of the Inner House.[5] It does not lie against answers by the Inner House to a case stated by an arbiter.[6] Appeals may be taken on grounds of fact or of law, though appeals on fact are not viewed with favour and the House is disinclined to differ on an issue of fact from the views of the

---

[95] *Fife Motor Auctions v. Perth and Kinross D.C.*, 1981 S.L.T. 106; *Humphries*, 1982 S.C. 79.
[96] For older cases see MacLaren, *Court of Session Practice*, 100 *et seq.*
[97] *Campbell-Wyndham-Long's Trs.*, 1962 S.C. 132.
[98] *Ferguson*, 1965 S.C. 16.
[99] *Bowie*, 1967 S.C. 36.
[1] *Boag*, 1967 S.C. 322.
[2] *Royal Bank v. Gillies*, 1987 S.L.T. 54.
[3] *Sloan*, 1991 S.L.T. 527.
[4] For an example, see *Gillies v. Glasgow Royal Infirmary*, 1960 S.C. 438.
[5] Leave is necessary in the case of an interlocutory judgment (*i.e.* one which does not finally dispose of the action) if the Division was unanimous. Application for leave to appeal is made by petition. See further, Appeal Directions and Standing Orders applicable to Appeals to the House of Lords, in *Parliament House Book*, Div. B.
[6] *McGregor v. Grampian R.C.*, 1991 S.L.T. 365.

judge who saw and heard the witnesses.[7] The House may also refuse to hear argument on a matter not argued before the Court of Session.[8]

An appeal takes the form of a petition to the House of Lords praying that an interlocutor, set out in the schedule to the petition, may be reversed, varied or altered, so that the petitioner may have such relief as may seem right. It must be signed by two counsel as being a proper case to be heard by way of appeal. The parties lodge a joint Statement of Facts and Issues, and the appellant lodges an Appendix of all the documents in the case, including pleadings, interlocutors, correspondence, etc. The opinions of the judges in the courts below are also printed or, if the case has been reported, copies of the report are lodged. Copies of the printed cases are exchanged between the agents and copies are bound in a volume containing both cases.[9]

The case is heard by at least three, and usually by five, Law Lords sitting formerly in the same legislative chamber as is used by the full House of Lords and nowadays in one of the committee rooms. Only the Lord Chancellor, if he sits, is robed.[10] At least two counsel are instructed but the argument is normally sustained by one senior counsel on each side (who for this appearance formerly had to wear full-bottomed wigs), but in cases of great length and complexity the argument on each side is divided, one counsel arguing certain points, the other following on other topics. Not more than two counsel will be heard on each side. Counsel for the appellant opens, and may reply briefly after the respondent has made his submissions.[11]

The House usually takes time to consider and gives judgment later. Since the sitting is nominally a sitting of the House as a legislative body, the question is put and the peers present (*i.e.* the Law Lords who heard the appeal) speak for or against the motion. In modern practice judgments are not usually delivered orally but are issued later in typescript.[12]

After judgment in the House the case returns to the Inner House, which *applies the judgment*, but if the judgment of the Inner House has not been simply affirmed, a petition must be presented to the Inner House craving it to apply the judgment of the House of Lords and to deal with expenses.

Sheriff Court Proceedings

Ordinary Causes

The general principles of the procedure already discussed in relation to the Court of Session apply also to the sheriff court, with certain variations

---

[7] *Flower v. Ebbw Vale Steel Co.* [1936] A.C. 206, 220; *Thomas v. Thomas*, 1947 S.C.(H.L.) 45; *Higgins v. Smith*, 1990 S.L.T. 663. See also *Martinez v. Grampian Health Board*, 1996 S.L.T. 69.

[8] *British Oxygen Co. v. South-West Scotland Electricity Board*, 1956 S.C.(H.L.) 112, 120.

[9] See *Practice Direction* [1964] 2 All E.R. 509; *Practice Note* [1991] 3 All E.R. 609.

[10] The Lord Chancellor has so many duties that he only sometimes sits to hear appeals. More usually, the senior Law Lord present presides.

[11] As to submitting in advance lists of authorities to be cited in argument, see *Practice Direction* [1967] 1 All E.R. 128.

[12] See *Practice Direction* [1963] 1 W.L.R. 1382; [1963] C.L.Y. 2777; [1977] C.L.Y. 3632.

of terminology and practice. Most proceedings are governed by the Ordinary Cause Rules issued by the Court of Session by Act of Sederunt.[13] An action is commenced by an Initial Writ, Petition or Summons[14] but it cannot be served on the defender without a warrant obtained from the sheriff-clerk: it does not pass the Signet. But the principles of pleading, the Open and Closed Records, the hearings on Procedure Roll and the conduct of proof follow closely Court of Session procedure. Jury trial in the sheriff court was abolished in 1980,[15] but in certain cases an action commenced in the sheriff court may be remitted to the Court of Session for disposal there.[16] Under various statutes proceedings take the form of a summary application which is commenced by a similar form of writ. There are some specialities in divorce proceedings. The sheriff must append a note to all interlocutors, except those of a formal nature, setting forth the grounds on which he has proceeded, and in a final judgment on the merits he must set out his findings in fact and in law separately.

Summary Causes

More material variations arise in respect of summary causes, that is, actions where the value of the cause does not exceed £1500. Most claims are for recovery of debts or recovery of possession of houses let. A summary cause is commenced by completing a standard printed form appropriate to the kind of claim, prescribed by the Summary Cause Rules[17] with annexed a statement of claim containing a concise statement of the facts which are the ground of action.[18] It is signed by the sheriff clerk. The action is dealt with throughout in a summary way. There are normally no written pleadings. The defender need appear only if he is defending the action. Evidence given at a proof is not recorded. In certain circumstances an ordinary action may be dealt with as a summary cause, or a summary cause be dealt with as an ordinary action.[19] The Summary Cause Rules allow a party in certain circumstances to be represented by a person who is neither an advocate nor a solicitor.[20]

Small Claims

A small claim, which is for a sum not exceeding £750, and certain other claims directed to be dealt with under this procedure, is initiated by

---

[13] Sheriff Courts (Scotland) Act 1971, s. 32; A.S. (Ordinary Cause Rules, Sheriff Court) 1993 (S.I. 1993 No. 1956).

[14] There is no fixed name for the first writ in a sheriff court action; it is sometimes called Initial Writ and sometimes Summons or Petition or Statement of Claim.

[15] Law Reform (Miscellaneous Provisions) (Scotland) Act 1980, s. 11.

[16] *Shaw v. Lanarkshire Health Board*, 1988 S.C.L.R. 13; *Mullan v. Anderson*, 1993 S.L.T. 835.

[17] See specimen in Appx. B.

[18] *G.U.S. Catalogue Order v. Oxborrow*, 1988 S.L.T.(Sh.Ct.) 2.

[19] Sheriff Courts (Scotland) Act 1971, ss. 35–38 and A.S. (Summary Cause Rules, Sheriff Court) 1976 (S.I. 1976 No. 476). Previously, a rather similar procedure applied in the Sheriff Small Debt Court. The Royal Commission on Legal Services in Scotland recommended replacement of the Summary Cause by a "small claims procedure" with a sheriff as adjudicator.

[20] Summary Case Rules, 17.

completing a summons in the shape of a prescribed printed form[21] which is served on the defender. It must give the defender fair notice of the claim. It is signed by the sheriff clerk and the copy served on the defender tells him what he has to do if he wishes to defend or to seek a time-to-pay direction. There are no written pleadings. A preliminary hearing is fixed at which a defender wishing to defend or seeking a time-to-pay direction must appear, failing which decree may be granted in absence. Such cases proceed with a minimum of formality and the rules of evidence are relaxed.[22]

In the sheriff court there are wide powers to transfer a case from an ordinary cause to a summary cause and conversely, and from a small claim to a summary cause or an ordinary cause and conversely. Procedure is regulated by the Small Claims Rules.[23] Some Ordinary Cause rules and some Summary Cause Rules apply also to small claims. A party to a small claim may be represented by a non-lawyer if the sheriff accepts him as a suitable and authorised person.

Appeal from Sheriff to Sheriff Principal

Appeal is competent from the judgment of the sheriff to the sheriff principal in many cases, including all final judgments, without leave, and in other cases with the leave of the sheriff.[24] It is taken by note of appeal signed by the appellant.

The sheriff principal hears oral argument on behalf of parties, based on the Record and transcript of evidence, if any, and may allow amendment of the Record, or further proof in the action. He will dispose of the appeal by adhering to the interlocutor of the sheriff, or recalling it and pronouncing a fresh one. As in the case of the sheriff, the sheriff principal must append to his interlocutor a note setting forth the grounds on which he has proceeded. Appeal on a sentence by a sheriff for contempt of court is competent only in the Court of Session or High Court.[25] No appeal lies when the sheriff was acting in an administrative rather than a judicial capacity.[26]

In summary causes appeal lies from a final judgment to the sheriff principal[27] on a point of law, by way of a stated case containing the sheriff's findings in fact and law and giving a note of his reason for his decision in law. Notice must be given of the points of law to be raised and no other point may be taken. Matters of fact cannot be raised on appeal.[28]

---

[21] Specimen in Appx. C.

[22] *McLaughlin v. Timber Terminal*, 1993 S.C.L.R. 176.

[23] Small Claims Rules, 1988: A.S. (Small Claims Rules) 1988 (S.I. 1988 No. 1976).

[24] Appeal proceedings may be televised with the sheriff principal's approval, and TV pictures, without sound, may be allowed with the consent of the sheriff concerned: [1993] C.L.Y. 5873.

[25] *Forbes v. Forbes*, 1994 S.L.T. 16.

[26] *East Kilbride District Council v. King*, 1994 S.C.L.R. 950.

[27] Sheriff Courts (Scotland) Act 1971, s. 38; *Rediffusion v. McIlroy*, 1986 S.L.T.(Sh.Ct.) 33.

[28] *Gilbey Vintners v. Perry*, 1978 S.L.T.(Sh.Ct.) 48; *McFall v. Lochgorm Warehouses*, 1978 S.L.T.(Sh.Ct.) 67.

In small claims appeal lies to the sheriff principal by note of appeal requesting a stated case, specifying the points of law on which the appeal is to proceed, which is lodged within 14 days. The sheriff prepares a stated case framing appropriate questions of law with a note of his reason for his decision in law, and argument thereon is heard by the sheriff principal. Save on cause shown no new point of law may be raised at the appeal.

Appeal from Sheriff Court to Court of Session and House of Lords

Unless where a particular statute expressly or by clear implication excludes review, appeal is competent to the Court of Session by note of appeal against final judgments of either sheriff or sheriff principal or against certain interlocutors, or in any case with leave,[29] save that in a case tried as a summary cause no appeal is competent unless the sheriff principal after final judgment by him on appeal, certifies the cause as suitable for appeal in the Court of Session,[30] and no appeal lies in a case heard as a small claim. When competent, appeal is by note of appeal. Further appeal to the House of Lords is competent, but only on grounds of law, and that even if further proof has been heard in the Court of Session.

DILIGENCE

When one party obtains a decree against another, as for payment of money as debt or damages, the decree may not be satisfied voluntarily, in which case resort must be had to one or more of the forms of diligence. Some forms of diligence may be used at an early stage in an action to force a debtor to appear, or to compel him to find security for the sum claimed against him pending the decision of the action, but diligence is most commonly used in execution of a judgment. The forms of diligence vary according as it is done against the person or the property of the debtor and according to the kind of property.

The usual basis for diligence is an *extract* of the decree of court, containing a warrant for execution, but diligence may also follow on any writ containing a clause of consent to registration for execution and recorded in the books of a court, which is equivalent to an extracted decree.

---

[29] See, *e.g. Kearney's Exrx. v. MacLeod and Parker*, 1965 S.C. 450. Thus, *e.g.* in *White & Carter (Councils) Ltd v. McGregor*, 1962 S.C.(H.L.) 1 an action was brought in the sheriff court and dismissed after debate; appeal was taken to the Court of Session which allowed a proof before answer; after proof the sheriff-substitute dismissed the action, and the Court of Session on appeal affirmed his decision. The House of Lords by 3 to 2 reversed the Court of Session and the sheriff-substitute. See also *Grant v. N.C.B.*, 1956 S.C.(H.L.) 48; *Designers and Decorators (Scotland) Ltd v. Ellis*, 1957 S.C.(H.L.) 69. If the sheriff made findings in fact and in law the appellant should intimate whether he accepts the findings in fact or not: *Marshall v. Sharp*, 1991 S.L.T. 114.

[30] Sheriff Courts (Scotland) Act 1971, s. 38.

Imprisonment for civil debt or failure to obey a decree is the only form of diligence against the person and is now very limited in application.

Moveable property belonging to the debtor but in the hands of a third party, such as money in a bank, may be attached by *arrestment* and may be taken by a subsequent action of *furthcoming*. Moveable property in the debtor's own hands may be taken in satisfaction of a decree by *poinding*[31] following by sale by auction. As a preliminary to poinding the defender must receive a *charge*, or formal requisition to pay, served by a messenger-at-arms (for a Court of Session decree) or sheriff-officer (for a sheriff court decree).[32]

Adjudication is the means of attaching heritable property and requires a special action in the Court of Session. Other forms of diligence which are less common are *inhibition* which prevents a party transacting to the creditor's prejudice, *poinding of the ground*, which attaches moveables on land belonging to the proprietor of the lands; *maills and duties*, which attaches the rents payable by a debtor's tenants to him, and *sequestration for rent* which entitles a landlord to have a tenant's goods sequestrated, valued and sold. Bankruptcy (or more properly *sequestration*) is not strictly a form of diligence but may be resorted to by a creditor who presents a petition for the sequestration of the debtor as a means of exacting payment of at least part of a claim. It is the legal process whereby a person who is unable to pay his debts in full may surrender, or have all his property transferred by the court, to a trustee, who realises the property and pays creditors proportionately to their claims, after certain preferential claims have been met.

II.—PROCEEDINGS IN SPECIAL COURTS AND TRIBUNALS

It is impossible to discuss briefly and generally the characteristic features of proceedings before special courts and tribunals, since they differ so very much *inter se*. They vary from special courts such as service courts-martial and the Scottish Land Court, which have formal rules of procedure, to tribunals where the greatest informality prevails. In every case the rules and practice of the particular judicial or quasi-judicial body must be looked for and followed. Thus it has been emphasised that in a referral from a children's hearing to the sheriff, the procedure applicable to such proceedings alone applies and none of the rules of civil or criminal procedure apply.[33] Similarly whether appeal lies, to whom, and in what form depends on the statutes and rules applicable to the particular kind of quasi-judicial body in question.

---

[31] Pronounced "pinding."
[32] For procedure see *New Day Furnishing Stores Ltd v. Curran*, 1974 S.L.T.(Sh.Ct.) 20; *Cantors v. Hardie*, 1974 S.L.T.(Sh.Ct.) 26; *Scottish Gas Board v. Johnstone*, 1974 S.L.T.(Sh.Ct.) 65.
[33] *McGregor v. D.*, 1977 S.C. 330.

III.—ARBITRATIONS

Procedure

The procedure in an arbitration is such as the parties may agree, and the degree of formality or informality will depend largely on whether issues of fact or of law bulk larger in the case. The arbiter must accept office and normally appoints a clerk to the arbitration. Counsel or solicitors may be instructed, there may be pleadings in the shape of a claim and answers, written or oral argument, a proof, an inspection of the premises or subject-matter of dispute or otherwise as may be required. The arbiter may consult an expert, such as an engineer, if such assistance is necessary.

The arbiter may submit a draft award or proposed findings to the parties, and allow them to lodge, and be heard on, representations regarding these proposed findings. He may also make an interim award. The final award or decree arbitral narrates the circumstances, the submission, and the procedure which followed, and then makes the final finding and decree, which once issued and delivered to the parties, is beyond recall and binding on them and their successors.

Appeal to the Courts

By accepting arbitration, parties voluntarily exclude the jurisdiction of the courts. In statutory arbitrations there may be an appeal to the courts by case stated,[34] and, subject to express provision to the contrary in an agreement to refer to arbitration, an arbiter or oversman may, on the application of a party, and must, if the Court of Session directs, at any stage in the arbitration state a case for the opinion of that court on a question of law arising in the arbitration.[35] Apart from that the courts will not interfere on the merits, however wrong the arbiter's decision may appear to be in fact or in law or in both, and there is no appeal. The whole object of arbitration is to exclude resort to the courts.

An arbiter's award may however be reduced by an action of reduction in court on the ground that he had an interest, unknown to one party, in the case, or if he proceeds *ultra fines compromissi*, that is, deals with a point beyond the scope of the reference to him, or if he has mistaken the point in issue, or has not exhausted the questions submitted to him, or if there has been corruption, bribery or falsehood, or such a serious error in procedure as amounts to a denial of a principle of natural justice, as, for example, failing to hear one party.[36]

---

[34] *e.g.* under the Agricultural Holdings (Scotland) Act 1991; see, *e.g. MacNab of MacNab v. Willison*, 1960 S.C. 83; *Forsyth-Grant v. Salmon*, 1961 S.C. 54; *Johnson v. Gill*, 1978 S.C. 74; *Grant v. Broadland Properties Estates Ltd*, 1997 S.L.T. 1030.

[35] Administration of Justice (Scotland) Act 1972, s. 3. *e.g. Aberdeen City Council v. Bredero Aberdeen Centre Ltd*, 1998 S.C. 269.

[36] On the need for an arbiter to be impartial, see *Fleming's Trs. v. Henderson*, 1962 S.L.T. 401.

IV.—ALTERNATIVE DISPUTE RESOLUTION

The cost of any kind of litigation has led to a demand for simpler and cheaper methods of resolving disputes. The Faculty of Advocates in 1994 named a panel of members offering parties involved in commercial disputes a new service in any of three forms, early neutral evaluation, mediation and a fast-track hearing of the dispute as a basis for agreement. This is intended to be a quick, flexible and cost-effective means of settling disputes without need for litigation or arbitration.

To try to minimise acrimony in family disputes, the Civil Evidence (Family Mediation) (Scotland) Act 1995 permits family mediation but excludes evidence thereof in subsequent family proceedings.

FURTHER READING

Remedies
Walker: *Law of Civil Remedies in Scotland.*

Court of Session Procedure
Anton: *Civil Jurisdiction in Scotland.*
Black: *An Introduction to Written Pleading.*
McEwan: *Pleading in Court.*
Mackay: *Practice of the Court of Session.*
　　　　Manual of Practice in the Court of Session.
MacLaren: *Court of Session Practice.*
Maxwell: *Court of Session Procedure.*
Mullen and Prosser: *Judicial Review in Scotland.*
Annual Reports: *Civil Judicial Statistics (Scotland).*

Sheriff Court Procedure
Dobie: *Sheriff Court Styles.*
Kearney: *Introduction to Ordinary Civil Procedure in the Sheriff Court.*
Lees: *Handbook of Pleading in the Sheriff Court.*
Macphail: *Sheriff Court Practice.*

Evidence
Walker and Walker: *Law of Evidence in Scotland.*

Diligence
Graham Stewart: *Law of Diligence.*
Maher and Cusine: *Law and Practice of Diligence.*

Expenses
Hastings: *Expenses in the Supreme and Sheriff Courts of Scotland.*
Maclaren: *Expenses in the Court of Session and Sheriff Court.*

Legal Aid
Stoddart: *Law and Practice of Legal Aid in Scotland.*

Arbitration
Hunter: *Law of Arbitration.*
Irons and Melville: *Arbitration.*

CHAPTER 13

THE ADMINISTRATION OF CRIMINAL JUSTICE

THE purpose of criminal proceedings is not so much to obtain a remedy for an injured person as, by the exercise of the power of organised society, to vindicate and enforce law and order, to maintain minimum standards of conduct and to prevent and suppress anti-social, amoral, dangerous, harmful or other detrimental conduct by punishing those who have infringed the code of conduct maintained by the criminal law.

The salient feature of criminal proceedings in Scotland is that public prosecution is the rule and private prosecution uncommon,[1] except in such cases as factory inspectors or officers of Customs and Excise, who are prosecuting in the public interest.[2] Government departments do not prosecute, but in case of need the Lord Advocate acts on their behalf. Nor do the police conduct prosecutions, but transmit information and evidence to the procurator-fiscal with a view to prosecution by him.

The system of public prosecution is directed by the Lord Advocate,[3] who is assisted by the Solicitor-General for Scotland and a number of Advocates-Depute appointed by the Lord Advocate from members of the Bar, known collectively as Crown counsel. There is a small permanent staff headed by the Crown Agent, in the Crown Office in Edinburgh, and permanent officials, the procurators-fiscal, are appointed in each sheriffdom to be responsible for the investigation and prosecution of crime in the sheriff and district courts of the sheriffdom, subject to the overriding control of the Crown Office.[4] It is ultimately the responsibility of the Lord Advocate, in practically all cases, to decide whether to prosecute, in what court, whether on indictment or summarily, and on what charge, though

---

[1] *J. & P. Coats v. Brown*, 1909 S.C. (J.) 29 and the account thereof by Lord Macmillan (who was counsel in the case) in *A Man of Law's Tale* at pp. 110–114; *McBain v. Crichton*, 1961 J.C. 25; *Trapp v. M.*, 1971 S.L.T.(Notes) 30; *Meehan v. Inglis*, 1975 J.C. 9; *X. v. Sweeney*, 1982 J.C. 70; *McDonald v. H.M. Advocate*, 1988 S.L.T. 713.

[2] *e.g. Griffith v. Ferrier*, 1952 J.C. 56; *Fishmongers' Co. v. Bruce*, 1980 S.L.T.(Notes) 35. In practice such cases are usually presented by the procurator-fiscal. See *Houston v. McDonald*, 1989 S.L.T. 276.

[3] On powers and duties, see *Dumfries C.C. v. Phyn* (1895) 22 R. 538. See also Normand, "The Public Prosecutor in Scotland" (1938) 54 L.Q.R. 345. On the privileged position of Lord Advocate and procurators-fiscal in conducting prosecutions, see *Hester v. MacDonald*, 1961 S.C. 370.

[4] Though the control by the Lord Advocate had been developing for a long time, it was only in 1927 that the procurator-fiscal service was made a branch of the Civil Service: Sheriff Courts and Legal Officers Act 1927.

most everyday offences can be dealt with without need to refer to him for instructions. Cases reported by procurators-fiscal are sent to the Crown Office and all High Court indictments are prepared in the Crown Office. There is a Procurator-Fiscal Service Book of Regulations issued to all procurators-fiscal to secure uniformity of practice. All prosecutors are independent of the judiciary and no judge can order one of them to do or not to do anything.

Solemn and Summary Procedure

The important distinction in criminal proceedings is that between solemn procedure (trial on *indictment* before a judge of the High Court of Justiciary and a jury, or before a sheriff principal or sheriff and a jury), and summary procedure (trial on *complaint* before a sheriff principal or sheriff, or magistrate, or one or more justices of the peace, in each case without a jury). This distinction depends mainly on the gravity of the particular crime in question and on whether the limited powers of sentence of a sheriff or magistrate seem adequate, if a conviction is obtained. Some serious crimes are triable on indictment only, but most may be tried in either manner depending on the circumstances and gravity of the case. The decision whether to prosecute on indictment or summarily is vested in the Crown officers. The course of procedure followed and the measure of punishment competent differs in the two cases. Crimes created by statute are frequently prescribed as being "punishable on summary complaint" or "punishable by a court of summary jurisdiction" only.

The High Court has exclusive jurisdiction in cases of treason, murder, rape, incest, deforcement of messengers, breach of duty by magistrates, and cases of certain statutory offences, and may try all crimes unless its jurisdiction is expressly or impliedly excluded by statute. Other serious crimes may be tried in the High Court or before a sheriff and jury. The sheriff court has jurisdiction over all crimes not within the exclusive competence of the High Court. District courts may try cases only if jurisdiction is conferred on them by statute expressly or by implication.[5]

In all courts, procedure is accusatorial, requiring each side to present evidence for the consideration of the judge and, if there is one, the jury, and not inquisitorial, the mode of procedure in which the judge conducts inquiry into the facts before the accused is charged.

A fundamental principle of all criminal procedure is that a person questioned or accused is presumed innocent and the onus of proof rests on the prosecution. Moreover, the standard of proof is proof beyond reasonable doubt, which is more demanding than the standard in civil cases.[6]

---

[5] *McPherson v. Boyd* (1907) 5 Adam 246; *Torrance v. Robertson*, 1946 J.C. 135.

[6] The following description of procedure deals with the main points only and is intended to enable the reader to read reports of cases with understanding.

PRELIMINARIES—INVESTIGATION AND APPREHENSION

A person believed to have committed a crime may be arrested on the spot,[7] or arrested after the police have made inquiries and obtained a warrant for his arrest as a person suspected. After arrest a suspect may be charged at once or after preliminary questioning, or he may be released. Once arrested a suspect should be cautioned to the effect that anything he says will be taken down and may be used in evidence. Failure to caution a suspect or interrogating him harshly has sometimes resulted in an alleged "confession" being held inadmissible at his trial.[8] Alternatively a person may be detained for a limited time to enable investigations to be carried out. He may be searched, fingerprinted and questioned but is not obliged to answer any questions.[9] Alternatively a person may be asked to come to a police station to be interviewed.[10] Such a person may be later detained and charged, or released.

Any person or body may bring a matter to the notice of the procurator-fiscal and in serious cases he participates in the investigation of an apparent crime, but in the majority of cases inquiries are made by the police and reported to the procurator-fiscal.

SOLEMN PROCEDURE

Petition

Solemn procedure is initiated by the procurator-fiscal presenting a petition to a sheriff, naming the accused, stating the charge and craving warrants to arrest the accused, search him and his premises, cite witnesses and, after examination, to commit the accused for further examination or until liberated in due course of law. The police also have common law and statutory powers of arrest without warrant in various circumstances. The Crown authorities may obtain warrant to have a special examination made of a suspect,[11] or a search of his house,[12] and—in emergency—examination may be made without warrant.[13]

---

[7] A private person may arrest a suspect where circumstances are strongly indicative of his having committed a crime: *Wightman v. Lees*, 1999 S.C.C.R. 664. The police have greater powers of arrest, in many cases without a warrant.

[8] *Rigg v. H.M. Advocate*, 1946 J.C. 1; *H.M. Advocate v. Chalmers*, 1954 J.C. 56; *Miln v. Cullen*, 1967 J.C. 21; *H.M. Advocate v. Brown*, 1966 S.L.T. 105; *Jones v. Milne*, 1975 S.L.T. 2; *Balloch v. H.M. Advocate*, 1977 J.C. 23; *H.M. Advocate v. Friel*, 1978 S.L.T.(Notes) 21; *Hartley v. H.M. Advocate*, 1979 S.L.T. 26. Whether the evidence should be admitted or not may be investigated in a "trial within a trial," *i.e.* a hearing of the evidence in the absence of the jury to determine whether it should be repeated to the jury.

[9] Criminal Justice (Scotland) Act 1980, ss. 2–3. See, *e.g. Grant v. H.M. Advocate*, 1990 S.L.T. 402.

[10] This is called "helping the police with their inquiries."

[11] *Hay v. H.M. Advocate*, 1968 J.C. 40.

[12] *Stewart v. Roach*, 1950 S.C. 318.

[13] *Bell v. Hogg*, 1967 J.C. 49.

First Examination

On being arrested an accused is entitled to have a solicitor summoned and to have an interview with him. A person arrested on a serious criminal charge must be brought before a magistrate, usually a sheriff, as soon as possible, for examination. First examination is now normally a brief and formal appearance. The proceedings are private. The charge is read and he is cautioned. Normally he makes no *plea* or *declaration* but, if he does, it is taken down and signed by him and by the sheriff and some of those present as witnesses. A witness may also make a declaration on oath and is not entitled subsequently to have it destroyed.[14] He may then be committed to prison for further examination, or committed for trial, or released on bail. If the Crown thereafter deserts the diet *simpliciter* or intimates that it is not proceeding with the prosecution the case is at an end and subsequent indictment is incompetent.[15]

Judicial Examination

The fiscal may have the accused brought to court for judicial examination. He is not put on oath and is warned that he need not answer any question; he is entitled to have his solicitor with him and consult him. He is questioned by the fiscal to elicit any explanation he may have of his involvement in the matters charged and if he has a reasonable explanation he will normally be anxious to put it forward but may decline to answer. The record of the judicial examination may be put in evidence at his subsequent trial.[16]

Bail

An accused, in all cases except treason and murder, is entitled to release on bail unless the Crown objects. It is then a question for the court's discretion whether to grant or refuse release on bail having regard to the nature of the crime. Bail was formerly the deposit of money to ensure that an accused appeared at court, forfeited if he did not. It now means release on conditions to be laid down by the court or the Lord Advocate,[17] to ensure that the accused appears at future court diets and does not commit offences while on bail. In special cases money may be required to be deposited.[18] The danger of the accused absconding or tampering with witnesses or committing further offences, and his criminal record are all

---

[14] *Coll., Petr.*, 1978 S.L.T. 58.

[15] *Thom v. H.M. Advocate*, 1976 J.C. 48.

[16] *e.g. Alexander v. H.M. Advocate*, 1989 S.L.T. 193; *Moran v. H.M. Advocate*, 1990 S.C.C.R. 40.

[17] There are four statutory conditions of bail: to appear at court when required, not to commit an offence while on bail, not to interfere with witnesses, and to be available for inquiries or report: Criminal Justice (Scotland) Act 1995, s. 1. It is an offence to breach any condition of bail; *ibid.* s. 2.

[18] Bail (Scotland) Act 1980; Criminal Justice (Scotland) Act 1995, ss. 1–5.

factors to be considered.[19] The grant or refusal of bail may be appealed to the High Court.[20]

Indictment

The case is then reported to the Crown Office and the accused's release, or the suitable mode of trial, ordered, and an *indictment*[21] is then prepared. It is at the instance of Her Majesty's Advocate, and must be served on the accused.[22] It sets out the crimes charged and lists the witnesses and productions, *i.e.* documents and articles to be produced, to be adduced at the trial. To enable him to prepare his defence, an accused may apply to the court for a commission and diligence to enable him to recover documents in the hands of third parties.[23] Statute provides that a person cannot be detained in custody for more than 80 days without an indictment being served on him, failing which he must be liberated,[24] that an accused may not be detained in custody under a warrant on a petition committing him for trial for more than 110 days without being brought to trial,[25] and that a person not in custody must have his trial on indictment commenced within one year from the date of first appearance on petition, failing which he must be freed.[26] The Lord Advocate may apply for an extension of the period,[27] and release from custody interrupts the running of the period even if an indictment has been served.[28] An accused who wishes to plead guilty and have the disposal of his case expedited may do so by letter to the Crown Agent.[29] The accused may then be sentenced.[30]

The Preliminary Diet

A person indicted had formerly to appear at two diets of trial, the first or pleading diet and the second or trial diet.[31] Now a preliminary diet is held on written notice to the court, usually by the accused or if the trial is to be in the sheriff court, a first diet is held to ascertain if both sides are ready to go to trial.[32] It usually takes the form of a debate. The accused

---

[19] *A.B. v. Dickson*, 1907 S.C.(J.) 111; *Mackintosh v. McGlinchy*, 1921 J.C. 75; *MacDonald v. Clifford*, 1952 J.C. 22; *MacLeod v. Wright*, 1959 J.C. 12.

[20] *Mackintosh, supra*; *MacLeod, supra*; *H.M. Advocate v. Renicks*, 1998 S.C.C.R. 417.

[21] Pronounced "inditement."

[22] Specimen form in Renton and Brown, *Criminal Procedure* (5th ed.), and Appx. D hereof.

[23] *H.M. Advocate v. Hasson*, 1971 J.C. 35.

[24] This is known as "the 80-day rule."

[25] This is known as "the 110-day rule."

[26] This is known as "the one-year rule." The lapse of this time does not exclude a complainer from seeking to present a bill for criminal letters against the accused, *i.e.* initiate a private prosecution: *C. v. Forsyth*, 1995 S.L.T. 905.

[27] Criminal Procedure (Scotland) Act 1975, s. 101; see, *e.g. H.M. Advocate v. Park*, 1967 J.C. 70; *Hartley v. H.M. Advocate*, 1970 J.C. 17; *H.M. Advocate v. McTavish*, 1974 S.L.T. 246; *H.M. Advocate v. Shevlin*, 1986 S.C.C.R. 462; *Rudge v. H.M. Advocate*, 1989 S.C.C.R. 105.

[28] *H.M. Advocate v. McCann*, 1977 J.C. 1.

[29] Criminal Procedure (Scotland) Act 1975, s. 102.

[30] *e.g. H.M. Advocate v. Cairns*, 1967 J.C. 37; *Mackie v. H.M. Advocate,* 1969 J.C. 20.

[31] The Criminal Justice (Scotland) Act 1980, s. 12 abolished the mandatory first diet.

[32] Criminal Justice (Scotland) Act 1995, s. 13.

may object to the *competency* of the proceedings or to the *relevancy* or legal sufficiency of the charge.[33] These objections raise issues of law only.[34] He has at this stage to tender any *plea in bar of trial* he wishes to put forward; these include that he was under the age of criminal responsibility, that he is presently *insane*, unable to plead and to give instructions for his defence, that a libel in the same form as the indictment and based on the same facts has previously been held irrelevant,[35] or that he already *tholed an assize, i.e.* been tried for the same offence. He had also at this stage to tender any *special defence* which he wished to rely on.[36] Special defences are probably limited to the pleas of *insanity at the time of committing the crime, alibi, i.e.* that he was not there but at another stated place, *incrimination, i.e.* that the crime was not committed by him but by another named person, and *self-defence*.[37]

An appeal may be taken from a preliminary diet to the High Court by note of appeal.[38]

The Trial Diet

At the trial diet, which is always called in the court which has jurisdiction to try the accused, unless the panel (as the accused is now called), when called on to plead, pleads guilty, a jury of 15 is empanelled, and the substance of the indictment read to it. The Crown and the accused may each challenge three jurors without giving a reason, and any others on cause shown, *e.g.* known enmity. There should be no questioning of prospective jurors as to facts which might prejudice them.[39] The clerk then reads to the jury the charge. It is then sworn and any special defence read to the jury. There is no opening speech and Crown counsel (High Court) or the procurator-fiscal (sheriff and jury court) proceeds at once to examine his witnesses. Each is in turn sworn by the presiding judge, examined-in-chief by the Crown counsel or procurator-fiscal, cross-examined by defence counsel and, if need be, re-examined by Crown counsel or the procurator-fiscal. Cross-examination may be selective and the defence need not cross-examine every witness on material points.[40] If

---

[33] *e.g. H.M. Advocate v. Mannion*, 1961 J.C. 69; *H.M. Advocate v. Cairns, supra*; *H.M. Advocate v. R.M.*, 1969 J.C. 52; *Cameron v. H.M. Advocate*, 1971 J.C. 50.

[34] Debates on difficult cases of competency or relevancy may be heard by three judges of the High Court, *e.g. H.M. Advocate v. Cairns*, 1967 J.C. 37; *H.M. Advocate v. McKenzie*, 1970 S.L.T. 81.

[35] *H.M. Advocate v. Mullen*, 1987 S.L.T. 475. See also, *Docherty v. H.M. Advocate*, 2000 J.C. 307.

[36] On preparation for trial and the practice of the Crown to give a measure of assistance to the defence, see *Smith v. H.M. Advocate*, 1952 J.C. 66; *Hasson v. H.M. Advocate*, 1971 J.C. 35.

[37] On special defences see *H.M. Advocate v. Kidd*, 1960 J.C. 61; *H.M. Advocate v. Hayes*, 1973 S.L.T. 202; *Lambie v. H.M. Advocate*, 1973 S.L.T. 219; *Brennan v. H.M. Advocate*, 1977 J.C. 38.

[38] *e.g. H.M. Advocate v. Harris*, 1993 S.L.T. 963 (heard by five judges); *Justice v. H.M. Advocate*, 1995 S.L.T. 1011.

[39] *McCadden v. H.M. Advocate*, 1986 S.L.T. 138.

[40] *McPherson v. Copeland*, 1961 J.C. 74.

the accused on judicial examination emitted a declaration, it is read to the jury at the end of the Crown evidence. The Crown must prove the facts necessary to convince the jury *beyond reasonable doubt* that the accused did the things charged. As in civil actions the evidence may be oral evidence of observation, expert evidence, real or circumstantial evidence[41] or written evidence, but the rules as to admission or rejection of evidence are more strictly applied than in civil cases. Importance attaches to corroboration; by Scots law every essential fact must be corroborated, *i.e.* the evidence must be supported by independent evidence from another witness or from facts and circumstances justifying an inference to the same effect.[42]

At the conclusion of the Crown case the presiding judge may, with the consent of the Lord Advocate or his representative prosecuting, if satisfied that there is no evidence to support a conviction, withdraw the case from the jury, or the panel's counsel may submit that there is no case to answer, in which case the judge must hear the submissions outwith the presence of the jury; if it succeeds the judge acquits the panel. Otherwise the defence witnesses are called and examined by defence counsel, cross-examined and, if need be, re-examined. If the panel gives evidence, he usually does so first, and from the witness-box, on oath. If the panel has put forward a special defence he must support it by evidence, but it is enough if he satisfies the jury *on balance of probabilities*. If his defence is a mere denial, he need not give evidence at all but merely argue that the Crown has failed to prove its case beyond reasonable doubt. A question which frequently causes difficulty is identification of the accused; is the man in the dock the one who was seen or heard to do the crime?[43] Neither panel nor witness may make any unsworn statement, nor make any statement except by way of evidence.[44] The evidence is recorded by a shorthand-writer and the judge makes notes for his own use.

Thereafter prosecuting and defence counsel successively address the jury, and the judge charges the jury, instructing them in the relevant law and on the points in issue.[45] He must instruct the jury that the onus of proof is throughout on the Crown, that all material factors in the evidence must be corroborated, that the jury must evaluate the evidence and decide which evidence to accept and which to reject, that before convicting the

---

[41] See, *e.g. H.M. Advocate v. Kidd*, 1960 J.C. 61; *Ryrie v. Campbell*, 1964 J.C. 33.

[42] *e.g. Sinclair v. MacLeod*, 1964 J.C. 19; *H.M. Advocate v. W.B.*, 1969 J.C. 72. There are exceptions; see, *e.g. Gerber v. B.R. Board*, 1969 J.C. 7.

[43] On identification see *Cameron v. H.M. Advocate*, 1959 J.C. 59; *Patterson v. Nixon*, 1960 J.C. 42; *Sinclair v. MacLeod*, 1964 J.C. 19; *Hay v. H.M. Advocate*, 1968 J.C. 40; *Muldoon v. Herron*, 1970 J.C. 30; *Temple v. H.M. Advocate*, 1971 J.C. 1.

[44] *Gilmour v. H.M. Advocate*, 1965 J.C. 45.

[45] *Hamilton v. H.M. Advocate*, 1938 J.C. 134; *Rubin v. H.M. Advocate*, 1984 S.C.C.R. 96; *King v. H.M. Advocate*, 1985 S.C.C.R. 322. For specimens of presiding judge's charge to a jury, see, *e.g. Bird v. H.M. Advocate*, 1952 J.C. 23; *H.M. Advocate v. Kidd*, 1960 J.C. 61.

jury must have been satisfied beyond reasonable doubt[46] of the panel's guilt, and as to the possible verdicts. He may have to instruct them as to a defence plea of insanity, diminished responsibility or alibi, or other special defence,[47] as to treating the evidence of certain witnesses with particular care, and may have to instruct them to return a verdict of not guilty on a count on which no legally adequate evidence has been adduced.[48] The panel may at any stage change his plea to one of "guilty as libelled" or to a modified plea of guilty, in which case the judge directs the jury to return a verdict of guilty in terms of the confession.[49] The prosecutor may at any stage abandon the prosecution in whole or in part, in which case the judge directs the jury to return a verdict of not guilty.

At the conclusion of the charge, the jury may give a verdict at once, or retire to the jury room to consider it. If the jury wish to ask questions or wish further directions from the judge, they should be brought back into court and further directions should be given in open court.[50] The jury verdict may be returned by a majority and may, unless they have been specially directed in law that one or another is not open to them, be any one of "guilty," "not guilty," or "not proven."[51] It is announced in reply to a question from the clerk of the court, by the chancellor (more commonly called foreman) of the jury. The verdict discloses whether the jury was unanimous or divided, but the size of the majority is not disclosed. Some jurors may have voted for each of these possible verdicts,[52] but the panel is liable to be convicted only if at least eight jurors vote for "guilty."[53] The verdict is recorded, read over to the jury, and their assent to its terms recorded. Thereafter, the verdict cannot be amended.[54] If there are several counts in the indictment, the jury must bring in a verdict on each count.

If the verdict is one of "not guilty" or "not proven", the accused is at once assoilzied from the charge and discharged. If the verdict is one of "guilty", prosecuting counsel moves his Lordship to pass sentence, without which no sentence can be passed,[55] and, if any previous convictions are relied on, lays before the presiding judge a copy of the notice of previous convictions previously served on the accused. If these are disputed they will have to be proved. Defending counsel may make a plea in bar of

---

[46] In civil cases the onus is on the pursuer to satisfy the court or jury on the balance of probabilities only: *Hendry v. Clan Line Steamers*, 1949 S.C. 320.

[47] The presiding judge or sheriff must direct the jury as to how to treat any special defence: *Donnelly v. H.M. Advocate,* 1977 S.L.T. 147.

[48] On charging juries, see *McKenzie v. H.M. Advocate*, 1959 J.C. 32; *McPhelim v. H.M. Advocate*, 1960 J.C. 17; *McCann v. H.M. Advocate,* 1960 J.C. 36.

[49] *H.M. Advocate v. Dunlop*, 1974 S.L.T. 242.

[50] *McColl v. H.M. Advocate*, 1989 S.L.T. 691; *Kerr v. H.M. Advocate*, 1992 S.L.T. 1031.

[51] On the Not Proven verdict, see J. G. Wilson, "Not Proven"; *McNicol v. H.M. Advocate*, 1964 J.C. 25.

[52] See *Lord Advocate v. Nicholson*, 1958 S.L.T.(Sh.Ct.) 17; *Kerr, supra*.

[53] *McPhelim v. H.M. Advocate*, 1960 J.C. 17, 22.

[54] *McGarry v. H.M. Advocate*, 1959 J.C. 30.

[55] See *Noon v. H.M. Advocate*, 1960 J.C. 52.

sentence, such as that the verdict is ambiguous, or that the accused has become insane. He then addresses the court in mitigation of punishment and may adduce witnesses (who should be sworn)[56] in support of his plea in mitigation, after which the presiding judge pronounces sentence. He may adjourn the case, but not for more than three weeks at a time, to consider what sentence is suitable or to permit of inquiries being made as to the accused's physical or mental condition or his suitability for particular kinds of punishment or treatment. If the trial has been before a sheriff and jury, the sheriff may remit the panel to the High Court for sentence if he thinks that any sentence which he can pronounce is inadequate.[57]

Appeal

A person convicted on indictment in the High Court or sheriff court[58] may appeal to the High Court of Justiciary sitting as Court of Criminal Appeal.[59] Appeal may be taken (a) against conviction, on any question of law alone, or (b) against sentence, unless the sentence is fixed by law or (c) against both conviction and sentence.[60] The appeal is initiated by completing and lodging within 14 days an intimation of intention to appeal, followed within six weeks by a note of appeal stating the grounds of appeal.[61] Full specification of the grounds of appeal must be stated and not merely a vague objection to the conviction.[62] The judge who presided at the trial must furnish a written report of his opinion on the case generally and on the grounds in the note of appeal. The appeal is considered first by a single judge of the High Court in chambers without the parties being present. He may grant leave to appeal, or refuse it in which case the appellant may appeal by letter against the refusal of leave to appeal, in which case the matter will be considered by the High Court in chambers without the parties being present, and leave granted or refused.[63] The appellant may be released on bail pending the appeal but such applications are not regarded favourably. If released on bail the period of liberation is not counted towards his period of sentence.

Sessions of the High Court are held in Edinburgh every few weeks for the disposal of appeals, and the Bench normally consists of the Lord Justice-General or Lord Justice-Clerk and two other Lords Commissioners of Justiciary, though a larger Bench may be convened to hear cases

---

[56] *Forbes v. H.M. Advocate*, 1963 J.C. 68.
[57] See, *e.g. H.M. Advocate v. Churchill*, 1963 J.C. 6.
[58] *i.e.* after trial before a sheriff and jury.
[59] Criminal Procedure (Scotland) Act 1995, s. 106.
[60] This applies only to treason and murder and formerly to capital murder.
[61] Criminal Justice (Scotland) Act, 1980, Sched. 2.
[62] *Boyd v. H.M. Advocate*, 1939 J.C. 6; *Reilly v. H.M. Advocate*, 1950 J.C. 52; Practice Note [1985] C.L.Y. 3876.
[63] [1995] C.L.Y. 5768.

of particular importance.[64] The appellant may present a written case, but usually oral argument is presented by counsel. The appellant may be present in court, in the custody of two warders, except in the case of appeals on law alone. The Crown is represented by one or more of the Advocates-Depute and sometimes by one of the Law Officers.

The court have before them the trial judge's notes and his report giving his opinion on the case or on any point arising therein and, if necessary, a transcript of the shorthand-writer's notes of the evidence and proceedings at the trial. They may order the production of documents or the attendance of further witnesses for examination, so long as the witnesses could not have been examined at the trial.[65] If fresh evidence is admitted the court must consider whether the jury verdict would necessarily have been different if it had heard both the evidence now adduced and that put before it at the trial.

Where the appeal is on a matter of law alone, counsel for the appellant proceeds at once with his argument, after which Crown counsel replies. In considering any criticism of the trial judge's charge, the court will have regard to the whole of it, not merely to some phrase.[66]

The court is empowered[67] to allow the appeal if they think that the verdict of the jury should be set aside on the ground that there was a miscarriage of justice. This covers an unreasonable verdict,[68] error in law in the proceedings[69] or misdirection by the trial judge.[70] If the court allow the appeal they quash the conviction and discharge the accused. The court may also allow an appeal but substitute a verdict of guilty of another charge, and impose a sentence therefor.[71] In other cases they dismiss the appeal, and the court may dismiss the appeal even if of the opinion that the point raised in the appeal might be decided in favour of the appellant, if they consider that no substantial miscarriage of justice has actually

---

[64] A notable instance is *Sugden v. H.M. Advocate*, 1934 J.C. 103. Appeals against sentence may be disposed of by two judges, Criminal Justice (Scotland) Act 1995, s. 43.

[65] As, for example, when it has only later been discovered that those witnesses had any knowledge of the facts in issue. See further, *Lowson v. H.M. Advocate*, 1943 J.C. 141; *Lennie v. H.M. Advocate*, 1946 J.C. 79; *Gallacher v. H.M. Advocate* 1951 J.C. 38.

[66] *Reynolds v. H.M. Advocate*, 1928 S.N. 103; *McEwan v. H.M. Advocate*, 1939 J.C. 26; *McPhelim v. H.M. Advocate*, 1960 J.C. 17.

[67] Criminal Procedure (Scotland) Act 1995, s. 118 as amended.

[68] This covers cases where the jury convicted on inadequate evidence, *e.g.* *Morton v. H.M. Advocate*, 1938 J.C. 50. The test is not whether the court agrees or disagrees with the jury's verdict, but whether the jury's verdict was so flagrantly wrong and unreasonable that no reasonable jury acting honestly under proper direction could have given it: *Webb v. H.M. Advocate*, 1927 J.C. 92.

[69] This includes irrelevancy of the indictment, wrongful admission or exclusion of evidence, and misdirection of the jury by the presiding judge, as by laying down the wrong rule of law, or failing to direct them on some matter.

[70] *e.g.* failure to direct the jury on onus of proof, or corroboration; *Stillie v. H.M. Advocate*, 1990 S.C.C.R. 719.

[71] *McKenzie v. H.M. Advocate*, 1959 J.C. 32.

occurred.[72] If the appeal is dismissed the court may reduce or alter the sentence.[73] The court now has power to order a retrial,[74] as when sitting as Courts-Martial Appeal Court,[75] and may allow fresh evidence to be led.[76]

The Court is frequently asked to allow an appeal because fresh evidence has emerged. The evidence must have been something which came to light after the trial and could not have been led at the trial. The appeal court may reject evidence which no reasonable jury would have regarded as credible or reliable,[77] but if it would have been credible and reliable it may allow the appeal and direct a retrial.[78]

Where the appeal is against sentence alone, a written note of appeal is lodged and counsel argues for reduction or variation; in practice Crown counsel do not exercise their right of reply, unless called on by the court. The court may quash the sentence and pass any other sentence legally allowed, or increase it,[79] or affirm the sentence and dismiss the appeal. All aspects of sentence are appealable. The Lord Advocate has power to appeal against a sentence as being unduly lenient.[80]

The remedy of advocation is competent to the Crown where an indictment is dismissed on a preliminary ground.

Where an accused has been acquitted the Lord Advocate may make a reference to the High Court for a ruling on a point of law, without prejudice to the acquittal.[81] In 1999, the Scottish Criminal Cases Review Commission, a body of persons appointed by the First Ministers, took over from the Secretary of State for Scotland[82] powers to consider alleged miscarriages of justice and refer cases meeting relevant criteria to the Appeal Court for review.

---

[72] This is known as "the proviso." It is intended to prevent convictions having to be quashed because of some trivial objection, which is valid, but does not at all disturb the rightness of the conviction. For the rather differently worded powers which regulate the court when sitting as Courts-Martial Appeal Court, see Court-Martial Appeal Act 1968, s. 12.

[73] *Connelly v. H.M. Advocate,* 1954 J.C. 90.

[74] In 1990 James McGhee was jailed for life for murder but an appeal succeeded. The court allowed a new trial and in 1991 McGhee was again convicted and jailed for life. Retrials have been allowed in several lesser cases. An accused convicted of culpable homicide on a charge of murder and, the conviction having been quashed on appeal and a retrial allowed, can be again indicted of murder: *H.M. Advocate v. Boyle,* 1993 S.L.T. 577, 1079, 1085.

[75] Criminal Appeal Act 1964, s. 6(5) and Sched. 1.

[76] *Slater v. H.M. Advocate,* 1928 J.C. 94; *Lowson v. H.M. Advocate,* 1943 J.C. 141; *Thompson v. H.M. Advocate,* 1968 J.C. 61; *Henderson v. H.M. Advocate,* 1970 J.C. 52; *Temple v. H.M. Advocate,* 1971 J.C. 1.

[77] *Tolmie v. H.M. Advocate,* 1998 S.L.T. 508.

[78] *Church v. H.M. Advocate,* 1996 S.L.T. 383; *Mitchell v. H.M. Advocate,* 1996 S.C.C.R. 477.

[79] *Boyle v. H.M. Advocate,* 1949 S.L.T.(Notes) 40; *Connelly v. H.M. Advocate,* 1954 J.C. 90; *Grant v. H.M. Advocate,* 1985 S.C.C.R. 431; *Donnelly v. H.M. Advocate,* 1988 S.C.C.R. 386.

[80] *H.M. Advocate v. Jamieson,* 1997 S.L.T. 955; *H.M. Advocate v. Hodgson,* 1998 S.C.C.R. 320; *H.M. Advocate v. Heron,* 1998 S.C.C.R. 449.

[81] Criminal Justice (Scotland) Act 1980, s. 37. See, *e.g. Lord Advocate's Reference No. 1 of 1983,* 1984 J.C. 52.

[82] Criminal Procedure (Scotland) Act 1995; *H.M. Advocate v. McPhee,* 1994 S.L.T. 1292; *H.M. Advocate v. Bell,* 1995 S.L.T. 350.

Appeal procedure does not affect the royal prerogative of mercy which may be exercised on the recommendation of the Secretary of State[83] and now of the First Minister.[84]

SUMMARY CRIMINAL PROCEDURE

Summary criminal procedure is followed by all courts in Scotland having criminal jurisdiction, other than the High Court of Justiciary,[85] when criminal jurisdiction is exercised by the sheriff or other inferior judge sitting alone and without a jury.[86] The sheriff court has jurisdiction to try all common law offences except murder, rape, incest and wilful fire-raising, and also statutory offences, except where that jurisdiction is expressly or impliedly excluded,[87] and certain crimes must be tried by the sheriff. Courts other than the sheriff court have jurisdiction to try minor common law crimes, but statutory offences only if the statute clearly confers such jurisdiction.[88] Apart from that principle and from the provisions of any relevant statute, it rests with the Lord Advocate and the procurators-fiscal to decide in which court a summary prosecution is to commence.

Alternatives to Prosecution

A fiscal may issue to a person reported a warning that his behaviour has been unacceptable and any repetition will result in prosecution. Or he may try to direct an offender to accepting guidance from a voluntary body such as Alcoholics Anonymous. Or in minor road traffic offences he may offer an accused the chance to pay a fixed penalty with or without endorsement of licence rather than be prosecuted.[89] Or, in offences triable by a district court the fiscal may offer alleged offenders an opportunity to pay a fine (a "fiscal fine") as an alternative to being prosecuted; refusal will result in prosecution.[90] For certain kinds of traffic offences, a police constable or traffic warden may give a fixed penalty notice to a person or attach it to the car. Failure to pay results in the penalty being recoverable as a fine.[91]

---

[83] *e.g. Hall v. H.M. Advocate,* 1998 S.C.C.R. 525; *Campbell v. H.M. Advocate,* 1998 J.C. 130.

[84] *H.M. Advocate v. Waddell,* 1976 S.L.T.(Notes) 61; *Gilmour v. H.M. Advocate,* 1989 S.L.T. 881. The Secretary of State's failure to recommend is not actionable: *Leitch v. Secretary of State for Scotland,* 1982 S.L.T.(Sh.Ct.) 76.

[85] These courts are the sheriff courts and district courts. Procedure is uniform for all these courts.

[86] The main procedural statute is the Criminal Procedure (Scotland) Act 1995 and the Criminal Justice (Scotland) Act 1995, replacing earlier Acts in similar terms, later substantially amended.

[87] *Wilson v. Hill,* 1943 J.C. 124.

[88] *McPherson v. Boyd,* 1907 S.C. (J.) 42; *Czajkowski v. Lewis,* 1956 J.C. 8.

[89] Road Traffic Offenders Act, 1988, ss. 75–77.

[90] Criminal Justice (Scotland) Act 1987, s. 56 and Fixed Penalty Order 1996 (S.I. 1996 No. 617).

[91] Road Traffic Offenders Act 1988, ss. 54–68.

Prosecution

Nearly all prosecutions in the sheriff court are initiated by the procurator-fiscal in the public interest, but some are initiated by other persons prosecuting in the public interest such as factory inspectors,[92] and some by private persons statutorily authorised to prosecute for statutory offences; this includes such as British Railways Board.[93] Prosecutions in the district court are initiated by the procurator-fiscal.

Initiation of Proceedings

In some cases an accused has been arrested and may be in custody, but is usually on bail or has merely been ordained to appear, sometimes under penalty, but he has frequently merely been reported by the police as having committed an offence and has never been in custody. There is no petition to a sheriff, judicial examination, declaration or committal for trial.

A contravention of a statutory prohibition must be prosecuted within six months unless the particular statute or order fixes a different period.

Complaint

Summary criminal proceedings are instituted by the service on the accused of a *complaint*[94] and, in the case of a statutory offence, a relative notice of the penalties to which the accused is liable on conviction. This runs in the name of the procurator-fiscal or other prosecutor[95] and states the substance of the charge against the accused, adding, in the case of a statutory contravention, that it is contrary to a specified section of a particular Act. If previous convictions are to be laid before the court by the prosecutor, notice is served separately of those on which it is intended to rely, but they are not disclosed to the judge until after conviction. The complaint is signed by the prosecutor.

In many cases of statutory contraventions such as road traffic offences, the accused pleads guilty by letter, in which case sentence may be pronounced in his absence.

When the complaint is called in court, the accused must personally plead to it, if he has not already done so by letter, and the trial may take place then but, as a rule, if he pleads not guilty, an adjourned diet is fixed for trial.

Prior to pleading, the accused may state objections to the competency or relevancy of the complaint[96] or pleas in bar of trial.[97] The complaint

---

[92] *e.g. Griffith v. Ferrier*, 1952 J.C. 56; *Simpson v. Hardie & Smith, Ltd*, 1968 J.C. 23.

[93] *e.g. Gerber v. British Railways Board*, 1969 J.C. 7.

[94] For specimen, see Appx. E.

[95] Certain officials, such as factory inspectors, may prosecute in their own names. A local authority has no title to institute a private prosecution: *McKinstry v. Lanark C.C.*, 1962 J.C. 16.

[96] See, *e.g. McLennan v. MacMillan*, 1964 J.C. 1; *Dean v. Menzies*, 1981 J.C. 23.

[97] On whether a special defence need be intimated in advance in summary procedure see *Adam v. MacNeill*, 1972 J.C. 1.

may accordingly be dismissed[98] or amended at this stage. The disposal of a plea to competency or relevancy may be appealed.[99]

Intermediate Diet

An intermediate diet may be held between service off the complaint and the trial diet to determine whether both sides will be ready for trial when the due date comes, so as to avoid citing witnesses unnecessarily.[1]

Trial

At the adjourned diet of trial the accused, who may be represented by counsel but usually is represented by a solicitor, or who may have elected to defend himself, is again called on personally to plead and many accused, at this stage, change their plea to one of guilty, or of guilty to a modified charge. If the accused pleads guilty and his plea is accepted by the procurator-fiscal, the sheriff proceeds to consider previous convictions, hears any plea in mitigation offered, and pronounces sentence. If the accused adheres to his plea of not guilty the trial proceeds; the proceedings are conducted fairly informally and summarily and only brief notes of the evidence are taken by the sheriff. The witnesses for the prosecution are called by the procurator-fiscal, and examined, cross-examined and re-examined in the usual way. At the close of the prosecution case the defence may submit that there is no case to answer. If this is upheld, the accused is acquitted. If it is rejected the case proceeds. The rejection of such a submission may be appealed.[2] If not, the accused himself, if he wishes, and any witnesses for the accused, give evidence. The rules of evidence are the same as in trials under solemn procedure. Thereafter, the procurator-fiscal and counsel or solicitor for the accused address the court. Objections to evidence may be taken in the course of the trial and must be noted, if requested, so as to be available for appeal. No previous conviction should be disclosed, even by implication, until the judge is satisfied that the charge has been proved.[3]

The judge must himself determine the credibility and veracity of witnesses and decide whether he finds the charge proved beyond reasonable doubt or not. The judge normally pronounces his finding at once; if it is "not guilty" or "not proven", the accused is liberated at once; if "guilty" any previous convictions, notice of which has been served on the accused, if they are admitted or proved, are laid before the sheriff; the accused or his counsel or solicitor may address the court in mitigation before sentence is pronounced.

---

[98] See, *e.g. Aitchison v. Bartlett*, 1963 J.C. 27.

[99] *e.g. Francis v. Cardle*, 1987 S.C.C.R. 1. See also *Milne v. Gauld*, 1986 S.L.T. 431.

[1] Criminal Justice (Scotland) Act 1995, s. 48; Criminal Procedure (Intermediate Diets) (Scotland) Act 1998.

[2] *Wingate v. McGlennan*, 1991 S.C.C.R. 133.

[3] *Bryce v. Gardiner*, 1951 J.C. 134; *MacGregor v. Macdonald*, 1952 J.C. 4; *Clark v. Connell*, 1952 J.C. 119.

The sentence is usually one of fine or imprisonment, and a fine is sometimes paid on the spot, but an accused is entitled, save exceptionally, to have time to pay or to be allowed to pay by instalments. In many road traffic cases, the sheriff must order the offender's driving licence to be endorsed and may, or must, order him to be disqualified from driving for a period. In some cases, the court is required to, and in other cases the sheriff decides to, defer sentence for a period, not exceeding three weeks, to obtain a social inquiry report from the local authority social work department to assist him in determining what sentence is appropriate.[4] In certain cases, the court must state and record in the minutes its reasons for imposing or refraining from imposing certain penalties.[5] The court may in its discretion fix any punishment within the limits of its competency, or may dismiss with an admonition, or without recording a conviction, or may make a probation order. There is no power to remit to the High Court for sentence. If the accused fails to pay the fine or any instalment, he is cited to the court again and a means inquiry held; that is, he is questioned by the sheriff as to the reasons for non-payment and he may be committed to prison or another arrangement made for payment, such as smaller instalments.

Review of Summary Trial Verdicts

There are six methods whereby the proceedings of courts of summary criminal jurisdiction may be reviewed.

The first is an appeal against decisions on the competency or relevancy of proceedings taken at a preliminary diet.[6]

Stated Case

Either party[7] may, on the final determination of a summary prosecution, apply to the court to state a case for the opinion of the High Court of Justiciary. A stated case may be obtained on very varied grounds, so as to cover practically every question which may have caused a miscarriage of justice, including objections to jurisdiction, competency, relevancy,[8] the admission or rejection of evidence, whether the findings in fact were warranted by the evidence, irregularities in procedure, oppressive conduct by the sheriff,[9] and the competency of sentence[10] (but not the amount of sentence).

---

[4] See, *e.g. Auld v. Herron*, 1969 J.C. 4.

[5] *e.g. Bruce v. Hogg*, 1966 J.C. 33; *Binnie v. Farrell*, 1972 J.C. 49.

[6] *e.g. Robertson v. Smith*, 1980 J.C. 1; *Dean v. Menzies*, 1981 J.C. 23, 26; *Sommerville* v. *Tudhope*, 1981 J.C. 58; *Walkingshaw v. Coid*, 1988 S.C.C.R. 454; *Lafferty v. Jessop*, 1989 S.L.T. 849. A fiscal can appeal against a sheriff's decision to seek a preliminary ruling on a point from the C.J.E.C.: *Wither v. Cowie*, 1990 S.C.C.R. 741.

[7] For an instance of stated case requested by the procurator-fiscal, see *MacDonald* v. *Cassidy*, 1959 J.C. 1.

[8] *e.g. Tudhope v. Sommerville*, 1981 S.L.T. 117.

[9] *e.g. McClung v. Cruickshank*, 1964 J.C. 64.

[10] *e.g. Kesson v. Heatly*, 1964 J.C. 40.

The party dissatisfied with the legal determination of the court applies to the judge to state and sign a case for the opinion of the High Court of Justiciary. It is competent for either party to ask for a stated case, so that the prosecutor may appeal against an acquittal on a matter of law.

The stated case is prepared by the sheriff[11] and each party may intimate any adjustments desired, the case being finally settled by the judge after hearing the parties. Review does not cover questions of fact but only questions of law (which includes legal inferences drawn from findings in fact and whether there was sufficient evidence to warrant a finding in fact). The case narrates the circumstances and what facts the judge found to be admitted or proved,[12] and states the judge's decision and disposal of the case on the basis of these findings of fact. It then states for the opinion of the High Court one or more questions of law[13] such as: "On the facts stated, was I entitled to convict the accused?" or "On the facts stated, was I entitled to reject the evidence of . . . ?" The question whether the inferior court was *right* in convicting is not a question of law for appeal, but a matter which the inferior court had to determine on the facts. The question really is whether the summary court erred in applying the law to the facts it had found admitted or proved, not whether it was right in finding those facts. In some cases it has been difficult to decide whether a question was one of fact, on which the summary court was final, or one of law and open to reconsideration by the High Court on appeal. If the appeal is against conviction and sentence, it is necessary to add a question on whether the sentence was excessive or inappropriate.

Stated cases are heard by the High Court of Justiciary, similarly composed as for a sitting as Court of Criminal Appeal.[14] The appellant is represented by counsel, and the procurator-fiscal by one or more Crown counsel. Legal argument is heard from both sides, one speech on each side, and the court usually disposes of the case at once. It may, however, remit the case with an opinion, or for amendment or clarification of the findings or the point in issue.

The High Court has wide powers[15] to affirm, reverse or alter the decision of the inferior court, to substitute a fine for imprisonment, to reduce either fine or imprisonment, to convict and sentence an accused or remit the case to the inferior court with instructions to convict and sentence, to quash the conviction, and so on. It may grant authority to bring a new prosecution. There is no further appeal and application to the *nobile officium* of the High Court is incompetent.[16]

---

[11] For specimen, see A.A. (Consolidation) 1988 (S.I. 1988, No. 10), Form 72.

[12] It is incorrect, as is sometimes done, to narrate some of the evidence; the inferior court should have made up its mind on what it held, on the evidence, to have been established.

[13] See *Drummond v. Hunter*, 1948 J.C. 109.

[14] In practice the judges of one or other of the Divisions of the Inner House of the Court of Session sit as High Court for about a week, hearing first criminal appeals and then stated cases and bills of suspension.

[15] Criminal Procedure (Scotland) Act 1975, s. 452.

[16] *Anderson v. H.M. Advocate*, 1974 S.L.T. 239.

Appeal against Sentence Only

If the prosecutor appeals against sentence he may do so only on a point of law, and does so by stated case. An accused who appeals against sentence only may do so by note of appeal, alleging a miscarriage of justice in that the sentence was excessive or inappropriate. The sheriff must submit a report. The High Court may affirm or quash the sentence imposed or quash the sentence and substitute another not heavier than the inferior court could have imposed.[17]

Bill of Suspension

Suspension is the procedure whereby an illegal or improper warrant, conviction or judgment issued by an inferior judge acting under summary criminal procedure[18] may be reviewed and set aside by the High Court. If the complainer is in custody the process becomes one of suspension and liberation. It is in general a remedy open to the person accused or convicted only and not to the prosecutor.[19] It is not a means of having reviewed the rightness of a conviction[20] but a means of having stopped proceedings which are in excess of jurisdiction, illegal or unwarrantable, incompetent or irrelevant, or where there is oppression or injustice or irregularity in the proceedings.[21]

The Bill of Suspension runs in name of the aggrieved party as complainer, against the prosecutor as respondent and resembles a civil petition in form, having a prayer for the suspension of the sentence complained of, and, where appropriate, for liberation from prison, a statement of facts in numbered paragraphs, and pleas-in-law.[22] The prosecutor normally lodges answers in the form of corresponding paragraphs and pleas-in-law. The facts in the Bill must relevantly aver grounds on which the sentence is challenged, and it is competent even though the sentence has been carried out.

The Bill is put out for hearing by three or more members of the High Court of Justiciary and legal argument is heard from counsel for the suspender and from Crown counsel. The facts are not investigated except so far as admitted by the respondent, but a remit may be made to the

---

[17] Criminal Justice (Scotland) Act 1980, s. 34; *Henry v. Docherty*, 1990 S.L.T. 301.

[18] It has no application to trials on indictment: *Outram v. Lees*, 1992 S.L.T. 32.

[19] The prosecutor's remedy is by advocation, *e.g. Macleod v. Levitt*, 1969 J.C. 16, though this may be invoked by both parties.

[20] *Moffat v. Skeen*, 1963 J.C. 84.

[21] Full list of grounds in Renton and Brown: see also *Henderson v. Forster*, 1944 J.C. 91; *Blair v. Hawthorn*, 1945 J.C. 4; *Gray v. Morrison*, 1954 J.C. 31; *McGinley and Dowds v. MacLeod*, 1963 J.C. 11; *Auld v. Herron*, 1969 J.C. 4; *Patrick v. Copeland*, 1969 J.C. 42; *Thompson v. Tudhope*, 1987 S.L.T. 247; *Wilson v. Lowe*, 1991 S.C.C.R. 77; *Frew v. O'Brien*, 1996 S.L.T. 282; *Sneddon v. Lees*, 1996 S.L.T. 294. Exceptionally, in *Loch Lomond Sailings Ltd v. Hawthorn*, 1962 J.C. 8, the court considered a bill of suspension brought by one other than the accused, whose property had been used in the crime and had been forfeited.

[22] For specimen, see Renton and Brown, para. 16.133.

inferior court to report on some matter. It is not a suitable process to challenge the sufficiency of the evidence for conviction or the admissibility of evidence, or otherwise to challenge the merits of a conviction, but only a means to object where some miscarriage of justice is alleged.

The High Court may pass the Bill, suspend the sentence and order repayment of any fine paid, may repel the reasons of suspension, refuse the Bill and let the sentence take effect, or may amend the conviction and sentence and, if necessary, remit the case to the inferior court. A Bill may be passed with authority to bring a fresh prosecution.[23] Expenses may be awarded, in full or modified.

Bill of Advocation

Advocation may be used by the accused but is normally used by the prosecutor. It is appropriate to seek review of irregularities in the preliminary stages of a case,[24] or where a lower court has dismissed an indictment or complaint as incompetent or irrelevant[25] or the judge has not dealt properly with a case,[26] or where there are problems after conviction.[27] If the Bill is presented by the accused, there has to have been a fundamental nullity or flagrant breach of fundamental principles of justice, but if presented by the prosecutor, it is enough to establish seriously mistaken dealing with the case below. Such a Bill is heard by the High Court in the same way as a Bill of Suspension.

Consent to Conviction Being Set Aside

When an appeal has been taken by stated case, suspension or otherwise and the prosecutor is not prepared to maintain the conviction, he may by minute consent to it being set aside. A judge of the High Court may set it aside or decline to do so; he may decline if there is no detailed explanation as to why the conviction is not being maintained.[28]

Petition to the Nobile Officium

The High Court, like the Court of Session, has inherent equitable power, which it may use to deal with extraordinary or unforeseen circumstances, or where there is no common law or statutory remedy[29] and no other mode of review appears competent or appropriate, for the

---

[23] *Brims v. Macdonald*, 1994 S.L.T. 922.

[24] *H.M. Advocate v. Thomson*, 1994 S.L.T. 354; *Khalid v. H.M. Advocate*, 1994 S.L.T. 357; *McKenna v. H.M. Advocate*, 1994 S.L.T. 362.

[25] *McFayden v. Stewart*, 1951 J.C. 164.

[26] *e.g. Skeen v. Sullivan*, 1980 S.L.T.(Notes) 11; *MacKenzie v. Maclean*, 1980 J.C. 89; *MacPherson*, 1989 S.C.C.R. 518; *H.M. Advocate v. Dow*, 1992 S.L.T. 577.

[27] *Valentine v. Parker*, 1992 S.C.C.R. 695; *Wilson v. Donald*, 1993 S.L.T. 31; *Gallagher*, 1996 S.C.C.R. 833.

[28] *MacRae v. Hingston*, 1992 S.L.T. 1197.

[29] *Wan Ping Nam v. German Minister of Justice*, 1972 J.C. 43; *Black*, 1991 S.C.C.R. 1.

avoidance of deadlock, injustice or oppression.[30] Either party may seek to invoke it. It is not an alternative to another mode of appeal, cannot be used to overcome or excuse failure to comply with statutory requirements,[31] such as to appeal within a stated time, and cannot be invoked after the dismissal of an appeal made in another form.[32]

OFFENCES COMMITTED BY CHILDREN

A child under the age of eight cannot in law be guilty of any offence. Special provision is made for dealing with children under 16.[33] No child may be prosecuted for any offence save on the instructions of the Lord Advocate or at his instance, and even then only in the High Court or sheriff court.[34] If a child is so prosecuted in the sheriff court, special provisions apply to keep the child away from adult criminals. In a case of murder the High Court will order a child or person under 18 to be detained during Her Majesty's pleasure. In other cases, a court may order a child to be detained, required to undergo residential training, put on probation, fined, admonished or discharged.

Most cases of delinquency are now dealt with by children's hearings. In each local authority area there has been established a Children's Panel made up of lay members appointed by the Secretary of State and removable by him. Groups of three members of the panel, including members of each sex, hold children's hearings in places dissociated from criminal courts and police stations. Each local authority has an officer called the Reporter, with deputies; they are of the staff of the Scottish Children's Reporter Administration; they need not be legally qualified.[35] The Reporter's function is to investigate cases of children likely to be in need of compulsory measures of care, not solely by reason of having committed offences,[36] and, if he thinks fit, to bring the child before a children's hearing.[37] If he proposes to do so he must give the child and its parent a statement of the grounds of referral and call for a report on the child from the local authority social work department.

---

[30] *Anderson v. H.M. Advocate*, 1974 S.L.T. 239; *Muirhead*, 1983 S.L.T. 208; *Gerrard*, 1984 S.L.T. 108; *Maclachlan*, 1987 S.C.C.R. 195; *Singh*, 1987 S.L.T. 63; *Gibbons*, 1988 S.L.T. 657; *Evans*, 1991 S.C.C.R. 160; *Outram v. Lees*, 1992 S.L.T. 32.

[31] *Berry*, 1985 S.C.C.R. 106; *Manson*, 1991 S.L.T. 96.

[32] *Fenton*, 1982 S.L.T. 164; *Perrie*, 1991 S.C.C.R. 475.

[33] The law is now contained in the Children (Scotland) Act 1995 and the Social Work (Scotland) Act 1968.

[34] In summary cases the Lord Advocate's instructions are presumed given unless this is challenged. Even then general instructions will suffice: *M. v. Dean*, 1974 S.L.T. 229. The commonest case is of a child committing an offence along with an adult.

[35] They are directed centrally by the Principal Reporter and the Scottish Children's Reporter Administration.

[36] For grounds for bringing before a hearing see 1968 Act, s. 32. See also Children's Hearings (Scotland) Rules 1971.

[37] Specimen citation in Appx. F.

At the hearing,[38] the child's parent has a right to be present at all stages and may be obliged to attend. Child and parent may be accompanied by a representative, who need not be legally qualified. Hearings are private and the public are excluded. The procedure is generally in the discretion of the chairman. The chairman must explain the grounds of referral alleged; if the child and his parent accept the grounds, the hearing proceeds; if they do not, the Reporter must apply to the sheriff for a finding as to whether the disputed grounds are established. Such an application is heard summarily, in chambers.[39] The sheriff may hold that none of the grounds for referral are established and dismiss the application and discharge the referral, or hold the grounds for referral established; he gives his decision orally. The sheriff may be called on to state a case for the opinion of the Court of Session.[40] The case then goes back to the hearing.

In considering a case, the hearing must discuss the case with the child, his parent and representative, and consider social inquiry and other available reports, and endeavour to obtain the views of the child and his parent on what arrangements would be in the best interests of the child. The chairman must inform the child, parent and representative of the decision and reasons for it. The disposal may be by discharging the referral and taking no further action, or by making a supervision requirement which may require the child to reside in a named residential establishment.[41] A supervision requirement places the child in the care of the local authority and, unless discharged or varied, lasts until the child is 18. The hearing may not deal with the child by admonition or fine, nor impose any penalty on the parent.

An appeal lies from any decision of a children's hearing to the sheriff, on the ground of error in law or irregularity in procedure, or that the disposal ordered is not appropriate, and is heard summarily, in chambers.[42] The sheriff must allow the appeal if he is satisfied that the decision of the hearing is not justified in all the circumstances of the case; he may

---

[38] For procedure see A.S. (Social Work) (Sheriff Court Procedure Rules) 1971; Grant, "Model Procedure for a Children's Hearing," 1974 S.L.T.(News) 229.

[39] Parents are competent and compellable witnesses: *McGregor v. T.*, 1975 S.L.T. 76. A deputy Reporter not legally qualified was held to have no right of audience: *Kennedy v. O.*, 1975 S.L.T. 235. See now Reporters (Conduct of Proceedings before the Sheriff) (Scotland) Regs. 1975 (S.I. 1975, No. 2251).

[40] e.g. *McGregor v. D.*, 1977 S.C. 330; *Constanda v. M*, 1997 S.C. 217. Where application is made to the sheriff and the grounds for referral are then accepted the sheriff should dismiss the application and remit to the Reporter: *Strathclyde Regional Council v. X.*, 1978 S.L.T.(Sh.Ct.) 46.

[41] *Aitken v. Aitken*, 1978 S.L.T. 183. In deciding on a disposal a hearing may act only on grounds accepted by the parent or held established by the court: *K. v. Finlayson*, 1974 S.L.T.(Sh.Ct.) 51.

[42] Appeal against a decision of a children's hearing is competent only when the decision is a final disposal of the referral: *H. v. McGregor*, 1973 S.L.T. 110. When hearing an appeal any change in circumstances since the decision was reached must be considered: *Kennedy v. B.*, 1973 S.L.T. 38; *D. v. Sinclair*, 1973 S.L.T.(Sh.Ct.) 47. On time see *S., Appellants*, 1979 S.L.T.(Sh.Ct.) 37. On procedure see *H. v. Mearns*, 1974 S.L.T. 184.

remit the case to a children's hearing for reconsideration, or may discharge the child. A further appeal lies to the Court of Session by way of stated case on a point of law, or in respect of any irregularity in the conduct of the case at the instance of the child and/or his parent or the Reporter.[43] There may be appeals on both the sheriff's finding of fact on the grounds of referral and on the disposal of the case. No appeal lies against a decision to impose a supervision requirement solely on the ground that the treatment prescribed is inappropriate.

All supervision requirements imposed by children's hearings are subject to at least annual review and the child or his parent may require a review after three months, after six months after a review has continued a previous requirement, or after three months after a review has varied a previous requirement. A local authority can require a review at any time. Review hearings are arranged by the Reporter and are conducted in the same way as an initial hearing. Supervision requirements cease to have effect when the child attains 18, and within three months before that date the local authority must have the Reporter arrange a hearing so that it may advise whether the child still requires supervision and guidance. The First Minister may terminate a supervision requirement at any time.

PUNISHMENT AND TREATMENT OF CRIMINALS

Many changes have been made in the methods of punishment and treatment in recent years and experiment and change is constantly going on, the emphasis being now on training and reformation of criminals, not on mere punishment.[44] In solemn procedure the prosecutor must make an express motion for sentence, and in summary procedure his motion is implied. A court may defer sentence to a later date, or adjourn the case for not more than three weeks at a time for inquiries or other reports on the accused's suitability for a particular sentence. During adjournment, the accused may be remanded in custody, released on bail or ordained to appear. Sentence must be pronounced orally, in open court, and the accused must be present, save where in a summary case, he has pleaded guilty by letter.

The sentence of death is now disused.[45] Persons convicted of murder are sentenced to life imprisonment, and the judge may recommend a minimum period which should elapse before the First Minister orders release

---

[43] See, *e.g. D. v. Kennedy*, 1974 S.L.T. 168.

[44] In 1959 a new Scottish Advisory Council on the Treatment of Offenders was set up to advise and assist the Secretary of State for Scotland. In 1996 a Criminal Justice Forum, chaired by the Secretary of State for Scotland, was established to address current issues in the criminal justice system. It includes judges and sheriffs, senior police officers and other persons involved with criminal justice. There is also a Standing Advisory Council on Employment of Prisoners, appointed by the Home Secretary and the Secretary of State for Scotland. There is an Institute of Criminology at Cambridge University to study the causes and prevention of crime, while research is also pursued in various other universities and by the Home Office Research Unit.

[45] Homicide Act 1957; Murder (Abolition of Death Penalty) Act 1965 (expiring on July 31, 1970, but continued by affirmative resolutions of both Houses of Parliament).

on licence.[46] An accused may appeal against the recommendation made and it may be altered.[47] The First Minister may not release a murderer on licence unless he has consulted the Lord Justice-General and the trial judge, if available. Persons under 18 convicted of murder are sentenced to be detained during Her Majesty's pleasure.

Transportation, penal servitude and imprisonment with hard labour have all been abolished. Imprisonment[48] may be imposed for such period as the court thinks fit or such period as may be authorised by any relevant statute. A sheriff acting under solemn procedure may not imprison for more than three years (though he may remit a case to the High Court for sentence) and, in summary procedure, unless statute authorises more, the maximum sentence is of three months' imprisonment, or six months if there is a previous conviction of dishonesty or personal violence. The district court may not imprison for more than 60 days. Sentences of imprisonment on multiple charges may be made consecutive or concurrent. The court cannot by making sentences consecutive exceed the period for which it could sentence on one complaint, but it can do so where there is more than one complaint.[49] A court passing a sentence of imprisonment must specify the date of commencement of the sentence; if the accused has been detained in custody on remand awaiting trial or sentence, the sentence must be backdated to not earlier than the start of detention or remand unless the judge declines to do so and states in court his reasons.[50] There are restrictions on imprisonment of adult first offenders[51] and a prohibition on imprisonment of persons under 21 who are instead sentenced to detention. There is also provision for supervision of prisoners after release.

The First Minister now has power[52] on the recommendation of the Parole Board for Scotland[53] to release on licence a person serving a sentence of imprisonment of at least four years, other than imprisonment for life, after that person has served one-third of his sentence or 12 months, whichever is greater. The licence may contain conditions and may

---

[46] *Draper*, 1997 S.L.T. 815; *Murray v. H.M. Advocate*, 2000 J.C. 102.

[47] *Casey v. H.M. Advocate*, 1994 S.L.T. 44.

[48] Scottish prisons are at Aberdeen, Castle Huntly, Cornton Vale (women), Dumfries, Edinburgh (Saughton), Friarton, Glasgow (Barlinnie), Glenochil, Greenock, Inverness, Kilmarnock, Longriggend, Low Moss, Noranside, Perth, Peterhead and Shotts. There are Young Offenders' Institutions at Dumfries, Glenochil and Polmont, and for girls, Cornton Vale, and a National Induction Unit at Shotts.

[49] *Nicholson v. Lees*, 1996 S.C.C.R. 551.

[50] Criminal Procedure (Sc.) Act 1995, s. 210 *Brooks v. H.M. Advocate*, 1994 S.L.T. 932.

[51] Criminal Procedure (Scotland) Act 1995, s. 204(2); *Winslow v. Farrell*, 1965 J.C. 49; *Auld v. Herron*, 1969 J.C. 4.

[52] Prisons (Scotland) Act 1989, ss. 18, 22, 28. See *Rea v. Parole Board for Scotland*, 1993 S.L.T. 1074.

[53] Constituted under s. 59 of Criminal Justice Act 1967. The Parole Board for Scotland has a chairman and eight members, including two sheriffs. See Parole Board (Scotland) Rules 1995 (S.I. 1995, No. 1273).

be revoked. A person sentenced to life imprisonment may, on the Parole Board's recommendation, be released on licence only after consultation with the Lord Justice-General and the trial judge, if available. Prisoners sentenced to more than four years' and less than 10 years' imprisonment qualify for automatic conditional release, if the Parole Board so recommends after half sentence.[54] Courts may recall persons convicted of another imprisonable offence during conditional release.

Pecuniary fines are commonly imposed in addition to, or instead of, imprisonment. The amount of any fine is within the court's discretion; in solemn procedure there is no limit on the amount of fine but, unless statute otherwise authorises, the sheriff court exercising summary jurisdiction, or a stipendiary magistrate, may not impose a fine of over the prescribed sum[55] and district courts not over level 4 on the standard scale.[56] In imposing a fine, a court must have regard for the offender's ability to pay a fine of the amount imposed. It should be related both to the gravity of the offence and to the offender's circumstances, such that he will feel it. Where an offender is fined, the fine may be paid at the Bar but he is entitled to have time to pay and to pay by agreed instalments. He may be put under social work supervision to assist him to pay. The court may at the same time impose the alternative, failing payment, of imprisonment for a period related by a statutory tariff to the sum unpaid. If the alternative is not imposed but the offender defaults in payment, he will be cited to a Means Inquiry Court,[57] which will hear his excuse and may modify the instalments, or may impose imprisonment for non-payment (which will frequently result in money being quickly found by a relative), or may make a supervised attendance order[58] requiring the offender to attend for from 10 to 60 hours, doing unpaid activity which may include work or instructional sessions, supervised by the social work department. Enforcement in case of default is on the same lines as for community service orders.

Courts also have power to defer sentence for a period, subject to conditions, such as of good behaviour or repayment of money taken,[59] or to admonish the offender,[60] or to grant him an absolute discharge,[61] or to

---

[54] Prisoners and Criminal Proceedings (Scotland) Act 1993; [1995] C.L.Y. 6238; *Elliot v. H.M. Advocate*, 1997 S.C.C.R. 111; *McEleny v. Carnegie*, 1998 S.C.C.R. 15.

[55] The prescribed sum is £5000 or such other sum as may be prescribed from time to time: Criminal Procedure (Scotland) Act 1995, s. 225(8), as amended.

[56] The standard scale is that set out in the Criminal Procedure (Scotland) Act 1995, s. 225 as amended, and, as at 2000, is as follows: level 1, £200; level 2, £500; level 3, £1000; level 4, £2500; level 5, £5000.

[57] A Means Inquiry Court consists of a sheriff or justice sitting alone; see, *e.g. Fraser v. Herron*, 1968 J.C. 1.

[58] Law Reform (Miscellaneous Provisions) (Scotland) Act 1990, s. 62 and Sched. 6.

[59] Criminal Procedure (Scotland) Act 1995, s. 202. If the condition in satisfied the offender is frequently admonished when the case is recalled. But see *Laing v. Heywood*, 1998 S.C.C.R. 458.

[60] *Ibid.*, s. 246. Admonition expresses disapproval and warning.

[61] *Ibid.*, s. 246.

put the offender on probation for between six months and three years.[62] The offender must consent. The standard probation order requires the offender to be of good behaviour and to conform to the directions of the supervising social worker, who will keep in regular contact with him and advise and guide him. A probation order may also contain conditions such as of paying compensation to the victim, undergoing psychological or psychiatric treatment, living at a specified place, finding security for good behaviour, undertaking unpaid work of benefit to the community attending an intensive programme of training or of taking other action towards rehabilitation. Breach of an order will result in the offender being recalled to court, fined for breach of the order or having the order varied or terminated and, in the latter case, the offender being sentenced for the original offence.

A court may also make a Community Service Order[63] ordering the offender, if considered suitable and it he consents to it, to undertake within 12 months between 80 and 300 hours of unpaid work of benefit to the community, such as cleaning up the environment, gardening or painting, as arranged and supervised by the social work department. An offender who defaults may be given additional hours or sentenced for the original offence.

A court may also require payment of compensation to the victim of the offence for loss or injury;[64] such orders must have regard to the offender's means and are enforceable in substantially the same way as fines.[65] These different regimes, particularly probation and community service, are not soft options but alternatives to imprisonment which require substantial efforts by offenders under firm supervision.

Before making a probation order or community service order, or imposing a first sentence of imprisonment on an offender aged over 20, or a sentence of detention of an offender aged 16–20, or disposing of an offender under 16 or one subject to a supervision requirement imposed by a Children's Hearing, a court must obtain and consider a social inquiry report prepared by a local authority social worker, and for this purpose it may adjourn the case before sentence for not more than 21 days.[66] Such reports give background information about the offender, his family, way of life and surrounding circumstances and frequently help the court to decide on an appropriate sentence.

---

[62] *Ibid.*, s. 228.

[63] Criminal Procedure (Scotland) Act 1995, s. 238; *Hewitt v. Vannet*, 1997 S.C.C.R. 530; *Gilbert v. Buchanan*, 1997 S.C.C.R. 642.

[64] Criminal Justice (Scotland) Act 1980, ss. 58–67; *Bruce v. Macleod*, 1998 S.L.T. 173; *Downie v. H.M. Advocate*, 1999 S.C.C.R. 375. A compensation order does not affect a victim's claim to the Criminal Injuries Compensation Board but money received is deducted from a C.I.C.B. award. It is not competent to make an order in favour of a charity which had not suffered from the crime: *H.M. Advocate v. Nelson*, 1996 S.L.T. 1073.

[65] *Robertson v. Lees*, 1992 S.C.C.R. 545.

[66] *Bain v. Wilson*, 1998 S.C.C.R. 457.

Courts have power to order forfeiture of property used in drug trafficking and confiscation of the proceeds of such business,[67] and forfeiture of motor vehicles used in committing the crime charged,[68] and to confiscate the proceeds of indictable offences and certain summary offences.[69]

Social work departments, frequently in co-operation with voluntary organisations, also provide Throughcare, assistance to offenders' families, victims of crime, children involved in court proceedings and others affected. During imprisonment, prison-based social workers seek to assist prisoners to tackle the causes of their misbehaviour. They also report on prisoners being considered for release by the Parole Board. They super-vise prisoners released on parole and enforce any special conditions, such as of undergoing treatment, required by the Parole Board, and provide the mandatory aftercare imposed on all offenders released after detention in a Young Offenders' Institution, and seek to assist them to resettle. Persons released from custody may also, within 12 months of release, voluntarily seek advice, guidance and assistance from social work departments. Local authority social work departments accordingly increasingly play an import-ant role in the criminal justice system.[70]

Young persons aged 16 to 21 may be discharged absolutely, admon-ished, put on probation for six months to three years, fined or required to find caution for good behaviour. In more serious cases they may be detained in a remand home for observation and examination, or for reports,[71] or sent to a detention centre or, for longer periods, a Young Offenders' Institution.[72] In cases of murder they must be detained during Her Majesty's pleasure.[73] Aftercare by a social worker is obligatory for young persons after release from Young Offenders' Institutions.

Minor penalties include admonition, or absolute discharge, or forfeiture of property used or intended to be used for any offence. In road traffic cases a licence may be endorsed or disqualification from driving be ordered.

---

[67] Criminal Justice (Scotland) Act 1987; Law Reform. (Misc. Prov.) (Sc.) Act 1990, s. 63.

[68] Criminal Procedure (Scotland) Act 1995, s. 87; *Reid v. Houston*, 1992 S.C.C.R. 442; *Carroll*, 1997 S.L.T. 481.

[69] Proceeds of Crime (Scotland) Act 1995; *Rowan v. H.M. Advocate*, 1998 S.L.T. 53; *Donnelly v. H.M. Advocate*, 1999 S.C.C.R. 508.

[70] The Scottish Office Social Work Services Group has issued a comprehensive *National Objectives and Standards for Social Work Services in the Criminal Justice System*. A new system was announced in 2000; see S.E. 1347/2000.

[71] Remand homes are provided by local authorities and "List D," formerly approved, schools by local authorities or other bodies, such as churches. The First Minister may regulate the constitution of the managers of an approved school, other than a local authority one.

[72] For the development of the system, see Fox, *The English Prison and Borstal Systems* 327 *et seq.* The Scottish Young Offender Institutions are at Cornton Vale, Dumfries, Glenochil and Polmont.

[73] Criminal Procedure (Scotland) Act 1995, s. 208.

Rehabilitation of Offenders

In certain cases if an offender is not reconvicted within a stated period his convictions are deemed spent and are ignored. The period depends on the gravity of the offence and convictions resulting in imprisonment, detention or custody for life, detention during Her Majesty's pleasure or imprisonment, youth custody or detention in excess of 30 months are never "spent."[74]

FURTHER READING

Solemn Criminal Procedure
Renton and Brown: *Criminal Procedure According to the Law of Scotland* (5th ed.).

Summary Criminal Procedure
Renton and Brown: *Criminal Procedure According to the Law of Scotland* (5th ed.).

Evidence
Stone: *Proof of Fact in Criminal Trials.*
     Cross-examination in Criminal Trials.
Walker and Walker: *Law of Evidence in Scotland.*

Punishment and Treatment
Annual Reports: *Criminal Statistics, Scotland.*
                Prisons in Scotland.
Fox: *The English Prison and Borstal System.*
Morris (ed.): *The Oxford History of the Prison.*
Nicholson: *Law and Practice of Sentencing in Scotland.*
Walker: *Crime and Punishment in Britain.*
Windlesham: *Responses to Crime*, 3 vols.

---

[74] Rehabilitation of Offenders Act 1974.

CHAPTER 14

THE MAKING OF NEW LAW

THE body of doctrines, principles and rules, and of exceptions and qualifications thereto, which constitutes the current content of the law is constantly being added to and modified. Consequently any statement in a textbook or judgment may be subsequently superseded or altered, and a perennial difficulty for the student or practitioner of law is to keep track of the constant changes and note how what he has hitherto understood to be the law on one point or another, or what is stated as the law in the latest available book, has been subsequently changed.

The Need for New Law

The need for new law and the alteration of old arises simply from the fact that society is not static. Views change on what the legal rule should be on particular topics, new situations develop such as the growth of motor traffic, calling for new controls, new forms of crime become prevalent, views change as to the proper disposal of convicted criminals, the grounds on which it should be permissible to terminate marriages, the persons who should be entitled to recover damages for the death of a breadwinner, the rights of illegitimate children, the need to limit hours of work in certain premises, and so on.

In brief, the constant changes in our society and in the world in which we live, brought about by changing ideas, changing social habits and patterns, scientific and technological changes, and developments in medical science, in commercial practices, in international relations, all bring about constant need to modify the rules of law at some point or another if they are not to be out of touch with the general feeling of the community on the matter and the needs of the situation. Frequently some event, a particular crime, or disaster, or discovery, or court case, or other particular event, exposes a gap or defect in the existing law and generates a public feeling in favour of, or even demand for, a change. Increasingly in the twentieth century there have been movements for the deliberate consideration of topics of law and their reform to make them more consistent with current needs and views, rather then to rely on merely *ad hoc* stoppings of gaps and correction of obvious defects.

Lawmaking by Judicial Decision

The superior court judges have no express power to alter the law or make new law[1] and judges at various times have disclaimed any law-making power,[2] but it is undeniable that in the exercise of their duty to apply the law to cases coming before them, and, in so doing, to state what they understand the rules to be, they frequently in effect make new law or modify the existing law. The judicial function is not merely to declare existing law, or apply it to another set of facts. It extends to reshaping it. Thus where a court overrules a prior decision,[3] or limits or extends the application of a rule as compared with previous decisions on that point, the judges are really making new law or at least altering, albeit in detail, an existing rule, particularly when one has regard to the principle of *stare decisis*, which makes their reformulation of a rule binding for the future. The effect of a decision may be far wider than the mere decision of the issue between the parties. Thus when *Donoghue* v. *Stevenson*[4] was decided, the House of Lords not only decided the case before them, but in substance laid down a new general principle, namely, that in future every manufacturer of goods had to take reasonable care for the safety of the ultimate consumer of his goods if there was no reasonable probability of the inspection of the goods between manufacture and consumption, and would be liable in damages if such a consumer were injured by reason of the original manufacturer's failure to have taken such care. This principle finally condemned a mistaken former view of the law, that if a defender did not owe a contractual or statutory duty to a pursuer, he owed no duty at all. This principle, laid down in the context of a bottled drink, and in the first instance applicable only thereto, has been extended by other decisions to clothing, vehicles, food and other commodities. Its limits are not yet settled.

Again, when a court decides that a particular rule of law, common law or statute, is to a particular effect and not what it was hitherto thought to be, it is hard to say that there has not been a making of new law. So, too, where a court decides what has hitherto been undecided, even though the decision is not startling or surprising, there can be said to be a change in the law; what was formerly thought to be the law has now been authoritatively declared to be the law. Law is indeed created and declared and sometimes modified by the very acts of finding it, stating it and applying it in cases.

There is a large personal element in judicial law-making; much depends on whether judges faced with a case, the decision in which may be far-

---

[1] Apart from powers to make or modify purely procedural rules, as by Act of Sederunt.

[2] *e.g. Willis v. Baddeley* [1892] 2 Q.B. 324, 326; *Harnett v. Fisher* [1927] 1 K.B. 402, 424; *Baylis v. Bishop of London* [1913] 1 Ch. 127, 137.

[3] Where the House of Lords overrules one of its own prior decisions, under the principle enunciated in 1966, it is quite plain that it is changing the law.

[4] 1932 S.C.(H.L.) 31. Similarly in England in *Hedley Byrne & Co. Ltd. v. Heller and Partners Ltd* [1964] A.C. 465 the House of Lords reached a decision which laid down a new principle with far-reaching implications, that the maker might be liable for the consequences of negligent misrepresentation.

reaching, are forward-looking or conservative, bold or timorous, and the attitudes of superior courts at various times have undoubtedly varied, depending on the composition of the courts.[5]

Limitations on Judicial Lawmaking

At the same time the severe limitations on judicial lawmaking are evident; the courts cannot lay down a rule for a set of facts by anticipation, but only if and when a case of such facts arises; they cannot deal with all such cases generally, but only with the one case which has arisen. And judges are very reluctant to state a rule more generally than the necessities of the case require them to do, so that it may be that the rule laid down is particular to that case, or class of case, and not a general rule at all. The power of the courts to alter any rule of law is dependent on the established conventions as to *stare decisis*, so that a court cannot alter the law on a point settled by a precedent binding on that court, though it may establish an exception or qualification if it can distinguish the precedent, and it may further define, or limit or extend the principle.[6] Still less can judicial lawmaking override any rule existing by virtue of legislation, however absurd or unjust the courts may consider the statutory rule. If it is applicable, it cannot be ignored or altered by the court.

Not least, a decision of a point cannot be made solely on the basis of what the judge thinks is desirable or right; he cannot ignore the existing law and his decision must be consistent with the existing body of law on similar and related points, and based on some recognised principle. Thus a judge cannot grant a divorce because husband and wife are incompatible in temperament, because the legally permitted grounds of divorce do not include that, but if the judge finds that the spouses were incompatible and as a consequence of incompatibility that the conduct of one was such as to be detrimental to the health of the other, he may find that that amounted to intolerable behaviour, which evidences irretrievable breakdown of marriage, which is the ground of divorce. In *MacLennan* v. *MacLennan*,[7] a judge was faced, for the first time in Britain, with the problem whether the allegation that a wife had had herself artificially inseminated with the

---

[5] Jaffé, *English and American Judges as Lawmakers* (1969); Stevens, *Law and Politics: the House of Lords as a Judicial Body, 1800–1976* (1979); Griffith, *The Politics of the Judiciary* (1977) discussed in Devlin, "Judges, Government and Politics" (1978) 41 M.L.R. 505.

[6] Thus in the years before 1948 the courts could not get rid of "the rule of common employment," to the effect that an employer was not liable to one employee for an accident caused by the fault of a fellow-employee in common employment with the injured man. This rule, established for Scotland by the House of Lords in *Bartonshill Coal Co.* v. *Reid* (1858) 3 Macq. 266, could only be, and was, criticised and distinguished in a series of cases and its application limited. It was finally abolished by the Law Reform (Personal Injuries) Act 1948, s. 1. See also Freeman, "Standards of Adjudication, Judicial Lawmaking and Prospective Overruling" (1973) 26 C.L.P. 166.

[7] 1958 S.C. 105; the argument was on the law only and it was never determined whether the wife's plea was justified in fact or not; see footnotes on p. 115 of the report.

semen of a donor (an unknown male) and had had a child in consequence, gave her husband grounds for divorce. It would have been blatant judicial legislation to hold that artificial insemination did so by itself. But could her conduct be held to amount to adultery? He might have held that impregnation by the unknown male's semen by medical intervention was equivalent to impregnation by the unknown male by normal physical intercourse, and therefore equally adultery. In fact he held that "adultery" involved extra-marital physical intercourse and that no conduct or insemination without physical intercourse, however morally wrongful, amounted to adultery. The decision therefore merely proceeded on the analysis and interpretation of the term "adultery," limiting it to what is generally understood by that term. The opposite view would have been such an extension of the term as to amount to judicial legislation, but might nevertheless have been right. Is the essence of "adultery" sexual infidelity to one's spouse or is it only physical coitus?

Accordingly, there are severe limitations on judicial lawmaking and only exceptionally can it go beyond redefinition, explanation, extension or qualification of existing principles, though even in these ways, particularly over a period of time, the courts can quite materially modify rules of law.

Lawmaking by Text-writers

From the sixteenth to the early nineteenth century some writings by some jurists have undoubtedly been creative and in effect made law or new law.[8] No jurist's statement of what the law should be, or, truly understood, is, on any unsettled point has any binding force today against a decision of a competent court, still less against legislation, though the writings of jurists in textbooks and periodicals of high reputation have sometimes been influential on courts and have been a factor in persuading a court to adopt a particular course of action or decision, and have thus indirectly played a part in shaping the law.[9] The text-writer has greater freedom than a judge in suggesting what is wrong with the law and how it should be modified, but less effect in that, unless his views are adopted by a court or a government department concerned, they will be completely ineffective, however sensible or carefully thought out.

Lawmaking by Legislation

The main mode of lawmaking and law-changing today is undoubtedly parliamentary legislation. This mode has the theoretical advantages that it can deal with a problem in general and not merely with a particular case which has arisen, that it can make changes by anticipation, instead of

---

[8] Walker, "The Province of Jurists Determined," 1991 J.R. 20.
[9] *e.g. Bradford v. Symondson* (1881) 7 Q.B.D. 456, 462; *Haynes v. Harwood* [1935] 1 K.B. 146; *Shenton v. Tyler* [1939] 1 Ch. 620; *Re Egerton's Will Trusts* [1956] Ch. 593; *Boys v. Chaplin* [1971] A.C. 356; *Qureshi v. Qureshi* [1971] 1 All E.R. 325; *Richards v. H.M. Advocate*, 1971 J.C. 29.

having to wait on a problem arising, that it can completely abrogate pre-existing and contrary rules, however long-established or well-settled, get rid of anomalies, absurdities and injustices, and can formulate the new rule in a general statement and in a verbally authoritative form.

In practice this very rarely happens, and much (far too much) legislation is piecemeal patching, dealing with particular problems rather than with the whole law on the subject, frequently merely adding to, or amending, or introducing an exception into, a substantial volume of existing legislation on the subject, so that the law on the topic consists, apart from cases, of many layers of legislation, each adding to or altering, but rarely completely restating or wholly superseding, rules in an earlier layer. Frequently, also, legislation proceeds by applying a rule earlier enacted for one subject to a new and different, and possibly unsuitable, further set of circumstances, or by making exceptions and qualifications to previous enactments. Amendment is too frequently by the addition or deletion of words, rather than by the complete replacement of a section in an earlier Act by a rewritten section. In the result, the state of the statute law on many topics is a patchwork of fragments of various statutes of different dates, a chaotic mess, wherein it is difficult, tedious and time-consuming to discover what words and fragments of sections appear to be still in force, let alone to determine whether they apply to, and what they mean in, particular circumstances.[10]

Initiatives for Legislation

The initiative for legislation comes from many sources.[11] Most legislation is introduced by or on behalf of the Government of the day and must be taken to relate to something regarded by the Cabinet as of sufficient importance in the Government's programme to justify parliamentary time being found for its discussion.[12] Some of this is essential annual legislation, such as the Finance Bill, the Consolidated Fund Bill, the Appropriation Bill (the first of which always makes some, and frequently important, drastic and extensive changes in the law of taxation), and the Expiring Laws Continuance Bill, without which various statutes passed for only limited periods would lapse. Some is legislation necessitated by current world affairs, international relations, or relations with some part of the Commonwealth or a colony. Some is more or less emergency legislation to cope with some crisis or special circumstances.

---

[10] *cf. Winslow v. Farrell*, 1965 J.C. 49, 52, *per* Lord Wheatley: "The . . . Act . . . has been extensively amended by the . . . Act. In view of the devious and complicated ways by which this original four subsections Act was amended, one wonders why the statute was not simply re-enacted in its new form. It is perhaps not surprising that mistakes may be made by a person seeking the goal of enlightenment while wandering through the maze of amendment, cross-reference, substitution and deletion."

[11] Jennings, *Parliament*, Chap. 7.

[12] Morrison, *Government and Parliament*, Chap. 11.

In the sphere of public law and the management of the national economy, the major initiating factor is the social, political and economic philosophy of the party in power at a given time. Thus the Acts which nationalised,[13] denationalised,[14] and renationalised the steel industry[15] were all passed because of the views of successive governments (of different political complexions) on whether the steel industry should be publicly or privately owned. Similarly, the transport industry has, since 1945, been a shuttlecock thrown backwards and forwards by legislation founded on different political theories. The result is a chaotic mess of legislation.

Then there are Bills sponsored by departments of state in the furtherance of departmental policy on housing or agriculture or education or whatever else is that department's responsibility, because every department constantly sees the need for alteration and what it thinks is improvement of the law on some topic within its responsibility. Some of these raise little or no matter of political philosophy. Practically every year some alteration requires to be made to the rules of social security, or assistance to local authorities, or the control of media and communications, or the like. Again, even when not seeking to make substantial changes, many government departments frequently have a number of small reforms which they would like enacted if parliamentary time can be found, and are consequently constantly in the queue for an opportunity to effect these changes.

Reactions to events

Some noteworthy events, a crime, accident, scandal or other happening, may reveal a gap in the law and prompt a government to take quick action in the hope of preventing repetition of the event.

Pressure Groups

Numerous groups of persons, professional associations, federations, societies, trade unions, charitable and philanthropic bodies and similar organisations of many kinds, are constantly pressing for legislation or legislative amendment of the law on some matter affecting their and their members' interests, in the interest of the furtherance or preservation of the rights of their members or of some interest which they have at heart.[16] They press their views on Ministers and their departments, M.P.s, on Royal Commissions and Committees considering the state of the law, and on any person who may be able to influence parliamentary action in the way they want. Many such groups have one or more of their own leading

---

[13] Iron and Steel Act 1949 (Labour Government).
[14] Iron and Steel Act 1953 (Conservative Government).
[15] Iron and Steel Act 1967 (Labour Government).
[16] S.E. Finer, *Anonymous Empire*.

members among M.P.s, or know a member who is sympathetic to their cause, and many of the members who ballot for the opportunity to introduce a Private Member's Bill are really doing so as the mouthpieces of some organisation, group or interest.

Pressure groups include sectoral commercial groups, such as motor manufacturers, single-issue pressure groups, charities, consumer groups, and professional pressurists employed by companies and interests.[17] Particularly powerful among pressure groups are the T.U.C. and the major trade unions.[18] Thus the Trade Disputes Acts 1906, 1913 and 1965 and the Trade Unions and Labour Relations Act 1974, were all passed as a result of strong pressure from the trade unions, to overrule, or at least modify, the results of judicial decisions[19] or legislation[20] regarded by the trade unions as trenching on what they thought their privileged legal position was or should be. Much of this was modified by the Employment Acts 1980, 1982 and 1988. Bills affecting industry or trade, employment, pensions or related topics are also objects of pressure by trade unions and M.P.s supported by them and sympathetic to their views, to secure that the law is changed in a manner beneficial, or at least minimally harmful, to the interests of trade unionists.

Other pressure groups include the Confederation of British Industry, the churches, the licensed trade, the motoring organisations, organisations of professional persons engaged in every kind of trade, profession, business, industrial or commercial undertaking, the farmers, the teachers, the doctors, those concerned for the protection of children, or animals, or birds, or the countryside, those representing disabled and handicapped persons, the old, the young, the widowed, the divorced, the homeless and every conceivable kind and group of individuals.[21] Some of these organisations may, of course, despite their names, actually represent and be supported by only a minority of the group for whose interests they campaign.

Private Members' Bills

Private Members' Bills[22] are accordingly sometimes expressions of the sponsoring members' own belief as to the desirability of some change in the law, which may be in some obscure detail, or may fundamentally affect

---

[17] Hennessy, *Whitehall*, 337.

[18] On this, see Mackintosh, *The British Cabinet*, 470; see also Harrison, *Trade Unions and the Labour Party since 1945*.

[19] *Taff Vale Ry. v. Associated Society of Railway Servants* [1901] A.C. 426; *Amalgamated Society of Railway Servants v. Osborne* [1910] A.C. 87; *Rookes v. Barnard* [1964] A.C. 1129.

[20] Industrial Relations Act 1971.

[21] See further, Christoff, *Capital Punishment and British Politics*; Wootton, *The Politics of Influence*; Eckstein, *Pressure Group Politics: The Case of the British Medical Association*.

[22] The monthly parts of *Current Law, s.v.* Parliament, list all Bills currently before Parliament, showing the stage of progress made to enactment, and marking those introduced by a private member as distinct from those sponsored by the Government.

some of the best-settled rules of law. Thus Private Members' Bills have several times altered the law of divorce[23] and other subjects affected in this way have been the death penalty for murder,[24] the medical termination of pregnancy,[25] and the provision of family planning advice by the National Health Service.[26] Frequently, however, a private member has taken up and is sponsoring a reform for which some pressure group or section of the community has been agitating, and he is as much, or more, the mouthpiece of that group as an independent legislator.[27] Numerous useful reforms, particularly in such fields as protection of animals, civic amenities, superannuation, and professional organisation of groups of persons, have sprung from measures originating in this way.

Technical Changes

In the more technical parts of the law, such as company law, conveyancing, bankruptcy, procedure, and the like, Parliament relies frequently on the reports and recommendations of Royal Commissions,[28] Departmental Committees,[29] the Law Commissions[30] or standing advisory committees.[31] At any given time there are usually, apart from permanent bodies, a dozen or more Commissions and Committees and similar bodies at work, gathering views, hearing evidence and suggestions, and formulating recommendations, which normally would require for their implementation some changes, sometimes far-reaching changes, in some branch or other of the law. The Cabinet or the Minister to whom the body reports has to decide whether and how far to accept the recommendations and, in the case of a Minister, he has then to fight for the opportunity to have the appropriate Bill drafted and launched on its parliamentary journey.

International Agreements

Some Bills are introduced into Parliament to give the force of law in the United Kingdom to a treaty or convention to which Her Majesty's Government in the United Kingdom has become a party. In the United Kingdom, with a few exceptions, treaties and conventions cannot receive

---

[23] The outstanding instance is Mr. (later Sir) A.P. Herbert's championing of the Bill which became the (English) Matrimonial Causes Act 1937. See the story recounted by him in *The Ayes Have It*. The Divorce (Scotland) Act 1964 was also a private member's measure.

[24] Murder (Abolition of Death Penalty) Act 1965. Despite the title the Act only suspended the death penalty until 1970.

[25] Abortion Act 1967.

[26] National Health Service (Family Planning) Act 1967.

[27] Jennings, *Parliament*, Chap. 11.

[28] See, *e.g.* The Royal Commission on Trade Unions and Employers' Organisations 1965–68 (Chairman: Lord Donovan: Cmnd. 3623, 1968).

[29] See, *e.g.* The Departmental Committee on the Sheriff Court in Scotland, 1963–67 (Chairman: Lord Justice-Clerk Grant; Report: Cmnd. 3248, 1967).

[30] On these bodies, see p. 586, *infra*.

[31] *e.g.* the Scottish Advisory Council on the Treatment of Offenders. See also P.E.P., *Advisory Committees in British Government*.

effect in municipal law unless adopted into the municipal law by statute.[32] Thus an international convention agreed at Warsaw in 1929, settling uniform rules as to the international carriage of goods by air, was adopted into British law by the Carriage by Air Act 1932, and when the convention was revised at The Hague in 1955, the revised version was enacted by the Carriage by Air Act 1961. So, too, certain rules relative to carriage by sea formulated by the International Convention on Maritime Law at Brussels in 1922 and 1923 were enacted by the Carriage of Goods by Sea Act 1924, and amendments contained in a protocol agreed internationally at Brussels in 1968 resulted in a revised Act in 1971. Similarly, the Diplomatic Privileges Act 1964 gave effect to a convention agreed at Vienna in 1961 on diplomatic immunities, and the Consular Relations Act 1968 gave effect to a Vienna Convention of 1963 on consular relations.

Lawmaking by Subordinate Legislation

In so far as legislative power has been delegated to Ministers and other authorities, any making or alteration of subordinate legislation by departments or other authorised bodies is legislative equally with direct legislation by Parliament.

Lawmaking by Other Means

In some spheres and to a limited extent, the law can be changed simply by practice. In the criminal law of Scotland the centralised control of prosecutions by the Lord Advocate and the Crown Office permits a modest amount of, what is in effect, change in the law of the land by the practice of prosecuting or not prosecuting certain kinds of conduct. Thus adultery once was criminal in Scotland but for so many years now has not been prosecuted as such that, though not formally declared non-criminal, it cannot now be regarded as a crime. The Inland Revenue has periodically announced "extra-statutory concessions," or intimations that it does not propose to treat as taxable certain receipts or benefits, though as a matter of law they might be taxable. There is a published pamphlet stating these concessions. Courts have frequently protested against this as departmental suspending of laws[33] or as showing that something is wrong with the taxing legislation[34] but the practice continues. It is highly objectionable and illegal, but it continues.

Difficulties and Defects of Changes in the Law

This constant process of changes in the law is not without its difficulties and disadvantages. In the first place, there is the constant and growing

---

[32] McNair, *Law of Treaties*, 81 *et seq.*

[33] Illegal under the Bill of Rights 1688.

[34] *Gleaner Co. Ltd v. Assessment Committee* [1922] 2 A.C. 169, 175; *Absalom v. Talbot* [1943] 1 All E.R. 589, 598; *I.R.C. v. Frere* [1965] A.C. 402, 429; *Bates v. I.R.C.* [1968] A.C. 483, 516; *Vestey v. I.R.C.* [1979] 2 All E.R. 225, 233.

difficulty of finding and keeping up to date with changes, and of understanding how the changes made have affected the pre-existing rules. Frequently, this is not at all clear. In the second place, new rules all too seldom completely supersede existing rules; more often they are superadded on the existing ones, replacing them in part, but to a large extent adding fresh conditions and a fresh layer of law on to a pile, already too thick, of Acts and decisions dealing with the topic. Again, changes not infrequently have unforeseen consequences, or repercussions on other parts of the law, possibly creating a lacuna or a fresh complication elsewhere.

Lawyers are frequently accused of not being interested in law reform, or of being apathetic or unenthusiastic about it, or of having sought to block and obstruct changes. This is not really fair, because there are many factors which make the experienced lawyer frequently less than enthusiastic for law reform in general or for particular proposed reforms. In the first place, an existing state of the law on any topic may be fairly well known, and its defects, difficulties and dangers have been uncovered. It is accordingly possible to predict with some confidence how the courts would apply the rules in question, and to advise an inquirer with some confidence. If the law is changed, a new set of rules have to be assimilated, their interpretations and applications worked out, and for a very substantial time the lawyer has only his own guess as a basis for advice to a client on a matter involving this point of law. Reasonable certainty and predictability of application are valuable qualities of law; they are frequently lost when the law is changed and the lawyer is reluctant to see them lost. Furthermore, long and painful experience of legislation and parliamentary law-changing has been that lacunae, mistakes, inconsistencies and other defects in the reforming legislation always occur and quite quickly become apparent in practice, so that a defective or out-of-date state of the law may have been exchanged for one defective in other respects. Thus *Adams v. Spencer*[35] revealed a lacuna in the Law Reform (Personal Injuries) Act 1948 which had to be corrected by the Law Reform (Personal Injuries) Amendment Act 1953.[36] A reforming Act may create an absurdity. Thus the Law Reform (Miscellaneous Provisions) Act 1971, s. 4, enacted that in assessing damages payable to a *widow* in respect of her husband's death, no account should be taken of her remarriage or prospect of remarriage. This may produce an absurd result.[37] The previous common law rule, that account should be taken of remarriage, applies to children[38] and to widowers. Lawyers sometimes complain, and with a great deal of justification, that Parliament always changes the law for the worse.

---

[35] 1951 S.C. 175.
[36] The matter is now covered by the Damages (Scotland) Act 1976.
[37] *McKinnon v. Reid*, 1975 S.C. 233.
[38] *Howitt v. Heads* [1972] All E.R. 491; *Thompson v. Price* [1973] 2 All E.R. 846.

Again, changes are frequently proposed and even carried through without any, or adequate, consideration of their repercussions on the law as a whole, and without regard to anomalies, difficulties and absurdities being created in other cases. Thus the Hire-Purchase Act 1964, ss. 27 to 29, introduced a rule about the passing to a purchaser of the right of property in a motor-vehicle sold to him but which was already the subject of a contract of hire-purchase, which rule is different from the rule applicable to any other kind of property subject to such a contract, different from the rule applicable to the sale of goods which are subject to other kinds of transactions such as hire or loan, and itself subject to exceptions where the hire-purchaser is a company, or the value of the car is over a stated sum, or the buyer is a "trade or finance purchaser." Is this a rule of law of which any modern community can be proud? Was the creation of this anomaly justified, or ever really thought out? The Consumer Credit Act 1974 has created a maze of nightmarish complexity, introduced incomprehensible jargon, and raised a great mass of uncertainties.

Not least, a change in the law may be proposed in the guise of reform with which some, or many, lawyers quite conscientiously disagree. Thus some would regard the abolition of civil jury trial as a desirable reform, but others would regard it as the destruction of a valuable civil right, an essential element of justice.[39] Some see the abolition of the death penalty for murder as a great advance, others as an utterly wrong and stupid step. Not every change in the law is a reform, or change for the better, and a good deal of so-called reform is prompted by angling for votes or similar unworthy motives. Some legislation is motivated by jealousy, greed or plain stupidity.

The way in which legislation is framed has provoked, and provokes, much criticism. In fairness to the draftsmen, the Bill may have been drafted in haste and under pressure, it is always extremely difficult to formulate complex ideas in clear though formal language, and quite impossible to foresee, and provide for, every kind of instance and practical case which may arise under the legislation. Moreover, the draftsman's work will be amended and tinkered with by many hands as well as by his own during the Bill's progress through Parliament, so that what finally emerges may have little resemblance to the draft as originally presented to the legislature.[40] Nevertheless, judicial complaints and criticisms abound[41]

---

[39] See the Report of the Committee on Civil Jury Trial (Cmnd. 851, 1959). The Committee was divided in opinion.

[40] Graham Harrison, "An Examination of the Main Criticisms of the Statute Book and of the Possibility of Improvement," 1935 J.S.P.T.L. 45; Ram, "Improvement of the Statute Book," 1951 J.S.P.T.L. 442.

[41] *e.g.* "It is not easy to penetrate the tangled confusion of these Acts of Parliament, and though we have entered the labyrinth together we have unfortunately found exit by different paths": *G.W. Ry. v. Bater* [1922] 2 A.C. 1, 11; " . . . to make some sort of path through the

and it would in many cases be surprising if Members of Parliament could themselves explain what they have enacted.

Frequently Acts seem to be badly planned. It is not easy to see why the Succession (Scotland) Act 1964 was so planned that a lawyer applying it must apply sections 1, 8, 9, 10 to 12 and 2 in that order![42] Apart from defects in drafting and the expression of the enacted law, the state of the statute law in Britain is a disgrace and the courts, the legal profession and the public are very ill-served by Parliament. Too frequently, different and even unconnected topics are dealt with in one Act. The law on one topic is sometimes altered by an Act dealing with quite a different topic. The statute law on any given topic is far too frequently scattered through many Acts, sometimes innovating substantially on the prior law, sometimes containing only verbal changes. Scotland and Scots law is particularly ill-served in that, on matters where the law is roughly the same in Scotland as in England, a fresh Act is normally drafted in terms applicable to England and English law with an "application to Scotland" section stating that certain parts of the Act are to apply to Scotland and that for certain words in the text certain other, Scottish, terms are to be substituted. That much of the law is a mess is Parliament's, and only Parliament's, fault. Particularly disgraceful is the chaotic muddle of injustices and incomprehensible verbiage which cumulatively amounts to our law of taxation.

Particularly objectionable, and the worst device of legislative technique of the twentieth century, is the Law Reform (Miscellaneous Provisions) Act,[43] which is the name given periodically to a piece of legislation which embodies a number of small, usually unconnected, reforming provisions. It is a most unsatisfactory method of law reform, as the provisions are usually not very significant and are disconnected from each other so that

---

labyrinth and jungle of these sections and schedules": *Parry v. Harding* [1925] 1 K.B. 111, 114; "It might be possible, but I doubt if it would be easy, to compress in the same number of lines more fertile opportunities for doubt and error": *L.C.C. v. Lees* [1939] 1 All E.R. 191, 194: "I have not the least idea what sub-sec. 8 means": *Bebb v. Frank* [1939] 1 K.B. 558, 568; " . . . the almost insuperable difficulty of applying the obscure and complicated provisions of these Acts": *Sharpe v. Nicholls* [1945] 1 K.B. 382, 384; " . . . another almost insoluble problem arising from this welter of legislation . . . "; *Vaughan v. Shaw* [1945] K.B. 400, 401; " . . . this chaotic series of Acts": *Cole v. Harris* [1945] K.B. 474, 478; "[The Rent Acts are] a byword for confused draftsmanship . . . ": *Joint Properties v. Williamson*, 1945 S.C. 68, 74; "The obscurity of the Act has been frequently and severely criticised; indeed I think this Act has a strong claim to the distinction of being the worst drafted Act on the Statute book": *Central Asbestos Co. v. Dodd* [1973] A.C. 518.

[42] A Committee on the Preparation of Legislation was appointed by Parliament in 1973 to review the form in which public Bills are drafted, with a view to greater simplicity and clarity in statute law.

[43] Acts under this title were passed in 1940, 1949, 1966, 1968, 1971, 1980, 1985 and 1990. Distinct from these are the Law Reform (Contributory Negligence) Act 1945, the Law Reform (Personal Injuries) Acts 1948 and 1953, the Law Reform (Limitation of Actions, etc.) Act 1954 (extensively amended by the Limitation Act 1963), the Law Reform (Damages and Solatium) Act 1962, and numerous other Acts making reforms in a particular field.

the reforming Act is difficult to remember in any context. Reform in this way is the worst kind of tinkering with and patching of the law and the provisions of such an Act, and their effect on the existing law, are readily overlooked and forgotten.

Modes of Legislative Reform

There are four modes of legislative reform of the law. The first is by passing Acts which in some way alter the pre-existing common law, or statute law, or both, on a particular matter, and this is a mode which has been employed in Scotland and England for centuries. More sophisticated, more difficult, more valuable and more important are the other three, namely, statute law revision, consolidation of legislation, and codification of the law.

Acts Altering Existing Law

Practically every Act in some way alters the existing common law, or statute law, or both. Its effect on common law can only be discerned by investigation of what the common law was; its effect on existing statute law is fairly evident from the Schedules of amendments and repeals appended to the Act, which are frequently lengthy. But the extent and precise effect of the alterations may not be apparent until a problem arises and the interpretation of the Act has to be determined.

A substantial amount of law reform by statute was effected between 1707 and the mid-twentieth century, notably in such fields as the structure and powers of the Court of Session[44] and the sheriff court, marriage and divorce, bankruptcy, entails and conveyancing. But Scotland has always suffered since 1707 from the ignorance of Parliament and the attitude of English departments of state that Scots law should be assimilated to English. This affected the Mercantile Law Amendment Act (Scotland) 1856, the Bills of Exchange Act 1882, and the Sale of Goods Act 1893 (now 1979).

Statute Law Revision

The process of statute law revision consists in repealing, and thereby expunging from the Statute Book, Acts which are spent or have served their purpose, or were enacted for a particular object which has been served, or have been superseded, or have been virtually repealed by, or are inconsistent with, some later enactment, or are otherwise obsolete. There were numerous projects for statute law revision and codification of the law in Scotland from 1425 onwards. The passing of Statute Law Revision Acts and Statute Law (Repeals) Acts to cut away such dead wood commenced

---

[44] Phillipson, *The Scottish Whigs and the Reform of the Court of Session, 1785–1830* (Stair Socy., 1990).

in 1856, and such Acts have been passed periodically since then.[45] A notable one was the Act of 1863, introduced by Lord Westbury in a speech explaining fully the principles on which such a Bill was founded.

In 1868 Lord Chancellor Cairns established the Statute Law Committee which supervised this work, and also the preparation and publication of a *Revised Edition of the Statutes* in 18 volumes, brought down to the end of the year 1878. The edition was completed by 1885 and by the omission of repealed Acts substituted 18 volumes for 118. Twelve more Statute Law Revision Acts were passed between 1887 and 1898 and the second edition of the *Statutes Revised* was published in 16 volumes from 1888 to 1901, containing the statute law as revised down to 1886. Subsequent supplementary volumes brought the law down to 1920. A third edition of the *Statutes Revised* in 32 volumes was published in 1950, stating the statute law as amended down to the end of 1948[46] and publication of a new looseleaf edition, entitled *Statutes in Force*, commenced in 1972.[47] The classification of the statutes as Public General and Local and Private also dates from 1868.[48]

The Statute Law Committee dealt originally only with English Acts prior to 1707 and British Acts thereafter, including Irish Acts down to 1800. In 1897 the committee was reinforced by three Scottish members and the revision of the pre-1707 Scots Acts was undertaken, resulting in the Statute Law Revision (Scotland) Act 1906 and the publication in 1908 of an edition of the Scots Acts still in force. A similar Act of 1964 was followed by the publication in 1965 of the *Acts of the Parliaments of Scotland, 1424–1707,*[49] setting out those Acts still in force as amended down to 1965.

The Statute Law Committee has also been responsible since 1870 for the publication annually of the *Chronological Table of the Statutes*, which sets out all the Scottish, English and United Kingdom statutes in chronological order, showing which and which parts have been repealed or amended, and by what later Act, and the annual *Index to the Statutes in Force* which indexes the provisions of all the statutes in force under wellknown legal heads and sub-heads. In 1996 the committee published a *Chronological Table of Local Legislation, 1797–1994* and the Private Bill Office of the House of Lords authorised publication of an *Index to the Local and Personal Acts, 1850–1995*.

In 1947 the committee was given the task of consolidating enactments and preparing editions of the *Statutes Revised* from which repealed and obsolete matter was omitted. It is now responsible for producing the *Statutes in Force*.

---

[45] See, *e.g.* Statute Law (Repeals) Acts 1971, 1975 and 1978.
[46] It does not contain pre-1707 Scots Acts.
[47] This does contain pre-1707 Scots Acts.
[48] Ilbert, *Legislative Methods and Forms*, 24–27, 65–67.
[49] HMSO, 1965.

Since 1965, statute law revision has become the responsibility of the Law Commission and the Scottish Law Commission, and since 1969 Statute Law (Repeals) Bills have largely replaced Statute Law Revision Bills. The Statute Law Committee and the editorial board of *Statutes in Force* has from 1991 been replaced by an Advisory Committee on Statute Law. The Chairman is the Lord Chancellor and it includes Scottish representatives.

Consolidation of Legislation

Consolidation of statute law consists in bringing together and amalgamating into one Act all the then existing legislation on a particular topic, and repealing and superseding the individual statutes. It had been done occasionally in England in the time of Elizabeth I, and James I appointed a commission in 1609 for the purpose, while Bacon made similar proposals in 1616 and two committees were appointed for the purpose under the Commonwealth.[50]

In 1826 Sir Robert Peel began a series of Acts which consolidated and amended parts of the English criminal law, while in 1833 a Royal Commission was appointed to digest the common law and statute law affecting crimes each into one statute. The commissioners made seven useful reports before they were dissolved in 1845. A second commission was appointed in 1845, made six reports, and survived until 1849.[51] About the same time was appointed Macaulay's commission for digesting and codifying the law of British India, the chief achievement of which was the Indian Penal Code enacted in 1860, and in 1861 seven English criminal law consolidation Acts were passed.

Particularly since about 1868, numerous consolidation Acts have been passed, mostly initiated by the Statute Law Committee, among the most notable being the massive Merchant Shipping Act of 1894.

Consolidation is one of the most valuable forms of law reform, because it enormously facilitates study, understanding and professional use of the statutes to have all the statutory matter on a particular topic available in one Act, and to be able to ignore the bits and pieces of legislation replaced thereby. It also greatly reduces the volume of the statute law. Thus the Police (Scotland) Act 1956 superseded and totally repealed 10 Acts, and amended or partially repealed 10 others. Along with the Police (Scotland) Act 1966 and certain lesser enactments it was itself consolidated into the Police (Scotland) Act 1967. The Rent (Scotland) Act 1971 superseded 14 Acts and parts of 14 more and was itself consolidated with other legislation in the Rent (Scotland) Act 1984. The Criminal Law (Consolidation) (Scotland) Act 1995 consolidated several enactments

---

[50] Ilbert, 43–47.
[51] Ilbert, 51–52; on the difficulties of consolidation, see Ilbert, 111–121.

relating to criminal law. Some other consolidating Acts have embodied the substance of, and replaced, considerably larger numbers of Acts.

The Consolidation of Enactments (Procedure) Act 1949 allowed a Bill designed primarily to consolidate various earlier Acts, but also including corrections and minor improvements, to be referred to a Joint Committee on Consolidation, etc. Bills and passed by an abbreviated procedure. It was largely replaced by a new procedure of consolidation with amendments proposed by either or both of the Law Commissions.[52]

Under the Companies Act 1981 an Order in Council may make amendments of the Companies Acts to facilitate consolidation of those Acts, which was achieved in 1985.

Codification

Codification[53] is the reduction of the law, or the law on a topic, to carefully formulated statutory form, comprising the substantial effect of both the pre-existing common law, declared by cases and formulated by jurists, and the pre-existing statute law, and intended to supersede all the pre-existing statements of the law, and possibly including material amendments and changes. In Scotland there were repeated projects for codification from 1425 onwards. Codification was the method of law restatement urged by Bentham and some of his followers in the early nineteenth century. In Europe, large-scale codification has been effected in many countries, and in most the major parts of the law are embodied in Civil Codes, Commercial Codes, Criminal Codes, and so on. Codes are never, however, all-embracing and some topics are found in statutes outside the main codes. Also, codification cannot stop the development of the law, and codes need to be amended and even replaced in the same way as statutes in this country. With its civilian bias, the codification of Scots law in the nineteenth century, had Scotland preserved her independence, would have been a natural development and would probably have presented no overwhelming difficulties, in view of the great work done by the jurists, particularly Erskine and Bell, in producing carefully formulated statements of the substance of the existing law. In the early nineteenth century Jeremy Bentham urged comprehensive codes based on the principle of utility. But the Anglo-American tradition has always been antagonistic to codification, though codification has been strongly urged in some parts of the United States.[54] In Britain, only in particular and limited areas has small-scale codification by statute been attempted.[55]

---

[52] House of Lords Standing Orders (1994) (Public Business) No. 49(4); House of Commons Standing Orders (1994) (Public Business) No. 123.

[53] See generally, Ilbert, 122 *et seq.*

[54] See Field, "Codification in the United States" (1889) 1 J.R. 18; Sweet, "The Recent Progress of Codification" (1891) 3 J.R. 97.

[55] Hunter, "Law Reform: The Meaning and the Methods," *Proc. 5th Commonwealth Law Conference* (1977) 1.

In 1853, following on the work of the Statute Law Commissioners, Lord Chancellor St. Leonards instructed the preparation of Bills for the codification of the criminal law, but none of the Bills prepared passed into law. In 1853 Lord Chancellor Cranworth, on succeeding St. Leonards, made ambitious proposals for a programme which he hoped might eventually result in a Code Victoria, and appointed a Board for the Revision of the Statute Law. This Board was later (1854) superseded by a Statute Law Commission consisting of judges and senior lawyers, including the then Lord Advocate and the then Solicitor-General for Scotland, and the first Statute Law Revision Act (1856) was based on their recommendations, while they stated that they had over 90 consolidating Bills prepared. In 1861 there were passed seven English Criminal Law Consolidation Acts based on the reports of the Commissioners of 1833 and 1849.[56] A Royal Commission was established in 1866 to consider the expediency of codification, but nothing resulted. Sir James Fitzjames Stephen, who had got passed for India a Criminal Procedure Code, an Evidence Act and a Contract Act,[57] drafted a Bill to codify the English law of evidence and a draft code of criminal law and procedure, and in 1878–83 several attempts were made to put through Parliament a Bill for codifying English criminal law and procedure but without success.

The Bills of Exchange Act 1882, the Partnership Act 1890, the Sale of Goods Act 1893 (now 1979) and the Marine Insurance Act 1906 are the only specimens of codification in British law, and each covers only a small part of the law even of the topic dealt with. All presuppose much common law not embodied in the Acts. All are probably as lucid and plain as statute can be, in marked contrast to many more modern Acts, and have been generally successful, in that they have required little amendment and not provoked much litigation on their interpretation, but only on whether the particular case is or is not covered by a particular section of the Act.

In the United States the Civil Code of Louisiana, based on the French Code, was passed in 1808, and since 1850 several states have adopted codes as part of their law.

While a codified system of law is the ultimate state which should be attained by the legal system of a developed and civilised country, the enactment of a code does not, and should not, stop legal development and change.[58] Provisions of any code will become out of date and will need to be replaced, revised or supplemented, while judicial and juristic interpretation, criticism and uncovering of errors and omissions will necessarily

---

[56] Ilbert, 53–60.

[57] On codification in India, see Ilbert, 129–155; Sweet, "The Anglo-Indian Codes" (1895) 7 J.R. 330.

[58] Experience in France has shown that though the Codes of 1803–1810 still stand, they have been amended and supplemented in many respects, and can be understood only in the light of interpretation. Since the Second World War a Commission for the reform of the Civil Code has been at work.

continue. Codification does not, and must not, end the development of a legal system.[59]

Planned Law Reform

In the twentieth century further conscious attempts have been made to achieve planned law reform.

In 1934 a Law Revision Committee was established in England. After the war it was reconstituted as the Law Reform Committee and a separate [English] Criminal Law Revision Committee was set up in 1959. There was also established in 1952 a Private International Law Committee. All these bodies consider and report on topics of law referred to them for consideration.[60] There is a standing Advisory Council on the Penal System, appointed in 1966, to make recommendations on the prevention of crime.

In Scotland, the Law Reform Committee for Scotland was established in 1954 and did useful work in reporting on topics referred to it by the Lord Advocate, and some of its reports formed the basis for reforming legislation.[61] With the creation of the Scottish Law Commission, the Law Reform Committee for Scotland was allowed to lapse into inactivity and it was later abolished.

The Law Commissions

A fresh stage in the move for law reform was reached by the passing in 1965 of the Law Commissions Act 1965,[62] which established the Law Commission and the Scottish Law Commission, each consisting of a Chairman and four other Commissioners appointed by the Lord Chancellor[63] for England and by the Secretary of State for Scotland and the Lord Advocate jointly for Scotland. From 1972, appointment was by the Lord Advocate alone. By section 3 it is the duty of each Commission "to take and keep under review all the law with which they are respectively concerned, with a view to its systematic development and reform, including in particular the codification of such law, the elimination of anomalies, the repeal of obsolete and unnecessary enactments, the reduction of the number of separate enactments and generally the simplification and modernisation of the law, and for that purpose—

---

[59] See further Cohn, "The German Attorney" (1960) I.C.L.Q. 586; Hahlo, "Here Lies the Common Law" (1967) 30 M.L.R. 241; Diamond, "Codification of the Law of Contract" (1968) 31 M.L.R. 361.

[60] See Winfield, "Law Reform" (1928) 44 L.Q.R. 289; Foster, "Law Revision" (1938) 2 M.L.R. 14; Wade, "The Machinery of Law Reform" (1961) 24 M.L.R. 1; Hutton, "The Mechanics of Law Reform" (1961) 24 M.L.R. 18; *Law Reform and the Law Commission* (1974).

[61] *e.g.* the Occupiers' Liability (Scotland) Act 1960; the Maintenance Orders (Reciprocal Enforcement) Act 1972. See *The Laws of Scotland*, Vol. 22, ss. 650–664.

[62] Analysed in Chorley and Dworkin, "The Law Commissions Act 1965" (1965) 28 M.L.R. 675.

[63] See Gardiner, "The Role of the Lord Chancellor in the Field of Law Reform" (1971) 87 L.Q.R. 326.

(*a*) to receive and consider any proposals for the reform of the law which may be made or referred to them;

(*b*) to prepare and submit to the [Lord Chancellor or the Secretary of State and the Lord Advocate] from time to time programmes for the examination of different branches of the law with a view to reform, including recommendations as to the agency (whether the Commission or another body) by which any such examination should be carried out;

(*c*) to undertake, pursuant to any such recommendations approved by the [Lord Chancellor or the Secretary of State for Scotland and the Lord Advocate], the examination of particular branches of the law and the formulation, by means of draft Bills or otherwise, of proposals for reform therein;

(*d*) to prepare from time to time at the request of the [Lord Chancellor or the Secretary of State for Scotland and the Lord Advocate] comprehensive programmes of consolidation and statute law revision, and to undertake the preparation of draft Bills pursuant to any such programme approved by the [Lord Chancellor or the Secretary of State and the Lord Advocate];

(*e*) to provide advice and information to government departments and other authorities or bodies concerned at the instance of the Government with proposals for the reform or amendment of any branch of the law;

(*f*) to obtain such information as to the legal system of other countries as appears to the Commissioners likely to facilitate the performance of any of their functions."

Programmes prepared by the Commissions and approved, any proposals for reform formulated by the Commissions pursuant to such programmes, and the annual reports of each Commission have to be laid before Parliament.

In pursuance of the Act there were appointed the [English] Law Commission under a High Court judge and the Scottish Law Commission under a Court of Session judge (Lord Kilbrandon)[64] with, in each case, four other Commissioners.

The creation of these bodies offers some prospect of more continuous and constructive thought being given to legal reforms, though the constant threat is that in the interest of uniformity the solution acceptable to England will always be adopted. The Commissions, separately and

---

[64] They later returned to judicial duties and were replaced by other judges, in Scotland in 1971 by Lord Hunter, in 1981 Lord Maxwell, in 1988 Lord Davidson and in 1995 Lord Gill. The two Chairmen serve whole-time, being seconded from the Bench; Lord Gill is to serve part-time. The other English Commissioners serve whole-time, but of the Scottish Commissioners two serve whole-time, and two serve part-time. Both Commissions have legally-qualified assistants and draftsmen.

together, have produced numerous reports, memoranda and proposals, many of which have been enacted.[65] They work generally by issuing memoranda, asking for comments thereon, then proceeding to Reports containing proposals. But their reforming work has been greatly interfered with by regular requests from Government for advice on UN, EU, Council of Europe and other conventions, and on proposals from other sources for legal reforms.

The major obstacle is that any proposals for reform, even if generally agreed to be desirable, must find a place in the legislative queue to await their turn for consideration by a Parliament already grossly overburdened with proposed legislation. Moreover, a reforming measure may well be talked out or emasculated or substantially destroyed in its passage through Parliament, or the most carefully prepared change rendered valueless by foolish amendments. Moreover, law reform is not a popular or vote-catching plank in a party political programme. Votes may be won by promises to nationalise an industry, or give higher social security benefits, but few will be captured by proposals to amend the law of conveyancing or bankruptcy or procedure. The plain fact is that, so long as Britain adheres to its present parliamentary system, the chances of satisfactory large-scale law reform seem negligible. It may be significant that the two major successful codifications of modern times, the French Civil Code of 1804 and the German Civil Code of 1900, were passed through their respective legislatures by autocratic governing régimes. Parliament is ill-suited to the consideration and approval of really large-scale restatements of law.[66]

Also the Scottish Law Commission has to face the obstacle that Whitehall departments, notably the Department of Trade and Industry, frequently want reforms which will accord with English principles or effect assimilation of Scots and English law.[67]

The enactment of Scottish criminal and private law is now a function of the Scottish Parliament and the important Abolition of Feudal Tenure etc. (Scotland) Act 2000[68] was the enactment of proposals of the Scottish Law Commission. But some topics may raise problems of legislative competence as being matters reserved to Westminster.[69] Section 36(3)(a) and (b) envisage special procedure for law reform Bills in the Scottish Parliament.

---

[65] *e.g.* Matrimonial Proceedings (Polygamous Marriages) Act 1972; Prescription and Limitation (Scotland) Act 1973. See also *The Laws of Scotland*, Vol. 22, ss. 667–697.

[66] See also Anton, "Obstacles to Codification," 1982 J.R. 15.

[67] For surveys of the work of the Scottish Law Commission see Lord Hunter, "Law Reform: The Scottish Law Commission," 1988 J.R. 158; E. M. Clive, "Family Law Reform in Scotland— Past Present and Future," 1989 J.R. 33; *The Laws of Scotland: Stair Memorial Encyclopaedia*, Vol. 22, paras. 667–697.

[68] asp. 5, 2000.

[69] See Scotland Act 1998, Sched. 4, para. 2 and Sched. 5.

International Unification of Rules of Law

Multilateral conventions have in several instances resulted in the adoption by several countries of common rules of internal law. Thus the Scandinavian countries have signed conventions unifying in their countries the rules relating to bankruptcy and the mutual recognition of judgments. The League of Nations entrusted to the International Institute for the Unification of Private Law, established by the Italian Government in Rome, the task of indicating on what lines ultimate unity of national legal systems might be sought, and proposals for the unification of the law of sale and related topics have been formulated.[70] This Institute is now linked with the United Nations and the Council of Europe. Conferences of Ministers of Justice of the countries which are members of the Council of Europe have also considered the possibilities of harmonising certain aspects of private law. A Commission on European Contract Law has been at work for a long time on drafting uniform principles of contract law.

In the particular sphere of international private law, attempts have been made at Hague Conferences on Private International Law to minimise the number of topics on which the approaches of different countries diverge or conflict as to the choice of law.[71] In 1951 the Hague Conference was put on a permanent footing by the establishment by charter of a permanent bureau, which works under the general direction of the Standing Governmental Commission of the Netherlands, established in 1897 with the object of promoting the codification of international private law, and of which the main functions are to examine and prepare proposals for the unification of the rules of international private law and to maintain contact with the Council of Europe and with governmental and non-governmental organisations. The United Kingdom has sent representatives since 1951 but hitherto has accepted only a few of the major conventions concluded by the Hague Conference, such as on the formal validity of wills[72] and on the recognition of divorces and legal separations.[73] The Scandinavian and the Benelux countries have also concluded smaller multilateral conventions on certain limited topics.

Legal Change by International or Supranational Authority

International organisations, such as the United Nations Organisation, have no powers to change, or require change in, the internal law of

---

[70] Gutteridge, "An International Code of the Law of Sale" (1933) 14 B.Y.I.L. 75. Conventions of 1964 were enacted into U.K. law by the Uniform Laws on International Sales Act 1967.

[71] Graveson, "The Hague Conference on Private International Law" (1953) 2 I.C.L.Q. 605; Van Hoogstraten, "The United Kingdom joins an Uncommon Market: The Hague Conference on Private International Law" (1963) 12 I.C.L.Q. 148; and see also 10 I.C.L.Q. 18; 14 I.C.L.Q. 528; 18 I.C.L.Q. 618; 42 I.C.L.Q. 553; 47 I.C.L.Q. 439.

[72] Implemented by the Wills Act 1963.

[73] Implemented by the Recognition of Divorces and Legal Separations Act 1971.

member countries. But accession to conventions negotiated under the auspices of the UN will frequently require changes in British law. Accession to conventions negotiated by the International Labour Organisation has prompted much legislation.

Similarly, conventions negotiated through the Council of Europe may require legislative implementation.

The Treaty of Paris of 1951 establishing the European Coal and Steel Community, and the two Treaties of Rome of 1957 establishing the European Economic Community and Euratom, have important law-changing powers. The Rome Treaty establishing the European Economic Community imposes certain rights and duties direct on member states which may override domestic laws so far as they are inconsistent with the terms of the Treaty. Thus by Article 189 the Council and the Commission may adopt Regulations which are binding in every respect and are directly applicable in each member state. Moreover, there are common rules for the regulation of competition, co-ordination of economic policies and the approximation of domestic laws to the extent necessary for the functioning of the Community, and a member cannot legislate in contravention of these rules. Thus Article 100 provides that the Council may issue directives for the approximation of such legislative and administrative provisions in member states as have a direct incidence on the establishment or functioning of the EU. There have been issued a series of directives on company law which have had to be implemented by British statutes. The Commission has also to consult with member states and promote collaboration particularly in respect of employment, labour law, social security, trade unions and collective bargaining. A considerable measure of harmonisation of the national legal systems of the member countries as to patents, trade marks and designs has been achieved. In 1989 the European Parliament resolved to move towards the harmonisation of the private law of the member states. The creation of a single contract law for all member states has been seen as essential for the working of the internal market and a so-called Land Commission produced in 1995 the first part of "The Principles of European Contract Law." The Unidroit Institute in Rome published its own "Principles of International Commercial Contracts" in 1994, and there have been other proposals. It is obvious that the admission of the United Kingdom to membership has enabled and will result increasingly in substantial changes in internal Scottish and English law to achieve the necessary harmonisation.[74] The powers of the EU indeed pose a major threat to the continued existence of Scots law and English law. It can be argued that unification of rules on any topic would contribute to greater unity among member states, but only at the cost of extinguishing national characteristics.

---

[74] See Bathurst and others, *Legal Problems of an Enlarged European Community.* For examples of results of EEC membership to date see Patents Act 1977 and Companies Act 1980.

Similarly, a convention on jurisdiction and the enforcement of judgments in civil and commercial matters agreed by the member states of the EC in 1968 was given effect to in the United Kingdom by the Civil Jurisdiction and Judgments Act 1982, which radically changed the law of Scotland and England on jurisdiction and the recognition and enforcement of judgments from courts in other member states.[75]

FURTHER READING

Abel-Smith and Stevens: *Lawyers and the Courts.*
Cardozo: *The Growth of the Law.*
      The Nature of the Judicial Process.
Farrar: *Law Reform and the Law Commission.*
Friedmann: *Law in a Changing Society.*
Finer: *Anonymous Empire.*
Gardiner and Martin (eds.): *Law Reform Now.*
Ilbert: *Legislative Methods and Forms.*
      The Mechanics of Law Making.
Jennings: *Parliament.*
Law Commission: *Annual Reports.*
Law Reform Committee for Scotland: *Reports.*
Morrison: *Government and Parliament.*
Potter: *Organised Groups in British National Politics.*
Scottish Law Commission: *Annual Reports.*
      Programmes Memoranda and Reports.
Stevens: *Law and Politics: the House of Lords as a Judicial Body, 1800–1976.*
Stewart: *British Pressure Groups.*
Statute Law Society: *Reports.*
The Laws of Scotland: Stair Memorial Encyclopaedia, Vol. 22: Sources of Law
      (General and Historical).
Thring: *Practical Legislation.*

---

[75] See also Civil Jurisdiction and Judgments Act 1991.

SPECIMEN OF CLOSED RECORD

0/999/2000
COURT OF SESSION,
SCOTLAND
May 1, 2000

CLOSED RECORD

In causa

GEORGE
WASHINGTON

against

MICHELANGELO
RUBENS

Gloag and Henderson,
W.S.

Solicitors for Pursuer

Kames and Hume, S.S.C.

Solicitors for Defender

October 30, 2000   Lord Dunedin

The Lord Ordinary on joint motion closes the Record and appoints the case to the Procedure Roll.

Andrew Dunedin

CLOSED RECORD

in the action at the instance of

GEORGE WASHINGTON,
residing at 123 Garden Place, Glasgow   — *Pursuer*

against

MICHELANGELO RUBENS,
345 London Street, Glasgow   — *Defender*

COURT OF SESSION, SCOTLAND

I. SUMMONS

GEORGE WASHINGTON, Retired school teacher, residing at 123 Garden Place, Glasgow

PURSUER

against

MICHELANGELO RUBENS, Fine Art Dealer, carrying on business at 345 London Street, Glasgow

DEFENDER

ELIZABETH THE SECOND, By the Grace of God, of the United Kingdom of Great Britain and Northern Ireland, and of Her other realms and territories, Queen, Defender of the Faith, Head of the Commonwealth, to the said Michelangelo Rubens,

Whereas by this Summons the pursuer craves the Lords of our Council and Session to pronounce a decree against you in terms of the conclusions appended hereto, We therefore charge you that, if you have any good reason why such decree should not be pronounced, you cause appearance to be entered on your behalf in the Office of the Court, 2 Parliament Square, Edinburgh, on the Calling of the Summons in Court, which will be not earlier than the twenty-first day from the date of service upon you of this Summons; and take warning that, if appearance is not so entered on your behalf, the pursuer may proceed to obtain decree against you in your absence.

This Summons is Warrant for Arrestment and Inhibition on the Dependence.

Given under our Signet at Edinburgh, Seventh day of May, Two Thousand.

W.M.Gloag,
543 St Vincent Street,
Edinburgh.

Solicitor for Pursuer

CONCLUSIONS

1. For payment by the defender to the pursuer of the sum of ONE HUNDRED AND FORTY-FOUR THOUSAND POUNDS (£144,000) STERLING, with interest thereon at the rate of eight per centum per annum from the date of the decree to follow hereon until payment.

2. For the expenses of the action.

II. CONDESCENDENCE for Pursuer and ANSWERS thereto for Defender

Cond. 1 The pursuer is a retired school teacher and resides at 123 Garden Place, Glasgow. The defender is a fine art dealer and carries on business at 345 London Street, Glasgow. The present action has as its object a right to damages for breach of a contract made and broken in Scotland and damages for a delict committed in Scotland. The Court of Session has jurisdiction. No proceedings are in subsistence before any other Court involving the parties hereto and the present cause of action. No agreement exists prorogating jurisdiction herein to any other Court.
Ans. 1 Admitted.

Cond. 2 In or about June 1995 the pursuer wished to sell an oil painting, entitled The Laird of Inversnecky, which had been in his home for many years. He had been informed by his father that it was by the school of Raeburn but not by that master himself and that it was valuable but probably not very valuable. He asked the defender if he would be interested in buying that said painting and the defender sent a representative, a Mr Tom Bloggs, to the pursuer's house where he examined the painting. Having done so, the said Mr Bloggs, as agent for the defender and acting within the scope of his authority for him, offered orally to buy the said painting for the sum of £6000. The pursuer orally accepted this offer. The defender later removed the said painting and paid the pursuer the sum of £6000. The defender's explanations in answer are denied.
Ans. 2 Admitted that in June 1995 the pursuer asked the defender if he would be interested in buying a painting entitled The Laird of Inversnecky, that Mr Tom Bloggs, acting on the defender's behalf, called at the pursuer's house and having inspected the said painting, orally offered to purchase it for £6000, which offer was accepted, and that the defender then removed the said painting and paid the pursuer £6000. *Quoad ultra* not known and not admitted. Explained that at the time of the said sale the defender and the said Mr Tom Bloggs honestly believed that the said painting was by an inferior painter in the style of Raeburn and that in these circumstances £6000 was a fair price.

Cond. 3 In June 1998 the pursuer's attention was drawn to a report that a long-lost painting by Raeburn had turned up in a London saleroom and had been sold by auction for £150,000. Inquiries by the pursuer have elicited that the painting was that of The Laird of Inversnecky, that it had been resold by the defender to Messrs Velasquez, 123 Bond Street, London, in 1997 for £80,000 and resold by Messrs Velasquez at auction in June 1998 for £150,000. The defender's averments in answer as to storage and insurance charges are not known and not admitted.
Ans. 3 Admitted that the defender sold the said painting in 1997 to the said Messrs Velasquez for £80,000. *Quoad ultra* not known and not admitted. Explained that while the defenders owned the said painting they incurred storage and insurance charges in respect of it which they reasonably estimate at £2000.

Cond. 4 The pursuer was not at any material time expert as to the authenticity or real market value of paintings. When the pursuer sold the said painting he acted under essential error as to its real market value. He believed that its fair market value was about £6000. If he had then known what he now knows he would not have sold it for less than £150,000. The defender's conduct in taking advantage of his ignorance has caused the pursuer a loss of £144,000, which is the sum sued for.

Ans. 4 Not known and not admitted that the pursuer was not at any material time expert as to the authenticity or real market value of paintings. Not known and not admitted that when he sold the said painting the pursuer was acting under essential error as to its real market value. *Quoad ultra* denied.

Cond. 5 Further, and in any event, when the defender bought the said painting as condescended on, he acted in breach of a duty owed to *inter alios*, the pursuer, in not having known or discovered the true value of the said painting when his representative examined it or not having discovered its true value before offering to buy it from the pursuer. In this duty he failed and by his offer he impliedly represented through his said employee that the sum offered was the true value of the said painting. This failure in duty caused the pursuer, who acted throughout in reliance on the defender's skill, experience and knowledge, to act under essential error and induced him to sell the said painting for a grossly inadequate sum. By his said misrepresentation the defender caused the pursuer a loss of £144,000, which is the sum sued for. With reference to the defender's averments in answer the defender was in breach of duty in allowing the said Mr Bloggs to negotiate for him and contract on his behalf if he was inadequately experienced in nineteenth-century painting.

Ans. 5 Denied that the defender owed to the pursuer any such duty of care as is averred. Denied that he was in breach of any duty of care to the pursuer. *Quoad ultra* denied. *Esto*, which is denied, the defender owed to the pursuer any such duty as is averred his said representative, in making the contract with the pursuer, acted in good faith but was inexperienced and, if he misrepresented the true value of the said painting, did so innocently.

Cond. 6 The pursuer has called on the defender to compensate him for having taken advantage of his essential error in buying the said painting from him at a grossly inadequate price, but he has refused to do so. The present action is accordingly necessary.

Ans. 6 Admitted that the pursuer has called on the defender to compensate him for having sold the said painting at a price which he now deems inadequate, and that the defender has refused to do so. Denied that the present action is necessary.

Cond. 7 Further, and in any event, the pursuer has called on the defender to pay him damages for having negligently misrepresented to him the true value of the said painting and caused him loss thereby, but he has refused to do so. The present action is accordingly necessary.

Ans. 7 Admitted that the pursuer has called on the defender to compensate him for having negligently misrepresented the true value of the said painting and that the defender has refused to do so. Denied that the present action is necessary.

III. PLEAS-IN-LAW for Pursuer

1. The Pursuer, having contracted with the Defender to sell him the painting, The Laird of Inversnecky, as condescended on, for an inadequate price, by reason of

his essential error as to the true value of the said painting, is entitled to compensation from him therefor.

2. The Pursuer, having contracted with the Defender to sell his painting for an inadequate sum by reason of the defender's negligent misrepresentation to him of its true value and having suffered loss thereby, is entitled to damages from him in compensation for his said loss.

IN RESPECT WHEREOF

W. M. Gloag, W.S.

543 St Vincent Street,
Edinburgh

Solicitor for Pursuer

IV. PLEAS-IN-LAW for Defender

1. The Pursuer's averments being irrelevant, *et separatim*, lacking in specification, the action should be dismissed.
2. The Pursuer's averments, so far as material, being unfounded in fact, the Defender should be assoilzied.
3. The Defender, not having taken advantage of the Pursuer's own essential error, is not liable to compensate him and should be assoilzied.
4. The Pursuer having contracted under unilateral error not induced in any way by any conduct of the Defender is not entitled to compensation from him and the Defender should be assoilzied.
5. The Defender not having misrepresented either negligently or at all to the Pursuer the true value of the said painting, is not liable to pay damages to him for any loss sustained in consequence of the sale of the said painting.
6. *Esto*, which is denied, the Defender owed any duty of care to the Pursuer not to misrepresent to him the true value of the said painting, any misrepresentation being innocent, the Defender is not liable to compensate the Pursuer for any loss sustained in consequence.
7. *Esto*, which is denied, the Defender is under any liability to compensate the Pursuer, the liability should be limited to £72,000 as the profit which he made on the resale of the said painting.
8. In any event, the sum sued for being excessive, decree should not be pronounced therefor.

IN RESPECT WHEREOF

Geo. J. Bell

V. INTERLOCUTORS

October 15, 2000   Act. Erskine. Alt. Bell. The Lord Ordinary, on joint motion, continues the adjustment of record to October 30.

A. DUNEDIN

October 30, 2000   Act. Erskine. Alt. Bell. The Lord Ordinary of consent closes the record and appoints the case to the Procedure Roll.

A. DUNEDIN

INITIAL WRIT IN SUMMARY CAUSE

(Prescribed by Summary Cause Rules, 1976, as amended)

Form Aa

SUMMARY CAUSE SUMMONS CLAIM FOR PAYMENT OF MONEY	**Official Use Only** Summons No. Return day Calling date

Sheriff Court (name, address and tel. no.) 1

Name and address of person making the claim (PURSUER) 2

Name and address of person from whom money is claimed (DEFENDER) 3

4 | **CLAIM**
1. The pursuer claims from the defender the sum of £... with interest on that sum at the rate of   % annually from the date of service and expenses.

5 | RETURN DAY   19

CALLING DATE   19   at   am

*Sheriff Clerk to delete as appropriate

The pursuer is authorised to serve a service copy summons in *Form Ab/Form Ac on the defender not less than 21 days before the Return Day shown in the box above. The summons is warrant for arrestment on the dependence.

Sheriff Clerk Depute   Date

Name, full address and tel. no. of pursuer's solicitor (if any)

6

NOTE:

The pursuer should complete boxes 1, 2, 3, 4 and 6 on this page, and the statement of claim on page 2.
The Sheriff Clerk will complete box 5.

599

STATE CLAIM HERE OR ATTACH A STATEMENT OF CLAIM
(to be completed by the pursuer)

1. The defender has refused or delayed to pay the sum claimed.

2. The details of the claim are*

*If necessary attach a separate sheet.

FOR OFFICIAL USE ONLY

DEFENCE OR STATEMENT OF DEFENCE

Form Ab

SUMMARY CAUSE SUMMONS DEFENDER'S COPY CLAIM OF PAYMENT OF MONEY WHERE TIME TO PAY DIRECTION MAY BE APPLIED FOR	**Official Use Only** Summons No.

Sheriff Court **1**
(name, address
and tel. no.)

Name and **2**
address of
person making
the claim
(PURSUER)

Name and **3**
address of
person from whom
money is claimed
(DEFENDER)

4 **CLAIM**

1. The pursuer claims from the defender the sum of £... (you will find details of the claim on page 2).
   and
2. The pursuer claims interest on that sum at the rate of % annually from the date on which this summons was served on you.
   and
3. The pursuer also claims from you the Court expenses.

5 | RETURN DAY | 19 |

| CALLING DATE | 19 at am |

CITATATION OF DEFENDER

Place   Date

, defender,
you are served with this summons. The pursuer has been authorised
by the Court to serve it on you.

SOLICITOR/SHERIFF OFFICER

Name, full address and tel. no. of pursuer's solicitor (if any)

6

NOTE:
The pursuer should complete boxes 1, 2, 3, 4 and 6 on this page, the statement of claim on page 2, and Section A on page 4 before service on the defender. The person serving the summons will complete box 5.

[Page 2]

STATEMENT OF CLAIM

1. The defender has refused or delayed to pay the sum claimed.

2. The details of the claim are*

*If necessary attach a separate sheet.

WHAT CAN I DO ABOUT THIS SUMMONS?

Decide whether you admit owing the money or not and what you want to do about it. Then look at the section on this page which covers your decision and follow the instructions in that section. You will find the RETURN DAY and the CALLING DATE on page 1. A leaflet "Guide to Summary Cause Procedure in the Sheriff Court" can be obtained from the sheriff clerk. If you wish further advice contact any Citizens Advice Bureau, Consumer Advice Centre or Trading Standards or Consumer Protection Department or a solicitor.

DO NOTHING
If you do nothing about this summons the court may order you to pay the pursuer the sum claimed including interest and expenses.

ADMIT THE CLAIM—and pay in full
If you want to avoid a court order against you, the whole sum claimed including interest and any expenses due should be paid **to the pursuer or his solicitor** in good time **before the return day.**

ADMIT THE CLAIM—and make written application to pay by instalments or by deferred lump sum
Complete and sign box 1 opposite on page 3 and section B on page 4, and return pages 3 and 4 to the court to arrive **on or before the return day.** If the pursuer does not accept your offer, the court will decide how the amount claimed is to be paid.

ADMIT THE CLAIM—and attend court to make application to pay by instalments or deferred lump sum
Complete and sign box 2 on page 3. Return pages 3 and 4 to the court to arrive **on or before the return day. You must attend or be represented at court on the calling date.** Your representative may be a solicitor or someone else having your authority. It may help you or your respresentative to bring pages 1 and 2 to the court. If you fail to return pages 3 and 4 as directed or if having returned them, you fail to attend or be represented, the court may decide the claim in your absence.

DENY THE CLAIM—and attend court to dispute the sum claimed or state a defence or challenge the jurisdiction of the court.

Complete and sign box 3 on page 3. Return pages 3 and 4 to the court to arrive **on or before the return day. You must attend or be represented at court on the calling date.** Your representative may be a solicitor or someone else having your authority. It may help you or your representative to bring pages 1 and 2 to the court. **If you fail to return pages 3 and 4 as directed or if having returned them, you fail to attend or be represented, the court may decide the claim in your absence.**

WRITTEN NOTE OF PROPOSED DEFENCE—You may also send to the court a written note of the defence you propose to state at the calling date. You can send this note at any time **before the date of the calling date.** However you must still attend or be represented at court on the calling date.

If you decide to send a note you must send a copy of it to the pursuer.

KEEP PAGES 1 AND 2—YOU MAY NEED THEM AT A LATER STAGE

[Page 3]

YOUR RESPONSE TO THE SUMMONS

CLAIM ADMITTED—Under the Debtors (Scotland) Act 1987

The Act gives you the right to apply to the court for a "time to pay direction" which is an order saying that you can pay any sum you are ordered to pay to the pursuer either in instalments or by deferred lump sum. A deferred lump sum means that you must pay all the amount at one time within a specified period set by the court.

In addition when making a "time to pay direction" the court may recall or restrict an arrestment made on your property by the pursuer in connection with the action or debt (for example your bank account may have been frozen).

If the court makes a "time to pay direction" a copy of the court order (called an extract decree) will be served on you by the pursuer telling you when payment should start or when it is you have to pay the lump sum.

If the court does not make a "time to pay direction" and makes an order for immediate payment against you, an order to pay (called a charge) may be served on you if you do not pay.

Box 1

> **ADMIT THE CLAIM—and make written application to pay by instalments or deferred lump sum**
>
> I do not intend to defend the case but admit the claim and wish to make a WRITTEN APPLICATION about payment.
>
> I have completed the application form in section B on page 4.
>
> Signature ....

Box 2

> **ADMIT THE CLAIM—INTENTION TO APPEAR**
>
> I admit the claim and INTEND TO APPEAR OR BE REPRESENTED IN COURT.
>
> Signature ....

Box 3

> **DENY THE CLAIM—INTENTION TO APPEAR**
>
> I do not admit the claim. I intend to appear or be represented in court to state my defence.
>
> *I intend to challenge the jurisdiction of the court.
> *I attach a note of my proposed defence which has been copied to the pursuer.
>
> Signature ....   *Delete as necessary.

> **PLEASE REMEMBER**
>
> Send pages 3 and 4 to the court to arrive **on or before the return day** if you have signed any of the responses above. If you have admitted the claim do not send payment to the court.

[Page 4]

	SHERIFF COURT (including address)	
SECTION A This section must be completed before service		Summons No. _____ Return day _____ Calling date _____
	COURT STAMP (OFFICIAL USE ONLY)	
Pursuer's full name and address		Defender's full name and address

SECTION B

**APPLICATION IN WRITING FOR A TIME TO PAY DIRECTION
UNDER THE DEBTORS (SCOTLAND) ACT 1987**
(payment by instalments or deferred lump sum)

CLAIM ADMITTED—I admit the claim and make application
(1) To pay by instalments of £...............

(Tick one box only)

EACH... WEEK ☐ FORTNIGHT ☐ MONTH ☐

OR

(2) To pay the sum ordered in one payment within .WEEKS/MONTHS

Signature ....

> **To help the Court please provide details of your financial position
> in the boxes below.**

If necessary attach a separate sheet

My outgoings are:	Weekly ☐	Fortnightly ☐	Monthly ☐
Rent/Mortgage	£		
Heating	£		
Food	£		
HP	£		
Other	£		
Total	£		

My income is:	Weekly ☐	Fortnightly ☐	Monthly ☐
Wages/Pensions	£		
Social Security	£		
Other	£		
Total	£		

Dependent children—how many ☐   Dependent relatives—how many ☐

Here list all capital (if any) for example value of house; amount in bank/
building society account, shares or other investments:

APPLICATION FOR RECALL OR RESTRICTION OF AN ARRESTMENT

I seek the recall or restriction of the arrestment of which the details are as
follows:—

Signature ....   Date ....

Form Ac

SUMMARY CAUSE SUMMONS DEFENDER'S COPY CLAIM FOR PAYMENT OF MONEY	**Official Use Only** Summons No.

Sheriff Court (name, address and tel. no.) **1**

Name and address of person making the claim (PURSUER) **2**

Name and address of person from whom money is claimed (DEFENDER) **3**

4 **CLAIM**
1. The pursuer claims from the defender the sum of £... (you will find details of the claim on page 2).
and
2. The pursuer claims interest on that sum at the rate of %
annually from the date on which this summons was served on you.
and
3. The pursuer also claims from you the Court expenses.

5

RETURN DAY	19
CALLING DATE	19 at am

CITATATION OF DEFENDER

Place   Date

                                              , defender,
you are served with this summons. The pursuer has been authorised by the Court to serve it on you.

SOLICITOR/SHERIFF OFFICER

Name, full address and tel. no. of pursuer's solicitor (if any)

6

NOTE:
The pursuer should complete boxes 1, 2, 3, 4 and 6 on this page, the statement of claim on page 2, and Section A on page 3 before service on the defender. The person serving the summons will complete box 5.

STATEMENT OF CLAIM

1. The defender has refused or delayed to pay the sum claimed.

2. The details of the claim are*

*If necessary attach a separate sheet.

WHAT CAN I DO ABOUT THIS SUMMONS?

Decide whether you admit owing the money or not and what you want to do about it. Then look at the section on this page which covers your decision and follow the instructions in that section. You will find the RETURN DAY and the CALLING DATE on page 1. A leaflet "Guide to Summary Cause Procedure in the Sheriff Court" can be obtained from the sheriff clerk. If you wish further advice contact any Citizens Advice Bureau, Consumer Advice Centre or Trading Standards or Consumer Protection Department or a solicitor.

DO NOTHING
If you do nothing about this summons the court may order you to pay the pursuer the sum claimed including interest and expenses.

ADMIT THE CLAIM—and pay in full
If you want to avoid a court order against you, the whole sum claimed including interest and any expenses due should be paid **to the pursuer or his solicitor** in good time **before the return day.**

DENY THE CLAIM—and attend court to dispute the sum claimed or state a defence or challenge the jurisdiction of the court.
Complete and sign box 3 on page 3. Return pages 3 and 4 [*sic*] to the court to arrive **on or before the return day. You must attend or be represented at court onthe calling date.** Your representative may be a solicitor or someone else having your authority. It may help you or your representative to bring pages 1 and 2 to the court. **If you fail to return pages 3 and 4 [*sic*]as directed or if having returned them, you fail to attend or be represented, the court may decide the claim in your absence.**

WRITTEN NOTE OF PROPOSED DEFENCE—You may also send to the court a written note of the defence you propose to state at the calling date. You can send this note at any time **before the date of the calling date.** However you must still attend or be represented at court on the calling date.
If you decide to send a note you must send a copy of it to the pursuer.

KEEP PAGES 1 AND 2—YOU MAY NEED THEM AT A LATER STAGE

[Page 3]

SHERIFF COURT (including address)

SECTION A
This section must be completed before service

Summons No. _____
Return day _____
Calling date _____

COURT STAMP
(OFFICIAL USE ONLY)

Pursuer's full name and address

Defender's full name and address

YOUR RESPONSE TO THE SUMMONS

SECTION B

DENY THE CLAIM—INTENTION TO APPEAR

I do not admit the claim.
I INTEND TO APPEAR OR BE REPRESENTED IN COURT TO STATE MY DEFENCE.

*I intend to challenge the jurisdiction of the court.
*I attach a note of my proposed defence which has been copied to the pursuer.

Signature .... *delete as necessary

PLEASE REMEMBER

Send this page to the court to arrive **on or before the return day** if you have signed Section B above.

If you have admitted the claim do not send any payment to the court.

INITIAL WRIT IN SMALL CLAIMS CAUSE

(Prescribed by Small Claims Rules, 1988, Appx.)

FORM 1

Form of summons in small claim for payment of money

SMALL CLAIM SUMMONS CLAIM FOR PAYMENT OF MONEY	**Official Use Only** Summons No.
	Return date
	Preliminary hearing date

			Name, full address and tel. no. of pursuer's solicitor (if any)	
Sheriff Court (name and address and tel. no.)	1			2

Name and address of person making the claim (PURSUER)	3	

Name and address of person from whom money is claimed (DEFENDER)	4	

5 | **CLAIM**
1. The pursuer claims from the defender the sum of £... with interest on that sum at the rate of   % annually from the date of service and expenses.

6

RETURN DATE	19		
PRELIMINARY HEARING DATE	19	at	am

The pursuer is authorised to serve (insert as appropriate form 2 or form 3), which is a service copy summons, on the defender not less that 21 days before the RETURN DATE shown in the box above. The summons is warrant for arrestment on the dependence (and for arrestment to found jurisdiction).

Sheriff Clerk Depute   Date..........................19......

The person making the claim (the pursuer) should complete boxes 1, 2, 3, 4 and 5 on this page and the statement of claim on page 2 and the sheriff clerk will complete box 6 when he receives this form from the pursuer.

(Page 2 of Form 1)

STATE CLAIM HERE OR ATTACH A STATEMENT OF CLAIM
(to be completed by the pursuer)

1. The defender has refused or delayed to pay the sum claimed.

2. The details of the claim are*

*If necessary attach a separate sheet.

FOR OFFICIAL USE ONLY

Defence (to be noted by the sheriff)

Disputed issues (to be noted by the sheriff)

APPENDIX D

SPECIMEN INDICTMENT—HIGH COURT OF JUSTICIARY

IN THE HIGH COURT OF JUSTICIARY

HER MAJESTY'S ADVOCATE against JOHN MILTON

JOHN MILTON, prisoner in the prison of Glasgow, you are Indicted at the instance of the Right Honourable GEORGE MACKENZIE, Her Majesty's Advocate, and the charge against you is that on January 1, 2000, about 2 o'clock a.m. in Hillhead Street, Glasgow, at a point in front of No. 63 Hillhead Street, you did discharge a Beretta pistol loaded with ball ammunition at BEN JONSON, residing at 63 Hillhead Street, Glasgow, aforesaid, and the said ball struck him in the left shoulder and wounded him to the danger of his life, and you did attempt to murder him.

List of productions
1. Beretta 9-mm. pistol.
2. Magazine for said pistol containing six live rounds.
3. Pistol ball extracted from the shoulder of the said Ben Jonson.

List of witnesses
1. Ben Jonson, unemployed, 63 Hillhead Street, Glasgow.
2. Cleopatra Antony, 63 Hillhead Street, Glasgow.
3. Robert Burns, excise officer, 70 Hillhead Street, Glasgow.
4. Charlotte Brontë, teacher, 72 Hillhead Street, Glasgow.
5. Percy B. Shelley, Police Constable B123, Strathclyde Police.
6. John Keats, Police Constable B456, Strathclyde Police.
7. Matthew Arnold, M.B. Police Surgeon, Strathclyde Police.
8. Isaac Newton, B.Sc., Forensic Physicist, Strathclyde Police.

THOMAS HOPE,

Advocate Depute.

APPENDIX E

SPECIMEN SUMMARY COMPLAINT—SHERIFF COURT

Under the Criminal Procedure (Scotland) Act 1995

In the Sheriff Court of Glasgow and Strathkelvin at Glasgow

THE COMPLAINT OF THE PROCURATOR FISCAL AGAINST

GLASGOW: February 20, 2000

WILLIAM SHAKESPEARE,   Date of birth: 3.4.66
123 Hathaway Street,
GLASGOW

The charges against you are that on December 31, 1999 in the common close at 129 Hathaway Street, Glasgow, You did

(1) conduct yourself in a disorderly manner, bawl, shout, curse and swear and commit a breach of the peace;

(2) date and place above libelled, you did resist, obstruct, molest and hinder Alfred Tennyson and William Wordsworth, both Constables, Strathclyde Police, then in the execution of their duty and did struggle violently with them;

CONTRARY to the Police (Scotland) Act 1956, Section 41(1)(*a*).

IVAN T. TERRIBULL,

Procurator-Fiscal Depute.

CITATION TO A CHILDREN'S HEARING

SOCIAL WORK (SCOTLAND) ACT 1968

To[1]:

You have been referred to a children's hearing[2]

You are required in terms of section 40(1) of the Social Work (Scotland) Act 1968 to attend the hearing

on (date)

at (time)

at (place)

Please read the Notes set out below

16 ALBION STREET,
GLASGOW G1 1JZ

. 19   . . . .
                                                                                for Reporter

NOTES

A children's hearing is a group of three people specially selected for their interest and concern in understanding and helping children who are in trouble. They meet to discuss with a child and his parents any difficulties that may have arisen, to discover the reasons for these difficulties and to find an answer which is in the best interests of the child. In some cases this may involve compulsory supervision or even removal from home. Further information on the hearing is set out in the leaflet entitled "To tell you about the Children's Hearing" a copy of which accompanies this notification.

When the children's hearing are discussing your case, they will want to find out your views and you may, if you wish, bring with you to the hearing someone to help you in discussing your difficulties and what might be done. The personal expenses of this representative (but not any fees) may be refunded if they are not less than fifteen pence (15p).

Your own personal expenses (but not any loss of earnings) in coming to the hearing may be refunded if those expenses, together with any expenses of your parent(s) in coming to the hearing are not less than fifteen pence (15p).

If you do not attend the hearing, steps may be taken, including possibly your detention, to make sure that you do appear before a hearing. If there is a very good reason, such as illness, why you will be unable to attend the hearing, you should contact the reporter immediately at 0141–227

---

1. Name and address of child   2. State shortly the purpose of the hearing, for example, "on the basis   3 Address of Reporter
                                         of the grounds of referral set out in the attached statement" or "for
                                         the purpose of reviewing the supervision requirement made on
                                         (date)"

(second page of citation)

Supervision requirement. (Rule 22)

SOCIAL WORK (SCOTLAND) ACT 1968

At[1]

A children's hearing for the Strathclyde Region in exercise of the powers conferred by section 44(1) of the Social Work (Scotland) Act 1968, being satisfied that[2]

is in need of compulsory measures of care require h   to reside in[3]

to be under the supervision of[4]

subject to the conditions noted below.

The operation of this supervision requirement is postponed until

. . . .
Chairman of the children's hearing

CONDITIONS REFERRED TO IN THE FOREGOING
SUPERVISION REQUIREMENT

†1. The child is required to observe the rules of conduct of the residential establishment.
†2. The requirement to reside is subject to the discretion of the managers of the residential establishment to grant leave of absence from time to time.
3.
etc.

. . . .
Chairman of the children's hearing

1. Place and date   3. Name of residential establishment
2. Name and address of child   4. Name of local authority or other supervisor.
† Where a supervision requirement requires a child to reside in a residential establishment conditions 1 and 2 shall be inserted
  in the supervision requirement.

INDEX